Summary of FORTRAN 77 Statements

STATEMENT	DESCRIPTION (Page in Text)	EXAMPLE OF USAGE
ENTRY	Specifies entry point in a subprogram (564)	ENTRY POLY (X)
EQUIVALENCE	Establishes sharing of memory locations by different variables in same program unit (559)	EQUIVALENCE (X, Y), (ALPHA, A, T(3))
EXTERNAL	Specifies externally defined subprograms that may be used as arguments (257)	EXTERNAL F, QUAD
FORMAT	Defines a list of descriptors (275, 292)	20 FORMAT (1X, 'ROOTS ARE', 2F8.3)
FUNCTION	Heading for a function subprogram (185)	FUNCTION AVE(X, N)
GO TO	Unconditionally transfers control to a specified statement (143)	GO TO 100
IMPLICIT	Used to establish a naming convention (552)	IMPLICIT REAL (L, N-Z), INTEGER (A-K)
INQUIRE	Determines properties of a file or of its connection to a unit number (522)	INQUIRE (EXIST = FLAG, NAME = FNAME)
INTEGER	Specifies integer type (59)	INTEGER X, CLASS, TABLE(10,20)
INTRINSIC	Specifies intrinsic functions that may be used as arguments (260)	INTRINSIC SIN, DSQRT
LOGICAL	Specifies logical type (102)	LOGICAL P, Q, TABLE(4,6)
Logical IF	Executes or bypasses a statement, depending on the truth or falsity of a logical expression (114)	IF (DISC .GT. 0) DISC = SQRT(DISC)
OPEN	Opens a file (303, 518)	OPEN(UNIT = 12, FILE = FNAME, STATUS = 'OLD')
PARAMETER	Defines parameters (60)	PARAMETER (LIM = 100, RATE = 1.5)
PAUSE	Interrupts program execution, program may be restarted (552)	PAUSE PAUSE 'PROGRAM PAUSE'
PRINT	Output statement (77, 275)	PRINT *, 'X = ', X PRINT * PRINT '(1X, 317)', M, N, M + N
PROGRAM	Program heading (82)	PROGRAM WAGES
READ	Input statement (78, 291, 301, 524)	READ *, ALPHA, BETA READ '(I5, F7.2)', NUM, Z READ (12, *, END = 20) HOURS, RATE
REAL	Specifies real type (59)	REAL NUM, GAMMA, MAT(10,10)
RETURN	Returns control from subprogram to calling program unit (187, 565)	RETURN RETURN 2
REWIND	Positions file at initial point (306, 527)	REWIND 12
SAVE	Save values of local variables in a subprogram for later references (196)	SAVE X, Y, NUM SAVE
Statement function	Function defined within a program unit by a single statement (197)	F(X,Y) = X**2 + Y**2
STOP	Terminates execution (557)	STOP STOP 'PROGRAM HALTS'
SUBROUTINE	Heading for subroutine subprogram (218)	SUBROUTINE CONVER (U, V, RHO, PHI)

WHILE, DO WHILE	First statement of a WHILE loop; not in standard FORTRAN 77 (138)	WHILE X > 0 DO DO WHILE X > 0
		  PRINT *, X PRINT *, X
		  X = X − .1 X = X − .1
		END WHILE END DO

WRITE	Output statement (298, 528)	WRITE (*,*) A, B, C WRITE (12,'(1X, 316)') N1, N2, N3

PREFACE

FORTRAN, now more than 30 years old, is a language that is used throughout the world to write programs for solving problems in science and engineering. Since its creation in the late 1950s, it has undergone a number of modifications that have made it a very powerful yet easy-to-use language. These modifications, however, led to a proliferation of different dialects of FORTRAN, which hindered program portability. Since some uniformity was desirable, the American National Standards Institute (ANSI) published the first FORTRAN standard in 1966. In the years following, extensions to this standard version of FORTRAN were developed, some of which came into common use. It became apparent that many of these features should be incorporated into a new standard. This updated ANSI FORTRAN standard (ANSI X3.9-1978), popularly known as FORTRAN 77, is the basis for this text. A new standard has recently been finalized and the version of FORTRAN—FORTRAN 90—specified by it has many new features. Thus at the end of each chapter and in Chapter 13 we describe some of these additions to the FORTRAN language.

FORTRAN is one of the most widely used programming languages for solving problems in science and engineering. This text emphasizes these applications in the examples and exercises. It contains more than 60 complete examples and over 250 exercises, both written and programming exercises, chosen from areas that are relevant to science and engineering students.

Although this book gives a complete presentation of FORTRAN 77, it is more than just a programming manual. It reflects our view that the main reason for learning a programming language is to use the computer to solve problems. The basic steps in program development are discussed and illustrated in the text: (1) problem analysis and specification, (2) algorithm development, (3) program coding, (4) program execution and testing, and (5) program maintenance. We also feel that an intelligent user of the computer must have some elementary understanding of the manner in which a computer operates, how it stores information, how it processes data, and what some of its capabilities and limitations are. For this reason the text also contains a brief sketch of the history of computers and a simple description of a computer system, including techniques for representing data and machine instructions in binary form.

The text also emphasizes the importance of good structure and style in programs. In addition to describing these concepts in general, it contains a large number of complete examples. Each of these consists of a description of the algorithm using pseudocode and/or flowcharts together with a program and sample run. These are intended to demonstrate good algorithm design and programming style. At the end of each chapter a Programming Pointers section summarizes the main points regarding structure and style as well as language features presented and some problems that beginning programmers may experience.

Like the first two editions, this text is intended for a first course in computing and assumes no previous experience with computers. It provides a comprehensive description of FORTRAN 77, and most of the material presented can be covered in a one-semester course. Each chapter progresses from the simpler features to the more complex ones; the more difficult material thus appears in the last sections of the chapters.

New to the Third Edition

Since publication of the first two editions, we have received a number of constructive comments and suggestions for improvements from instructors and students and we have incorporated many of these into the third edition. The significant changes in the new edition include the following:

- Topics have been rearranged so that concepts of structured programming and modular design (including functions and procedures) are introduced earlier and used throughout the text.
- Discussion of the basic control structures has been improved.
- The presentation of arrays has been simplified and expanded.
- More examples of an engineering and/or scientific nature have been added.
- Detailed consideration of the character type and string processing has been moved to a later chapter in the text.
- Special FORTRAN 90 sections at chapter ends and a new chapter describe the new features of FORTRAN 90.

Supplementary Materials

A number of supplementary materials are available from the publisher. These include the following:

- An instructor's manual containing lecture notes and transparency masters.
- A solutions manual.
- Data disks containing all the sample programs and data files used in the text.
- A disk containing all the exercises in the text.
- A test bank, both in printed form and on disk.

Acknowledgments

We express our sincere appreciation to all who helped in any way in the preparation of this text. We especially thank our erudite editor David Johnstone, whose professional competence has kept us on course, whose words of en-

LARRY NYHOFF
SANFORD LEESTMA
Department of Mathematics and Computer Science
Calvin College, Grand Rapids, Michigan

FORTRAN 77
for Engineers and
Scientists

THIRD EDITION

Macmillan Publishing Company
NEW YORK

Maxwell Macmillan Canada
TORONTO

Maxwell Macmillan International
NEW YORK   OXFORD   SINGAPORE   SYDNEY

Editor: David Johnstone
Production Supervisor: Ron Harris
Production Manager: Sandra Moore
Text Designer: Natasha Sylvester
Cover Designer: Natasha Sylvester

This book was set in CRT Times Roman by Waldman Graphics, printed
by Hawkins Printing Co., and bound by Hawkins Printing Co. The
cover was printed by Phoenix Color Corp.

Macmillan Publishing Company
866 Third Avenue, New York, New York 10022

Macmillan Publishing Company is part of the
Maxwell Communication Group of Companies.

Maxwell Macmillan Canada, Inc.
1200 Eglinton Avenue East
Suite 200
Don Mills, Ontario M3C 3N1

Library of Congress Cataloging-in-Publication Data

Nyhoff, Larry R.
    Fortran 77 for engineers and scientists / Larry Nyhoff, Sanford
Leestma.--3rd ed.
        p.   cm.
    Includes indexes.
    ISBN 0-02-388655-2
    1. FORTRAN 77 (Computer program language) I. Leestma,
Sanford. II. Title. III. Title: Fortran seventy seven for engineers
and scientists.
QA76.73.F25N9   1992
005.13'3--dc20
                                              90-28109
                                                CIP

Printing: 4 5 6 7 8   Year: 2 3 4 5 6 7 8 9 0 1

FORTRAN 77

**for Engineers
and Scientists**

couragement have kept us going, and whose friendship over the years has made textbook writing for Macmillan an enjoyable experience. We must also thank our punctilious production supervisor Ronald Harris, whose attention to details and deadlines has compensated for our lack thereof and whose encouraging words and kind admonitions (when needed) have prodded us to action; working without him is almost unthinkable. And we cannot fail to note the many hours spent by Sheryl Lanser in preparing the manuscript and computer disks, making corrections, proofreading, and doing a multitude of other tasks, always with patience and a cheerful spirit; we thank her so much for all that she has done. We also appreciate the preparation of engineering examples and exercises by Lawrence J. Genalo of Iowa State University for use in the last two editions and for reviewing these editions. The comments and suggestions made by the following reviewers of the second and third editions were also valuable, and their work is much appreciated: Susan M. Simons, Memphis State University; Robert D. Slonneger, West Virginia University; Thomas A. Lackey, Lawrence Institute of Technology; Paul Sand, University of New Hampshire; Asghar Bhatti, University of Iowa; Val Tareski, North Dakota State University; Bernhard Weinberg, Michigan State University; and Thomas D. L. Walker, Virginia Polytechnic Institute and State University. And, of course, we must once again pay homage to our wives Shar and Marge, whose love and understanding have kept us going through another year of textbook writing, and to our kids, Jeff and Dawn, Jim, Julie, Joan, Michelle and Paul, Sandy, and Michael, for not complaining about the times that their needs and wants were slighted by our busyness. Above all, we give thanks to God for giving us the opportunity, ability, and stamina to prepare another new edition of this text.

L. N.
S. L.

CONTENTS

1

Introduction and History

I wish these calculations had been executed by steam.

CHARLES BABBAGE

For, contrary to the unreasoned opinion of the ignorant, the choice of a system of numeration is a mere matter of convention.

BLAISE PASCAL

The modern electronic computer is one of the most important products of the twentieth century. It is an essential tool in many areas, including business, industry, government, science, and education; indeed, it has touched nearly every aspect of our lives. The impact of this twentieth-century information revolution brought about by the development of high-speed computing systems has been nearly as widespread as the impact of the nineteenth-century industrial revolution. This chapter summarizes the history of computer systems and briefly describes their components.

1.1 History of Computing Systems

There are two important concepts in the history of computation: the **mechanization of arithmetic** and the concept of a **stored program** for the automatic control of computations. We shall focus our attention on some of the devices that have implemented these concepts.

A variety of computational devices were used in ancient civilizations. One of the earliest, which might be considered a forerunner of the modern computer, is the **abacus** (Figure 1.1), which has movable beads strung on rods to count and make computations. Although its exact origin is unknown, the abacus was used by the Chinese perhaps three to four thousand years ago and is still used today.

1

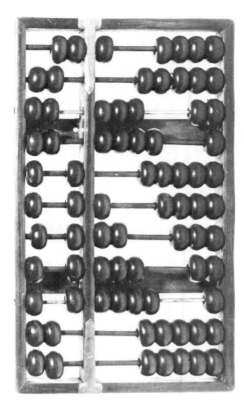

Figure 1.1 Abacus.

The ancient British stone monument **Stonehenge** (Figure 1.2a), located in southern England was built between 1900 and 1600 B.C. and evidently was an astronomical calculator used to predict the changes of the seasons. Five hundred years ago, the Inca Indians of South America used a system of knotted cords called **quipus** (Figure 1.2b) to count and record divisions of land among the various tribal groups. In Western Europe, **Napier's bones** (Figure 1.2c) and tables of **logarithms** were designed by the Scottish mathematician John Napier (1550–1617) to simplify calculations. These led to the invention of the **slide rule** (Figure 1.2d).

In 1642, the young French mathematician **Blaise Pascal** (1623–1662) invented one of the first mechanical adding machines (Figure 1.3). This device used a system of gears and wheels similar to that used in odometers and other modern counting devices. **Pascal's adder** could both add and subtract and was invented to calculate taxes. Pascal's announcement of his invention reveals the labor-saving motivation for its development:

> Dear reader, this notice will serve to inform you that I submit to the public a small machine of my invention, by means of which you alone may, without any effort, perform all the operations of arithmetic, and may be relieved of the work which has often times fatigued your spirit, when you have worked with the counters or with the pen. As for simplicity of movement of the operations, I have so devised it that, although the operations of arithmetic are in a way opposed the one to the other—as addition to subtraction, and multiplication to division—nevertheless they are all performed on this ma-

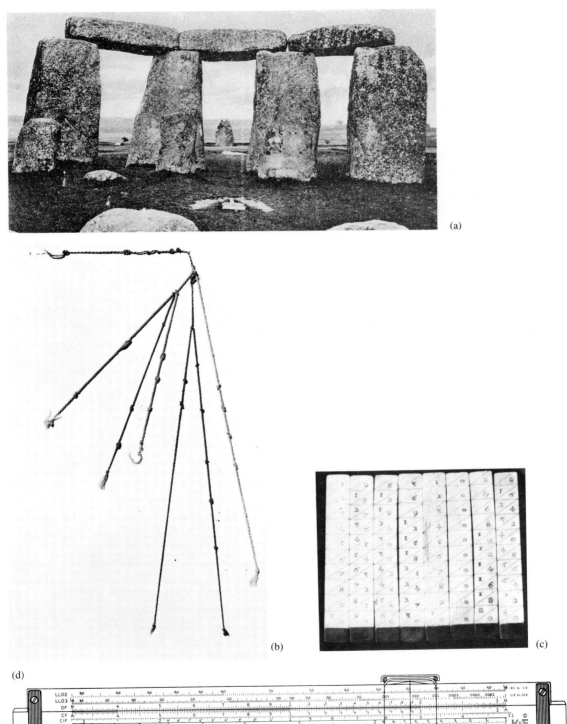

Figure 1.2 (a) Stonehenge. (b) Quipus. (Courtesy of the American Museum of Natural History) (c) Napier's bones. (Courtesy of the Smithsonian Institution.) (d) Slide rule.

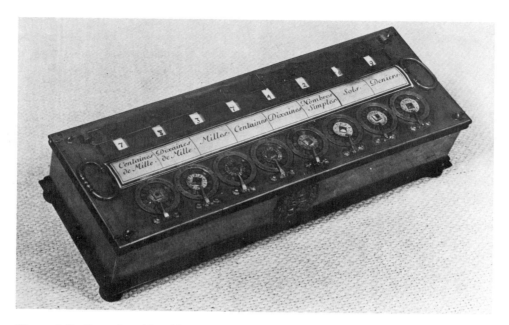

Figure 1.3   Pascal's adder. (Courtesy of IBM.)

chine by a single movement. The facility of this movement of operation is very evident since it is just as easy to move one thousand or ten thousand dials, all at one time, if one desires to make a single dial move, although all accomplish the movement perfectly. The most ignorant find as many advantages as the most experienced. The instrument makes up for ignorance and for lack of practice, and even without any effort of the operator, it makes possible shortcuts by itself, whenever the numbers are set down.

Although Pascal built more than fifty of his adding machines, his commercial venture failed because the devices could not be built with sufficient precision for practical use.

In the 1670s, the German mathematician **Gottfried Wilhelm von Leibniz** (1646–1716) produced a machine that was similar in design to Pascal's but somewhat more reliable and accurate (Figure 1.4). Leibniz's calculator could perform all four of the basic arithmetic operations: addition, subtraction, multiplication, and division.

A number of other mechanical calculators followed that further refined the designs of Pascal and Leibniz. By the end of the nineteenth century, these calculators had become important tools in science, business, and commerce.

As noted earlier, the second idea to emerge in the history of computing was the concept of a stored program to control the calculations. One early example of an automatically controlled device is the weaving loom (Figure 1.5) invented by the Frenchman **Joseph Marie Jacquard** (1752–1834). This automatic loom, introduced at a Paris exhibition in 1801, used metal cards punched with holes to position threads for the weaving process. A collection of these cards made up a program that directed the loom. Within a decade, eleven thousand of these machines were in use in French textile plants, resulting in

Figure 1.4 Leibniz's calculator. (Courtesy of IBM.)

what may have been the first incidence of unemployment caused by automation. Indeed, unemployed workers rioted and destroyed several of the new looms and cards. Jacquard wrote: ''The iron was sold for iron, the wood for wood, and I its inventor delivered up to public ignominy.'' The **Jacquard loom** is still used today, although modern versions are controlled by programs stored on magnetic tape rather than punched cards.

Figure 1.5 Jacquard loom. (Courtesy of IBM.)

These two concepts, mechanized calculation and stored program control, were combined by the English mathematician **Charles Babbage** (1792–1871), who began work in 1822 on a machine that he called the **Difference Engine** (Figure 1.6a). This machine was designed to compute polynomials for the preparation of mathematical tables. Babbage continued his work until 1833 with support from the British government, which was interested in possible military applications of the Difference Engine. But Babbage later abandoned this project, because the metal-working technology of that time was not sufficiently advanced to manufacture the required precision gears and linkages. Babbage was not discouraged, however, but designed a more sophisticated machine that he called his **Analytical Engine** (Figure 1.6b). This machine had several special-purpose components that were intended to work together. The "mill" was supposed to carry out the arithmetic computations; the "store" was the machine's memory for storing data and intermediate results; and other components were designed for the input and output of information and for the transfer of information between components. The operation of this machine was to be fully automatic, controlled by punched cards, an idea based on Jacquard's earlier work. In fact, as Babbage himself observed: "The analogy of the Analytical Engine with this well-known process is nearly perfect." **Ada Augusta,** Lord George Byron's daughter and the countess of Lovelace, understood how the device was to work and supported Babbage. Considered by some to be the first programmer, Lady Lovelace described the similarity of Jacquard's and Babbage's inventions: "The Analytical Engine weaves algebraic patterns just as the Jacquard loom weaves flowers and leaves." Although Babbage's machine was not built during his lifetime, it is nevertheless part of the history of computing because many of the concepts of its design are used in modern computers.

A related development in the United States was the census bureau's use of punched-card systems to help compile the 1890 census (Figure 1.7). These systems, designed by **Herman Hollerith,** a young mathematician employed by the bureau, used electrical sensors to interpret the information stored on the punched cards. In 1896, Hollerith left the census bureau and formed his own tabulating company, which in 1924 became the International Business Machines Corporation (IBM).

The development of computing devices continued at a rapid pace in the United States. Some of the pioneers in this effort were Howard Aiken, John Atanasoff, J. P. Eckert, J. W. Mauchly, and John von Neumann. Repeating much of the work of Babbage, Aiken designed a system consisting of several mechanical calculators working together. This work, which was supported by IBM, led to the invention in 1944 of the electromechanical **Mark I** computer (Figure 1.8). This machine is the best-known computer built before 1945 and may be regarded as the first realization of Babbage's Analytical Engine.

The first fully electronic computer was developed by **John Atanasoff** at Iowa State University. With the help of his assistant, **Clifford Berry,** he built a prototype in 1939 and completed the first working model in 1942 (Figure 1.9a). The best known of the early electronic computers was the **ENIAC** (Electronic Numerical Integrator and Computer), constructed in 1946 by J. P. Eckert and J. W. Mauchly at the Moore School of Electrical Engineering of the University of Pennsylvania (Figure 1.9b). This extremely large machine contained

(a)

(b)

Figure 1.6 (a) Babbage's Difference Engine. (b) Babbage's Analytical Engine. (Courtesy of IBM.)

Figure 1.7 Hollerith equipment. (Courtesy of IBM.)

Figure 1.8 Mark I. (Courtesy of IBM.)

(a)

(b)

Figure 1.9 (a) Atanasoff-Berry computer. (Courtesy of Iowa State University.) (b) ENIAC. (Courtesy of Sperry Corporation.)

over 18,000 vacuum tubes and 1500 relays and nearly filled a room 20 feet by 40 feet in size. It could multiply numbers approximately one thousand times faster than the Mark I could, though it was quite limited in its applications and was used primarily by the Army Ordnance Department to calculate firing tables and trajectories for various types of shells. Eckert and Mauchly later left the University of Pennsylvania to form the Eckert-Mauchly Computer Corporation, which built the **UNIVAC** (Universal Automatic Computer), the first commercially available computer designed for both scientific and business applications. The first UNIVAC was sold to the census bureau in 1951.

The instructions, or program, that controlled the ENIAC's operation were entered into the machine by rewiring some parts of the computer's circuits. This complicated process was very time-consuming, sometimes taking several people several days, and during this time, the computer was idle. In other early computers, the instructions were stored outside the machine on punched cards or some other medium and were transferred into the machine one at a time for interpretation and execution. A new scheme, developed by Princeton mathematician John von Neumann and others, used internally stored commands. The advantages of this stored program concept are that internally stored instructions can be processed more rapidly and, more important, that they can be modified by the computer itself while computations are taking place. The stored program concept makes possible the general-purpose computers so commonplace today.

The actual physical components used in constructing a computer system are its **hardware.** Several generations of computers can be identified by the type of hardware used. The ENIAC and UNIVAC are examples of **first-generation** computers, which are characterized by their extensive use of vacuum tubes. Advances in electronics brought changes in computing systems, and in 1958, IBM introduced the first of the **second-generation** computers, the IBM 7090. These computers were built between 1959 and 1965 and used transistors in place of vacuum tubes. Consequently, these computers were smaller and less expensive, required less power, generated far less heat, and were more reliable than their predecessors. The **third-generation** computers that followed used integrated circuits and introduced new techniques for better system utilization, such as multiprogramming and time-sharing. The IBM System/360 introduced in 1964 is commonly accepted as the first of this generation of computers. Computers of the 1980s, commonly called **fourth-generation** computers, use very large-scale integrated circuits (VLSI) on silicon chips and other microelectronic advances to shrink their size and cost still more while enlarging their capability. A typical memory chip is equivalent to many thousands of transistors, is smaller than a baby's fingernail, weighs a small fraction of an ounce, requires only a trickle of power, and costs but a few dollars. Such miniaturization has made possible the development of the personal computers so popular today (Figure 1.10). One of the pioneers in the development of transistors, Robert Noyce, contrasted the microcomputers of the 1970s with the ENIAC:

> An individual integrated circuit on a chip perhaps a quarter of an inch square now can embrace more electronic elements than the most complex piece of electronic equipment that could be built in 1950. Today's microcomputer, at a cost of perhaps $300, has more computing capacity than the first electronic computer, ENIAC. It is twenty times faster, has a larger memory, consumes the power of a light bulb rather than that of a locomotive, occupies 1/30,000

Figure 1.10
A modern personal computer.
(Courtesy of IBM.)

the volume and costs 1/10,000 as much. It is available by mail order or at your local hobby shop.

Someone else noted that if progress in the automotive industry had been as rapid as in computer technology since 1960, today's automobile would have an engine that is less than 0.1 inch in length, would get 120,000 miles to a gallon of gas, have a top speed of 240,000 miles per hour, and would cost $4.00.

The stored program concept was a significant improvement over manual programming methods, but early computers were still difficult to use because of the complex coding schemes required for the representation of programs and data. Consequently, in addition to improved hardware, computer manufacturers began to develop collections of programs known as **system software,** which make computers easier to use. One of the more important advances in this area was the development of **high-level languages,** which allow users to write programs in a language similar to natural language. A program written in a high-level language is known as a **source program.** For most high-level languages, the instructions that make up a source program must be translated into **machine language,** that is, the language used directly by a particular computer in all its calculations and processing. This machine language program is called an **object program.** The programs that translate source programs into object programs are called **compilers.** Another part of the system software, the **operating system,** controls the translation of the source program, allocates storage for the program and data, and carries out many other supervisory functions. In particular, it acts as an interface between the user and the machine. The operating system interprets commands given by the user and then directs the appropriate system software and hardware to carry them out.

One of the first high-level languages to gain widespread acceptance was **FORTRAN** (**FOR**mula **TRAN**slation), which was developed for the IBM 704 computer by **John Backus** and a team of thirteen other programmers at IBM over a three-year period (1954–1957). The group's first report on the completed language included the following comments:

> The programmer attended a one-day course on FORTRAN and spent some more time referring to the manual. He then programmed the job in four hours, using 47 FORTRAN statements. These were compiled by the 704 in six minutes, producing about 1000 instructions. He ran the program and found the output incorrect. He studied the output and was able to localize his error in a FORTRAN statement he had written. He rewrote the offending statement, recompiled, and found that the resulting program was correct. He estimated that it might have taken three days to code the job by hand, plus an unknown time to debug it, and that no appreciable increase in speed of execution would have been achieved thereby.

As computer hardware improved, the FORTRAN language also was refined and extended. By 1962 it had undergone its fourth revision, and in 1977 there appeared the fifth revision, known as FORTRAN 77. More recently, an extensive revision known as FORTRAN 90 has been prepared and approved, and compilers to support this new version of FORTRAN are being developed. The American National Standards Institute (ANSI), which establishes standards for programming languages, has decided that there will be two American standards for FORTRAN, FORTRAN 77 and FORTRAN 90, while International Standards Organization (ISO) groups have decided that FORTRAN 90 will be the only international FORTRAN standard. Many other high-level languages have also been developed—BASIC, COBOL, Pascal, Modula-2, C, and Ada, to name but a few. As with FORTRAN, there has been a considerable effort to standardize several of these languages so that programs written in a higher-level language are "portable," that is, so that they can be processed on several different machines with little or no alteration.

In summary, the history of computation and computational aids began several thousands of years ago, and in some cases, the theory underlying such devices progressed much more rapidly than did the technical skills required to produce working models. Although the modern electronic computer with its mechanized calculation and automatic program control has its roots in the mid-nineteenth-century work of Charles Babbage, the electronic computer is a fairly recent development. The rapid changes that have marked its progression since its inception in 1945 can be expected to continue into the future.

1.2 Computing Systems

In our discussion of the history of computing, we noted that Babbage designed his Analytical Engine as a system of several separate components, each with its own function. This general scheme was incorporated in many later computers and is, in fact, a common feature of most modern computers. In this section we briefly describe the major components of a modern computing system.

The heart of any computing system is its **central processing unit,** or **CPU.** The CPU controls the operation of the entire system, performs the arithmetic and logic operations, and stores and retrieves instructions and data. The instructions and data are stored in a high-speed **memory unit**, and the **control unit** fetches these instructions from memory, decodes them, and directs the system to execute the operations indicated by the instructions. Those operations that are arithmetical or logical in nature are carried out using special registers and circuits of the **arithmetic–logic unit (ALU)** of the CPU.

The memory unit is called the **internal** or **main** or **primary memory** of the computer system. It is used to store the instructions and data of the programs being executed. Most computing systems also contain components that serve as **external** or **auxiliary** or **secondary memory.** Common forms of this type of memory are magnetic disks and magnetic tapes. These **peripheral devices** provide long-term storage for large collections of information. The rate of transfer of information to and from them is considerably slower than that for internal memory.

Other peripherals are used to transmit instructions, data, and computed results between the user and the CPU. These are the **input/output devices**, which have a variety of forms, such as terminals, scanners, voice input devices, printers, and plotters. Their function is to convert information from an external form understandable to the user to a form that can be processed by the computer system, and vice versa.

Figure 1.11 shows the relationship between these components in a computer system. The arrows indicate how information flows through the system.

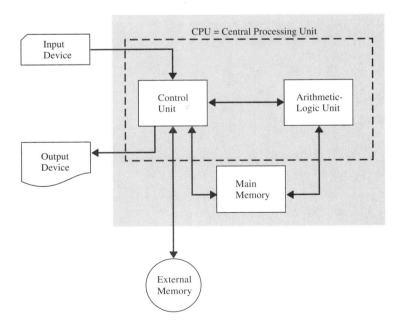

Figure 1.11 Major components of a computing system.

1.3 Internal Representation

The devices that comprise the memory unit of a computer are two-state devices. If one of the states is interpreted as 0 and the other as 1, then it is natural to use a **binary scheme,** using only the two binary digits (**bits**) 0 and 1 to represent information in a computer. These two-state devices are organized into groups called **bytes,** each of which contains a fixed number of these devices, usually eight, and thus can store a fixed number of bits. Memory is commonly measured in bytes, and a block of $2^{10} = 1024$ bytes is called **1K** of memory. Thus, a 512K memory usually refers to a memory that consists of $512 \times 2^{10} = 2^9 \times 2^{10} = 2^{19} = 524,288$ bytes, or, equivalently, $2^{19} \times 2^3 = 2^{22} = 4,194,304$ bits (1 byte = 8 bits).

A larger grouping of bits and bytes is into **words.** Word sizes vary with computers, but common sizes are 16 bits (= 2 bytes) and 32 bits (= 4 bytes). Each word or byte is identified by an **address** and can be directly accessed using this address. This makes it possible to store information in a specific memory location and then to retrieve it later. To understand how this is done, we must first examine the binary number system.

The number system that we are accustomed to using is a decimal or **base-10** number system, which uses the digits 0, 1, 2, 3, 4, 5, 6, 7, 8, and 9. The significance of these digits in a numeral depends on the positions that they occupy in that numeral. For example, in the numeral

$$485$$

the digit 4 is interpreted as

$$4 \text{ hundreds}$$

and the digit 8 as

$$8 \text{ tens}$$

and the digit 5 as

$$5 \text{ ones}$$

Thus, the numeral 485 represents the number four-hundred eighty-five and can be written in **expanded form** as

$$(4 \times 100) + (8 \times 10) + (5 \times 1)$$

or

$$(4 \times 10^2) + (8 \times 10^1) + (5 \times 10^0)$$

The digits that appear in the various positions of a decimal (base-10) numeral thus represent coefficients of powers of 10.

Similar positional number systems can be devised using numbers other than 10 as a base. The **binary** number system uses 2 as the base and has only two digits, 0 and 1. As in a decimal system, the significance of the bits in a binary numeral is determined by their positions in that numeral. For example, the binary numeral

$$101$$

can be written in expanded form (using decimal notation) as

$$(1 \times 2^2) + (0 \times 2^1) + (1 \times 2^0)$$

that is, the binary numeral 101 has the decimal value

$$4 + 0 + 1 = 5$$

Similarly, the binary numeral 111010 has the decimal value

$$(1 \times 2^5) + (1 \times 2^4) + (1 \times 2^3) + (0 \times 2^2) + (1 \times 2^1) + (0 \times 2^0)$$
$$= 32 + 16 + 8 + 2$$
$$= 58$$

When necessary, to avoid confusion about which base is being used, it is customary to write the base as a subscript for nondecimal numerals. Using this convention, we could indicate that 5 and 58 have the binary representations just given by writing

$$5 = 101_2$$

and

$$58 = 111010_2$$

Two other nondecimal numeration systems are important in the consideration of computer systems: **octal** and **hexadecimal.** The octal system is a base-8 system and uses the eight digits 0, 1, 2, 3, 4, 5, 6, and 7. In an octal numeral such as

$$1703_8$$

the digits represent coefficients of powers of 8; this numeral is, therefore, an abbreviation for the expanded form

$$(1 \times 8^3) + (7 \times 8^2) + (0 \times 8^1) + (3 \times 8^0)$$

and thus has the decimal value

$$512 + 448 + 0 + 3 = 963$$

A hexadecimal system uses a base of 16 and the digits 0, 1, 2, 3, 4, 5, 6, 7, 8, 9, A (10), B (11), C (12), D (13), E (14), and F (15). The hexadecimal numeral

$$5E4_{16}$$

has the expanded form

$$(5 \times 16^2) + (14 \times 16^1) + (4 \times 16^0)$$

TABLE 1.1

Decimal	Binary	Octal	Hexadecimal
0	0	0	0
1	1	1	1
2	10	2	2
3	11	3	3
4	100	4	4
5	101	5	5
6	110	6	6
7	111	7	7
8	1000	10	8
9	1001	11	9
10	1010	12	A
11	1011	13	B
12	1100	14	C
13	1101	15	D
14	1110	16	E
15	1111	17	F
16	10000	20	10
17	10001	21	11
18	10010	22	12
19	10011	23	13
20	10100	24	14
21	10101	25	15
22	10110	26	16
23	10111	27	17
24	11000	30	18
25	11001	31	19
26	11010	32	1A
27	11011	33	1B
28	11100	34	1C
29	11101	35	1D
30	11110	36	1E
31	11111	37	1F

which has the decimal value

$$1280 + 224 + 4 = 1508$$

Table 1.1 displays the decimal, binary, octal, and hexadecimal representations for the first 31 nonnegative integers.

When an integer value such as 5 or 58 must be stored in the computer's memory, the binary representation of that value is typically stored in one memory word. To illustrate, consider a computer whose word size is sixteen, and suppose that the integer value 58 is to be stored. A memory word is selected, and a sequence of sixteen bits formed from the binary representation 111010 of 58 is stored there:

Memory

| 0 | 0 | 0 | 0 | 0 | 0 | 0 | 0 | 0 | 0 | 1 | 1 | 1 | 0 | 1 | 0 |

Negative integers must also be stored in a binary form in which the sign of the integer is part of the representation. There are several ways that this can be done, but one of the most common is the **two's complement** representation. In this scheme, positive integers are represented in binary form as just described, with the leftmost bit set to 0 to indicate that the value is positive. The representation of a negative integer $-n$ is obtained by first finding the binary representation of n, complementing it, that is, changing each 0 to 1 and each 1 to 0, and then adding 1 to the result. For example, the two's complement representation of -58 using a string of sixteen bits is obtained as follows:

1. Represent 58 by a 16-bit binary numeral:

$$0000000000111010$$

2. Complement this bit string:

$$1111111111000101$$

3. Add 1:

$$1111111111000110$$

Note that the leftmost bit in this two's complement representation of a negative integer will always be 1, indicating that the number is negative.

The fixed word size limits the range of the integers that can be stored internally. For example, the largest positive integer that can be stored in a 16-bit word is

$$0111111111111111_2 = 2^{15} - 1 = 32767$$

and the smallest negative integer is

$$1000000000000000_2 = -2^{15} = -32768$$

The range of integers that can be represented using a 32-bit word is

$$10000000000000000000000000000000_2 = -2^{31} = -2147483648$$

through

$$01111111111111111111111111111111_2 = 2^{31} - 1 = 2147483647$$

Representation of an integer outside the allowed range would require more bits than can be stored in a single word, a phenomenon known as **overflow.** This limitation may be partially overcome by using more than one word to store an integer. Although this technique enlarges the range of integers that can be stored exactly, it does not resolve the problem of overflow; the range of representable integers is still finite.

Numbers that contain decimal points are called **real numbers** or **floating point numbers.** In the decimal representation of such numbers, each digit is the coefficient of some power of 10. Digits to the left of the decimal point are coefficients of nonnegative powers of 10, and those to the right are coefficients of negative powers of 10. For example, the decimal numeral 56.317 can be written in expanded form as

$$(5 \times 10^1) + (6 \times 10^0) + (3 \times 10^{-1}) + (1 \times 10^{-2}) + (7 \times 10^{-3})$$

or, equivalently, as

$$(5 \times 10) + (6 \times 1) + \left(3 \times \frac{1}{10}\right) + \left(1 \times \frac{1}{100}\right) + \left(7 \times \frac{1}{1000}\right)$$

Digits in the binary representation of a real number are coefficients of powers of two. Those to the left of the **binary point** are coefficients of non-negative powers of two, and those to the right are coefficients of negative powers of two. For example, the expanded form of 110.101 is

$$(1 \times 2^2) + (1 \times 2^1) + (0 \times 2^0) + (1 \times 2^{-1})$$
$$+ (0 \times 2^{-2}) + (1 \times 2^{-3})$$

and thus has the decimal value

$$4 + 2 + 0 + \frac{1}{2} + 0 + \frac{1}{8} = 6.625$$

There is some variation in the schemes used for storing real numbers in computer memory, but one common method is the following. The binary representation

$$110.101_2$$

of the real number 6.625 can be written equivalently as

$$0.110101_2 \times 2^3$$

Typically, one part of a memory word (or words) is used to store a fixed number of bits of the **mantissa** or **fractional part** 0.110101_2, and another part to store the **exponent** $3 = 11_2$. For example, if the leftmost eleven bits in a 16-bit word are used for the mantissa and the remaining five bits for the exponent, 6.625 could be stored as

$$\boxed{0\,|\,1\,|\,1\,|\,0\,|\,1\,|\,0\,|\,1\,|\,0\,|\,0\,|\,0\,|\,0\,|\,0\,|\,0\,|\,0\,|\,1\,|\,1}$$

mantissa   exponent

where the first bit in each part is reserved for the sign.

Because the binary representation of the exponent may require more than the available number of bits, we see that the overflow problem discussed in connection with the integer representation may also occur when storing a real number. Also, there obviously are some real numbers whose mantissas have more than the allotted number of bits; consequently, some of these bits will be lost when storing such numbers. In fact, most real numbers do not have finite binary representations and thus cannot be stored exactly in any computer. For example, the binary representation of the real number 0.7 is

$$(0.10110011001100110\ldots)_2$$

where the block 0110 is repeated indefinitely. If only the first eleven bits are stored and all remaining bits are truncated, then the stored representation of 0.7 is

$$0.10110011000_2$$

which has the decimal value 0.69921875. If the binary representation is rounded to eleven bits, then the stored representation for 0.7 is

$$0.10110011001_2$$

which has the decimal value 0.700195312. In either case, the stored value is not exactly 0.7. This error, called **roundoff error**, can be reduced, but not eliminated, by using a larger number of bits to store the binary representation of real numbers.

Computers store and process not only numeric data but also boolean or logical data (false or true), character data, and other types of nonnumeric information. Storing logical values is easy; false can be encoded as 0, true as 1, and these bits stored. The schemes used for the internal representation of character data are based on the assignment of a numeric code to each of the char-

TABLE 1.2   Character Codes

	ASCII		EBCDIC	
Character	**Decimal**	**Binary**	**Decimal**	**Binary**
A	65	01000001	193	11000001
B	66	01000010	194	11000010
C	67	01000011	195	11000011
D	68	01000100	196	11000100
E	69	01000101	197	11000101
F	70	01000110	198	11000110
G	71	01000111	199	11000111
H	72	01001000	200	11001000
I	73	01001001	201	11001001
J	74	01001010	209	11010001
K	75	01001011	210	11010010
L	76	01001100	211	11010011
M	77	01001101	212	11010100
N	78	01001110	213	11010101
O	79	01001111	214	11010110
P	80	01010000	215	11010111
Q	81	01010001	216	11011000
R	82	01010010	217	11011001
S	83	01010011	226	11100010
T	84	01010100	227	11100011
U	85	01010101	228	11100100
V	86	01010110	229	11100101
W	87	01010111	230	11100110
X	88	01011000	231	11100111
Y	89	01011001	232	11101000
Z	90	01011010	233	11101001

acters in the character set. Several standard coding schemes have been developed, such as **ASCII** (American Standard Code for Information Interchange) and **EBCDIC** (Extended Binary Coded Decimal Interchange Code). Table 1.2 shows these codes for capital letters. A complete table of ASCII and EBCDIC codes for all characters is given in Appendix A.

Characters are represented internally using these binary codes. A byte consisting of eight bits can thus store the binary representation of one character, and a 16-bit word consisting of two bytes can store two characters. For example, the character string HI can be stored in a single 16-bit word with the code for H in the left byte and the code for I in the right byte; with ASCII code, the result would be as follows:

$$\boxed{0}\boxed{1}\boxed{0}\boxed{0}\boxed{1}\boxed{0}\boxed{0}\boxed{0}\boxed{0}\boxed{1}\boxed{0}\boxed{0}\boxed{1}\boxed{0}\boxed{0}\boxed{1}$$

$$\underbrace{\qquad}_{H} \quad \underbrace{\qquad}_{I}$$

Memory words of size 32 (bits) are usually divided into four bytes and thus can store four characters. Character strings of a length greater than the number of bytes in a word are usually stored in two or more consecutive memory words.

We have now seen how various types of data can be stored in a computer's memory. Program instructions for processing data must also be stored in memory. As an example, suppose that three values $8 = 1000_2$, $24 = 11000_2$, and $58 = 111010_2$ have been stored in memory locations with addresses 4, 5, and 6 and that we want to multiply the first two values, add the third, and store the result in memory word 7.

Address	Memory	
0		
1		
2		
3		
4	0000000000001000	← 8
5	0000000000011000	← 24
6	0000000000111010	← 58
7		← Result

To perform this computation, the following instructions must be executed:

1. Fetch the contents of memory word 4 and load it into the accumulator register of the ALU.
2. Fetch the contents of memory word 5 and compute the product of this value and the value in the accumulator.
3. Fetch the contents of memory word 6 and add this value to the value in the accumulator.
4. Store the contents of the accumulator in memory word 7.

In order to store these instructions in computer memory, they must be represented in binary form. The addresses of the data value present no problem, as they can easily be converted to binary addresses:

$$4 = 100_2$$
$$5 = 101_2$$
$$6 = 110_2$$
$$7 = 111_2$$

The operations load, multiply, add, store, and other basic machine instructions are represented by numeric codes, called **opcodes;** for example,

$$LOAD = 16 = 10000_2$$
$$STORE = 17 = 10001_2$$
$$ADD = 35 = 100011_2$$
$$MULTIPLY = 36 = 100100_2$$

Using part of a word to store the opcode and another part for the address of the **operand,** we could represent our sequence of instructions in **machine language** as

1. 0001000000000100
2. 0010010000000101
3. 0010001100000110
4. 0001000100000111

   opcode   operand

These instructions can then be stored in four (consecutive) memory words. When the program is executed, the control unit will fetch each of these instructions, decode it to determine the operation and the address of the operand, fetch the operand, and then perform the required operation, using the ALU if necessary.

Programs for early computers had to be written in such machine language. Later it became possible to write programs in **assembly language,** which uses mnemonics (names) in place of numeric opcodes and variable names in place of numeric addresses. For example, the preceding sequence of instructions might be written in assembly language as

1. LOAD A
2. MULT B
3. ADD C
4. STORE X

An **assembler,** part of the system software, translates such assembly language instructions into machine language.

Today, most programs are written in a high-level language such as FORTRAN, and a **compiler** translates each statement in this program into a sequence of basic machine (or assembly) language instructions.

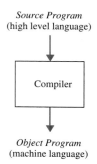

Source Program
(high level language)

Compiler

Object Program
(machine language)

For example, for the preceding problem, the programmer could write the FORTRAN statement

$$X = A * B + C$$

which instructs the computer to multiply the values of A and B, add the value of C, and assign the value to X. The compiler would then translate this statement into the sequence of four machine (or assembly) language instructions considered earlier.

As the preceding diagram indicates, a compiler translates the entire source program into an equivalent object program consisting of machine language instructions. After this translation is complete, this object program is executed by the computer. Some languages are processed using an **interpreter** rather than a compiler. An interpreter also examines a source program statement by statement. However, after each statement is translated, the resulting machine language instructions are immediately executed before the next statement is examined; no object program is actually produced. Still another approach is to compile the source program into simple machine-independent language called **intermediate code.** The resulting program may be either interpreted or compiled. In any case, the original source program in a high-level language must be translated into strings of 0s and 1s that represent machine instructions.

Exercises

1. Describe the importance of each of the following persons to the history of computing:

   (a) Charles Babbage   (b) Blaise Pascal
   (c) John von Neumann   (d) Herman Hollerith
   (e) Joseph Jacquard   (f) Gottfried Wilhelm von Leibniz
   (g) John Atanasoff

2. Describe the importance of each of the following devices to the history of computing:

   (a) ENIAC   (b) Analytical Engine
   (c) Jacquard loom   (d) UNIVAC
   (e) Mark I

3. Distinguish the four different generations of computers.

4. Briefly define each of the following terms:

(a) stored program concept	**(b)** FORTRAN
(c) Pascal	**(d)** CPU
(e) ALU	**(f)** peripheral devices
(g) bit	**(h)** byte
(i) word	**(j)** overflow
(k) roundoff error	**(l)** ASCII
(m) EBCDIC	**(n)** source program
(o) object program	**(p)** compiler
(q) assembler	**(r)** assembly language
(s) machine language	

5. Convert each of the following unsigned binary numerals to base 10:

(a) 1001	**(b)** 110010
(c) 1000000	**(d)** 111111111111111 (fifteen 1's)
(e) 1.1	**(f)** 1010.10101

6. Convert each of the following octal numerals to base 10:

(a) 123	**(b)** 2705	**(c)** 10000
(d) 77777	**(e)** 7.2	**(f)** 123.45

7. Convert each of the following hexadecimal numerals to base 10:

(a) 12	**(b)** 1AB	**(c)** ABC
(d) FFF	**(e)** 8.C	**(f)** AB.CD

8. Conversion from octal representation (see Exercise 6) to binary representation is easy, as we need only replace each octal digit with its three-bit binary equivalent. For example, to convert 617_8 to binary, replace 6 with 110, 1 with 001, and 7 with 111, to obtain 110001111_2. Convert each of the octal numerals in Exercise 6 to binary numerals.

9. Imitating the conversion scheme in Exercise 8, convert each of the hexadecimal numerals in Exercise 7 to binary numerals.

10. To convert a binary numeral to octal, place the digits in groups of three, starting from the binary point—or from the right end if there is no binary point—and replace each group with the corresponding octal digit. For example, $10101111_2 = 010\ 101\ 111_2 = 257_8$. Convert each of the binary numerals in Exercise 5 to octal numerals.

11. Imitating the conversion scheme in Exercise 10, convert each of the binary numerals in Exercise 5 to hexadecimal numerals.

12. One method for finding the **base-b** representation of a whole number given in base-10 notation is to divide the number repeatedly by b until a quotient of zero results. The successive remainders are the digits from right to left of the base-b representation. For example, the binary representation of 26 is 11010_2, as the following computation shows:

$$
\begin{array}{r}
0 \ \text{R} \ 1 \\
2\overline{)1} \ \text{R} \ 1 \\
2\overline{)3} \ \text{R} \ 0 \\
2\overline{)6} \ \text{R} \ 1 \\
2\overline{)13} \ \text{R} \ 0 \\
2\overline{)26}
\end{array}
$$

Convert each of the following base-10 numerals to (i) binary, (ii) octal, (iii) hexadecimal:

(a) 27   (b) 99   (c) 314   (d) 5280

13. To convert a decimal fraction to its base-b equivalent, repeatedly multiply the fractional part of the number by b. The integer parts are the digits from left to right of the base-b representation. For example, the decimal numeral 0.6875 corresponds to the binary numeral 0.1011_2, as the following computation shows:

$$
\begin{array}{r|l}
 & .6875 \\
 & \times \quad 2 \\
\hline
1 & .375 \\
 & \times \ 2 \\
\hline
0 & .75 \\
 & \times 2 \\
\hline
1 & .5 \\
 & \times 2 \\
\hline
1 & .0
\end{array}
$$

Convert the following base-10 numerals to (i) binary, (ii) octal, (iii) hexadecimal:

(a) 0.5   (b) 0.25   (c) 0.625
(d) 16.0625   (e) 8.828125

14. Even though the base-10 representation of a fraction may terminate, its representation in some other base need not terminate. For example, the following computation shows that the binary representation of 0.7 is $(0.1011001100110011001100110 \ldots)_2$, where the block of bits 0110 is repeated indefinitely. This representation is commonly written as $0.1\overline{0110}_2$.

$$
\begin{array}{r|l}
 & .7 \\
 & \times \ 2 \\
\hline
1 & .4 \leftarrow \\
 & \times \ 2 \\
\hline
0 & .8 \\
 & \times \ 2 \\
\hline
1 & .6 \\
 & \times \ 2 \\
\hline
1 & .2 \\
 & \times \ 2 \\
\hline
0 & .4
\end{array}
$$

Convert the following base-10 numerals to (i) binary, (ii) octal, (iii) hexadecimal:

(a) 0.3   **(b)** 0.6   **(c)** 0.05   **(d)** $0.\overline{3} = 0.33333 \ldots = 1/3$

15. Find the decimal value of each of the following 16-bit integers, assuming a two's complement representation:

(a) 0000000001000000   **(b)** 1111111111111110
(c) 1111111110111111   **(d)** 0000000011111111
(e) 1111111100000000   **(f)** 1000000000000001

16. Find the 16-bit two's complement representation for each of the following integers:

(a) 255   **(b)** 1K
(c) -255 **(d)** -256
(e) -34567_8 **(f)** $-3ABC_{16}$

17. Assuming two's complement representation, what range of integers can be represented in 8-bit words?

18. Assuming an 11-bit mantissa and a 5-bit exponent, as described in the text, and assuming that two's complement representation is used for each, indicate how each of the following real numbers would be stored in a 16-bit word if extra bits in the mantissa are (i) truncated or (ii) rounded:

(a) 0.375   **(b)** 37.375
(c) 0.03125   **(d)** 63.84375
(e) 0.1   **(f)** 0.01

19. Using the tables for ASCII and EBCDIC in Appendix A, indicate how each of the following character strings would be stored in 2-byte words using (i) ASCII or (ii) EBCDIC:

(a) TO   **(b)** FOUR   **(c)** AMOUNT
(d) ETC.   **(e)** J. DOE   **(f)** A#*4−C

20. Using the instruction mnemonics and opcodes given in the text, write a sequence of (a) assembly language and (b) machine language instructions equivalent to the FORTRAN statement

$$X = (A + B) * C$$

For the machine language instructions, assume that the values of A, B, and C are stored in memory words 15, 16, and 17, respectively, and the value of X is to be stored in memory word 23.

21. Repeat Exercise 20 for the FORTRAN statement

$$X = (A + B) * (C + D)$$

assuming that the value of D is stored in memory word 18.

2 Program Development

People always get what they ask for; the only trouble is that they never know, until they get it, what it actually is that they have asked for.

ALDOUS HUXLEY

The main reason that people learn programming languages is to use the computer as a problem-solving tool. At least four steps can be identified in the computer-aided problem-solving process:

1. Problem analysis and specification.
2. Algorithm development.
3. Program coding.
4. Program execution and testing.

In this chapter we describe and illustrate each of these steps. In the last section, we discuss one additional step that is particularly important in the **life cycle** of programs developed in real-world applications:

5. Program maintenance.

2.1 Problem Analysis and Specification

Because the initial description of a problem may be somewhat vague and imprecise, the first step in the problem-solving process is to review the problem carefully in order to determine its **input**—what information is given and which items are important in solving the problem—and its **output**—what information must be produced to solve the problem. Input and output are the two major parts of the problem's **specification**, and for a problem that appears in a programming text, they are usually not too difficult to identify. In a real-world problem encountered by a professional programmer, however, the specification of the problem often includes other items, such as those described in Section

2.5, and considerable effort may be required to formulate it completely. In this section we illustrate this first step of the problem-solving process with three simple examples.

PROBLEM 1: Radioactive Decay. John Doe is a nuclear physicist at Dispatch University and is conducting research with the radioactive element polonium. The half-life of polonium is 140 days; that is, the amount of polonium that remains after 140 days is one half of the original amount. John would like to know how much polonium will remain after running his experiment for 180 days if 10 milligrams are present initially.

Identifying the input and output of this problem is easy:

Input	Output
Initial amount: 10 mg	Amount remaining
Half-life: 140 days	
Time period: 180 days	

The other given items of information—the physicist's name, the name of the university, the name of the particular radioactive element—are not relevant (at least not to this problem) and so can be ignored.

Determining the residual amount of polonium can be done by hand or by using a calculator and does not warrant the development of a computer program for its solution. A program written to solve this particular problem would probably be used just once; because if the experiment runs longer, or if there is a different initial amount, or if a radioactive element with a different half-life is used, we have a new problem requiring the development of a new program. This is obviously a waste of effort, since it is clear that each such problem is a special case of the more general problem of finding the residual amount of a radioactive element at any time, given any initial amount and the half-life for that element. Thus a program that solves the general problem can be used in a variety of situations and is consequently more useful than is one designed for solving only the original special problem.

One important aspect of problem analysis, therefore, is **generalization.** The effort involved in later phases of the problem-solving process demands that the program eventually developed be sufficiently flexible, that it solve not only the given specific problem but also related problems of the same kind with little, if any, modification required. In this example, therefore, the specification of the problem would be better formulated in general terms:

Input	Output
Initial amount	Amount remaining
Half-life	
Time period	

PROBLEM 2: Pollution Indices. The level of air pollution in the city of Dogpatch is measured by a pollution index. Readings are made at 12:00 P.M. at three locations: the Abner Coal Plant, downtown at the corner of Daisy

Avenue and 5th Street, and at a randomly selected location in a residential area. The average of these three readings is the pollution index, and a value of 50 or greater for this index indicates a hazardous condition, whereas values lower than 50 indicate a safe condition. Because this index must be calculated daily, the Dogpatch Environmental Statistician would like a program that calculates the pollution index and then determines the appropriate condition, safe or hazardous.

The relevant given information consists of three pollution readings and the cutoff value used to distinguish between safe and hazardous conditions. A solution to the problem consists of the pollution index and a message indicating the condition. Generalizing so that any cutoff value, not just 50, can be used, we could specify the problem as follows:

Input	Output
Three pollution readings	Pollution index = the average of the pollution readings
Cutoff value to distinguish between safe and hazardous condition	Condition: safe or hazardous

PROBLEM 3: Mean Time to Failure. One important statistic that is used in measuring the reliability of a component in a circuit is the *mean time to failure*, which can be used to predict the circuit's lifetime. This is especially important in situations in which repair is difficult or even impossible, such as a computer circuit in a space satellite. Suppose that an engineering laboratory has been awarded a contract by NASA to evaluate the reliability of a particular component for a future space probe to Jupiter. As part of this evaluation, an engineer at this laboratory has tested several of these circuits and recorded the time at which each failed. She now wishes to develop a program to process this data and determine the mean time to failure.

The input for this problem is obviously a collection of failure times for the component being tested, and the output is clearly the average or mean of these times. To calculate this mean, we must know how many tests were conducted, but this information is not given in the statement of the problem. We cannot assume, therefore, that it is part of the input, and so the program will have to be flexible enough to process any number of measurements. A specification of the input and output for this problem thus might be

Input	Output
A collection of numeric values (number unknown)	The number of values The mean of the values

2.2 Algorithm Development

Once a problem has been specified, a procedure to produce the required output from the given input must be designed. Because the computer is a machine possessing no inherent problem-solving capabilities, this procedure must be formulated as a detailed sequence of simple steps. Such a procedure is called an **algorithm.**

The steps that comprise an algorithm must be organized in a logical and clear manner so that the program that implements this algorithm will be similarly well structured. **Structured algorithms** and **programs** are designed using three basic methods of control:

1. **Sequential:**   Steps are performed in a strictly sequential manner, each step being executed exactly once.
2. **Selection:**   One of a number of alternative actions is selected and executed.
3. **Repetition:**   One or more steps is performed repeatedly.

These three structures appear to be very simple, but in fact they are sufficiently powerful that any algorithm can be constructed using them.

Programs to implement algorithms must be written in a language that the computer can understand. It is natural, therefore, to describe algorithms in a language that resembles the language used to write computer programs, that is, in a "pseudoprogramming language" or, as it is more commonly called, **pseudocode.**

Unlike the definitions of high-level programming languages such as FORTRAN, there is no set of rules that defines precisely what is and what is not pseudocode. It varies from one programmer to another. Pseudocode is a mixture of natural language and symbols, terms, and other features commonly used in high-level languages. Typically one finds the following features in the various pseudocodes in use:

1. The usual computer symbols are used for arithmetic operations: + for addition, − for subtraction, * for multiplication, / for division, and ** for exponentiation.
2. Symbolic names (variables) are used to represent the quantities being processed by the algorithm.
3. Some provision is made for including comments. This is often done by enclosing each comment line between special symbols such as asterisks (*).
4. Certain key words that are common in high-level languages may be used: for example, *Read* or *Enter* to indicate input operations, and *Display, Print,* or *Write* for output operations.
5. Indentation is used to indicate certain key blocks of instructions.

Some programmers also use graphical representations of algorithms in addition to or in place of pseudocode descriptions. A number of such representations have been developed over the years, but probably the most common one and surely the one used for the longest time is the **flowchart**, a diagram that uses symbols like those shown in Figure 2.1. The various steps of the algorithm are placed in a box of the appropriate shape, and the order in which these steps are to be carried out is indicated by connecting them with arrows called **flow lines.** Although flowcharts have fallen out of favor in some circles, beginning programmers usually find that their two-dimensional nature, as opposed to the one-dimensional nature of a pseudocode description, makes it easier to visualize and understand the structure of the algorithm. For this reason,

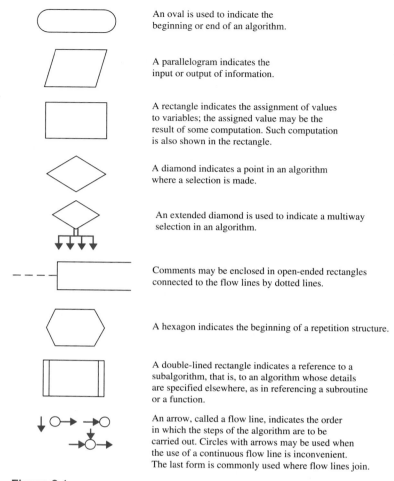

An oval is used to indicate the beginning or end of an algorithm.

A parallelogram indicates the input or output of information.

A rectangle indicates the assignment of values to variables; the assigned value may be the result of some computation. Such computation is also shown in the rectangle.

A diamond indicates a point in an algorithm where a selection is made.

An extended diamond is used to indicate a multiway selection in an algorithm.

Comments may be enclosed in open-ended rectangles connected to the flow lines by dotted lines.

A hexagon indicates the beginning of a repetition structure.

A double-lined rectangle indicates a reference to a subalgorithm, that is, to an algorithm whose details are specified elsewhere, as in referencing a subroutine or a function.

An arrow, called a flow line, indicates the order in which the steps of the algorithm are to be carried out. Circles with arrows may be used when the use of a continuous flow line is inconvenient. The last form is commonly used where flow lines join.

Figure 2.1

therefore, many of the algorithms in this book will have both pseudocode descriptions and flow diagrams.

The structure of an algorithm is also sometimes displayed in a **structure diagram** that shows the various tasks that must be performed and their relation to one another. These diagrams are especially useful in describing algorithms for more complex problems and will be described in more detail in Section 2.5. In this section we restrict our attention to the three simple examples introduced in the preceding section. Using these examples, we illustrate the three basic control structures—sequence, selection, and repetition—and how to present algorithms using both pseudocode and flowcharts.

PROBLEM 1: Radioactive Decay—Sequential Structure. As we noted in the preceding section, the input for Problem 1 consists of the initial amount of some radioactive element, its half-life, and a time period. The output to be produced is the amount of the substance that remains at the end of the specified time period.

The first step in an algorithm for solving this problem is to obtain the values for the input items—initial amount, half-life, and time period. Next we must determine how to use this information to calculate the amount of the substance remaining after the given time period. The half-life of polonium is 140 days, and if we assume that the initial amount of polonium is 10 mg, then after 140 days, or one half-life,

$$10 \times .5$$

milligrams remain. At the end of 280 days or two half-lives, the amount of polonium remaining is one half of this amount,

$$(10 \times .5) \times .5$$

which can also be written

$$10 \times (.5)^2$$

Similarly, the amount of polonium at the end of 420 days or three half-lives is

$$10 \times (.5)^3$$

The general formula for the amount of the substance remaining is

$$\text{Amount remaining} = \text{initial amount} \times (.5)^{\text{time/half-life}}$$

Thus, the second step in our algorithm is to perform this calculation for the data entered in Step 1. Finally, the value of the amount remaining must be displayed.

This rather lengthy description of the algorithm can be summarized in pseudocode as follows:

ALGORITHM FOR RADIOACTIVE DECAY PROBLEM

```
* This algorithm calculates the amount RESID of a radioactive    *
* substance that remains after a specified TIME for a given initial    *
* amount INIT and a given half-life HFLIFE.    *
```

1. Enter INIT, HFLIFE, and TIME.
2. Calculate
         RESID = INIT * (.5) ** (TIME / HFLIFE).
3. Display RESID.

A flowchart representation of this algorithm clearly displays its sequential structure.

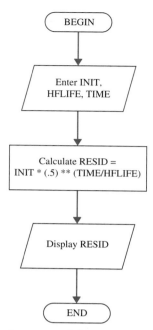

This algorithm uses only sequential control; the steps are executed in order, from beginning to end, with each step being performed exactly once. For other problems, however, the solution may require that some of the steps be performed in some situations and bypassed in others. This is illustrated by our second example.

PROBLEM 2: Pollution Index—Selection Structure. Recall that for Problem 2, the input consists of three pollution readings and a cutoff value that distinguishes between safe and hazardous conditions. The output to be produced consists of the pollution index, which is the average of the three readings, and a message indicating the appropriate condition.

Once again, the first step in an algorithm to solve this problem is to obtain values for the input items—the three pollution readings and the cutoff value. The next step is to calculate the pollution index by averaging the three readings. Now, one of two possible actions must be selected. Either a message indicating a safe condition or a message indicating a hazardous condition must be displayed. The appropriate action is selected by comparing the pollution index with the cutoff value. In the pseudocode description of this algorithm, this selection is indicated by

> If INDEX < CUTOFF then
> > Display 'Safe condition'
> Else
> > Display 'Hazardous condition'

ALGORITHM FOR POLLUTION INDEX PROBLEM

* This algorithm reads three pollution levels, LEVEL1, LEVEL2, and *
* LEVEL3, and a CUTOFF value. It then calculates the pollution   *
* INDEX. If the value of INDEX is less than CUTOFF, a message   *

* indicating a safe condition is displayed; otherwise, a message   *
* indicating a hazardous condition is displayed.   *

1. Enter LEVEL1, LEVEL2, LEVEL3, and CUTOFF.
2. Calculate

$$\text{INDEX} = \frac{\text{LEVEL1} + \text{LEVEL2} + \text{LEVEL3}}{3}.$$

3. If INDEX < CUTOFF then
    Display 'Safe condition'
  Else
    Display 'Hazardous condition'

The following flowchart representation of this algorithm shows that its basic overall structure is sequential but that one of the steps in this sequential execution is a selection. The highlighted region of the diagram clearly shows the two alternatives, one of which must be selected according to the truth or falsity of the condition INDEX < CUTOFF; a diamond-shaped box like that shown is commonly used to indicate that a selection must be made.

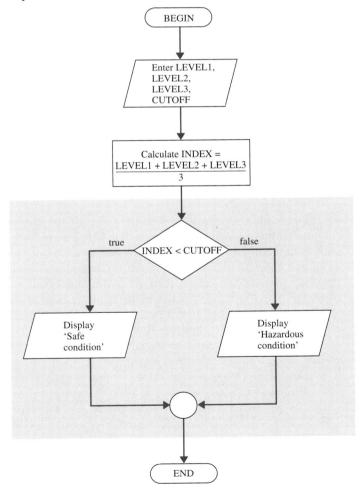

In addition to the sequential processing and selection illustrated in the preceding two examples, the solution of other problems may require that a step or a collection of steps be repeated. This is illustrated in our third example.

PROBLEM 3: Mean Time to Failure—Repetition Structure. In Problem 3, the input is a set of numbers, each representing the time until a component in a circuit failed. The output is the number of data values and their average, which is then the mean time to failure for this component.

In developing algorithms to solve problems like this, one useful method is to begin by considering how the problem could be solved without the use of a computer, say by using pencil and paper and/or a calculator. To solve this problem in this manner, we would enter the values one at a time, counting each value as it is entered and adding it to the sum of the preceding values. We see that the procedure will thus involve two quantities:

1. A counter that is incremented by 1 each time a data value is entered.
2. A running sum of the data values.

Data Value	COUNT	SUM
	0	0.0
3.4	1	3.4
4.2	2	7.6
6.0	3	13.6
5.5	4	19.1
.	.	.
.	.	.
.	.	.

The procedure begins with 0 as the value of the counter and 0.0 as the initial value of the sum. At each stage, a data value is entered, the value of the counter is incremented by 1, and the data value is added to the sum, producing a new sum. These steps are repeated until eventually all the data values have been processed, and the sum is then divided by the count to obtain the mean value.

When solving this problem by hand, it is clear when the last data value has been entered, but if this procedure is to be performed by a program, some method is needed to indicate that all of the data values have been processed. A common technique is to signal this by entering an artificial value called a **flag**, which is distinct from any possible valid data item. This value is not processed as a regular data value but serves only to terminate the repetition.

A pseudocode description of this algorithm is

ALGORITHM TO CALCULATE MEAN TIME TO FAILURE

* Algorithm to read failure times, count them, and find the mean time *
* to failure (MEAN). FAILTM represents the current failure time *
* entered, COUNT is the number of failure times, and SUM is their *
* sum. Values are read until an end-of-data flag is encountered. *

1. Set COUNT to 0.
2. Set SUM to 0.0.
3. Enter first value for FAILTM.
4. While FAILTM is not the end-of-data flag, do the following:
    a. Increment COUNT by 1.
    b. Add FAILTM to SUM.
    c. Enter next value for FAILTM.
5. Calculate MEAN = SUM / COUNT.
6. Display MEAN and COUNT.

In this algorithm, the repetition is indicated by

While FAILTM is not the end-of-data flag, do the following:
    a. Increment COUNT by 1.
    b. Add FAILTM to SUM.
    c. Enter next value for FAILTM.

This specifies that statements a, b, and c are to be repeated as long as the value of FAILTM is not the end-of-data flag. Thus, when the flag signaling the end of data is entered, this repetition is terminated, and the remaining statements of the algorithm are performed.

The following flowchart gives a graphical representation of the structure of this algorithm. It is clear that its overall structure is sequential but that one of the steps in this sequence is a repetition structure, as indicated by the highlighted region in the diagram. We will indicate repetition by placing a hexagon containing the information that controls the repetition at the beginning of the steps to be repeated and an arrow from the last of these statements back to the hexagon. The ''exit'' flow line labeled ''false'' shows where execution is to continue when repetition is terminated:

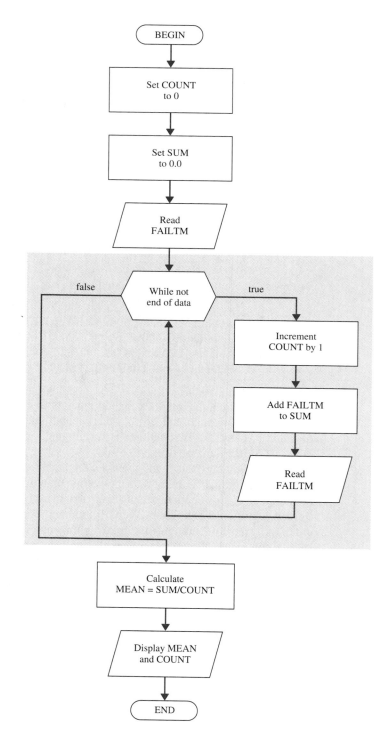

2.3 Program Coding

The first two steps of the problem-solving process are extremely important, because the remaining phases will be much more difficult if the first two steps are skipped or are not done carefully. On the other hand, if the problem has been carefully analyzed and if complete and clear algorithms have been developed, the third step of program coding is usually straightforward.

Coding is the process of expressing an algorithm in a programming language. In the second step of the problem-solving process, algorithms may be described in a natural language or pseudocode, but a program that implements an algorithm must be written in the vocabulary of a programming language and must conform to the **syntax**, or grammatical rules, of that language. This text is concerned with the vocabulary and syntax of the programming language FORTRAN. In this section we introduce some elementary features of this language and give an example of a simple FORTRAN program. These features will be discussed in detail in subsequent chapters.

Variables. In the three examples in the preceding section, we used names to identify various quantities. These names are called *variables*. In the first example, the variables INIT, HFLIFE, and TIME represent the initial amount of a radioactive substance, its half-life, and time, respectively. The output in this example is the amount of the substance remaining after the specified time and is represented by the variable RESID. In the second example, the variables are LEVEL1, LEVEL2, LEVEL3, CUTOFF, and INDEX, and in the third example, the variables are FAILTM, COUNT, SUM, and MEAN.

In standard FORTRAN, variable names must begin with a letter, which may be followed by up to five letters or digits. For example, INIT, HFLIFE, TIME, RESID, LEVEL1, LEVEL2, LEVEL3, CUTOFF, INDEX, FAILTM, COUNT, SUM, and MEAN are valid FORTRAN variable names, and each name suggests what the variable represents. *Meaningful variable names should always be used because they make the program easier to read and understand.*

Types. In the examples we have been considering, two types of numbers are used. The value of COUNT in the third example and perhaps also the values of LEVEL1, LEVEL2, LEVEL3, and CUTOFF in the second example are integers, whereas the values of INIT, HFLIFE, TIME, and RESID in the first example, INDEX in the second example, and FAILTM, SUM, and MEAN in the third are real; that is, they may have fractional parts. FORTRAN distinguishes between these two types of numeric data, and the types of values that each variable may have must be declared. This may be done by placing statements of the form

```
INTEGER list1
REAL     list2
```

at the beginning of the program, where *list1* is a list of the variable names of integer type and *list2* is a list of variable names of real type. Thus, the types of the FORTRAN variables in the first example can be declared by

```
REAL INIT, HFLIFE, TIME, RESID
```

those in the second example by

```
INTEGER LEVEL1, LEVEL2, LEVEL3, CUTOFF
REAL INDEX
```

and those in the third example by

```
INTEGER COUNT
REAL FAILTM, SUM, MEAN
```

Operations. Addition and subtraction are denoted in FORTRAN by the usual + and − symbols. Multiplication is denoted by ∗ and division by /. Exponentiation is denoted by ∗∗.

Assignment. Assignment of a value to a variable is denoted by = in FORTRAN programs. For example, the assignment statement

```
RESID = INIT * .5 ** (TIME / HFLIFE)
```

assigns the value of the expression

```
INIT * .5 ** (TIME / HFLIFE)
```

to the variable RESID.

Input/Output. In the pseudocode description of an algorithm in the preceding section, the words *Read* and *Enter* are used for input operations, and *Display*, *Print*, and *Write* are used for output operations. The FORTRAN statement used for input is the READ statement. A simple form of this statement is

```
READ *, list
```

where *list* is a list of variables for which values are to be read. For example, the statement

```
READ *, INIT, HFLIFE, TIME
```

reads values for the variables INIT, HFLIFE, and TIME from some input device.

A simple output statement in FORTRAN is the PRINT statement of the form

```
PRINT *, list
```

or the WRITE statement of the form

```
WRITE (*, *) list
```

where *list* is a list of items to be displayed. For example, the statement

```
PRINT *, 'AMOUNT REMAINING = ', RESID
```

displays the label

```
AMOUNT REMAINING =
```

followed by the value of the variable RESID.

Comments. Comment lines can also be incorporated into FORTRAN programs. Any line that is completely blank or that contains the letter C or an asterisk (∗) in the first position of the line is a comment line.

Program Composition. Figure 2.2 shows a FORTRAN program for the algorithm to solve the radioactive decay problem considered earlier in this chapter; also shown is a sample run of the program. The program begins with the PROGRAM statement

```
PROGRAM DECAY
```

which marks the beginning of the program and associates the name DECAY with it.

The first step in the algorithm is an input instruction to enter values for the variables INIT, HFLIFE, and TIME:

1. Enter INIT, HFLIFE, and TIME.

This is translated into two statements in the program:

```
PRINT *, 'ENTER INITIAL AMOUNT, HALF-LIFE, AND TIME'
READ *, INIT, HFLIFE, TIME
```

The PRINT statement is used to prompt the user that the input values are to be entered. The READ statement actually assigns the three values entered by the user to the three variables INIT, HFLIFE, and TIME. Thus, in the sample run shown, when the user enters

```
10, 140, 700
```

the value 10 is assigned to INIT, 140 to HFLIFE, and 700 to TIME.

The next step in the algorithm

2. Calculate RESID = INIT ∗ .5 ∗∗ (TIME / HFLIFE).

easily translates into the FORTRAN assignment statement

```
RESID = INIT * .5 ** (TIME / HFLIFE)
```

The output instruction

3. Display RESID.

is translated into the FORTRAN statement

```
PRINT *, 'AMOUNT REMAINING =', RESID
```

The end of the program is indicated by the FORTRAN statement

```
END
```

This statement terminates execution of the program.

```
      PROGRAM DECAY
**************************************************
* This program calculates the amount of a       *
* radioactive substance that remains after      *
* a specified time, given an initial amount      *
* and its half-life.  Variables used are:        *
*      INIT    :  initial amount of substance    *
*      HFLIFE  :  half-life of substance         *
*      TIME    :  time at which the amount        *
*                 remaining is calculated         *
*      RESID   :  amount remaining               *
**************************************************

      REAL INIT, HFLIFE, TIME, RESID

      PRINT *, 'ENTER INITIAL AMOUNT, HALF-LIFE, AND TIME'
      READ *, INIT, HFLIFE, TIME
      RESID = INIT * .5 ** (TIME / HFLIFE)
      PRINT *, 'AMOUNT REMAINING =', RESID
      END
```

Sample run:

```
ENTER INITIAL AMOUNT, HALF-LIFE, AND TIME
10, 140, 700
AMOUNT REMAINING =    0.312500
```

Figure 2.2

2.4 Program Execution and Testing

The fourth step in using the computer to solve a problem is to execute and test the program. The procedure for submitting a program to a computer varies from one system to another; the details regarding your particular system can be obtained from your instructor, computer center personnel, or user manuals supplied by the manufacturer.

Access to the computer system must first be obtained. In the case of a personal computer, this may only mean turning on the machine and inserting the appropriate diskette in the disk drive. For a larger system, some **login** procedure may be required to establish contact between a remote terminal and the computer. Once access has been gained, the program must be entered, often using an **editor** provided as part of the system's software.

Once the program has been entered, it is compiled and executed by giving appropriate system commands. If no errors are detected during compilation, the resulting object program can be executed, and output like the following will appear on the screen:

```
ENTER INITIAL AMOUNT, HALF-LIFE, AND TIME
10, 140, 700
AMOUNT REMAINING =     0.312500
```

The program displays a message prompting the user for three input values, and after these values are entered, the desired output value is calculated and displayed.

In this example, we illustrated the **interactive mode** of processing, in which the user enters data values 10, 140, and 700 during program execution (from the keyboard), and the output produced by the program is displayed directly to the user (usually on a video screen). Another mode of operation is **batch processing.** In this mode, the user must prepare a file containing the program, the data, and certain command lines and submit it to the system. Then the execution proceeds without any user interaction.

In this example, the program was entered, compiled, and executed without error. Usually, however, a programmer will make some errors when designing the program or when attempting to enter and execute it. Errors may be detected at various stages of program processing and may cause the processing to be terminated. For example, an incorrect system command will be detected early in the processing and will usually prevent compilation and execution of the program. Errors in the program's syntax, such as incorrect punctuation or misspelled key words, will be detected during compilation. (On some systems, syntax errors may be detected while the program is being entered.) Such errors are called **syntax errors** or **compile-time errors** and usually make it impossible to complete the compilation and execution of the program. For example, if the output statement that displays the residual amount of radioactive substance were mistakenly written as

```
PRINT *, 'AMOUNT REMAINING = , RESID
```

without a quotation mark after the equals sign, an attempt to compile and execute the program might result in a message like the following, signaling a ''fatal'' error:

```
MAIN decay:
"error.f", line 19: Error: unbalanced quotes
```

Less severe errors may generate ''warning'' messages, but the compilation will continue, and execution of the resulting object program will be attempted.

Other errors, such as an attempt to divide by zero in an arithmetic expression, may not be detected until execution of the program has begun. Such errors are called **run-time errors.** The error messages displayed by your particular system can be found in the user manuals supplied by the manufacturer. In any case, the errors must be corrected by replacing the erroneous statements with correct ones, and the modified program must be recompiled and then reexecuted.

Errors that are detected by the computer system are relatively easy to identify and correct. There are, however, other errors that are more subtle and difficult to identify. These are **logical errors** that arise in the design of the algorithm or in the coding of the program that implements the algorithm. For example, if the statement

```
RESID = INIT * .5 ** (TIME / HFLIFE)
```

in the program of Figure 2.2 were mistakenly entered as

```
RESID = INIT * .5 * (TIME / HFLIFE)
```

with the exponentiation symbol (**) replaced by the symbol for multiplication (*), the program would still be syntactically correct. No error would occur during the compilation or execution of the program. But the results produced by the program would be incorrect because an incorrect formula would have been used to calculate the residual amount of the substance. Thus, if the values 10, 140, and 700 were entered for the variables INIT, HFLIFE, and TIME, respectively, the output produced by the program would be

```
AMOUNT REMAINING =     25.000000
```

instead of the correct output

```
AMOUNT REMAINING =     0.312500
```

as shown in the sample run in Figure 2.1.

Because it may not be obvious whether the results produced by a program are correct, *it is important that the user run a program several times with input data for which the correct results are known in advance.* For the preceding example, it is easy to calculate by hand the correct answer for values such as 100, 5, and 10 for INIT, HFLIFE, and TIME, respectively, in order to check the output produced by the program. This process of **program validation** is extremely important because *a program cannot be considered to be correct until it has been validated with several sets of test data.* The test data should be carefully selected so that each part of the program is checked.

2.5 Software Engineering

Programming and problem solving is an art in that it requires a good deal of imagination, ingenuity, and creativity. But it is also a science in that certain techniques and methodologies are commonly used. The term **software engineering** has come to be applied to the study and use of these techniques.

As we noted in the introduction to this chapter, the **life cycle** of software, that is, programs, consists of five basic phases:

1. Problem analysis and specification.
2. Algorithm development.
3. Program coding.
4. Program execution and testing.
5. Program maintenance.

In the preceding sections we described the first four phases and illustrated them with some examples.We deliberately kept these examples simple, however, so that we could emphasize the main ideas without getting lost in a maze of details. But in real-world applications and in problems later in this text, these phases may be considerably more complex. In this section we reexamine each of these phases and describe some of the additional questions and complications that face professional programmers, together with some of the software engineering techniques used in dealing with them.

Problem Analysis and Specification. Like the exercises and problems in most programming texts, the examples we have considered thus far were quite simple and, we hope, clearly stated. Analysis of these problems to identify the input and output is, therefore, quite easy. This is not the case, however, with most real-world problems, which are often stated vaguely and imprecisely, because the person posing the problem does not fully understand it. For example, the president of a land development company might request a programmer to ''use the computer to estimate costs for constructing Celestial Condominiums.''

In these situations, many questions must be answered in order to complete the problem's specifications. Some of these answers are required to describe more completely the problem's input and output. What information is available regarding the construction project? How is the program to access this data? Has the information been validated, or must the program provide error checking? In what format should the output be displayed? Must reports be generated for company executives, zoning boards, environmental agencies, and/or other governmental agencies?

Other questions deal more directly with the required processing. Are employees paid on an hourly or a salaried basis, or are there some of each? What premium, if any, is paid for overtime? What items must be withheld—for federal, state, and city income taxes, retirement plans, insurance, and the like— and how are they to be computed? What materials are required? What equipment will be needed?

Many other questions must be answered before the specification of the problem is complete and before the design of the algorithms and programs can begin. Will the users of the program be technically sophisticated, or must the program be made very user friendly to accommodate novice users? How often will the program be used? What are the response time requirements? What is the expected life of the program; that is, how long will it be used, and what changes can be expected in the future? What hardware and software are available?

Although this list is by no means exhaustive, it does indicate the wide range of information that must be obtained in analyzing and specifying the problem. In some situations this is done by a **systems analyst,** whereas in others it is part of the programmer's responsibility.

Algorithm Development. The solution of a complex problem may require so many steps in the final algorithm that they cannot all be anticipated at the outset. To attack such problems, a **top-down** approach is commonly used. We begin by identifying the major tasks to be performed to solve the problem and arranging them in the order in which they are to be carried out. These tasks and their relation to one another can be displayed in a one-level **structure diagram.** For example, a first structure diagram for the problem might have the form

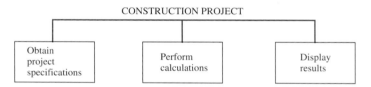

Usually one or more of these first-level tasks is still quite complex and must be divided into subtasks. For example, in the construction problem, some of the input data pertains to personnel requirements. Other data items refer to material requirements, and still others to equipment needs. Consequently, the task ''Obtain project specifications'' can be subdivided into three subtasks:

1. Obtain personnel requirements.
2. Obtain equipment requirements.
3. Obtain materials requirements.

Similarly, the task ''Perform calculations'' may be split into three subtasks:

1. Calculate personnel cost.
2. Calculate equipment cost.
3. Calculate materials cost.

In a structure diagram, these subtasks are placed on a second level below the corresponding main task, as pictured in Figure 2.3. These subtasks may require further division into still smaller subtasks, resulting in additional levels, as illustrated in Figure 2.4. This **successive refinement** continues until each subtask is sufficiently simple that the design of an algorithm for that subtask is straightforward.

This **divide-and-conquer** approach can thus be used to break up a complex problem into a number of simpler subproblems. This allows the programmer to design and test an algorithm and a corresponding program **module** for each subproblem independently of the others. For very large projects a team

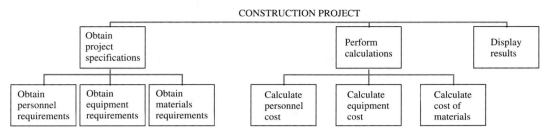

Figure 2.3

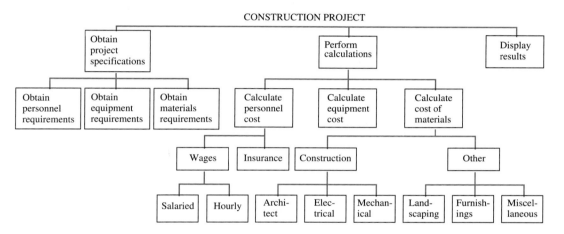

Figure 2.4

approach might be used in which the low-level subtasks are assigned to different programmers. The individual program modules they develop are eventually combined into one complete program that solves the original problem.

Program Coding. The first decision that must be made when translating an algorithm into a program is what programming language to use. This obviously depends on the languages available to the programmer, but other factors also influence the decision. The problem may have characteristics that make one language more appropriate than another. For example, if the problem involves scientific computations requiring extended precision and/or complex arithmetic, FORTRAN may be the most suitable language. Problems that involve a large amount of file input/output and report generation can perhaps best be handled in COBOL. And applications in artificial intelligence that require making logical inferences might best be written in PROLOG.

Regardless of which language is used, certain programming practices contribute to the development of *correct, readable, and understandable programs.*

One principle is that *programs should be well structured.* Two helpful guidelines in this regard are to

- *Use a top-down approach when developing a program for a complex problem.* Divide the problem into simpler and simpler subproblems, and develop individual subprograms to solve these subproblems.
- *Strive for simplicity and clarity.* Avoid clever programming tricks intended only to demonstrate the programmer's ingenuity or to produce code that executes only slightly more efficiently.

A second principle is that *each program unit should be documented.* In particular:

- *Each program unit should include opening documentation.* Comments should be included at the beginning of each program (subroutine, function) to explain what it does, how it works, any special algorithms it uses, and so on, and they may also include such items of information as the name of the programmer, the date the program was written and when it was last modified, and references to books and manuals that give additional information about the program. In addition, it is a good practice to explain the variables that are being used in the program.
- *Comments should also be used to explain key program segments and/ or segments whose purpose or design is not obvious.* However, too many detailed or unnecessary comments clutter the program and only make it more difficult to read and understand.
- *Meaningful identifiers should be used.* For example, the statement

```
DIST = RATE * TIME
```

is more meaningful than

```
D = R * T
```

or

```
X7 = R * ZEKE
```

Don't use "skimpy" abbreviations just to save a few keystrokes. Also, avoid "cute" identifiers, as in

```
HOWFAR = GOGO * SQUEAL
```

A third principle has to do with a program's appearance. *A program should be formatted in a style that enhances its readability.* The following are some guidelines for good program style:

- *Use spaces between the items in a statement, so as to make it more readable,* for example, before and after each operator ($+$, $-$, $=$, etc.).
- *Insert a blank line between sections of a program and wherever appropriate in a sequence of statements to set off blocks of statements.*
- *Adhere rigorously to alignment and indentation guidelines to emphasize*

the relationship between various parts of the program. For example, indent those statements that make up the body of a loop.

It is often difficult for beginning programmers to appreciate the importance of practicing good programming habits that lead to the design of programs that are readable and understandable. The reason for this is that programs developed in an academic environment are often quite different from those developed in real-world situations, in which program style and form are critical. Student programs are usually quite small (seldom more than a few hundred lines of code); are executed and modified only a few times (almost never, once they have been handed in); are rarely examined in detail by anyone other than the student and the instructor; and are not developed within the context of severe budget restraints. Real-world programs, on the other hand, may be very large (several thousand lines of code); are developed by teams of programmers; are commonly used for long periods of time and thus require maintenance if they are to be kept current and correct; and are often maintained by someone other than the original programmer. As hardware costs continue to decrease and programmer costs increase, it becomes even more important to write programs that can be easily read and understood by others.

Program Execution and Testing.   Obviously, the most important characteristic of any program is that it be *correct.* No matter how well structured, how well documented, or how nice the program looks, if it does not produce correct results, it is worthless. As we have seen, the fact that a program executes without producing any error messages is no guarantee that it is correct. The results produced may be erroneous because of logical errors that the computer system cannot detect. It is the responsibility of the programmer to test each program in order to ensure that it is correct. (See Section 4.10 for more about program testing.)

Program Maintenance.   The life cycle of a program written by a student programmer normally ends with the fourth phase; that is, once the program has been written, executed, and tested, the assignment is complete. Programs in real-world applications, however, will likely be used for a number of years and will probably require some modification as time passes. Especially in large programs developed for complex projects, there will usually be obscure bugs that do not become apparent until after the program has been placed in use. Correcting these flaws is obviously one aspect of program maintenance. It may also be necessary to modify the program in order to improve its performance, add new features, and so on. Other modifications may be required owing to changes in the computer hardware and/or the system software such as the operating system. External factors may also force program modification; for example, changes in the tax laws may mean revising part of a payroll program.

Software maintenance is, in fact, a major component of the life cycle of a program and may account for as much as 80 percent of its total cost. This fact, combined with the fact that most program maintenance is done by someone not involved in the original design, makes it mandatory that the programmer do his or her utmost to design a program that is readable, documented, and well structured so that it is easy to understand and modify.

Exercises

1. Consider the following algorithm:

1. Initialize X to 0, Y to 5, Z to 25.
2. While X $\leq$ 4 do the following:
   a. Set Y $=$ Z $-$ Y, A $=$ X $+$ 1, and then increment X by 1.
   b. If A $>$ 1 then
              Set Z $=$ Z $-$ 5, A $=$ A^2, and then set B $=$ Z $-$ Y.
3. Display A, B, X, Y, and Z.

Complete the following **trace table** for this algorithm, which displays the labels of the statements in the order in which they are executed and the values of the variables at each stage:

Statement	A	B	X	Y	Z
1	?	?	0	5	25
2	"	"	"	"	"
2-a	1	"	1	20	"
2-b	"	"	"	"	"
2-a	2	"	2	5	"
$\vdots$	$\vdots$	$\vdots$	$\vdots$	$\vdots$	$\vdots$
3	"	"	"	"	"

(? $=$ undefined)

2. Construct a trace table similar to that in Exercise 1 for the following algorithm, assuming that the value entered for A is (a) 0.1, (b) 0.3, (c) 1.0:

1. Enter A.
2. While A $\leq$ 0.3 do the following:
   a. Increment A by 0.1.
   b. If A $\neq$ 0.3 then do the following:
      i. Set S and X to 0, T to 1.
      ii. While T $\leq$ 6 do the following:
         (a) Add T to X and then increment T by 2.
   c. Else do the following:
      i. Set T to 0, X to 1, and S $=$ 3 $*$ S.
      ii. While T $\leq$ 5 do the following:
         (a) Increment T by 1 and then set X $=$ X $*$ T.
   d. Display A, S, and X.

3. Construct a trace table similar to that in Exercise 1 for the following algorithm, assuming the data values shown in the table are entered for b, h, and k:

1. Initialize I, A, and X to 0.
2. While I < 4 do the following:
   a. Increment I by 1.
   b. Enter b, h, k.
   c. If k ≥ 1 then do the following:
      i. Set A = $\dfrac{bh}{2}$.
     ii. If k ≥ 2 then do the following:
        (a) Set X = $\dfrac{bh^3}{36}$.
   d. Display I, b, h, A, and X.

b	h	k
3	6	1
4	3	2
5	2	0
2	6	2

For each of the problems described in Exercises 4 through 17, identify both the information that must be produced to solve the problem and the given information that will be useful in obtaining the solution. Then design an algorithm to solve the problem.

4. Calculate and display the radius, circumference, and area of a circle with a given diameter.

5. Three resistors are arranged in parallel in the following circuit:

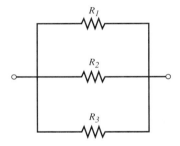

Calculate and display the combined resistance

$$\dfrac{1}{\dfrac{1}{R_1} + \dfrac{1}{R_2} + \dfrac{1}{R_3}}$$

for given values of R_1, R_2, and R_3.

6. The boiling point of water is 212° on the Fahrenheit scale and 100° on the Celsius scale. The freezing point of water is 32° on the Fahrenheit scale and 0° on the Celsius scale. Assuming a linear relationship ($F = a \cdot C + b$) between these two temperature scales, convert a temperature of C degrees on the Celsius scale to the corresponding Fahrenheit temperature, and display the Fahrenheit temperature.

7. Calculate and display the largest and the smallest of three given voltage readings.

8. Calculate and display the largest number, the smallest number, and the range (largest number − smallest number) for any given set of numbers between two values LOWLIM and UPLIM.

9. A certain city classifies a pollution index of less than 35 as pleasant, 35 through 60 as unpleasant, and above 60 as hazardous. The city's pollution control officer desires a program that will accept several values of the pollution index and produce the appropriate classification for each.

10. Suppose that a professor gave a quiz to her class and compiled a list of scores ranging from 50 through 100. She intends to use only three grades: A if the score is 90 or above, B if it is below 90 but above or equal to 75, and C if it is below 75. She would like a program to assign the appropriate letter grades to the numeric scores.

11. A car manufacturer wants to determine average noise levels for the ten different models of cars the company produces. Each can be purchased with one of five different engines. Design an algorithm to enter the noise levels (in decibels) that were recorded for each possible model and engine configuration, and to calculate the average noise level for each model as well as the average noise level over all models and engines.

12. (a) Develop an algorithm to approximate the value of e^x using the infinite series

$$e^x = \sum_{n=0}^{\infty} \frac{x^n}{n!}$$

(b) Construct a trace table for your algorithm, and trace the value of n, x^n, $n!$, each term $x^n/n!$, and the value of the sum of all terms up through the current one for $n = 0, 1, \ldots, 10$, and $x = 0.8$.

13. The "divide-and-average" algorithm for approximating the square root of any positive number A is as follows: For any initial approximation X that is positive, find a new approximation by calculating the average of X and A/X, that is,

$$\frac{X + A/X}{2}$$

Repeat this procedure with X replaced by this new approximation, stopping when X and A/X differ in absolute by some specified error allowance, such as .00001.

14. The quadratic equation $Ax^2 + Bx + C = 0$ has no real roots if the discriminant $B^2 - 4AC$ is negative; it has one real root, $-B/2A$, if the discriminant is zero; and it has two real roots given by the quad-

ratic formula

$$\frac{-B \pm \sqrt{B^2 - 4AC}}{2A}$$

if the discriminant is positive. A program is to be developed to solve several different quadratic equations or to indicate that there are no real roots.

15. Dispatch Die-Casting currently produces 200 castings per month and realizes a profit of $300 per casting. The company now spends $2000 per month on research and development and has a fixed operating cost of $20,000 per month that does not depend on the amount of production. If the company doubles the amount spent on research and development, it is estimated that production will increase by 20 percent. The company president would like to know, beginning with the current status and successively doubling the amount spent on research and development, at what point the net profit will begin to decline.

16. Consider a cylindrical reservoir with a radius of 10.0 feet and a height of 40.0 feet that is filled and emptied by a 12-inch diameter pipe. The pipe has a 1000.0-foot-long run and discharges at an elevation 20.0 feet lower than the bottom of the reservoir. The pipe has been tested and has a roughness factor of 0.0130.

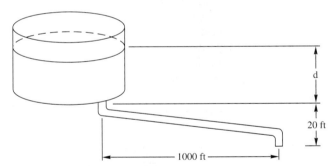

Several formulas have been developed experimentally to determine the velocity of flow fluids through such pipes. One of these, the *Manning formula*, is

$$V = \frac{1.486}{N} R^{2/3}S^{1/2}$$

where

V = velocity in feet per second
N = roughness coefficient
R = hydraulic radius = $\left(\dfrac{\text{cross-sectional area}}{\text{wetted perimeter}}\right)$
S = slope of the energy gradient
$\left(= \dfrac{d + 20}{1000} \text{ for this problem}\right)$

The rate of fluid flow is equal to the cross-sectional area of the pipe multiplied by the velocity.

Design an algorithm to enter the reservoir's height, roughness coefficient, hydraulic radius, and pipe radius, and then estimate the time required to empty the reservoir. Do this by assuming a constant flow rate for 5-minute segments.

17. A 100.0-lb sign is hung from the end of a horizontal pole of negligible mass. The pole is attached to the building by a pin and is supported by a cable, as shown. The pole and cable each are 6.0 feet long.

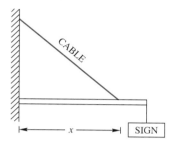

Design an algorithm to find the appropriate place (indicated by x in the diagram) to attach the cable to the pole so that the tension in the cable will be minimized. The equation governing static equilibrium tells us that

$$\text{Tension} = \frac{100 \cdot 6 \cdot 6}{x\sqrt{36 - x^2}}$$

Calculate the tension for x starting at 1.0 and incrementing it by 0.1 until the approximate minimum value is located.

18. Enter and execute the following FORTRAN program on your computer system, but with the name, course name, and date replaced with your name and course name and the current date.

```
      PROGRAM ARITH
*****************************************************************
*  John Doe              CPSC 141C          January 1, 1991 *
*                        ASSIGNMENT #1                        *
*  Program to add two numbers X and Y giving SUM             *
*****************************************************************

      REAL X, Y, SUM

      X = 3.14
      Y = 2.057
      SUM = X + Y
      PRINT *, 'SUM OF', X, ' AND', Y, ' IS', SUM
      END
```

19. For the program in Exercise 18, make the following changes and execute the modified program:

(a) Change 3.14 to 17.2375 in the statement that assigns a value to X.

(b) Change the variable names X and Y to ALPHA and BETA throughout.

(c) Insert the comment

```
*** Calculate the sum
```

before the statement SUM = X + Y.

(d) Insert the following comment and statement before the PRINT statement:

```
*** Now calculate the difference
      DIFF = ALPHA - BETA
```

change the REAL statement to

```
REAL ALPHA, BETA, SUM, DIFF
```

and add the following statement after the PRINT statement:

```
PRINT *, 'DIFF. OF', ALPHA, BETA, ' IS', DIFF
```

Also change the comments in lines 2 and 3, as appropriate.

20. Using the program in Figure 2.2 as a guide, write a FORTRAN program for the circle problem in Exercise 4. Note that asterisks indicating a comment line are placed in the first position of the line. In standard FORTRAN, all other statements must begin in position 7 and may not extend beyond position 72.

21. Proceed as in Exercise 20, but for the resistance problem in Exercise 5.

22. Proceed as in Exercise 20, but for the temperature conversion problem in Exercise 6.

3

Basic FORTRAN

Algorithms + Data Structures = Programs

NIKLAUS WIRTH

Kindly enter them in your note-book. And, in order to refer to them conveniently, let's call them A, B, and Z.

The tortoise in LEWIS CARROLL'S
What the Tortoise Said to Achilles.

In language, clarity is everything.

CONFUCIUS

The programming language FORTRAN, developed in the 1950s, was one of the first high-level languages. Since its introduction it has undergone several revisions, so that today there are a number of different versions of FORTRAN in use. In an attempt to minimize the differences among these versions, the American National Standards Institute (ANSI) has established standards for the FORTRAN language. One of the recent ANSI FORTRAN standards is known as **FORTRAN 77**, and it is this commonly used version of FORTRAN that forms the basis for this text. However, a new standard for FORTRAN known as FORTRAN 90 has recently appeared that adds a number of new features to the language. These features are summarized in special sections at the end of each chapter.

3.1 Data + Algorithms = Programs

Two important concepts emerge from our examination of the first two steps of the problem-solving process: **data** and **algorithms**. Every problem involves processing data, and this data may be of various types. It may be numeric data representing times or temperatures, or character data representing names, or logical data used in designing a circuit, and so on. Consequently, a program for solving a problem must be written in a language that can store and process various data types.

FORTRAN is designed to handle six types of data. Four of these are numeric types—integer, real, double precision, and complex—which are used to store and process various kinds of numbers. It also provides a character type for storing and processing strings of characters and a logical type for storing and processing data whose values are either .FALSE. or .TRUE. . In this chapter we will restrict our attention mainly to integer, real, and character types; the logical data type is considered in Chapter 4 and the double precision and complex types are considered in Chapter 9.

The second important aspect of solving a problem is the development of algorithms to process the input data and produce the required output. A program for solving a problem must be written in a language that provides operations for processing data and instructions that carry out the steps of the algorithm. For example, FORTRAN provides basic arithmetic operations for numeric computations, input and output instructions for entering and displaying data, instructions for implementing the basic control structures, and so on.

Since the two basic aspects of problem solving, data and algorithms, cannot be separated, a program for solving a problem must incorporate both aspects; that is, some part of the program must specify the data that is being processed, and another part must contain the instructions to do the processing. A FORTRAN program contains a **specification part** in which are declared the names and types of constants and variables used to store input and output values as well as intermediate results. This is followed by an **execution part**, which contains the statements that carry out the steps of the algorithm.

The general form of a FORTRAN program is

> heading
> specification part
> execution part

The first statement of a FORTRAN program is its **heading.** This statement marks the beginning of the program and gives it a name. The heading is normally followed by **opening documentation** in the form of comments that describe the nature and purpose of the program, the variables it uses, and other relevant information such as the date the program was written and the name of the programmer. Each of the parts of a program is described in detail in the following sections.

3.2 Program Format

Although some versions of FORTRAN allow considerable flexibility in the actual program format, standard FORTRAN has rather strict rules that dictate where the various parts of a program unit are to be placed. These rules are summarized in the following diagram:

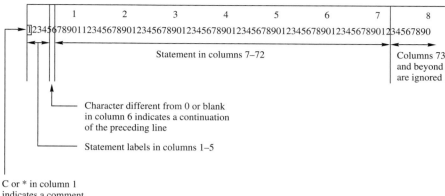

The positions within a line are called **columns** and are numbered 1, 2, 3, . . . , 80. All FORTRAN statements must be positioned in columns 7 through 72; characters that appear in columns 73 and beyond are ignored. If a statement requires a **statement label,** this label must appear in columns 1 through 5. Statement labels must be integers in the range 1 through 99999.

Occasionally it may not be possible to write a complete FORTRAN statement using only columns 7 through 72 of a line. In this case, the statement may be continued on another line or lines (up to a maximum of 19), provided that a **continuation indicator** is placed in column 6 of the line(s) on which the statement is continued. This continuation indicator may be any alphabetic or numeric character other than a zero or a space. A zero or a space in column 6 indicates the first line of a statement.

Lines that contain only blanks or that have the letter C or an asterisk (∗) in column 1 represent **comment lines.** Comments are not executed but, rather, appear only in the listing of the program unit. In standard FORTRAN, comments themselves may not be continued from one line to another by using a continuation indicator in column 6; instead, all comments must begin with a C or ∗ in column 1.

3.3   Constants and Variables

As we noted in Section 3.1, data is an important aspect of programming, and a problem may involve several different types of data. In this section we describe integer, real, and character constants in FORTRAN and how the types of variables used to store these constants are declared.

Constants.   **Constants** are quantities whose values do not change during program execution. In FORTRAN they may be of numeric (integer, real, double precision, complex), character, or logical type.

An **integer constant** is a string of digits *that does not include commas or a decimal point; negative integer constants must be preceded by a negative sign, but a plus sign is optional for nonnegative integers.* Thus

$$0$$
$$137$$
$$-2516$$
$$+17745$$

are valid integer constants, whereas the following are invalid for the reasons indicated:

5,280	(Commas are not allowed in numeric constants.)
16.0	(Integer constants may not contain decimal points.)
− −5	(Only one algebraic sign is allowed.)
7 −	(The algebraic sign must precede the string of digits.)

Another numeric data type is the **real** type, also known as **single precision** data. Constants of this type may be represented as ordinary decimal numbers or in exponential notation. *In the decimal representation of real constants, a decimal point must be present, but no commas are allowed.* Negative real constants must be preceded by a negative sign, but the plus sign is optional for nonnegative reals. Thus

$$1.234$$
$$-.01536$$
$$+56473.$$

are valid real constants, whereas the following are invalid for the reasons indicated:

12,345	(Commas are not allowed in numeric constants.)
63	(Real constants must contain a decimal point.)

The scientific representation of a real constant consists of an integer or decimal number, representing the mantissa or fractional part, followed by an exponent written as the letter E *with an integer constant following.* For example, the real constant 337.456 may also be written as

3.37456E2

which means 3.37456×10^2, or it may be written in a variety of other forms, such as

0.337456E3
337.456E0
33745.6E − 2
337456E − 3

Character constants, also called **strings,** are sequences of symbols chosen from the FORTRAN character set. The ANSI standard character set for FORTRAN is given in the following table:

Character	Meaning
blank	blank or space
0, . . . , 9	digits
A, . . . , Z	uppercase letters
$	dollar sign
'	apostrophe (single quote)
(	left parenthesis
)	right parenthesis
*	asterisk
+	plus sign
−	minus sign
/	slash
,	comma
.	period
:	colon
=	equals sign

Many versions of FORTRAN also include lowercase letters and other special symbols in their character sets. *The sequence of characters that comprise a character constant must be enclosed in apostrophes* (single quotes), and the number of such characters is the **length** of the constant. For example,

'PDQ123-A'

is a character constant of length 8;

'JOHN Q. DOE'

is a character constant of length 11, because blanks are characters and are thus included in the character count. *If an apostrophe is to be one of the characters of a constant, it must be entered as a pair of apostrophes:*

'DON''T'

is thus a character constant consisting of the five characters D, O, N, ', and T.

Identifiers. **Identifiers** are names given to programs, constants, variables, and other entities in a program or subprogram. In standard FORTRAN, *identifiers must begin with a letter, which may be followed by up to five letters or digits.* Thus

    MASS
    RATE
    VELOC
    ALPHA1

are valid FORTRAN identifiers, but the following are invalid for the reasons indicated:

    TOOLONG   (Identifiers must consist of at most six characters.)

R2-D2   (Only letters and digits are allowed in variable names.)
6FEET   (Names must begin with a letter.)

One should always use identifiers that are as meaningful as possible, so that the name suggests what the identifier represents.

Variables. In mathematics, a symbolic name is often used to refer to a quantity. For example, the formula

$$A = l \cdot w$$

is used to calculate the area (denoted by A) of a rectangle with a given length (denoted by l) and a given width (denoted by w). These symbolic names, A, l, and w, are called **variables.** If specific values are assigned to l and w, this formula can be used to calculate the value of A, which then represents the area of a particular rectangle.

When a variable is used in a FORTRAN program, the compiler associates it with a particular memory location. The value of a variable at any time is the value stored in the associated memory location at that time.

The type of a FORTRAN variable must be one of the aforementioned six data types, and the type of each variable determines the type of value that may be assigned to that variable. It is therefore necessary to declare the type of each variable in a FORTRAN program. This can be done by using **type statements.** *These type statements must appear in the specification part of the program.*

The type statements used to declare real variables and integer variables have the form

REAL *list*
INTEGER *list*

where *list* is a list of variable names, separated by commas, whose types are being declared real or integer, respectively. Thus, the statements

```
REAL MASS, VELOC
INTEGER COUNT, FACTOR, SUM
```

declare MASS and VELOC to be of real type, and COUNT, FACTOR, and SUM to be of integer type.

The type statement used to declare character variables has the form

CHARACTER∗*n*, *list*

where *list* is a list of variable names typed as character and *n* is an integer constant specifying the length of character constants to be assigned to the variables in this list. The names in the list must be separated by commas; however, the comma separating the length descriptor ∗*n* from the list is optional. In fact, the length descriptor ∗*n* itself is optional, and if omitted, the length for the variables in the list is 1. For example, the type statement

```
CHARACTER*10 ALPHA, BETA, IOTA
```

declares ALPHA, BETA, and IOTA to be character variables and specifies that the length of any character constant assigned to any of these variables is 10. The type statement

```
CHARACTER INIT, FIRST
```

declares INIT and FIRST to be character variables with values of length 1.

A length descriptor may also be attached to any of the individual variables in the list of a CHARACTER statement. In this case, this length specification for that variable overrides the length specification given for the list. The statement

```
CHARACTER*10 FNAME, LNAME*20, INIT*1, STREET, CITY
```

declares that FNAME, LNAME, INIT, STREET, and CITY are character variables and that the length of values for FNAME, STREET, and CITY is 10, the length of values for LNAME is 20, and values of INIT have length 1.

For any variable whose type is not *explicitly* specified in a type statement, FORTRAN will *implicitly* assign it a type according to its **naming convention:** All variables whose names begin with I, J, K, L, M, or N are integer variables, whereas all those whose names begin with any other letter are real variables. (This naming convention may be modified using the IMPLICIT statement described in Chapter 12.)

It is important that variables of a given type be used in a manner that is appropriate to that data type, since otherwise the program may fail to execute correctly. *It is therefore important to declare explicitly the type of each variable used in a program.* This practice encourages one to think carefully about each of these variables, what each represents, what type of values it will have, what operations will be performed with it, and so on.

Named Constants: The PARAMETER Statement. Certain constants occur so often that they are given names. For example, the name ''pi'' is commonly given to the constant 3.14159 . . . and ''e'' to the base 2.71828 . . . of natural logarithms. FORTRAN allows the programmer to assign identifiers to constants in a **PARAMETER statement** in the program's specification part. This statement has the form

$$\text{PARAMETER } (param_1 = const_1, \ldots, param_n = const_n)$$

where $param_1, \ldots, param_n$ are parameter names and $const_1, \ldots, const_n$ are constants or expressions involving only constants and previously defined parameters. Such statements must be preceded by type statements that specify the types of the parameters.

For example, the statements

```
REAL PI, E, TWOPI
PARAMETER (PI = 3.14159, E = 2.71828, TWOPI = 2.0 * PI)
INTEGER LIMIT
PARAMETER (LIMIT = 100)
CHARACTER*6 UNITS
PARAMETER (UNITS = 'METERS')
```

associate the names PI, E, and TWOPI with the real constants 3.14159, 2.71828, and 6.28318, respectively, LIMIT with the integer 100, and UNITS with the character string 'METERS'. These names can then be used anywhere in the program that the corresponding constant value can be used (except as noted later in the text.) For example, a statement such as

```
XCOORD = RATE * COS(TWOPI * TIME)
```

is equivalent to

```
XCOORD = RATE * COS(6.28318 * TIME)
```

but the first form is preferable as it is more readable and does not require modification if a different value with more or fewer significant digits is required for PI.

Another way that named constants can make programs easier to read and to modify is by using them to avoid "magic numbers." To illustrate, suppose that the statements

```
CHANGE = (0.1758 - 0.1257) * POPUL
POPUL = POPUL + CHANGE
```

appear at one point in a program and the statements

```
POPINC = 0.1758 * POPUL
POPDEC = 0.1257 * POPUL
```

appear later. In these statements, the constants 0.1758 and 0.1257 magically appear, without explanation. If they must be changed, it will be necessary for someone to search through the program to determine what they represent and which are the appropriate ones to change, and to locate all the places where they appear. To make the program more understandable and to minimize the number of statements that must be changed when other values are required, it is better to associate these constants with names, as in

```
REAL BIRTH, DEATH
PARAMETER (BIRTH = 0.1758, DEATH = 0.1257)
```

(or to assign them to variables) and then use these names in place of the magic numbers:

```
CHANGE = (BIRTH - DEATH) * POPUL
POPUL = POPUL * CHANGE
          .
          .
          .
POPINC = BIRTH * POPUL
POPDEC = DEATH * POPUL
```

Readability is improved and the flexibility of the program is increased, because if these constants must be changed, one need only change the PARAMETER statement.

Variable Initialization: The DATA Statement. It is important to note that in standard FORTRAN, *all variables are initially undefined.* Although some compilers may initialize a variable with a particular value (e.g., 0 for numeric variables), this is not required. It should be assumed that all variables are initially undefined, and they therefore should be initialized in the program.

This initialization can be done at compile time using a DATA statement of the form

$$\text{DATA } list_1/data_1/, \; list_2/data_2/, \; \ldots, \; list_k/data_k/$$

where each $list_i$ is a list of variable names separated by commas, and each $data_i$ is a list of constants that are used to initialize the variables in $list_i$. DATA statements may appear in the execution part of a program, but it is standard practice to place them after the PARAMETER and type statements in the specification part.

For example, to initialize the values of variables W, X, Y, and Z to 1.0, 2.5, 7.73, and -2.956, respectively, we could use the statements

```
REAL W, X, Y, Z
DATA W, X, Y, Z /1.0, 2.5, 7.73, -2.956/
```

The DATA statement could also be written as

```
DATA W /1.0/, X, Y /2.5, 7.73/, Z /-2.956/
```

or in a variety of other forms.

A list of *n* variables all may be initialized with the same value by preceding the value with *n*∗. Here *n* must be an integer constant or parameter. For example, to initialize ZETA to 1.2, M and N to 3, and each of A, B, C, and D to 3.14, the following statements could be used:

```
REAL ZETA, A, B, C, D
INTEGER M, N
DATA ZETA, M, N, A, B, C, D /1.2, 2*3, 4*3.14/
```

Exercises

1. Which of the following are legal FORTRAN identifiers?

(a) XRAY	**(b)** X-RAY	**(c)** PRESSURE
(d) R2D2	**(e)** 3M	**(f)** CARB14
(g) PS.175	**(h)** X	**(i)** 4
(j) N/4	**(k)** M$	**(l)** ZZZZZZ
(m) ANGLE	**(n)** AGNLE	**(o)** ANGEL
(p) X AXIS	**(q)** A+	**(r)** Z0000Z

2. Classify each of the following as an integer constant, a real constant, or neither:

   (a) 12   (b) 12.   (c) '12'
   (d) 8 + 4   (e) -3.7   (f) 3.7-
   (g) 1,024   (h) +1   (i) $3.98
   (j) 0.357E4   (k) 24E0   (l) E3
   (m) FIVE   (n) 3E.5   (o) .000001
   (p) 1.2 * 10

3. Which of the following are legal character constants?

   (a) 'X'   (b) RATE'
   (c) '$1.98'   (d) '3.14159'
   (e) 'OHM''S LAW'   (f) 'ISN''T'
   (g) 'CONSTANT'   (h) 'A''B''C'
   (i) 'RESULTANT FORCE:'   (j) 'NEWTON'S'
   (k) '12 + 34'   (l) '''S LAW'

4. Write type statements to declare

   (a) TEMP, PRESS, and VOLUME to be of real type.
   (b) ZETA to be of integer type.
   (c) MU to be of real type.
   (d) TIME and DIST to be of integer type.
   (e) STRA, STRB, and STRC to be of character type with values of length 10.
   (f) NAME1 and NAME2 to be of character type with values of length 20 and NAME3 of character type with values of length 10.
   (g) NAME, STREET, CITY, and STATE to be of character type with values of length 20, 30, 15, and 2, respectively.

5. Assuming the standard FORTRAN naming convention, classify each of the following as integer variable, a real variable, or neither:

   (a) GAUSS   (b) FORTRAN   (c) H
   (d) I   (e) LIST   (f) TABLE
   (g) D3   (h) 3D   (i) DISTANCE
   (j) DISTNCE   (k) H20   (l) CHAR
   (m) LOGIC   (n) DIGIT   (o) TWO
   (p) DOUBLE

6. For each of the following, write type statements and PARAMETER statements to name each given constant with the specified name:

   (a) 1.25 with the name RATE.
   (b) 32 with the name GRAV.
   (c) 1.2E12 with EARTH and 1.5E10 with MARS.
   (d) 100 with CBOIL and 212 with FBOIL.
   (e) 1.0E-5 with EPSIL, 0.001 with DELTAX, 500 with NUMINT.
   (f) 'CPSC 141' with COURSE.

    (g) 'CPSC' with DEPT and 141 with CNUMB.

    (h) 'FE2O3' with FORMUL, 'FERRIC OXIDE' with NAME, and .182 with SPHEAT.

    (i) 12713 with IDNUMB, 'J. SMITH' with IDNAME, and 12.75 with RATE.

7. For each of the following, write type statements and DATA statements to declare each variable to have the specified type and initial value:

    (a) RATE1 and RATE2 to be real variables with initial values of 1.25 and 2.33, respectively.

    (b) NUM1 and NUM2 to be integer variables with initial values of 10 and 20, respectively.

    (c) DIST1, DIST2, DIST3, and DIST4 to be real variables, each with the initial value of 0.0.

    (d) LIM1, LIM2, LIM3, LIM4, LIM5, and LIM6 to be integer variables with initial values of 10, 10, 10, 20, 20, and 30, respectively.

    (e) SUM1 and SUM2 to be real variables, each with an initial value of 0.0; SIZE1, SIZE2, SIZE3, and SIZE4 to be integer variables with initial values of 100, 100, 100, and 500, respectively; and ALPHA, BETA, and GAMMA to be real variables with initial values of 0.00001, 2.5E6, and 12.34, respectively.

    (f) DEPT to be a character variable with initial value 'CPSC' and COURS1, COURS2 to be integer variables with initial values 141 and 142.

    (g) CH1, CH2, CH3, CH4, and CH5 to be character variables of length 1, each with the initial value 'X'.

    (h) UNITS1, UNITS2, UNITS3, and UNITS4 to be character variables with initial values 'FEET', 'FEET', 'INCHES', and 'CENTIME-TERS', respectively, NUM1, NUM2, NUM3, NUM4, NUM5, and NUM6 to be integer variables with values 0, 0, 0, 0, 1, and 1, respectively, and RATE1, RATE2, RATE3, and RATE4 to be real variables with values 0.25, 1.5, 1.5, and 2.0, respectively.

3.4 Arithmetic Operations and Functions

In the preceding section we considered variables and constants of various types. These variables and constants can be processed by using operations and functions appropriate to their types. In this section we discuss the arithmetic operations and functions that are used with numeric data.

In FORTRAN, **addition** and **subtraction** are denoted by the usual $(+)$ and minus $(-)$ signs. **Multiplication** is denoted by an asterisk $(*)$. This symbol must be used to denote every multiplication; thus, to multiply N by 2, we must use $2 * N$ or $N * 2$, not 2N. **Division** is denoted by a slash (/), and **exponentiation** is denoted by a pair of asterisks $(**)$. For example, the quantity $B^2 - 4AC$ is written as

```
B ** 2 - 4 * A * C
```

in a FORTRAN program.

An expression containing these operations is evaluated in accordance with the following **priority rules:**

1. *All exponentiations are performed first; consecutive exponentiations are performed from right to left.*
2. *All multiplication and divisions are performed next, in the order in which they appear from left to right.*
3. *The additions and subtractions are performed last, in the order in which they appear from left to right.*

The following examples illustrate this order of evaluation:

```
2 ** 3 ** 2 = 2 ** 9 = 512
10 - 8 - 2 = 2 - 2 = 0
10 / 5 * 2 = 2 * 2 = 4
2 + 4 / 2 = 2 + 2 = 4
2 + 4 ** 2 / 2 = 2 + 16 / 2 = 2 + 8 = 10
```

The standard order of evaluation can be modified by using parentheses to enclose subexpressions within an expression. These subexpressions are evaluated first in the standard manner, and the results are then combined to evaluate the complete expression. If the parentheses are "nested," that is, if one set of parentheses is contained within another, the computations in the innermost parentheses are performed first.

For example, consider the expression

```
(5 * (11 - 5) ** 2) * 4 + 9
```

The subexpression 11 − 5 is evaluated first, producing

```
(5 * 6 ** 2) * 4 + 9
```

Next, the subexpression 5 ∗ 6 ∗∗ 2 is evaluated in the standard order, giving

```
180 * 4 + 9
```

Now the multiplication is performed, giving

```
720 + 9
```

and the addition produces the final result

```
729
```

Expressions containing two or more operations must be written carefully to ensure that they will be evaluated in the order intended. Even though parentheses may not be required, they should be used freely to clarify the intended order of evaluation and to write complicated expressions in terms of simpler subexpressions. However, parentheses must balance; that is, they must occur in pairs, as an unpaired parenthesis will result in an error.

The symbols + and − can also be used as **unary operators;** for example, +X and −(A + B) are allowed. But unary operators must be used carefully, because standard FORTRAN *does not allow two operators to follow in succession.* (Note that ∗∗ is interpreted as a single operator rather than two operators in succession.) For example, the expression N ∗ −2 is not allowed; rather, it must be written as N ∗ (−2). The unary operations have the same low priority as the corresponding binary operations.

When two constants or variables of the same type are combined using one of the four basic arithmetic operations (+, −, ∗, /), the result has the same type as the operands. For example, the sum of the integers 3 and 4 is the integer 7, whereas the sum of the real numbers 3.0 and 4.0 is the real number 7.0. This distinction may seem unimportant until one considers the division operation. Division of the real constant 9.0 by the real constant 4.0,

$$9.0 \ / \ 4.0$$

produces the real quotient 2.25, whereas dividing the integer 9 by the integer 4,

$$9 \ / \ 4$$

produces the integer quotient 2, which is equal to the integer part of the real quotient 2.25. Similarly, if N has the value 2 and X has the value 2.0, the real division

$$1.0 \ / \ X$$

yields .5, whereas the integer division

$$1 \ / \ N$$

yields 0.

It is also possible to combine an integer quantity with a real quantity using these arithmetic operations. Expressions involving different types of numeric operands are **mixed-mode expressions.** When an integer quantity is combined with a real one, the integer quantity is converted to its real equivalent, and the result is of real type. The following examples illustrate the evaluation of some mixed-mode expressions; note that type conversion does not take place until necessary:

```
1.0 / 4 → 1.0 / 4.0 → 0.25
3.0 + 8 / 5 → 3.0 + 1 → 3.0 + 1.0 → 4.0
3 + 8.0 / 5 → 3 + 8.0 / 5.0 → 3 + 1.6 → 3.0 + 1.6 → 4.6
```

These last two examples show why *mixed-mode expressions must be used with care.* The two expressions 3.0 + 8 / 5 and 3 + 8.0 / 5 seem to be algebraically equal but are in fact unequal because of the differences in real and integer arithmetic.

These differences also affect the manner in which exponentiations are performed. If the exponent is an integer quantity, exponentiation is carried out using repeated multiplication. The following examples illustrate:

```
2 ** 3 → 2 * 2 * 2 → 8
(-4.0) ** 2 → (-4.0) * (-4.0) → 16.0
1.5 ** 2 → 1.5 * 1.5 → 2.25
```

If, however, the exponent is a real quantity, exponentiation is performed using logarithms. For example,

```
2.0 ** 3.0
```

is evaluated as

$$e^{3.0\ln(2.0)}$$

which will not be exactly 8.0 because of roundoff errors that arise in storing real numbers and because the exponentiation and logarithm functions produce only approximate values. Another consequence of this method of performing exponentiation is that a negative quantity raised to a real power is undefined because the logarithms of negative values are not defined. Consequently, $(-4.0) ** 2.0$ will be undefined, even though $(-4.0) ** 2$ is evaluated as $(-4.0) * (-4.0) = 16.0$. These examples show why a *real exponent should never be used in place of an integer exponent.*

There are, however, computations in which real exponents are appropriate. For example, in mathematics, $7^{1/2}$ denotes $\sqrt{7}$, the square root of 7. In FORTRAN this operation of extracting roots can be performed using exponentiation with real exponents. Thus, to compute the square root of 7, we could write 7 ** 0.5, 7 ** (1.0 / 2.0) or even 7 ** (1.0 / 2). (Note, however, that 7 ** (1 / 2) yields 7 ** 0 = 1.) In general, the Nth root of X can be computed by using

```
X ** (1.0 / N)
```

for any positive-valued X.

Because many computations involve the square root of a real quantity, FORTRAN provides a special **function** to implement this operation. This function is denoted by SQRT and is used by writing

```
SQRT(argument)
```

where *argument* is a *real-valued* constant, variable, or expression. For example, to calculate the square root of 7, we would write

```
SQRT(7.0)
```

but not SQRT(7). IF B ** 2 − 4 * A * C is a nonnegative real-valued expression, its square root can be calculated by writing

```
SQRT(B ** 2 - 4 * A * C)
```

TABLE 3.1 Some FORTRAN Functions

Function	Description	Type of Argument(s)*	Type of Value
ABS(x)	Absolute value of x	Integer or real	Same as arguments
COS(x)	Cosine of x radians	Real	Real
EXP(x)	Exponential function	Real	Real
INT(x)	Integer part of x	Real	Integer
LOG(x)	Natural logarithm of x	Real	Real
MAX($x_1, \ldots, x_n$)	Maximum of $x_1, \ldots, x_n$	Integer or real	Same as arguments
MIN($x_1, \ldots, x_n$)	Minimum of $x_1, \ldots, x_n$	Integer or real	Same as arguments
MOD(x, y)	x (mod y); $x - \text{INT}(x/y) * y$	Integer or real	Same as arguments
NINT(x)	x rounded to nearest integer	Real	Integer
REAL(x)	Conversion of x to real type	Integer	Real
SIN(x)	Sine of x radians	Real	Real
SQRT(x)	Square root of x	Real	Real

* In several cases, the arguments (and values) may be of double precision or complex types. See Table 9.1.

If the value of the expression B ** 2 $-$ 4 * A * C is negative, an error will result because the square root of a negative number is not defined. To calculate the square root of an integer variable NUM it is necessary first to convert its value to a real value before using SQRT:

```
SQRT(REAL(NUM))
```

There are several other functions provided in FORTRAN; some of the more commonly used functions are listed in Table 3.1. To use any of these functions, we simply give the function name followed by the argument(s) enclosed in parentheses. In each case, the argument(s) must be of the type specified for that function in the table.

Exercises

1. Find the value of each of the following expressions:

    (a) 9 - 5 - 3
    (b) 2 ** 3 + 3 / 5
    (c) 2.0 / 4
    (d) 2 + 3 ** 2
    (e) (2 + 3) ** 2
    (f) 3 ** 2 ** 3
    (g) (3 ** 2) ** 3
    (h) 3 ** (2 ** 3)
    (i) (3 ** 2 ** 3)
    (j) 25 ** 1 / 2
    (k) -3.0 ** 2
    (l) 12.0 / 1.0 * 3.0
    (m) ((2 + 3) ** 2) / (8 - (2 + 1))
    (n) (2 + 3 ** 2) / (8 - 2 + 1)

(o) `(2.0 + 3 ** 2) / (8 - 2 + 1)`

(p) `SQRT(6.0 + 3.0)`

2. Given that TWO = 2.0, TRI = 3.0, FOUR = 4.0, IJK = 8, INK = 5, find the value for each of the following:

   (a) `TWO + TRI * TRI`
   (b) `INK / 3`
   (c) `(TRI + TWO / FOUR) ** 2`
   (d) `IJK / INK * 5.1`
   (e) `FOUR ** 2 / TWO ** 2`
   (f) `INK ** 2 / TWO ** 2`
   (g) `SQRT(TWO + TRI + FOUR)`

3. Write FORTRAN expressions equivalent to the following:

   (a) $10 + 5B - 4AC$
   (b) Three times the difference $4 - N$ divided by twice the quantity $M^2 + N^2$
   (c) The square root of $A + 3B^2$
   (d) The cube root of X (calculated as X to the one-third power)
   (e) $A^2 + B^2 - 2AB \cos T$
   (f) The natural logarithm of the absolute value of $\dfrac{X - Y}{X + Y}$

3.5   The Assignment Statement

The **assignment statement** is used to assign values to variables and has the form

   variable = expression

where *expression* may be a constant, another variable to which a value has previously been assigned, or a formula to be evaluated. For example, suppose that XCOORD and YCOORD are real variables and NUMBER and TERM are integer variables, as declared by the following statements:

```
REAL XCOORD, YCOORD
INTEGER NUMBER, TERM
```

These declarations associate memory locations with these variables. This might be pictured as follows, where the question marks indicate that these variables are initially undefined:

XCOORD	?
YCOORD	?
NUMBER	?
TERM	?

Now consider the following assignment statements:

```
XCOORD = 5.23
YCOORD = SQRT(25.0)
NUMBER = 17
TERM = NUMBER / 3 + 2
XCOORD = 2.0 * XCOORD
```

The first assignment statement assigns the real constant 5.23 to the real variable XCOORD, and the second assigns the real constant 5.0 to the real variable YCOORD. The next assignment statement assigns the integer constant 17 to the integer variable NUMBER; the variable TERM is still undefined.

XCOORD	5.23
YCOORD	5.0
NUMBER	17
TERM	?

This means that until the contents of these memory locations are changed, these values are substituted for the variable names in any subsequent expression containing these variables. Thus, in the fourth assignment statement, the value 17 is substituted for the variable NUMBER; the expression NUMBER / 3 + 2 is evaluated, yielding 7; and this value is then assigned to the integer variable TERM; the value of NUMBER is unchanged.

XCOORD	5.23
YCOORD	5.0
NUMBER	17
TERM	7

In the last assignment statement, the variable XCOORD appears on both sides of the assignment operator (=). In this case, the current value 5.23 for XCOORD is used in evaluating the expression 2.0 * XCOORD, yielding the value 10.46; this value is then assigned to XCOORD. The old value 5.23 is lost because it has been replaced with the new value 10.46.

XCOORD	10.46
YCOORD	5.0
NUMBER	17
TERM	7

Because there are different types of numeric variable and constants, it is possible to have not only mixed-mode arithmetic, as described in the preceding section, but also mixed-mode assignment. This occurs when the type of variable to be assigned a value is different from that of the value being assigned.

If an integer-valued expression is assigned to a real variable, the value is converted to a real constant and then assigned to the variable. Thus, if the integer variable N has the value 9, and ALPHA and BETA are real variables, the statements

```
ALPHA = 3
BETA = (N + 3) / 5
```

assign the real constant 3.0 to ALPHA and the real constant 2.0 to BETA.

In the case of a real-valued expression assigned to an integer variable, the fractional part of the expression value is truncated, and the integer part is assigned to the variable. For example, if the real variable X has the value 5.75, and I, KAPPA, and MU are integer variables, the statements

```
I = 3.14159
KAPPA = X / 2.0
MU = 1.0 / X
```

assign the integer constants 3, 2, and 0 to the variables I, KAPPA, and MU, respectively. As this example shows, *mixed-mode assignments must be used with care* because the fractional part of the value being assigned is lost.

An assignment statement may also be used to assign a value to a character variable. To illustrate, suppose that the character variables STR, TRUN, and PAD are declared by the type statement

```
CHARACTER*5 STR, TRUN, PAD*10
```

The assignment statement

```
STR = 'ALPHA'
```

assigns the value 'ALPHA' to STR. In this example, the declared length of the variable is equal to the length of the corresponding value assigned to this variable. *If, however, the lengths do not match, the values are padded with blanks or truncated as necessary.* If the declared length of the variable is greater than the length of the value being assigned, trailing blanks are added to the value; thus the statement

```
PAD = 'PARTICLE'
```

assigns the value 'PARTICLEƀƀ' to the variable PAD (where ƀ denotes a blank character). If the declared length of the variable is less than the length of the value being assigned, that value is truncated to the size of the variable, and the leftmost characters are assigned; thus, the statement

```
TRUN = 'TEMPERATURE'
```

assigns the value 'TEMPE' to the variable TRUN.

In every assignment statement, the variable to be assigned a value must appear on the left side of the assignment operator (=), and a legal expression must appear on the right. For example, if we assume the declarations

```
INTEGER M, N
REAL X
```

then the following are not valid FORTRAN statements, for the reasons indicated:

Statement	Error
5 = N	Variable names must be on the left of the equals sign.
X + 3.5 = 4.26	Numeric expressions may not appear on the left of the equals sign.
N = 'FIVE'	Character constants may not be assigned to a numeric variable.
N = '2' + '3'	'2' + '3' is not a legal expression.
M = N = 1	N = 1 is not a legal expression.

It is important to remember that *the assignment statement is not a statement of algebraic equality; rather, it is a* replacement *statement.* Some beginning programmers forget this and write the assignment statement

```
A = B
```

when the statement

```
B = A
```

is intended. These two statements produce very different results, as the first assigns the value of B to A, leaving A unchanged,

$$
\begin{array}{cc}
A & 8.5 \\
B & 9.37
\end{array}
\quad \xrightarrow{A = B} \quad
\begin{array}{cc}
A & 9.37 \\
B & 9.37
\end{array}
$$

and the second assigns the value of A to B, leaving A unchanged.

$$
\begin{array}{cc}
A & 8.5 \\
B & 9.37
\end{array}
\quad \xrightarrow{B = A} \quad
\begin{array}{cc}
A & 8.5 \\
B & 8.5
\end{array}
$$

To illustrate further that an assignment statement is a replacement statement, suppose that DELTA and RHO are integer variables with values 357 and 59, respectively. The following statements interchange the values of DELTA and RHO, using the auxiliary variable TEMP:

```
INTEGER DELTA, RHO, TEMP
        .
        .
        .
TEMP = DELTA
DELTA = RHO
RHO = TEMP
```

As another example, consider the statement

```
SUM = SUM + X
```

Such a statement, in which the same variable appears on both sides of the assignment operator, often confuses beginning programmers. Execution of this statement causes the values of SUM and X to be substituted for these variables to evaluate the expression SUM + X, and the resulting value is then assigned to SUM. The following diagram illustrates this statement for the case in which the real variables SUM and X have the values 132.5 and 8.4, respectively.

SUM | 132.5 | SUM = SUM + X   →   SUM | 140.9 |
X | 8.4 | X | 8.4 |

Note that the old value of the variable SUM is lost because it was replaced with a new value.

Another statement in which the same variable appears on both sides of the assignment operator is

```
COUNT = COUNT + 1
```

This statement implements the operation "increment COUNT by 1." When it is executed, the current value of COUNT is substituted for this variable to evaluate the expression COUNT + 1, and this new value is then assigned to COUNT. For example, if COUNT has the value 3, the value of COUNT + 1 is 3 + 1 = 4, which is then assigned as the new value for COUNT:

COUNT | 3 | COUNT = COUNT + 1   →   COUNT | 4 |

Note once again that the old value of the variable has been lost because it was replaced with a new value.

Exercises

1. Assuming the declarations

```
INTEGER N
REAL PI, ALPHA
```

determine which of the following are valid FORTRAN assignment statements. If they are not valid, explain why they are not.

(a) `PI = 3.141592`   (b) `3 = N`
(c) `N        = N+    1`   (d) `N+1 = N`
(e) `ALPHA = 1`   (f) `ALPHA = '1'`
(g) `ALPHA = ALPHA`

2. Given that TWO $=$ 2.0, TRI $=$ 2.0, FOUR $=$ 3.0, NUM $=$ 8, and MIX $=$ 5 and that the following declarations have been made

```
REAL TWO, TRI, FOUR, X
INTEGER NUM, MIX, J
```

find the value assigned to the given variable for each of the following, or indicate why the statement is not valid:

(a) `X = (TWO + TRI) ** TRI`
(b) `X = (TRI + TWO / FOUR) ** 2`
(c) `X = NUM / MIX + 5.1`
(d) `J = NUM / MIX + 5.1`
(e) `X = MIX ** 2 / NUM ** 2`
(f) `J = MIX ** 2 / NUM ** 2`
(g) `NUM = NUM + 2`
(h) `X = SQRT(TRI ** 2 + FOUR ** 2)`
(i) `NUM = ABS(TRI - 4.5)`
(j) `J = MAX(INT(FOUR / 3), MIX)`

3. Given that the following declarations have been made

```
CHARACTER*10 ALPHA, BETA*5, GAMMA*1, DELTA*4
```

and that DELTA $=$ 'FOUR', find the value assigned to the given variable for each of the following, or indicate why the statement is not valid.

(a) `GAMMA = 1`
(b) `GAMMA = '1'`
(c) `ALPHA = 'ONETWO'`
(d) `ALPHA = '12'`
(e) `BETA = 'DON'T'`
(f) `BETA = 'DON''T'`
(g) `BETA = 'ABCDEFGHIJKLMNOPQRSTUVWXYZ'`
(h) `BETA = '123,456,789'`
(i) `ALPHA = DELTA`
(j) `GAMMA = DELTA`

4. Write a FORTRAN assignment statement for each of the following that calculates the given expression and assigns the result to the specified variable:

(a) RATE times TIME to DIST

(b) $\sqrt{A^2 + B^2}$ to C

(c) $\dfrac{1}{\dfrac{1}{R1} + \dfrac{1}{R2} + \dfrac{1}{R3}}$ to RESIST

(d) P times $(1 + R)^N$ to VALUE

(e) Area of triangle (one-half base times height) of base B and height H to AREA

(f) 5/9 of the difference $F - 32$ to C (conversion of Fahrenheit to Celsius)

(g) $\dfrac{2V^2 \sin A \cos A}{G}$ to RANGE

5. For each of the following, give values for the integer variables I, J, and K and the real variable X for which the two expressions are not equal:

   (a) I * (J / K) and I * J / K

   (b) X * I / J and X * (I / J)

   (c) (I + J) / K and I / K + J / K

3.6   List-Directed Input/Output

In the preceding section, we considered the assignment statement, which enables us to calculate the values of expressions and store the results of these computations by assigning them to variables. An assignment statement does not, however, display these results on some output device, nor does it allow the user to enter new values during execution. For example, if a projectile is launched from an initial height of HGHT0 with an initial vertical velocity of VELOC0 and a vertical acceleration of ACCEL, then the equations

```
HGHT = 0.5 * ACCEL * TIME ** 2 + VELOC0 * TIME + HGHT0
```

and

```
VELOC = ACCEL * TIME + VELOC0
```

give the height (HGHT) and the vertical velocity (VELOC) at any TIME after launch. The program in Figure 3.1 assigns the value -9.807 (m/sec^2) to ACCEL, 150.0 (m) to HGHT0, 100.0 (m/sec) to VELOC0, and 5.0 (sec) to TIME and then computes the corresponding values of HGHT and VELOC.

```
      PROGRAM PROJEC
************************************************************************
* This program calculates the velocity and height of a projectile    *
* given its initial height, initial velocity, and constant           *
* acceleration.  Variables used are:                                  *
*      HGHT0   :  initial height                                      *
*      HGHT    :  height at any time                                  *
*      VELOC0  :  initial vertical velocity                           *
*      VELOC   :  vertical velocity at any time                       *
*      ACCEL   :  vertical acceleration                               *
*      TIME    :  time elapsed since projectile was launched          *
************************************************************************
```

Figure 3.1

Figure 3.1   (continued)

```
REAL HGHT0, HGHT, VELOC0, VELOC, ACCEL, TIME

ACCEL = -9.807
HGHT0 = 150.0
VELOC0 = 100.0
TIME = 5.0
HGHT = 0.5 * ACCEL * TIME ** 2  +  VELOC0 * TIME  +  HGHT0
VELOC = ACCEL * TIME + VELOC0
END
```

The values of HGHT and VELOC are calculated as desired, but they are stored only internally and are not displayed to the user. Moreover, if the same calculation is to be done for the same acceleration but with values 100.0 for HGHT0, 90.0 for VELOC0, and 4.3 for TIME, then several statements must be modified, as shown in Figure 3.2, and the program executed again.

```
      PROGRAM PROJEC
************************************************************************
* This program calculates the velocity and height of a projectile    *
* given its initial height, initial velocity, and constant           *
* acceleration.  Variables used are:                                 *
*      HGHT0   :  initial height                                     *
*      HGHT    :  height at any time                                 *
*      VELOC0  :  initial vertical velocity                          *
*      VELOC   :  vertical velocity at any time                      *
*      ACCEL   :  vertical acceleration                              *
*      TIME    :  time elapsed since projectile was launched         *
************************************************************************

      REAL HGHT0, HGHT, VELOC0, VELOC, ACCEL, TIME

      ACCEL = -9.807
      HGHT0 = 100.0
      VELOC0 = 90.0
      TIME = 4.3
      HGHT = 0.5 * ACCEL * TIME ** 2  +  VELOC0 * TIME  +  HGHT0
      VELOC = ACCEL * TIME + VELOC0
      END
```

Figure 3.2

The output statement that we consider in this section provides a method for easily displaying information. We also consider an input statement to provide a convenient way of assigning values from an external source during execution of the program.

FORTRAN provides two types of input/output statements. In the first type, the programmer must explicitly specify the format in which the data is presented for input or, in the case of output, the precise format in which it is to be displayed. In the second type of input/output, certain predetermined standard formats that match the types of items in the input/output list are automatically provided by the compiler. It is this second type, known as **list-directed input/output,** that is considered in this section.

List-Directed Output. The simplest list-directed output statement has the form

PRINT *, *output-list*

where *output-list* is a single expression or a list of expressions separated by commas. Each of these expressions is a constant, a variable, or a formula. For example, to display some of the relevant information from the preceding example, we might add two PRINT statements, as shown in Figure 3.3. Execution of the program will produce output similar to that shown. Note that each PRINT statement produces a new line of output. The exact format and spacing used to display these values are compiler dependent; for example, in some systems, real values might be displayed in scientific notation, and the number of spaces in an output line might be different from that shown.

```
      PROGRAM PROJEC
************************************************************************
* This program calculates the velocity and height of a projectile    *
* given its initial height, initial velocity, and constant           *
* acceleration.  Variables used are:                                  *
*      HGHT0   :  initial height                                      *
*      HGHT    :  height at any time                                  *
*      VELOC0  :  initial vertical velocity                           *
*      VELOC   :  vertical velocity at any time                       *
*      ACCEL   :  vertical acceleration                               *
*      TIME    :  time elapsed since projectile was launched          *
************************************************************************

      REAL HGHT0, HGHT, VELOC0, VELOC, ACCEL, TIME

      ACCEL = -9.807
      HGHT0 = 100.0
      VELOC0 = 90.0
      TIME = 4.3
      HGHT = 0.5 * ACCEL * TIME ** 2  +  VELOC0 * TIME  +  HGHT0
      VELOC = ACCEL * TIME + VELOC0
      PRINT *, 'AT TIME ', TIME, ' THE VERTICAL VELOCITY IS ', VELOC
      PRINT *, 'AND THE HEIGHT IS ', HGHT
      END
```

Figure 3.3

Figure 3.3 (continued)

Sample run:

```
AT TIME     4.30000 THE VERTICAL VELOCITY IS     47.8299
AND THE HEIGHT IS     396.334
```

In some situations, one or more blank lines in the output improve readability. A blank line can be displayed by a PRINT statement of the form

PRINT *

in which the output list is empty. Note that the comma that normally follows the asterisk is also omitted. Execution of each statement of this form causes a single blank line to be displayed.

List-Directed Input. The simplest form of the list-directed input statement is

READ *, *input-list*

where *input-list* consists of a single variable or a list of variables separated by commas. Execution of this READ statement causes the transfer of values from some external source (keyboard, card reader, file) and the assignment of these values to the variables in the input list. For example, the statement

```
READ *, HGHT0, VELOC0, TIME
```

assigns values to the variables HGHT0, VELOC0, and TIME. Therefore, this single READ statement replaces the three assignment statements used to assign values to these variables in the preceding examples. The modified program is shown in Figure 3.4.

```
      PROGRAM PROJEC
************************************************************************
* This program calculates the velocity and height of a projectile    *
* given its initial height, initial velocity, and constant           *
* acceleration.  Variables used are:                                  *
*     HGHT0   :  initial height                                       *
*     HGHT    :  height at any time                                   *
*     VELOC0  :  initial vertical velocity                            *
*     VELOC   :  vertical velocity at any time                        *
*     ACCEL   :  vertical acceleration                                *
*     TIME    :  time elapsed since projectile was launched           *
************************************************************************
```

Figure 3.4

Figure 3.4 (continued)

```
REAL HGHT0, HGHT, VELOC0, VELOC, ACCEL, TIME

ACCEL = -9.807
READ *, HGHT0, VELOC0, TIME
HGHT = 0.5 * ACCEL * TIME ** 2  +  VELOC0 * TIME  +  HGHT0
VELOC = ACCEL * TIME + VELOC0
PRINT *, 'AT TIME ', TIME, ' THE VERTICAL VELOCITY IS ', VELOC
PRINT *, 'AND THE HEIGHT IS ', HGHT
END
```

The values assigned to the variables in the input list may be prepared in advance and saved in a file and read from this file during program execution. This is the typical procedure followed in a batch mode of operation. In an interactive mode the values may be entered by the user during program execution. In both modes, all columns of the input line may be used, and the following rules apply:

1. A new line of data is processed each time a READ statement is executed.
2. If there are fewer entries in a line of input data than there are variables in the input list, successive lines of input are processed until values for all variables in the list have been obtained.
3. If there are more entries in a line of input data than there are variables in the input list, the first data values are used, and all remaining values are ignored.
4. The entries in each line of input data must be constants and of the same type as the variables to which they are assigned. (However, an integer value may be assigned to a real variable, with automatic conversion taking place.)
5. Consecutive entries in a line of input data must be separated by a comma or by one or more spaces.

For example, to assign the values 100.0, 90.0, and 4.3 to the variables HGHT0, VELOC0, and TIME, respectively, in the statement

```
READ *, HGHT0, VELOC0, TIME
```

the following line of input data could be used:

```
100.0, 90.0, 4.3
```

Spaces could be used as separators in place of the commas,

```
100.0 90.0 4.3
```

or more than one line of data could be used:

```
100.0 90.0
4.3
```

Character values can also be read using list-directed input, but they must be enclosed in single quotes. Truncation or blank padding is done when necessary, as described earlier for assignment statements. For example, if UNITS1 and UNITS2 have been declared by

```
CHARACTER*8 UNITS1, UNITS2
```

then entering the values

```
'METER', 'CENTIMETER'
```

in response to the statement

```
READ *, UNITS1, UNITS2
```

assigns the value 'METERƀƀƀ' to UNITS1 (where ƀ denotes a blank) and the value 'CENTIMET' to UNITS2.

In a batch mode of operation, lines of input data together with the program and certain command lines are placed in a file prepared by the user. When a READ statement is encountered, the values from these data lines are retrieved automatically and assigned to the variables in the input list.

In an interactive mode of operation, the values assigned to variables in an input list are entered during program execution. In this case, when a READ statement is encountered, program execution is suspended while the user enters values for all the variables in the input list. Program execution then automatically resumes. Because execution is interrupted by a READ statement and because the correct number and types of values must be entered before execution can resume, *it is good practice to provide some message to prompt the user when it is necessary to enter data values.* This is accomplished by preceding each READ statement with a PRINT statement that displays the appropriate prompts. The program in Figure 3.5 illustrates this by prompting the user when values for HGHT0, VELOC0, and TIME are to be entered; it is a modification of the program in Figure 3.4.

```
      PROGRAM PROJEC
*******************************************************************************
* This program calculates the velocity and height of a projectile    *
* given its initial height, initial velocity, and constant           *
* acceleration.  Variables used are:                                 *
*      HGHT0   :  initial height                                     *
*      HGHT    :  height at any time                                 *
*      VELOC0  :  initial vertical velocity                          *
*      VELOC   :  vertical velocity at any time                      *
*      ACCEL   :  vertical acceleration                              *
*      TIME    :  time elapsed since projectile was launched         *
*******************************************************************************
```

Figure 3.5

Figure 3.5 (continued)

```
REAL HGHT0, HGHT, VELOC0, VELOC, ACCEL, TIME

ACCEL = -9.807
PRINT *, 'ENTER THE INITIAL HEIGHT AND VELOCITY:'
READ *, HGHT0, VELOC0
PRINT *, 'ENTER TIME AT WHICH TO CALCULATE HEIGHT AND VELOCITY:'
READ *, TIME
HGHT = 0.5 * ACCEL * TIME ** 2  +  VELOC0 * TIME  +  HGHT0
VELOC = ACCEL * TIME + VELOC0
PRINT *, 'AT TIME ', TIME, ' THE VERTICAL VELOCITY IS ', VELOC
PRINT *, 'AND THE HEIGHT IS ', HGHT
END
```

Sample runs:

```
ENTER THE INITIAL HEIGHT AND VELOCITY:
100.0 90.0
ENTER TIME AT WHICH TO CALCULATE HEIGHT AND VELOCITY:
4.3
AT TIME      4.30000 THE VERTICAL VELOCITY IS      47.8299
AND THE HEIGHT IS      396.334


ENTER THE INITIAL HEIGHT AND VELOCITY:
150.0 100.0
ENTER TIME AT WHICH TO CALCULATE HEIGHT AND VELOCITY:
5.0
AT TIME      5.00000 THE VERTICAL VELOCITY IS      50.9650
AND THE HEIGHT IS      527.412


ENTER THE INITIAL HEIGHT AND VELOCITY:
150.0 100.0
ENTER TIME AT WHICH TO CALCULATE HEIGHT AND VELOCITY:
0
AT TIME    0. THE VERTICAL VELOCITY IS      100.0000
AND THE HEIGHT IS      150.000


ENTER THE INITIAL HEIGHT AND VELOCITY:
150.0 100.0
ENTER TIME AT WHICH TO CALCULATE HEIGHT AND VELOCITY:
21.79
AT TIME      21.7900 THE VERTICAL VELOCITY IS      -113.695
AND THE HEIGHT IS      0.797852
```

3.7 Program Composition

In Section 3.1 we noted that a FORTRAN program has the form

heading
specification part
execution part

The **program heading** has the form

    PROGRAM *name*

where *name* is a legal FORTRAN identifier; that is, it consists of up to six
letters or digits, the first of which must be a letter. This name must be distinct
from all other names in the program and should be chosen to indicate the
purpose of the program. Thus, the first statement in the program of Figure 3.5
to calculate the height and velocity of a projectile is

    PROGRAM PROJEC

Although the PROGRAM statement is optional, it should be used to identify
the program and to distinguish it from other program units such as function
subprograms, subroutine subprograms, and block data subprograms, which are
described later.

Following the PROGRAM statement there should be **opening documentation** that explains the purpose of the program, clarifies the choice of variable
names, and provides other pertinent information about the program. This documentation consists of comment lines, which are blank lines or lines having
the letter C or an asterisk (∗) in the first position of the line. Comment lines
are not considered to be program statements and may be placed anywhere in
the program. Such comment lines can be used to clarify the purpose and structure of key parts of the program. Program documentation is invaluable when
revisions and modifications are made in the future, especially when they are
made by persons other than the original programmer.

The **specification part** of a program must appear next. This part contains
type statements like

    REAL HGHT0, HGHT, VELOC0, VELOC, ACCEL, TIME

whose purpose is to specify the type of each of the variables used in the
program. The type statements we have considered thus far have the form

    REAL *list*

for declaring real variables,

    INTEGER *list*

for declaring integer variables and

    CHARACTER∗*n* *list*

for declaring character variables. Others will be considered in later chapters.

The specification part may also contain PARAMETER statements that may be used to associate names with constants to be used in the program. These statements have the form

PARAMETER ($param_1 = const_1, \ldots, param_n = const_n$)

Data statements of the form

DATA $list_1/data_1/, list_2/data_2/, \ldots, list_k/data_k/$

may be included to initialize the values of variables at compile time. They must appear after all PARAMETER and type statements.

FORTRAN statements are classified as either executable or nonexecutable. **Nonexecutable statements** provide information that is used during compilation of a program, but they do not cause any specific action to be performed during execution. For example, the PROGRAM statement, PARAMETER statements, DATA statements, and type statements are nonexecutable statements.

Executable statements do specify actions to be performed during execution of the program. Assignment statements and input/output statements are examples. Executable statements are placed in the last part of a FORTRAN program, its **execution part**, which has the form

statement-1
statement-2
.
.
.
END

Note that the last statement in this part and thus the last statement of every program must be the **END statement.** This statement indicates to the compiler the end of the program; it also halts execution of the program and thus is an executable statement.

3.8   Example: Acidity of a Diluted Mixture

In this chapter we have introduced several FORTRAN statements, operations, and functions and have considered how they are used in a FORTRAN program. In this section we present an example illustrating each of the steps of the problem-solving process. The FORTRAN program that results uses only those statements that we have considered thus far.

Suppose that the manufacturing process for castings at a certain plant includes cooling each casting in a water bath, followed by cleaning it by immersion in an acid bath. When the casting is transferred from the water bath to the acid bath, a certain amount of water accompanies it, thereby diluting the acid. When the casting is removed from the acid bath, the same amount of this diluted mixture is also removed; thus the volume of the liquid in the acid bath remains constant, but the acidity decreases each time a casting is immersed. We wish to design a program to determine the acidity of the liquid in the acid bath after a given number of castings are immersed and to determine when the acidity falls below some lower limit at which the mixture becomes too diluted to clean the castings.

The input to the program consists of the volume of the acid bath, the amount of water that is mixed with the acid when a casting is transferred from the water bath, the number of castings immersed, and the lower limit on the acidity. The output must include a measure of the acidity after the specified number of castings have been immersed and the number of castings that may be immersed before the acidity falls below the specified lower limit.

To solve this problem, we observe that if A is the original amount of acid and W is the amount of water that is mixed in at each stage, the proportion of acid in the mixture when the first casting is immersed is

$$\frac{A}{A + W}$$

When this casting is removed from the acid bath, the amount of acid in the diluted mixture is

$$\left(\frac{A}{A + W}\right) \cdot A$$

This means that when the second casting is immersed, the proportion of acid in the mixture becomes

$$\frac{\left(\dfrac{A}{A + W}\right) \cdot A}{A + W}$$

which can be written as

$$\left(\frac{A}{A + W}\right)^2$$

In general, the proportion of acid in the diluted mixture after n castings have been immersed is given by

$$\left(\frac{A}{A + W}\right)^n$$

This provides the formula needed to solve the first part of the problem.

For the second part, if L denotes the lower limit on acidity, we must determine the least value of n for which

$$\left(\frac{A}{A + W}\right)^n < L$$

Taking logarithms, we find that this inequality is equivalent to

$$n > \frac{\log L}{\log A - \log(A + W)}$$

and the desired value of n is thus the least integer greater than the expression on the right side.

Selecting names for the quantities involved that are somewhat self-explanatory, we arrive at the following algorithm to solve this problem:

ALGORITHM FOR ACID DILUTION PROBLEM

* This algorithm determines the acidity of a diluted mixture in an   *
* acid bath after a given number of castings are immersed in it and   *
* also determines how often the mixture can be used before its   *
* acidity falls below some lower limit. ACID represents the amount   *
* of acid in the mixture, WATER is the amount of water added with   *
* each immersion, and CONCEN is the proportion of acid in the   *
* mixture. The number of castings is NCASTS, and LIMIT is the   *
* lower limit on acidity.   *

1. Enter ACID, WATER, and NCASTS.
2. Calculate CONCEN = (ACID / (ACID + WATER)) ** NCASTS.
3. Display CONCEN.
4. Enter LIMIT.
5. Calculate $NCASTS = 1 + \dfrac{\log(LIMIT)}{\log(ACID) - \log(ACID + WATER)}$.
6. Display NCASTS.

Figure 3.6 shows the structure of this algorithm as a flowchart.

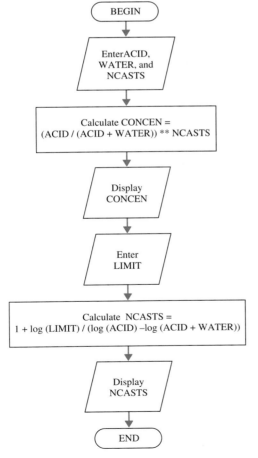

Figure 3.6

The program in Figure 3.7 implements this algorithm. Note the inclusion of the variable directory in the opening documentation of the program to explain what each variable represents. Several sample runs using test data to verify that the program is correct are also shown.

```
        PROGRAM DILUTE
*******************************************************************
* Program to determine the acidity of a diluted mixture in an acid   *
* bath after a given number of castings are immersed in it, and to   *
* determine how often the mixture can be used before its acidity falls *
* below some specified lower limit.  Variables used are:          *
*       ACID    :  amount of acid in the mixture               *
*       WATER   :  amount of water added with each casting immersion *
*       CONCEN  :  proportion of acid in the mixture            *
*       NCASTS  :  number of castings                          *
*       LIMIT   :  lower limit on acidity                       *
*******************************************************************

        INTEGER NCASTS
        REAL ACID, WATER, CONCEN, LIMIT

        PRINT *, 'ENTER ORIGINAL AMOUNT OF ACID, AMOUNT OF WATER ADDED'
        PRINT *, 'AND THE NUMBER OF CASTINGS'
        READ *, ACID, WATER, NCASTS
        CONCEN = (ACID / (ACID + WATER)) ** NCASTS
        PRINT *, 'THE PROPORTION OF ACID IN THE MIXTURE AFTER'
        PRINT *, NCASTS, ' IMMERSIONS IS ', CONCEN
        PRINT *, 'NOW ENTER THE LOWER LIMIT ON THE ACIDITY'
        READ *, LIMIT
        NCASTS = 1 + LOG(LIMIT) / (LOG(ACID) - LOG(ACID + WATER))
        PRINT *, NCASTS, ' CASTINGS CAN BE IMMERSED BEFORE THE ACIDITY'
        PRINT *, 'FALLS BELOW THIS LIMIT'
        END
```

Sample run #1:

```
ENTER ORIGINAL AMOUNT OF ACID, AMOUNT OF WATER ADDED
AND THE NUMBER OF CASTINGS
100, 100, 1
THE PROPORTION OF ACID IN THE MIXTURE AFTER
   1 IMMERSIONS IS    0.500000
NOW ENTER THE LOWER LIMIT ON THE ACIDITY
.9
   1 CASTINGS CAN BE IMMERSED BEFORE THE ACIDITY
FALLS BELOW THIS LIMIT
```

Figure 3.7

Figure 3.7 (continued)

Sample run #2:

```
ENTER ORIGINAL AMOUNT OF ACID, AMOUNT OF WATER ADDED
AND THE NUMBER OF CASTINGS
100, 100, 2
THE PROPORTION OF ACID IN THE MIXTURE AFTER
   2 IMMERSIONS IS    0.250000
NOW ENTER THE LOWER LIMIT ON THE ACIDITY
.1
   4 CASTINGS CAN BE IMMERSED BEFORE THE ACIDITY
FALLS BELOW THIS LIMIT
```

Sample run #3:

```
ENTER ORIGINAL AMOUNT OF ACID, AMOUNT OF WATER ADDED
AND THE NUMBER OF CASTINGS
90, 10, 2
THE PROPORTION OF ACID IN THE MIXTURE AFTER
   2 IMMERSIONS IS    0.810000
NOW ENTER THE LOWER LIMIT ON THE ACIDITY
.7
   4 CASTINGS CAN BE IMMERSED BEFORE THE ACIDITY
FALLS BELOW THIS LIMIT
```

Sample run #4:

```
ENTER ORIGINAL AMOUNT OF ACID, AMOUNT OF WATER ADDED
AND THE NUMBER OF CASTINGS
400, .05, 190
THE PROPORTION OF ACID IN THE MIXTURE AFTER
   190 IMMERSIONS IS    0.976541
NOW ENTER THE LOWER LIMIT ON THE ACIDITY
.75
   2303 CASTINGS CAN BE IMMERSED BEFORE THE ACIDITY
FALLS BELOW THIS LIMIT
```

Exercises

1. Write a program to read the lengths of the two legs of a right triangle and to calculate and print the area of the triangle (one-half the product of the legs) and the length of the hypotenuse (square root of the sum of the squares of the legs).

2. The Pythagorean theorem states that the sum of the squares of the sides of a right triangle is equal to the square of the hypotenuse. Thus, for a right triangle with sides 3 and 4, the length of the hypotenuse is 5. Similarly, a right triangle with sides 5 and 12 has a hypotenuse

of 13, and a right triangle with sides 8 and 15 has a hypotenuse of 17. Triples of integers such as 3, 4, 5, or 5, 12, 13, or 8, 15, 17, which represent the two sides and the hypotenuse of a right triangle, are called *Pythagorean triples*. There are infinitely many such triples, and they all can be generated by the formulas

$$side1 = m^2 - n^2$$

$$side2 = 2mn$$

$$hypotenuse = m^2 + n^2$$

where m and n are positive integers and $m > n$. Write a program that reads values for m and n and then calculates the Pythagorean triple that is generated by these formulas.

3. Write a program to read values for the three sides a, b, and c of a triangle and then to calculate its perimeter and its area. These should be printed together with the values of a, b, and c using appropriate labels. (For the area, you might use Hero's formula for the area of a triangle:

$$area = \sqrt{s(s - a)(s - b)(s - c)}$$

where s is one-half the perimeter.)

4. The current in an alternating current circuit that contains resistance, capacitance, and inductance in series is given by

$$I = \frac{E}{\sqrt{R^2 + (2\pi fL - 1/2\pi fC)^2}}$$

where I = current (amperes), E = voltage (volts), R = resistance (ohms), L = inductance (henrys), C = capacitance (farads), and f = frequency (hertz). Write a program that reads values for the voltage, resistance, capacitance, and frequency and then calculates and displays the current.

5. At t seconds after firing, the horizontal displacement x and the vertical displacement y in feet are given by

$$x = v_0 t \cos \theta$$

$$y = v_0 t \sin \theta - 16t^2$$

where v_0 is the initial velocity (ft/sec), and θ is the angle at which the rocket is fired. Write a program that reads values for v_0, θ, and t, calculates x and y using these formulas, and displays these values.

6. The speed in miles per hour of a satellite moving in a circular orbit about a celestial body is given approximately by

$$speed = \sqrt{\frac{C}{D}}$$

where C is a constant depending on the celestial body and D is the distance from the center of the celestial body to the satellite (in miles). Write a program that reads the value of the constant C for a celestial body and a value for D and that then displays the speed of the satellite. Run the program with the following values: (earth) $C = 1.2E12$; (moon) $C = 1.5E10$; (Mars) $C = 1.3E11$.

7. One set of *polar coordinates* of a point in a plane is given by (r, θ), where r is the length of the ray from the origin to the point and θ is the measure of an angle from the positive x axis to this ray.

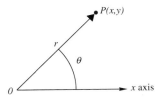

Write a program that reads polar coordinates for a point and calculates and displays its rectangular coordinates (x, y) obtained by using the formulas

$$x = r \cos \theta$$

$$y = r \sin \theta$$

8. The equation of the curve formed by a hanging cable weighing w pounds per foot of length can be described by

$$y = a \cosh \frac{x}{a}$$

where $a = H/w$, with H representing the horizontal tension pulling on the cable at its low point, and cosh is the hyperbolic cosine function defined by

$$\cosh u = \frac{e^u + e^{-u}}{2}$$

Write a program that reads values of w, H, and x and calculates and displays the corresponding value of y.

9. Write a program to convert a measurement given in feet to the equivalent number of (a) yards, (b) feet, (c) inches, (d) centimeters, and (e) meters. (1 foot = 12 inches, 1 yard = 3 feet, 1 inch = 2.54 centimeters, 1 meter = 100 centimeters.) Read the number of feet, and print, with appropriate labels, the number of yards, number of feet, number of inches, number of centimeters, and number of meters.

10. The formula for the volume of an oblate spheroid, such as the earth, is

$$V = \frac{4}{3} \pi a^2 b$$

where a and b are the half-lengths of the major and minor axes, respectively. Write a program that reads values for a and b and then calculates and displays the volume. Use your program to find the volume of the earth for which the values of a and b are 3963 miles and 3950 miles, respectively.

11. In order for a shaft with an allowable shear strength of S lbs/in^2 to transmit a torque of T in-lbs, it must have a diameter of at least D inches, where D is given by

$$D = \sqrt[3]{\frac{16T}{S}}$$

If P horsepower is applied to the shaft at a rotational speed of N rpm, the torque is given by

$$T = 63000\, \frac{P}{N}$$

Write a program that reads values for P, N, and S and calculates the torque developed and the required diameter to transmit that torque. Run your program with the following inputs:

P (hp)	N (rpm)	S (psi)
20	1500	5000
20	50	5000
270	40	6500

12. The period of a pendulum is given by the formula

$$P = 2\pi \sqrt{\frac{L}{g}\left(1 + \frac{1}{4}\sin^2\left(\frac{\alpha}{2}\right)\right)}$$

where

$g = 980$ cm/sec^2
$L = $ pendulum length
$\alpha = $ angle of displacement

Write a program to read values for L and α and to calculate the period of a pendulum having this length and angle of displacement. Run your program with the following inputs:

L (cm)	α (degrees)
120	15
90	20
60	5
74.6	10
83.6	12

13. A containing tank is to be constructed that will hold 500 cubic meters of oil when filled. The shape of the tank is to be a cylinder (including a base) surmounted by a cone, whose height is equal to its radius. The material and labor costs to construct the cylindrical portion of the tank are $300 per square meter, and the costs for the conical top are $400 per square meter. Write a program that calculates the heights of the cylinder and the cone for a given radius that is input and that also calculates the total cost of constructing the tank. Starting with a radius of 4.0 meters and incrementing by various (small) step sizes, run your program several times to determine the dimensions of the tank that will cost the least.

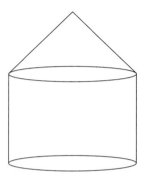

14. Write a program to read the thickness, density, and outside radius of a hollow ball and to calculate its volume and the mass. Starting with a value 0.2 cm, run your program several times to find the largest wall thickness of a copper ball (density $= .0089$ kg/cm^3) with an outside radius of 50.0 cm that will float in water. (For the ball to float, its volume must be at least 1000 times its mass.)

15. The declining balance formula for calculating depreciation is

$$V_N = V_0(1 - R)^N$$

where

$V_N =$ the value after N years
$V_0 =$ the initial value
$R =$ the rate of depreciation
$N =$ the number of years

Write a program to read values for V_0, R, and N and to calculate the depreciated value. Run the program several times to find the depreciated value of a new machine just purchased by Dispatch Die-Casting for $50,000 at the end of each year of its useful life. Assume that the rate of depreciation is 12 percent and that the usual life of the machine is five years.

16. The castings produced at Dispatch Die-Casting must be shipped in special containers that are available in four sizes—huge, large, medium, and small—that can hold 50, 20, 5, and 1 casting, respectively. Write a program that reads the number of castings to be shipped and displays the number of containers needed to send the shipment most efficiently. The output for input value 598 should be similar to the following:

```
CONTAINER    NUMBER
   HUGE        11
   LARGE        2
   MEDIUM       1
   SMALL        3
```

17. The length of the line segment joining two points $P_1(x_1, y_1)$ and $P_2(x_2, y_2)$ is given by

$$\sqrt{(x_2 - x_1)^2 + (y_2 - y_1)^2}$$

and the midpoint of the segment has the coordinates

$$\left(\frac{x_1 + x_2}{2}, \frac{y_1 + y_2}{2}\right)$$

The slope of the line through P_1 and P_2 is given by

$$\frac{y_2 - y_1}{x_2 - x_1}$$

(provided $x_1 \neq x_2$), and the slope-intercept equation of this line is

$$y = mx + b$$

where m is the slope and b is the y intercept; b can be calculated by

$$b = y_1 - mx_1$$

The perpendicular bisector of the line segment joining P_1 and P_2 is the line through the midpoint of this segment and having slope $-1/m$ (provided $m \neq 0$). Write a program that reads the coordinates of two points, P_1 and P_2, with distinct x coordinates and distinct y coordinates and calculates and displays the length of the segment P_1P_2, the midpoint of the segment, the slope of the line through P_1 and P_2, its y intercept, its slope-intercept equation, and the equation of the perpendicular bisector of P_1P_2.

18. Write a program that will read a student's number, his or her old grade point average (GPA) and old number of course credits (e.g., 30179, 3.29, 19) and then print these with appropriate labels. Then read the course credit and grade for each of four courses; for example, C1 = 1.0, G1 = 3.7, C2 = 0.5, G2 = 4.0, and so on. Calculate

number of old honor points =
                    (old # of course credits) * (old GPA)

number of new honor points = C1 * G1 + $\cdots$ + C4 * G4
total # of new course credits = C1 + C2 + C3 + C4

$$\text{current GPA} = \frac{\text{\# of new honor points}}{\text{\# of new course credits}}$$

Print the current GPA with an appropriate label. Then calculate

cumulative GPA =
$$\frac{(\text{\# of old honor points}) + (\text{\# of new honor points})}{(\text{\# of old course credits}) + (\text{\# of new course credits})}$$

and print this with a label.

Programming Pointers

In this section we consider some aspects of program design and suggest guidelines for good programming style. We also point out some errors that may occur when writing FORTRAN programs.

Program Design

1. *Programs cannot be considered correct until they have been validated using test data.* Test all programs with data for which the results are known or can be checked by hand calculation.

2. *Programs should be readable and understandable.*

   - *Use meaningful variable names that suggest what each variable represents.* For example,

     ```
     DIST = RATE * TIME
     ```

     is more meaningful than

     ```
     D = R * T
     ```

     or

     ```
     Z7 = ALPHA * X
     ```

     Also, avoid "cute" identifiers, as in

     ```
     HOWFAR = GOGO * SQUEAL
     ```

   - *Do not use "magic numbers" that suddenly appear without explanation*, as in the statement

     ```
     OUTPUT = 0.1237 * AMOUNT + 1.34E-5
     ```

     If these numbers must be changed, someone must search through the program to determine what they represent and which ones should be changed, and to locate all their occurrences. It is thus better to associate them with named constants, as in

     ```
     REAL RATE, ERROR
     PARAMETER (RATE = 0.1758, ERROR = 1.34E-5)
     ```

or assign them to variables, as in

```
REAL RATE, ERROR
DATA RATE, ERROR /0.1758, 1.34E-5/
```

● *Use comments to describe the purpose of a program, the meaning of variables, and the purpose of key program segments.* However, do not clutter the program with needless comments; for example, the comment in

```
* ADD 1 TO COUNT
      COUNT = COUNT + 1
```

is not helpful in explaining the statement that follows it and so should be omitted.

● *Label all output produced by a program.* For example,

```
PRINT *, 'RATE = ', RATE, ' TIME = ', TIME
```

produces more informative output than does

```
PRINT *, RATE, TIME
```

3. *Programs should be efficient.* For example, duplicate computations, as in

```
ROOT1 = (-B + SQRT(B * B - 4 * A * C)) / (2 * A)
ROOT2 = (-B - SQRT(B * B - 4 * A * C)) / (2 * A)
```

should be avoided. It is not efficient to calculate the value of B * B − 4 * A * C or its square root twice; instead, calculate it once, assign it to a variable, and then use this variable in these calculations.

4. *Programs should be general and flexible.* They should solve a class of problems rather than one specific problem. It should be relatively easy to modify a program to solve a related problem without changing much of the program. Avoiding the use of magic numbers, as described in Programming Pointer 2, is important in this regard.

Potential Problems

1. *Do not confuse* I *or* l (*lowercase "ell"*) *and* 1 *or* 0 (*zero*) *and* O (*the letter "oh"*). For example, the statement

```
PROGRAM DILUTE
```

produces an error, because the numeral 0 is used in place of the letter O. Many programmers distinguish between these in handwritten programs by writing the numeral 0 as Ø.

2. *When preparing a FORTRAN program, do not let any statement extend past column 72.* Most FORTRAN compilers will ignore any characters beyond column 72, which can easily lead to errors caused by incomplete statements. For example, if one uses

```
PRINT *, 'FOR THE X-VALUE ', X, ' THE CORRESPONDING Y-VALUE IS ', Y
```

in a program where the last character (Y) is in column 73, an error message such as the following may result:

```
PRINT *, 'FOR THE X-VALUE ', X, ' THE CORRESPONDING Y-VALUE IS ',
        *** Input/output list is incomplete
```

3. *String constants must be enclosed in single quotes.* If either the beginning or the ending quote is missing, an error will result. An apostrophe is represented in a string constant as a pair of apostrophes, for example,

```
'ISN''T'
```

4. *String constants should not be broken at the end of a line.* All character positions through column 72 of a line are read, and so unintended blanks may be produced in a string constant. For example, the statement

```
 PRINT *, 'ENTER THE VALUES ON SEPARATE LINES.  SEPARATE
+ THEM BY COMMAS
```

produces the output

```
ENTER THE VALUES ON SEPARATE LINES.  SEPARATE     THEM BY COMMAS.
```

5. *All multiplications must be indicated by* ∗. For example, 2 ∗ N is valid, but 2N is not.

6. *Division of integers produces an integer.* For example, 1 / 2 has the value 0. Similarly, if N is an integer variable greater than 1, 1/N will have the value 0.

7. *Parentheses within expressions must be paired.* For each left parenthesis there must be a matching right parenthesis.

8. *All variables are initially undefined.* Although some compilers may initialize variables to specific values (e.g., 0 for numeric variables), it should be assumed that all variables are initially undefined. For example, the statement Y = X + 1 usually produces a ''garbage'' value for Y if X has not previously been assigned a value.

9. *Initialization by means of DATA statements is done only once, during compilation, before execution of the program begins.* In particular, this means that the variables are not reinitialized while the program is being executed. Programming Pointer 8 in Chapter 4 shows why this is a potential problem.

10. *A value assigned to a variable must be of a type that is appropriate to the type of the variable.* Thus entering the value 2.7 for an integer variable NUMBER in the statement

```
READ *, NUMBER
```

may generate an error message. However, an integer value read for a real variable is automatically converted to real type.

11. *Mixed-mode assignment must be used with care.* For example, if A, B, and C are real variables but NUMBER is an integer variable, the statement

```
NUMBER = -B + SQRT(B ** 2 - 4 * A * C)
```

calculates the real value of the expression on the right side correctly but then assigns only the integer part to NUMBER. This happens, for example, when the types of these variables are determined by FORTRAN's naming convention.

12. *In assignment statements and in list-directed input, if a character value being assigned or read has a length greater than that specified for the character variable, the rightmost characters are truncated. If the value has a length less than that of the variable, blanks are added at the right.* Thus, if STRING is declared by

```
CHARACTER*10 STRING
```

the statement

```
STRING = 'ABCDEFGHIJKLMNO'
```

will assign the string 'ABCDEFGHIJ' to STRING, and

```
STRING = 'ABC'
```

will assign the string 'ABCbbbbbbb' to STRING. An acronym sometimes used to remember this is

> ● **APT:** For **A**ssignment (and list-directed input), both blank-**P**adding and **T**runcation occur on the right.

13. *The types of all variables should be declared in type statements.* Any variable whose type is not explicitly specified will have its type determined by the FORTRAN naming convention. Thus, if the variable NUMBER has not been declared to be of real type, the function reference SQRT(NUMBER) causes an error, since SQRT requires a real argument and NUMBER is of integer type according to the naming convention. If A, B, C, and NUMBER have not been declared, execution of the statement

```
NUMBER = -B + SQRT(B ** 2 - 4 * A * C)
```

produces the result described in the Programming Pointer 11. According to FORTRAN's naming conventions, A, B, and C are real variables, and so the real value of the expression on the right side is calculated correctly, but only its integer part is assigned to NUMBER because the naming convention specifies that it is an integer variable.

14. *A comma must precede the input/output list in input/output statements of the form*

> READ *, *input-list*
> PRINT *, *output-list*

Program Style

In the examples in this text, we adopt certain style guidelines for FORTRAN programs, and you should write your programs in a similar style. The following standards are used (others are described in the Programming Pointers of subsequent chapters).

1. When a statement is continued from one line to another, indent the continuation line(s).

2. Document each program with comment lines at the beginning of the program to explain the purpose of the program and what the variables represent. You should also include in this documentation your name, date, course number, assignment number, and so on.

3. Break up long expressions into simpler subexpressions.

4. Insert a blank comment line between the opening documentation and the specification statements at the beginning of the program and between these statements and the rest of the program.

5. To improve readability, insert a blank space between items in a FORTRAN statement such as before and after assignment operators and arithmetic operators.

FORTRAN 90 Features

Several variations of and extensions to the features of FORTRAN 77 described in this chapter have been provided in FORTRAN 90. This section briefly describes the most important ones.

Program Format

- Free-form source code is allowed. There is no special significance attached to the various columns of a line. Statements may begin in any column.
- Lines may extend up to 132 characters.
- More than one statement may be placed on a line. A semicolon is used to separate such statements.

● In-line comments are allowed. Such comments begin with an exclamation point (!) and extend to the end of the line; for example,

```
CELS = 5.0/9.0 * (FAHR - 32.0) ! Convert to Celsius
```

● Continuation of a statement is indicated by using an ampersand (&) as the last nonblank character in the line being continued or the last nonblank character before the exclamation mark that marks the beginning of a comment. Up to 39 continuation lines are allowed.

Constants and Variables

● Variables may be initialized in type specification statements; for example, the type statement

```
REAL :: RATE = 7.25
```

or

```
REAL RATE = 7.25
```

declares RATE to be a real variable with initial value 7.25.
● Parameters can be declared and defined in a single type statement. For example, the type statement

```
REAL, PARAMETER :: PI = 3.14159
```

declares PI to be a real parameter associated with the constant 3.14159.
● A KIND = clause may be used in a type statement to specify the range of integer constants or the precision of real constants. Two intrinsic functions, SELECTED_REAL_KIND and KIND, are provided to determine kind type parameters. For example, either of the type statements

```
REAL (KIND = SELECTED_REAL_KIND(10)) :: X, Y
```

or

```
REAL (KIND = KIND(0.0123456789)) :: X, Y
```

declares that X and Y are real variables whose values are to have at least ten decimal digits of precision.

The intrinsic function PRECISION can be used to determine the precision of a real value; for example, the function reference PRECISION(X) returns the value 10. See Chapter 9 for more details.
● Integer values may have binary, octal, or hexadecimal representations in DATA statements. Such representations consist of the binary, octal, or hexadecimal digits enclosed in quotes (single or double) and preceded by B, O, or Z, respectively; for example, the binary representation B'1001' of the integer 9 may be used in a DATA statement.
● Strings may be enclosed in either single (') or double ('') quotes.
● Identifiers may consist of up to 31 letters, digits, or underscores (_); the first character must be a letter. For example, AREA_OF_CIRCLE is a valid FORTRAN identifier.

● A modified form of the IMPLICIT statement, IMPLICIT NONE, cancels the naming convention, with the result that the types of all named constants and variables (and functions) *must be* specified explicitly in type statements.

Arithmetic Operations and Functions

● Several new arithmetic functions have been added.

Program Composition

● A FORTRAN program may have a subprogram section that immediately precedes the END statement.

4

Structured Programming

A journey of a thousand miles begins with a single step.

ANCIENT PROVERB

Then Logic would take you by the throat, and force you to do it!

Achilles in LEWIS CARROLL'S
What the Tortoise Said to Achilles

But what has been said once can always be repeated.

ZENO OF ELEA

In Chapter 2 we described several software engineering techniques that assist in the design of programs that are easy to understand and whose logical flow is easy to follow. Such programs are more likely to be correct when first written than are poorly structured programs; and if they are not correct, the errors are easier to find and correct. Such programs are also easier to modify, which is especially important, since such modifications may be required long after the program was originally written and are often made by someone other than the original programmer.

We noted that one important software engineering principle is that algorithms and programs should be structured. In a **structured program**, the logical flow is governed by three basic control structures, **sequence, selection,** and **repetition.** In this chapter we show how these basic control structures are implemented in FORTRAN.

4.1 Sequential Structure: Statement Sequences

Sequential structure, as illustrated in the following diagram, simply refers to the execution of a sequence of statements in the order in which they appear so that each statement is executed exactly once. All the sample programs in Chapter 3 are "straight-line" programs in which the only control used is sequential.

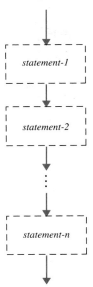

In a FORTRAN program, a sequential structure is implemented as a list of statements:

statement-1
statement-2

.

.

.

statement-n

To illustrate, consider the sequence of statements

```
PRINT *, 'ENTER TWO NUMBERS:'
READ *, NUM1, NUM2
SUM = NUM1 + NUM2
PRINT *, 'SUM = ', SUM
```

When executed, this sequence first displays the prompt "ENTER TWO NUMBERS:", and then reads values for NUM1 and NUM2. After this, the value of SUM is calculated, and then the label "SUM =" is displayed, followed by the value of SUM.

4.2   The LOGICAL Data Type

Several of the control structures in FORTRAN that are used to implement selection and repetition structures involve logical expressions. Consequently, before we can describe these control structures, we must examine in more detail the LOGICAL data type.

Recall that there are two **logical constants** in FORTRAN:

.TRUE.

and

.FALSE.

and logical variables may have only these values. Note the periods that must appear as part of these logical constants. A **logical variable** is declared using a LOGICAL type statement of the form

LOGICAL *list*

where *list* is a list of variables being typed as logical. Like all type statements, this type statement must appear in the specification part of the program. For example,

```
LOGICAL ENDATA, SORTED, NEG, SATUR
```

declares that ENDATA, SORTED, NEG, and SATUR are logical variables.

Logical expressions may be either **simple** or **compound**. Simple logical expressions are logical constants or logical variables or **relational expressions** of the form

expression-1 relational-operator expression-2

where both *expression-1* and *expression-2* are numeric or character or logical expressions, and the *relational-operator* may be any of the following:

Symbol	Meaning
.LT.	Is less than
.GT.	Is greater than
.EQ.	Is equal to
.LE.	Is less than or equal to
.GE.	Is greater than or equal to
.NE.	Is not equal to

The periods must appear as parts of these relational symbols, because they serve to distinguish a logical expression such as X.EQ.Y from the variable XEQY.

The following are examples of simple logical expressions:

```
.TRUE.
ENDATA
X .LT. 5.2
B ** 2 .GE. 4 * A * C
NUMBER .EQ. -999
```

If X has the value 4.5, the logical expression X .LT. 5.2 is true. If NUMBER has the value 400, the logical expression NUMBER .EQ. -999 is false.

When using the relational operators .EQ. and .NE., it is important to remember that *many real values cannot be stored exactly* (see Section 1.3). *Consequently, logical expressions formed by comparing real quantities with .EQ. are often evaluated as false, even though these quantities are algebraically equal.* This is illustrated by the program at the end of this section.

For character data, a **collating sequence** is used to establish an ordering for the character set. This sequence varies from one machine to another, but in all cases, the letters are in alphabetical order, and the digits are in numerical order. Thus

```
'A' .LT. 'F'
'6' .GT. '4'
```

are true logical expressions. Two strings are compared character by character using this collating sequence. For example, for a logical expression of the form

   string1 .LT. *string2*

if the first character of *string1* is less than the first character of *string2* (that is, precedes it in the collating sequence), then *string1* is less than *string2*. Thus,

```
'CAT' .LT. 'DOG'
```

is true since 'C' .LT. 'D' is true. If the first characters of *string1* and *string2* are the same, the second characters are compared; if these characters are the same, the third characters are compared, and so on. Thus,

```
'CAT' .LT. 'COW'
```

is true, since A is less then O. Similarly,

```
'JUNE' .GT. 'JULY'
```

is true, since N is greater than L. If the two strings have different lengths, blanks are appended to the shorter string, resulting in two strings of equal length to be compared. For example, the logical expression

```
'CAT' .LT. 'CATTLE'
```

or equivalently

```
'CATƀƀ' .LT. 'CATTLE'
```

(where ƀ denotes a blank) is true because a blank character precedes all letters.

Compound logical expressions are formed by combining logical expressions using the **logical operators**

.NOT.
.AND.
.OR.
.EQV.
.NEQV.

These operators are defined as follows:

Logical Operator	Logical Expression	Definition
.NOT.	.NOT. P	.NOT. P is true if P is false and is false if P is true.
.AND.	P .AND. Q	*Conjunction* of P and Q: P .AND. Q is true if both P and Q are true; it is false otherwise.
.OR.	P .OR. Q	*Disjunction* of P and Q: P .OR. Q is true if P or Q or both are true; it is false otherwise.
.EQV.	P .EQV. Q	*Equivalence* of P and Q: P .EQV. Q is true if both P and Q are true or both are false; it is false otherwise.
.NEQV.	P .NEQV. Q	*Nonequivalence* of P and Q: P .NEQV. Q is the negation of P .EQV. Q; it is true if one of P or Q is true and the other is false; it is false otherwise.

These definitions are summarized by the following **truth tables**, which display all the possible values for P and Q and the corresponding values of the logical expression:

P	.NOT. P
.TRUE.	.FALSE.
.FALSE.	.TRUE.

P	Q	P .AND. Q	P .OR. Q	P .EQV. Q	P .NEQV. Q
.TRUE.	.TRUE.	.TRUE.	.TRUE.	.TRUE.	.FALSE.
.TRUE.	.FALSE.	.FALSE.	.TRUE.	.FALSE.	.TRUE.
.FALSE.	.TRUE.	.FALSE.	.TRUE.	.FALSE.	.TRUE.
.FALSE.	.FALSE.	.FALSE.	.FALSE.	.TRUE.	.FALSE.

In a logical expression containing several of these operators, the operations are performed in the order .NOT., .AND., .OR., .EQV. (or .NEQV.). Parentheses may be used to indicate those subexpressions that should be evaluated first. For example, given the logical variables NEG, SATUR, and ENDATA, we can form logical expressions such as

```
SATUR .AND. NEG
.NOT. SATUR .AND. NEG
SATUR .AND. (NEG .OR. ENDATA)
```

The first expression, SATUR .AND. NEG, is true only in the case that both
SATUR and NEG are true. In the second example, the subexpression .NOT.
SATUR is evaluated first, and this result is then combined with the value of
NEG, using the operator .AND. The entire expression is therefore true only in
the case that SATUR is false and NEG is true. In the last example, the subexpression NEG .OR. ENDATA is evaluated first; the possible values it may
have are displayed in the following truth table:

SATUR	NEG	ENDATA	SATUR .AND. (NEG .OR. ENDATA)
.TRUE.	.TRUE.	.TRUE.	.TRUE.
.TRUE.	.TRUE.	.FALSE.	.TRUE.
.TRUE.	.FALSE.	.TRUE.	.TRUE.
.TRUE.	.FALSE.	.FALSE.	.FALSE.
.FALSE.	.TRUE.	.TRUE.	.TRUE.
.FALSE.	.TRUE.	.FALSE.	.TRUE.
.FALSE.	.FALSE.	.TRUE.	.TRUE.
.FALSE.	.FALSE.	.FALSE.	.FALSE.

This value is then combined with the value of SATUR using the operator
.AND.:

SATUR	NEG	ENDATA	SATUR .AND. (NEG .OR. ENDATA)	
.TRUE.	.TRUE.	.TRUE.	.TRUE.	.TRUE.
.TRUE.	.TRUE.	.FALSE.	.TRUE.	.TRUE.
.TRUE.	.FALSE.	.TRUE.	.TRUE.	.TRUE.
.TRUE.	.FALSE.	.FALSE.	.FALSE.	.FALSE.
.FALSE.	.TRUE.	.TRUE.	.FALSE.	.TRUE.
.FALSE.	.TRUE.	.FALSE.	.FALSE.	.TRUE.
.FALSE.	.FALSE.	.TRUE.	.FALSE.	.TRUE.
.FALSE.	.FALSE.	.FALSE.	.FALSE.	.FALSE.

When a logical expression contains several operators, some of which are
relational operators and others are logical operators, the order in which they
are performed is

1. Relational operators (.GT., .GE., .EQ., .NE., .LT., .LE.)
2. .NOT.
3. .AND.
4. .OR.
5. .EQV. and .NEQV.

Parentheses may be used in the usual way to modify this order. For example,
if the integer variable N has the value 4, the logical expression

```
N**2 + 1 .GT. 10 .AND. .NOT. N .LT. 3
```

or with parentheses inserted to improve readability,

```
(N**2 + 1 .GT. 10) .AND. .NOT. (N .LT. 3)
```

is true. The logical expression

        N .EQ. 3 .OR. N .EQ. 4

is valid and is true, whereas

        N .EQ. 1 .OR. 2

is not, since this would be evaluated as

        (N .EQ. 1) .OR. 2

and 2 is not a logical expression to which .OR. can be applied.
An assignment statement of the form

   logical-variable = logical-expression

can be used to assign a value to a logical variable. Thus,

        SATUR = .TRUE.

is a valid assignment statement; it assigns the value true to SATUR. Likewise,

        NEG = SATUR

is a valid assignment statement and assigns the value of SATUR to the logical
variable NEG. The assignment statement

        ENDATA = (NUMBER .EQ. -999)

is also valid and assigns the value true to the logical variable ENDATA if the
value of the relational expression (NUMBER .EQ. -999) is true, that is, if
NUMBER has the value –999, and assigns the value false otherwise.
   Logical values can be displayed using list-directed output. A logical value
is displayed as only a T or an F, usually preceded by a space. For example, if
A, B, and C are logical variables with the values true, false, and false, respectively, the statement

        PRINT *, A, B, C, .TRUE. .OR. A, A .AND. B

produces

        _T_F_F_T_F

as output.
   Logical values can also be read using list-directed input. In this case, the
input values consist of optional blanks followed by an optional period followed
by T or F, which may be followed by other characters. The value of true or

false is assigned to the corresponding variable according to whether the first
letter encountered is T or F. For example, for the statements

```
LOGICAL A, B, C
READ *, A, B, C
```

the following data could be entered:

```
.T., .F., .FALSE
```

The values assigned to A, B, and C would be true, false, and false, respectively.
This would also be the case if the following data were entered:

```
.T., .FALL, .FLASE
```

As we noted earlier, when the relational operators .EQ. and .NE. are used
to compare numeric quantities, it is important to remember that *many real
values cannot be stored exactly* (see Section 1.3). *Consequently, logical expressions formed by comparing real quantities with* .EQ. *may be evaluated as
false, even though these quantities are algebraically equal.* The program in
Figure 4.1 demonstrates this by showing that for some real values X, the value
of Y computed by

```
Y = X * (1.0 / X)
```

is not 1. In this program, the assignment statement

```
EQUALS = (Y .EQ. 1.0)
```

calculates the value of the logical expression Y .EQ. 1.0 and assigns this value
to the logical variable EQUALS. The value of this expression and thus the
value assigned to EQUALS is the logical constant .TRUE. if the value of Y is
equal to 1.0 and is .FALSE. otherwise.

```
      PROGRAM APPROX
*******************************************************************
*     Program to show inexact representation of reals.  A real number X *
*     is entered, the value of X * (1.0 / X) is assigned to Y, and the  *
*     value of the logical expression Y .EQ. 1.0 is then calculated,    *
*     assigned to the logical variable EQUALS, and displayed.           *
*******************************************************************

      REAL X, Y
      LOGICAL EQUALS
```

Figure 4.1

Figure 4.1 (continued)

```
PRINT *, 'ENTER REAL NUMBER'
READ *, X
Y = X * (1.0 / X)
PRINT *, 'X = ', X, '        Y = X * (1 / X) = ', Y
PRINT *, '1.0 - Y = ', 1.0 - Y
EQUALS = (Y .EQ. 1.0)
PRINT *, 'Y EQUALS 1?  ', EQUALS
END
```

Sample runs:

```
ENTER REAL NUMBER
.5
X =     0.500000      Y = X * (1 / X) =     1.00000
1.0 - Y =   0.
Y EQUALS 1?     T

ENTER REAL NUMBER
6.39631
X =       6.39631      Y = X * (1 / X) =     1.000000
1.0 - Y =     5.96046E-08
Y EQUALS 1?    F

ENTER REAL NUMBER
15.7981
X =       15.7981      Y = X * (1 / X) =     1.000000
1.0 - Y =     5.96046E-08
Y EQUALS 1?    F
```

4.3 Example: Logical Circuits

As an application of logical expressions, consider the following logical circuit, called a **binary half-adder,** which can be used to add two binary digits:

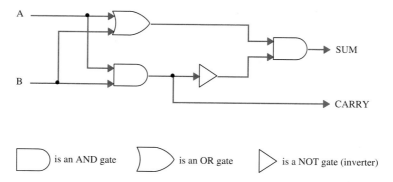

This circuit is designed to accept two inputs, A and B, and produce two outputs, SUM and CARRY. It contains four basic electronic components called **gates,** two AND gates, one OR gate, and one NOT gate (also called an *inverter*). The inputs to these gates are pulses of current applied to the lines leading into the gates, and the outputs are pulses of current on the lines emanating from the gates. In the case of an AND gate, an output pulse is produced only if there are pulses on both input lines. An OR gate produces an output pulse only if there is an input pulse on at least one of the input lines. A NOT gate is designed to produce an output pulse only when there is no incoming pulse. If we associate the logical expression ''a pulse is present'' with each line, that is, if we interpret .TRUE. as the presence of a pulse and .FALSE. as the absence of a pulse, then the logical operators .AND., .OR., and .NOT. can be used to model AND, OR, and NOT gates, respectively.

Logical expressions can thus be used to model logical circuits. For example, the output SUM in the circuit for a binary half-adder can be represented by the logical expression

    (A .OR. B) .AND. .NOT. (A .AND. B)

and the logical expression for the output CARRY is

    A .AND. B

The values of these logical expressions are displayed in the following truth table:

A	B	CARRY	SUM
.TRUE.	.TRUE.	.TRUE.	.FALSE.
.TRUE.	.FALSE.	.FALSE.	.TRUE.
.FALSE.	.TRUE.	.FALSE.	.TRUE.
.FALSE.	.FALSE.	.FALSE.	.FALSE.

If we now take the value .FALSE. to represent the binary digit 0 and .TRUE. to represent the binary digit 1, then the preceding truth table can be written as

A	B	CARRY	SUM
1	1	1	0
1	0	0	1
0	1	0	1
0	0	0	0

If we interpret SUM and CARRY as the sum and carry bits produced when two binary digits are added as specified by the addition table

+	0	1
0	0	1
1	1	10

then we see that this circuit does in fact carry out this addition correctly.

The program in Figure 4.2 reads values for the inputs A and B and calculates and displays the values of the two outputs, SUM and CARRY. Note that if we identify the binary digits 0 and 1 with false and true, respectively, the program's output can be interpreted as a demonstration that $1 + 1 = 10$ (SUM = 0, CARRY = 1), $1 + 0 = 01$, $0 + 1 = 01$, and $0 + 0 = 00$. This program, therefore, correctly implements binary addition of one-bit numbers.

```
      PROGRAM HADDER
************************************************************************
* Program to calculate the outputs from a logical circuit that       *
* represents a binary half-adder.  Variables used are:               *
*     A, B  : the two logical inputs to the circuit                  *
*     SUM, CARRY : the two logical outputs                           *
************************************************************************

      LOGICAL A, B, SUM, CARRY

      PRINT *, 'ENTER LOGICAL INPUTS A AND B:'
      READ *, A, B
      SUM = (A .OR. B) .AND. .NOT. (A .AND. B)
      CARRY = A .AND. B
      PRINT *, 'CARRY, SUM = ', CARRY, SUM
      END
```

Sample runs:

```
ENTER LOGICAL INPUTS A AND B:
T T
CARRY, SUM = T F

ENTER LOGICAL INPUTS A AND B:
T F
CARRY, SUM = F T

ENTER LOGICAL INPUTS A AND B:
F T
CARRY, SUM = F T

ENTER LOGICAL INPUTS A AND B:
F F
CARRY, SUM = F F
```

Figure 4.2

Exercises

1. Assuming that M and N are integer variables with the values -5 and 8, respectively, and that X, Y, and Z are real variables with the values

-3.56, 0, and 44.7, respectively, find the values of the following logical expressions:

(a) `M .LE. N`
(b) `2 * ABS(M) .LE. 8`
(c) `X * X .LT. SQRT(Z)`
(d) `NINT(Z) .EQ. (6 * N - 3)`
(e) `(X .LE. Y) .AND. (Y .LE. Z)`
(f) `.NOT. (X .LT. Y)`
(g) `.NOT. ((M .LE. N) .AND. (X + Z .GT. Y))`
(h) `.NOT. (M .LE. N) .OR. .NOT. (X + Z .GT. Y)`
(i) `.NOT. ((M .GT. N) .OR. (X .LT. Z)) .EQV.`
　　`((M .LE. N) .AND. (X .GE. Z))`
(j) `.NOT. ((M .GT. N) .AND. (X .LT. Z)) .NEQV.`
　　`((M .LE. N) .AND. (X .GE. Z))`

2. Assuming that A, B, and C are logical variables, use truth tables to display the values of the following logical expressions for all possible values of A, B, and C:

(a) `A .OR. .NOT. B`
(b) `.NOT. (A .AND. B)`
(c) `.NOT. A .OR. .NOT. B`
(d) `A .AND. .TRUE. .OR. (1 + 2 .EQ. 4)`
(e) `A .AND. (B .OR. C)`
(f) `(A .AND. B) .OR. (A .AND. C)`

3. Write logical expressions to express the following conditions:

(a) X is greater than 3.
(b) Y is strictly between 2 and 5.
(c) R is negative and Z is positive.
(d) ALPHA and BETA both are positive.
(e) ALPHA and BETA have the same sign (both are negative or both are positive).
(f) $-5 < X < 5$.
(g) A is less than 6 or is greater than 10.
(h) P = Q = R.
(i) X is less than 3, or Y is less than 3, but not both.

4. Given the logical variables A, B, and C, write a logical expression that is

(a) true if and only if A and B are true and C is false.
(b) true if and only if A is true and at least one of B or C is true.
(c) true if and only if exactly one of A and B is true.

5. In a certain region, pesticide can be sprayed from an airplane only if the temperature is at least 70 degrees, the relative humidity is between 15 and 35 percent, and the wind speed is at most 10 miles per hour. Write a program that accepts three numbers representing temperature,

relative humidity, and wind speed; assigns the value true or false to the logical variable PESTOK according to these criteria; and displays this value.

6. A *binary full-adder* has three inputs: the two bits A and B being added and a "carry-in" bit CIN (representing the carry bit that results from adding the bits to the right of A and B in two binary numbers). It can be constructed from two binary half-adders and an OR gate:

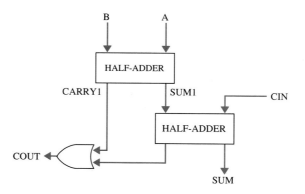

(a) Write logical expressions for
   (i) SUM1 and CARRY1 in terms of A and B.
   (ii) SUM and COUT in terms of CIN, SUM1, and CARRY1.
(b) Write a program to implement this binary full-adder, and use it to verify the results shown in the following table:

A	B	CIN	SUM	COUT
0	0	0	0	0
0	0	1	1	0
0	1	0	1	0
0	1	1	0	1
1	0	0	1	0
1	0	1	0	1
1	1	0	0	1
1	1	1	1	1

7. An *adder* to calculate binary sums of two-bit numbers

$$\begin{array}{r} A2 \; A1 \\ + \; B2 \; B1 \\ \hline COUT \; S2 \; S1 \end{array}$$

where S1 and S2 are the sum bits and COUT is the carry-out bit can be constructed from a binary half-adder and a binary full-adder:

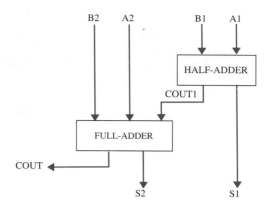

(a) Write logical expressions for
  (i) S1 and COUT1 in terms of A1 and B1.
  (ii) S2 and COUT in terms of A2, B2, and COUT1.
(b) Write a program to implement this adder and use it to demonstrate that $00 + 00 = 000$, $01 + 00 = 001$, $01 + 01 = 010$, $10 + 01 = 011$, $10 + 10 = 100$, $11 + 10 + 101$, and $11 + 11 = 110$.

8. Write a program that reads triples of real numbers and assigns the appropriate value of true or false to the following logical variables:

TRIANG:	True if the real numbers can represent lengths of the sides of a triangle, and false otherwise (the sum of any two of the numbers must be greater than the third).
EQUIL:	True if TRIANG is true and the triangle is equilateral (the three sides are equal).
ISOS:	True if TRIANG is true and the triangle is isosceles (at least two sides are equal).
SCAL:	True if TRIANG is true and the triangle is scalene (no two sides are equal).

The output from your program should have a format like the following:

```
ENTER 3 LENGTHS:
2, 3, 3
TRIANG IS:   T
EQUIL IS:    F
ISOS IS:     T
SCAL IS:     F
```

4.4 The IF Selection Structure

A selection structure makes possible the selection of one of several alternative actions, depending on the value of a logical expression. In the simplest selection structure, a sequence of statements (also called a block of statements) is executed or bypassed, depending on whether a given logical expression is true or false. This is illustrated in the following diagram:

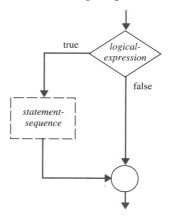

This selection structure is implemented in FORTRAN by using an **IF construct** (also called a **block IF statement**) of the form

IF (*logical-expression*) THEN
    statement-sequence
END IF

If the logical expression is true, the specified sequence of statements is executed; otherwise, it is bypassed and execution continues with the next statement in the program (following the END IF). For example, in the IF construct

```
IF (X .GE. 0) THEN
    Y = X * X
    Z = SQRT(X)
END IF
```

the logical expression X .GE. 0 is evaluated, and if it is true, Y is set equal to the square of X and Z equal to the square root of X; otherwise, these assignment statements are not executed. Note that *the logical expression in an IF construct must be enclosed in parentheses.*

FORTRAN also provides a simplified form of the IF construct that can be used if the statement sequence consists of a single statement. This short form is called a **logical IF statement** and has the form

IF (*logical-expression*) *statement*

For example, in the logical IF statement

```
IF (1.5 .LE. X .AND. X .LE. 2.5) PRINT *, X
```

if $1.5 \leq X \leq 2.5$, the value of X is printed; otherwise, the PRINT statement is bypassed. In either case, execution continues with the next statement in the program.

In the preceding selection structure, the selection is made between (1) executing a given sequence of statements and (2) bypassing these statements. In the two-way selection pictured in the following diagram, the selection is made between (1) executing one sequence (block) of statements and (2) executing a different sequence (block) of statements.

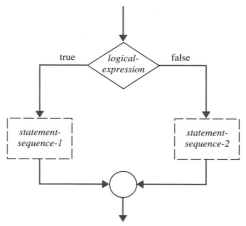

This selection structure is implemented in FORTRAN by an IF construct that allows the programmer not only to specify the sequence of statements to be selected for execution when the logical expression is true but also to indicate an alternative statement sequence for execution when it is false. This IF construct has the form

IF (*logical-expression*) THEN
    statement-sequence-1
ELSE
    statement-sequence-2
END IF

If the logical expression is true, *statement-sequence-1* is executed and *statement-sequence-2* is bypassed. Otherwise, *statement-sequence-1* is bypassed, and *statement-sequence-2* is executed. In either case, execution continues with the next statement following the END IF statement that terminates the IF construct, unless, of course, execution is terminated or control is transferred elsewhere by one of the statements in the statement sequence selected.

As an example of this form of an IF construct, consider the problem of calculating the values of the following piecewise continuous function:

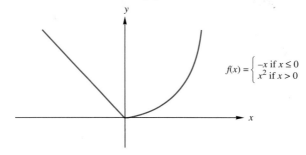

$$f(x) = \begin{cases} -x & \text{if } x \le 0 \\ x^2 & \text{if } x > 0 \end{cases}$$

An IF construct containing an ELSE clause makes this easy:

```
IF (X .LE. 0) THEN
    FVAL = -X
ELSE
    FVAL = X ** 2
END IF
```

Another problem that requires this type of selection structure is the pollution index problem considered in Chapter 2. In this problem, a pollution index is calculated, and if this index is less than some cutoff value, a message indicating a safe condition must be displayed; if not, a message indicating a hazardous condition must be displayed. This selection is indicated in the algorithm for solving this problem (see Section 2.2) by

If INDEX < CUTOFF then
    Display 'Safe condition'
Else
    Display 'Hazardous condition'

and is implemented in the FORTRAN program in Figure 4.3 by the following IF construct:

```
IF (INDEX .LT. CUTOFF) THEN
    PRINT *, 'SAFE CONDITION'
ELSE
    PRINT *, 'HAZARDOUS CONDITION'
END IF
```

```
      PROGRAM POLLUT
*********************************************************************
* Program that reads 3 pollution LEVELS, calculates a pollution    *
* INDEX as their average, and then displays a "safe condition"     *
* message if this index is less than some CUTOFF value, otherwise  *
* displays a "hazardous condition" message.                        *
*********************************************************************

      INTEGER CUTOFF, LEVEL1, LEVEL2, LEVEL3, INDEX
      PARAMETER (CUTOFF = 50)

      PRINT *, 'ENTER 3 POLLUTION READINGS:'
      READ *, LEVEL1, LEVEL2, LEVEL3
      INDEX = (LEVEL1 + LEVEL2 + LEVEL3) / 3
      IF (INDEX .LT. CUTOFF) THEN
          PRINT *, 'SAFE CONDITION'
      ELSE
          PRINT *, 'HAZARDOUS CONDITION'
      END IF
      END
```

Figure 4.3

Figure 4.3 (continued)

Sample runs:

```
ENTER 3 POLLUTION READINGS:
55, 39, 48
SAFE CONDITION

ENTER 3 POLLUTION READINGS:
68, 49, 57
HAZARDOUS CONDITION
```

As another illustration of using an IF construct to implement a two-alternative selection structure, consider the problem of solving the quadratic equation

$$Ax^2 + Bx + C = 0$$

by using the quadratic formula to obtain the roots

$$\frac{-B \pm \sqrt{B^2 - 4AC}}{2A}$$

In this problem, the input values are the coefficients A, B, and C of the quadratic equation, and the output is the pair of real roots or a message indicating that there are no real roots (in case $B^2 - 4AC$ is negative). An algorithm for solving a quadratic equation is the following:

**ALGORITHM FOR SOLVING QUADRATIC
EQUATIONS—VERSION 1**

```
* This algorithm solves quadratic equations Ax² + Bx + C = 0    *
* using the quadratic formula. If the discriminant DISC =        *
* B² − 4AC is positive, the pair of real roots ROOT1 and ROOT2   *
* is calculated; otherwise, a message is displayed indicating that *
* there are no real roots.                                        *
```

1. Enter A, B, and C.
2. Calculate DISC = B ** 2 − 4 * A * C.
3. If DISC < 0 then do the following:
   a. Display DISC.
   b. Display a message that there are no real roots.
   Else do the following:
   a. Calculate DISC = $\sqrt{\text{DISC}}$.
   b. Calculate ROOT1 = (−B + DISC) / (2 * A).
   c. Calculate ROOT2 = (−B − DISC) / (2 * A).
   d. Display ROOT1 and ROOT2.

Figure 4.4 displays the structure of this algorithm in flowchart form.

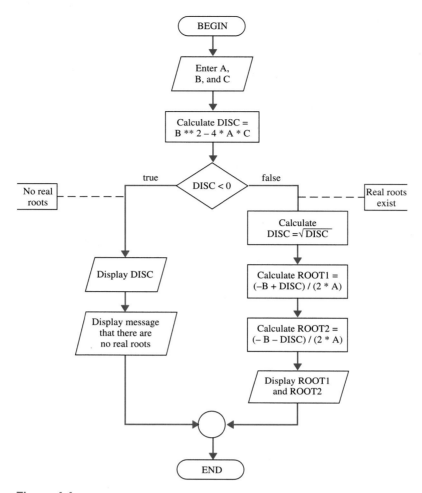

Figure 4.4

The program in Figure 4.5 implements this algorithm. Note the indentation of the statements in the IF construct. Although not required, it is good programming style to set off these statements in this manner to emphasize that they constitute a single block.

```
      PROGRAM QUAD1
*****************************************************************************
* Program to solve a quadratic equation using the quadratic formula.    *
* Variables used are:                                                   *
*      A, B, C       : the coefficients of the quadratic equation       *
*      DISC          : the discriminant, B ** 2 - 4 * A * C             *
*      ROOT1, ROOT2  : the two roots of the equation                    *
*****************************************************************************
```

Figure 4.5

Figure 4.5   (continued)

```
REAL A, B, C, DISC, ROOT1, ROOT2

PRINT *, 'ENTER THE COEFFICIENTS OF THE QUADRATIC EQUATION'
READ *, A, B, C
DISC = B ** 2 - 4.0 * A * C
IF (DISC .LT. 0) THEN
     PRINT *, 'DISCRIMINANT IS', DISC
     PRINT *, 'THERE ARE NO REAL ROOTS'
ELSE
     DISC = SQRT(DISC)
     ROOT1 = (-B + DISC) / (2.0 * A)
     ROOT2 = (-B - DISC) / (2.0 * A)
     PRINT *, 'THE ROOTS ARE', ROOT1, ROOT2
END IF
END
```

Sample runs:

```
ENTER THE COEFFICIENTS OF THE QUADRATIC EQUATION
1, -5, 6
THE ROOTS ARE     3.00000     2.00000


ENTER THE COEFFICIENTS OF THE QUADRATIC EQUATION
1, 0, -4
THE ROOTS ARE     2.00000    -2.00000


ENTER THE COEFFICIENTS OF THE QUADRATIC EQUATION
1, 0, 4
DISCRIMINANT IS    -16.0000
THERE ARE NO REAL ROOTS


ENTER THE COEFFICIENTS OF THE QUADRATIC EQUATION
3.7, 16.5, 1.7
THE ROOTS ARE   -0.105528    -4.35393
```

The sequence(s) of statements in an IF construct may themselves contain other IF constructs. In this case, the second IF construct is said to be **nested** within the first. For example, suppose the right branch of the earlier piecewise continuous function is modified so that the function becomes constant for $x \geq 1$:

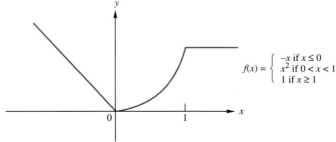

$$f(x) = \begin{cases} -x & \text{if } x \leq 0 \\ x^2 & \text{if } 0 < x < 1 \\ 1 & \text{if } x \geq 1 \end{cases}$$

The earlier IF construct for evaluating this function can be modified by inserting another IF construct within the ELSE block:

```
IF (X .LE. 0) THEN
    FVAL = -X
ELSE
    IF (X .LT. 1.0) THEN
        FVAL = X ** 2
    ELSE
        FVAL = 1.0
END IF
```

As another example of a nested IF construct, consider again the quadratic equation problem. If there are real roots of the equation, we wish to determine whether these roots are distinct or repeated. The following algorithm can be used:

ALGORITHM FOR SOLVING QUADRATIC EQUATIONS—VERSION 2

* This algorithm solves quadratic equations $Ax^2 + Bx + C = 0$ *
* using the quadratic formula. The distinct real roots ROOT1 and   *
* ROOT2 are calculated if the discriminant DISC $= B^2 - 4AC$ is   *
* positive; if it is zero, the repeated real root ROOT1 is calculated; if *
* it is negative, a message is displayed indicating that there are no   *
* real roots.   *

1. Enter A, B, and C.
2. Calculate DISC $= B ** 2 - 4 * A * C$.
3. If DISC < 0 then do the following:
      a. Display DISC.
      b. Display a message that there are no real roots.
   Else do the following:
     IF DISC $= 0$ then do the following:
       a. Calculate ROOT1 $= -B / (2 * A)$.
       b. Display ROOT1.
     Else do the following:
       a. Calculate DISC $= \sqrt{DISC}$.
       b. Calculate ROOT1 $= (-B + DISC) / (2 * A)$.
       c. Calculate ROOT2 $= (-B - DISC) / (2 * A)$.
       d. Display ROOT1 and ROOT2.

The nesting of the IF construct based on the condition DISC $= 0$ within the outer construct based on the condition DISC < 0 is clearly seen in the flowchart in Figure 4.6, which shows the structure of this algorithm.

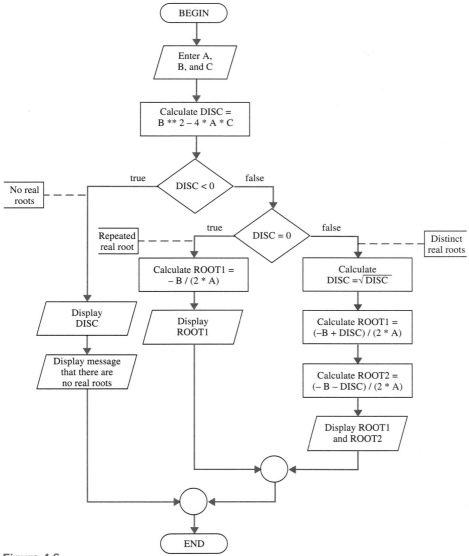

Figure 4.6

The program in Figure 4.7 implements this algorithm. Note again the indentation used to indicate the blocks in the IF statements.

```
      PROGRAM QUAD2
*********************************************************************
* Program to solve a quadratic equation using the quadratic formula.  *
* Variables used are:                                                 *
*     A, B, C      : the coefficients of the quadratic equation       *
*     DISC         : the discriminant, B ** 2 - 4 * A * C             *
*     ROOT1, ROOT2 : the two roots of the equation                    *
*********************************************************************
```

Figure 4.7

Figure 4.7 (continued)

```
REAL A, B, C, DISC, ROOT1, ROOT2

PRINT *, 'ENTER THE COEFFICIENTS OF THE QUADRATIC EQUATION'
READ *, A, B, C
DISC = B ** 2 - 4.0 * A * C
IF (DISC .LT. 0) THEN
    PRINT *, 'DISCRIMINANT IS', DISC
    PRINT *, 'THERE ARE NO REAL ROOTS'
ELSE
    IF (DISC .EQ. 0) THEN
        ROOT1 = -B / (2.0 * A)
        PRINT *, 'REPEATED ROOT IS', ROOT1
    ELSE
        DISC = SQRT(DISC)
        ROOT1 = (-B + DISC) / (2.0 * A)
        ROOT2 = (-B - DISC) / (2.0 * A)
        PRINT *, 'THE ROOTS ARE', ROOT1, ROOT2
    END IF
END IF
END
```

Sample runs:

```
ENTER THE COEFFICIENTS OF THE QUADRATIC EQUATION
1, 5, 6
THE ROOTS ARE    -2.00000    -3.00000


ENTER THE COEFFICIENTS OF THE QUADRATIC EQUATION
1, 4, 4
REPEATED ROOT IS    -2.00000


ENTER THE COEFFICIENTS OF THE QUADRATIC EQUATION
4, 1, 2
DISCRIMINANT IS    -31.0000
THERE ARE NO REAL ROOTS
```

The selection structures considered thus far involved selecting one of two alternatives. It is also possible to use the IF construct to design selection structures that contain more than two alternatives. For example, consider again the piecewise continuous function defined by

$$f(x) = \begin{cases} -x & \text{if } x \le 0 \\ x^2 & \text{if } 0 < x < 1 \\ 1 & \text{if } x \ge 1 \end{cases}$$

This definition really consists of three alternatives and was implemented earlier using an IF construct of the form

```
IF (logical-expression-1) THEN
    statement-sequence-1
ELSE
    IF (logical-expression-2) THEN
        statement-sequence-2
    ELSE
        statement-sequence-3
    END IF
END IF
```

But such compound IF constructs that implement selection structures with many alternatives can become quite complex, and the correspondence between the IFs, ELSEs and END IFs may not be clear if indentation is not used properly.

An alternative method of implementing a **multialternative selection structure** is to use ELSE IF statements within an IF construct so that it has the form

```
IF (logical-expression-1) THEN
    statement-sequence-1
ELSE IF (logical-expression-2) THEN
    statement-sequence-2
ELSE IF (logical-expression-3) THEN
    statement-sequence-3

        .
        .
        .

ELSE
    statement-sequence-n
END IF
```

which we might call an **IF–ELSE IF construct.** The logical expressions are evaluated to determine the first true logical expression; the associated sequence of statements is executed; and execution then continues with the next statement following the END IF statement (unless one of these statements transfers control elsewhere or terminates execution). If none of the logical expressions is true, the statement sequence associated with the ELSE statement is executed, and execution then continues with the statement following the END IF statement (unless it is terminated or transferred to some other point by a statement in this block). This IF construct thus implements an *n*-way selection structure in which exactly one of *statement-sequence-1*, *statement-sequence-2*, ... , *statement-sequence-n* is executed.

The ELSE statement and its corresponding sequence of statements may be omitted in this structure. In this case, if none of the logical expressions is true, execution continues with the statement following the END IF.

As an example of an IF–ELSE IF construct, the three-part definition of the preceding function $f(x)$ could be evaluated by

```
IF (X .LE. 0) THEN
    FVAL = -X
ELSE IF (X .LT. 1.0) THEN
    FVAL = X ** 2
ELSE
    FVAL = 1.0
END IF
```

To illustrate further the use of an IF–ELSE IF construct to implement a multialternative selection structure, consider the following alternative description of the algorithm for solving quadratic equations:

ALGORITHM FOR SOLVING QUADRATIC EQUATIONS—VERSION 3

* This algorithm solves quadratic equations $Ax^2 + Bx + C = 0$ *
* using the quadratic formula. A multialternative selection structure is *
* used to select one of the following actions: *
* DISC < 0: Display a message that there are no real roots   *
* DISC = 0: Calculate repeated real root ROOT1   *
* DISC > 0: Calculate distinct real roots ROOT1 and ROOT2   *
* where DISC is the discriminant $B^2 - 4AC$.   *

1. Enter A, B, and C.
2. Calculate DISC = B ** 2 − 4 * A * C.
3. If DISC < 0 then do the following:
    a. Display DISC.
    b. Display a message that there are no real roots.
   Else if DISC = 0 then do the following:
    a. Calculate ROOT1 = − B / (2 * A).
    b. Display ROOT1.
   Else do the following:
    a. Calculate DISC = $\sqrt{\text{DISC}}$.
    b. Calculate ROOT1 = (− B + DISC) / (2 * A).
    c. Calculate ROOT2 = (− B − DISC) / (2 * A).
    d. Display ROOT1 and ROOT2.

The flowchart in Figure 4.8 that displays the structure of this algorithm clearly shows the three-way selection structure in step 3. The program in Figure 4.9 uses an IF–ELSE IF construct to implement this three-way selection structure.

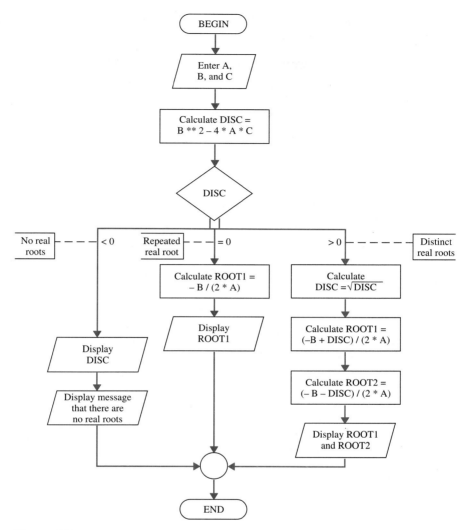

Figure 4.8

```
      PROGRAM QUAD3
***********************************************************************
* Program to solve a quadratic equation using the quadratic formula.  *
* Variables used are:                                                 *
*     A, B, C      : the coefficients of the quadratic equation       *
*     DISC         : the discriminant, B ** 2 - 4 * A * C             *
*     ROOT1, ROOT2 : the two roots of the equation                    *
***********************************************************************
```

Figure 4.9

Figure 4.9 (continued)

```
REAL A, B, C, DISC, ROOT1, ROOT2

PRINT *, 'ENTER THE COEFFICIENTS OF THE QUADRATIC EQUATION'
READ *, A, B, C
DISC = B ** 2 - 4.0 * A * C
IF (DISC .LT. 0) THEN
    PRINT *, 'DISCRIMINANT IS', DISC
    PRINT *, 'THERE ARE NO REAL ROOTS'
ELSE IF (DISC .EQ. 0) THEN
    ROOT1 = -B / (2.0 * A)
    PRINT *, 'REPEATED ROOT IS', ROOT1
ELSE
    DISC = SQRT(DISC)
    ROOT1 = (-B + DISC) / (2.0 * A)
    ROOT2 = (-B - DISC) / (2.0 * A)
    PRINT *, 'THE ROOTS ARE', ROOT1, ROOT2
END IF
END
```

There are three other statements in FORTRAN that may be used to form multialternative selection structures: the arithmetic IF statement, the computed GO TO statement, and the assigned GO TO statement. These statements are less commonly used than are the other control statements and are described in Chapter 12.

Exercises

1. Write FORTRAN program segments for the following:

   (a) If CODE $= 1$, read X and Y, and calculate and print the sum of X and Y.
   (b) If A is strictly between 0 and 5, set B equal to $1 / A^2$; otherwise set B equal to A^2.
   (c) Display the message 'LEAP YEAR' if the integer variable YEAR is the number of a leap year. (A leap year is a multiple of 4, and if it is a multiple of 100, it must also be a multiple of 400.)
   (d) Assign a value to COST corresponding to the value of DIST given in the following table:

DIST	COST
0 through 100	5.00
More than 100 but not more than 500	8.00
More than 500 but less than 1000	10.00
1000 or more	12.00

2. Write IF constructs to evaluate the following functions:

   (a) The output of a simple d-c generator; the shape of the curve is the absolute value of the sine function. (100 V is the maximum voltage.)

   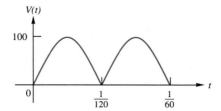

   (b) A rectified half-wave; the curve is a sine function for half the cycle and zero for the other half. (Maximum current is 5 amp.)

   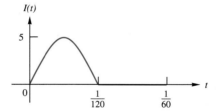

   (c) Sawtooth; the graph consists of two straight lines. The maximum voltage of 100 V occurs at the middle of the cycle.

   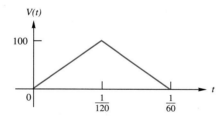

   (d) The excess pressure $p(t)$ in a sound wave whose graph is as follows:

   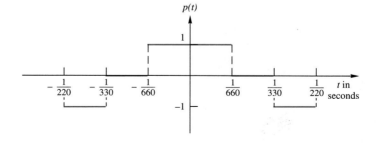

3. A certain city classifies a pollution index of less than 35 as "pleasant," 35 through 60 as "unpleasant," and above 60 as "hazardous." Write

a program that accepts a real number representing a pollution index and displays the appropriate classification of it.

4. Write a program to read one of the codes 1 for circle, 2 for square, or 3 for equilateral triangle, and a number representing the radius of the circle, side of the square, or side of the triangle, respectively. Then calculate and display the area and the perimeter of that geometric figure with appropriate labels. (See Exercise 3 in Section 3.8.)

5. Modify the program in Figure 4.9 for solving quadratic equations so that when the discriminant is negative, the complex roots of the equation are displayed. If the discriminant D is negative, these roots are given by

$$\frac{-B \pm \sqrt{-D}i}{2A}$$

where $i^2 = -1$.

6. Write a program that reads values for the coefficients A, B, C, D, E, and F of the equations

$$Ax + By = C$$
$$Dx + Ey = F$$

of two straight lines. Then determine whether the lines are parallel (slopes are equal) or intersect and, if they intersect, whether the lines are perpendicular (product of slopes is equal to -1).

7. Write a program that reads the coordinates of three points and then determines whether they are collinear.

8. Suppose the following formulas give the safe loading L in pounds per square inch for a column with slimness ratio S:

$$L = \begin{cases} 16500 - .475S^2 & \text{if } S < 100 \\ \dfrac{17900}{2 + (S^2/17900)} & \text{if } S \geq 100 \end{cases}$$

Write a program that reads a slimness ratio and then calculates the safe loading.

9. Suppose that charges by a gas company are based on consumption according to the following table:

Gas Used	Rate
First 70 cubic meters	$5.00 minimum cost
Next 100 cubic meters	5.0¢ per cubic meter
Next 230 cubic meters	2.5¢ per cubic meter
Above 400 cubic meters	1.5¢ per cubic meter

Write a program in which the meter reading for the previous month and the current meter reading are entered, each a four-digit number and each representing cubic meters, and that then calculates the amount of the bill. *Note:* The current reading may be less than the previous one; for example, the previous reading may have been 9897, and the current one is 0103.

4.5   Repetition Structure: DO Loops

The third basic control structure is a **repetition structure** or **loop** that makes possible the repeated execution of one or more statements. This repetition must be controlled so that these statements are executed only a finite number of times. There are two basic types of repetition structures:

1. *Loops controlled by a counter* in which the body of the loop is executed once for each value of some control variable in a specified range of values.
2. *Loops controlled by a logical expression* in which the decision to continue or to terminate repetition is determined by the truth or falsity of some logical expression.

In FORTRAN a repetition of the first type is called a **DO loop** and is implemented using the **DO** and **CONTINUE statements**. This structure has one of the forms

> DO *n, control-variable = initial-value, limit*
> > *statement-sequence*
> *n* CONTINUE

> DO *n, control-variable = initial-value, limit, step-size*
> > *statement-sequence*
> *n* CONTINUE

Here *n* is a statement number that is a positive integer of up to five digits; *initial-value*, *limit,* and *step-size* are integer or real (or double precision) expressions; and *step-size* must be nonzero. The comma following the statement number *n* is optional, and we omit it in our examples of this structure. The first form of a DO loop is equivalent to a DO loop of the second form in which the value of *step-size* is 1.

A DO loop in which the step size is positive implements the repetition structure shown in Figure 4.10(a). As the flowchart shows, when a DO loop is executed, the control variable is assigned the initial value, and the sequence of statements, called the **body of the loop,** is executed unless the initial value is greater than the limit. After the body of the loop has been executed, the control variable is incremented by the step size, and if this new value does not exceed the limit, the body of the DO loop is executed again. Execution of the DO loop terminates when the value of the control variable exceeds the limit. Note that if the initial value is greater than the limit, the body of the loop is never executed.

DO loops will be represented in flowcharts as shown in Figure 4.10(b), to emphasize that they are repetition structures. The hexagon at the beginning of

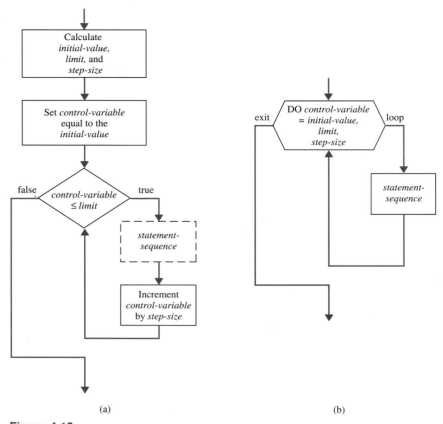

(a)   (b)

Figure 4.10

the loop is intended to include the initialization, testing, and incrementing, which are shown explicitly in Figure 4.10(a).

To illustrate, consider the DO loop

```
      DO 10 NUMBER = 1, 9
          PRINT *, NUMBER, NUMBER **2
   10 CONTINUE
```

where NUMBER is of integer type. In this example, NUMBER is the control variable, the initial value is 1, the limit is 9, and the step size is 1. When this DO loop is executed, the initial value 1 is assigned to NUMBER, and the PRINT statement is executed. The value of NUMBER is then increased by 1, and because this new value 2 is less than the limit 9, the PRINT statement is executed again. This repetition continues as long as the value of the control variable NUMBER is less than or equal to the limit 9. Thus, the output produced by this DO loop is

```
1  1
2  4
3  9
4  16
5  25
6  36
7  49
8  64
9  81
```

If the step size in a DO loop is negative, the control variable is decremented rather than incremented, and repetition continues as long as the value of the control variable is greater than or equal to the limit. This is illustrated in Figure 4.11. Note that if the initial value is less than the limit, the body of the loop is never executed.

For example, consider the DO loop

```
DO 10 NUMBER = 9, 1, -1
    PRINT *, NUMBER, NUMBER **2
10 CONTINUE
```

The control variable NUMBER is assigned the initial value 9, and because this value is greater than the limit 1, the PRINT statement is executed. The value

Figure 4.11

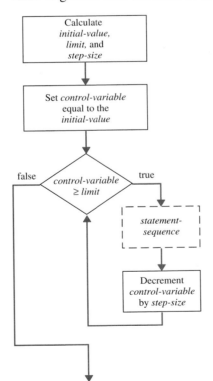

of NUMBER is then decreased to 8, and because this new value is greater than the limit, the PRINT statement is executed again. This process continues as long as the value of NUMBER is greater than or equal to the limit 1. Thus the output produced is

```
9 81
8 64
7 49
6 36
5 25
4 16
3 9
2 4
1 1
```

The initial values of the control variable, the limit, and the step size are determined before repetition begins and cannot be changed during execution of the DO loop. Within the body of the DO loop, the values of variables that specify the initial value, the limit, and the step size may change, but this does not affect the number of repetitions.[1] Also, the statements within a DO loop may use the value of the control variable , but *they must not modify the value of the control variable.* (See Potential Problem 6 in the Programming Pointers at the end of this chapter.) Upon exit from a DO loop, the control variable retains its value, and so this value may be used later in the program.

The initial value, the limit, and the step size in a DO loop may be variables or expressions. To illustrate, consider the declarations

```
REAL FIRSTX, LASTX, DELTAX, X, Y
```

and the statements

```
      READ *, FIRSTX, LASTX, DELTAX
      DO 10 X = FIRSTX, LASTX, DELTAX
         Y = EXP(-X) * SIN(X)
         PRINT *, X, Y
   10 CONTINUE
```

The values read for FIRSTX, LASTX, and DELTAX are the initial value, limit, and step size, respectively, for the DO loop. The program in Figure 4.12 uses these statements to print a table of points on the damped vibration curve

$$y = e^{-x} \sin x$$

---

[1] The number of repetitions is calculated as the larger of the value 0 and the integer part of

$$\frac{limit - initial\text{-}value + step\text{-}size}{step\text{-}size}$$

```
       PROGRAM VIBRAT
*******************************************************************
* Program to print a table of points on the curve                *
*              -x                                                 *
*        y = e  *  sin x                                          *
* Variables used are:                                            *
*     X, Y           : coordinates of the point                  *
*     FIRSTX, LASTX  : lower and upper limits on X               *
*     DELTAX         : step size                                 *
*******************************************************************

       REAL X, Y, FIRSTX, LASTX, DELTAX

       PRINT *, 'ENTER LOWER AND UPPER LIMITS ON X AND STEP SIZE'
       READ *, FIRSTX, LASTX, DELTAX
       PRINT *, '         X                Y'
       PRINT *, ' ==========================='
       DO 10 X = FIRSTX, LASTX, DELTAX
          Y = EXP(-X) * SIN(X)
          PRINT *, X, Y
10     CONTINUE
       END
```

Sample run:

```
ENTER LOWER AND UPPER LIMITS ON X AND STEP SIZE
1, 3, .25
         X                Y
 ===========================
     1.00000    0.309560
     1.25000    0.271889
     1.50000    0.222571
     1.75000    0.170991
     2.00000    0.123060
     2.25000    8.20083E-02
     2.50000    4.91256E-02
     2.75000    2.43988E-02
     3.00000    7.02595E-03
```

Figure 4.12

The body of a DO loop may contain another DO loop. In this case, the second DO loop is said to be **nested** within the first DO loop. As an example, consider the program in Figure 4.13 that calculates and displays products of the form M * N for M ranging from 1 through LASTM and N ranging from 1 through LASTN for integers M, N, LASTM, and LASTN. The table of products is generated by the DO loop

```
       DO 20 M = 1, LASTM
          DO 10 N = 1, LASTN
             PROD = M * N
             PRINT *, M, N, PROD
10        CONTINUE
20 CONTINUE
```

In the sample run, both LASTM and LASTN are assigned the value 4. The control variable M is assigned its initial value 1, and the DO loop

```
DO 10 N = 1, LASTN
   PROD = M * N
   PRINT *, M, N, PROD
10 CONTINUE
```

is executed. This calculates and displays the first four products, $1 * 1$, $1 * 2$, $1 * 3$, and $1 * 4$. The value of M is then incremented by 1, and the preceding DO loop is executed again. This calculates and displays the next four products, $2 * 1$, $2 * 2$, $2 * 3$, and $2 * 4$. The control variable M is then incremented to 3, producing the next four products, $3 * 1$, $3 * 2$, $3 * 3$, and $3 * 4$. Finally, M is incremented to 4, giving the last four products, $4 * 1$, $4 * 2$, $4 * 3$, and $4 * 4$.

```
      PROGRAM MULT
*********************************************************************
* Program to calculate and display a list of products of two numbers.  *
* Variables used are:                                                  *
*     M, N          : the two numbers being multiplied                 *
*     PROD          : their product                                    *
*     LASTM, LASTN  : the last values of M and N                       *
*********************************************************************

      INTEGER M, N, LASTM, LASTN, PROD

      PRINT *, 'ENTER THE LAST VALUES OF THE TWO NUMBERS'
      READ *, LASTM, LASTN
      PRINT *, '  M  N  M * N'
      PRINT *, '============='
      DO 20 M = 1, LASTM
         DO 10 N = 1, LASTN
            PROD = M * N
            PRINT *, M, N, PROD
10       CONTINUE
20    CONTINUE
      END
```

Sample run:

```
ENTER THE LAST VALUES OF THE TWO NUMBERS
4, 4
```

Figure 4.13

Figure 4.13 (continued)

```
M   N   M * N
==============
1   1   1
1   2   2
1   3   3
1   4   4
2   1   2
2   2   4
2   3   6
2   4   8
3   1   3
3   2   6
3   3   9
3   4   12
4   1   4
4   2   8
4   3   12
4   4   16
```

4.6 The While Repetition Structure

A DO loop can be used to implement a repetition structure in which the number of iterations is determined before the loop is executed. In some cases, a repetition structure is required in which repetition is controlled by some logical expression and continues while this logical expression remains true, terminating when it becomes false. Such a repetition structure is called a **while loop** and is pictured in Figure 4.14(a). It will be represented in flowcharts as shown in the second Figure 4.14(b) to emphasize that it is a repetition structure.

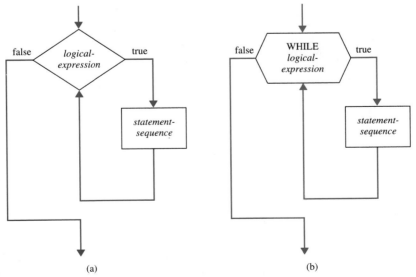

(a)   (b)

Figure 4.14

To illustrate the use of a while loop, consider the following problem:

For a given value of LIMIT, what is the smallest positive integer NUMBER for which the sum

$$1 + 2 + ... + NUMBER$$

is greater than LIMIT, and what is the value of this sum?

The following algorithm solves this problem:

ALGORITHM FOR SUMMATION PROBLEM

* Algorithm to find the smallest positive NUMBER for which the   *
* sum $1 + 2 + \cdots + NUMBER$ is greater than some specified   *
* value LIMIT.   *

1. Enter LIMIT.
2. Set NUMBER equal to 0.
3. Set SUM equal to 0.
4. While SUM ≤ LIMIT, do the following:
    a. Increase NUMBER by 1.
    b. Add NUMBER to SUM.
5. Display NUMBER and SUM.

Figure 4.15 displays the structure of this algorithm in flowchart form.

As the diagrams in Figure 4.14 indicate, the logical expression in a while loop is evaluated *before* repetition, and this loop is therefore sometimes called a **pretest loop** or a "test-at-the-top" loop. If the logical expression that controls repetition is false initially, the body of the loop is not executed. Thus, in the preceding summation algorithm, if the value -1 is entered for LIMIT, the body of the while loop is bypassed, and execution continues with the display instruction that follows the while loop; the value 0 will be displayed for both NUMBER and SUM.

As another illustration of a while loop, we reconsider Problem 3 of Chapter 2 in which failure times of some device are to be read and counted and the mean time to failure is to be calculated. Since the number of failure times is not known in advance, some method must be devised to determine when all of the data values have been read. As suggested in Section 2.2, we will append to the data an artificial data value called an **end-of-data flag,** which is distinct from any possible data item. As each data item is read, it is checked to determine whether it is this end-of-data flag. If it is not, the value is processed. When the end-of-data flag is read, it must not be processed as a regular data value, but, rather, should serve only to terminate repetition.

This scheme can be implemented by using a while loop:

1. Read first data value.
2. While the data value is not the end-of-data flag, do the following:
    a. Process the data value.
    b. Read the next data value.

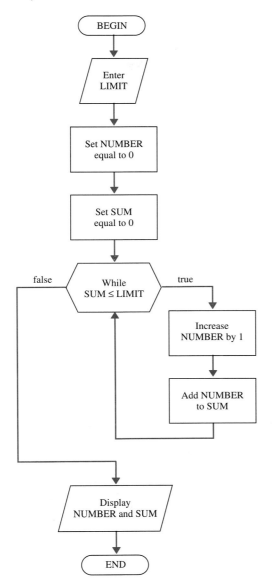

Figure 4.15

Note that the first data value must be read before the while loop so that the logical expression that controls repetition can be evaluated. If this data value is not the end-of-data flag, the body of the while loop is entered and the value is processed. The next data value must then be read and checked to determine whether it is the end-of-data flag. If it is not, the value is processed. When the end-of-data flag is eventually read, the while loop will be exited without processing this artificial data value.

This standard technique for reading and processing data values is used in the algorithm given in Section 2.2 for solving this problem:

ALGORITHM TO CALCULATE MEAN TIME TO FAILURE

```
* Algorithm to read failure times, count them, and find the mean time  *
* to failure (MEAN). FAILTM represents the current failure time        *
* entered, COUNT is number of failure times, and SUM is their sum.     *
* Values are read until the end-of-data flag is encountered.           *
```

1. Set COUNT to 0.
2. Set SUM to 0.
3. Enter first value for FAILTM.
4. While FAILTM is not the end-of-data flag, do the following:
   a. Increment COUNT by 1.
   b. Add FAILTM to SUM.
   c. Enter next value for FAILTM.
5. Calculate MEAN = SUM / COUNT.
6. Display MEAN and COUNT.

Here, statements a, b, and c are to be repeated as long as the value of FAILTM is not some end-of-data flag entered by the user. When it is, so that the value of the logical expression "FAILTM is not the end-of-data flag" becomes false, repetition terminates, and execution continues with statement 5.

A while statement that implements this important control structure is not included in standard FORTRAN, but it is a common extension that is available in many versions of FORTRAN and will be included in FORTRAN 90. In the next section we consider a DO WHILE statement and show how it can be used in programs that implement the algorithms presented in this section. In Section 4.8 we show how while loops can be implemented in standard FORTRAN, and in later programs in this text, all while loops will be implemented in this manner because we wish to conform to the standard. But each while loop in the examples will be clearly marked with a comment to indicate where a DO WHILE statement could be used.

4.7 The DO WHILE Statement[2]

The DO WHILE statement that is provided in many versions of FORTRAN commonly has one of the following forms:

DO WHILE (*logical-expression*)
    statement-sequence
END DO
	WHILE (*logical-expression*) DO
	    statement-sequence
	END WHILE

---

[2] Both Sections 4.7 and 4.8 discuss implementations of while loops. If your version of FORTRAN provides a DO WHILE statement, you may wish to study Section 4.7 and omit Section 4.8. Note, however, that using a DO WHILE statement makes a program less *portable*, as it cannot be compiled correctly by FORTRAN compilers that do not support this extension.

When this statement is executed, the logical expression is evaluated; if it is true, the sequence of statements that comprise the *body* of the while loop is executed. The logical expression is then reevaluated, and if it is still true, these statements are executed again. This process of evaluating the logical expression and executing the specified statements is repeated as long as the logical expression is true. When it becomes false, repetition is terminated. This means that execution of the statements within the DO WHILE statement must eventually cause the logical expression to become false, since otherwise an **infinite loop** would result.

The program in Figure 4.16 implements the summation algorithm of the preceding section for finding the smallest positive integer NUMBER for which the sum $1 + 2 + \cdots + $ NUMBER is greater than some specified value LIMIT. It uses the DO WHILE statement

```
DO WHILE (SUM .LE. LIMIT)
   NUMBER = NUMBER + 1
   SUM = SUM + NUMBER
END DO
```

to implement the while loop

While SUM $\leq$ LIMIT, do the following:
   a. Increase NUMBER by 1.
   b. Add NUMBER to SUM.

in this algorithm.

Because the logical expression in a DO WHILE statement is evaluated before the repetition begins, the statements that comprise the body of the while loop are not executed if this expression is initially false. This is demonstrated in the last sample run, in which the value -1 is entered for LIMIT. The DO WHILE statement causes an immediate transfer of control to the last PRINT statement which displays the value 0 for both NUMBER and SUM.

```
      PROGRAM ADDER1
*******************************************************************
* Program that uses a WHILE statement to find the smallest positive   *
* integer NUMBER for which the sum 1 + 2 + ... + NUMBER is greater     *
* than some specified LIMIT.  Variables used are:                      *
*     NUMBER : the current number being added                          *
*     SUM    : the sum 1 + 2 + ... + NUMBER                            *
*     LIMIT  : the value which SUM is to exceed                        *
*******************************************************************
```

Figure 4.16

Figure 4.16 (continued)

```
      INTEGER NUMBER, SUM, LIMIT

* Read LIMIT and initialize NUMBER and SUM

      PRINT *, 'ENTER VALUE 1 + 2 + ... + ? IS TO EXCEED'
      READ *, LIMIT
      NUMBER = 0
      SUM = 0

* While SUM does not exceed LIMIT, increment NUMBER and add to SUM

      DO WHILE (SUM .LE. LIMIT)
         NUMBER = NUMBER + 1
         SUM = SUM + NUMBER
      END DO

* Print the results

      PRINT *, '1 + ... +', NUMBER, ' =', SUM, ' >', LIMIT
      END
```

Sample runs:

```
ENTER VALUE 1 + ... + ? IS TO EXCEED
10
1 + ... +  5 =  15 >  10

ENTER VALUE 1 + ... + ? IS TO EXCEED
10000
1 + ... +  141 =  10011 >  10000

ENTER VALUE 1 + ... + ? IS TO EXCEED
-1
1 + ... +  0 =  0 >  -1
```

In the first sample run of Figure 4.16, in which the value 10 is entered for LIMIT, the body of the while loop is executed five times, as indicated in the following table, which traces its execution:

NUMBER	SUM	SUM .LE. LIMIT	Action
0	0	.TRUE.	Execute body of while loop
1	1	.TRUE.	Execute body of while loop
2	3	.TRUE.	Execute body of while loop
3	6	.TRUE.	Execute body of while loop
4	10	.TRUE.	Execute body of while loop
5	15	.FALSE.	Terminate repetition

A similar trace table for the second sample run would show that the loop body is executed 141 times. A trace table for the third sample run shows that the loop body is not executed because the logical expression SUM .LE. LIMIT that controls repetition is initially false:

NUMBER	SUM	SUM .LE. LIMIT	Action
0	0	.FALSE.	Terminate repetition. That is, bypass loop body.

As another example, we reconsider the problem of calculating the mean time to failure of some device. The program in Figure 4.17 implements the algorithm given in the preceding section for solving this problem. It uses the statements

```
PRINT *, 'ENTER FAIL TIME OF -999 OR LESS TO STOP'
PRINT *, 'ENTER FAIL TIME'
READ *, FAILTM

DO WHILE (FAILTM .GT. -999)
   COUNT = COUNT + 1
   SUM = SUM + FAILTM
   PRINT *, 'ENTER FAIL TIME'
   READ *, FAILTM
END DO
```

to implement the following instructions in the algorithm:

3. Enter first value for FAILTM.
4. While FAILTM is not the end-of-data flag, do the following:
    a. Increment COUNT by 1.
    b. Add FAILTM to SUM.
    c. Read next value for FAILTM.

```
      PROGRAM FAIL1
*******************************************************************
* Program to read a list of failure times, count them, and find the  *
* mean time to failure.  Values are read until an end-of-data flag    *
* (any value less than or equal to -999) is read.  Variables used are: *
*     FAILTM  :  the current fail time read                          *
*     COUNT   :  the number of fail time readings                    *
*     SUM     :  sum of fail times                                   *
*     MEAN    :  the mean time to failure                            *
*******************************************************************
```

Figure 4.17

Figure 4.17   (continued)

```
      INTEGER COUNT
      REAL FAILTM, SUM, MEAN

* Initialize SUM and COUNT, and read 1-st fail time

      SUM = 0
      COUNT = 0
      PRINT *, 'ENTER FAIL TIME OF -999 OR LESS TO STOP'
      PRINT *, 'ENTER FAIL TIME'
      READ *, FAILTM

* While not end-of-data, count, sum, and read fail times

      DO WHILE (FAILTM .GT. -999)
         COUNT = COUNT + 1
         SUM = SUM + FAILTM
         PRINT *, 'ENTER FAIL TIME'
         READ *, FAILTM
      END DO

* Calculate and display mean time to failure

      MEAN = SUM / COUNT
      PRINT *
      PRINT *, 'NUMBER OF FAIL TIME READINGS:', COUNT
      PRINT *, 'MEAN TIME TO FAILURE:', MEAN
      END
```

Sample run:

```
ENTER FAIL TIME OF -999 OR LESS TO STOP
ENTER FAIL TIME
127
ENTER FAIL TIME
123.5
ENTER FAIL TIME
155.4
ENTER FAIL TIME
99
ENTER FAIL TIME
117.3
ENTER FAIL TIME
201.5
ENTER FAIL TIME
-999

NUMBER OF FAIL TIME READINGS:  6
MEAN TIME TO FAILURE:    137.283
```

4.8   Implementing While Loops in Standard FORTRAN[3]

As we noted earlier, standard FORTRAN does not include a WHILE statement. Nevertheless, this important control structure can be implemented in standard FORTRAN by using a **GO TO statement** within an IF construct. The GO TO statement is a branching statement and has the form

GO TO *statement-number*

where *statement-number* is the number of an executable statement. The GO TO statement alters the usual sequential execution so that the statement with the specified number is executed next.

A while loop can thus be implemented by a program segment of the form

n IF (*logical-expression*) THEN
       statement-sequence
    GO TO *n*
    END IF

Repeated execution of the statements in the body of the while loop must eventually cause the logical expression to become false, as an **infinite loop** results otherwise.

The program in Figure 4.18 implements the summation algorithm of the preceding section for finding the smallest positive integer NUMBER for which the sum $1 + 2 + \cdots + $ NUMBER is greater than some specified value LIMIT. It uses the statements

```
10 IF (SUM .LE. LIMIT) THEN
       NUMBER = NUMBER + 1
       SUM = SUM + NUMBER
   GO TO 10
   END IF
```

to implement the while loop

While SUM $\leq$ LIMIT, do the following:
   a. Increase NUMBER by 1.
   b. Add NUMBER to SUM.

in this algorithm.

Because the logical expression in a while loop is evaluated before the repetition begins, the statements that comprise the body of the while loop are not executed if this expression is initially false. This is demonstrated in the last sample run, where the value -1 is entered for LIMIT. The while loop causes an immediate transfer of control to the last PRINT statement that displays the value 0 for both NUMBER and SUM.

---

[3] Both Sections 4.7 and 4.8 discuss implementations of while loops. If your version of FORTRAN provides a DO WHILE statement, you may wish to study Section 4.7 and omit Section 4.8. Note, however, that using a DO WHILE statement makes a program less *portable*, as it cannot be compiled correctly by FORTRAN compilers that do not support this extension.

```
      PROGRAM ADDER2
************************************************************************
* Program to find the smallest positive integer NUMBER for which the  *
* sum 1 + 2 + ... + NUMBER is greater than some specified value LIMIT. *
* Variables used are:                                                  *
*      NUMBER : the current number being added                         *
*      SUM    : the sum 1 + 2 + ... + NUMBER                           *
*      LIMIT  : the value which SUM is to exceed                       *
************************************************************************

      INTEGER NUMBER, SUM, LIMIT

* Read LIMIT and initialize NUMBER and SUM

      PRINT *, 'ENTER VALUE 1 + 2 + ... + ? IS TO EXCEED'
      READ *, LIMIT
      NUMBER = 0
      SUM = 0

* While SUM does not exceed LIMIT, increment NUMBER and add to SUM

10    IF (SUM .LE. LIMIT) THEN
          NUMBER = NUMBER + 1
          SUM = SUM + NUMBER
      GO TO 10
      END IF

* Print the results

      PRINT *, '1 + ... +', NUMBER, ' =', SUM, ' >', LIMIT
      END
```

Sample runs:

```
ENTER VALUE 1 + ... + ? IS TO EXCEED
10
1 + ... +   5 =   15 >   10

ENTER VALUE 1 + ... + ? IS TO EXCEED
10000
1 + ... +   141 =   10011 >   10000

ENTER VALUE 1 + ... + ? IS TO EXCEED
-1
1 + ... +   0 =   0 >   -1
```

Figure 4.18

In the first sample run of Figure 4.18 in which the value 10 is entered for LIMIT, the body of the while loop is executed five times, as indicated in the following table, which traces its execution:

NUMBER	SUM	SUM .LE. LIMIT	Action
0	0	.TRUE.	Execute body of while loop
1	1	.TRUE.	Execute body of while loop
2	3	.TRUE.	Execute body of while loop
3	6	.TRUE.	Execute body of while loop
4	10	.TRUE.	Execute body of while loop
5	15	.FALSE.	Terminate repetition

A similar trace table for the second sample run would show that the loop body is executed 141 times. A trace table for the third sample run shows that the loop body is not executed because the logical expression SUM .LE. LIMIT that controls repetition is initially false:

NUMBER	SUM	SUM .LE. LIMIT	Action
0	0	.FALSE.	Terminate repetition. That is, bypass loop body.

As another example, we reconsider the problem of calculating the mean time to failure of some device. The program in Figure 4.19 implements the algorithm given in the Section 4.6 for solving this problem. It uses the statements

```
      PRINT *, 'ENTER FAIL TIME OF -999 OR LESS TO STOP'
      PRINT *, 'ENTER FAIL TIME'
      READ *, FAILTM

   10 IF (FAILTM .GT. -999) THEN
         COUNT = COUNT + 1
         SUM = SUM + FAILTM
         PRINT *, 'ENTER FAIL TIME'
         READ *, FAILTM
      GO TO 10
      END IF
```

to implement the following instructions in the algorithm:

3. Enter first value for FAILTM.
4. While FAILTM is not the end-of-data flag, do the following:
   a. Increment COUNT by 1.
   b. Add FAILTM to SUM.
   c. Read next value for FAILTM.

```
      PROGRAM FAIL2
*****************************************************************************
* Program to read a list of failure times, count them, and find the     *
* mean time to failure.  Values are read until an end-of-data flag       *
* (any value less than or equal to -999) is read.  Variables used are:   *
*     FAILTM  :  the current fail time read                              *
*     COUNT   :  the number of fail time readings                        *
*     SUM     :  sum of fail times                                       *
*     MEAN    :  the mean time to failure                                *
*****************************************************************************

      INTEGER COUNT
      REAL FAILTM, SUM, MEAN

* Initialize SUM and COUNT, and read 1-st fail time

      SUM = 0
      COUNT = 0
      PRINT *, 'ENTER FAIL TIME OF -999 OR LESS TO STOP'
      PRINT *, 'ENTER FAIL TIME'
      READ *, FAILTM

* While not end-of-data, count, sum, and read fail times

10    IF (FAILTM .GT. -999) THEN
          COUNT = COUNT + 1
          SUM = SUM + FAILTM
          PRINT *, 'ENTER FAIL TIME'
          READ *, FAILTM
      GO TO 10
      END IF

* Calculate and display mean time to failure

      MEAN = SUM / COUNT
      PRINT *
      PRINT *, 'NUMBER OF FAIL TIME READINGS:', COUNT
      PRINT *, 'MEAN TIME TO FAILURE:', MEAN
      END
```

Sample run:

```
ENTER FAIL TIME OF -999 OR LESS TO STOP
ENTER FAIL TIME
127
ENTER FAIL TIME
123.5
ENTER FAIL TIME
155.4
ENTER FAIL TIME
99
```

Figure 4.19

Figure 4.19 (continued)

```
ENTER FAIL TIME
117.3
ENTER FAIL TIME
201.5
ENTER FAIL TIME
-999

NUMBER OF FAIL TIME READINGS:  6
MEAN TIME TO FAILURE:    137.283
```

4.9   A Posttest Repetition Structure

A while loop is a **pretest** loop in which the logical expression that controls the repetition is evaluated *before* the body of the loop is executed. Sometimes, however, it is appropriate to use a **posttest** or "test-at-the-bottom" loop in which the termination test is made *after* the body of the loop is executed. Such a structure is pictured in Figure 4.20 and can be implemented in FORTRAN with a program segment of the form

> *n* CONTINUE
>   *statement-sequence*
>   IF (*logical-expression*) GO TO *n*

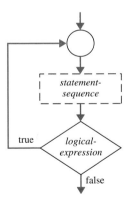

Figure 4.20

To illustrate a posttest loop, we reconsider the problem of calculating the mean of a set of failure times. An alternative to using a "dummy" data value to signal the end of data is to ask the user repeatedly if there are more data items. And because there ordinarily will be at least one data item, it seems natural to check the termination condition at the bottom of the loop. Thus the algorithm given earlier can be modified as follows:

MODIFIED ALGORITHM TO CALCULATE
MEAN TIME TO FAILURE

* Algorithm to read failure times, count them, and find the mean time *
* to failure (MEAN). FAILTM represents the current failure time   *
* entered, COUNT is number of failure times, and SUM is their sum.   *
* Values are read until the user enters 0 as the value for RESPON.   *

1. Set COUNT to 0.
2. Set SUM to 0.
3. Repeat the following until RESPON = 0:
    a. Read next value for FAILTM.
    b. Increment COUNT by 1.
    c. Add FAILTM to SUM.
    d. Read RESPON (0 to stop, 1 to continue).
4. Calculate MEAN = SUM / COUNT.
5. Display MEAN and COUNT.

For this algorithm it is appropriate to implement the posttest loop with the statements

```
10 CONTINUE
        PRINT *, 'ENTER FAIL TIME'
        READ *, FAILTM
        COUNT = COUNT + 1
        SUM = SUM + FAILTM
        PRINT *, 'MORE (0 = NO, 1 = YES)?'
        READ *, RESPON
    IF (RESPON .NE. 0) GO TO 10
```

as shown in the program of Figure 4.21.

```
      PROGRAM FAIL3
***********************************************************************
* Program to read a list of failure times, count them, and find the  *
* mean time to failure.  Values are read until the user indicates that*
* there is no more data.  Variables used are:                         *
*     FAILTM  :  the current fail time read                           *
*     COUNT   :  the number of fail time readings                     *
*     SUM     :  sum of fail times                                    *
*     MEAN    :  the mean time to failure                             *
*     RESPON  :  user response                                        *
***********************************************************************

      INTEGER COUNT, RESPON
      REAL FAILTM, SUM, MEAN
```

Figure 4.21

Figure 4.21 (continued)

```
* Initialize SUM and COUNT

      SUM = 0
      COUNT = 0

* Read fail times, count and sum them until there are no more

10      CONTINUE
          PRINT *, 'ENTER FAIL TIME'
          READ *, FAILTM
          COUNT = COUNT + 1
          SUM = SUM + FAILTM
          PRINT *, 'MORE (0 = NO, 1 = YES)'
          READ *, RESPON
        IF (RESPON .NE. 0) GO TO 10

* Calculate and display mean time to failure

      MEAN = SUM / COUNT
      PRINT *
      PRINT *, 'NUMBER OF FAIL TIME READINGS:', COUNT
      PRINT *, 'MEAN TIME TO FAILURE:', MEAN
      END
```

Sample run:

```
ENTER FAIL TIME
127
MORE (0 = NO, 1 = YES)
1
ENTER FAIL TIME
123.5
MORE (0 = NO, 1 = YES)
1
ENTER FAIL TIME
155.4
MORE (0 = NO, 1 = YES)
1
ENTER FAIL TIME
99
MORE (0 = NO, 1 = YES)
1
ENTER FAIL TIME
117.3
MORE (0 = NO, 1 = YES)
1
ENTER FAIL TIME
201.5
MORE (0 = NO, 1 = YES)
0

NUMBER OF FAIL TIME READINGS:  6
MEAN TIME TO FAILURE:    137.283
```

It is appropriate to use a posttest loop when we want to ensure that the body of the loop will be executed at least once. In a pretest loop, the body of the loop may never be executed. The exercises explore in more detail the difference between these two repetition structures.

4.10 Program Testing and Debugging Techniques: An Example

In Section 2.4 we noted that three types of errors may occur when developing a program to solve a problem: syntax or compile-time errors, run-time errors, and logical errors. **Syntax errors** such as incorrect punctuation, unbalanced parentheses, and misspelled key words are detected during the program's compilation, and an appropriate error message is usually displayed. **Run-time errors** such as division by zero and integer overflow are detected during the program's execution, and again, a suitable error message is often displayed. These two types of errors are, for the most part, relatively easy to correct, since the system error messages often indicate the type of error and where it occurred. **Logical errors**, on the other hand, are usually more difficult to detect, since they arise in the design of the algorithm or in coding the algorithm as a program, and in most cases, no error messages are displayed to assist the programmer in identifying such errors.

The Programming Pointers at the ends of the chapters of this book include warnings about some of the more common errors. As programs become increasingly complex, however, the logical errors that may occur are more subtle and consequently more difficult to identify and correct. In this section we consider an example of a program that contains logical errors and describe techniques that are useful in detecting them.

Suppose that as a programming exercise, students were asked to write a program to read a list of positive integers representing noise levels (in decibels) in an automobile under various conditions and to determine the range, that is, the difference between the largest and the smallest values. The following program heading, opening documentation, and variable declarations were given, and the students were asked to write the rest of the program:

```
PROGRAM RANGE
********************************************************************
*       Program to read a list of noise levels in decibels and    *
*       determine the range of values. A negative noise level is   *
*       used to signal the end of data. Variables used are:        *
*       NOISE  :  the current noise level being processed          *
*       LARGE  :  the largest value read so far                    *
*       SMALL  :   "  smallest   "      "   "   "                   *
********************************************************************

        INTEGER NOISE, LARGE, SMALL
```

One attempted solution was the following (in which the statements have been numbered for easy reference):

```
(1)         PRINT *, 'ENTER NOISE LEVELS IN DECIBELS (INTEGERS).'
(2)         PRINT *, 'ENTER ZERO OR A NEGATIVE VALUE TO STOP.'
```

```
         * Initialize largest noise level with a small value
         * and smallest with a very large value

(3)              LARGE = 0
(4)              SMALL = 999

         * While NOISE is not the end of data flag do:

(5)  10      IF (NOISE .GT. 0) THEN
(6)              PRINT *, 'NOISE LEVEL?'
(7)              READ *, NOISE
(8)              IF (NOISE .GT. LARGE) THEN
(9)                  LARGE = NOISE
(10)             ELSE IF (NOISE .LT. SMALL) THEN
(11)                 SMALL = NOISE
(12)             END IF
(13)         GO TO 10
(14)         END IF

(15)         PRINT *, 'RANGE OF NOISE LEVELS =', LARGE - SMALL, ' DECIBELS'
(16)         END
```

Execution of the program produced

```
         ENTER NOISE LEVELS IN DECIBELS (INTEGERS).
         ENTER ZERO OR A NEGATIVE VALUE TO STOP.
         RANGE OF NOISE LEVELS = -999 DECIBELS
```

Since the user was not allowed to enter any data, it is clear that the body of the while loop was not entered. This suggests that the logical expression NOISE .GT. 0 that controls repetition was initially false, thus causing immediate termination.

This is in fact what happened. Because the student did not ensure that NOISE had been assigned a value before the beginning of the while loop in line 5 was encountered, NOISE had an undefined value when the logical expression NOISE .GT. 0 was evaluated. (The student did not heed the warning in Potential Problem 8 in the Programming Pointers of Chapter 3!) The particular system on which the program was executed used a value of 0 for NOISE, making this logical expression false and causing the while loop to terminate immediately.

To remedy the situation, the student inserted the assignment statement NOISE = 1 ahead of the IF construct to force an entrance into the while loop:

```
(1)          PRINT *, 'ENTER NOISE LEVELS IN DECIBELS (INTEGERS).'
(2)          PRINT *, 'ENTER ZERO OR A NEGATIVE VALUE TO STOP.'

         * Initialize largest noise level with a small value
         * and smallest with a very large value

(3)          LARGE = 0
(4)          SMALL = 999
(5)          NOISE = 1

         * While NOISE is not the end of data flag do:

(6)  10      IF (NOISE .GT. 0) THEN
(7)              PRINT *, 'NOISE LEVEL?'
```

```
(8)          READ *, NOISE
(9)          IF (NOISE .GT. LARGE) THEN
(10)            LARGE = NOISE
(11)         ELSE IF (NOISE .LT. SMALL) THEN
(12)            SMALL = NOISE
(13)         END IF
(14)      GO TO 10
(15)      END IF
(16)      PRINT *, 'RANGE OF NOISE LEVELS =', LARGE - SMALL, ' DECIBELS'
(17)      END
```

This "quick and dirty patch" fixed the problem of premature termination of the while loop, and execution of this revised program produced

```
ENTER NOISE LEVELS IN DECIBELS (INTEGERS).
ENTER ZERO OR A NEGATIVE VALUE TO STOP.
NOISE LEVEL?
94
NOISE LEVEL?
102
NOISE LEVEL?
88
NOISE LEVEL?
-1
RANGE OF NOISE LEVELS = 103 DECIBELS
```

Data values were read and processed, terminating when the end-of-data flag -1 was read. The correct range for this set of noise levels is 14, however, and not 103 as computed by the program.

In the exercises of Section 2.5, **trace tables** were used to trace the execution of an algorithm. These trace tables may also be used to locate logical errors in a program by constructing manually a trace table of the segment of the program that is suspect. This technique is also known as **desk checking** and consists of recording in a table, step by step, the values of all or certain key variables in the program segment. In this example, the following trace table for the loop in statements 6 through 15 might be obtained:

Statements	NOISE	LARGE	SMALL	
	1	0	999	← Initial Values
6	1	0	999	
7–8	94	94	999	First pass through the loop
9–10	94	94	999	
6	94	94	999	
7–8	102	94	999	Second pass through the loop
9–10	102	94	999	
6	102	102	999	
7–8	88	102	88	Third pass through the loop
11–12	88	102	88	
6	102	102	999	
7–8	−1	102	88	Fourth pass through the loop
11–12	−1	102	−1	

The last line in this trace table shows why the range is incorrect: The value of SMALL became -1 on the last pass through the loop because the value -1 used to signal the end of data was read and processed as a noise level.

The execution of a program segment can also be traced automatically by inserting temporary output statements or by using special system-debugging software to display the values of key variables at selected stages of program execution. For example, we might insert the statement

```
PRINT *, 'NOISE LEVEL', NOISE
```

after the READ statement to echo the data values as they are entered, and the statement

```
PRINT *, 'LARGEST', LARGE, ' SMALLEST', SMALL
```

at the bottom of the loop to display the values of these variables at the end of each pass through the loop. The resulting output then is

```
ENTER NOISE LEVELS IN DECIBELS (INTEGERS).
ENTER ZERO OR A NEGATIVE VALUE TO STOP.
NOISE LEVEL?
94
NOISE LEVEL   94
LARGEST   94   SMALLEST   999
NOISE LEVEL?
102
NOISE LEVEL   102
LARGEST   102   SMALLEST   999
NOISE LEVEL?
88
NOISE LEVEL   88
LARGEST   102   SMALLEST   88
NOISE LEVEL?
-1
NOISE LEVEL   -1
LARGEST   102   SMALLEST   -1
RANGE OF NOISE LEVELS =   103 DECIBELS
```

This technique must not be used indiscriminately, however, since incorrect placement of such temporary debugging statements may display output that is not helpful in locating the source of the error. Also, if too many such statements are used, so much output may be produced that it will be difficult to isolate the error.

Either a manual or an automatic tracing of this program reveals that the source of difficulty is that the value -1 used to signal the end of data was processed as an actual noise level. A first reaction might be to fix this error by using an IF statement to keep this from happening:

```
IF (NOISE .GT. 0) THEN
   IF (NOISE .GT. LARGE) THEN
      LARGE = NOISE
   ELSE IF (NOISE .LT. SMALL) THEN
      SMALL = NOISE
   END IF
END IF
```

Patches like this one and the one used earlier are not recommended, however, because they often fail to address the real source of the problem and make the program unnecessarily complicated and messy.

The real source of difficulty in the preceding example is that the student did not use the correct technique for reading and processing data. As we noted in Section 4.6, when an end-of-data flag is used to signal the end of data, the correct approach is to read the first data value before the while loop is entered, to ensure that the logical expression that controls repetition is evaluated correctly the first time. This would solve the problem in the student's first version of the program. Also, as we noted, subsequent data values should be read at the "bottom" of the while loop so that they are compared with the end-of-data flag *before* they are processed in the next pass through the loop.

Using this standard technique for reading and processing data, the student rewrote his program as follows:

```
(1)          PRINT *, 'ENTER NOISE LEVELS IN DECIBELS (INTEGERS).'
(2)          PRINT *, 'ENTER ZERO OR A NEGATIVE VALUE TO STOP.'

      * Initialize largest noise level with a small value
      * and smallest with a very large value

(3)          LARGE = 0
(4)          SMALL = 999
(5)          PRINT *, 'NOISE LEVEL?'
(6)          READ *, NOISE

      * While NOISE is not the end of data flag do:

(7) 10       IF (NOISE .GT. 0) THEN
(8)              IF (NOISE .GT. LARGE) THEN
(9)                  LARGE = NOISE
(10)             ELSE IF (NOISE .LT. SMALL) THEN
(11)                 SMALL = NOISE
(12)             END IF
(13)             PRINT *, 'NOISE LEVEL?'
(14)             READ *, NOISE
(15)         GO TO 10
(16)         END IF

(17)         PRINT *, 'RANGE OF NOISE LEVELS =', LARGE - SMALL, ' DECIBELS'
(18)         END
```

A sample run with the same data values now produces the correct output:

```
ENTER NOISE LEVELS IN DECIBELS (INTEGERS).
ENTER ZERO OR A NEGATIVE VALUE TO STOP.
NOISE LEVEL?
94
NOISE LEVEL?
102
NOISE LEVEL?
88
NOISE LEVEL?
-1
RANGE OF NOISE LEVELS =  14 DECIBELS
```

The student may now be tempted to conclude that the program is correct. However, to establish one's confidence in the correctness of a program, it is necessary to test it with several sets of data. For example, the following sample run reveals that the program still contains a logical error:

```
ENTER NOISE LEVELS IN DECIBELS (INTEGERS).
ENTER ZERO OR A NEGATIVE VALUE TO STOP.
NOISE LEVEL?
88
NOISE LEVEL?
94
NOISE LEVEL?
102
NOISE LEVEL?
-1
RANGE OF NOISE LEVELS =  -897 DECIBELS
```

Tracing the execution of the while loop produces the following:

Statements	NOISE	LARGE	SMALL	
	88	0	999	← Initial Values
7–9	88	88	999	} First pass through the loop
12–15	94	88	999	
7–9	94	94	999	} Second pass through the loop
12–15	102	94	999	
7–9	102	102	999	} Third pass through the loop
12–15	−1	102	999	

This trace table reveals that the value of SMALL never changes, suggesting that the statement

```
SMALL = NOISE
```

is never executed. The reason is that the logical expression NOISE .GT. LARGE is true for each data value because these values are entered in increasing order; consequently, the ELSE IF statement is never executed. This error can be corrected by using two IF constructs in place of the single IF–ELSE IF construct:

```
IF (NOISE .GT. LARGE) THEN
   LARGE = NOISE
END IF
IF (NOISE .LT. SMALL) THEN
   SMALL = NOISE
END IF
```

or using logical IF statements

```
IF (NOISE .GT. LARGE) LARGE = NOISE
IF (NOISE .LT. SMALL) SMALL = NOISE
```

The resulting program is then correct but is not as efficient as it could be, because the logical expressions in both of these IF statements must be evaluated on each pass through the loop. A more efficient alternative is described in the exercises.

In summary, logical errors may be very difficult to detect, especially in more complex programs, and it is very important that test data be carefully selected so that each part of the program is thoroughly tested. The program should be executed with data values entered in several different orders, with large data sets and small data sets, with extreme values, and with ''bad'' data. For example, entering the noise levels in increasing order revealed the existence of a logical error in the program considered earlier. Also, even though the last version of the program will produce correct output if legitimate data values are read, the output

```
RANGE OF NOISE LEVELS = -999 DECIBELS
```

would be produced if a negative value were entered immediately. Although it may not be necessary to guard against invalid data input in student programs, those written for the public domain—especially programs used by computer novices—should be as **robust** as possible and should not ''crash'' or produce ''garbage'' results when unexpected data values are read.

When a logical error is detected, a trace table is an effective tool for locating the source of the error. Once it has been found, the program must be corrected and then tested again. It may be necessary to repeat this cycle of testing, tracing, and correcting many times before the program produces correct results for a wide range of test data, thereby allowing us to be reasonably confident of its correctness. It is not possible, however, to check a program with every possible set of data, and thus obscure bugs may still remain. In some applications, this may not be critical, but in others, for example, in programs used to guide a space shuttle, errors cannot be tolerated. Certain formal techniques have been developed for proving that a program is correct and will always be executed correctly (assuming no system malfunction), but a study of these techniques is beyond the scope of this introductory text.

4.11   Examples: Numerical Integration, Series Evaluation, Least Squares Line

EXAMPLE 1: Numerical Integration.   One problem in which numerical methods are often used is that of approximating the area under the graph of a nonnegative function $y = f(x)$ from $x = a$ to $x = b$, thus obtaining an approximate value for the integral

$$\int_a^b f(x)\, dx$$

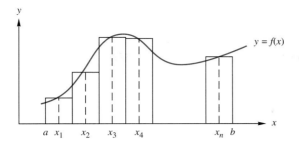

Figure 4.22

One simple method is to divide the interval $[a, b]$ into n subintervals each of length $\Delta x = (b - a) / n$ and then to form rectangles with these subintervals as bases and with altitudes given by the values of of the function at the midpoints (or left or right endpoints) $x_1, x_2, \ldots, x_n$ of the subintervals. This is illustrated in Figure 4.22. The sum of the areas of these rectangles

$$f(x_1) \, \Delta x + f(x_2) \, \Delta x + \cdots + f(x_n) \, \Delta x$$

which is the same as

$$[f(x_1) + f(x_2) + \cdots + f(x_n)] \, \Delta x$$

or, written more concisely using Σ (sigma) notation,

$$\left[\sum_{i=1}^{n} f(x_i) \right] \Delta x$$

is then an approximation of the area under the curve.

Figure 4.22 illustrates this method for a curve lying above the x axis. It may also be used to approximate the integral of a function whose graph falls below the x axis. In this case, the integral does not give the total area between the curve and the axis but, rather, gives the area of the region(s) above the axis minus the area of the region(s) below the axis.

The program in Figure 4.23 uses this rectangle method to approximate an integral. The endpoints A and B of the interval of integration and the number N of subintervals are read during execution. It implements the algorithm whose structure is shown in the flowchart in Figure 4.24.

```
       PROGRAM AREA
**********************************************************************
* Program to approximate the integral of a function over the interval  *
* [A,B] using the rectangle method with altitudes chosen at the        *
* midpoints of the subintervals.  Variables used are:                  *
*      A, B    : the endpoints of the interval of integration          *
*      N       : the number of subintervals used                       *
*      I       : counter                                               *
*      DELX    : the length of the subintervals                        *
*      X       : the midpoint of one of the subintervals               *
*      Y       : the value of the function at X                        *
*      SUM     : the approximating sum                                 *
**********************************************************************
```

Figure 4.23

Figure 4.23 (continued)

```
      REAL A, B, X, DELX, Y, SUM
      INTEGER N, I

      PRINT *, 'ENTER THE INTERVAL ENDPOINTS AND THE # OF SUBINTERVALS'
      READ *, A, B, N
      DELX = (B - A) / REAL(N)

* Initialize the approximating SUM and set X equal to
* the midpoint of the first subinterval

      SUM = 0
      X = A + DELX / 2.0

* Now calculate and display the sum

      DO 10 I = 1, N

*         Calculate the value of the function at X
          Y = X ** 2 + 1.0

          SUM = SUM + Y
          X = X + DELX
10    CONTINUE
      SUM = DELX * SUM
      PRINT *, 'APPROXIMATE VALUE USING ', N, ' SUBINTERVALS IS ', SUM
      END
```

Sample runs:

```
ENTER THE INTERVAL ENDPOINTS AND THE # OF SUBINTERVALS
0, 1, 10
APPROXIMATE VALUE USING    10 SUBINTERVALS IS     1.33250


ENTER THE INTERVAL ENDPOINTS AND THE # OF SUBINTERVALS
0, 1, 20
APPROXIMATE VALUE USING    20 SUBINTERVALS IS     1.33313


ENTER THE INTERVAL ENDPOINTS AND THE # OF SUBINTERVALS
0, 1, 100
APPROXIMATE VALUE USING   100 SUBINTERVALS IS      1.33332
```

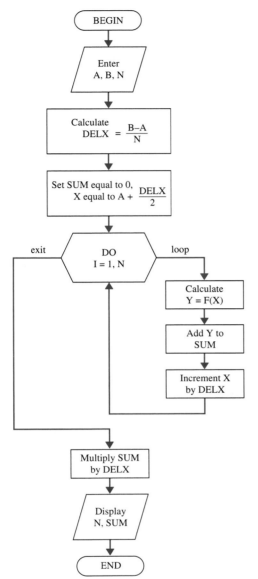

Figure 4.24

EXAMPLE 2: Series Evaluation. The cosine of an angle X measured in radians may be computed using the infinite series

$$\cos (X) = 1 - \frac{X^2}{2!} + \frac{X^4}{4!} - \cdots + (-1)^N \frac{X^{2N}}{(2N)!} + \cdots$$

$$= \sum_{N=0}^{\infty} \frac{(-1)^N X^{2N}}{(2N)!}$$

Programming languages such as FORTRAN that provide trigonometric functions like cosine, exponential functions, logarithmic functions, and so on as predefined functions use series representations like this to calculate values of these functions. In this section we develop a program that calculates the approximate values of cos(X) for user-supplied values of X using this series.

The input for this problem will consist of the angle in degrees whose cosine is to be calculated. The user will also input two values NMAX and EPSIL that will be used to determine how many terms of the series are to be used in computing the approximation. A repetition structure is then used to sum these terms, and the repetition is to terminate when the number of terms that have been included reaches NMAX or when the absolute value of the next term is less than some small positive real number EPSIL. When repetition is terminated, the value of the running sum is displayed as the approximate value of the cosine of the angle entered by the user; if the number of terms is NMAX, an appropriate message should also be displayed.

An algorithm for computing this approximate value of the cosine function is

ALGORITHM FOR APPROXIMATING THE COSINE FUNCTION

```
* This algorithm calculates the approximate value of cos(X) using    *
* its infinite series. NMAX is the maximum number of terms of the    *
* series to be used. EPSIL is the desired accuracy. TERM is a        *
* term in the series, and SUM is the sum of the first N terms.       *
```

1. Enter XDEG = angle in degrees.
2. Enter NMAX and EPSIL.
3. Multiply XDEG by $\pi/180$ to give the angle X in radians.
4. Initialize N to 1, TERM to 1, and SUM to 1.
5. While $|\text{TERM}| \geq$ EPSIL and N $<$ NMAX, do the following:
   a. Multiply TERM by $\dfrac{-X^2}{(2N - 1) \cdot (2N)}$.
   b. Add TERM to SUM.
   c. Increment N by 1.
6. Display SUM.
7. If N = NMAX, then display an appropriate message indicating that the desired precision may not have been achieved.

The flowchart in Figure 4.25 displays the structure of this algorithm and shows clearly the three basic control structures. The main logical flow is sequential, but one of the steps is a repetition structure that repeats execution of a sequence of four instructions, and the last step is a selection structure. The program in Figure 4.26 implements this algorithm.

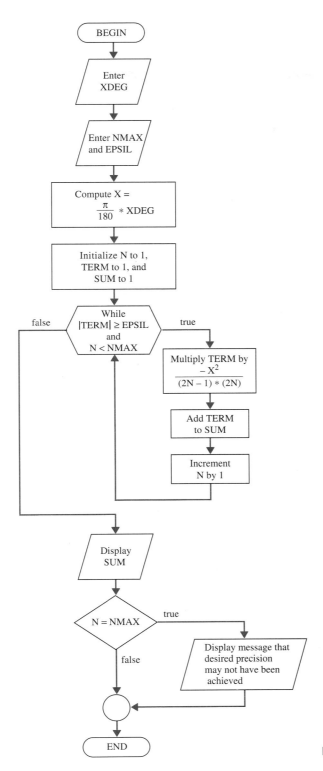

Figure 4.25

```
      PROGRAM COSINE
***********************************************************************
* Program to calculate approximate values of the cosine function using *
* a series representation.  Identifiers used are:                     *
*      NMAX    : Upper limit on the number of terms to use            *
*      EPSIL   : desired accuracy (stop when |term| < EPSIL)          *
*      XDEG    : angle in degrees                                     *
*      X       : angle in radians                                     *
*      TERM    : current term                                         *
*      N       : number of terms                                      *
*      SUM     : sum of terms                                         *
*      PI      : the constant pi                                      *
***********************************************************************

      INTEGER NMAX, N
      REAL PI, EPSIL, XDEG, X, TERM, SUM
      PARAMETER (PI = 3.141593)

* Get angle in degrees, desired accuracy, and limit on number of terms;
* convert angle to radians, and initialize things

      PRINT *, 'ENTER ANGLE (IN DEGREES)'
      READ *, XDEG
      PRINT *, 'ENTER LIMIT ON NUMBER OF TERMS'
      READ *, NMAX
      PRINT *, 'ENTER DESIRED ACCURACY (I.E., STOP WHEN |TERM| IS ',
     +         'SMALLER THAN THIS)'
      READ *, EPSIL
      X = (PI / 180.0) * XDEG
      N = 1
      TERM = 1.0
      SUM = 1.0

* While |TERM| >= EPSIL and N < NMAX, generate next term and
* and add it to SUM

10    IF ((ABS(TERM) .GE. EPSIL) .AND. (N .LT. NMAX)) THEN
          TERM = (-TERM) * X**2 / REAL((2*N - 1) * (2*N))
          SUM = SUM + TERM
          N = N + 1
      GO TO 10
      END IF

* Display value and reason for termination if necessary

      PRINT *, 'COS(', XDEG, ' DEGREES) IS APPROXIMATELY', SUM
      IF (N .EQ. NMAX) THEN
          PRINT *, 'SERIES EVALUATION TERMINATED AFTER ', NMAX, ' TERMS'
          PRINT *, 'SO THIS VALUE MAY NOT BE VERY ACCURATE.'
      END IF
      END
```

Figure 4.26

Figure 4.26　(continued)

Sample runs:

```
ENTER ANGLE (IN DEGREES)
45
ENTER LIMIT ON NUMBER OF TERMS
10
ENTER DESIRED ACCURACY (I.E., STOP WHEN |TERM| IS SMALLER THAN THIS)
.000001
COS(   45.0000 DEGREES) IS APPROXIMATELY   0.707107

ENTER ANGLE (IN DEGREES)
60
ENTER LIMIT ON NUMBER OF TERMS
7
ENTER DESIRED ACCURACY (I.E., STOP WHEN |TERM| IS SMALLER THAN THIS)
.000001
COS(   60.0000 DEGREES) IS APPROXIMATELY   0.500000

ENTER ANGLE (IN DEGREES)
90
ENTER LIMIT ON NUMBER OF TERMS
5
ENTER DESIRED ACCURACY (I.E., STOP WHEN |TERM| IS SMALLER THAN THIS)
.000001
COS(   90.0000 DEGREES) IS APPROXIMATELY   2.46064E-05
SERIES EVALUATION TERMINATED AFTER   5 TERMS
SO THIS VALUE MAY NOT BE VERY ACCURATE.
```

EXAMPLE 3: Least Squares Line.　Suppose the following data was collected in an experiment to measure the effect of temperature on resistance:

Temperature (°C)	Resistance (ohms)
20.0	761
31.5	817
50.0	874
71.8	917
91.3	1018

The plot of this data in Figure 4.27 indicates a linear relationship between temperature and resistance. We wish to find the equation of the line that "best fits" this data.

In general, whenever the relation between two quantities x and y appears to be roughly linear, that is, when a plot of the points (x, y) indicates that they tend to fall along a straight line, one can ask for the equation

$$y = mx + b$$

of a best-fitting line for these points. Such a **regression equation** can then be used to predict the value of y by evaluating the equation for a given value of x.

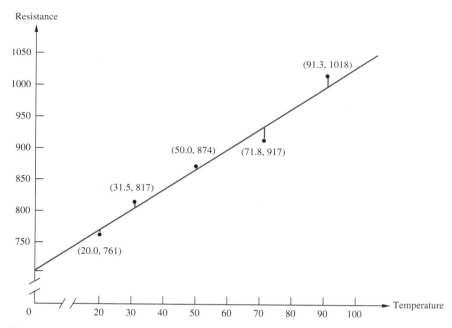

Figure 4.27

A standard method for finding the **regression coefficients** m and b is the **method of least squares**, so named because it produces the line $y = mx + b$, for which the sum of the squares of the deviations of the observed y values from the predicted y values (using the equation) is as small as possible (see Figure 4.27). This least squares line has the equation $y = mx + b$, where

$$\text{slope} = m = \frac{(\Sigma xy) - (\Sigma x)\bar{y}}{(\Sigma x^2) - (\Sigma x)\bar{x}}$$

$$y \text{ intercept} = b = \bar{y} - m\bar{x}$$

where

Σx is the sum of the x values.
Σx^2 is the sum of the squares of the x values.
Σxy is the sum of the products xy of corresponding x and y values.
$\bar{x}$ and $\bar{y}$ are the means of the x and y values, respectively.

The program in Figure 4.28 finds the equation of the least squares line for a given set of data points. Note that in this program a while loop controlled by an end-of-data condition is used to read the data values and to calculate the necessary sums. It implements the following algorithm:

ALGORITHM FOR LEAST SQUARES LINE

```
* Algorithm to find the equation of the least squares line for a set    *
* of COUNT data points (X, Y). SLOPE is its slope, and YINT is its      *
* y intercept. SUMX, SUMY, SUMX2, and SUMXY are the sums                *
* of the Xs, the Ys, the squares of the Xs, and the products X*Y.       *
* XMEAN and YMEAN are the means of the Xs and the Ys,                   *
* respectively.                                                         *
```

1. Initialize COUNT, SUMX, SUMY, SUMX2, AND SUMXY all to 0.
2. Read the first data point X, Y.

   * Dummy end-of-data values are entered to terminate input *

3. While X and Y are not the end-of-data values, do the following:
   a. Increment COUNT by 1.
   b. Add X to SUMX.
   c. Add X^2 to SUMX2.
   d. Add Y to SUMY.
   e. Add X*Y to SUMXY.
   f. Read next data point X, Y.

4. Calculate

$$XMEAN = \frac{SUMX}{COUNT}$$

and

$$YMEAN = \frac{SUMY}{COUNT}$$

5. Calculate

$$SLOPE = \frac{SUMXY - SUMX*YMEAN}{SUMX2 - SUMX*XMEAN}$$

and

$$YINT = YMEAN - SLOPE * XMEAN$$

6. Display SLOPE and YINT.

```
      PROGRAM LSQUAR
***************************************************************
* Program to find the equation of the least squares line for a set  *
* of data points.  Variables used are:                              *
*     X, Y     : (X,Y) is the observed data point                   *
*     COUNT    : number of data points                              *
*     SUMX     : sum of the X's                                     *
*     SUMX2    : sum of the squares of the X's                      *
*     SUMY     : sum of the Y's                                     *
*     SUMXY    : sum of the products X*Y                            *
*     XMEAN    : mean of the X's                                    *
*     YMEAN    : mean of the Y's                                    *
*     SLOPE    : slope of least squares line                        *
*     YINT     : y-intercept of the line                            *
***************************************************************

      INTEGER COUNT
      REAL X, Y, SUMX, SUMX2, SUMY, SUMXY, XMEAN, YMEAN, SLOPE, YINT
```

Figure 4.28

Figure 4.28 (continued)

```
* Initialize counter and the sums to 0 and read first data point

        COUNT = 0
        SUMX = 0
        SUMX2 = 0
        SUMY = 0
        SUMXY = 0
        PRINT *, 'ENTER POINT (-999, -999 TO STOP)'
        READ *, X, Y

* While there is more data, calculate the necessary sums
* and read the next data point (X, Y)

10      IF ((X .NE. -999.) .AND. (Y .NE. -999.)) THEN
            COUNT = COUNT + 1
            SUMX = SUMX + X
            SUMX2 = SUMX2 + X ** 2
            SUMY = SUMY + Y
            SUMXY = SUMXY + X * Y
            PRINT *, 'ENTER NEXT POINT'
            READ *, X, Y
        GO TO 10
        END IF

* Find equation of least squares line

        XMEAN = SUMX / COUNT
        YMEAN = SUMY / COUNT
        SLOPE = (SUMXY - SUMX * YMEAN) / (SUMX2 - SUMX * XMEAN)
        YINT = YMEAN - SLOPE * XMEAN
        PRINT *
        PRINT *, 'EQUATION OF LEAST SQUARES LINE IS Y = MX + B, WHERE'
        PRINT *, 'SLOPE = M =        ', SLOPE
        PRINT *, 'Y-INTERCEPT = B =', YINT
        END
```

Sample run:

```
ENTER POINT (-999, -999 TO STOP)
20.0, 761
ENTER NEXT POINT
31.5, 817
ENTER NEXT POINT
50.0, 874
ENTER NEXT POINT
71.8, 917
ENTER NEXT POINT
91.3, 1018
ENTER NEXT POINT
-999, -999

EQUATION OF LEAST SQUARES LINE IS Y = MX + B, WHERE
SLOPE = M =          3.33658
Y-INTERCEPT = B =    700.828
```

Exercises

1. Write in pseudocode the algorithm for approximating an integral given by the flowchart of Figure 4.24 in Example 1 of Section 4.11.

2. Display in a flowchart the structure of the algorithm for calculating a least squares line given in Example 3 of Section 4.11.

3. Write FORTRAN program segments to
   (a) Print the first 100 positive integers using a DO loop.
   (b) Branch to statement 50 if the value of X is negative or greater than 10.
   (c) Print the value of X and decrease X by 0.5 as long as X is positive.
   (d) Read values for A, B, and C and print their sum, repeating this procedure while none of A, B, or C is negative.
   (e) Print the square roots of the first 25 odd positive integers.
   (f) Calculate and print the squares of consecutive positive integers until the difference between a square and the preceding one is greater than 50.
   (g) Print a list of points (X, Y) on the graph of the equation $Y = X^3 - 3X + 1$ for X ranging from -2 to 2 in steps of .1.

4. Suppose that the pretest loop in the summation algorithm in Section 4.6 were replaced by a posttest loop so that the statements in the programs of Figures 4.16 and 4.18 that implement this algorithm were replaced by

```
      PRINT *, 'ENTER VALUE 1 + ... + ? IS TO EXCEED'
      READ *, LIMIT
      NUMBER = 0
      SUM = 0

*     Increment NUMBER and add it to SUM
*     until SUM exceeds LIMIT

10    CONTINUE
         NUMBER = NUMBER + 1
         SUM = SUM + NUMBER
      IF (SUM .LE. LIMIT) GO TO 10

*     Print the results

      PRINT *, '1 + ... + ', NUMBER, ' =', SUM, ' >', LIMIT
      END
```

   Would the resulting program produce the same results as those in Figures 4.16 and 4.18?

5. (a) Design an algorithm that uses a posttest loop to count the number of digits in a given integer.
   (b) Write FORTRAN statements to implement the algorithm in part (a).

(c) Rewrite the algorithm in part (a) so that it uses a pretest loop.
(d) Write FORTRAN statements to implement the algorithm in part (c).
(e) Which of these repetition structures seems more natural, and why?

6. The velocity of a falling parachutist might be approximated by the equation

$$V(t) = \frac{gm}{c}(1 - e^{(-c/m)t})$$

where g is the acceleration due to gravity, c is the drag coefficient, and m is the parachutist's mass. Modify the program in Figure 4.23 to approximate the distance the parachutist falls from time $t = A$ to time $t = B$. (Distance is the integral of the velocity.) Use values of 9.8 (m/sec^2), 12.4 (kg/sec), and 81.7 (kg) for g, c, and m, respectively.

7. Write a program to implement the algorithm displayed in the flowchart of Figure 4.29.

8. Write a program for the "divide-and-average" algorithm for calculating square roots described in Exercise 13 of Chapter 2.

9. Write a program to read the data values shown in the following table, calculate the miles per gallon in each case, and print the values with appropriate labels:

Miles Traveled	Gallons of Gasoline Used
231	14.8
248	15.1
302	12.8
147	9.25
88	7
265	13.3

10. Write a program to implement the algorithm for estimating the time required to empty the reservoir described in Exercise 16 of Chapter 2.

11. If a loan of A dollars, which carries a monthly interest rate of R (expressed as a decimal), is to be paid off in N months, then the monthly payment P will be

$$P = A\left[\frac{R(1 + R)^N}{(1 + R)^N - 1}\right]$$

During this time period, some of each monthly payment will be used to repay that month's accrued interest, and the rest will be used to reduce the balance owed.

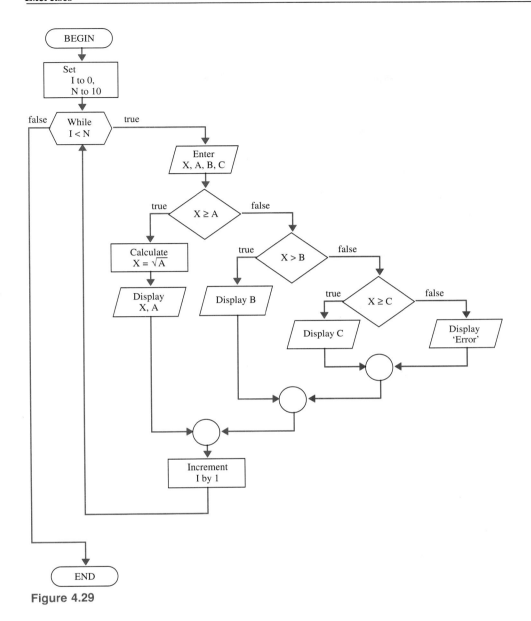

Figure 4.29

Write a program to print an *amortization table* that displays the payment number, the amount of the monthly payment, the interest for that month, the amount of the payment applied to the principal, and the new balance. Use your program to produce an amorization table for a loan of $50,000 to be repaid in 36 months at 1 percent per month.

12. **(a)** Write a program that solves the noise-level range problem discussed in Section 4.10 but is more efficient than those described

in the text. (*Hint:* Initialize LARGE and SMALL to the first data value.)

(b) For each of the following data sets, construct a trace table for the repetition structure used in your program and determine the range of noise levels that will be computed by your program:

(i) 88, 109, 94, -1

(ii) 88, 94, 102, -1

(iii) 102, 94, 88, -1

(iv) 88, -1

(v) -1

13. Write a program to read a set of numbers, count them, and find and print the largest and smallest numbers in the list and their positions in the list.

14. Write a program to read a set of numbers, count them, and calculate the mean, variance, and standard deviation of the set of numbers. The *mean* and *variance* of numbers $x_1, x_2, \ldots, x_n$ can be calculated using the following formulas:

$$\text{mean} = \frac{1}{n} \sum_{i=1}^{n} x_i \qquad \text{variance} = \frac{1}{n} \sum_{i=1}^{n} x_i^2 - \frac{1}{n^2} \left(\sum_{i=1}^{n} x_i \right)^2$$

The *standard deviation* is the square root of the variance.

15. The following is the initial part of the sequence of *Fibonacci numbers:* 1, 1, 2, 3, 5, 8, 13, 21, ... , where each number after the first two is the sum of the two preceding numbers. One property of this sequence is that the ratios of consecutive Fibonacci numbers (1/1, 1/2, 2/3, 3/5, ...) approach the "golden ratio"

$$\frac{\sqrt{5} - 1}{2}$$

Write a program to calculate all the Fibonacci numbers less than 5000 and the decimal values of the ratios of consecutive Fibonacci numbers.

16. Suppose that a ball dropped from a building bounces off the pavement and that on each bounce it returns to a certain constant percentage of its previous height. Write a program to read the height from which the ball was dropped and the percentage of rebound. Then repeatedly let the ball bounce, and print the height of the ball at the top of each bounce, the distance traveled during that bounce, and the total distance traveled thus far, terminating when the height of the ball is almost zero (less than some small positive value).

17. Suppose that at a given time, genotypes AA, AB, and BB appear in the proportions x, y, and z, respectively, where $x = .25$, $y = .5$, and $z = .25$. If individuals of type AA cannot reproduce, then the prob-

ability that one parent will donate gene A to an offspring is

$$p = \frac{1}{2}\left(\frac{y}{y + z}\right)$$

since $y/(y + z)$ is the probability that the parent is of type AB, and 1/2 is the probability that such a parent will donate gene A. Then the proportions x', y', z' of AA, AB, and BB, respectively, in the succeeding generation are given by

$$x' = p^2, \, y' = 2p(1 - p), \, z' = (1 - p)^2$$

and the new probability is given by

$$p' = \frac{1}{2}\left(\frac{y'}{y' + z'}\right)$$

Write a program to calculate and print the generation number and the proportions of AA, AB, and BB under appropriate headings until the proportions of both AA and AB are less than some small positive value.

18. Suppose that two hallways, one 8 feet wide and the other 10 feet wide, meet at a right angle and that a ladder is to be carried around the corner from the narrower hallway into the wider one. Using the similar triangles in the following diagram we see that

$$L = x + \frac{10x}{\sqrt{x^2 - 64}}$$

Write a program that initializes x to 8.1 and then increments it by 0.1 to find to the nearest 0.1 foot the length of the longest ladder that can be carried around the corner. (*Note:* This length is the same as the *minimum* value of the distance L.)

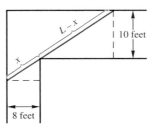

19. Two measures of central tendency other than the (arithmetic) mean (defined in Exercise 14) are the *geometric mean* and the *harmonic mean* defined for a list of positive numbers $x_1, x_2, \ldots, x_n$ as follows:

$$\text{geometric mean} = \sqrt[n]{x_1 \cdot x_2 \cdot \, \cdots \, \cdot x_n}$$

$$= \text{the } n\text{th root of the product of the numbers}$$

$$\text{harmonic mean} = \frac{n}{\dfrac{1}{x_1} + \dfrac{1}{x_2} + \cdots + \dfrac{1}{x_n}}$$

Write a program that reads a list of numbers, counts them, and calculates their arithmetic mean, geometric mean, and harmonic mean. These values should be printed with appropriate labels.

20. The infinite series

$$\sum_{k=0}^{\infty} \frac{1}{k!}$$

converges to the number e. (For a positive integer k, $k!$, read "k factorial," is the product of the integers from 1 through k ; 0! is defined to be 1.) The nth *partial sum* of such a series is the sum of the first n terms of the series; for example,

$$\frac{1}{0!} + \frac{1}{1!} + \frac{1}{2!} + \frac{1}{3!}$$

is the fourth partial sum. Write a program to calculate and print the first 10 partial sums of this series.

21. In Example 1 of Section 4.11 we considered the numerical approximation of integrals using rectangles. As Figure 4.30 indicates, a better approximation can usually be obtained by using trapezoids rather than rectangles.

The sum of the areas of these trapezoids is given by

$$\sum_{i=1}^{n} [f(x_{i-1}) + f(x_i)] \frac{\Delta x}{2}$$

which can also be written

$$\frac{\Delta x}{2} [f(x_0) + 2f(x_1) + 2f(x_2) + \cdots + 2f(x_{n-1}) + f(x_n)]$$

or

$$\Delta x \left[\frac{f(a) + f(b)}{2} + \sum_{i=1}^{n-1} f(x_i) \right]$$

Write a program to approximate an integral using this *trapezoidal method*.

Figure 4.30

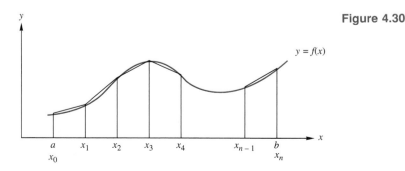

22. Another method of numerical integration that generally produces better approximations than does the rectangle method described in Example 1 of Section 4.11 or the trapezoidal method described in Exercise 21 is based on the use of parabolas and is known as *Simpson's Rule*. In this method, the interval [a, b] is divided into an even number n of subintervals, each of length Δx, and the sum

$$\frac{\Delta x}{3} [f(x_0) + 4f(x_1) + 2f(x_2) + 4f(x_3)$$
$$+ 2f(x_4) + \cdots + 2f(x_{n-2}) + 4f(x_{n-1}) + f(x_n)]$$

is used to approximate the integral of f over the interval [a, b]. Write a program to approximate an integral using Simpson's Rule.

23. In Example 3 of Section 4.11 we considered the problem of fitting a line to a set of data points. In some situations, a better fit is obtained by using an exponential function

$$y = ae^{bx}$$

To determine the constants a and b, one common method is to take logarithms

$$\ln y = \ln a + bx$$

and then use the method of least squares to find values of the constants b and ln a. Write a program that uses this method to fit an exponential curve to a set of data points. Run it for the values in the following table, which gives the barometric pressure readings, in millimeters of mercury, at various altitudes.

Altitude (meters) x	Barometric Pressure (millimeters) y
0	760
500	714
1000	673
1500	631
2000	594
2500	563

24. Related to the least squares method (see Example 3 of Section 4.11) is the problem of determining whether there is a linear relationship between two quantities x and y. One statistical measure used in this connection is the *correlation coefficient*. It is equal to 1 if there is a perfect positive linear relationship between x and y, that is, if y increases linearly as x increases. If there is a perfect negative linear relationship between x and y, that is, if y decreases linearly as x increases, then the correlation coefficient has the value -1. A value of zero for the correlation coefficient indicates that there is no linear relationship between x and y, and nonzero values between -1 and 1 indicate a partial linear relationship between the two quantities. The correlation coefficient for a set of n pairs of x and y values is calculated by

$$\frac{n(\Sigma xy) - (\Sigma x)(\Sigma y)}{\sqrt{(n\Sigma x^2 - (\Sigma x)^2)(n\Sigma y^2 - (\Sigma y)^2)}}$$

where

Σx is the sum of all the x values.
Σy is the sum of all the y values.
Σx^2 is the sum of the squares of the x values.
Σy^2 is the sum of the squares of the y values.
Σxy is the sum of the products xy of corresponding x and y values.

Write a program to calculate the correlation coefficient of a set of data points. Run it for the data points used in the sample run in Figure 4.18 and for several data sets of your own.

Programming Pointers

Program Design

1. *All programs can be written using the three control structures considered in this chapter: sequential, repetition, and selection.*

2. *Multialternative selection structures can be implemented more efficiently with an IF–ELSE IF construct than with a sequence of IF statements.* **For example, using the statements**

```
IF (SCORE .LT. 60) GRADE = 'F'
IF ((SCORE .GE. 60) .AND. (SCORE .LT. 70)) GRADE = 'D'
IF ((SCORE .GE. 70) .AND. (SCORE .LT. 80)) GRADE = 'C'
IF ((SCORE .GE. 80) .AND. (SCORE .LT. 90)) GRADE = 'B'
IF (SCORE .GE. 90) GRADE = 'A'
```

is less efficient than using

```
IF (SCORE .LT. 60) THEN
    GRADE = 'F'
ELSE IF (SCORE .LT. 70) THEN
    GRADE = 'D'
ELSE IF (SCORE .LT. 80) THEN
    GRADE = 'C'
ELSE IF (SCORE .LT.90) THEN
    GRADE = 'B'
ELSE
    GRADE = 'A'
END IF
```

In the first case, all of the IF statements are executed for each score processed, and three of the logical expressions are compound expressions. In the second case, each logical expression is simple, and not all of the expressions are evaluated for each score; for example, for a score of 65, only the logical expressions SCORE .LT. 60 and SCORE LT. 70 are evaluated.

3. *The* GO TO *statement should ordinarily be used only in standard repetition structures (while loops and posttest loops). Indiscriminate use of* GO TO *makes the logic of the program difficult to follow and is symptomatic of a poorly designed program.*

Potential Problems

1. *Periods must be used in the relational operators* .LT., .GT., .EQ., .LE., .GE., *and* .NE. *and in the logical operators* .NOT., .AND., .OR., .EQV., *and* .NEQV..

2. *Parentheses must enclose the logical expression in an* IF *construct or* IF *statement.*

3. *Real quantities that are algebraically equal may yield a false logical expression when compared with* .EQ. *because most real values are not stored exactly.* For example, even though the two real expressions $X * (1.0 / X)$ and 1.0 are algebraically equal, the logical expression $X * (1.0 / X)$ .EQ. 1.0 is usually false. Thus, if two real values RNUM1 and RNUM2 are subject to the roundoff error caused by inexact representation, it is usually not advisable to check whether they are equal. Rather, one should check whether the absolute value of their difference is small:

```
IF (ABS(RNUM1 - RNUM2) .LT. ERRTOL) THEN
                 .
                 .
                 .
```

where ERRTOL is some small positive real value such as 1E-6.

4. *Each* IF *construct must be closed with an* END IF *statement.*

5. *It should be assumed that all subexpressions are evaluated when determining the value of a compound logical expression.* Suppose, for example, that we write an IF construct of the form

```
IF ((X .GE. 0) .AND. (SQRT(X) .LT. 5.0)) THEN
    PRINT *, 'SQUARE ROOT IS LESS THAN 5'
                 .
                 .
                 .
    END IF
```

in which the subexpression X .GE. 0 is intended to prevent an attempt to calculate the square root of a negative number when X is negative. Some FORTRAN compilers may evaluate the subexpression X. GE. 0 and, if it is false, may not evaluate the second subexpression, SQRT(X) .LT. 5.0. Other compilers evaluate both parts, and thus an error results when X is negative. This error can be avoided by rewriting the construct as

```
IF (X .GE. 0) THEN
  IF (SQRT(X) .LT. 5.0) THEN
    PRINT *, 'SQUARE ROOT IS LESS THAN 5'
            .
            .
            .
  END IF
END IF
```

6. *The control variable in a DO loop may not be modified within the loop. Modifying the initial value, limit, or step size does not affect the number of repetitions.* For example, the statements

```
    K = 5
    DO 10 I = 1, K
        PRINT *, K
        K = K - 1
10  CONTINUE
```

produce the output

```
5
4
3
2
1
```

Modifying the control variable I, as in the following DO loop

```
    DO 10 I = 1, 5
        PRINT *, I
        I = I - 1
10  CONTINUE
```

is an error and produces a message such as

```
A CONTROL VARIABLE MAY NOT BE ALTERED IN A DO LOOP
```

One consequence is that nested DO loops must have different control variables.

7. *The statements within a while loop controlled by a logical expression must eventually cause the logical expression to become false, because otherwise an infinite loop will result.* For example, if X is a real variable, the statements

```
    X = 0.0
*   While X is not equal to 1, print its value and
*   increment it
```

```
10 IF (X .NE. 1.0) THEN
      PRINT *, X
      X = X + 0.3
   GO TO 10
   END IF
```

produce an infinite loop.

Output:

```
0.000000
0.300000
0.600000
0.900000
1.200000
1.500000
1.800000
   .
   .
   .
```

Since the value of X is never equal to 1.0, repetition is not terminated. In view of Potential Problem 3, the statements

```
   X = 0.0
*  While X is not equal to 1, print its value and
*  increment it

10 IF (X .NE. 1.0) THEN
      PRINT *, X
      X = X + 0.2
   GO TO 10
   END IF
```

may also produce an infinite loop.

Output:

```
0.000000
0.200000
0.400000
0.800000
1.000000
1.200000
1.400000
1.600000
   .
   .
   .
```

Since X is initialized to 0 and 0.2 is added to X five times, X should have the value 1. However, the logical expression X .NE. 1.0 may remain true because most real values are not stored exactly.

8. *Data statements initialize variables at compile time, not during execution.* This is important to remember when a program processes sev-

eral sets of data and uses variables that must be initialized to certain values before processing each data set. To illustrate, consider the following program:

```
         INTEGER NUMBER, SUM
         DATA SUM /0/

         READ *, NUMBER
******While there is more data do the following:
10       IF (NUMBER .NE. -8888) THEN

**********While NUMBER is not -999 do the following:

20           IF (NUMBER .NE. -999) THEN
                 SUM = SUM + NUMBER
                 READ *, NUMBER
             GO TO 20
             END IF
             PRINT *, 'SUM = ', SUM
         GO TO 10
         END IF
         END
```

If the following data is entered

```
10
20
30
-999
0
15
25
-999
-8888
```

the output produced will be

```
SUM =        60
SUM =       100
```

When the second set of numbers is processed, SUM is not reset to 0, because the DATA statement does this at compile time, not during execution. This problem cannot be solved by simply attaching a label to the DATA statement and then branching to it, because DATA statements are not executable. The obvious solution is to insert the statement

```
SUM = 0
```

after statement 10 and delete the DATA statement.

Program Style

In this text, we use the following conventions for formatting the statements considered in this chapter:

1. *The body of a loop should be indented.*

```
*************** DO-loops ***************
    DO ### variable = init, limit, step
        statement-1
                .
                .
                .
        statement-n
### CONTINUE


********** WHILE loops **********
    DO WHILE (logical-expression)
        statement-1
                .
                .
                .
        statement-n
    END DO

### IF (logical-expression) THEN
        statement-1
                .
                .
                .
        statement-n
    GO TO ###
    END IF


*************** Posttest loops ***************
### CONTINUE
        statement-1
                .
                .
                .
        statement-n
    IF (logical-expression) GO TO ###
```

2. *The statement sequence(s) within an* **IF** *construct should be indented.*

```
IF logical-expression
    statement-1
            .
            .
            .
    statement-n
ELSE
    statement-n+1
            .
            .
            .
    statement-m
END IF
```

FORTRAN 90 Features

The control structures described in this chapter have been carried over into FORTRAN 90 with a few extensions:

- Symbolic forms of the relational operators are allowed:

Relational Operator	Symbol
.LT.	<
.GT.	>
.EQ.	= =
.LE.	< =
.GE.	> =
.NE.	<>

- IF and IF–ELSE IF constructs may be named by attaching a label at the beginning and the end of the construct so that it has the form

    name : IF (*logical-expression*) THEN
    .
    .
    .
    END IF *name*

for example,

```
UPDATE: IF (X > LARGEST) THEN
          LARGEST = X
          POSITION = N
        END IF UPDATE
```

The name may also be attached to any ELSE IF and ELSE statements appearing in the construct; for example,

```
TEST: IF (DISCRIMINANT > 0) THEN
        PRINT *, 'DISTINCT REAL ROOTS'
      ELSE IF (DISCRIMINANT = 0) THEN TEST
        PRINT *, 'ONE (REPEATED) REAL ROOT'
      ELSE TEST
        PRINT *, 'COMPLEX ROOTS'
      END IF TEST
```

- A CASE construct can be used to implement certain multialternative selection structures. It has the form

    SELECT CASE (*selector*)
      CASE (*label-list-1*)
        statement-sequence-1

CASE (*label-list-2*)
   statement-sequence-2
     .
     .
     .
CASE (*label-list-n*)
   statement-sequence-n
END SELECT

where the *selector* is an integer, character, or logical expression, and each of the *label-list-i* is a list of one or more possible values of the selector, enclosed in parentheses, or is the word DEFAULT. The values in this list may have any of the forms

value
value-1 : *value-2*
value-1 :
: *value-2*

to denote a single *value*, the range of values from *value-1* through *value-2*, the set of all values greater than or equal to *value-1*, or the set of all values less than or equal to *value-2*, respectively. When this CASE construct is executed, the selector is evaluated; if this value is in *label-list-i*, *statement-sequence-i* is executed, and execution continues with the statement following the END SELECT statement. If the value is not in any of the lists of values, the sequence of statements associated with DEFAULT is executed, if there is such a statement sequence, and continues with the statement following the CASE construct otherwise. A name may also be attached to a CASE construct:

SELECT CASE (*selector*) *name*
   .
   .
   .
END SELECT *name*

An example of a CASE construct is the following:

```
SELECT CASE (DISTANCE)
   CASE (0:99)
     FARE = 5
   CASE (100:300)
     FARE = 10
   DEFAULT
     PRINT *, 'DISTANCE', DISTANCE, ' OUT OF RANGE'
END CASE
```

It assigns the value 5 to FARE if the value of the integer variable DISTANCE is in the range 0 through 99, the value 10 if DISTANCE is in the range 100 through 300, and displays an out-of-range message otherwise.

- DO loops may have either of the forms

  > DO *control-variable* = *initial-value, limit, step-size*
  >   *statement-sequence*
  > END DO

  or

  > DO *n, control-variable* = *initial-value, limit, step-size*
  >   *statement-sequence*
  > *n*   CONTINUE

  where in both cases, the *step-size* is optional, and the comma after *n* in the second form is optional.

- Like IF constructs, DO constructs may have names attached; for example,

  ```
  OUTER:     DO I = 1, 10
                 .
                 .
                 .
      INNER: DO J = 1, 20
                 .
                 .
                 .
      END DO   INNER
                 .
                 .
                 .
  END DO OUTER
  ```

- While loops are implemented with DO constructs of the form

  > DO WHILE (*logical-expression*)
  >   *statement-sequence*
  > END DO

  which are executed in the manner described in Section 4.7. This form of the DO construct may also have a name attached as described for DO loops.

- Loop-forever repetition structures can be implemented with DO constructs of the form

  > DO
  >   *statement-sequence*
  > END DO

  or

  > DO *n*
  >   *statement-sequence*
  > *n*   CONTINUE

In this case, one of the statements within the body of the loop must cause termination, or an infinite loop will result. An EXIT statement of the form

    EXIT

or

    EXIT *name*

is provided for this purpose; in the second form, *name* is a name attached to the DO construct containing the EXIT statement. For example,

```
DO
  .
  .
  .
  IF (N .EQ. 0) EXIT
  .
  .
  .
END DO
```

● A CYCLE statement of the form

    CYCLE

or

    CYCLE *name*

can be used to terminate the current pass through a loop and proceed to the next iteration. In the second form, *name* is the name attached to the DO construct in which the CYCLE statement appears.

5

Introduction to Subprograms and Modular Programming

Great things can be reduced to small things, and small things can be reduced to nothing.

CHINESE PROVERB

From a little distance one can perceive an order in what at the time seemed confusion.

F. SCOTT FITZGERALD

All the best work is done the way ants do things—by tiny but untiring and regular additions.

LAFCADIO HEARN

The problems we have considered thus far have been simple enough that algorithms for their complete solution are quite straightforward. As we noted in Chapter 2, more complex problems are best solved using a **top-down** approach that uses a **divide-and-conquer** strategy to divide a problem into a number of simpler subproblems. Each of these subproblems is then considered individually, and in some cases it may be necessary to divide them further until the resulting subproblems are simple enough that algorithms for their solution can be easily designed. The complete algorithm for the original problem is then described in terms of these subalgorithms. **Subprograms** or **modules** can be written to implement each of these subalgorithms, and these subprograms can be combined to give a complete program that solves the original problem. In FORTRAN these subprograms are **functions** and **subroutines** whose execution is controlled by some other program unit, either the main program or some other subprogram.

Because the program units in this modular style of programming are independent of one another, the programmer can write each module and test it without worrying about the details of the other modules. This makes it considerably easier to locate an error, because it often occurs in the module most recently written and added to the program and the effects of these modules are easily isolated. Programs developed in this manner are also usually easier to understand because each program unit can be studied independently of the other program units.

5.1   Function Subprograms

The FORTRAN language provides many **library,** or **intrinsic, functions.** These library functions include not only the numeric functions introduced in Chapter 3 but also a number of other numeric functions, as well as character and logical functions. Table 5.1 gives a complete list of the standard FORTRAN numeric library functions; others are described in Chapters 9 and 10 and in Appendix D.

As we have seen, any of these functions may be used to calculate some value in an expression by giving its name followed by the actual arguments to which it is to be applied, enclosed in parentheses. For example, if ALPHA, NUM1, NUM2, SMALL, BETA, and X are declared by

```
INTEGER NUM1, NUM2, SMALL
REAL ALPHA, BETA, X
```

then the statements

```
PRINT *, ABS(X)
ALPHA = ANINT(100.0 * BETA) / 100.0
SMALL = MIN(0, NUM1, NUM2)
```

display the absolute value of X, assign to ALPHA the value of BETA rounded to the nearest hundredth, and assign to SMALL the smallest of the three integers 0, NUM1, and NUM2.

In some programs it is convenient for the user to define additional functions. Such **user-defined functions** are possible in FORTRAN, and once defined, they are used in the same way as are the library functions. The most common and useful way to do this is to use **function subprograms.** They are called subprograms because they are separate program units external to any other program unit (main program or other subprogram) that references them. Thus, once a subprogram has been prepared and saved in a user's library, it may be used in any program, simply by attaching it to that program.

The syntax of a function subprogram is similar to that of a FORTRAN (main) program:

    function heading
    specification part
    execution part

The **function heading** is a **FUNCTION statement** of the form

    FUNCTION *name(formal-argument-list)*

Table 5.1   Standard FORTRAN Numeric Library Functions

FORTRAN Function	Description	Type of Arguments*	Type of Value
ABS(x)	Absolute value of x	I, R, DP C	Same as argument R
ACOS(x)	Arccosine (in radians) of x	R, DP	Same as argument
AINT(x)	Value resulting from truncation of fractional part of x	R, DP	Same as argument
ANINT(x)	x rounded to the nearest integer INT(x + .5) if x ≥ 0 INT(x − .5) if x < 0	R, DP	Same as argument
ASIN(x)	Arcsine (in radians) of x	R, DP	Same as argument
ATAN(x)	Arctangent (in radians) of x	R, DP	Same as argument
ATAN2(x, y)	Arctangent (in radians) of x / y	R, DP	Same as argument
COS(x)	Cosine of x (in radians)	R, DP, C	Same as argument
COSH(x)	Hyperbolic cosine of x	R, DP	Same as argument
DIM(x, y)	x − y if x ≥ y 0 if x < y	I, R, DP	Same as argument
EXP(x)	Exponential function e^x	R, DP, C	Same as argument
INT(x)	Conversion of x to integer type; sign of x or real part of x times the greatest integer ≤ ABS(x)	I, R, DP, C	I
LOG(x)	Natural logarithm of x	R, DP, C	Same as argument
LOG10(x)	Common (base 10) logarithm of x	R, DP	Same as argument
MAX(x_1, . . . , x_n)	Maximum of x_1, . . . , x_n	I, R, DP	Same as arguments
MIN(x_1, . . . , x_n)	Minimum of x_1, . . . , x_n	I, R, DP	Same as arguments
MOD(x, y)	x (mod y); x − INT(x / y) * y	I, R, DP	Same as arguments
NINT(x)	x rounded to the nearest integer [see ANINT(x)]	R, DP	I
REAL(x)	Conversion of x to real type (Sections 9.1 and 9.2)	I, R, DP, C	R
SIGN(x, y)	Transfer of sign: ABS(x) if y ≥ 0 −ABS(x) if y < 0	I, R, DP	Same as arguments
SIN(x)	Sine of x (in radians)	R, DP, C	Same as argument
SINH(x)	Hyperbolic sine of x	R, DP	Same as argument
SQRT(x)	Square root of x	R, DP, C	Same as argument
TAN(x)	Tangent of x (in radians)	R, DP	Same as argument
TANH(x)	Hyperbolic tangent of x	R, DP	Same as argument

*I = integer, R = real, DP = double precision, C = complex. Types of arguments in a given function reference must be the same.

where *name* is the name of the function and may be any legal FORTRAN identifier. The type of the function value is the type specified for the function name in the specification part (or in the heading itself as described later). The *formal-argument-list* is an identifier or a list (possibly empty) of identifiers separated by commas. These variables are called **formal** or **dummy arguments** and are used to pass information to the function subprogram.

The specification part of a function subprogram has the same form as the specification part of a FORTRAN program with the additional stipulation that it (or the function heading itself) must include a specification of the type of the function. Similarly, the execution part of a function subprogram has the same form as the execution part of a FORTRAN program with the additional stipulation that it must include at least one statement that assigns a value to the identifier that names the function. Normally, this is done with an assignment statement of the form

$name = expression$

where *expression* may be any expression involving constants, the formal arguments of the function, other variables already assigned values in this subprogram, as well as references to other functions. The last statement of the execution part must be

END

The value of the function is returned to the program unit that references the function when this END statement or a **RETURN statement** of the form

RETURN

is executed.

To illustrate, suppose we wish to use the function

$$f(x, y) = \begin{cases} x + 1 & \text{if } x < y \\ x^n + y^n & \text{if } x \geq y \end{cases}$$

where x and y are real numbers and n is an integer. A function subprogram to implement this function will have three formal arguments, X, Y, and N, and so an appropriate function heading is

```
FUNCTION F(X, Y, N)
```

Since X and Y must be of type REAL, N of type INTEGER, and the function is to return real values, the specification part of this function subprogram is

```
REAL F, X, Y
INTEGER N
```

The complete function subprogram is

```
FUNCTION F(X, Y, N)

REAL F, X, Y
INTEGER N

IF (X .LT. Y) THEN
    F = X + 1
ELSE
    F = X ** N + Y ** N
END IF
END
```

If this subprogram is attached to a program, it can be referenced in the same manner as are other functions we have considered. The arguments in a function reference are called **actual arguments.** When a function is referenced, the values of these actual arguments become the values of the corresponding formal arguments and are used in computing the value of the function. For example, if ALPHA, BETA, and GAMMA have been declared to be real variables and the values of ALPHA and BETA are 4.0 and 3.0, respectively, then in the statement

```
GAMMA = F(ALPHA, BETA, 2)
```

the values of the actual arguments ALPHA and BETA become the values of the formal arguments X and Y, respectively, and the actual argument 2 becomes the value of the formal argument N. The value of the function

$$4.0^2 + 3.0^2 = 25.0$$

is then computed and assigned to GAMMA.

Because of this association between actual arguments and formal arguments, *the number and type of the actual arguments must agree with the number and type of the formal arguments.* To illustrate, consider the type specification statements

```
INTEGER I
REAL F, A, B, C
LOGICAL L
```

The function reference in

```
PRINT *, F(A, B + C, I)
```

is legal, but those in the statements

```
C = F(A, 2)
Z = F(A, B, L)
```

are not, because the first function reference has an incorrect number of arguments, and in the second the argument L is not the correct type.

As another example, consider again the problem of approximating the definite integral of a function. In Example 1 of Section 4.11 we approximated the integral

$$\int_a^b (x^2 + 1)\, dx$$

using the rectangle method. In the program in Figure 4.23, we used the expression X ** 2 + 1 to calculate the function values within the loop that accumulated the areas of approximating rectangles.

Although this program correctly calculated the approximate value of the integral, it is preferable to separate the definition of the function from the part of the program that calculates the approximation of the integral. The program in Figure 5.1 is a modification of the program in Figure 4.23 that uses a function subprogram to define the function to be integrated.

```
      PROGRAM AREA
*******************************************************************
* Program to approximate the integral of a function over the interval *
* [A,B] using the rectangle method with altitudes chosen at the       *
* midpoints of the subintervals.  Identifiers used are:               *
*     A, B   : the endpoints of the interval of integration           *
*     N      : the number of subintervals used                        *
*     I      : counter                                                 *
*     DELX   : the length of the subintervals                         *
*     X      : the midpoint of one of the subintervals                *
*     F      : the function being integrated                          *
*     SUM    : the approximating sum                                  *
*******************************************************************

      REAL F, A, B, X, DELX, SUM
      INTEGER N, I

      PRINT *, 'ENTER THE INTERVAL ENDPOINTS AND THE # OF SUBINTERVALS'
      READ *, A, B, N
      DELX = (B - A) / REAL(N)

* Initialize the approximating SUM and set X equal to
* the midpoint of the first subinterval

      SUM = 0
      X = A + DELX / 2.0

* Now calculate and display the sum

      DO 10 I = 1, N
          SUM = SUM + F(X)
          X = X + DELX
10    CONTINUE
      SUM = DELX * SUM
      PRINT *, 'APPROXIMATE VALUE USING ', N, ' SUBINTERVALS IS ', SUM
      END

**F(X)********************************************
* Function subprogram that defines the integrand *
*************************************************

      FUNCTION F(X)

      REAL X, F

      F = X**2 + 1.0
      END
```

Figure 5.1

Figure 5.1   (continued)

Sample runs:

```
ENTER THE INTERVAL ENDPOINTS AND THE # OF SUBINTERVALS
0, 1, 10
APPROXIMATE VALUE USING    10 SUBINTERVALS IS      1.33250

ENTER THE INTERVAL ENDPOINTS AND THE # OF SUBINTERVALS
0, 1, 20
APPROXIMATE VALUE USING    20 SUBINTERVALS IS      1.33313

ENTER THE INTERVAL ENDPOINTS AND THE # OF SUBINTERVALS
0, 1, 100
APPROXIMATE VALUE USING    100 SUBINTERVALS IS      1.33332
```

To use this program to approximate the integral of a different function such as

$$f(x) = \begin{cases} 1 & \text{if } x < 0 \\ 1 - x^2 & \text{if } 0 \le x \le 1 \\ \ln x & \text{if } x > 1 \end{cases}$$

we need only replace the function subprogram with one that defines this function. Figure 5.2 illustrates.

```
      PROGRAM AREA
************************************************************************
* Program to approximate the integral of a function over the interval  *
* [A,B] using the rectangle method with altitudes chosen at the        *
* midpoints of the subintervals.  Identifiers used are:                *
*     A, B   : the endpoints of the interval of integration            *
*     N      : the number of subintervals used                         *
*     I      : counter                                                 *
*     DELX   : the length of the subintervals                          *
*     X      : the midpoint of one of the subintervals                 *
*     F      : the function being integrated                           *
*     SUM    : the approximating sum                                   *
************************************************************************

      REAL F, A, B, X, DELX, SUM
      INTEGER N, I
                .
                .
                .

      END
```

Figure 5.2

Figure 5.2 (continued)

```
**F(X) ********************************************
* Function subprogram that defines the integrand *
*************************************************

      FUNCTION F(X)

      REAL X, F

      IF (X .LT. 0) THEN
          F = 1.0
      ELSE IF (X .LE. 1.0) THEN
          F = 1.0 - X ** 2
      ELSE
          F = LOG(X)
      END IF
      END
```

Sample runs:

```
ENTER THE INTERVAL ENDPOINTS AND THE # OF SUBINTERVALS
-1, 0, 1
APPROXIMATE VALUE USING    1 SUBINTERVALS IS      1.00000

ENTER THE INTERVAL ENDPOINTS AND THE # OF SUBINTERVALS
-2, 2, 50
APPROXIMATE VALUE USING   50 SUBINTERVALS IS      3.05123

ENTER THE INTERVAL ENDPOINTS AND THE # OF SUBINTERVALS
-2, 2, 100
APPROXIMATE VALUE USING  100 SUBINTERVALS IS      3.05313
```

Some function subprograms may require the use of constants and/or variables in addition to the formal arguments. These **local identifiers** are declared in the specification part of the subprogram, which has the same form as the specification part of the main program. To illustrate, consider the *factorial function*. The factorial of a nonnegative integer n is denoted by $n!$ and is defined by

$$n! = \begin{cases} 1 & \text{if } n = 0 \\ 1 \times 2 \times 3 \times \cdots \times n & \text{if } n > 0 \end{cases}$$

A function subprogram to define this function will have one integer parameter N, but it will also need a local variable I to use as a control variable in a DO loop that computes N!. The complete function subprogram is

```
**FACTOR*************************************************
* Function to calculate the factorial N! of N which *
* is 1 if N = 0, 1 * 2 *   * N if N > 0.   It        *
* uses I as a counter.                               *
********************************************************

      FUNCTION FACTOR (N)

      INTEGER FACTOR, N, I

      FACTOR = 1
      DO 10 I = 2, N
         FACTOR = FACTOR * I
   10 CONTINUE
      END
```

The program in Figure 5.4 uses this subprogram in calculating values of the **Poisson probability function**, which is the probability function of a random variable such as the number of radioactive particles striking a given target in a given period of time, the number of flaws in a given length of magnetic tape, or the number of failures in an electronic device during a given time period. This function is defined by

$$P(n) = \frac{\lambda^n \cdot e^{-\lambda}}{n!}$$

where

λ = the average number of occurrences of the phenomenon per time period.

n = the number of occurrences in that time period.

For example, if the average number of particles passing through a counter during 1 millisecond in a laboratory experiment is 3 ($\lambda = 3$), then the probability that exactly five particles enter the counter ($n = 5$) in a given millisecond will be

$$P(5) = \frac{3^5 \cdot e^{-3}}{5!} = 0.1008$$

The program in Figure 5.4 reads values for N and LAMBDA, references the function POISS, which calculates the Poisson probability, and displays this probability. The value of N! is obtained by the function POISS from the function subprogram FACTOR. This program implements the algorithm whose structure is shown in Figure 5.3. Note the use of double-lined rectangles to indicate references to subprograms.

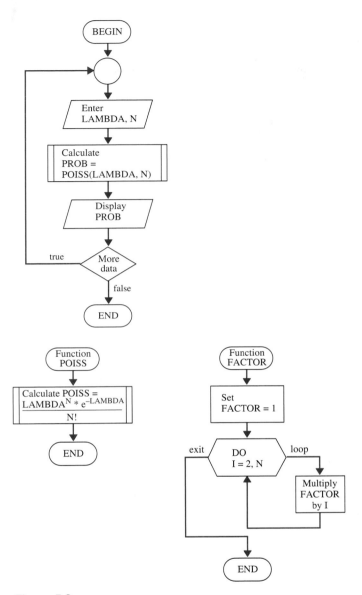

Figure 5.3

```
      PROGRAM PROBAB
************************************************************************
* Program to calculate the Poisson probability function using the     *
* function subprogram POISS.  Identifiers used are:                   *
*      LAMBDA : average # of occurrences of phenomenon per time period *
*      N      : number of occurrences in a time period                *
*      PROB   : Poisson probability                                   *
*      POISS  : function subprogram to calculate Poisson probability  *
************************************************************************

      REAL LAMBDA, POISS, PROB
      INTEGER N

      PRINT *, 'THIS PROGRAM CALCULATES THE POISSON PROBABILITY FOR'
      PRINT *, 'LAMBDA = AVERAGE # OF OCCURRENCES PER TIME PERIOD'
      PRINT *, 'N = # OF OCCURRENCES FOR WHICH PROBABILITY TO BE FOUND'
      PRINT *, 'ENTER LAMBDA AND N (NEGATIVE VALUES TO STOP)'
      READ *, LAMBDA, N

* While LAMBDA >= 0 do the following

10    IF (LAMBDA .GE. 0) THEN
          PROB = POISS(LAMBDA, N)
          PRINT *, 'POISSON PROBABILITY = ', PROB
          PRINT *
          PRINT *, 'ENTER LAMBDA AND N (NEGATIVE VALUES TO STOP)'
          READ *, LAMBDA, N
      GO TO 10
      END IF

      END


**POISS*****************************************************************
* Function to calculate the Poisson probability                       *
*                         N    -LAMBDA                                *
*                   LAMBDA * e                                        *
*         POISS(N) = ------------------                               *
*                         N!                                          *
* Function FACTOR is called to calculate N!                          *
************************************************************************

      FUNCTION POISS(LAMBDA, N)

      INTEGER N, FACTOR
      REAL POISS, LAMBDA

      POISS = (LAMBDA ** N * EXP(-LAMBDA)) / FACTOR(N)
      END
```

Figure 5.4

Figure 5.4 (continued)

```
**FACTOR*********************************************************************
* Function to calculate the factorial N! of N which is 1 if N = 0,     *
* 1 * 2 * ... * N for N > 0.  It uses variable I as a  counter.        *
****************************************************************************

      FUNCTION FACTOR(N)

      INTEGER FACTOR, N, I

      FACTOR = 1
      DO 10 I = 2, N
         FACTOR = FACTOR * I
10    CONTINUE
      END
```

Sample run:

```
THIS PROGRAM CALCULATES THE POISSON PROBABILITY FOR
LAMBDA = AVERAGE # OF OCCURRENCES PER TIME PERIOD
N = # OF OCCURRENCES FOR WHICH PROBABILITY TO BE FOUND
ENTER LAMBDA AND N (NEGATIVE VALUES TO STOP)
3, 5
POISSON PROBABILITY =       1.00819E-01

ENTER LAMBDA AND N (NEGATIVE VALUES TO STOP)
4, 6
POISSON PROBABILITY =       1.04196E-01

ENTER LAMBDA AND N (NEGATIVE VALUES TO STOP)
-1, -1
```

The order in which subprograms are arranged following the main program is irrelevant. Thus, in Figure 5.4, the subprogram FACTOR could just as well precede the subprogram POISS. Notice that there is no conflict between statement numbers and identifiers in different program units; for example, both the main program and the subprogram FACTOR have a statement numbered 10. Similarly, if the main program or the subprogram POISS declared and used the identifier I, used as a control variable in FACTOR, no conflict would result, because these are independent program units connected only via the function names and the arguments.

Normally when control returns from a subprogram, all **local variables** in the subprogram, that is, variables declared within the subprogram that are not arguments, become undefined. (Exceptions include variables initialized by a DATA statement within that subprogram that are not redefined and variables in common blocks, as described in Section 5.6.) In particular, this means that the values of such variables are not available in subsequent references to the subprogram. If it is necessary to save their values from one execution of the subprogram to the next, this can be accomplished by listing their names in a

SAVE statement of the form

    SAVE *list*

If *list* is omitted, all variables in the subprogram will be saved. The program in Figure 5.9 of the next section illustrates the use of the SAVE statement.

As another example of function subprograms, consider the following:

```
CHARACTER*20 STRING, LSTR, RSTR
LOGICAL INBETW
      .
      .
      .
IF (INBETW(STRING, LSTR, RSTR)) THEN
      .
      .
      .
END


**INBETW*****************************************
* Function that returns true or false according *
* to whether or not string STR is between or    *
* equal to strings LS and RS                     *
*************************************************

FUNCTION INBETW(STR, LS, RS)

CHARACTER*20 STR, LS, RS
LOGICAL INBETW

INBETW = (LS .LE. STR) .AND. (STR .LE. RS)
END
```

We could also specify the type and lengths of the formal arguments STR, LS, and RS using the **assumed length specifier** (∗) in the statement

```
CHARACTER*(*) STR, LS, RS
```

In this case, the lengths of STR, LS, and RS are taken to be the same as the lengths of the corresponding actual arguments STRING, LSTR, and RSTR, respectively. Thus, STR, LS, and RS are assumed to be of length 20.

As illustrated in the examples, *the type of a function must be declared both in the subprogram defining the function and in each program unit that references the function.* The declaration in the subprogram can be made in one of two ways. The first method is to declare the function type in the specification part of the subprogram, as we have done in our examples thus far and as illustrated in the following:

```
FUNCTION PHI(X, Y)
INTEGER PHI
REAL X, Y
   .
   .
   .
END
```

```
FUNCTION TRUN(STRING, N)
CHARACTER*15 STRING, TRUN*10
INTEGER N
       .
       .
       .
END
```

In the last example, we could specify the type and length of the function TRUN and/or the formal arguments STRING using the assumed length specifier (*) as follows:

```
FUNCTION TRUN(STRING, N)
CHARACTER*(*) STRING, TRUN
INTEGER N
```

In this case, the length of TRUN is the length specified in the program unit referencing the function, and the length of STRING is the length of the corresponding actual argument.

The second method of declaring the type of a function is to use a modified form of the function heading in which the type of the function is placed before the word FUNCTION. Thus, the preceding examples could also be written

```
INTEGER FUNCTION PHI(X, Y)
REAL X, Y

CHARACTER*10 FUNCTION TRUN(STRING, N)
CHARACTER*15 STRING
INTEGER N
```

or using the assumed length specifier in the last example,

```
CHARACTER*(*) FUNCTION TRUN(STRING, N)
CHARACTER*(*) STRING
INTEGER N
```

In addition to function subprograms, FORTRAN provides another method for defining functions, namely, by using **statement functions.** A statement function is appropriate when the function can be defined by means of a single expression and when it does not change from one execution of the program to another. A statement function is defined by a single statement of the form

name(formal-argument-list) = expression

The *expression* may contain constants, variables, formulas, or references to library functions, to previously defined statement functions, or to functions defined by subprograms, but not references to the function being defined. *Such statement functions must appear in the program unit in which the functions are referenced, and they must be placed at the end of the specification part.*

To illustrate, consider a program that requires the hypotenuse of some right triangles at various places in the program. The following type specification statement and statement function might be placed at the end of the specification part:

```
REAL A, B, HYPO
HYPO(A, B) = SQRT(A ** 2 + B ** 2)
```

and the function HYPO could then be used in the same manner as all other functions. A program that requires the logical *exclusive or* operation XOR might define it as a statement function:

```
LOGICAL P, Q, XOR
XOR(P, Q) = (P .OR. Q) .AND. .NOT. (P .AND. Q)
```

The program in Figure 5.5, which is a modification of the program in Figure 4.2, uses this statement function to calculate the SUM bit in a half-adder.

```
      PROGRAM HADDER
*********************************************************************
* Program to calculate the outputs from a logical circuit that      *
* represents a binary half-adder.  Variables used are:              *
*      A, B  : the two logical inputs to the circuit                *
*      SUM, CARRY : the two logical outputs                         *
*********************************************************************
      LOGICAL P, Q, XOR, A, B, SUM, CARRY
      XOR(P, Q) = (P .OR. Q) .AND. .NOT. (P .AND. Q)

      PRINT *, 'ENTER LOGICAL INPUTS A AND B:'
      READ *, A, B
      SUM = XOR(A, B)
      CARRY = A .AND. B
      PRINT *, 'CARRY, SUM = ', CARRY, SUM
      END
```

Figure 5.5

Exercises

1. Write a statement function RANGE that calculates the range between two integers, that is, the larger integer minus the smaller one.

2. Write a real-valued statement function ROUND that has a real argument AMOUNT and an integer argument N and returns the value of AMOUNT rounded to N places. For example, the function references ROUND(10.536, 0), ROUND(10.536, 1), and ROUND(10.536, 2) should give the values 11.0, 10.5, and 10.54, respectively.

3. The number of bacteria in a culture can be estimated by

$$N \cdot e^{kt}$$

where N is the initial population, k is a rate constant, and t is time. Write a statement function to calculate the number of bacteria present at time t for given values of k and N; use it in a program that reads values for the initial population, the rate constant, and the time (e.g., 1000, 0.15, 100) and displays the number of bacteria at that time.

4. Write a program to accept a temperature and the letter C or F, indicating that it is Celsius or Fahrenheit, respectively, and that then uses an appropriate function to convert the temperature to the other scale. (One of the conversion formulas is $F = \frac{9}{5}C + 32$.)

5. Using statement functions to define the logical functions

$$\sim p \wedge \sim q \qquad (\text{not } p \text{ and not } q)$$

and

$$\sim(p \vee q) \qquad (\text{not } (p \text{ or } q))$$

write a program to calculate and print truth tables for these logical expressions.

6. Write a logical-valued function that determines whether a character is one of the digits 0 through 9. Use it in a program that reads several characters and checks to see whether each is a digit.

7. Write a statement function that has as arguments the coordinates of two points $P_1(x_1, y_1)$ and $P_2(x_2, y_2)$ and returns the distance $\sqrt{(x_2 - x_1)^2 + (y_2 - y_1)^2}$ between P_1 and P_2. Use the function in a program that reads the coordinates of several triples of points and determines whether they can be the vertices of a triangle. (The sum of the lengths of each pair of sides must be greater than the length of the third side.)

8. If an amount of A dollars is borrowed at an annual interest rate r (expressed as a decimal) for y years and n is the number of payments to be made per year, then the amount of each payment is given by

$$\frac{r \cdot A/n}{1 - \left(1 + \dfrac{r}{n}\right)^{-n \cdot y}}$$

Define a statement function to calculate these payments. Use it in a program that reads several values for the amount borrowed, the interest rate, the number of years, and the number of payments per year and, for each set of values, displays the corresponding payment.

9. (a) Write a real-valued function NGRADE that accepts a letter grade and returns the corresponding numeric value (A = 4.0, B = 3.0, C = 2.0, D = 1.0, F = 0.0).

  (b) Write a character-valued function LGRADE that assigns a letter grade to an integer score using the following grading scale:

90–100: A

80–89: B

70–79: C

60–69: D

Below 60: F

  (c) Use these functions in a program that reads several scores and, for each, displays the corresponding letter grades and numeric value.

10. Write a program to calculate *binomial coefficients*

$$\binom{n}{k} = \frac{n!}{k!(n-k)!}$$

using a function subprogram to calculate factorials. Let n run from 1 through 10, and for each such n, let k run from 0 through n.

11. Suppose that in an experiment the probability that a certain outcome will occur is p; then $1 - p$ is the probability that it will not occur. The probability that out of n independent trials the desired outcome will occur exactly k times is given by

$$\binom{n}{k} p^k (1-p)^{n-k}$$

Write a program to calculate this probability for several values of n and k, using a function subprogram to calculate factorials.

12. The *power series*

$$1 + x + \frac{x^2}{2!} + \frac{x^3}{3!} + \cdots = \sum_{n=0}^{\infty} \frac{x^n}{n!}$$

converges to e^x for all values of x. Write a function subprogram that uses this series to calculate values for e^x to five-place accuracy (that is, using terms up to the first one that is less than 10^{-5} in absolute value) and that uses a function subprogram to calculate factorials. Use these subprograms in a main program to calculate and print a table of values for the function

$$\cosh(x) = \frac{e^x + e^{-x}}{2}$$

and also the corresponding values of the library function COSH for $x = -1$ to 1 in increments of 0.1.

13. A more efficient procedure for evaluating the power series in Exercise 12 is to observe that if $a_n = x^n/n!$ and $a_{n+1} = x^{n+1}/(n + 1)!$ are two consecutive terms of the series, then

$$a_{n+1} = \frac{x}{n + 1} a_n$$

Write a function subprogram to calculate e^x using the series of Exercise 12 and using this relationship between consecutive terms. Then use this in a main program to print a table of values for the function

$$\sinh(x) = \frac{e^x - e^{-x}}{2}$$

and the corresponding values of the library function SINH for $x = -2$ to 2 in increments of 0.1.

14. The *greatest common divisor* of two integers a and b, not both of which are zero, is the largest positive integer that divides both a and b. The *Euclidean algorithm* for finding this greatest common divisor of a and b, GCD(a, b), is as follows: If $b = 0$, GCD(a, b) is a. Otherwise, divide a by b to obtain quotient q and remainder r, so that $a = bq + r$. Then GCD(a, b) = GCD(b, r). Replace a by b and b by r and repeat this procedure. Because the remainders are decreasing, eventually a remainder of 0 will result. The last nonzero remainder is then GCD(a, b). For example:

$$1260 = 198 \cdot 6 + 72 \qquad \text{GCD}(1260, 198) = \text{GCD}(198, 72)$$
$$198 = 72 \cdot 2 + 54 \qquad\qquad\qquad\qquad = \text{GCD}(72, 54)$$
$$72 = 54 \cdot 1 + 18 \qquad\qquad\qquad\qquad = \text{GCD}(54, 18)$$
$$54 = 18 \cdot 3 + 0 \qquad\qquad\qquad\qquad = 18$$

Note: If either a or b is negative, replace it with its absolute value.

Write a function subprogram to calculate the GCD of two integers. Then use it in a program that calculates the GCD of any finite set of integers using the following:

If $d = \text{GCD}(a_1, \ldots, a_n)$, then

$$\text{GCD}(a_1, \ldots, a_n, a_{n+1}) = \text{GCD}(d, a_{n+1})$$

For example:

$$\text{GCD}(1260, 198) = 18$$
$$\text{GCD}(1260, 198, 585) = \text{GCD}(18, 585) = 9$$
$$\text{GCD}(1260, 198, 585, 138) = \text{GCD}(9, 138) = 3$$

15. A *prime number* is an integer $n > 1$ whose only positive divisors are 1 and n itself. Write a logical-valued function that determines whether n is a prime number. Use it in a program that reads several integers, uses the function to determine whether each is a prime, and displays each number with the appropriate label 'IS PRIME' or 'IS NOT PRIME'.

16. Write a program to approximate $f'(a)$, the value of the derivative of f at a, for f defined by a statement function, and a given number a. The *derivative of f at a* is given by

$$f'(a) = \lim_{h \to 0} \frac{f(a + h) - f(a)}{h}$$

Calculate values of the difference quotient

$$\frac{f(a + h) - f(a)}{h}$$

for various values of h approaching 0, say first for $h = 1/2^n$, and then for $h = -1/2^n$, as n runs from 0 to 15.

17. (a) Write a function DAYSIN that returns the number of days in a given month and year. (See Exercise 1(c) of Section 4.4, which describes which years are leap years.)
    (b) Write a function NDAYS that returns the number of days between two given dates.
    (c) A person's biorhythm index on a given day is the sum of the values of his or her physical, intellectual, and emotional cycles. Each of these cycles begins at birth and forms a sine curve having an amplitude of 1 and periods of 23, 33, and 28 days, respectively. Write a program that accepts the current date, a person's name, and his or her birthdate and then calculates the biorhythm index for that person. (See Exercise 1(c) of Section 4.4 regarding leap years.)

5.2 Examples: Root Finding, Numerical Solutions of Differential Equations, Simulation

EXAMPLE 1: Root Finding. In many applications, it is necessary to find a **zero** or **root** of a function f, that is, a number c for which

$$f(c) = 0$$

For some functions f, it may be very difficult or even impossible to find this value c exactly. Examples include the function

$$f(v) = 50 \cdot 10^{-9}(e^{40v} - 1) + v - 20$$

which may arise in a problem of determining the dc operating point in an electrical circuit, or the function

$$f(x) = x \tan x - a$$

for which a zero must be found to solve some heat conduction problems.

For such functions, an iterative numerical method is used to find an approximate zero. One method that is often used for differentiable functions is **Newton's method.** This method consists of taking an initial approximation x_1 to the zero and constructing the tangent line to the graph of f at point $P_1(x_1, f(x_1))$. The point x_2 at which this tangent line crosses the x axis is the second approximation to the zero. Another tangent line may be constructed at point $P_2(x_2, f(x_2))$, and the point x_3 where this tangent line crosses the x axis is the third approximation. For many functions, this sequence of approximations $x_1, x_2, x_3, \ldots$ converges to the zero, provided that the first approximation is sufficiently close to the zero. The following diagram illustrates Newton's method:

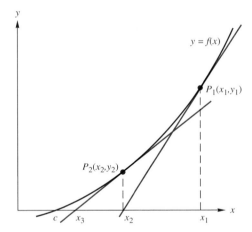

If x_n is an approximation to the zero of f, then the formula for obtaining the next approximation x_{n+1} by Newton's method is

$$x_{n+1} = x_n - \frac{f(x_n)}{f'(x_n)}$$

where f' is the derivative of f. Note that Newton's method will fail if $f'(x_n)$ is 0 at some approximation x_n.

Figure 5.6 shows a flowchart for Newton's method, and the program in Figure 5.7 uses this method to find an approximate zero of the function

$$f(x) = x - \cos x$$

Function subprograms are used to define this function and its derivative:

$$f'(x) = 1 + \sin x$$

The program reads an initial approximation to a zero of f and generates and displays successive approximations using Newton's method as long as

$$|f(x)| \geq \epsilon$$

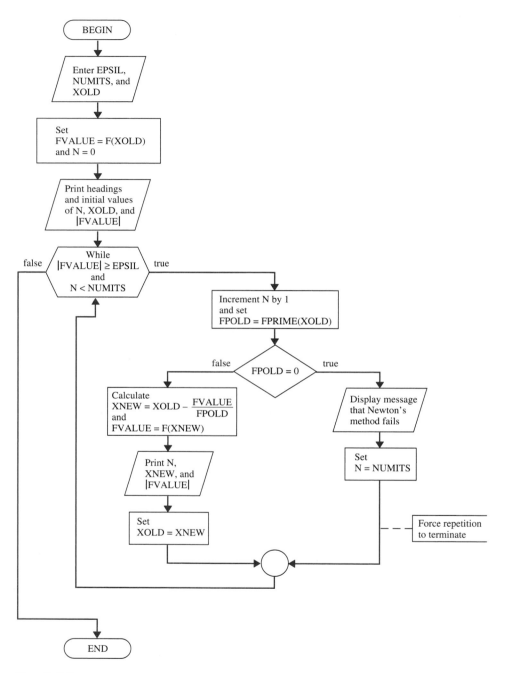

Figure 5.6

for some small positive number ϵ (denoted in the program by EPSIL). If the number of iterations exceeds an upper limit NUMITS (in case of divergence), execution is terminated.

```
      PROGRAM NEWTON
************************************************************************
* Program to find an approximate zero of a function F using Newton's  *
* method.  Variables used are:                                        *
*     XOLD    : previous approximation (initially the first one)      *
*     FPOLD   : value of the derivative of F at XOLD                   *
*     XNEW    : the new approximation                                 *
*     FVALUE  : value of F at an approximation                        *
*     EPSIL   : repetition stops when ABS(FVALUE) is less than EPSIL  *
*     NUMITS  : limit on number of iterations                         *
*     N       : number of iterations                                  *
************************************************************************

      INTEGER NUMITS, N
      REAL XOLD, FPOLD, XNEW, EPSIL,  F, FPRIME, FVALUE

* Get termination values EPSIL & NUMITS and initial approximation

      PRINT *, 'ENTER EPSILON, LIMIT ON # OF ITERATIONS, AND'
      PRINT *, 'THE INITIAL APPROXIMATION'
      READ *, EPSIL, NUMITS, XOLD
      FVALUE = F(XOLD)
      N = 0
      PRINT *, '   N        X(N)      ABS(F(X(N)))'
      PRINT *, '================================='
      PRINT *, 0, XOLD, ABS(FVALUE)

* Iterate using Newton's method while ABS(FVALUE) is greater
* than or equal to EPSIL and N has not reached NUMITS.
* Terminate if the derivative is 0 at some approximation.

10    IF ((ABS(FVALUE) .GE. EPSIL) .AND. (N .LT. NUMITS)) THEN
         N = N + 1
         FPOLD = FPRIME(XOLD)
         IF (FPOLD .EQ. 0) THEN
            PRINT *, 'NEWTON''S METHOD FAILS -- DERIVATIVE = 0'
*           Force repetition to terminate
            N = NUMITS
         ELSE
            XNEW = XOLD - (FVALUE / FPOLD)
            FVALUE = F(XNEW)
            PRINT *, N, XNEW, ABS(FVALUE)
            XOLD = XNEW
         END IF
      GO TO 10
      END IF
      END
```

Figure 5.7

Figure 5.7 (continued)

```
**F(X)******************************************
* Function for which a zero is being found *
***********************************************

      FUNCTION F(X)

      REAL X, F

      F = X - COS(X)
      END

**FPRIME(X)*****************************
* The derivative of the function f *
***************************************

      FUNCTION FPRIME(X)

      REAL X, FPRIME

      FPRIME = 1 + SIN(X)
      END
```

Sample run:

```
ENTER EPSILON, LIMIT ON # OF ITERATIONS, AND
THE INITIAL APPROXIMATION
1E-5, 20, 1.0
  N       X(N)       ABS(F(X(N)))
==============================
  0     1.00000    0.459698
  1     0.750364   1.89230E-02
  2     0.739113   4.64916E-05
  3     0.739085   0.
```

EXAMPLE 2: Numerical Solutions of Differential Equations. Equations that involve derivatives or differentials are called **differential equations.** These equations arise in a large number of problems in science and engineering. For many differential equations, it is very difficult or even impossible to find the exact solution, but it may be possible to find an approximate solution using a numerical method. There are many such methods, and in this example we describe two of the simpler ones.

Suppose we wish to approximate the solution of the **first-order differential equation**

$$y' = f(x, y)$$

satisfying the **initial condition**

$$y(x_0) = y_0$$

The **Euler method** for obtaining an approximation solution over some interval $[a, b]$ where $a = x_0$ is as follows:

EULER'S METHOD

1. Select an x increment Δx.
2. For $n = 0, 1, 2, \ldots$, do the following:
   a. Set $x_{n+1} = x_n + \Delta x$.
   b. Find the point $P_{n+1}(x_{n+1}, y_{n+1})$ on the line through $P_n(x_n, y_n)$ with slope $f(x_n, y_n)$.
   c. Display y_{n+1}, which is the approximate value of y at x_{n+1}.

The following diagram illustrates Euler's method:

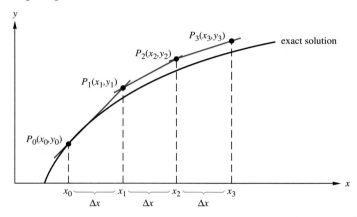

The program in Figure 5.8 uses Euler's method to obtain an approximate solution for

$$y' = 2xy$$

$$y(0) = 1$$

Sample runs with $a = 0$, $b = .5$, $\Delta x = .2$, and $a = 0$, $b = .5$, $\Delta x = .05$ are shown.

```
      PROGRAM EULER
********************************************************************
* Program that uses Euler's method to obtain an approximate solution  *
* to a first order differential equation. of the form:                *
*                       Y' = F(X, Y)                                  *
* Variables used are:                                                 *
*      X      : current X-value                                       *
*      XNEXT  : next X-value (X + DELTAX)                             *
*      Y      : approximate Y-value corresponding to X                *
*      DELTAX : X-increment used                                      *
*      NVALS  : number of iterations                                  *
*      N      : counts iterations                                     *
********************************************************************

      REAL X, Y, XNEXT, DELTAX, F
      INTEGER N, NVALS
```

Figure 5.8

Figure 5.8 (continued)

```
* Get given information

      PRINT *, 'ENTER X0 AND Y0, X-INCREMENT TO USE, AND'
      PRINT *, 'THE NUMBER OF VALUES TO CALCULATE.'
      READ *, X, Y,  DELTAX, NVALS
      PRINT *, 'X(', 0, ') =', X
      PRINT *, ' Y(', 0, ') =', Y

* Iterate with Euler's method

      DO 10 N = 1, NVALS
          XNEXT = X + DELTAX
          Y = Y + F(X,Y) * (XNEXT - X)
          X = XNEXT
          PRINT *, 'X(', N, ') =', X
          PRINT *, ' Y(', N, ') =', Y
10    CONTINUE
      END


**F(X, Y)*************************************************
* The function F in differential equation Y' = F(X, Y) *
*******************************************************

      FUNCTION F(X, Y)

      REAL X, Y, F

      F = 2.0 * X * Y
      END
```

Sample runs:

```
ENTER X0 AND Y0, X-INCREMENT TO USE, AND
THE NUMBER OF VALUES TO CALCULATE.
0, 1, .2, 5
X(  0) =  0.
 Y(  0) =    1.00000
X(  1) =  0.200000
 Y(  1) =    1.00000
X(  2) =  0.400000
 Y(  2) =    1.08000
X(  3) =  0.600000
 Y(  3) =    1.25280
X(  4) =  0.800000
 Y(  4) =    1.55347
X(  5) =  1.00000
 Y(  5) =    2.05058
```

Figure 5.8   (continued)

```
ENTER X0 AND Y0, X-INCREMENT TO USE, AND
THE NUMBER OF VALUES TO CALCULATE.
0, 1, .05, 10
X(  0) =  0.
 Y(  0) =    1.00000
X(  1) =    5.00000E-02
 Y(  1) =    1.00000
X(  2) =    1.00000E-01
 Y(  2) =    1.00500
X(  3) =  0.150000
 Y(  3) =    1.01505
X(  4) =  0.200000
 Y(  4) =    1.03028
X(  5) =  0.250000
 Y(  5) =    1.05088
X(  6) =  0.300000
 Y(  6) =    1.07715
X(  7) =  0.350000
 Y(  7) =    1.10947
X(  8) =  0.400000
 Y(  8) =    1.14830
X(  9) =  0.450000
 Y(  9) =    1.19423
X( 10) =  0.500000
 Y( 10) =    1.24797
```

For the differential equation and initial condition considered in the preceding example, the exact solution is:

$$y = e^{x^2}$$

In this case, therefore, we can compare the approximate y values with the exact values to see how well Euler's method does.

x	$y = e^{x^2}$
0.0	1.00000
0.1	1.01005
0.2	1.04081
0.3	1.09417
0.4	1.17351
0.5	1.28401

Comparing these values with the approximate y values in the sample runs of Figure 5.8, we note that the accuracy of Euler's method did improve when a smaller x increment was used. However, if one uses Euler's method over a larger range of x values, the error in the y values can grow rapidly; for example, if we had used 40 iterations in the second sample run, the approximate y value for $x = 2$ would have been 39.0929, but the exact y value is 54.5982.

One of the most popular and most accurate numerical methods for solving a first-order differential equation is the following **Runge–Kutta method:**

RUNGE–KUTTA METHOD

1. Select an x increment Δx.
2. The approximate solution y_{n+1} at $x_{n+1} = x_0 + (n + 1)\Delta x$ for $n = 0, 1, 2, \ldots$, is given by

$$y_{n+1} = y_n + \frac{1}{6}(K_1 + 2K_2 + 2K_3 + K_4)$$

where

$$K_1 = \Delta x \cdot f(x_n, y_n)$$

$$K_2 = \Delta x \cdot f\left(x_n + \frac{\Delta x}{2}, y_n + \frac{K_1}{2}\right)$$

$$K_3 = \Delta x \cdot f\left(x_n + \frac{\Delta x}{2}, y_n + \frac{K_2}{2}\right)$$

$$K_4 = \Delta x \cdot f(x_n + \Delta x, y_n + K_3)$$

A program implementing the Runge–Kutta method is left as an exercise.

EXAMPLE 3: Simulation. The term **simulation** refers to modeling a dynamic process and using this model to study the behavior of the process. This model may consist of an equation or a set of equations that describe the process. For example, an equation of the form $A(t) = A_0(.5)^{t/h}$ was used in Section 2.1 to model the radioactive decay of polonium, and linear systems are used in Example 2 of Section 8.4 to model an electrical network. In many problems, the process being studied involves **randomness**, for example, Brownian motion, arrival of airplanes at an airport, and number of defective parts manufactured by a machine. Computer programs that simulate such processes use a **random number generator,** which is a subprogram that produces a number selected ''at random'' from some fixed range in such a way that a sequence of these numbers tends to be uniformly distributed over the given range. Although it is not possible to develop an algorithm that produces truly random numbers, there are some methods that produce sequences of **pseudorandom numbers** that are adequate for most purposes.

Many system libraries provide a random number generator that produces random real numbers uniformly distributed over the range 0 to 1. The numbers produced by such a generator can be used to generate random real numbers in other ranges or to generate random integers. To demonstrate how this is done, suppose that the random number generator is implemented as a function RAND having one integer argument. The expression

```
A + (B - A) * RAND(N)
```

can be used to generate random real numbers in the range A to B, and the expression

```
M + INT(K * RAND(N))
```

can be used to generate random integers in the range M through M + K − 1.

As an illustration, suppose that a slab of material is used to shield a nuclear reactor and that a particle entering the shield follows a random path by moving forward, backward, left, or right with equal likelihood, in jumps of one unit. A change of direction is interpreted as a collision with an atom in this shield. Suppose that after 10 such collisions, the particle's energy is dissipated and that it dies within the shield, provided that it has not already passed back inside the reactor or outside through the shield. A program is to be written to simulate particles entering this shield and to determine what percentage of them gets through it.

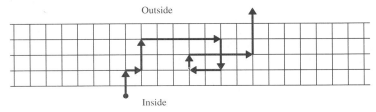

An algorithm for this simulation is

**ALGORITHM TO SIMULATE SHIELDING
OF NUCLEAR REACTOR**

```
* Algorithm to simulate particles entering a shield and to determine    *
* how many reach the outside. The particles are assumed to move         *
* forward, backward, left, and right with equal likelihood and to die   *
* within the shield if a certain number of collisions (changes of       *
* direction) have occurred. A random number generator is assumed.       *
```

1. Read the thickness (THICK) of the shield, the limit on the number of collisions (LIMCOL), and the number (N) of particles to simulate.
2. Read a SEED for the random number generator.
3. Initialize COUNT to 0 (number of particles reaching the outside).
4. Do the following for I = 1 to N:
   a. Initialize FORW to 1 (net units forward), OLDDIR to 0 (previous direction of particle), and COLLIS to 0 (number of collisions).
   b. Repeat the following until particle reaches the outside of the shield (FORW ≥ THICK), returns inside the reactor (FORW ≤ 0) or dies within the shield (COLLIS ≥ LIMCOL):
      i. Generate a random integer 1, 2, 3, or 4 for the direction DIR.
      ii. If DIR ≠ OLDDIR, increment COLLIS by 1 and set OLDDIR equal to DIR.
      iii. If DIR = 1, increment FORW by 1.
         Else if DIR = 2, decrement FORW by 1.
   c. If FORW = THICK, increment COUNT by 1.
5. Display 100 * COUNT / N.

The program in Figure 5.9 implements this algorithm. It uses the function subprogram RAND to generate random real numbers in the range 0 to 1, which are then transformed into random integers 1, 2, 3, or 4, corresponding to the four directions forward, backward, left, and right, respectively. For best results, the initial argument for this function RAND should be an odd integer.[1]

[1] For details of the *congruential method* of generating random numbers and other techniques, see Donald Knuth, *The Art of Computer Programming, Seminumerical Algorithms*, vol. 2 (Reading, Mass.: Addison-Wesley, 1981).

```
      PROGRAM SHIELD
*****************************************************************
* This program uses the random number generator  RAND  to simulate    *
* particles entering a shield and to determine what percentage reaches *
* the outside.  The particles are assumed to move forward, backward,   *
* left, and right with equal likelihood and to die within the shield   *
* if a certain number of collisions (changes of direction) have        *
* occurred. Variables used are:                                        *
*      THICK  : thickness of shield                                    *
*      LIMCOL : limit on # of collisions (before energy dissipated)    *
*      DIR    : a random integer 1, 2, 3, or 4 representing direction  *
*      OLDDIR : previous direction of particle                         *
*      COLLIS : # of collisions (changes of direction)                 *
*      FORW   : net units forward traveled                             *
*      N      : # of particles simulated                               *
*      COUNT  : # of particles reaching outside of shield              *
*      SEED   : a seed for RAND                                        *
*      I      : index variable                                         *
*****************************************************************
      INTEGER THICK, LIMCOL, DIR, OLDDIR, COLLIS, FORW, N, COUNT,
     +         SEED, I
      REAL RAND

      PRINT *, 'ENTER THICKNESS OF SHIELD, LIMIT ON # OF COLLISIONS,'
      PRINT *, 'AND THE NUMBER OF PARTICLES TO SIMULATE'
      READ *, THICK, LIMCOL, N
      PRINT *, 'SEED FOR RANDOM NUMBER GENERATOR'
      READ *, SEED
      COUNT = 0

* Begin the simulation

      DO 20 I = 1, N
         FORW = 1
         OLDDIR = 0
         COLLIS = 0
```

Figure 5.9

Figure 5.9 (continued)

```
*          Repeat the following until particle reaches outside of
*          shield, returns inside reactor, or dies within shield

10        CONTINUE
              DIR = 1 + 4 * RAND(SEED)
              IF (DIR .NE. OLDDIR) THEN
                  COLLIS = COLLIS + 1
                  OLDDIR = DIR
              END IF
              IF (DIR .EQ. 1) THEN
                  FORW = FORW + 1
              ELSE IF (DIR .EQ. 2) THEN
                  FORW = FORW - 1
              END IF
          IF ((FORW .LT. THICK) .AND. (FORW .GT. 0) .AND.
     +        (COLLIS .LT. LIMCOL)) GO TO 10

          IF (FORW .EQ. THICK) THEN
              COUNT = COUNT + 1
          END IF
20        CONTINUE

          PRINT 30, 100 * COUNT / REAL(N)
30        FORMAT(1X, F6.2, '% OF THE PARTICLES ESCAPED')
          END

**RAND**********************************************************
* This function generates a random real number in the interval from   *
* 0 to 1.  The variable M is initially the seed supplied by the       *
* user;  thereafter, it is the random integer generated on the pre-   *
* ceding call to the function and saved using the SAVE statement.     *
* NOTE:  The constants 2147483647 and .4656613E-9 used in this sub-   *
* program are appropriate when it is executed on a machine having     *
* 32-bit memory words.  For a machine having M-bit words, these two   *
* constants should be replaced by the values of  2**M - 1  and        *
* 1/(2**M - 1) , respectively.                                        *
******************************************************************

          FUNCTION RAND(K)

          INTEGER K, M, CONST1
          REAL RAND, CONST2
          PARAMETER (CONST1 = 2147483647, CONST2 = .4656613E-9)
          SAVE
          DATA M /0/

          IF (M .EQ. 0) M = K
          M = M * 65539
          IF (M .LT. 0) M = (M + 1) + CONST1
          RAND = M * CONST2
          END
```

Figure 5.9 (continued)

Sample runs:

```
ENTER THICKNESS OF SHIELD, LIMIT ON # OF COLLISIONS,
AND THE NUMBER OF PARTICLES TO SIMULATE
4, 5, 100
SEED FOR RANDOM NUMBER GENERATOR
5773
 11.00% OF THE PARTICLES ESCAPED

ENTER THICKNESS OF SHIELD, LIMIT ON # OF COLLISIONS,
AND THE NUMBER OF PARTICLES TO SIMULATE
8, 10, 500
SEED FOR RANDOM NUMBER GENERATOR
5773
 0.60% OF THE PARTICLES ESCAPED
```

Most random number generators generate random numbers having a **uniform distribution**, but they can also be used to generate random numbers having other distributions. The **normal distribution** is especially important because many physical processes can be modeled by it. For example, the heights and weights of people, the lifetime of light bulbs, the tensile strength of steel produced by a machine, and, in general, the variations in parts produced in almost any manufacturing process have normal distributions. The normal distribution has the following familiar bell-shaped curve, where μ is the mean of the distribution, σ is the standard deviation, and approximately two thirds of the area under the curve lies between $\mu - \sigma$ and $\mu + \sigma$.

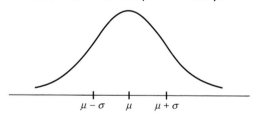

A normal distribution having $\mu = 0$ and $\sigma = 1$ is called a **standard normal distribution**, and random numbers having approximately this distribution can be generated quite easily from a uniform distribution with the following algorithm:

ALGORITHM FOR THE STANDARD NORMAL DISTRIBUTION

* Algorithm to generate random numbers having an approximate   *
* standard normal distribution from a uniform distribution.   *

1. Set SUM equal to 0.
2. Do the following 12 times:
   a. Generate a random number X from a uniform distribution.
   b. Add X to SUM.
3. Calculate Z = SUM − 6.

The numbers Z generated by this algorithm have an approximate standard normal distribution. To generate random numbers Y having a normal distribution with mean μ and standard deviation σ, we simply add the following step to the algorithm:

4. Calculate $Y = \mu + \sigma * Z$.

Implementing this algorithm as a program is left as an exercise.

Exercises

1. Another method for finding an approximate zero of a function is the *bisection method*. If f is a continuous function between $x = a$ and $x = b$—that is, if there is no break in the graph of $y = f(x)$ between these two values—and if $f(a)$ and $f(b)$ are of opposite signs, then f must have at least one zero between $x = a$ and $x = b$. To locate such a zero, or at least an approximation to it, we first bisect the interval $[a, b]$ and determine in which half f changes sign. Repeating this process gives a sequence of smaller and smaller subintervals, each of which contains a zero of the function. The process can be terminated when a small interval, say of length less than 0.0001, is obtained or f has the value 0 at one of the endpoints.

   Define a function to compute $x - \cos x$, and then write a program to find a zero of this function in the interval $[0, \pi/2]$.

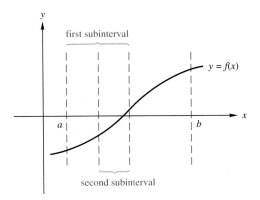

2. The Cawker City Cookie Company can purchase a new microcomputer for \$4,440 or by paying \$141.19 per month for the next 36 months. You are to determine what annual interest rate is being charged in the monthly payment plan.

   The equation that governs this calculation is the *annuity formula*

$$A = P \cdot \left(\frac{(1 + I)^N - 1}{I(1 + I)^N} \right)$$

   where A is the amount borrowed, P is the monthly payment, I is the monthly interest rate (annual rate/12), and N is the number of payments. In this problem, this equation is to be solved for I. Write a program that uses Newton's method or the bisection method (see Exercise 1) to find an approximate solution by finding an approximate zero of the function

$$F(x) = A - P \cdot \left(\frac{(1 + x)^N - 1}{x(1 + x)^N} \right)$$

3. In level flight, the total drag on the Cawker City Cookie Company jet is equal to the sum of parasite drag (D_P) and the drag due to lift (D_L) which are given by

$$D_P = \frac{\sigma f V^2}{391} \quad \text{and} \quad D_L = \frac{1245}{\sigma e} \left(\frac{W}{b} \right)^2 \frac{1}{V^2}$$

where V is velocity (mph), W is weight (15,000 lbs), b is the span (40 ft), e is the wing efficiency rating (0.80), f = parasite drag area (4 ft^2), and σ = (air density at altitude)/(air density at sea level) = 0.533 at 20,000 ft (for standard atmosphere). Write a program that uses Newton's method or the bisection method (see Exercise 1) to find the constant velocity V needed to fly at minimum drag (level flight), which occurs when $D_P = D_L$. (*Hint:* Consider the function $F(V) = D_P(V) - D_L(V)$.)

4. Write a program to implement the Runge–Kutta method for solving differential equations as described in Example 2 of Section 5.2. Run the program using the differential equation given in Example 2.

5. Suppose that an object at a certain temperature T_0 is dropped into a liquid at a lower temperature T_s. If the amount of liquid is quite large and is stirred, we can assume that the object's heat will spread quickly enough through the liquid so that the temperature of the liquid will not change appreciably. We can then assume that the object loses heat at a rate proportional to the difference between its temperature and the temperature of the liquid. Thus, the differential equation that models this problem is

$$T' = k(T - T_s)$$

where $T(t)$ is the temperature of the object at time t, k is the constant of proportionality, and

$$T(0) = T_0$$

is the initial condition. The exact solution of this differential equation can be shown to be

$$T = T_s + (T_0 - T_s)e^{-kt}$$

Write a program that uses the Runge–Kutta method (see Example 2 of Section 5.2) to obtain an approximate solution. Run the program with $T_s = 70$, $T_0 = 300$, and $k = .19$ for $t = 0$ to $t = 20$ with various t increments. Print a table of approximate T values, exact T values, and the differences between them.

Simulation Exercises

6. The tensile strength of a certain metal component has an approximate normal distribution with a mean of 10,000 pounds per square inch and a standard deviation of 100 pounds per square inch. Specifications require that all components have a tensile strength greater than 9800; all others must be scrapped. Write a program that uses the algorithm in Example 3 of Section 5.2 to generate 1000 normally distributed random numbers representing the tensile strength of these components, and determine how many must be rejected.

7. Modify the shield program in Example 3 of Section 5.2 to allow the particle to travel in any direction rather than simply left, right, forward, or backward. Choose a direction (angle) at random, and let the particle travel a fixed (or perhaps random) distance in that direction.

8. Write a program to simulate the random path of a particle in a box. A direction (angle) is chosen at random, and the particle travels a fixed (or random) distance in that direction. This procedure is repeated until the particle either passes out through the top of the box or collides with one of the sides or the bottom and stops. Calculate the average number of times the particle escapes from the box and the average number of jumps needed for it to get out.

Some modifications are as follows: Use a two-dimensional box if a three-dimensional one seems too challenging. Let the particle bounce off the sides or the bottom of the box at the same angle with which it hits rather than stop when it collides with these boundaries.

9. The classic *drunkard's walk problem:* Over an eight-block line, the home of an intoxicated chap is at block eight, and a pub is at block one. Our poor friend starts at block n, $1 < n < 8$ and wanders at random, one block at a time, either toward or away from home. At any intersection, he moves toward the pub with a certain probability, say 2/3, and toward home with a certain probability, say 1/3. Having gotten either home or to the pub, he remains there. Write a program to simulate 500 trips in which he starts at block two, another 500 in which he starts at block three, and so forth up to block seven. For each starting point, calculate and print the percentage of the time he ends up at home and the average number of blocks he walked on each trip.

10. The famous *Buffon Needle problem* is as follows: A board is ruled with equidistant parallel lines, and a needle whose length is equal to the distance between these lines is dropped at random on the board. What is the probability that it crosses one of these lines? The answer to this problem is $2/\pi$. Write a program to simulate this experiment and obtain an estimate for π.

11. An unusual method for approximating the area under a curve is the *Monte Carlo technique.* As illustrated in the following figure, consider a rectangle that has base $[a, b]$ and height m, where $m \geq f(x)$ for all x in $[a, b]$. Imagine throwing q darts at rectangle $ABCD$ and counting the total number p that hit the shaded region. For a large number of throws, we would expect

$$\frac{p}{q} \sim \frac{\text{area of shaded region}}{\text{area of rectangle } ABCD}$$

Write a program to calculate areas using this Monte Carlo method. To simulate throwing the darts, generate two random numbers, X from $[a, b]$ and Y from $[0, m]$, and consider point (X, Y) as being where the dart hits.

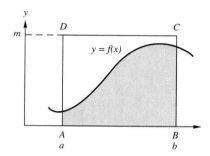

5.3 Subroutine Subprograms

Subroutine subprograms, like function subprograms, are program units designed to perform a particular task. They differ from function subprograms, however, in the following respects:

1. Functions are designed to return a single value to the program unit that references them. Subroutines often return more than one value, or they may return no value at all but simply perform some task such as displaying a list of instructions to the user.
2. Functions return values via function names; subroutines return values via arguments.
3. A function is referenced by using its name in an expression, whereas a subroutine is referenced by a CALL statement.

The syntax of subroutine subprograms is similar to that of function subprograms and thus to that of FORTRAN (main) programs:

    subroutine heading
    specification part
    execution part

The **subroutine heading** is a **SUBROUTINE** statement of the form

    SUBROUTINE *name (formal-argument-list)*

Here *name* represents the name given to the subroutine and may be any legal FORTRAN name, but no type is associated with the name of a subroutine;

formal-argument-list has the same form as for function subprograms. These formal or dummy arguments are used to transfer values to and from the subroutine. If there are no formal arguments, the parentheses in the SUBROUTINE statement may be omitted.

A subroutine is referenced by a **CALL statement** of the form

CALL *name(actual-argument-list)*

where *name* is the name of the subroutine being called, and *actual-argument-list* contains the variables, constants, or expressions that are the actual arguments. The number of actual arguments must equal the number of formal arguments, and each actual argument must agree in type with the corresponding formal argument. If there are no actual arguments, the parentheses in the subroutine reference may be omitted.

As a simple illustration, suppose we wish to develop a subroutine that accepts from the main program an angular measurement in degrees, minutes, and seconds and displays it as an equivalent number of degrees. For example, the value $100° \, 30' \, 36''$ is to be displayed as

```
100 DEGREES, 30 MINUTES, 36 SECONDS
IS EQUIVALENT TO
100.510 DEGREES
```

This subroutine will have three formal arguments, all of type INTEGER, one representing the number of degrees, the second the number of minutes, and the third the number of seconds. Thus, an appropriate heading for this subroutine is

```
SUBROUTINE PRNDEG(DEG, MIN, SEC)
```

where DEG, MIN, and SEC must be declared of type INTEGER in the specification part of this subroutine. The complete subroutine subprogram is

```
**PRNDEG*************************************************
* Subroutine to display a measurement of DEG degrees,  *
* MIN minutes and SEC seconds as the equivalent        *
* degree measure                                       *
********************************************************

      SUBROUTINE PRNDEG(DEG, MIN, SEC)

      INTEGER DEG, MIN, SEC

      PRINT *, DEG, ' DEGREES', MIN, ' MINUTES',
     +          SEC, ' SECONDS'
      PRINT *, 'IS EQUIVALENT TO '
      PRINT *, DEG + REAL(MIN)/60.0 + REAL(SEC)/3600.0,
     +          ' DEGREES'

      END
```

This subprogram is referenced in the program in Figure 5.10 by the CALL statement

```
CALL PRNDEG(DEGS, MINUTS, SECONS)
```

This statement causes the values of the actual arguments DEGS, MINUTS, and SECONS to be passed to the formal parameters DEG, MIN, and SEC, respectively, and initiates execution of the subroutine. When the end of the subroutine is reached, execution resumes with the statement following this CALL statement in the main program.

```
      PROGRAM ANGLE1
***********************************************************************
* Program demonstrating the use of a subroutine subprogram PRNDEG to  *
* display an angle in degrees.  Variables used are:                   *
*      DEGS   : degrees in the angle measurement                      *
*      MINUTS : minutes in the angle measurement                      *
*      SECONS : seconds in the angle measurement                      *
*      RESPON : user response to more-data question                   *
***********************************************************************

      INTEGER DEGS, MINUTS, SECONS, RESPON

* Read and convert angles until user signals no more data

10    CONTINUE
         PRINT *, 'ENTER DEGREES, MINUTES, AND SECONDS'
         READ *, DEGS, MINUTS, SECONS
         CALL PRNDEG(DEGS, MINUTS, SECONS)
         PRINT *
         PRINT *, 'MORE ANGLES (0 = NO, 1 = YES)'
         READ *, RESPON
      IF (RESPON .NE. 0) GO TO 10
      END


**PRNDEG*********************************************
* Subroutine to display a measurement of DEG degrees, *
* MIN minutes, and SEC seconds as the equivalent      *
* degree measure                                      *
*****************************************************

      SUBROUTINE PRNDEG(DEG, MIN, SEC)

      INTEGER DEG, MIN, SEC

      PRINT *, DEG, ' DEGREES', MIN, ' MINUTES',
     +         SEC, ' SECONDS'
      PRINT *, 'IS EQUIVALENT TO '
      PRINT *, DEG + REAL(MIN)/60.0 + REAL(SEC)/3600.0,
     +            ' DEGREES'
      END
```

Figure 5.10

Figure 5.10   (continued)

Sample run:

```
ENTER DEGREES, MINUTES, AND SECONDS
100, 30, 36
  100 DEGREES   30 MINUTES   36 SECONDS
IS EQUIVALENT TO
   100.510 DEGREES

MORE ANGLES (0 = NO, 1 = YES)
1
ENTER DEGREES, MINUTES, AND SECONDS
360, 0, 0
  360 DEGREES   0 MINUTES   0 SECONDS
IS EQUIVALENT TO
    360.000 DEGREES

MORE ANGLES (0 = NO, 1 = YES)
1
ENTER DEGREES, MINUTES, AND SECONDS
1, 1, 1
  1 DEGREES   1 MINUTES   1 SECONDS
IS EQUIVALENT TO
    1.01694 DEGREES

MORE ANGLES (0 = NO, 1 = YES)
0
```

The specification part of subroutine PRNDEG contains only type statements that specify the types of the formal parameters. In general, however, a subroutine subprogram's specification part has the same structure as the specification part of a FORTRAN program and thus may include other declarations. For example, suppose we wish to develop a subroutine DEGPRN to accept the measure of an angle in either radians or degrees and then display it in a degrees–minutes–seconds format. This subroutine will have two formal arguments, one real argument that is the measure of the angle and the other a logical argument that indicates whether or not radian measure has been used. An appropriate subroutine heading might thus be

```
SUBROUTINE DEGPRN(ANGLE, RADIAN)
```

where ANGLE will be declared to be of type REAL and RADIAN of type LOGICAL in the subroutine's specification part. If ANGLE is measured in radians, it will be necessary to find its degree equivalent by multiplying ANGLE by $180/\pi$. Thus we define a real parameter PI within the subroutine and declare a real local variable DANGLE to store this angle. The integer variables DEGS, MINUTS, and SECONS are also used to store degrees, minutes, and seconds, respectively. The complete subprogram is

```
**DEGPRN***************************************************
* Subroutine to display an angular measurement ANGLE in   *
* either radians or degrees in a degrees-minutes-seconds  *
* format.  RADIAN is true or false according to whether   *
* ANGLE is given in radians or degrees.  Local            *
* identifiers used are:                                   *
*     PI     : the constant pi                            *
*     DANGLE : the degree equivalent of ANGLE             *
*     DEGS   : the number of degrees                      *
*     MINUTS : the number of minutes                      *
*     SECONS : the number of seconds                      *
***********************************************************

      SUBROUTINE DEGPRN(ANGLE, RADIAN)

      REAL ANGLE, PI, DANGLE
      LOGICAL RADIAN
      INTEGER DEGS, MINUTS, SECONS
      PARAMETER (PI = 3.14159)

* First get the degree equivalent of the angle

      IF (RADIAN) THEN
          PRINT *, ANGLE, ' RADIANS'
          DANGLE = (180.0 / PI) * ANGLE
      ELSE
          PRINT *, ANGLE, ' DEGREES'
          DANGLE = ANGLE
      END IF
      PRINT *, 'IS EQUIVALENT TO'

* Now determine the number of degrees, minutes, and seconds

      DEGS = INT(DANGLE)
      DANGLE = DANGLE - REAL(DEGS)
      DEGS = MOD(DEGS, 360)
      DANGLE = 60.0 * DANGLE
      MINUTS = INT(DANGLE)
      DANGLE = DANGLE - REAL(MINUTS)
      SECONS = INT(DANGLE * 60.0)
      PRINT *, DEGS, ' DEGREES,', MINUTS, ' MINUTES,',
     +            SECONS, ' SECONDS'

      END
```

This program in Figure 5.11 reads values for ANGLE and RADIAN and then passes these values to the formal arguments having the same names in subroutine DEGPRN by means of the CALL statement

```
CALL DEGPRN(ANGLE, RADIAN)
```

Note that although in the preceding example we used different names for the actual arguments and the corresponding formal arguments, this is not necessary, as this example illustrates.

```
      PROGRAM ANGLE2
*****************************************************************
* Program demonstrating the use of a subroutine subprogram DEGPRN to  *
* display an angle measured in radians or degrees in degrees-minutes- *
* seconds format.  Variables used are:                                *
*     ANGLE  : angle measurement                                      *
*     RADIAN : true if radian measure, else false                     *
*     RESPON : user response to more-data question                    *
*****************************************************************

      REAL ANGLE
      LOGICAL RADIAN
      INTEGER RESPON

* Read and convert angles until user signals no more data

10    CONTINUE
          PRINT *, 'ENTER ANGLE AND T IF IN RADIANS, F IF NOT'
          READ *, ANGLE, RADIAN
          CALL DEGPRN(ANGLE, RADIAN)
          PRINT *
          PRINT *, 'MORE ANGLES (0 = NO, 1 = YES)'
          READ *, RESPON
      IF (RESPON .NE. 0) GO TO 10
      END


**DEGPRN******************************************************
* Subroutine to display an angular measurement ANGLE in       *
* either radians or degrees in a degrees-minutes-seconds      *
* format.  RADIAN is true or false according to whether       *
* ANGLE is given in radians or degrees.  Local                *
* identifiers used are:                                       *
*     PI     : the constant pi                                *
*     DANGLE : the degree equivalent of ANGLE                 *
*     DEGS   : the number of degrees                          *
*     MINUTS : the number of minutes                          *
*     SECONS : the number of seconds                          *
*************************************************************

      SUBROUTINE DEGPRN(ANGLE, RADIAN)

      REAL ANGLE, PI, DANGLE
      LOGICAL RADIAN
      INTEGER DEGS, MINUTS, SECONS
      PARAMETER (PI = 3.14159)

* First get the degree equivalent of the angle

      IF (RADIAN) THEN
          PRINT *, ANGLE, ' RADIANS'
          DANGLE = (180.0 / PI) * ANGLE
      ELSE
          PRINT *, ANGLE, ' DEGREES'
          DANGLE = ANGLE
      END IF
      PRINT *, 'IS EQUIVALENT TO'
```

Figure 5.11

Figure 5.11   (continued)

```
* Now determine the number of degrees, minutes, and seconds

      DEGS = INT(DANGLE)
      DANGLE = DANGLE - REAL(DEGS)
      DEGS = MOD(DEGS, 360)
      DANGLE = 60.0 * DANGLE
      MINUTS = INT(DANGLE)
      DANGLE = DANGLE - REAL(MINUTS)
      SECONS = INT(DANGLE * 60.0)
      PRINT *, DEGS, ' DEGREES,', MINUTS, ' MINUTES,',
     +          SECONS, ' SECONDS'

      END
```

Sample run:

```
ENTER ANGLE AND T IF IN RADIANS, F IF NOT
3.14159 T
     3.14159 RADIANS
IS EQUIVALENT TO
  180 DEGREES,   0 MINUTES,   0 SECONDS

MORE ANGLES (0 = NO, 1 = YES)
1
ENTER ANGLE AND T IF IN RADIANS, F IF NOT
555.55 F
    555.550 DEGREES
IS EQUIVALENT TO
  195 DEGREES,   32 MINUTES,   59 SECONDS

MORE ANGLES (0 = NO, 1 = YES)
Y
ENTER ANGLE AND T IF IN RADIANS, F IF NOT
1 T
     1.00000 RADIANS
IS EQUIVALENT TO
   57 DEGREES,   17 MINUTES,   44 SECONDS

MORE ANGLES (0 = NO, 1 = YES)
0
```

In the preceding examples, the subroutine subprograms do not calculate and return values to the main program; they only display the information passed to them. As an illustration of a subroutine that does return values, consider the problem of converting the polar coordinates (r, θ) of a point P to rectangular coordinates (x, y). The first polar coordinate r is the distance from the origin to P, and the second polar coordinate θ is the angle from the positive x axis to the ray joining the origin with P.

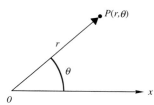

The formulas that relate the polar coordinates to the rectangular coordinates for a point are

$$x = r \cos \theta$$

$$y = r \sin \theta$$

Because the subprogram that performs this conversion must return *two* values, it is natural to use a subroutine subprogram like the following to accomplish this:

```
**CONVER********************************************
* Subroutine to convert polar coordinates (R,THETA) *
* to rectangular coordinates (X, Y)                 *
***************************************************

      SUBROUTINE CONVER(R, THETA, X, Y)

      REAL R, THETA, X, Y

      X = R * COS(THETA)
      Y = R * SIN(THETA)
      END
```

This subroutine can be referenced by the CALL statement

```
CALL CONVER(RCOORD, TCOORD, XCOORD, YCOORD)
```

where RCOORD, TCOORD, XCOORD, and YCOORD are real variables. When this CALL statement is executed, the actual arguments RCOORD, TCOORD, XCOORD, and YCOORD are associated with the formal arguments R, THETA, X, and Y, respectively, so that the corresponding arguments have the same values:

Actual Parameters				Formal Parameters
RCOORD	$\longleftrightarrow$	1.000000	$\longleftrightarrow$	R
TCOORD	$\longleftrightarrow$	1.570000	$\longleftrightarrow$	THETA
XCOORD	$\longleftrightarrow$	????????	$\longleftrightarrow$	X
YCOORD	$\longleftrightarrow$	????????	$\longleftrightarrow$	Y

These values are used to calculate the rectangular coordinates X and Y, and these values are then the values of the corresponding actual arguments XCOORD and YCOORD.

Actual Parameters				Formal Parameters
RCOORD	$\longleftrightarrow$	1.000000	$\longleftrightarrow$	R
TCOORD	$\longleftrightarrow$	1.570000	$\longleftrightarrow$	THETA
XCOORD	$\longleftrightarrow$	7.96274E$-$04	$\longleftrightarrow$	X
YCOORD	$\longleftrightarrow$	1.000000	$\longleftrightarrow$	Y

The program in Figure 5.12 reads values for RCOORD and TCOORD, calls the subroutine CONVER to calculate the corresponding rectangular coordinates, and displays these coordinates.

```
      PROGRAM POLAR
***********************************************************************
* This program accepts the polar coordinates of a point & displays   *
* the corresponding rectangular coordinates.  The subroutine CONVER is *
* used to effect the conversion.  Variables used are:                *
*      RCOORD, TCOORD : polar coordinates of a point                 *
*      XCOORD, YCOORD : rectangular coordinates of a point           *
*      RESPON : user response to more-data question                  *
***********************************************************************

      REAL RCOORD, TCOORD, XCOORD, YCOORD
      INTEGER RESPON

* Read and convert coordinates until user signals no more data

10    CONTINUE
         PRINT *, 'ENTER POLAR COORDINATES (IN RADIANS)'
         READ *, RCOORD, TCOORD
         CALL CONVER(RCOORD, TCOORD, XCOORD, YCOORD)
         PRINT *, 'RECTANGULAR COORDINATES:'
         PRINT *, XCOORD, YCOORD
         PRINT *
         PRINT *, 'MORE POINTS TO CONVERT (0 = NO, 1 = YES)?'
         READ *, RESPON
      IF (RESPON .NE. 0) GO TO 10
      END


**CONVER*************************************************************
* Subroutine to convert polar coordinates (R,THETA) to rectangular  *
* coordinates (X,Y).                                                 *
********************************************************************

      SUBROUTINE CONVER(R, THETA, X, Y)

      REAL R, THETA, X, Y

      X = R * COS(THETA)
      Y = R * SIN(THETA)
      END
```

Sample run:

```
ENTER POLAR COORDINATES (IN RADIANS)
1.0, 0
RECTANGULAR COORDINATES:
    1.00000  0.

MORE POINTS TO CONVERT (0 = NO, 1 = YES)?
1
```

Figure 5.12

Figure 5.12 (continued)

```
ENTER POLAR COORDINATES (IN RADIANS)
0, 1.0
RECTANGULAR COORDINATES:
   0.  0.

MORE POINTS TO CONVERT (0 = NO, 1 = YES)?
1
ENTER POLAR COORDINATES (IN RADIANS)
1.0, 1.57
RECTANGULAR COORDINATES:
     7.96274E-04   1.000000

MORE POINTS TO CONVERT (0 = NO, 1 = YES)?
1
ENTER POLAR COORDINATES (IN RADIANS)
4.0, 3.14159
RECTANGULAR COORDINATES:
   -4.00000    1.01407E-05

MORE POINTS TO CONVERT (0 = NO, 1 = YES)?
0
```

The linkage of actual arguments with formal arguments is accomplished by associating corresponding arguments with the same memory locations. To illustrate, in the preceding program, the type statement

```
REAL RCOORD, TCOORD, XCOORD, YCOORD
```

associates memory locations with the four variables RCOORD, TCOORD, XCOORD, and YCOORD.

                                    Memory
                                    Locations
         RCOORD ◄──► [   ]

         TCOORD ◄──► [   ]

         XCOORD ◄──► [   ]

         YCOORD ◄──► [   ]

When the READ statement is executed, values are stored in the memory locations associated with RCOORD and TCOORD; the variables XCOORD and YCOORD are undefined, as indicated by the question mark in the following diagram:

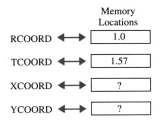

                                    Memory
                                    Locations
         RCOORD ◄──► [1.0   ]

         TCOORD ◄──► [1.57   ]

         XCOORD ◄──► [?   ]

         YCOORD ◄──► [?   ]

When the CALL statement

```
CALL CONVER(RCOORD, TCOORD, XCOORD, YCOORD)
```

is executed, the formal parameters R, THETA, X, and Y of subroutine CON-VER are associated with the existing memory locations of the corresponding actual arguments RCOORD, TCOORD, XCOORD, and YCOORD:

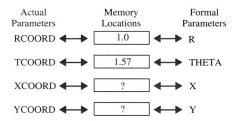

When the subroutine CONVER is executed, values are calculated for X and Y, and because XCOORD and YCOORD are associated with the same memory locations as X and Y, these values are also the values of X and Y:

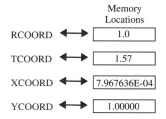

When execution of the subroutine is completed, the association of memory locations with the formal arguments R, THETA, X, and Y is terminated, and these formal parameters become undefined. The values of the corresponding actual parameters RCOORD, TCOORD, XCOORD, and YCOORD are retained, of course, in the memory locations associated with them by the type statement when the program was compiled.

	Memory Locations
RCOORD ⟷	1.0
TCOORD ⟷	1.57
XCOORD ⟷	7.967636E-04
YCOORD ⟷	1.00000

    This method of linking together the actual and formal arguments so that information can be transmitted between them is accomplished by making available to the subprogram the *addresses* of the memory locations in which the values of the actual arguments are stored. It is thus appropriately named **call by address** (or **call by reference**). If both the actual argument and the formal argument are variables, then as we have seen, this call-by-address technique causes both of these variables to refer to the same memory location. Because *corresponding pairs of actual and formal arguments are associated with the same memory locations,* changing the value of the formal argument in the subprogram also changes the value of the corresponding actual argument.

If the actual argument in a subroutine call is an expression, its value is placed in a temporary memory location by the processor, and the address of this location is made available to the subprogram. The values of the variables and constants that comprise the expression are not changed by any processing that takes place in the subprogram, even though the value of the formal argument corresponding to the expression may change. *Enclosing an actual argument that is a variable in parentheses protects it from being modified because it is then treated as an expression and its value is not changed by a subprogram.*

The association of arguments for function subprograms is the same as for subroutine subprograms. Ordinarily, however, we do not use arguments of a function to return values to another program unit but, rather, use the function name. Nevertheless, *it is important to remember that changing the values of formal arguments within a subprogram, whether it is a subroutine or a function, does, in fact, change the values of the corresponding actual arguments that are variables.*

Exercises

1. Write a subroutine subprogram that displays the name of a month whose number is passed to it.

2. Write a subroutine subprogram SWITCH that interchanges the values of two integer variables. For example, if A has the value 3 and B has the value 4, then the statement CALL SWITCH(A, B) causes A to have the value 4 and B the value 3.

3. Write a program that reads the diameters and heights of several right circular cylinders and displays the circumference, total surface area (including the ends), and the volume of each. The circumference should be calculated by a statement function, the surface area by a function subprogram, and the volume in a subroutine subprogram.

4. Consider a simply supported beam to which a single concentrated load is applied:

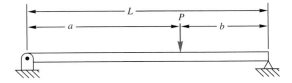

For $a \geq b$, the maximum deflection is given by

$$\text{MAX} = \frac{-Pb(L^2 - b^2)^{3/2}}{9\sqrt{3}\ EIL}$$

the deflection at the load by

$$\text{LDEF} = \frac{-Pa^2b^2}{3EIL}$$

and the deflection at the center of the beam by

$$\text{CEN} = \frac{-Pb(3^2 - 4b^2)}{48EI}$$

where P is the load, E is the modulus of elasticity, and I is the moment of inertia. For $a \leq b$, simply replace b with a and a with b in the preceding equations.

    Write a program that produces a table of values for MAX, LDEF, and CEN as the load position is moved along the beam in 6-in increments. It should use function or subroutine subprograms to calculate these values. Run your program with the following values: $L = 360$ inches, $P = 24{,}000$ pounds, $E = 30 \times 10^6$ psi, and $I = 795.5$ in^4.

5. The *greatest common divisor* GCD(A, B) of two integers A and B, not both of which are zero, can be calculated by the Euclidean algorithm described in Exercise 14 of Section 5.1. The *least common multiple* of A and B, LCM(A, B), is the smallest nonnegative integer that is a multiple of both A and B and can be calculated using

$$\text{LCM(A, B)} = \frac{|A * B|}{\text{GCD(A, B)}}$$

Write a program that reads two integers, calls a subroutine that calculates and returns their greatest common divisor and least common multiple, and displays these two values.

6. Write a program that reads a positive integer and then calls a subprogram that displays its prime factorization, that is, a subprogram that expresses a positive integer as a product of primes or indicates that it is a prime (see Exercise 15 of Section 5.1 for the definition of a prime number).

7. Write a program that reads two positive integers n and b and calls a subprogram to calculate and display the base-b representation of n. Assume that b is not greater than 10 (see Exercise 12 of Chapter 1 for one method of converting from base 10 to another base).

8. Write a program that reads a positive integer *n* and then calls a subprogram to display the hexadecimal (base-16) representation of *n*. The symbols A, B, C, D, E, and F should be used for 10, 11, 12, 13, 14, and 15, respectively (see Section 1.3 and the preceding exercise).

9. One simple method of calculating depreciation is the *straight-line* method. If the value of the asset being depreciated is AMOUNT dollars and is to be depreciated over NYEARS years, then AMOUNT/ NYEARS dollars is depreciated in each year. Write a program that reads the current year and values for AMOUNT and NYEARS, calls a subprogram to calculate the annual depreciation, and displays this value.

10. Another method of calculating depreciation is the *sum-of-the-years-digits* method. To illustrate, suppose that $30,000 is to be depreciated over a five-year period. We first calculate the sum $1 + 2 + 3 + 4 + 5 = 15$. Then 5/15 of $30,000 ($10,000) is depreciated the first year, 4/15 of $30,000 ($8,000) is depreciated the second year, 3/15 the third year, and so on. Write a program that reads the current year, an amount to be depreciated, and the number of years over which it is to be depreciated. It should then call a subroutine that displays a depreciation table that shows each year number and the amount to be depreciated for that year, beginning with the current year and continuing for the specified number of years.

    A possible addition to your program: To find how much is saved in taxes, assume a fixed tax rate over these years, and assume that the amounts saved in taxes by claiming the depreciation as a deduction are invested and earn interest at some fixed annual rate.

11. Another method of calculating depreciation is the *double-declining balance* method. For an asset with value AMOUNT dollars that is to be depreciated over NYEARS years, 2/NYEARS times the undepreciated balance is depreciated annually. Because in each year only a fraction of the remaining balance is depreciated, the entire amount would never be depreciated. Consequently, it is permissible to switch to the straight-line method (Exercise 9) at any time. Write a program that reads values for AMOUNT, NYEARS, and the year in which to switch to the straight-line method and that calls a subroutine to print a table showing the year number and the amount to be depreciated.

    A possible addition to your program: Calculate the tax savings as described in the previous exercise.

12. Proceed as in Exercise 11, but print one table giving the amount to be depreciated each year, assuming that we switch in year 1 (use the straight-line method for all NYEARS years), and another table giving

the amount to be depreciated each year, assuming that we switch in year 2, and so on.

13. Write a subroutine that calculates the amount of city income tax and the amount of federal income tax to be withheld from an employee's pay for one pay period. Assume that the city income tax withheld is computed by taking 1.15 percent of gross pay on the first $15,000 earned per year and that the federal income tax withheld is computed by taking the gross pay less $15 for each dependent claimed and multiplying it by 20 percent.

Use this subroutine in a program that for each of several employees reads his or her employee number, number of dependents, hourly pay rate, city income tax withheld to date, federal tax withheld to date, and hours worked for this pay period and that calculates and prints the employee number, gross pay and net pay for this pay period, the amount of city income tax and the amount of federal income tax withheld for this pay period, and the total amounts withheld through this pay period.

5.4 Examples of Modular Programming and Top-Down Design: Beam Deflection and Checking Academic Standing

In the introduction to this chapter, we claimed that one of the advantages of subprograms is that they enable a programmer to develop programs in a **modular** fashion. This means that the major tasks to be performed by the program can be identified and that individual subprograms for these tasks can then be designed and tested. Programs written in this manner are not only easier to develop and test and easier to understand but are also easier to modify, since individual modules can be added, deleted, or altered. In this section we illustrate this technique of modular programming by developing two programs. The first program is a rather simple **menu-driven** beam deflection calculator, and the second is a more complex program for checking academic standing.

EXAMPLE 1: Beam Deflection. The analysis of beams is an important part of the structural analysis carried out before the construction of a building begins. One frequently used type of beam is a *cantilever beam*, which has one end fixed and the other end free. The deflection at the free end of the beam depends on the beam's loading conditions. Three of the many possible loading cases are shown in the following diagrams. In these diagrams, W is the total load, δ is the deflection caused by the load, x is the distance from the free end of the beam, l is the length of the beam, a and b are the lengths as shown, and w is the unit load in the uniform loading cases.

1. end load, W

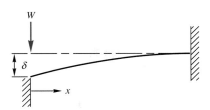

2. intermediate load, W

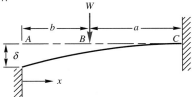

3. uniform load, $W = wl$

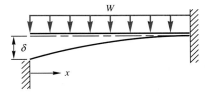

We assume that all forces are coplanar, that the beam is in static equilibrium, and that the mass of the beam may be neglected. With these assumptions, the following equations can be used to calculate the deflections for the three load cases:

1. $\delta = [-W / (6EI)][x^3 - 3l^2x + 2l^3]$
2. $\delta = [-W / (6EI)][-a^3 + 3a^2l - 3a^2x]$ from A to B
   $\delta = [-W / (6EI)][(x - b)^3 - 3a^2(x - b) + 2a^3]$ from B to C
3. $\delta = [-W / (24EIl)][x^4 - 4l^3x + 3l^4]$

Here E is the modulus of elasticity, which depends on the material of which the beam is made, and I is the moment of inertia, which depends on the cross section of the beam. In this example we consider an I beam made of steel where $I = 4.15 \times 10^{-8}$ and $E = 2.05 \times 10^{11}$.

The fact that the calculation of the deflection δ is different in the three cases suggests that separate subroutines be used to do the calculations in each of the cases. The flowcharts in Figure 5.13 show the structures of these three subroutines.

The main program will read the beam information, including the modulus of elasticity, the moment of inertia, and the length of the beam, and also the number of points along the beam along which the deflection is to be calculated. The user will then select an option from a menu, and the appropriate subroutine will be called to calculate the deflection in this case at the number of equally

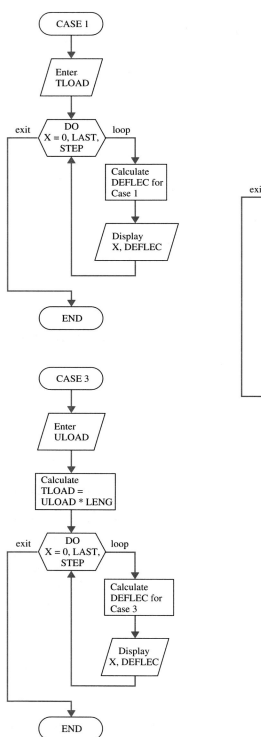

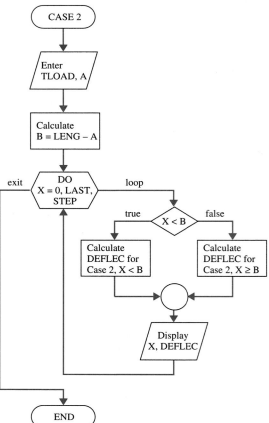

Figure 5.13

spaced points specified by the user. The execution part of the main program will thus have the form

```
*  Get beam information

         PRINT *, 'ENTER MODULUS OF ELASTICITY, MOMENT OF INERTIA'
      +            ' LENGTH OF THE BEAM'
         PRINT *,' AND NUMBER OF POINTS TO USE',
         READ *, ELAST, INERT, LENG, NUMPTS
         DELTAX = LENG / REAL(NUMPTS)

*  Repeat the following until user selects option 0 to stop

10       CONTINUE
            PRINT *,
            PRINT *, 'SELECT ONE OF THE FOLLOWING OPTIONS'
            PRINT *, '0 : STOP'
            PRINT *, '1 : END LOAD'
            PRINT *, '2 : INTERMEDIATE LOAD'
            PRINT *, '3 : UNIFORM LOAD'
            READ *, OPTION
            IF (OPTION .EQ. 0) THEN
                PRINT *, 'DONE PROCESSING FOR THIS BEAM'
            ELSE IF (OPTION .EQ 1) THEN
                CALL CASE1(ELAST, INERT, LENG, STEP, NUMPTS)
            ELSE IF (OPTION .EQ 2) THEN
                CALL CASE2(ELAST, INERT, LENG, STEP, NUMPTS)
            ELSE IF (OPTION .EQ 3) THEN
                CALL CASE3(ELAST, INERT, LENG, STEP, NUMPTS)
            ELSE
                PRINT *, 'NOT A VALID OPTION'
            END IF
         IF (OPTION .NE. 0) GO TO 10
         END
```

Figure 5.14 shows the complete program, consisting of a main program and three subroutine subprograms, CASE1, CASE2, and CASE3. These subroutines implement the algorithms shown in flowchart form in Figure 5.13. Although the final program is given here, it could well be developed in a piecewise manner by writing and testing only some of the subroutines before writing the others. For example, we might develop and test subroutine CASE1 before working on the other two subroutines. The undeveloped subroutines could simply have empty execution parts that consist only of the END statement. Usually, however, they are **program stubs** that at least signal execution of these subprograms, for example,

```
PRINT *, 'EXECUTING CASE2'
END
```

In some cases they might also produce temporary printouts to assist in checking other subprograms. Example 2 in this section illustrates the use of such program stubs.

```
      PROGRAM BEAM
*********************************************************************
* This program calculates deflections in a cantilevered beam       *
* under a given load. Three different loading conditions are       *
* analyzed.                                                        *
*                                                                  *
*   Case #1 : a single point load at the free end of the beam      *
*   Case #2 : a single point load at an interior point             *
*   Case #3 : load uniformly distributed along the beam            *
*                                                                  *
*      ELAST  : modulus of elasticity                              *
*      INERT  : moment of inertia                                  *
*      LENG   : length of the beam                                 *
*      NUMPTS : number of divisions at which deflections are found *
*      DELTAX : distance between points                            *
*      OPTION : option selected by the user                        *
*********************************************************************

      INTEGER NUMPTS, OPTION
      REAL ELAST, INERT, LENG, DELTAX

* Get beam information

      PRINT *, 'ENTER MODULUS OF ELASTICITY, MOMENT OF INTERTIA,',
     +         ' LENGTH OF THE BEAM'
      PRINT *, 'AND NUMBER OF POINTS TO USE:'
      READ *, ELAST, INERT, LENG, NUMPTS
      DELTAX = LENG / REAL(NUMPTS)

* Repeat the following until user selects option 0 to stop

10    CONTINUE
         PRINT *
         PRINT *, 'SELECT ONE OF THE FOLLOWING OPTIONS'
         PRINT *, '0 : STOP'
         PRINT *, '1 : END LOAD'
         PRINT *, '2 : INTERMEDIATE LOAD'
         PRINT *, '3 : UNIFORM LOAD'
         READ *, OPTION
         IF (OPTION .EQ. 0) THEN
             PRINT *, 'DONE PROCESSING FOR THIS BEAM'
         ELSE IF (OPTION .EQ. 1) THEN
             CALL CASE1(ELAST, INERT, LENG, DELTAX, NUMPTS)
         ELSE IF (OPTION .EQ. 2) THEN
             CALL CASE2(ELAST, INERT, LENG, DELTAX, NUMPTS)
         ELSE IF (OPTION .EQ. 3) THEN
             CALL CASE3(ELAST, INERT, LENG, DELTAX, NUMPTS)
         ELSE
             PRINT *, 'NOT A VALID OPTION'
         END IF
      IF (OPTION .NE. 0) GO TO 10
      END
```

Figure 5.14

Figure 5.14 (continued)

```
**CASE1************************************************************
*       TLOAD   : total load                                     *
*       I       : control variable used in DO loop               *
*       X       : distance from the free end of the beam         *
*       DEFLEC  : deflection at distance X                        *
*       TEMP    : temporary variable used in calculation of DEFLEC *
******************************************************************

        SUBROUTINE CASE1(ELAST, INERT, LENG, DELTAX, NUMPTS)

        REAL ELAST, INERT, LENG, DELTAX, TLOAD, X, DEFLEC, TEMP
        INTEGER NUMPTS, I

        PRINT *, 'ENTER TOTAL LOAD:'
        READ *, TLOAD
        X = 0.0
        DO 10 I = 1, NUMPTS
            TEMP = X**3 - 3.0 * LENG**2 * X + 2.0 * LENG**3
            DEFLEC = (-TLOAD / (6.0 * ELAST * INERT)) * TEMP
            PRINT *, 'AT DISTANCE', X, ' DEFLECTION = ', DEFLEC
            X = X + DELTAX
10      CONTINUE
        END


**CASE2************************************************************
*       TLOAD   : total load                                     *
*       A,B     : distances along the beam                        *
*       I       : control variable used in DO loop               *
*       X       : distance from the free end of the beam         *
*       DEFLEC  : deflection at distance X                        *
*       TEMP    : temporary variable used in calculation of DEFLEC *
******************************************************************

        SUBROUTINE CASE2(ELAST, INERT, LENG, DELTAX, NUMPTS)

        REAL ELAST, INERT, DELTAX, TLOAD, A, B, X, DEFLEC, TEMP
        INTEGER NUMPTS, I

        PRINT *, 'ENTER TOTAL LOAD AND DISTANCE A:'
        READ *, TLOAD, A
        B = LENG - A
        X = 0.0
        DO 10 I = 1, NUMPTS
            IF (X .LT. B) THEN
                TEMP = -A**3 + 3.0 * A**2 * LENG - 3.0 * A**2 * X
            ELSE
                TEMP = (X - B)**3 - 3.0 * A**2 * (X - B) + 2.0 * A**3
            END IF
            DEFLEC = (-TLOAD / (6.0 * ELAST * INERT)) * TEMP
            PRINT *, 'AT DISTANCE', X, ' DEFLECTION = ', DEFLEC
            X = X + DELTAX
10      CONTINUE
        END
```

Figure 5.14 (continued)

```
**CASE3********************************************************
*      ULOAD  : unit load when uniformly distributed          *
*      TLOAD  : total load                                    *
*      I      : control variable used in DO loop              *
*      X      : distance from the free end of the beam        *
*      DEFLEC : deflection at distance X                      *
*      TEMP   : temporary variable used in calculation of DEFLEC *
**************************************************************

       SUBROUTINE CASE3(ELAST, INERT, LENG, DELTAX, NUMPTS)

       REAL ELAST, INERT, DELTAX, ULOAD, TLOAD, X, TEMP
       INTEGER NUMPTS, I

       PRINT *, 'ENTER UNIT LOAD:'
       READ *, ULOAD
       TLOAD = ULOAD * LENG
       X = 0.0
       DO 10 I = 1, NUMPTS
           TEMP = X**4 - 4.0 * LENG**3 * X + 3.0 * LENG**4
           DEFLEC = (-TLOAD / (24.0 * ELAST * INERT * LENG)) * TEMP
           PRINT *, 'AT DISTANCE', X, ' DEFLECTION = ', DEFLEC
           X = X + DELTAX
10     CONTINUE
       END
```

Sample run:

```
ENTER MODULUS OF ELASTICITY, MOMENT OF INTERTIA, LENGTH OF THE BEAM
AND NUMBER OF POINTS TO USE:
2.05E11 4.15E-8 1.0 10

SELECT ONE OF THE FOLLOWING OPTIONS
0 : STOP
1 : END LOAD
2 : INTERMEDIATE LOAD
3 : UNIFORM LOAD
1
ENTER TOTAL LOAD:
125.0
AT DISTANCE  0. DEFLECTION =     -4.89764E-03
AT DISTANCE  0.100000 DEFLECTION =    -4.16544E-03
AT DISTANCE  0.200000 DEFLECTION =    -3.44794E-03
AT DISTANCE  0.300000 DEFLECTION =    -2.75982E-03
AT DISTANCE  0.400000 DEFLECTION =    -2.11578E-03
AT DISTANCE  0.500000 DEFLECTION =    -1.53051E-03
AT DISTANCE  0.600000 DEFLECTION =    -1.01871E-03
AT DISTANCE  0.700000 DEFLECTION =    -5.95063E-04
AT DISTANCE  0.800000 DEFLECTION =    -2.74268E-04
AT DISTANCE  0.900000 DEFLECTION =    -7.10156E-05
```

Figure 5.14 (continued)

```
SELECT ONE OF THE FOLLOWING OPTIONS
0 : STOP
1 : END LOAD
2 : INTERMEDIATE LOAD
3 : UNIFORM LOAD
2
ENTER TOTAL LOAD AND DISTANCE A:
125.0, 0.5
AT DISTANCE   0. DEFLECTION =     -1.53051E-03
AT DISTANCE   0.100000 DEFLECTION =     -1.34685E-03
AT DISTANCE   0.200000 DEFLECTION =     -1.16319E-03
AT DISTANCE   0.300000 DEFLECTION =     -9.79528E-04
AT DISTANCE   0.400000 DEFLECTION =     -7.95866E-04
AT DISTANCE   0.500000 DEFLECTION =     -6.12205E-04
AT DISTANCE   0.600000 DEFLECTION =     -4.30992E-04
AT DISTANCE   0.700000 DEFLECTION =     -2.64472E-04
AT DISTANCE   0.800000 DEFLECTION =     -1.27339E-04
AT DISTANCE   0.900000 DEFLECTION =     -3.42834E-05

SELECT ONE OF THE FOLLOWING OPTIONS
0 : STOP
1 : END LOAD
2 : INTERMEDIATE LOAD
3 : UNIFORM LOAD
3
ENTER UNIT LOAD:
125.0
AT DISTANCE   0. DEFLECTION =     -1.83661E-03
AT DISTANCE   0.100000 DEFLECTION =     -1.59179E-03
AT DISTANCE   0.200000 DEFLECTION =     -1.34783E-03
AT DISTANCE   0.300000 DEFLECTION =     -1.10693E-03
AT DISTANCE   0.400000 DEFLECTION =     -8.72759E-04
AT DISTANCE   0.500000 DEFLECTION =     -6.50468E-04
AT DISTANCE   0.600000 DEFLECTION =     -4.46665E-04
AT DISTANCE   0.700000 DEFLECTION =     -2.69431E-04
AT DISTANCE   0.800000 DEFLECTION =     -1.28318E-04
AT DISTANCE   0.900000 DEFLECTION =     -3.43446E-05

SELECT ONE OF THE FOLLOWING OPTIONS
0 : STOP
1 : END LOAD
2 : INTERMEDIATE LOAD
3 : UNIFORM LOAD
0
DONE PROCESSING FOR THIS BEAM
```

EXAMPLE 2: Checking Academic Standing. At several places in this text we have indicated that large and complex problems can best be solved using **top-down design.** In this approach, a **divide-and-conquer** strategy is used in which the original problem is divided into a number of simpler subproblems. Each of these subproblems can then be solved independently, perhaps using this same divide-and-conquer strategy to divide them into still simpler subproblems. This refinement process continues until the subproblems are simple enough that algorithms can be easily developed to solve them. Subprograms are then written to implement these algorithms, and these subprograms are combined with a main program into a complete program that solves the original problem. Because this software engineering technique is so important and because we have now considered subprograms in some detail, it is appropriate to illustrate the use of this technique to solve a relatively complex problem.

Suppose that the School of Engineering at a certain university wants a program for its secretarial staff that can be used to determine the academic standing of its students. The academic standing of each student is to be checked at the end of each of the first three years of the student's academic career and is based on two criteria: the number of hours that the student has successfully completed and his or her cumulative grade point average (GPA). To be in good standing, the student must have completed at least 25 hours with a minimum GPA of 1.7 by the end of the first year. At the end of the second year, 50 hours must have been completed with a cumulative GPA of 1.85 or higher, and at the end of the third year, 85 hours must have been completed with a minimum cumulative GPA of 1.95.

The program should display the student's number, class, cumulative hours, GPA for the current year, and cumulative GPA, as well as an indication of his of her academic standing. At the end of this report, the program should also display the total number of students processed, the number who are in good standing, and the average current GPA for all students. The information to be supplied to the program is the student's number, class level, hours accumulated, cumulative GPA, and hours and grades for courses taken during the current year.

Since this program will be used by personnel who are generally not regular users of a computer system, instructions should be displayed each time the program is used. The first subroutine will be designed to carry out this task. The second task is to read the given information for each student, calculate the relevant statistics, and determine academic standing. The final task is to generate and display the desired summary statistics after all the student information has been processed. The following outline, along with the structure diagram, summarizes this analysis:

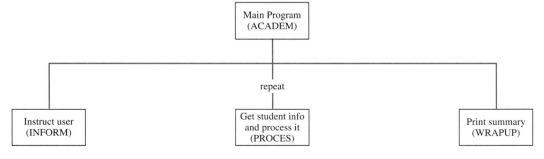

Input Data

Student's number.
Class level (1, 2, or 3).
Cumulative hours.
Cumulative GPA.
Hours and grade for each course completed in the current year.

Output Data

Student's number
Current GPA.
Updated cumulative hours and cumulative GPA.
Indication of academic standing.
Number of students processed.
Number of students in good standing.
Average of all current GPAs.

LEVEL 1 ALGORITHMS FOR ACADEMIC-STANDING PROBLEM

* Algorithm to determine academic standing for engineering students *
* based on hours of course work completed and cumulative grade   *
* point average.   *

1. Provide instructions to the user.
2. Repeat the following until there is no more data:
   Read the given information for a student, calculate statistics,
   determine academic standing, and display report.
3. Calculate and display summary statistics.

The three tasks we have identified can be implemented as three subroutines, INFORM, PROCES, and WRAPUP. The procedure INFORM simply displays instructions to the user; thus, since it requires no information from other program units, it has no formal arguments. The subroutine WRAPUP, which prints the summary, requires the total number of students (NUMSTU), the total number who are in good standing (NUMGS), and the sum of all the current GPAs (GPASUM). These values must be calculated by the subroutine PROCES and shared with WRAPUP. Thus, the entire program has the form

```
PROGRAM ACADEM

INTEGER NUMSTU, NUMGS, RESPON
REAL GPASUM
DATA NUMSTU, NUMGS, GPASUM / 0, 0, 0.0 /

CALL INFORM
*      Repeat the following until no more data
10     CONTINUE
           CALL PROCES(NUMSTU, NUMGS, GPASUM)
           PRINT *
           PRINT *
           PRINT *, 'MORE (0 = NO, 1 = YES)?'
           READ *, RESPON
       IF (RESPON .NE. 0) GO TO 10

       CALL WRAPUP(NUMSTU, NUMGS, GPASUM)
       END
```

Since the subprogram PROCES is central to the entire program, we begin with its development. We can identify three main subtasks. The first is to read the information for a student and calculate the relevant statistics. The second subtask is to use these statistics to determine whether the student is in good standing. The third subtask is to generate a report displaying some of these statistics and an indication of academic standing. The refined structure of our complete program thus is

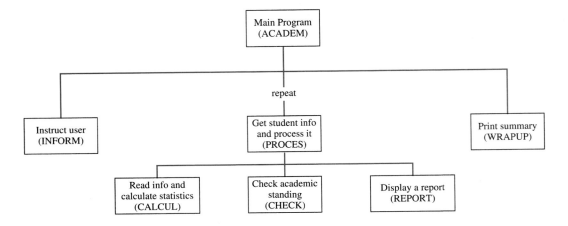

We will use the second-level subprograms CALCUL, CHECK, and REPORT to carry out these subtasks.

The development of subroutine CALCUL for reading student information and calculating statistics is relatively straightforward, and an algorithm is as follows:

LEVEL 2 ALGORITHM FOR CALCUL

```
* Algorithm to read a student's number (SNUMB), class level        *
* (CLASS), cumulative hours (CUMHRS), and cumulative GPA            *
* (CUMGPA) and then to calculate the student's current GPA         *
* (CURGPA) and update the student's cumulative hours and cumulative *
* GPA, the count of students (NUMSTU), and the sum of all GPAs      *
* (GPASUM).                                                         *
```

1. Read SNUMB, CLASS, CUMHRS, and CUMGPA for student.
2. Calculate the number of honor points the student already has earned:

$$OLDPTS = CUMHRS * CUMGPA$$

3. Initialize NEWHRS and NEWPTS to 0.
4. Read HOURS of credit and numeric GRADE for first course taken by student.
5. While the end-of-data flag has not been read do the following:
   a. Add HOURS to NEWHRS.
   b. Add HOURS * GRADE to NEWPTS.
   c. Read HOURS of credit and GRADE for next course.
6. Calculate student's current GPA; 0 if student took no new courses; else

$$CURGPA = NEWPTS / NEWHRS$$

7. Update cumulative hours for student by adding NEWHRS to CUMHRS.
8. Calculate student's cumulative GPA:

$$CUMGPA = \frac{OLDPTS + NEWPTS}{CUMHRS}$$

9. Increment NUMSTU by 1 and add CURGPA to GPASUM.

The subroutine CALCUL is now easy to write. Note that because values of SNUMB, CLASS, CUMHRS, CUMGPA, CURGPA, NUMSTU, and GPA-SUM must be shared with other program units, they must be formal arguments for this subroutine.

Once the subroutine CALCUL has been written, it can be incorporated into the total program and tested before the other subprograms are developed, as shown in Figure 5.15. We simply insert output statements in the undeveloped subprograms to signal when they are called. In this program, the execution parts of subroutines INFORM, WRAPUP, and PROCES contain **program stubs** to signal their execution, and REPORT produces a temporary printout to enable us to verify the correctness of CALCUL. The subroutine CALCUL is in its final form, as is the main program.

```
      PROGRAM ACADEM
*******************************************************************
* Program to determine academic standing of engineering students *
* according to two criteria:  cumulative hours and cumulative gpa.*
* It also counts the total # of students checked, and the # found to *
* be in good standing and calculates the average current gpa for all *
* students.  Variables used are:                                 *
*     NUMSTU : total number of students                          *
*     NUMGS  : number in good standing                           *
*     RESPON : user response to more-data inquiry                *
*     GPASUM : sum of all current GPAs                           *
*******************************************************************

      INTEGER NUMSTU, NUMGS, RESPON
      REAL GPASUM
      DATA NUMSTU, NUMGS, GPASUM /3*0/

      CALL INFORM

*     Repeat the following until no more data
10    CONTINUE
          CALL PROCES(NUMSTU, NUMGS, GPASUM)
          PRINT *
          PRINT *, 'MORE (0 = NO, 1 = YES)?'
          READ *, RESPON
      IF (RESPON .NE. 0) GO TO 10

      CALL WRAPUP(NUMSTU, NUMGS, GPASUM)
      END
```

Figure 5.15

Figure 5.15 (continued)

```
**INFORM*********************************************************************
      SUBROUTINE INFORM

      PRINT *, '*********** INFORM CALLED ***********'
      END


**PROCES*********************************************************************
* Accepts student information, determines academic standing, and        *
* maintains counts of # processed and # in good standing, and a sum     *
* of current GPAs.  Variables used are:                                 *
*     NUMSTU : total number of students                                 *
*     NUMGS  : number in good standing                                  *
*     GPASUM : sum of all current GPAs                                  *
*     SNUMB  : student's number                                         *
*     CLASS  : student's class                                          *
*     CUMHRS : student's cumulative hours                               *
*     CUMGPA : student's cumulative GPA                                 *
*     CURGPA : student's current GPA                                    *
*     GOODST : indicates whether student is in good standing            *
****************************************************************************


      SUBROUTINE PROCES(NUMSTU, NUMGS, GPASUM)

      INTEGER NUMSTU, NUMGS, SNUMB, CLASS
      REAL GPASUM, CUMHRS, CUMGPA, CURGPA
      LOGICAL GOODST

      CALL CALCUL(SNUMB, CLASS, NUMSTU, CUMHRS, CUMGPA, CURGPA,
     +            GPASUM)
      CALL CHECK
      CALL REPORT(SNUMB, CLASS, CUMHRS, CURGPA, CUMGPA)
      END

**WRAPUP*********************************************************************
      SUBROUTINE WRAPUP(NUMSTU, NUMGS, GPASUM)

      PRINT *, '*********** WRAPUP CALLED ***********'
      END
```

Figure 5.15 (continued)

```
**CALCUL**************************************************************
* Subroutine to read a student's number (SNUMB), CLASS, cumulative    *
* hours (CUMHRS), and cumulative gpa (CUMGPA); then read HOURS and     *
* GRADE for courses taken during the current year, and calculate      *
* current GPA (CURGPA), update cumulative hours cumulative GPA, and    *
* count (NUMSTU) of students processed.  HOURS = 0 and GRADE = 0 are   *
* used to signal the end of data for a student.  Other local variables *
* used are:                                                            *
*     NEWHRS : total hours earned during current year                  *
*     NEWPTS : honor points earned in current year                     *
*     OLDPTS : honor points earned in past years                       *
**********************************************************************

      SUBROUTINE CALCUL(SNUMB, CLASS, NUMSTU, CUMHRS, CUMGPA,
     +                  CURGPA, GPASUM)

      INTEGER SNUMB, NUMSTU, CLASS
      REAL CUMHRS, CUMGPA, CURGPA, GPASUM, HOURS, GRADE, NEWHRS,
     +     NEWPTS, OLDPTS

      PRINT *,'ENTER STUDENT NUMBER, CLASS, CUM. HOURS, CUM. GPA:'
      READ *, SNUMB, CLASS, CUMHRS, CUMGPA
      OLDPTS = CUMHRS * CUMGPA
      NEWHRS = 0.0
      NEWPTS = 0.0
      PRINT *, 'HOURS AND GRADE?'
      READ *, HOURS, GRADE

* While HOURS > 0.0 do the following
10    IF (HOURS .GT. 0.0) THEN
          NEWHRS = NEWHRS + HOURS
          NEWPTS = NEWPTS + HOURS * GRADE
          PRINT *, 'HOURS AND GRADE?'
          READ *, HOURS, GRADE
      GO TO 10
      END IF

      IF (NEWHRS .EQ. 0.0) THEN
          CURGPA = 0.0
      ELSE
          CURGPA = NEWPTS / NEWHRS
      END IF
      GPASUM = GPASUM + CURGPA
      CUMHRS = CUMHRS + NEWHRS
      CUMGPA = (OLDPTS + NEWPTS) / CUMHRS
      NUMSTU = NUMSTU + 1
      END

**CHECK***************************************************************
      SUBROUTINE CHECK

      PRINT *, '********** CHECK CALLED **********'
      END
```

Figure 5.15 (continued)

```
**REPORT*************************************************************
      SUBROUTINE REPORT(SNUMB, CLASS, CUMHRS, CURGPA, CUMGPA)

      INTEGER SNUMB, CLASS
      REAL CUMHRS, CURGPA, CUMGPA

      PRINT *, '********** REPORT CALLED **********'
***** Temporary printout *****
      PRINT *, 'SNUMB: ', SNUMB
      PRINT *, 'CLASS: ', CLASS
      PRINT *, 'CUM. HOURS: ', CUMHRS
      PRINT *, 'CURR. GPA:  ', CURGPA
      PRINT *, 'CUM. GPA:   ', CUMGPA
      END
```

Sample run:

```
********** INFORM CALLED **********
ENTER STUDENT NUMBER, CLASS, CUM. HOURS, CUM. GPA:
1234 1 0 0
HOURS AND GRADE?
5 3.0
HOURS AND GRADE?
4 3.0
HOURS AND GRADE?
3.5 3.0
HOURS AND GRADE?
4 3.0
HOURS AND GRADE?
3 3.0
HOURS AND GRADE?
2 3.0
HOURS AND GRADE?
0 0
********** CHECK CALLED **********
********** REPORT CALLED **********
SNUMB:    1234
CLASS:    1
CUM. HOURS:     21.5000
CURR. GPA:      3.00000
CUM. GPA:       3.00000

MORE (0 = NO, 1 = YES)?
0
********** WRAPUP CALLED **********
```

The sample run of this program indicates that the subroutine CALCUL is correct. Therefore, we may now turn to developing the other subprograms. A further analysis of the subtask of determining the student's academic standing reveals that two criteria are used: an hours condition and a GPA condition. The two corresponding subtasks are shown in the following refined structure diagram. These can be conveniently implemented as logical-valued function subprograms HRSCHK and GPACHK that return the value .TRUE. or .FALSE., depending on whether the student satisfies the corresponding criteria to be in good standing. Replacing the temporary version of CHECK and the reference to it in the execution part of subroutine PROCES in the preceding program produces the refined program in Figure 5.16. Note that we have also modified the temporary version of REPORT and the reference to it in order to display the value of GOODST, the number of students in good standing.

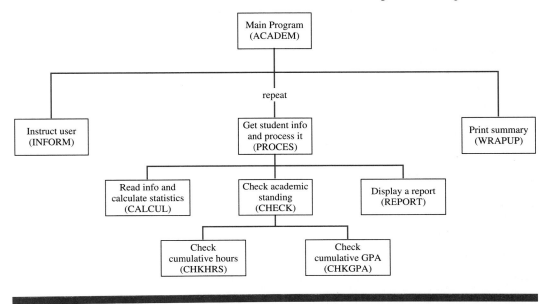

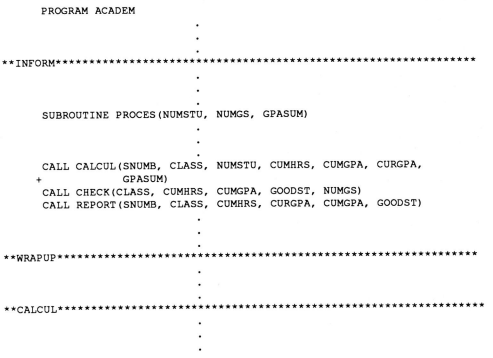

```
      PROGRAM ACADEM
                            .
                            .
                            .
**INFORM*************************************************************
                            .
                            .
                            .
      SUBROUTINE PROCES(NUMSTU, NUMGS, GPASUM)
                            .
                            .
                            .
      CALL CALCUL(SNUMB, CLASS, NUMSTU, CUMHRS, CUMGPA, CURGPA,
     +            GPASUM)
      CALL CHECK(CLASS, CUMHRS, CUMGPA, GOODST, NUMGS)
      CALL REPORT(SNUMB, CLASS, CUMHRS, CURGPA, CUMGPA, GOODST)
                            .
                            .
                            .
**WRAPUP*************************************************************
                            .
                            .
                            .
**CALCUL*************************************************************
                            .
                            .
                            .
```

Figure 5.16

Figure 5.16 (continued)

```
**CHECK*****************************************************************
* Subroutine to check academic standing.  Two criteria are used:    *
* cumulative hours and cumulative GPA.  Functions HRSCHK and GPACHK  *
* are used to check these.  CLASS, CUMHRS, and CUMGPA are the class, *
* cumulative hours, and cumulative GPA for the student being checked. *
* GOODST is true or false according to whether or not the student is *
* found to be in good standing, and NUMGS is the count of students who *
* are in good standing.                                             *
**********************************************************************

      SUBROUTINE CHECK(CLASS, CUMHRS, CUMGPA, GOODST, NUMGS)

      INTEGER CLASS, NUMGS
      REAL CUMHRS, CUMGPA
      LOGICAL GOODST, HRSCHK, GPACHK

      IF ((CLASS .LT. 1) .OR. (CLASS .GT. 3)) THEN
          PRINT *, '*** ILLEGAL CLASS CODE ***'
          GOODST = .FALSE.
      ELSE
          GOODST = HRSCHK(CLASS, CUMHRS) .AND. GPACHK(CLASS, CUMGPA)
      END IF
      IF (GOODST) THEN
          NUMGS = NUMGS + 1
      END IF
      END


**REPORT***************************************************************
                          .
                          .
                          .
      LOGICAL GOODST
                          .
                          .
                          .
      PRINT *, 'GOOD STANDING: ', GOODST
      END


**HRSCHK***************************************************************
* Check cumulative hours (CUMHRS) of student in CLASS.  Return true  *
* or false according to whether he/she has accumulated enough hours.  *
**********************************************************************

      LOGICAL FUNCTION HRSCHK(CLASS, CUMHRS)

      INTEGER CLASS
      REAL CUMHRS, FRESH, SOPH, JUNIOR
      PARAMETER (FRESH = 25.0, SOPH = 50.0, JUNIOR = 85.0)

      IF (CLASS .EQ. 1) THEN
          HRSCHK = (CUMHRS .GE. FRESH)
      ELSE IF (CLASS .EQ. 2) THEN
          HRSCHK = (CUMHRS .GE. SOPH)
      ELSE
          HRSCHK = (CUMHRS .GE. JUNIOR)
      END IF
      END
```

Figure 5.16 (continued)

```
**GPACHK*********************************************************
* Check cumulative GPA (CUMGPA) of student in CLASS.  Return true    *
* or false according to whether his/her GPA is high enough.          *
****************************************************************

       LOGICAL FUNCTION GPACHK(CLASS, CUMGPA)

       INTEGER CLASS
       REAL CUMGPA, GPA1, GPA2, GPA3
       PARAMETER (GPA1 = 1.7, GPA2 = 1.85, GPA3 = 1.95)

       IF (CLASS .EQ. 1) THEN
           HRSCHK = (CUMGPA .GE. GPA1)
       ELSE IF (CLASS .EQ. 2) THEN
           HRSCHK = (CUMGPA .GE. GPA2)
       ELSE
           HRSCHK = (CUMGPA .GE. GPA3)
       END IF
       END
```

Sample run:

```
********** INFORM CALLED **********
ENTER STUDENT NUMBER, CLASS, CUM. HOURS, CUM. GPA:
1234 1 0 0
HOURS AND GRADE?
5 3.0
HOURS AND GRADE?
4 3.0
HOURS AND GRADE?
3.5 3.0
HOURS AND GRADE?
4 3.0
HOURS AND GRADE?
3 3.0
HOURS AND GRADE?
2 3.0
HOURS AND GRADE?
0 0
********** REPORT CALLED **********
SNUMB:    1234
CLASS:    1
CUM. HOURS:      21.5000
CURR. GPA:       3.00000
CUM. GPA:        3.00000
GOOD STANDING:    F

MORE (0 = NO, 1 = YES)?
1
ENTER STUDENT NUMBER, CLASS, CUM. HOURS, CUM. GPA:
55555 5 0 0
HOURS AND GRADE?
3 3.0
HOURS AND GRADE?
0 0
```

Figure 5.16 (continued)

```
*** ILLEGAL CLASS CODE ***
********** REPORT CALLED **********
SNUMB:   55555
CLASS:   5
CUM. HOURS:     24.5000
CURR. GPA:      3.00000
CUM. GPA:       0.367347
GOOD STANDING:   F


MORE (0 = NO, 1 = YES)?
0
********** WRAPUP CALLED **********
```

Because the newly added subprograms appear to be correct, we proceed to develop the remaining subprograms REPORT, INFORM, and WRAPUP. The final version of the complete program is shown in Figure 5.17.

```
          PROGRAM ACADEM
*********************************************************************
* Program to determine academic standing of engineering students    *
* according to two criteria:  cumulative hours and cumulative gpa.   *
* It also counts the total # of students checked, and the # found to *
* be in good standing and calculates the average current gpa for all *
* students.  Variables used are:                                     *
*     NUMSTU : total number of students                              *
*     NUMGS  : number in good standing                               *
*     RESPON : user response to more-data inquiry                    *
*     GPASUM : sum of all current GPAs                               *
*********************************************************************

          INTEGER NUMSTU, NUMGS, RESPON
          REAL GPASUM
          DATA NUMSTU, NUMGS, GPASUM /3*0/

          CALL INFORM

*     Repeat the following until no more data
10    CONTINUE
          CALL PROCES(NUMSTU, NUMGS, GPASUM)
          PRINT *
          PRINT *, 'MORE (0 = NO, 1 = YES)?'
          READ *, RESPON
      IF (RESPON .NE. 0) GO TO 10

          CALL WRAPUP(NUMSTU, NUMGS, GPASUM)
          END
```

Figure 5.17

Figure 5.17 (continued)

```
**INFORM*****************************************************************
*                   Display instructions to the user                  *
***********************************************************************

      SUBROUTINE INFORM

      PRINT *, 'YOU WILL FIRST BE ASKED TO ENTER THE STUDENT''S'
      PRINT *, 'NUMBER, CLASS, CUMULATIVE HOURS, AND CUMULATIVE GPA.'
      PRINT *, 'ENTER THESE WITH AT LEAST ONE SPACE OR COMMA',
     +          ' SEPARATING THEM.'
      PRINT *
      PRINT *, 'YOU WILL THEN BE ASKED TO ENTER THE NUMBER OF HOURS AND'
      PRINT *, 'THE NUMERIC GRADE EARNED FOR EACH OF THE COURSES THE'
      PRINT *, 'STUDENT TOOK DURING THE CURRENT YEAR.  SEPARATE THE'
      PRINT *, 'NUMBER OF HOURS FROM THE GRADE BY AT LEAST ONE SPACE'
      PRINT *, 'OR BY A COMMA.  ENTER 0 FOR HOURS AND 0 FOR GRADES WHEN'
      PRINT *, 'YOU ARE FINISHED ENTERING THE INFORMATION FOR EACH',
     +          ' STUDENT.'
      PRINT *
      PRINT *
      PRINT *
      PRINT *
      END


**PROCES****************************************************************
* Accepts student information, determines academic standing, and      *
* maintains counts of # processed and # in good standing, and a sum   *
* of current GPAs.  Variables used are:                               *
*    NUMSTU : total number of students                                *
*    NUMGS  : number in good standing                                 *
*    GPASUM : sum of all current GPAs                                 *
*    SNUMB  : student's number                                        *
*    CLASS  : student's class                                         *
*    CUMHRS : student's cumulative hours                              *
*    CUMGPA : student's cumulative GPA                                *
*    CURGPA : student's current GPA                                   *
*    GOODST : indicates whether student is in good standing           *
***********************************************************************

      SUBROUTINE PROCES(NUMSTU, NUMGS, GPASUM)

      INTEGER NUMSTU, NUMGS, SNUMB, CLASS
      REAL GPASUM, CUMHRS, CUMGPA, CURGPA
      LOGICAL GOODST

      CALL CALCUL(SNUMB, CLASS, NUMSTU, CUMHRS, CUMGPA, CURGPA,
     +            GPASUM)
      CALL CHECK(CLASS, CUMHRS, CUMGPA, GOODST, NUMGS)
      CALL REPORT(SNUMB, CLASS, CUMHRS, CURGPA, CUMGPA, GOODST)
      END
```

Figure 5.17 (continued)

```
**WRAPUP*****************************************************************
*            Subroutine to print some summary statistics             *
***********************************************************************

      SUBROUTINE WRAPUP(NUMSTU, NUMGS, GPASUM)

      PRINT *
      PRINT *
      PRINT *, '************************************************************'
      PRINT *, '*                 SUMMARY STATISTICS                     *'
      PRINT *, '************************************************************'
      PRINT *
      PRINT *, 'NUMBER OF STUDENTS PROCESSED:   ', NUMSTU
      PRINT *, 'AVERAGE CURRENT GPA OF STUDENTS: ', GPASUM/NUMSTU
      PRINT *, 'NUMBER IN GOOD STANDING:        ', NUMGS
      END


**CALCUL*****************************************************************
* Subroutine to read a student's number (SNUMB), CLASS, cumulative   *
* hours (CUMHRS) and cumulative gpa (CUMGPA); then read HOURS and    *
* GRADE for courses taken during the current year, and calculate     *
* current GPA (CURGPA), update cumulative hours cumulative GPA, and   *
* count (NUMSTU) of students processed.  HOURS = 0 and GRADE = 0 are  *
* used to signal the end of data for a student.  Other local variables *
* used are:                                                          *
*     NEWHRS : total hours earned during current year                *
*     NEWPTS : honor points earned in current year                   *
*     OLDPTS : honor points earned in past years                     *
***********************************************************************

      SUBROUTINE CALCUL(SNUMB, CLASS, NUMSTU, CUMHRS, CUMGPA,
     +               CURGPA, GPASUM)

      INTEGER SNUMB, NUMSTU, CLASS
      REAL CUMHRS, CUMGPA, CURGPA, GPASUM, HOURS, GRADE, NEWHRS,
     +     NEWPTS, OLDPTS

      PRINT *,'ENTER STUDENT NUMBER, CLASS, CUM. HOURS, CUM. GPA:'
      READ *, SNUMB, CLASS, CUMHRS, CUMGPA
      OLDPTS = CUMHRS * CUMGPA
      NEWHRS = 0.0
      NEWPTS = 0.0
      PRINT *, 'HOURS AND GRADE?'
      READ *, HOURS, GRADE
```

Figure 5.17 (continued)

```
* While HOURS > 0.0 do the following
10      IF (HOURS .GT. 0.0) THEN
            NEWHRS = NEWHRS + HOURS
            NEWPTS = NEWPTS + HOURS * GRADE
            PRINT *, 'HOURS AND GRADE?'
            READ *, HOURS, GRADE
        GO TO 10
        END IF

        IF (NEWHRS .EQ. 0.0) THEN
            CURGPA = 0.0
        ELSE
            CURGPA = NEWPTS / NEWHRS
        END IF
        GPASUM = GPASUM + CURGPA
        CUMHRS = CUMHRS + NEWHRS
        CUMGPA = (OLDPTS + NEWPTS) / CUMHRS
        NUMSTU = NUMSTU + 1
        END

**CHECK*********************************************************
* Subroutine to check academic standing.  Two criteria are used: *
* cumulative hours and cumulative GPA.  Functions HRSCHK and GPACHK *
* are used to check these.  CLASS, CUMHRS, and CUMGPA are the class, *
* cumulative hours, and cumulative GPA for the student being checked. *
* GOODST is true or false according to whether or not the student is *
* found to be in good standing, and NUMGS is the count of students who *
* are in good standing.                                          *
***************************************************************

        SUBROUTINE CHECK(CLASS, CUMHRS, CUMGPA, GOODST, NUMGS)

        INTEGER CLASS, NUMGS
        REAL CUMHRS, CUMGPA
        LOGICAL GOODST, HRSCHK, GPACHK

        IF ((CLASS .LT. 1) .OR. (CLASS .GT. 3)) THEN
            PRINT *, '*** ILLEGAL CLASS CODE ***'
            GOODST = .FALSE.
        ELSE
            GOODST = HRSCHK(CLASS, CUMHRS) .AND. GPACHK(CLASS, CUMGPA)
        END IF
        IF (GOODST) THEN
            NUMGS = NUMGS + 1
        END IF
        END
```

Figure 5.17 (continued)

```
**REPORT*******************************************************************
*            Display the statistics for a given student            *
*************************************************************************

       SUBROUTINE REPORT(SNUMB, CLASS, CUMHRS, CURGPA, CUMGPA, GOODST)

       INTEGER SNUMB, CLASS
       REAL CUMHRS, CURGPA, CUMGPA
       LOGICAL GOODST

       PRINT *
       PRINT *, '***** REPORT FOR STUDENT', SNUMB, ' *****'
       PRINT *, 'CLASS:               ', CLASS
       PRINT *, 'CUMULATIVE HOURS: ', CUMHRS
       PRINT *, 'CURRENT GPA:      ', CURGPA
       PRINT *, 'CUMULATIVE  GPA:  ', CUMGPA
       IF (GOODST) THEN
           PRINT *, 'IN GOOD STANDING'
       ELSE
           PRINT *, '*** NOT IN GOOD STANDING ***'
       END IF
       PRINT *, '*****************************************'
       END


**HRSCHK*******************************************************************
* Check cumulative hours (CUMHRS) of student in CLASS.  Return true  *
* or false according to whether he/she has accumulateD enough hours.  *
*************************************************************************

       LOGICAL FUNCTION HRSCHK(CLASS, CUMHRS)

       INTEGER CLASS
       REAL CUMHRS, FRESH, SOPH, JUNIOR
       PARAMETER (FRESH = 25.0, SOPH = 50.0, JUNIOR = 85.0)

       IF (CLASS .EQ. 1) THEN
           HRSCHK = (CUMHRS .GE. FRESH)
       ELSE IF (CLASS .EQ. 2) THEN
           HRSCHK = (CUMHRS .GE. SOPH)
       ELSE
           HRSCHK = (CUMHRS .GE. JUNIOR)
       END IF
       END
```

Figure 5.17 (continued)

```
**GPACHK*******************************************************
* Check cumulative GPA (CUMGPA) of student in CLASS.  Return true   *
* or false according to whether his/her GPA is high enough.         *
***************************************************************

        LOGICAL FUNCTION GPACHK(CLASS, CUMGPA)

        INTEGER CLASS
        REAL CUMGPA, GPA1, GPA2, GPA3
        PARAMETER (GPA1 = 1.7, GPA2 = 1.85, GPA3 = 1.95)

        IF (CLASS .EQ. 1) THEN
            HRSCHK = (CUMGPA .GE. GPA1)
        ELSE IF (CLASS .EQ. 2) THEN
            HRSCHK = (CUMGPA .GE. GPA2)
        ELSE
            HRSCHK = (CUMGPA .GE. GPA3)
        END IF
        END
```

Sample run:

```
YOU WILL FIRST BE ASKED TO ENTER THE STUDENT'S
NUMBER, CLASS, CUMULATIVE HOURS, AND CUMULATIVE GPA.
ENTER THESE WITH AT LEAST ONE SPACE OR COMMA SEPARATING THEM.

YOU WILL THEN BE ASKED TO ENTER THE NUMBER OF HOURS AND
THE NUMERIC GRADE EARNED FOR EACH OF THE COURSES THE
STUDENT TOOK DURING THE CURRENT YEAR.  SEPARATE THE
NUMBER OF HOURS FROM THE GRADE BY AT LEAST ONE SPACE
OR BY A COMMA.  ENTER 0 FOR HOURS AND 0 FOR GRADES WHEN
YOU ARE FINISHED ENTERING THE INFORMATION FOR EACH STUDENT.

ENTER STUDENT NUMBER, CLASS, CUM. HOURS, CUM. GPA:
1234 1 0 0
HOURS AND GRADE?
5 3.0
HOURS AND GRADE?
4 3.0
HOURS AND GRADE?
3.5 3.0
HOURS AND GRADE?
4 3.0
HOURS AND GRADE?
3 3.0
HOURS AND GRADE?
2 3.0
HOURS AND GRADE?
0 0
```

Figure 5.17 (continued)

```
***** REPORT FOR STUDENT  1234 *****
CLASS:                1
CUMULATIVE HOURS:      21.5000
CURRENT GPA:           3.00000
CUMULATIVE  GPA:       3.00000
*** NOT IN GOOD STANDING ***
*******************************************

MORE (0 = NO, 1 = YES)?
1
ENTER STUDENT NUMBER, CLASS, CUM. HOURS, CUM. GPA:
3333 2 30 3.3
HOURS AND GRADE?
5 3.3
HOURS AND GRADE?
5 4.0
HOURS AND GRADE?
5 2.7
HOURS AND GRADE?
5 3.0
HOURS AND GRADE?
3 3.7
HOURS AND GRADE?
0 0

***** REPORT FOR STUDENT  3333 *****
CLASS:                2
CUMULATIVE HOURS:      53.0000
CURRENT GPA:           3.30870
CUMULATIVE  GPA:       3.30377
IN GOOD STANDING
*******************************************

MORE (0 = NO, 1 = YES)?
1
ENTER STUDENT NUMBER, CLASS, CUM. HOURS, CUM. GPA:
4444 3 60 2.0
HOURS AND GRADE?
5 1.0
HOURS AND GRADE?
5 1.3
HOURS AND GRADE?
4 0.7
HOURS AND GRADE?
3 0.7
HOURS AND GRADE?
5 1.0
HOURS AND GRADE?
0
0
```

Figure 5.17 (continued)

```
***** REPORT FOR STUDENT  4444 *****
CLASS:           3
CUMULATIVE HOURS:    82.0000
CURRENT GPA:         0.972727
CUMULATIVE  GPA:     1.72439
*** NOT IN GOOD STANDING ***
*****************************************

MORE (0 = NO, 1 = YES)?
0

*********************************************************
*              SUMMARY STATISTICS                       *
*********************************************************

NUMBER OF STUDENTS PROCESSED:     3
AVERAGE CURRENT GPA OF STUDENTS:     2.42714
NUMBER IN GOOD STANDING:          1
```

5.5 Functions and Subroutines as Arguments

In our examples of subprograms thus far, the actual arguments have been constants, variables, or expressions, but FORTRAN also permits function names and subroutine names as arguments for other subprograms. In this case, the name of the subprogram being used as an actual argument must be listed in an EXTERNAL or INTRINSIC statement in the program unit in which it is used as an actual argument.

The **EXTERNAL statement** has the form

EXTERNAL *name1, name2, . . .*

where *name1, name2, . . .* are the names of *user-written* subprograms to be used as arguments. The EXTERNAL statement must appear in the specification part of the program unit in which *name1, name2, . . .* are being used as actual arguments.

To illustrate the use of a user-defined function as an argument, consider a function subprogram DEFINT that approximates an integral

$$\int_a^b f(x)\ dx$$

using the rectangle method in Example 1 of Section 4.11 (see also Figures 5.1 and 5.2). We wish to use this subprogram in another program to calculate the integral of the function POLY(x), defined by POLY(x) = $x^2 + 3x + 2$, for $0 \le x \le 4$. We indicate that POLY is to be an argument by using an

EXTERNAL statement, and we define POLY in a function subprogram (*not* as a statement function), as shown in Figure 5.18:

```
      PROGRAM APPROX
*************************************************************************
* Program to approximate the integral of a function over the interval  *
* [A,B] using the rectangle method.  This approximation is calculated   *
* by the function subprogram DEFINT; the integrand, the interval of     *
* integration, and the # of subintervals are passed as arguments to     *
* DEFINT.  Identifiers used are:                                        *
*     A, B  : the endpoints of the interval of integration             *
*     POLY   : the integrand                                            *
*     SUBS   : the number of subintervals used                         *
*************************************************************************

      REAL A, B, DEFINT, POLY
      INTEGER SUBS
      EXTERNAL POLY

      PRINT *, 'ENTER THE INTERVAL ENDPOINTS AND THE # OF SUBINTERVALS'
      READ *, A, B, SUBS
      PRINT *, 'RECTANGLE APPROXIMATION WITH',  SUBS,
     +         ' SUBINTERVALS IS', DEFINT(POLY, A, B, SUBS)
      END

**DEFINT***************************************************************
* Function to calculate the rectangle approximation of the integral   *
* of the function F over the interval [A,B] using N subintervals.     *
* Altitudes of rectangles are chosen at the midpoints of the         *
* subintervals.  Local variables used are:                           *
*     I     : counter                                                *
*     DELX  : the length of the subintervals                         *
*     X     : midpoint of one of the subintervals                    *
**********************************************************************

      FUNCTION DEFINT(F, A, B, N)

      INTEGER N, I
      REAL DELX, X, DEFINT, F, A, B

      DELX = (B - A) / N
      DEFINT = 0
      X = A + DELX / 2
      DO 10 I = 1, N
          DEFINT = DEFINT + F(X)
          X = X + DELX
10    CONTINUE
      DEFINT = DEFINT * DELX
      END
```

Figure 5.18

Figure 5.18 (continued)

```
**POLY*******************************************************************
*                              The integrand                           *
************************************************************************

       FUNCTION POLY(X)

       REAL X, POLY
       POLY = X ** 2 + 3 * X + 2
       END
```

Sample run:

```
ENTER THE INTERVAL ENDPOINTS AND THE # OF SUBINTERVALS
0, 4, 50
RECTANGLE APPROXIMATION WITH  50 SUBINTERVALS IS    53.3312
```

To approximate the integral of the sine function from 0 to .5, we can simply change the definition of POLY to

```
       POLY = SIN(X)
```

and reexecute the program. An alternative is to delete the function subprogram POLY and to pass the library function SIN as an argument to DEFINT, provided that we indicate that it is to be an argument by listing it in an INTRINSIC statement, as shown in the program of Figure 5.19.

```
       PROGRAM APPROX
************************************************************************
* Program to approximate the integral of a function over the interval *
* [A,B] using the rectangle method.  This approximation is calculated *
* by the function subprogram DEFINT; the integrand, the interval of   *
* integration, and the # of subintervals are passed as arguments to   *
* DEFINT.  Identifiers used are:                                      *
*     A, B  : the endpoints of the interval of integration           *
*     SIN   : the integrand (library function)                        *
*     SUBS  : the number of subintervals used                         *
************************************************************************

       REAL A, B, DEFINT
       INTEGER SUBS
       INTRINSIC SIN

       PRINT *, 'ENTER THE INTERVAL ENDPOINTS AND THE # OF SUBINTERVALS'
       READ *, A, B, SUBS
       PRINT *, 'RECTANGLE APPROXIMATION WITH',  SUBS,
      +        ' SUBINTERVALS IS', DEFINT(SIN, A, B, SUBS)
       END
```

Figure 5.19

Figure 5.19 (continued)

```
**DEFINT**************************************************************
* Function to calculate the rectangle approximation of the integral  *
* of the function F over the interval [A,B] using N subintervals.    *
* Altitudes of rectangles are chosen at tne midpoints of the         *
* subintervals.  Local variables used are:                           *
*     I     : counter                                                *
*     DELX  : length of the subintervals                             *
*     X     : midpoint of one of the subintervals                    *
*********************************************************************

      FUNCTION DEFINT(F, A, B, N)

      INTEGER N, I
      REAL DELX, X, DEFINT

      DELX = (B - A) / N
      DEFINT = 0
      X = A + DELX / 2
      DO 10 I = 1, N
          DEFINT = DEFINT + F(X)
          X = X + DELX
10    CONTINUE
      DEFINT = DEFINT * DELX
      END
```

Sample run:

```
ENTER THE INTERVAL ENDPOINTS AND THE # OF SUBINTERVALS
0, 0.5, 20
RECTANGLE APPROXIMATION WITH  20 SUBINTERVALS IS    0.122421
```

In our discussion of the FORTRAN intrinisic functions, we have in most cases used the *generic* names of these functions. These generic names simplify references to the functions, as the same function may be used with more than one type of argument. Intrinsic functions may, however, also be referenced by *specific* names, as indicated in the table of Appendix D. These specific names— but not the generic names—of the FORTRAN intrinsic functions may be used as arguments in a subprogram reference, provided that they have been listed in an **INTRINSIC statement.** This statement has the form

INTRINSIC *fun1, fun2, . . .*

·where *fun1, fun2, . . .* are specific names of intrinsic library functions to be used as actual arguments in a subprogram reference. Of the functions listed in Appendix D, LGE, LGT, LLE, LLT, INT, REAL, DBLE, CMPLX, ICHAR, CHAR, MAX, and MIN may not be used as actual arguments of a subprogram. The INTRINSIC statement must appear in the specification part of the program unit in which *fun1, fun2, . . .* are being used as actual arguments.

User-written subroutine subprograms may also be used as arguments in subprogram references. Like function subprograms, their names must be listed in an EXTERNAL statement in the program unit in which their names are used as actual arguments.

5.6   The COMMON Statement

As illustrated in Section 5.4, large programming projects are usually developed as a collection of program units, each of which is designed to perform a particular part of the total processing required. Usually each of these program units must access a common set of data. Although *sharing this information via argument lists is preferred* (as we have done in the preceding sections), it is also possible to establish certain common memory areas in which this data can be stored and accessed *directly* by each of the program units. These common regions are established using the COMMON statement introduced in this section. Additional details regarding the COMMON statement are found in Chapter 12.

It must be emphasized, however, that *although common regions can be used to share data among program units, it is usually unwise to do so*, because this practice destroys the independence of these program units and thus makes modular programming more difficult. If several program units share a common area and one of these program units changes the value of a variable that has been allocated memory in this common region, the value of that variable is changed in all of the other program units. Consequently, it is difficult to determine the value of that variable at any particular point in the program.

Blank Common.   One form of the **COMMON statement** establishes a common region to which no name is assigned. This region is thus called **blank** or **unnamed common.** The form of the COMMON statement for this is

COMMON *list*

where *list* is a list of variables separated by commas. These variables are allocated memory locations in blank common in the order in which they are listed. The COMMON statement must appear in the specification part of a program unit.

When COMMON statements are used in different program units, the first item in each list is allocated the first memory location in blank common. These items are thus associated, because they refer to the same memory location. Successive items in the list are similarly associated because they are allocated successive memory locations in the common region.

The following restrictions apply to items that are allocated memory locations in blank common:

1. Associated items must be of the same type.
2. If they are of character type, they should be of the same length.
3. They may not be initialized in DATA statements (a BLOCK DATA subprogram, as described in Section 12.4, can be used for this purpose).
4. They may not be used as formal arguments in the subprogram in which the COMMON statement appears.

5. Numeric and character variables (or arrays) may not both be allocated memory locations from blank common.

To illustrate, suppose that one program unit contains the statements

```
REAL A, B
INTEGER M, N
COMMON A, B, M, N
```

These four variables are allocated memory locations in the common region in the following order:

Variable	Blank Common Location
A	#1
B	#2
M	#3
N	#4

If another program unit contains the statements

```
REAL W, X
INTEGER I, J
COMMON W, X, I, J
```

then W, X, I, and J are also allocated the first four memory locations in the common region:

Variable	Blank Common Location
W	#1
X	#2
I	#3
J	#4

It follows that these eight variables are then associated in the following manner:

Variable	Blank Common Location	Variable
A	#1	W
B	#2	X
M	#3	I
N	#4	J

As a simple illustration of the use of COMMON, the program in Figure 5.12 can be written as shown in Figure 5.20. Notice that no arguments are listed in the CALL statement or in the subroutine heading. The COMMON statements associate the variables RCOORD, TCOORD, XCOORD, and

YCOORD in the main program with the variables R, THETA, X, and Y, respectively in the subprogram CONVER.

```
      PROGRAM POLAR
*****************************************************************
* This program accepts the polar coordinates of a point & displays  *
* the corresponding rectangular coordinates.  The subroutine CONVER is *
* used to effect the conversion; a COMMON statement is used to    *
* associate variables in the main program with variables in CONVER.  *
* Variables used are:                         *
*    RCOORD, TCOORD : polar coordinates of a point        *
*    XCOORD, YCOORD : rectangular coordinates of a point     *
*****************************************************************

      INTEGER RESPON
      REAL RCOORD, TCOORD, XCOORD, YCOORD
      COMMON RCOORD, TCOORD, XCOORD, YCOORD

* Read and convert coordinates until user signals no more data

10    CONTINUE
         PRINT *, 'ENTER POLAR COORDINATES (IN RADIANS)'
         READ *, RCOORD, TCOORD
         CALL CONVER
         PRINT *, 'RECTANGULAR COORDINATES:'
         PRINT *, XCOORD, YCOORD
         PRINT *
         PRINT *, 'MORE POINTS TO CONVERT (0 = NO, 1 = YES)?'
         READ *, RESPON
      IF (RESPON .NE. 0) GO TO 10

      END


**CONVER********************************************************
* Subroutine to convert polar coordinates (R,THETA) to rectangular  *
* coordinates (X,Y).                         *
*****************************************************************

      SUBROUTINE CONVER

      REAL R, THETA, X, Y
      COMMON R, THETA, X, Y

      X = R * COS(THETA)
      Y = R * SIN(THETA)
      END
```

Figure 5.20

In the preceding examples we used different names for the same common locations. Although this is legal, the association between elements in different program units is much clearer if the same names are used in each program unit. This is especially important if there are a large number of program units and/or a large number of shared variables.

Named Common. In some situations it may be preferable to share one set of variables among some program units and to share another set among other program units. But this sharing is not possible using the form of COMMON statement considered thus far, as it establishes a single common region. It is possible, however, using a form of the COMMON statement that establishes common regions that are **named.** This form is

COMMON /*name1*/ *list1* /*name2*/ *list2* . . .

where each of *name1*, *name2*, . . . is the name of a list of items (namely, those in *list1*, *list2*, . . . , respectively) that are to be associated with the items in a block having the same name in another program unit. This association must be complete; that is, there must be a one-to-one correspondence between the items in associated blocks.

For example, suppose that the variables A, B, L, and M are to be shared by the main program and a subroutine GAMMA, and the variables A, B, N1, N2, N3 shared by the main program and the subroutine BETA. The following program scheme would be appropriate:

```
REAL A, B
INTEGER L, M, N1, N2, N3
COMMON /FIRST/ A, B /SECOND/ L, M /THIRD/ N1, N2, N3
       .
       .
       .
END

SUBROUTINE GAMMA
REAL A, B
INTEGER L, M
COMMON /FIRST/ A, B /SECOND/ L, M
       .
       .
       .
END

SUBROUTINE BETA
REAL A, B
INTEGER N1, N2, N3
COMMON /FIRST/ A, B /THIRD/ N1, N2, N3
       .
       .
       .
END
```

It is possible to use a single COMMON statement to establish both named and unnamed common regions. In this case, the unnamed region is "named" by a blank (or no space at all) between the slashes (thus the name "blank"

COMMON). In the preceding example, therefore, we could also have used

```
REAL A, B
INTEGER L, M, N1, N2, N3
COMMON // A,B /SECOND/ L, M /THIRD/ N1, N2, N3
             .
             .
             .

END

SUBROUTINE GAMMA
REAL A, B
INTEGER L, M
COMMON // A, B /SECOND/ L, M
             .
             .
             .

END

SUBROUTINE BETA
REAL A, B
INTEGER N1, N2, N3
COMMON // A, B /THIRD/ N1, N2, N3
             .
             .
             .

END
```

Exercises

1. Write a menu-driven program that allows the user to convert measurements from either miles to kilometers (1 mile = 1.60935 kilometers) or feet to meters (1 foot = 0.3048 meter), or from degrees Fahrenheit to degrees Celsius ($C = 5/9(F - 32)$). Use subroutines to implement the various options. A sample run of the program should proceed somewhat as follows:

```
Available options are:
0. Display this menu.
1. Convert miles to kilometers.
2. Convert feet to meters.
3. Convert degrees Fahrenheit to degrees Celsius.
4. Quit.

Enter an option (0 to see menu):
3
Enter degrees Fahrenheit:
212
This is equivalent to   100.000 degrees Celsius.

Enter an option (0 to see menu):
0
Available options are:
0. Display this menu.
1. Convert miles to kilometers.
```

```
2. Convert feet to meters.
3. Convert degrees Fahrenheit to degrees Celsius.
4. Quit.

Enter an option (0 to see menu):
1
Enter miles:
10
This is equivalent to   16.0935 kilometers.

Enter an option (0 to see menu):
2
Enter number of feet:
1
This is equivalent to   0.3048 meters.

Enter an option (0 to see menu):
4
```

2. Write a menu-driven program that allows the user to select one of the following methods of depreciation:

   1. Straight-line (see Exercise 9 in Section 5.3).
   2. Sum-of-the-years-digits (see Exercise 10 in Section 5.3).
   3. Double-declining balance (see Exercise 11 in Section 5.3).

   Design the program to be modular, using subprograms to implement the various options.

3. (Project) Many everyday situations involve *queues* (waiting lines): at supermarket checkout lanes, at ticket counters, at bank windows, and so on. Consider the following example: An airport has one runway. Each airplane takes three minutes to land and two minutes to take off. On the average, in one hour, eight planes land and eight take off. Assume that the planes arrive randomly. (Delays make the assumption of randomness quite reasonable.) There are two types of queues: airplanes waiting to land and airplanes waiting to take off. Because it is more expensive to keep a plane airborne than to have one waiting on the ground, we assume that an airplane waiting to land has priority over one waiting to take off.

   Write a computer simulation of this airport's operation. To simulate landing arrivals, generate a random number corresponding to a one-minute interval; if it is less than 8/60, then a "landing arrival" occurs and joins the queue of planes waiting to land. Generate another random number to determine whether a "takeoff" arrival occurs; if so, it joins the takeoff queue. Next, check to determine whether the runway is free. If so, first check the landing queue, and if planes are waiting, allow the first airplane in the landing queue to land; otherwise, consider the queue of planes waiting to take off. Have the program calculate the average queue lengths and the average time an airplane spends in a queue. For this exercise, you might simulate a 24-hour day. You might also investigate the effect of varying arrival and departure rates to simulate prime and slack times of the day, or what happens if the amount of time it takes to land or take off is increased or decreased.

4. Design a subprogram whose arguments are a function f and the endpoints of an interval known to contain a zero of the function and that uses the bisection method described in Exercise 1 of Section 5.2 to find an approximation to this zero. Use this subprogram in a program to find a zero of the function $f(x) = x - \cos x$ in the interval $[0, \pi/2]$.

5. Proceed as in Exercise 4, but use *Newton's method* (see Example 1 of Section 5.2) instead of the bisection method. Both the function and its derivative should be passed as arguments to the root-finding subprogram.

Programming Pointers

Program Design

1. *Programs for solving complex problems should be designed in a modular fashion.* The problem should be divided into simpler subproblems so that subprograms can be written to solve each of them.

2. *Information should be shared among program units by using argument lists rather than common regions.* The use of common regions destroys the independence of program units and thus hinders modular design.

Potential Problems

1. *When a subprogram is referenced, the number of actual arguments must be the same as the number of formal arguments, and the type of each actual argument must agree with the type of the corresponding formal argument.* For example, consider the declarations

```
INTEGER NUM1, NUM2, PYTHAG, K, L, M
PYTHAG(NUM1, NUM2) = NUM1 ** 2 + NUM2 ** 2
```

The function references

```
PYTHAG(K, L, M)
```

and

```
PYTHAG(K, 3.5)
```

are then incorrect. In the first case, the number of actual arguments does not agree with the number of formal arguments, and in the second, the real value 3.5 cannot be associated with the integer argument NUM2.

2. *Information is shared among different program units only via the arguments and the function name for function subprograms (or via com-*

mon regions). Thus, if the value of a variable in one program unit is needed by another program unit, it must be passed as an argument (or by using a common region), as this variable is not otherwise accessible to the other program unit. One consequence is that *local variables—* those not used as arguments or listed in COMMON statements—as well as statement labels in one program unit may be used in another program unit without conflict.

3. *When control returns from a subprogram, all local variables in that subprogram become undefined unless a SAVE statement is used.*

4. *The type of a function must be declared both in the function subprogram and in the program unit that references the function.*

5. *Corresponding actual arguments and formal arguments are associated with the same memory locations. Therefore, if the value of one of the formal arguments is changed in a subprogram, the value of the corresponding actual argument also changes.* For example, if the function F is defined by the function subprogram

```
FUNCTION F(X, Y)
REAL F, X, Y

F = X ** 2 - 2.5 * Y + 3.7 * Y ** 2
X = 0
END
```

then when the function is referenced in the main program by a statement such as

```
ALPHA = F(BETA, GAMMA)
```

where ALPHA, BETA, and GAMMA are real variables, the value of the function is assigned to ALPHA, but BETA is also set equal to zero, since it corresponds to the formal argument X, whose value is changed in the subprogram. *The value of a constant cannot be changed* in this manner, however. For example, the function reference

```
F(2.0, GAMMA)
```

does not change the value of the constant 2.0 to zero. Values of constants and expressions that are used as actual arguments in a subprogram reference are placed in temporary memory locations, and it is the contents of these memory locations that are changed. *If a variable name is enclosed in parentheses in the actual argument list, then this argument is treated as an expression, and thus the value of that variable cannot be changed by a subprogram reference.* For example, the function reference

```
F((BETA), GAMMA)
```

does not change the value of BETA.

7. *User-defined functions used as actual arguments in a subprogram reference must be defined by function subprograms, not statement functions, and must be listed in an* EXTERNAL *statement in the program unit that contains that reference.*

8. *Specific names, but not generic names, of library functions may be used as actual arguments in a subprogram reference, provided that they are listed in an* INTRINSIC *statement in the program unit that contains that reference.*

9. *Items that are allocated memory locations in a common region are subject to the following restrictions:*

   - Associated items must be of the same type.
   - Associated items of character type should have the same length.
   - Numeric items and character items cannot be allocated memory locations in the same common region.
   - They may not be initialized in DATA statements.
   - They may not be used as formal arguments in the subprogram in which the COMMON statement appears.

Program Style

1. *Subprograms should be documented in the same manner as the main program is.* The documentation should include a brief description of the processing carried out by the subprogram, the values passed to it, the values returned by it, and what the arguments and local variables represent.

2. *Subprograms are separate program units, and the program format should reflect this fact.* In this text, we

   - Insert a blank comment line before and after each subprogram to set it off from other program units.
   - Follow the stylistic standards described in earlier chapters when writing subprograms.

3. *In the formal argument list of a subroutine, it is usually considered good practice to list arguments whose values are passed to the subroutine (input arguments) before arguments whose values are returned by the subroutine (output arguments).*

FORTRAN 90 Features

FORTRAN 90 has added a number of new features that facilitate modular programming, including the following:

● A number of new intrinsic functions and subroutines have been added. Among the predefined numeric functions are:

CEILING: CEILING(X) is the least integer greater than or equal to the real value X.

FLOOR: FLOOR(X) is the greatest integer less than or equal to the real value X.

Some of the predefined subroutines are:

RANDOM: CALL RANDOM(X) returns a random real number X in the interval (0, 1).

RANDOMSEED: CALL RANDOMSEED initializes the random number generator.

● Function and subroutine subprograms may be declared to be recursive by attaching the word RECURSIVE as a prefix to the subprogram heading. For a recursive function, a RESULT clause must also be attached to the function heading to specify that an identifier other than the function name will be used for the function result. To illustrate, the following recursive function can be used to calculate N factorial = $1 \times 2 \times \cdots \times N$, usually denoted by N!:

```
RECURSIVE FUNCTION FACTORIAL(N) RESULT (FACT)

    INTEGER FACTORIAL, RESULT, N

    IF (N. LE. 1) THEN
        FACT = 1
    ELSE
        FACT = N * FACTORIAL(N - 1)
    END IF
END
```

● Program units may contain internal procedures. These have the same forms as function and subroutine subprograms except that they may not themselves contain internal procedures. A CONTAINS statement in a program unit signals that internal procedure definitions follow. These must be placed at the end of the execution part of that program unit. Internal procedures may be referenced in the same manner as (external) function and subroutine subprograms, but only within the program unit that contains them.

● A formal argument of a subprogram may be declared to be an IN argument, an OUT argument, or an INOUT argument by using an INTENT clause in a modified form of the type statement that specifies the type of that argument; for example,

```
REAL, INTENT(IN) :: R, THETA
REAL, INTENT(OUT) :: X, Y
```

IN arguments may not be modified within the subprogram; OUT arguments are intended to return values to the corresponding actual arguments, which must therefore be variables; INOUT arguments are intended both to receive and to return values.

● Explicit interfaces with a subprogram may be provided by means of an interface block of the form

> INTERFACE
>> *interface-body*
> END INTERFACE

where *interface-body* is a copy of the heading and specification part of the subprogram followed by an END statement. For example, the function DEFINT of Figure 5.18 could be written

```
REAL FUNCTION DEFINT(F, A, B, N)
   ! Calculates the rectangle approximation of the
   ! integral of the function F over the interval
   ! [A, B] using N subintervals.
   INTERFACE
      REAL FUNCTION F(X)
         REAL, INTENT(IN) :: X
      END FUNCTION F
   END INTERFACE
   REAL, INTENT(IN) :: A, B
   INTEGER, INTENT(IN) :: N
   REAL DELX, X
   INTEGER I
          .
          .
          .
END FUNCTION DEFINT
```

● Any formal argument of a subprogram may be declared to be optional by including an OPTIONAL attribute in the type statement that specifies the type of that argument; for example,

```
SUBROUTINE SUB(FIRST, SECOND, THIRD, FOURTH)

   INTEGER, OPTIONAL :: SECOND, FOURTH
   INTEGER FIRST, THIRD
```

This subroutine can then be called with a statement of the form

```
CALL SUB(F, S, T, FO)
```

or

```
CALL SUB(F, S, T)
```

if the fourth argument is not needed. If, however, we wish to use actual arguments corresponding to FIRST, THIRD, and FOURTH, we must use keyword forms for the actual argument corresponding to THIRD and FOURTH:

```
CALL SUB(F, THIRD = T, FOURTH = FO)
```

and we can, in fact, use keyword forms for all the arguments, and these can be in any order; for example,

```
CALL SUB(FIRST = F, FOURTH = FO, THIRD = T)
```

If optional or keyword arguments are used, then an explicit interface to the subprogram must also be provided by means of an interface block.

- An interface block of the form

> INTERFACE OPERATOR (*operator*)
>   *interface-block for function-1*
>   *interface-block for function-2*
>   .
>   .
>   .
>
> END INTERFACE

may be used to define or overload the specified *operator*, which must be an intrinsic operator ($+$, $-$, $*$, $/$, $<$, .LT., ...) or a period followed by one of more letters followed by another period (e.g., .IN. and .NEGATIVE.). The specified functions implement the operation being defined. For binary operations they must have two arguments, while unary operations require one argument. For example, suppose that EXCLUSIVE_OR is an external function subprogram and that the specification part of some other program unit contains the interface block

```
INTERFACE OPERATOR (.XOR.)
  FUNCTION EXCLUSIVE_OR(P, Q)
    LOGICAL EXCLUSIVE_OR, P, Q
  END FUNCTION EXCLUSIVE_OR
END INTERFACE
```

If, A, B, and C are logical variables in this program unit, the statement

```
C = A .XOR. B
```

is equivalent to the statement

```
C = EXCLUSIVE_OR(A, B)
```

If two or more functions are used to implement the operator, their formal argument lists must be sufficiently dissimilar that an application of *operator* to actual operands determines exactly one of the functions for execution.

- An interface block of the form

> INTERFACE OPERATOR ASSIGN ($=$)
>   *interface-block for subroutine-1*
>   *interface-block for subroutine-2*
>   .
>   .
>   .
>
> END INTERFACE

may be used in a similar manner to extend the assignment operator ($=$) to other data types. The specified subroutines, each of which must have two arguments, implement assignment statements of the form

> *argument-1* $=$ *argument-2*

If two or more subroutines are used to extend $=$, their formal argument lists must be sufficiently dissimilar in type that exactly one of them will be selected for execution.

- An interface block of the form

> INTERFACE *generic-name*
> *interface-block for subprogram-1*
> *interface-block for subprogram-2*
>
> .
> .
> .
>
> END INTERFACE

may be used to define a subprogram name *generic-name* that may be used to reference any of *subprogram-1, subprogram-2,* ... (all functions or all subroutines). The formal argument lists of these subprograms must be sufficiently dissimilar in number and/or type that a reference to *generic-name* with a list of actual arguments determines exactly one of *subprogram-1, subprogram-2,* ... for execution.

- A third kind of program unit, a *module*, is provided for packaging definitions and declarations of parameters, variables, types, and subprograms so that they can be used by other program units. Modules are described in Section 13.1.

6

Input/Output

When I read some of the rules for speaking and writing the English language correctly . . . I think
Any fool can make a rule
And every fool will mind it.

H. THOREAU

In Chapter 3 we noted that there are two types of input/output statements in FORTRAN, **list directed** and **formatted** (or more precisely, user formatted). In our discussion thus far, we have restricted our attention to list-directed input/output. This method is particularly easy to use, as the format for the input or output of data is automatically supplied by the compiler. It does not, however, permit the user to control the precise format of the data. For example, using list-directed output, one cannot specify that real values are to be displayed with only two digits to the right of the decimal point, even though this might be appropriate in some applications. The precise form of the output can be specified, however, using the formatted output statement introduced in this chapter.

Sometimes input data has a predetermined form, and the programmer must design the program to read this data. This can be accomplished by using the formatted input statement, also introduced in this chapter.

Finally, if the volume of input data is large, a **file** is usually prepared, and during program execution, data is read from it rather than entered by the user. In this chapter we introduce some statements for processing files.

List-directed input/output can be viewed as a special case of formatted input/output. Thus, some additional features of list-directed input/output are also considered in this chapter.

6.1 Formatted Output

There are two output statements in FORTRAN, the PRINT statement and the WRITE statement. The **PRINT statement** is the simpler of the two and has the form

PRINT *format-specifier, output-list*

Here *output-list* is a single expression or a list of expressions separated by commas; it may also be empty, in which case the comma preceding the list is omitted. The *format-specifier* specifies the format in which the values of the expressions in the output list are to be displayed. A large part of this section is devoted to the design of these format specifiers.

A format specifier may be

1. An asterisk (*).
2. A character constant or a character variable (or expression or array) whose value specifies the format for the output.
3. The label of a FORMAT statement.

As we saw in Chapter 3, an asterisk indicates list-directed output whose format is determined by the types of expressions in the output list. This is adequate when the precise form of the output is not important. However, for reports and other kinds of output in which results must appear in a precise form, list-directed formatting is not adequate, and so format specifiers of type 2 or 3 must be used.

In the second type of format specifier, the formatting information is given as a character string of the form

'*(list of format descriptors)*'

that is, a character string that consists of format descriptors, separated by commas and enclosed in parentheses.

In the third type of format specifier, the formatting information is supplied by a **FORMAT statement** whose label is specified. This statement has the form

FORMAT(*list of format descriptors*)

In the second and third types of format specifiers, the format descriptors specify precisely the format in which to display the items in the output list. For example, some output statements that could be used to display the value 17 of the integer variable NUMBER and the value 10.25 of the real variable TEMP are the following:

```
PRINT *, NUMBER, TEMP
PRINT '(1X, I5, F8.2)', NUMBER, TEMP
PRINT 20, NUMBER, TEMP
```

where statement 20 is the statement

```
20 FORMAT(1X, I5, F8.2)
```

In these statements, 1X, I5, and F8.2 are format descriptors that specify the format in which the values of NUMBER and TEMP are to be displayed. As we know, list-directed output like that produced by the first statement is compiler dependent but might appear as follows:

```
|__17___10.25000
```

The output produced by the second and third forms is not compiler dependent and appears as follows:

```
|___17___10.25
```

(If control characters are not in effect, there will be one additional space at the beginning of this output line.)

There are many format descriptors that may be used in format specifiers. Table 6.1 gives a complete list of these descriptors. In this section we consider those most commonly used: I, F, E, character strings, A, T, X, and /, deferring the others to Section 6.7.

Control Characters. In many computer systems, the first character of each line of output is used to control the vertical spacing. If this character is a

Table 6.1

Format Descriptor			Use
Iw		I$w.m$	Integer data
F$w.d$			Real data in decimal notation
E$w.d$		E$w.dEe$	Double precision data
G$w.d$			F or E input/output, depending on the value of the item
A		Aw	Character data
'$x \ldots x$'		nH$x \ldots x$	Character strings
Lw			Logical data
Tc	TLn	TRn	Tab descriptors
nX			Horizontal spacing
/			Vertical spacing
:			Format scanning control
S	SP	SS	Sign descriptors
kP			Scale factor
BN		BZ	Blank interpretation

w: positive integer constant specifying the field width.
m: nonnegative integer constant specifying the minimum number of digits to be displayed.
d: nonnegative integer constant specifying the number of digits to the right of the decimal point.
e: nonnegative integer constant specifying the number of digits in an exponent.
x: character.
c: positive integer constant representing a column number.
n: positive integer constant specifying the number of columns.
k: nonnegative integer constant specifying a scale factor.

control character, it is used only to effect the appropriate printer control and is not printed. The standard control characters with their effects are as follows:

Control Character	Effect
blank	Normal spacing: Advance to the next line before printing
0	Double spacing: Skip one line before printing
1	Advance to top of next page before printing
+	Overprint the last line printed.

Some systems may implement other control characters and may also use such characters to control the output to devices other than the printer. Consequently, if some character other than a standard control character appears in the first position of a line, the resulting output will depend on the computer system being used. The details regarding the use of control characters by your particular system can be obtained from the system manuals, your instructor, or computer center personnel.

In the case of list-directed output, a blank is automatically inserted at the beginning of each output line as a control character. This blank then produces normal spacing and in most systems is not printed.

In the case of formatted output, some attention must be paid to printer control, because otherwise the output may not be what the user intended. To illustrate, suppose that control characters are in effect, and consider the following statements:

```
    PRINT 20, N
 20 FORMAT(I3)
```

The format descriptor I3 specifies that the value to be printed is an integer and is to be printed in the first three positions of a line. If the value of N is 15, the three positions are filled with ‍b15 (where ‍b denotes a blank). Because the blank appears in the first position, it is interpreted as a control character. This produces normal spacing and displays the value 15 in the first two positions of a new line, as follows:

|15

If, however, the value of N is 150, the first three positions are filled with 150. The character 1 in the first position is again interpreted as a control character. It is not printed, but rather the value 50 is printed at the top of a new page:

‾50

When control characters are in effect, it is a good practice to use the first print position of each output line to indicate explicitly what printer control is desired. This can be done by making the first descriptor of each format specifier one of the following:

1X or ' ' for normal spacing
'0' for double spacing
'1' for advancing to a new page
'+' for overprinting

We follow this practice in the examples in this text.

Integer Output—The I Descriptor. The I descriptor used to describe the format in which integer data is to be displayed has the form

$$r\mathrm{I}w \quad \text{or} \quad r\mathrm{I}w.m$$

where

I   denotes integer data.
w   is an integer constant indicating the width of the field in which the data is to be displayed, that is, the number of spaces to be used in displaying it.
r   is an integer constant called a *repetition indicator*, indicating the number of such fields; for example, 4I3 is the same as I3, I3, I3, I3; if there is only one such field, the number 1 need not be given.
m   is the minimum number of digits to be printed.

Integer values are *right justified* in fields of the specified sizes; that is, each value is printed so that its last digit appears in the rightmost position of the field. For example, if the values of the integer variables NUM, L, and KAPPA are

```
NUM = 3
L = 5378
KAPPA = -12345
```

then the statements

```
PRINT '(1X, 2I5, I7, I10)', NUM, NUM - 3, L, KAPPA
```

or

```
      PRINT 30, NUM, NUM - 3, L, KAPPA
30 FORMAT(1X, 2I5, I7, I10)
```

produce the following output:

```
|____3____0___5378_____-12345
```

The statements

```
PRINT '(1X, 2I5.2, I7, I10.7)', NUM, NUM - 3, L, KAPPA
PRINT '(1X, 2I5.0, I7, I10)', NUM, NUM - 3, L, KAPPA
```

or

```
      PRINT 31, NUM, NUM - 3, L, KAPPA
      PRINT 32, NUM, NUM - 3, L, KAPPA
   31 FORMAT(1X, 2I5.2, I7, I10.7)
   32 FORMAT(1X, 2I5.0, I7, I10)
```

produce

```
|___03___00___5378__-0012345
|____3_____5378_____-12345
```

If an integer value (including a minus sign if the number is negative) requires more spaces than are allowed by the field width specified by a descriptor, the field is filled with asterisks. Thus, the statement

```
      PRINT 40, NUM, NUM - 3, L, KAPPA
   40 FORMAT(1X, 4I3)
```

produces

```
|__3__0******
```

Real Output—The F Descriptor. One of the descriptors used to describe the format of real (floating point) data has the form

$$rFw.d$$

where

F   denotes real (floating point) data.

w is an integer constant indicating the *total width of the field* in which the data is to be displayed.

d is an integer constant indicating the number of digits to the right of the decimal point.

r is the repetition indicator, an integer constant indicating the number of such fields; again, if there is to be only one such field, the number 1 need not be used.

Real values are printed *right justified* in the specified fields. For a descriptor F$w.d$, if the corresponding real value has more than d digits to the right of the decimal point, it is *rounded* to d digits. If it has fewer than d digits, the remaining positions are filled with zeros. In most systems, values less than 1 in magnitude are displayed with a zero to the left of the decimal point (for example, 0.123 rather than .123).

For example, to display the values of the integer variables IN and OUT and the values of the real variables A, B, and C as given by

```
        IN = 625
        OUT = -19
        A = 7.5
        B = .182
        C = 625.327
```

we can use the statements

```
        PRINT '(1X, 2I4, 2F6.3, F8.3)', IN, OUT, A, B, C
```

or

```
          PRINT 50, IN, OUT, A, B, C
       50 FORMAT(1X, 2I4, 2F6.3, F8.3)
```

The resulting output is

```
| 625 -19 7.500 0.182 625.327
```

To provide more space between the numbers and to round each of the real values to two decimal places, we can use the format specification

```
        (1X, 2I10, 3F10.2)
```

This displays the numbers right justified in fields containing ten spaces, as follows:

```
|        625       -19      7.50      0.18    625.33
```

As with the I descriptor, if the real number being output requires more spaces than are allowed by the field width specified in the descriptor, the entire field is *filled with asterisks*. For example,

```
        REAL BETA
        BETA = -567.89
        PRINT 55, 123.4
        PRINT 55, BETA
     55 FORMAT(1X, F5.2)
```

produces

```
| *****
| *****
```

It should be noted that for a descriptor F$w.d$, one should have

$$w \geq d + 3$$

to allow for the sign of the number, the first digit, and the decimal point.

Real Output—The E Descriptor. Real data may also be output in scientific notation using a descriptor of the form

$$rEw.d \quad \text{or} \quad rEw.dEe$$

where

E   indicates that the data is to be output in scientific notation.

w is an integer constant that indicates the total width of the field in which the data is to be displayed.

d is an integer constant indicating the number of decimal digits to be displayed.

r is the repetition indicator, an integer constant indicating the number of such fields; it need not be used if there is only one field.

e is the number of positions to be used in displaying the exponent.

Although some details of the output are compiler dependent, real values are usually printed in *normalized form*—a minus sign, if necessary, followed by one leading zero, then a decimal point followed by d significant digits, and E with an appropriate exponent in the next four spaces for the first form or e spaces for the second form. For example, if values of real variables A, B, C, and D are given by

```
REAL A, B, C, D
A = .12345E8
B = .0237
C = 4.6E-12
D = 76.1684E12
```

the statements

```
      PRINT 60, A, B, C, D
60 FORMAT(1X, 2E15.5, E15.4, E13.4)
```

produce output like the following:

```
|_____0.12345E+08____0.23700E-01_____0.4600E-11___-0.7617E+14
```

As with the F descriptor, a field is *asterisk filled* if it is not large enough for the value to be printed. It should also be noted that for a descriptor E$w.d$ one should have

$$w \geq d + 7$$

or for the second form E$w.dEe$

$$w \geq d + e + 5$$

to allow space for the sign of the number, a leading zero, a decimal point, and E with the exponent.

Logical Output.   An L descriptor is used for formatted output of logical values. This format descriptor has the form

$$rLw$$

where

  w is an integer constant specifying the field width.
  r is the repetition indicator, an integer constant specifying the number of such fields. It may be omitted if there is only one field.

The output field consists of $w - 1$ spaces followed by a T or an F. For example, if A, B, and C are logical variables given by

```
LOGICAL A, B, C

A = .TRUE.
B = .FALSE.
C = .FALSE.
```

the statements

```
      PRINT 30, A, B, C, A .OR. C
30 FORMAT(1X, L4, L2, 2L5)
```

or

```
PRINT '(1X, L4, L2, 2L5)', A, B, C, A .OR. C
```

produce

    |___T_F____F____T

Character Output. Character constants may be displayed by including them in the list of descriptors of a format specifier. For example, if X and Y have the values .3 and 7.9, respectively, the statements

```
      PRINT 70, X, Y
70 FORMAT (1X, 'X =', F6.2, ' Y =', F6.2)
```

or

```
PRINT '(1X, "X =", F6.2, " Y =", F6.2)', X, Y
```

produce as output

    |X_=__0.30_Y_=__7.90

Character data may also be displayed by using an A format descriptor of the form

  rA   or rAw

where

  w (if used) is an integer constant specifying the field width.

r   is the repetition indicator, an integer constant indicating the number
      of such fields; it may be omitted if there is only one field.

In the first form, the field width is determined by the length of the character
value being displayed. In the second form, if the field width exceeds the length
of the character value, that value is *right justified* in the field. In contrast with
numeric output, however, if the length of the character value exceeds the specified field width, the output consists of the *leftmost w* characters. For example,
the preceding output would also be produced if the labels were included in the
output list, as follows:

```
     PRINT 71, 'X =', X, ' Y =', Y
  71 FORMAT(1X, A, F6.2, A, F6.2)
```

or

```
  PRINT '(1X, A, F6.2, A, F6.2)', 'X =', X, ' Y =', Y
```

Placing labels in the output list rather than in the format specifier allows the
format specifier to be reused to print other labels and values, as in

```
   PRINT 71, 'MEAN IS', XMEAN,
  +          'WITH STANDARD DEVIATION', STDEV
```

Positional Descriptors—X and T.   Two format descriptors can be used to
provide spacing in an output line. An X descriptor can be used to insert blanks
in an output line. It has the form

   nX

where *n* is a positive integer constant that specifies the number of blanks to be
inserted.
   The T descriptor has the form

   T*c*

where *c* is an integer constant denoting the number of the space on a line at
which a field is to begin. This descriptor functions much like a tab key on a
typewriter and causes the next output field to begin at the specified position
on the current line. One difference is that the value of *c* may be less than the
current position; that is, "tabbing backward" is possible.[1]
   As an illustration of these descriptors, suppose that NUMBER is an integer
variable, and consider the output statement

```
  PRINT 75, 'JOHN Q. DOE', 'CPSC', NUMBER
```

together with either of the following FORMAT statements:

---

[1] In some systems, a runtime error occurs if *c* is less than the current position.

```
75 FORMAT(1X, A11, 3X, A4, 2X, I3)
```

or

```
75 FORMAT(1X, A11, T16, A4, 2X, I3)
```

If NUMBER has the value 141, the output produced is

```
|JOHN_Q._DOE___CPSC__141
```

Note that the descriptor 2X in either FORMAT statement can be replaced by T22 or that the pair of descriptors 2X, I3 can be replaced by the single descriptor I5. This same output is produced by the statements

```
    PRINT 75, 'JOHN Q. DOE', NUMBER, 'CPSC'
75 FORMAT(1X, A11, T22, I3, T16, A4)
```

which use the backward-tabbing feature of the T descriptor.

Repeating Groups of Format Descriptors.   As we have seen, it is possible to repeat some format descriptors by preceding them with a *repetition indicator*. For example,

```
3F10.2
```

is the same as

```
F10.2, F10.2, F10.2
```

It is also possible to repeat a group of descriptors by enclosing the group in parentheses and then preceding the left parenthesis with a repetition indicator. For example, the FORMAT statement

```
80 FORMAT(1X, A, F6.2, A, F6.2)
```

can be written more compactly as

```
80 FORMAT(1X, 2(A, F6.2))
```

Similarly, the format statement

```
81 FORMAT(1X, I10, F10.2, I10, F10.2, I10, F10.2, E15.8)
```

can be shortened to

```
81 FORMAT(1X, 3(I10, F10.2), E15.8)
```

Additional levels of groups are permitted. For example, the format statement

```
82 FORMAT(1X, E18.2, I3, A, I3, A, E18.2, I3, A,
   +        I3, A, F8.4)
```

can be written more compactly as

```
82 FORMAT(1X, 2(E18.2, 2(I3, A)), F8.4)
```

The Slash (/) Descriptor. A single output statement can be used to display values on more than one line, with different formats, by using a slash (/) descriptor. The slash causes output to begin on a new line. It can also be used repeatedly to skip several lines. It is not necessary to use a comma to separate a slash descriptor from other descriptors. For example, the statements

```
      PRINT 85, 'VALUES'
      PRINT *
      PRINT *
      PRINT 86, N, A, M, B
      PRINT 87, C, D
   85 FORMAT(1X, A)
   86 FORMAT(1X, 2(I10, F10.2))
   87 FORMAT(1X, 2E15.7)
```

can be combined in the pair of statements

```
      PRINT 88, 'VALUES', N, A, M, B, C, D
   88 FORMAT(1X, A /// 1X, 2(I10, F10.2) / 1X, 2E15.7)
```

(Note the descriptors 1X following the slashes to indicate the control characters for the new output lines.) If the values of N, A, M, B, C, and D are given by

```
N = 5173
A = 617.2
M = 7623
B = 29.25
C = 37.555
D = 5.2813
```

then in both cases the resulting output is

```
VALUES

       5173    617.20       7623     29.25
  0.3755500E+02  0.5281300E+01
```

Scanning the Format. When a formatted output statement is executed, the corresponding format specifier is scanned from left to right in parallel with the output list to locate the appropriate descriptors for the output items. The type of the descriptors should match the type of the values being displayed; for example, a real value should not be displayed with an I descriptor. If the values of all the items in the output list have been displayed before all the descriptors have been used, scanning of the format specifier continues. Values of character constants are displayed, and the positioning specified by slash, X, and T descriptors continues until one of the following is encountered:

1. The right parenthesis signaling the end of the list of format descriptors.
2. An I, F, E, or A (or L or G or D) descriptor.
3. A colon.

In cases 2 and 3, all remaining descriptors in the format specifier are ignored. To illustrate, consider the statements

```
      PRINT 100, I, J
100 FORMAT(1X, I5, 3I6)
      PRINT 105, X, Y
105 FORMAT(1X, F5.1, F7.0, F10.5)
      PRINT 110, 'BUMPER', 'HEADLIGHT'
110 FORMAT(1X, 5(' ITEM IS ', A10))
      PRINT 115, 'BUMPER', 'HEADLIGHT'
115 FORMAT(1X, 5(: ' ITEM IS ', A10))
```

If I and J are integer variables with values I = 1 and J = 2 and X and Y are real variables with values given by X = 5.6 and Y = 7.8, these statements produce the output

```
     1     2
   5.6     8.
  ITEM IS     BUMPER  ITEM IS  HEADLIGHT  ITEM IS
  ITEM IS     BUMPER  ITEM IS  HEADLIGHT
```

Note that like the slash, the colon descriptor need not be separated from other descriptors by a comma.

If the list of descriptors is exhausted before the output list is, a new line of output is begun, and the format specifier or part of it is rescanned. If there are no internal parentheses within the format specifier, the rescanning begins with the first descriptor. For example, the statements

```
      INTEGER M1, M2, M3, M4, M5

      M1 = 1
      M2 = 2
      M3 = 3
      M4 = 4
      M5 = 5
      PRINT 120, M1, M2, M3, M4, M5
120 FORMAT(1X, 2I3)
```

produce the output

```
   1  2
   3  4
   5
```

If the format specifier does contain internal parentheses, rescanning begins at the left parenthesis that matches the last-but-one right parenthesis; any repetition counter preceding this format group is in effect. Thus, if integer variables K, L1, L2, and L3 have values

```
K = 3
L1 = 21
L2 = 22
L3 = 23
```

and real variables X, Y1, Y2, and Y3 have values

```
X = 4.0
Y1 = 5.5
Y2 = 6.66
Y3 = 7.77
```

the statements

```
        PRINT 125, K, X, L1, Y1, L2, Y2, L3, Y3
    125 FORMAT(1X, I5, F10.3 / (1X, I10, F12.2))
```

produce the output

```
----3-----4.000-------
--------21--------5.50
--------22--------6.66
--------23--------7.77
```

Thus it is possible to specify a special format for the first output items and a different format for subsequent items by enclosing the last format descriptors in parentheses. In this example, when the right parenthesis of the FORMAT statement is encountered after printing the value of Y1, a new line is begun, and the descriptors following the second left parenthesis are reused to print the values of L2 and Y2 and then again on a new line for L3 and Y3.

6.2   Example: Printing Tables of Computed Values

In some of the sample programs of Chapter 4, the output was displayed in a table format. For example, the output produced in the sample run of the program in Figure 4.12 was

```
          X              Y
    ==========================
        1.00000    0.309560
        1.25000    0.271889
        1.50000    0.222571
        1.75000    0.170991
        2.00000    0.123060
        2.25000     8.20083E-02
        2.50000     4.91256E-02
        2.75000     2.43988E-02
        3.00000     7.02595E-03
```

One unpleasant feature of this table is that the last four values in the second column are printed in scientific notation, whereas all the others are printed in decimal format. Note also that all the values are displayed with five or six digits to the right of the decimal point, even though two or three might be sufficient for our purposes. With list-directed output, however, the format of the output cannot be controlled by the user.

Positioning headings for the columns of a table above the values in the columns can also be rather difficult, as the user cannot control the format or the spacing of these values. It may be necessary to change the output statements and reexecute the modified program several times before the appearance of the output is satisfactory.

The format descriptors in this section make it quite easy to control the format of the output and correct placement of items such as table headings is also considerably easier than with list-directed output. The program in Figure 6.1 demonstrates this. It reads a value for an integer LAST and then prints a table of values of N, the square and the cube of N, and its square root for N = 1, 2, . . . , LAST.

```
      PROGRAM TABLE
**************************************************************************
* Program demonstrating the use of formatted output to print a table  *
* of values of N, the square and cube of N, and the square root of N  *
* for N = 1, 2, ..., LAST where the value of LAST is read during      *
* execution.                                                          *
**************************************************************************

      INTEGER N, LAST

      PRINT *, 'ENTER LAST NUMBER TO BE USED'
      READ *, LAST

*     Print headings

      PRINT 100, 'NUMBER', 'SQUARE', '  CUBE', 'SQ. ROOT'
100   FORMAT(// 1X, A8, T11, A8, T21, A8, T31, A10 / 1X, 40('='))

*     Print the table

      DO 10 N = 1, LAST
          PRINT 110, N, N**2, N**3, SQRT(REAL(N))
110       FORMAT(1X, I6, 2I10, 2X, F10.4)
10    CONTINUE
      END
```

Sample run:

```
ENTER LAST NUMBER TO BE USED
10
```

Figure 6.1

Figure 6.1 (continued)

NUMBER	SQUARE	CUBE	SQ. ROOT
1	1	1	1.0000
2	4	8	1.4142
3	9	27	1.7321
4	16	64	2.0000
5	25	125	2.2361
6	36	216	2.4495
7	49	343	2.6458
8	64	512	2.8284
9	81	729	3.0000
10	100	1000	3.1623

Exercises

1. Assuming that the following declarations and assignments

```
INTEGER NUMBER
REAL ALPHA
LOGICAL P, Q

NUMBER = 12345
ALPHA = 87.6543
P = .TRUE.
Q = .FALSE.
```

have been made, describe the output that will be produced by the following statements (assume that control characters are in effect):

(a)   `PRINT *, 'COMPUTER SCIENCE -- EXERCISE 6.2'`

(b)   `PRINT *, NUMBER, NUMBER + 1`

(c)   `PRINT *, 'ALPHA = ', ALPHA, ' NUMBER =', NUMBER`

(d)   `PRINT *`

(e)   `PRINT '('' COMPUTER SCIENCE -- EXERCISE'', F4.1)',`
          `+        3 * 2.1 - 0.1`

(f)   `PRINT 10, 6.2`
      `10 FORMAT(' COMPUTER SCIENCE -- EXERCISE', F5.2)`

(g)   `PRINT 20, 'COMPUTER SCIENCE', 6.2`
      `20 FORMAT(1X, A, F4.1)`

(h)   `PRINT 30, 'EXERCISE', 6.2`
      `30 FORMAT('1COMPUTER SCIENCE --', A10, F6.3)`

(i)   `PRINT 40, 'EXERCISE', 6.2`
      `40 FORMAT('COMPUTER SCIENCE --', A2, F3.1)`

(j)   PRINT 50, NUMBER, NUMBER + 1, ALPHA, ALPHA + 1,
       +   ALPHA + 2
       50 FORMAT('0', 2I7, F10.5, F10.3, F10.0)

(k)   PRINT '(1X, I5, 4X, I4, T20, I6)', NUMBER,
       +   NUMBER + 1, NUMBER + 2

(l)   PRINT 60, NUMBER, ALPHA, NUMBER + 1, ALPHA + 1
       60 FORMAT(1X, I5, F7.4 / I5, E12.5)

(m)   PRINT 70, NUMBER, ALPHA, NUMBER + 1, ALPHA + 1
       70 FORMAT(1X, I10, F10.3)

(n)   PRINT 80, NUMBER, ALPHA, NUMBER + 1, ALPHA + 1
       80 FORMAT(1X, I10, F10.2, '---')

(o)   PRINT 90, NUMBER, ALPHA, NUMBER + 1, ALPHA + 1
       90 FORMAT(1X, I10, F10.2 : '---')

(p)   PRINT '(1X, I1, '' = 0 IS '', L1)', 1, Q

(q)   PRINT 100, NUMBER, 12346, Q
       100 FORMAT(1X, I5, ' = ', I5, ' IS', L2, 'ALSE')

(r)   PRINT 110, NUMBER, '=', 12345, (NUMBER .EQ. 12345)
       110 FORMAT(1X, I5, A2, I6, / 1X, 'IS', L3)

(s)   PRINT 120, NUMBER, ALPHA, NUMBER, ALPHA
       120 FORMAT(/// 2(1X,I6 // 1X,F6.2) /// ' ******')

(t)   PRINT 130, NUMBER, ALPHA, NUMBER, ALPHA, NUMBER, ALPHA
       130 FORMAT(1X, I6, F7.2, (1X, I5, F6.1))

(u)   PRINT 140, NUMBER, ALPHA, NUMBER, ALPHA, NUMBER, ALPHA
       140 FORMAT (1X, I6, F7.2, (I5, F6.1))

(v)   PRINT 150, 'THE END'
       150 FORMAT(1X, 10 ('*'), A, 10 ('*'))

2. Write a program that reads two three-digit integers and then calculates and prints their sum and their difference. The output should be formatted to appear as follows:

```
    456          456
  + 123        - 123
  - - - - -    - - - - -
    579          333
```

3. Write a program that reads two three-digit integers and then calculates and prints their product, and the quotient and the remainder that result when the first is divided by the second. The output should be formatted to appear as follows:

```
    739              61   R    7
  X  12            - - - -
  - - - - -    12 ) 739
    8868
```

4. Write a program that reads two three-digit integers and then prints their product in the following format:

```
        749
   X    381
   ------
        749
      5992
    2247
   ------
   285369
```

Execute the program with the following values: 749 and 381; −749 and 381; 749 and −381; −749 and −381; 999 and 999.

5. Suppose that a certain culture of bacteria has a constant growth rate r, so that if there are n bacteria present, the next generation will have $n + r \cdot n$ bacteria. Write a program to read the original number of bacteria, the growth rate, and an upper limit on the number of bacteria and then to print a table with appropriate headings that shows the generation number, the increase in the number of bacteria from the previous generation, and the total number of bacteria in that generation, for each generation number from 1 up through the first generation for which the number of bacteria exceeds the specified upper limit.

6.3 Formatted Input

We have seen that input is accomplished in FORTRAN by a **READ statement**. This statement has two forms, the simpler of which is

READ *format-specifier, input-list*

where *input-list* is a single variable or a list of variables separated by commas and *format-specifier* specifies the format in which the values for the items in the input list are to be entered. As in the case of output, the format specifier may be

1. An asterisk (*).
2. A character constant or a character variable (or expression or array) whose value specifies the format for the input.
3. The label of a FORMAT statement.

The most commonly used form of the READ statement is that in which the format specifier is an asterisk. As we saw in Chapter 3, this form indicates list-directed input in which the format is determined by the types of variables in the input list. In all situations except those in which the data have a specific predetermined form, list-directed input should be adequate. When the data items are of a predetermined form, it may be necessary to use a format specifier of type 2 or 3 to read this data.

As in the case of output, the format specifier may be a character constant or variable (or expression or array) whose value has the form

'(*list of format descriptors*)'

or the label of a FORMAT statement of the form

FORMAT(*list of format descriptors*)

The format descriptors are essentially the same as those discussed for output in the preceding section. Character constants, however, may not appear in the list of format descriptors, and the colon separator is not relevant to input.

Integer Input. Integer data can be read using the I descriptor of the form

*r*I*w*

where *w* indicates the width of the field, that is, the number of columns to be read, and *r* is the repetition indicator specifying the number of such fields. To illustrate, consider the following example:

```
      INTEGER I, J, K
      READ '(I6, I4, I7)', I, J, K
```

or

```
      READ 5, I, J, K
    5 FORMAT(I6, I4, I7)
```

For the values of I, J, and K to be read correctly, the numbers should be entered as follows: the value for I in the first six columns, the value for J in the next four columns, and the value for K in the next seven columns, with each value right justified within its field. Thus, if the values to be read are

    I: − 123
    J: 45
    K: 6789

the data may be entered as follows:

    ___-123__45___6789

If the format specification were changed to

    (I4, I2, I4)

the data should be entered as

    -123456789

with no intervening blanks. Here the first four columns are read for I, the next two columns for J, and the next four columns for K.

Blanks within a field read with an I descriptor can be interpreted as zeros, or they can be ignored. If they are interpreted as zeros, integer values must be right justified within their fields, as in the first example, if they are to be read correctly. Had they been entered as

    ‾123‾45‾6789‾‾‾‾

I would have been assigned the value -1230, J the value 4506, and K the value 7890000. If blanks are ignored, the location of an integer value within its field is irrelevant. We assume in the examples of this text that *blank columns within numeric fields are ignored*, since this agrees with the ANSI standard. (The BZ and BN descriptors described in Section 6.7 can be used to specify which of the two interpretations is to apply.)

Real Input.   One of the descriptors used to input real data is the F descriptor of the form

    rF$w.d$

where w indicates the width of the field to be read, d is the number of digits to the right of the decimal point, and r is the repetition counter.
    There are two ways that real data may be entered:

1. The numbers may be entered with no decimal points.
2. The decimal point may be entered as part of the input value.

In the first case, the d specification in the format descriptor F$w.d$ automatically positions the decimal point so that there are d digits to its right. For example, if we wish to enter the following values for real variables A, B, C, D, and E

    A: 6.25
    B: -1.9
    C: 75.0
    D: .182
    E: 625.327

we can use the statements

```
      READ 10, A, B, C, D, E
   10 FORMAT(F3.2, 2F3.1, F3.3, F6.3)
```

or

```
    READ '(F3.2, 2F3.1, F3.3, F6.3)', A, B, C, D, E
```

and enter the data in the following form:

    625‾19750182625327

Of course, we can use wider fields, for example,

```
    (F4.2, 2F4.1, 2F8.3)
```

and enter the data in the form

```
_625_-19_750_____182__625327
```

with the values right justified within their fields.

In the second method of entering real data, the position of the decimal point in the value entered overrides the position specified by the descriptor. Thus, if the number to be read is 9423.68, an appropriate descriptor is F6.2 if the number is entered without a decimal point and F7.2, or F7.1, or F7.0, and so on, if the number is entered with a decimal point. For example, the preceding values for A, B, C, D, and E can be read using the statements

```
    READ 15, A, B, C, D, E
15 FORMAT(4F5.0, F8.0)
```

with the data entered in the following form:

```
_6.25_-1.9__75.__182_625.327
```

Note that each field width must be large enough to accommodate the number entered, including the decimal point and the sign.

Real values entered in E notation can also be read using an F descriptor. Thus for the FORMAT specification

```
(5F10.0)
```

the data of the preceding example could also have been entered as

```
____.625E1_____-1.9_____75.0___18.2E-2_6.25327E2
```

In this case, the E need not be entered if the exponent is preceded by a sign. The following would therefore be an alternative method for entering the preceding data:

```
____.625+1_____-1.9_____75.0____18.2-2_6.25327+2
```

The E descriptor may also be used in a manner similar to that for the F descriptor.

Character Input. Character data can be read using an A descriptor of the form

```
    rA    or    rAw
```

where r is a repetition indicator, and in the second form w is the width of the field to be read. In the first form, the width of the field read for a particular variable in the input list is the length specified for that variable in the CHARACTER statement.

When a READ statement whose input list contains a character variable is executed, *all* characters in the field associated with the corresponding A descriptor are read. For example, if the line of data

```
FOURSCORE_AND_SEVEN_YEARS_AGO
```

is read by the statements

```
      CHARACTER*6 STRA, STRB
      READ 20, STRA, STRB
20 FORMAT(2A)
```

the value

```
FOURSC
```

is assigned to STRA and

```
ORE AN
```

to STRB.

Note that six columns were read for each of STRA and STRB, as this is their declared length. If the following line of data

```
AB1!!34!AN,APPLE_A_DAY
```

is entered, the values assigned to STRA and STRB would be

```
AB1''3
```

and

```
4'AN,A
```

respectively.

If the format statement

```
20 FORMAT(2A6)
```

were used, the same values would be assigned to STRA and STRB. If, however, the format statement

```
20 FORMAT(A2, A12)
```

were used, the value assigned to STRA would be

```
ABɞɞɞɞ
```

(where ɞ denotes a blank) and the value assigned to STRB would be

```
AN,APP
```

Note that in the case of STRB, a field of size 12 was read but the *rightmost* six characters were assigned. (See Programming Pointer 4 at the end of this chapter.)

Logical Input. Logical data can be read using an L descriptor of the form

rLw

where r is a repetition indicator and w is the width of the field to be read. The input value consists of optional blanks followed by an optional period followed by a T for true or an F for false; any characters following T or F are ignored. For example, if the line of data

```
 .TRUE   TWO.F FT
```

is read by the statements

```
      LOGICAL A, B, C, D, E

      READ 40, A, B, C, D, E
   40 FORMAT(2L6, 3L2)
```

or

```
      READ '(2L6, 3L2)', A, B, C, D, E
```

then A, B, and E are assigned the value true, and C and D the value false.

Skipping Columns of Input. The positional descriptors X and T may be used in the format specifier of a READ statement to skip over certain columns of data. For example, if we wish to assign the following values to the integer variables I, J, and K:

I: 4
J: 56
K: 137

by entering data in the form

```
I = 4   J = 56  K = 137
```

the following statements may be used:

```
      READ 20, I, J, K
   20 FORMAT(3X, I2, 6X, I3, 5X, I4)
```

or

```
   20 FORMAT(T4, I2, T12, I3, T20, I4)
```

Columns of data are also skipped if the end of the input list is encountered before the end of the data line has been reached. To illustrate, if the statements

```
      READ 25, NUM1, X
      READ 25, NUM2, Y
   25 FORMAT(I5, F7.0)
```

are used to read values for the integer variables NUM1 and NUM2 and real variables X and Y from the following data lines:

```
   ___17___3.56___34___13.4
   _9064_570550_3199_47____
```

the values assigned to NUM1 and X are

```
   NUM1:   17
      X:   3.56
```

and the values assigned to NUM2 and Y are

```
   NUM2:   9064
      Y:   570550.
```

All other information on these two lines is ignored.

Multiple Input Lines.   Recall that a new line of data is required each time a READ statement is executed. A new line of data is also required whenever a slash (/) is encountered in the format specifier for the READ statement. This may be used in case one wishes to separate some of the data entries by blank lines, remarks, and the like, which are to be skipped over by the READ statement. For example, the following data:

```
   AMOUNT_TO_BE_PRODUCED_____
   585.00_____
   REACTION_RATE_____
   (THIS_ASSUMES_CONSTANT_TEMPERATURE)
   5.75_____
```

can be read by a single READ statement, and the values 585.00 and 5.75 assigned to AMOUNT and RATE, respectively, in the following manner:

```
   REAL AMOUNT, RATE

      READ 30, AMOUNT, RATE
   30 FORMAT(/ F6.0 /// F4.0)
```

or

```
      READ '(/ F6.0 /// F4.0)', AMOUNT, RATE
```

The first slash causes the first line to be skipped, so that the value 585.00 is read for AMOUNT; the three slashes then cause an advance of three lines, so that 5.75 is read for RATE.

A new line is also required if all descriptors have been used and there still are variables remaining in the input list for which values must be read. In this case, the format specifier is rescanned, as in the case of output. Thus, the statements

```
      INTEGER I, J, K, L, M

      READ 35, I, J, K, L, M
   35 FORMAT(3I8)
```

require two lines of input, the first containing the values of I, J, and K and the second, the values of L and M.

6.4   The WRITE Statement and the General READ Statement

The PRINT and READ statements used thus far are simple FORTRAN input/output statements. In this section we consider more general input/output statements, the WRITE statement and the general form of the READ statement.

The WRITE Statement.   The **WRITE statement** has a more complicated syntax than does the PRINT statement, but it is a more general output statement. It has the form

> WRITE (*control-list*) *output-list*

where *output-list* has the same syntax as in the PRINT statement and *control-list* may include items selected from the following:

1. A unit specifier indicating the output device.
2. A format specifier.
3. Other items that are especially useful in file processing. (These are considered in Chapter 11.)

The control list must include a unit specifier and, except for the more advanced applications described in Chapter 11, a format specifier as well. The **unit specifier** is an integer expression whose value designates the output device, or it may be an asterisk, indicating the standard output device (usually a terminal or printer). The unit specifier may be given in the form

> UNIT = *unit-specifier*

or simply

> *unit-specifier*

If the UNIT = clause is not used, the unit specifier must be the first item in the control list.

The **format specifier** may be given in the form

FMT = *format-specifier*

or simply

format-specifier

where *format-specifier* may be of any of the forms allowed in the PRINT statement. If the format specifier without the FMT = clause is used, then it must be the second item in the control list, and the UNIT = clause must also be omitted for the unit specifier.

To illustrate the WRITE statement, suppose that the values of GRAV and WEIGHT are to be displayed on an output device having unit number 6. The statement

```
WRITE (6, *) GRAV, WEIGHT
```

or any of the following equivalent forms

```
WRITE (6, FMT = *) GRAV, WEIGHT

WRITE (UNIT = 6, FMT = *) GRAV, WEIGHT

WRITE (NOUT, *) GRAV, WEIGHT

WRITE (UNIT = NOUT, FMT = *) GRAV, WEIGHT
```

where NOUT is an integer variable with value 6, produce list-directed output to this device. If this device is the system's standard output device, the unit number 6 may be replaced by an asterisk in any of the preceding statements; for example,

```
WRITE (*, *) GRAV, WEIGHT
```

and each of these is equivalent to the short form

```
PRINT *, GRAV, WEIGHT
```

Formatted output of these values can be produced by statements like the following:

```
    WRITE (6, '(1X, 2F10.2)') GRAV, WEIGHT

    WRITE (6, FMT = '(1X, 2F10.2)') GRAV, WEIGHT

    WRITE (6, 30) GRAV, WEIGHT
30  FORMAT(1X, 2F10.2)

    WRITE (UNIT = 6, FMT = 30) GRAV, WEIGHT
30  FORMAT(1X, 2F10.2)
```

The program in Figure 6.2 displays tables of numbers together with their squares, cubes, and square roots. It is a modification of the program in Figure 6.1 in which the PRINT statements have been replaced by WRITE statements.

```
      PROGRAM TABLE
***********************************************************************
* Program demonstrating the use of formatted output to print a table  *
* of values of N, the square and cube of N, and the square root of N  *
* for N = 1, 2, ..., LAST where the value of LAST is read during      *
* execution.                                                          *
***********************************************************************

      INTEGER N, LAST

      WRITE (*, *) 'ENTER LAST NUMBER TO BE USED'
      READ *, LAST

*     Print headings

      WRITE (*, 100) 'NUMBER', 'SQUARE', '  CUBE', 'SQ. ROOT'
100   FORMAT(// 1X, A8, T11, A8, T21, A8, T31, A10 / 1X, 40('='))

*     Print the table

      DO 10 N = 1, LAST
          WRITE (*, 110) N, N**2, N**3, SQRT(REAL(N))
110       FORMAT(1X, I6, 2I10, 2X, F10.4)
10    CONTINUE

      END
```

Sample run:

```
ENTER LAST NUMBER TO BE USED
10


    NUMBER    SQUARE      CUBE    SQ. ROOT
    ========================================
         1         1         1      1.0000
         2         4         8      1.4142
         3         9        27      1.7321
         4        16        64      2.0000
         5        25       125      2.2361
         6        36       216      2.4495
         7        49       343      2.6458
         8        64       512      2.8284
         9        81       729      3.0000
        10       100      1000      3.1623
```

Figure 6.2

The General READ Statement. The general form of the **READ statement** is

>   READ (*control-list*) input-list

where *control-list* may include items selected from the following:

1. A unit specifier indicating the input device.
2. A format specifier.
3. An IOSTAT = clause or an END = clause to detect an input error or an end-of-file condition, as described in the next section.
4. Other items that are particularly useful in processing files. (These are considered in Chapter 11.)

As an illustration of the general form of the READ statement, suppose that values for CODE, TIME, and RATE are to be read using the input device 5. The statement

```
READ (5, *) CODE, TIME, RATE
```

or any of the following equivalent forms

```
READ (5, FMT = *) CODE, TIME, RATE

READ (UNIT = 5, FMT = *) CODE, TIME, RATE

READ (IN, *) CODE, TIME, RATE

READ (UNIT = IN, FMT = *) CODE, TIME, RATE
```

where IN has the value 5, can be used. If this device is the system's standard input device, an asterisk may be used in place of the device number in any of the preceding unit specifications; for example,

```
READ (*, *) CODE, TIME, RATE
```

Formatted input is also possible with the general READ statement; for example,

```
READ (5, '(I6, 2F6.2)') CODE, TIME, RATE
```

or

```
READ (UNIT = 5, FMT = '(I6, 2F6.2)') CODE, TIME, RATE
```

or

```
READ (UNIT = 5, FMT = 10) CODE, TIME, RATE
```

or

```
READ (5, 10) CODE, TIME, RATE
```

where 10 is the number of the following FORMAT statement:

```
10 FORMAT(I6, 2F6.2)
```

6.5 Introduction to File Processing

Up to this point we have assumed that the data for the sample programs was entered from the keyboard during program execution and that the output was displayed on the screen. This is usually adequate if the amounts of input/output data are relatively small. However, applications involving large data sets may be processed more conveniently if the data is stored in a file for later processing, for example, by a program as it reads input data from this file or by a printer as it produces a hard copy of the output. Files are usually stored on magnetic tape or magnetic disk or some other form of external (secondary) memory. Magnetic tape is coated with a substance that can be magnetized and stores information for computer processing in somewhat the same way that an audio tape stores sound information. Information can be written to or read from a tape using a device called a **tape drive**. A magnetic disk is also coated with a substance that can be magnetized. Information is stored on such disks in tracks arranged in concentric circles and is written to or read from a disk using a **disk drive**. This device transfers information by means of a read/write head that is positioned over one of the tracks of the rotating disk.

In general, any collection of data items that is input to or output by a program is called a **file**, and each line of data in the file is called a **record**. In this section we consider the characteristics of files and some of the FORTRAN statements used in processing them. (Others are described in Chapter 11.)

Each record of a file to be used as an input file must have the entries arranged in a form suitable for reading by a READ statement. These records are read during program execution, just like a line of data entered by the user. For example, if the variables CODE, TEMP, and PRESS are declared by

```
INTEGER CODE
REAL TEMP, PRESS
```

and the values for these variables are to be read from a file using a list-directed READ statement, this data file might have the following form:

```
37, 77.5, 30.39
22, 85.3, 30.72
1, 100.0, 29.95
78, 99.5, 29.01
      .
      .
      .
```

If the values are to be read using the format specifier

```
(I2, 2F8.0)
```

the file might have the form

```
37____77.5___30.39
22____85.3___30.72
_1___100.0___29.95
78____99.5___29.01
              .
              .
              .
```

whereas the format specifier

    (I2, F4.1, F4.2)

would be appropriate for the file

```
37_7753039
22_8533072
_110002995
78_9952901
    .
    .
    .
```

Opening Files. Before a file can be used for input or output in a FORTRAN program, it must be "opened." This can be accomplished using an **OPEN statement** of the form

    OPEN (*open-list*)

where *open-list* includes

1. A unit specifier indicating a unit number connected to the file being opened.
2. A FILE = clause giving the name of the file being opened.
3. A STATUS = clause specifying whether the file is a new or an old file.

(Other items that may be included are described in Chapter 11.)

The unit specifier has the form

    UNIT = *integer-expression*

or simply

    integer-expression

where the value of *integer-expression* is a nonnegative number that designates the unit number to be connected to this file. Reference to this file by a READ or WRITE statement will be by means of this unit number.

The FILE = clause has the form

    FILE = *character-expression*

where the value of *character-expression* (ignoring trailing blanks) is the name of the file to be connected to the specified unit number.

The STATUS = clause has the form

STATUS = *character-expression*

where the value of *character-expression* (ignoring trailing blanks) is

'OLD'

or

'NEW'

OLD means that the file already exists in the system. NEW means that the file does not yet exist and is being created by the program; execution of the OPEN statement creates an empty file with the specified name and changes its status to OLD.

Closing Files. The **CLOSE statement** has a function opposite to that of the OPEN statement and is used to disconnect a file from its unit number. This statement has the form

CLOSE (*close-list*)

where *close-list* must include a unit specifier and may include other items as described in Chapter 11. After a CLOSE statement is executed, the closed file may be reopened by means of an OPEN statement; the same unit number may be connected to it, or a different one may be used. All files that are not explicitly closed by means of a CLOSE statement are automatically closed when the END statement (or a STOP statement) is executed.

File Input/Output. Once a file has been connected to a unit number, data can be read from or written to that file using the general forms of the READ and WRITE statements in which the unit number appearing in the control list is the same as the unit number connected to the file. For example, to read values for CODE, TEMP, and PRESS from a file named INFO, the statement

```
OPEN (UNIT = 12, FILE = 'INFO', STATUS = 'OLD')
```

opens the file, and the statement

```
READ (12, *) CODE, TEMP, PRESS
```

reads the values.

Similarly, a file named REPORT to which values of CODE, TEMP, and PRESS are to be written can be created by

```
OPEN (UNIT = 13, FILE = 'REPORT', STATUS = 'NEW')
```

Values can then be written to this file with statement like

```
WRITE (13, '(1X, I3, F7.0, F10.2)') CODE, TEMP, PRESS
```

or

```
      WRITE (13, 30) CODE, TEMP, PRESS
30 FORMAT(1X, I3, F7.0, F10.2)
```

Each execution of a READ statement causes an entire record to be read and then positions the file so that the next execution of a READ (WRITE) statement causes values to be read from (written to) the next record in the file. Similarly, execution of a WRITE statement writes an entire record into the file and then positions the file so that the next execution of a WRITE (READ) statement produces output to (input from) the next record in the file.

The IOSTAT = Clause. In the preceding section, we noted that the control list of a general READ statement may contain an **IOSTAT = clause** to detect an end-of-file condition or an input error. This clause has the form

IOSTAT = *status-variable*

where *status-variable* is an integer variable. When the READ statement is executed, this variable is assigned

1. A positive value if an input error occurs.
2. A negative value if the end of data is encountered but no input error occurs.
3. Zero if neither an input error nor the end of data occurs.

In the first case, the value is usually the number of an error message in a list found in the system manuals. For example, if EOF is an integer variable, a while loop of the following form can be used to read and process values for CODE, TEMP, and PRESS from a file, terminating repetition when the end of the file is reached:

```
   * While there is more data
         READ (12, *, IOSTAT = EOF) CODE, TEMP, PRESS
   10    IF (EOF .GE. 0) THEN
            COUNT = COUNT + 1
                .
                .
                .
            SUMP = SUMP + PRESS
            READ (12, *, IOSTAT = EOF) CODE, TEMP, PRESS
         GO TO 10
         END IF
```

The END = Clause. An alternative method of detecting an end-of-file condition is to use an **END = clause** in the control list of a general READ statement.

END = *statement-number*

where *statement-number* is the number of an executable statement that is the next statement to be executed when the end of data is encountered. For example, the statement

```
READ (12, *, END = 20) CODE, TEMP, PRESS
```

can be used within a loop to read values for CODE, TEMP, and PRESS from a file. When the end of this file is reached, control transfers to statement 20, which marks the end of the loop:

```
*  Read and process data until the end of the file
*  is encountered

10      CONTINUE
           READ (12, *, END = 20) CODE, TEMP, PRESS
           COUNT = COUNT + 1
                  .
                  .
                  .
           SUMP = SUMP + PRESS
        GO TO 10
20      CONTINUE
```

File-Positioning Statements. There are several FORTRAN statements that may be used to position a file. Two of these statements are

REWIND *unit*

and

BACKSPACE *unit*

where *unit* is the unit number connected to the file.

The **REWIND statement** positions the file at its initial point, that is, at the beginning of the first record of the file. The **BACKSPACE statement** causes the file to be positioned at the beginning of the preceding record. If the file is at its initial point, these statements have no effect.

6.6 Examples: Time, Temperature, Pressure, and Volume Readings; Run-Time Formatting

EXAMPLE 1: Time, Temperature, Pressure, and Volume Readings.
Suppose that a device monitoring a process records time, temperature, pressure, and volume and stores this data in a file. Each record in this file contains

Time in columns 1–4.
Temperature in columns 5–8.
Pressure in columns 9–12.
Volume in columns 13–16.

The value for time is an integer representing the time at which the measurements were taken. The values for temperature, pressure, and volume are real numbers but are recorded with no decimal point. Each must be interpreted as a real value having a decimal point between the third and fourth digits.

A program is to be designed to read the values for the temperature and volume, print these values in tabular form, and display the equation of the least squares line determined by these values (see Section 4.11). Figure 6.3 shows the program along with a listing of the input file and the output produced by the program.

```
        PROGRAM TEMVOL
************************************************************************
* Program to read temperatures and volumes from a file containing     *
* time, temperature, pressure, and volume readings made by some       *
* monitoring device.  The temperature and volume measurements are     *
* displayed in tabular form, and the equation of the least squares    *
* line y = mx + b (x = temperature, y = volume) is calculated.        *
* Variables used are:                                                 *
*      FNAME    : name of data file                                   *
*      EOF      : end-of-file indicator                               *
*      TEMP     : temperature recorded                                *
*      VOLUME   : volume recorded                                     *
*      COUNT    : count of (TEMP, VOLUME) pairs                       *
*      SUMT     : sum of temperatures                                 *
*      SUMT2    : sum of squares of temperatures                      *
*      SUMV     : sum of volumes                                      *
*      SUMTV    : sum of the products TEMP * VOLUME                    *
*      TMEAN    : mean temperature                                    *
*      VMEAN    : mean volume                                         *
*      SLOPE    : slope of the least squares line                     *
*      YINT     : y-intercept of the line                             *
************************************************************************

        INTEGER COUNT, EOF
        CHARACTER*20 FNAME
        REAL TEMP, VOLUME, SUMT, SUMT2, SUMV, SUMTV, TMEAN, VMEAN,
     +       SLOPE, YINT
        DATA COUNT, SUMT, SUMT2, SUMV, SUMTV /0, 4*0.0/

* Open the file as unit 15, set up the input and output
* formats, and print the table heading.

        PRINT *, 'ENTER NAME OF DATA FILE:'
        READ '(A)', FNAME
        OPEN (UNIT = 15, FILE = FNAME, STATUS = 'OLD')
100     FORMAT(4X, F4.1, T13, F4.1)
110     FORMAT(1X, A11, A10)
120     FORMAT(1X, F8.1, F12.1)
        PRINT *
        PRINT 110, 'TEMPERATURE', 'VOLUME'
        PRINT 110, '===========', '======'
```

Figure 6.3

Figure 6.3 (continued)

```
* While there is more data, read temperatures and volumes,
* display each in the table, and calculate the necessary sums

      READ (UNIT = 15, FMT = 100, IOSTAT = EOF) TEMP, VOLUME
10    IF (EOF .GE. 0) THEN
          PRINT 120, TEMP, VOLUME
          COUNT = COUNT + 1
          SUMT = SUMT + TEMP
          SUMT2 = SUMT2 + TEMP ** 2
          SUMV = SUMV + VOLUME
          SUMTV = SUMTV + TEMP * VOLUME
          READ (UNIT = 15, FMT = 100, IOSTAT = EOF) TEMP, VOLUME
      GO TO 10
      END IF

* Find equation of least squares line

      TMEAN = SUMT / COUNT
      VMEAN = SUMV / COUNT
      SLOPE = (SUMTV - SUMT * VMEAN) / (SUMT2 - SUMT * TMEAN)
      YINT = VMEAN - SLOPE * TMEAN
      PRINT 130, SLOPE, YINT
130   FORMAT(//1X, 'EQUATION OF LEAST SQUARES LINE IS'
      +        /1X, '      Y =', F5.1, 'X + ', F5.1,
      +        /1X, 'WHERE X IS TEMPERATURE AND Y IS VOLUME')

      CLOSE (15)
      END
```

Listing of file TEMP-VOL-FILE used in sample run:

```
1200034203221015
1300038803221121
1400044803241425
1500051303201520
1600055503181665
1700061303191865
1800067503232080
1900072103282262
2000076803252564
2100083503272869
2200088903303186
```

Figure 6.3   (continued)

Sample run:

```
ENTER NAME OF DATA FILE:
TEMP-VOL-FILE

   TEMPERATURE     VOLUME
   ===========     ======
        34.2       101.5
        38.8       112.1
        44.8       142.5
        51.3       152.0
        55.5       166.5
        61.3       186.5
        67.5       208.0
        72.1       226.2
        76.8       256.4
        83.5       286.9
        88.9       318.6

EQUATION OF LEAST SQUARES LINE IS
     Y =   3.8X + -39.8
WHERE X IS TEMPERATURE AND Y IS VOLUME
```

EXAMPLE 2: Run-Time Formatting. In most of our examples of formatted input/output we used a FORMAT statement. As we noted, however, a format specifier may also be a character expression whose value is the list of format descriptors. For example, the statement

```
PRINT '(1X, F8.1, F12.1)', TEMP, VOLUME
```

is equivalent to the pair of statements

```
    PRINT 120, TEMP, VOLUME
120 FORMAT(1X, F8.1, F12.1)
```

A character variable could also be used:

```
CHARACTER*40 FORM
      .
      .
      .
FORM = '(1X, F8.1, F12.1)'
PRINT FORM, TEMP, VOLUME
```

A list of format descriptors can also be read at run-time and assigned to a character variable like FORM which can then be used as a format specifier. This makes it possible to change the format used for input or output each time a program is run without having to modify the program itself. This is illustrated in the program of Figure 6.4, which is like that in Figure 6.3 except that it only displays tables of the temperature and volume readings.

Two sample runs are shown. The first uses the data file given earlier

```
1200034203221015
1300038803221121
1400044803241425
1500051303201520
1600055503181665
1700061303191865
1800067503232080
1900072103282262
2000076803252564
2100083503272869
2200088903303186
```

in which the fifth through eighth digits constitute the temperatures, and the last four digits are the volumes. Decimal points must be positioned so there is one digit to its right in both cases. Thus an appropriate format specifier is

```
(4X, F4.1, T13, F4.1)
```

The second data file is

```
12:00PM
34.2 32.2 101.5
1:00PM
33.8 32.2 112.1
2:00PM
44.8 32.4 142.5
3:00PM
51.3 32.0 152.0
4:00PM
55.5 31.8 166.5
5:00PM
61.3 31.9 186.5
6:00PM
67.5 32.3 208.0
7:00PM
72.1 32.8 226.2
8:00PM
76.8 32.5 256.4
9:00PM
83.5 32.7 286.9
10:00PM
88.9 33.0 318.6
```

for which an appropriate format specifier is

```
(/F5.0, 5X, F6.0)
```

When the program is executed, the user enters the name of the file (FNAME) and the appropriate format specifier (FORM) for that file.

```
      PROGRAM TEMVOL
*************************************************************************
* Program to read temperatures and volumes from a file containing    *
* time, temperature, pressure, and volume readings made by some      *
* monitoring device and display the temperature and volume           *
* measurements in tabular form.  Variables used are:                 *
*      FNAME    : name of data file                                  *
*      EOF      : end-of-file indicator                              *
*      FORM     : input format specifier                             *
*      TEMP     : temperature recorded                               *
*      VOLUME   : volume recorded                                    *
*************************************************************************

      CHARACTER*50 FORM, FNAME*20
      INTEGER EOF
      REAL TEMP, VOLUME

* Open the file as unit 15, read the input format,
* and print the table heading.

      PRINT *, 'ENTER NAME OF DATA FILE:'
      READ '(A)', FNAME
      OPEN (UNIT = 15, FILE = FNAME, STATUS = 'OLD')
      PRINT*, 'ENTER INPUT FORMAT FOR ', FNAME
      READ '(A)', FORM
110   FORMAT(1X, A11, A10)
120   FORMAT(1X, F8.1, F12.1)
      PRINT *
      PRINT 110, 'TEMPERATURE', 'VOLUME'
      PRINT 110, '===========', '======'

* While there is more data, read temperatures and volumes,
* displaying each in the table.

      READ (UNIT = 15, FMT = FORM, IOSTAT = EOF) TEMP, VOLUME
10    IF (EOF .GE. 0) THEN
          PRINT 120, TEMP, VOLUME
          READ (UNIT = 15, FMT = FORM, IOSTAT = EOF) TEMP, VOLUME
      GO TO 10
      END IF

      CLOSE (15)
      END
```

Figure 6.4

Figure 6.4 (continued)

Sample runs:

```
ENTER NAME OF DATA FILE:
TEMP-VOL-FILE-1
ENTER INPUT FORMAT FOR TEMP-VOL-FILE-1
(4X, F4.1, T13, F4.1)
TEMPERATURE      VOLUME
===========      ======
       34.2      101.5
       38.8      112.1
       44.8      142.5
       51.3      152.0
       55.5      166.5
       61.3      186.5
       67.5      208.0
       72.1      226.2
       76.8      256.4
       83.5      286.9
       88.9      318.6

ENTER NAME OF DATA FILE:
TEMP-VOL-FILE-2
ENTER INPUT FORMAT FOR TEMP-VOL-FILE-2
(/F5.0, 5X, F6.0)
TEMPERATURE      VOLUME
===========      ======
       34.2      101.5
       38.8      112.1
       44.8      142.5
       51.3      152.0
       55.5      166.5
       61.3      186.5
       67.5      208.0
       72.1      226.2
       76.8      256.4
       83.5      286.9
       88.9      318.6
```

6.7 Miscellaneous Input/Output Topics

In this chapter we have described several of the more commonly used format descriptors. These descriptors are used to specify the precise format of output produced by a formatted PRINT or WRITE statement and to specify the format of values to be read by a formatted READ statement. In this section we describe a number of less commonly used format descriptors, as well as some additional features of list-directed input that were not mentioned in Chapter 3.

The G Descriptor. In addition to the E and F descriptors for the input and output of real data, a G descriptor of the form

$$rGw.d \qquad \text{or} \qquad rGw.dEe$$

may be used. A real value that is output using a G descriptor is displayed using an F or E descriptor, depending on the magnitude (absolute value) of the real number.

Intuitively, the G descriptor functions like an F descriptor for values that are neither very large nor very small, but like an E descriptor otherwise. More precisely, suppose that a real quantity has a value that if expressed in normalized scientific notation would have the form

$$\pm 0.d_1 d_2 \ldots d_n \times 10^k$$

and this value is to be displayed using a $Gw.d$ descriptor. If $0 \le k \le d$, this value is output in "F form" with a field width of $w - 4$ followed by four blanks. If, however, k is negative or greater than d, it is output using an $Ew.d$ descriptor. In either case, a total of d significant digits are displayed. The following examples illustrate:

Value	G Descriptor	Output Produced
0.123456	G12.6	0.123456____
0.123456E1	G11.6	1.23456____
0.123456E5	G11.6	12345.6____
0.123456E6	G11.6	123456.____
0.123456E7	G12.6	0.123456E+07

Although the G descriptor is intended primarily for real output, it may also be used for real input in a manner similar to that of the F descriptor.

Scale Factors. To permit more general usage of the E, F, G, and D descriptors, they may be preceded by scale factors of the form

$$n\text{P}$$

where n is an integer constant. In the case of output, a descriptor of the form

$$n\text{P}Fw.d$$

causes the displayed value to be multiplied by 10^n. For the E (and D) descriptor,

$$n\text{P}Ew.d \qquad \text{or} \qquad n\text{P}Ew.dEe$$

causes the fractional part of the displayed value to be multiplied by 10^n and the exponent to be decreased by n. For the G descriptor, a scale factor has an effect only if the value being output is in a range that causes it to be displayed in E form, and in this case the effect of the scale factor is the same as that described for the E descriptor.

To illustrate the use of scale factors, suppose that the values of the integer variable N and the real variables X, Y, and Z are given by

N: 27
X: -93.2094

Y: -0.0076
Z: 55.3612

and consider the following statements:

```
      PRINT 1, N, X, Y, Z
      PRINT 2, N, X, Y, Z
      PRINT 3, N, X, Y, Z
    1 FORMAT(1X, I2, 2F11.3, E12.4)
    2 FORMAT(1X, I2, 1P2F11.3, 3PE12.4)
    3 FORMAT(1X, I2, -1P2F11.3, E12.4)
```

The output produced by these statements is

```
27_____-93.209_____-0.008__0.5536E+02
27____-932.094_____-0.076__553.61E-01
27_____-9.321_____-0.001__0.0554E+03
```

As the last FORMAT statement demonstrates, once a scale factor has been given in a format specifier, it holds for all E, F, G, and D descriptors that follow it in the same format specifier. If a subsequent scale factor of zero is desired in that format specifier, it must be specified by 0P.

In the case of input, scale factors may be used with the descriptors for real data in much the same manner as they were for output. The only difference is that if a real value is input in E form, the scale factor has no effect. For example, for the statements

```
      REAL A, B, C
      READ 15, A, B, C
   15 FORMAT(2PF6.0, -2PF6.0, F6.0)
```

if the data

```
___1.1___1.1___1.1
```

are read, the following assignments are made:

A: 110.0
B: .011
C: .011

(The scale factor -2 remains in effect for the last descriptor.) If the data was entered in the form

```
1.1E0___1.1_1.1E0
```

the assignment would be

A: 1.1
B: .011
C: 1.1

The BN and BZ Descriptors. As we observed in Section 6.2, blanks within a numeric input field may be interpreted as zeros, or they may be ignored. Which interpretation is to be used may be specified by the programmer by including a BN or BZ descriptor in the format specifier. If a BN (''Blank Null'') or BZ (''Blank Zero'') descriptor is encountered during a scan of the list of descriptors, all blanks in fields determined by subsequent numeric descriptors in that format specifier are ignored or interpreted as zero, respectively. In all cases, a numeric field consisting entirely of blanks is interpreted as the value 0.

To illustrate, consider the following data line:

```
5̲3̲7̲_ _6̲.̲2̲5̲8̲E̲3̲_
```

If NUM is an integer variable and ALPHA is a real variable, the statements

```
      READ 40, NUM, ALPHA
   40 FORMAT(BZ, I5, F8.0)
```

assign the following values to NUM and ALPHA:

```
   NUM:    53700
   ALPHA:  6.258E30
```

since the BZ descriptor causes the two blank columns in the field corresponding to the I5 descriptor and the single blank column in the field corresponding to the F8.0 descriptor to be interpreted as zeros. On the other hand,

```
      READ 41, NUM, ALPHA
   41 FORMAT(BN, I5, F8.0)
```

assign the values

```
   NUM:    537
   ALPHA:  6.258E3
```

since the BN descriptor causes these same blank columns to be ignored. The statements

```
      READ 42, NUM, ALPHA
   42 FORMAT(BZ, I5, BN, F8.0)
```

assign the values

```
   NUM:    53700
   ALPHA:  6.258E3
```

The S, SP, and SS Descriptors. The S, SP, and SS descriptors may be used to control the output of plus ($+$) signs in a numeric output field. If the SP (''Sign Positive'') descriptor appears in a format specifier, all positive numeric values output by the statement are preceded by a $+$ sign. On the other hand, the SS ("Sign Suppress") descriptor suppresses the output of all such $+$ signs. An S descriptor may be used to restore control to the computer system, which has the option of displaying or suppressing a $+$ sign.

The H Descriptor. We have seen that character constants may be displayed by including them in the list of descriptors of a format specifier; for example,

```
(1X, 'FOR', I5, ' SAMPLES, THE AVERAGE IS', F8.2)
```

Strings may also be displayed by using a Hollerith descriptor of the form

nH*string*

where n is the number of characters in *string*. Thus, the preceding format specifier can also be written

```
(1X, 3HFOR, I5, 24H SAMPLES, THE AVERAGE IS, F8.2)
```

The TL and TR Descriptors. The TL and TR descriptors are positional descriptors of the form

TLn and   TRn

where n is a positive integer constant. They indicate that input or output of the next data value is to occur n positions to the left or right, respectively, of the current position. Thus a descriptor of the form TLn causes a backspace of n positions. In the case of input, this makes it possible to read the same input value several times. For example, for the data line

123

the statements

```
      INTEGER NUM
      REAL ALPHA, BETA

      READ 50, NUM, ALPHA, BETA
   50 FORMAT(I3, TL3, F3.1, TL3, F3.2)
```

assign the integer value 123 to NUM, the real value 12.3 to ALPHA, and the real value 1.23 to BETA:

NUM: 123
ALPHA: 12.3
BETA: 1.23

In the case of output, a descriptor of the form TLn causes a backspace of n positions on the current output line. However, subsequent descriptors may cause characters in these n positions to be replaced rather than overprinted. For both input and output, a descriptor of the form TRn functions in exactly the same manner as does nX.

List-directed Input. In a data line, consecutive commas with no intervening characters except blanks represent **null values,** which leave unchanged the corresponding variables in the input list of a list-directed READ statement. If the variables have previously been assigned values, the values are not changed; if they have not been assigned values, the variables remain undefined. A slash in a data line terminates the input and leaves unchanged the values of the remaining variables in the input list.

If the same value is to be read for r consecutive variables in the input list, this common value may be entered in the corresponding data line in the form

   r∗value

A repeated null value may be indicated by

   r∗

In this case, the corresponding r consecutive items in the input list are unchanged.

The following examples illustrate these conventions for list-directed input. They are not used in list-directed output, except that a given processor has the option of displaying

   r∗value

for successive output items that have the same value.

Statement	Data Entered	Result
READ *, J, K, A, B	1,,,2.3	J = 1. K and A are unchanged. B = 2.3.
READ *, J, K, A, B,	,,,,	J, K, A, and B all are unchanged.
READ *, J, K, A, B	1,2/	J = 1. K = 2. A and B are unchanged.
READ *, J, K, A, B	/	J, K, A, and B all are unchanged.
READ *, J, K, A, B	2*1, 2*2.3	J = 1 and K = 1. A = 2.3 and B = 2.3.
READ *, J, K, A ,B	1, 2*, 2.3	J = 1. K and A are unchanged. B = 2.3.

In the third and fourth examples, any values following the slash would be ignored.

Exercises

1. For each of the following READ statements, show how the data should be entered so that X, Y, I, J, P, Q, and C are assigned the values 123.77, 6.0, 77, 550, .TRUE., .FALSE., and 'FORTRAN' respectively:

    (a)   `READ *, I, J, X, Y`

    (b)   `READ 5, I, J, X, Y`
         `5 FORMAT(2I3, 2F6.0)`

    (c)   `READ 6, I, J, X, Y`
         `6 FORMAT(I3, F7.0, 2X, I5, T20, F5.0)`

    (d)   `READ 7, I, J, X, Y`
         `7 FORMAT(2I3, F5.2, F1.0)`

    (e)   `READ 8, I, X, J, Y`
         `8 FORMAT(I5, F6.0)`

    (f)   `READ 9, I, X, J, Y`
         `9 FORMAT(I2, F5.2 / I3, F2.1)`

    (g)   `READ 10, X, Y, I, J`
         `10 FORMAT(F5.2, 1X, F1.0, T4, I2, T9, I3)`

    (h)   `READ 11, P, Q`
         `11 FORMAT(2L1)`

    (i)   `READ 12, P, Q`
         `12 FORMAT(L5, L6)`

    (j)   `READ 13, X, I, P, Y, J, Q`
         `13 FORMAT(2(F5.2, I3, L1))`

    (k)   `READ 14, X, I, P, Y, J, Q`
         `14 FORMAT(F6.2 / I5 / L2 // F6.0, I6 / L6)`

    (l)   `READ *, C, J, P`

    (m)   `READ '(A, I2, L6)', C, I, P`

    (n)   `READ 15, C, I, P`
         `15 FORMAT(A7, I3, L5)`

    (o)   `READ 16, C, I, P`
         `16 FORMAT(A10, I10, L10)`

2. Describe the output that will be produced if the following program is executed with the specified input data:

```
PROGRAM COLUMN

INTEGER N, I
REAL R, DELTAR, R1, S1
```

```
            READ (5, 100) N, R, DELTAR
            PRINT 110

            DO 10 I = 1, N
                R1 = R + DELTAR*(I - 1)
                IF (R1 .LT. 120.0) THEN
                    S1 = 17000.0 - 0.485*R1**2
                ELSE
                    S1 = 18000.0 / (1.0 + R1**2/18000.0)
                END IF

                IF (MOD(I, 2) .EQ. 0) THEN
                    PRINT 120, I, R1, S1
                END IF
      10    CONTINUE

     100    FORMAT(/ I5, 2F10.4)
     110    FORMAT('1', T3, 'INDEX', T14, 'S RATIO', T30,
           +        'LOAD')
     120    FORMAT('0', 2X, I2, 2(5X, F10.3))

            END
```

Input data:

```
    12345678901234567890123456789O:   Column numbers
         4      100.0      100000
```

3. Angles are commonly measured in degrees, minutes ('), and seconds(''). There are 360 degrees in one complete revolution, 60 minutes in one degree, and 60 seconds in one minute. Write a program that reads two angular measurements, each in the form

   *ddd*D*mm'ss''*

   where *ddd, mm,* and *ss* are the number of degrees, minutes, and seconds, respectively, and then calculates and displays their sum. Use this program to verify each of the following:

   ```
   74D29'13" + 105D8'16" = 179D37'29"
   7D14'55" + 5D24'55" = 12D39'50"
   20D31'19" + 0D31'30" = 21D2'49"
   122D17'48" + 237D42'12" = 0D0'0"
   ```

4. Write a program that will read a student's number, his or her old GPA, and old number of course credits, followed by the course credit and grade for each of four courses. Calculate and print the current and cumulative GPAs with appropriate labels. See Exercise 18 of Section 3.8 for details of the calculations.) Design the program so that it will accept data entered in the form

   ```
   SNUMB 24179 GPA 3.25 CREDITS 19.0 _____
   CREDITS/GRADES 1.0 3.7 0.5 4.0 1.0 2.7 1.0 3.3
   ```

5. Write a program that reads the time, temperature, pressure, and volume readings from a data file like that described Example 1 of Section 6.6, converts the time from military to ordinary time (e.g., 0900 is 9:00 A.M., 1500 is 3:00 P.M.), calculates the average temperature, average pressure, and average volume, and displays a table like the following:

```
    TIME        TEMPERATURE        PRESSURE        VOLUME
============================================================
  12:00 PM         34.2             32.2           101.5
     .               .                .              .
     .               .                .              .
     .               .                .              .
  10:00 PM         88.9             33.0           318.6
============================================================
  AVERAGES           ?                ?              ?
```

(with the ?s replaced by the appropriate averages).

For the following exercises, see Appendix B for a description of USERS-FILE, STUDENT-FILE, and INVENTORY-FILE.

6. Write a program to search USERS-FILE to find and display the resource limit for a specified user's identification number.

7. Write a program to read STUDENT-FILE and produce a report for all freshmen with GPAs below 2.0. This report should include the student's number and cumulative GPA, with appropriate headings.

8. Write a program to search INVENTORY-FILE to find an item with a specified stock number. If a match is found, display the unit price, the item name, and the number currently in stock; otherwise, display a message indicating that the item was not found.

9. At the end of each month, a report is produced that shows the status of the account of each user in USERS-FILE. Write a program to accept the current date and produce a report of the following form, in which the three asterisks (***) indicate that the user has already used 90 percent or more of the resources available to him or her.

```
            USER ACCOUNTS-6/30/91

                 RESOURCE   RESOURCES
     USER-ID      LIMIT       USED
     -------      -----       ----
      10101       $750      $380.81
      10102       $650      $598.84***
                    .
                    .
                    .
```

10. Write a program to read STUDENT-FILE and calculate

(a) The average cumulative GPA for all male students.
(b) The average cumulative GPA for all female students.

Programming Pointers

In this chapter we considered formatted input/output and introduced files. Some of the key points to remember when using these features are the following:

1. *When control characters are in effect, the first print position of each output line should be used to indicate explicitly what printer control is desired.* In some computer systems, control characters are always in effect; in others, they are not unless a specific system command or compiler option is used.

2. *Formatted output of a numeric value produces a field filled with asterisks if the output requires more spaces than allowed by the specified field width.* For formatted output of real numbers with a descriptor of the form F$w.d$, one should always have

$$w \geq d + 3$$

and for an E descriptor of the form E$w.d$

$$w \geq d + 7$$

3. *For formatted input, blanks within a numeric field may be interpreted as zeros by some systems and ignored by others.* (The BZ and BN descriptors described in Section 6.7 may be used to specify explicitly which interpretation is to be used.)

4. *For formatted input/output, characters are truncated or blanks are added, depending on whether the field width is too small or too large. For input, truncation occurs on the left and blank padding on the right; for output, truncation occurs on the right and blank padding on the left.* The acronyms sometimes used to remember this are

- **POT: P**adding on the left with blanks occurs for formatted **O**utput, or **T**runcation of rightmost characters occurs.
- **TIP: T**runcation of leftmost characters occurs for formatted **I**nput, or **P**adding with blanks on the right occurs.

These are analogous to that in Potential Problem 12 in the Programming Pointers of Chapter 3 for assignment of character values:

- **APT:** For **A**ssignment (and list-directed input), both blank-**P**adding and **T**runcation occur on the right.

To illustrate, suppose STRING is declared by

```
CHARACTER*10 STRING
```

If STRING = 'ABCDEFGHIJ'

then the output produced by the statements

```
     PRINT 10, STRING
     PRINT 20, STRING
 10 FORMAT(1X, A5)
 20 FORMAT(1X, A15)
```

is

```
 ABCDE
 ƀƀƀƀƀABCDEFGHIJ
```

For the formatted input statement

```
 READ 10, STRING
```

if the value entered is

```
 ABCDE
```

(which might be followed by any other characters), the value assigned to STRING is ABCDEƀƀƀƀƀ. For the statement

```
 READ 20, STRING
```

entering the data

```
 ABCDEFGHIJKLMNO
```

assigns the value FGHIJKLMNO to STRING.

FORTRAN 90 Features

- Additional format descriptors have been added. For example, integer descriptors of the form Bw, $Bw.m$, Ow, $Ow.m$, Zw, and $Zw.m$ can be used to display integers in binary, octal, and hexadecimal form, respectively. An *engineering* descriptor EN is used in the same manner as is the E descriptor, except that the exponent is constrained to be a multiple of 3 and a nonzero mantissa is greater than or equal to 1 and less than 1000. The G descriptor can also be used with integer, logical, and character types, and in these cases, it follows the rules of the I, L, and A descriptors.

- A repetition indicator may be used with the slash descriptor; for example, 3/ is equivalent to /// in a format specifier.

- An ADVANCE = clause may appear in the control list of a general READ or WRITE statement; ADVANCE = 'NO' causes nonadvancing input/output, whereas ADVANCE = 'YES' is the default condition and causes an advance to a new line of input or output after the i/o statement has been executed. Nonadvancing output is useful in displaying prompts for interactive input; for example,

```
 WRITE (*, *, ADVANCE = 'NO') 'Enter next number: '
 READ *, NUMBER
```

- A NAMELIST feature can be used to read or display an annotated list of values. This is acccomplished by grouping the items together in a NAMELIST declaration of the form

> NAMELIST /*group-name*/ *variable-list*

in the specification part of a program unit, for example,

```
NAMELIST /POINT/ XCOORD, YCOORD
```

To read or display the variables in a namelist group, a general READ or WRITE statement is used that contains no input/ouput list and in which the format specifier is replaced by the namelist *group-name* or by a clause of the form NML = *group-name* ; for example,

```
READ (*, NML = POINT)
WRITE (*, NML = POINT)
```

Data for namelist input has the form

> &*group-name variable-1* = *value-1*, *variable-2* = *value-2*, ... /

for example,

```
&POINT XCOORD = 1.5, YCOORD = 3.78 /
```

Data for namelist output has this same form; for example, the statement

```
WRITE (*, POINT)
```

might produce as output

```
&POINT XCOORD = 1.50000, YCOORD = 3.78000 /
```

7

One-Dimensional Arrays

In Chapter 3 we introduced the six predefined FORTRAN data types, four for processing numeric data—integer, real, double precision, and complex—one for processing character data, and one for processing logical data. These data types are called **simple** types because a data value of one of these types is atomic; that is, it consists of a single item that cannot be subdivided. In many situations, however, it is necessary to process a collection of values that are related in some way, for example, a list of test scores, a collection of measurements resulting from some experiment, or a matrix. Processing such collections using only simple data types can be extremely cumbersome, and for this reason, most high-level languages include special features for structuring such data. FORTRAN 77 provides one **structured** data type, the array, and in this chapter we consider one-dimensional arrays.

7.1 Introduction to Arrays; Subscripted Variables

In many of our examples, a collection of data values was processed by reading the data values one at a time and processing each item individually, for example, reading a failure time and assigning it to a variable, counting it, and adding it to a running sum. When the value was no longer needed, a new value was read for the same variable, counted and added to the running sum, and the process was repeated again and again. There are many problems, however, in which the collection of data items must be processed several times. To illustrate, suppose that a program is to be developed to

1. Read a list of failure times for some item.
2. Find the mean time to failure.
3. Print a list of failure times greater than the mean.
4. Sort the list so that the failure times are in ascending order.

The following are two possible solutions:

Solution 1: Use one variable for each failure time. Suppose, for example, that there are 50 failure times. We might use 50 different variables, FAIL1, FAIL2, . . . , FAIL50, thus creating 50 different memory locations to store the failure times:

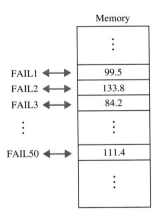

While this approach might be practical if we have only a few data values to process, it is obviously very cumbersome and awkward for large data sets, as the following program skeleton demonstrates:

```
PROGRAM FAILS

REAL FAIL1, FAIL2, FAIL3, FAIL4, FAIL5
+      FAIL6, FAIL7, FAIL8, FAIL9, FAIL10,
           .
           .
           .
+      FAIL46, FAIL47, FAIL48, FAIL49, FAIL50,
+      MEANFT
```

```
* Read the failure times

      READ *, FAIL1, FAIL2, FAIL3, FAIL4, FAIL5,
     +         FAIL6, FAIL7, FAIL8, FAIL9, FAIL10,
                        .
                        .
                        .
     +         FAIL46, FAIL47, FAIL48, FAIL49, FAIL50


* Calculate the mean time to failure

      MEANFT = (FAIL1 + FAIL2 + FAIL3 + FAIL4 + FAIL5
     +          + FAIL6 + FAIL7 + FAIL8 + FAIL9 + FAIL10
                        .
                        .
                        .
     +          + FAIL46 + FAIL47 + FAIL48 + FAIL49
     +          + FAIL50) / 50.0
      PRINT *, 'MEAN TIME TO FAILURE = ', MEANFT


* Display failure times above the mean

          IF (FAIL1 .GT. MEANFT) THEN
             PRINT *, FAIL1
          END IF
          IF (FAIL2 .GT. MEANFT) THEN
             PRINT *, FAIL2
          END IF
          IF (FAIL3 .GT. MEANFT) THEN
             PRINT *, FAIL3
          END IF
                 .
                 .
                 .
          IF (FAIL50 .GT. MEANFT) THEN
             PRINT *, FAIL50
          END IF
* After about 200 lines of code, sort them?
* There must be a better way!

          END
```

Solution 2: Use a data file. If we do not use 50 different memory locations to store all of the failure times, then we are forced to read the values several times. Reentering them again and again so that the required processing can be carried out is obviously not practical. Instead we might prepare a data file containing the failure times and read the values from it, as described in Chapter 6, rewinding the file each time we need to read through the list of times.

```
      PROGRAM FAILS

      REAL FAILTM, SUM, MEANFT
      INTEGER NTIMES, I
```

```
* Read and count the failure times

            OPEN (UNIT = 10, FILE = 'TIMESFILE', STATUS = 'OLD')
            NTIMES = 0
10          CONTINUE
                READ (10, *, END = 20) FAILTM
                NTIMES = NTIMES + 1
            GO TO 10
20          CONTINUE

* Calculate the mean time to failure

            REWIND (UNIT = 10)
            SUM = 0
            DO 30 I = 1, NTIMES
                READ (10, *) FAILTM
                SUM = SUM + FAILTM
30          CONTINUE
            MEANFT = SUM / NTIMES
            PRINT *, 'MEAN TIME TO FAILURE =', MEANFT

* Display failure times above the mean

            REWIND (UNIT = 10)
            DO 40 I = 1, NTIMES
                READ (10, *) FAILTM
                IF (FAILTM .GT. MEANFT) THEN
                    PRINT *, FAILTM
                END IF
40          CONTINUE

* Sort them???   Hm-m-m-m

            END
```

Although this program is more manageable than that in Solution 1, it is not a good solution to the problem because files are usually stored in secondary memory, from which data retrieval is rather slow.

Solution 3: Use an array. To solve this problem efficiently, we need a **data structure** to store and organize the entire collection of failure times, as in Solution 2. However, because of the slowness of file input/output, we need the values stored in main memory, as in Solution 1. Also, many kinds of list processing, such as sorting, cannot be done efficiently if the data items can be retrieved only **sequentially**, that is, when an item can be accessed only by searching from the beginning of the list. What is needed instead is a **direct access** structure that allows a data item to be stored or retrieved directly by specifying its location in the structure, so that it takes no longer to access the item in location 50 than to access that in location 5. And we prefer that the structure be stored in main memory so that storage and retrieval are fast. One such data structure is an **array** in which a fixed number of data items, all of the same type, are organized in a sequence and direct access to each item is possible by specifying its position in this sequence.

If an array is to be used in a FORTRAN program to solve the mean-time-to-failure problem, the computer must first be instructed to reserve a sequence of 50 memory locations for the failure times. For example, the specification statements

```
DIMENSION FAILTM(1:50)
REAL FAILTM
```

or

```
DIMENSION FAILTM(50)
REAL FAILTM
```

instruct the compiler to establish an array with name FAILTM consisting of 50 memory locations in which values of type REAL can be stored:

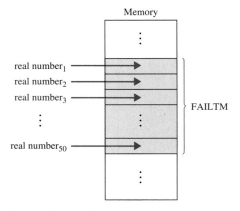

In the program we can then refer to this entire array of real numbers by using the **array variable** FAILTM, but we can also access each individual element or **component** of the array by means of a **subscripted variable** formed by appending a **subscript** (or **index**) enclosed in parentheses to the array variable. This subscript specifies the position of an array component. Thus, FAILTM(1) refers to the first component of the array FAILTM, FAILTM(2) to the second component, and so on. The preceding specification statements thus not only reserve a block of memory locations in which to store the elements of the array FAILTM, but they also associate the subscripted variables FAILTM(1), FAILTM(2), FAILTM(3), ... , FAILTM(50) with these locations:

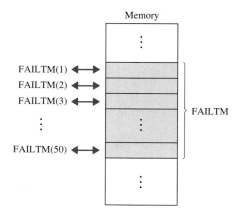

This same array could be declared by including the dimensioning information in the type statement itself,

```
REAL FAILTM(1:50)
```

or

```
REAL FAILTM(50)
```

Each subscripted variable FAILTM(1), FAILTM(2), ... , FAILTM(50) names an individual memory location and hence can be used in much the same way as a simple variable can. For example, the assignment statement

```
FAILTM(4) = 177.8
```

stores the value 177.8 in the fourth location of the array FAILTM, and the output statement

```
PRINT *, FAILTM(10)
```

displays the value stored in the tenth location of the array FAILTM.

An important feature of the notation used for arrays is that the subscript attached to the array name may be an integer variable or expression. For example, the statements

```
IF (FAILTM(N) .LT. 100.0) THEN
    PRINT *, FAILTM(N), ' EARLY FAILURE'
END IF
```

retrieves the Nth item of the array FAILTM, compares it with 100.0, and prints it with the message 'EARLY FAILURE' if it is less than 100.0. The statements

```
IF (FAILTM(I) .GT. FAILTM(I + 1)) THEN
    TEMP = FAILTM(I)
    FAILTM(I) = FAILTM(I + 1)
    FAILTM(I + 1) = TEMP
END IF
```

interchange the values of FAILTM(I) and FAILTM(I + 1) if the first is greater than the second.

Using an array reference in which the subscript is a variable or an expression in a loop that changes the value of the subscript on each pass through the loop is a convenient way to process each item in the array. Thus,

```
        DO 10 I = 1, 50
            IF (FAILTM(I) .LT. 100.0) THEN
                PRINT *, FAILTM(I), ' EARLY FAILURE'
            END IF
    10 CONTINUE
```

retrieves each item of the array FAILTM in sequence, beginning with

FAILTM(1), compares it with 100.0, and prints it with the message 'EARLY FAILURE' if it is less than or equal to 100.0. The effect, therefore, is the same as if we write a sequence of 50 IF constructs, comparing each element of the array FAILTM with 100.0:

```
IF (FAILTM(1) .LT. 100.0) THEN
    PRINT *, FAILTM(1), ' EARLY FAILURE'
END IF
IF (FAILTM(2) .LT. 100.0) THEN
    PRINT *, FAILTM(2), ' EARLY FAILURE'
END IF
IF (FAILTM(3) .LT. 100.0) THEN
    PRINT *, FAILTM(3), ' EARLY FAILURE'
END IF
                    .
                    .
                    .
IF (FAILTM(50) .LT. 100.0) THEN
    PRINT *, FAILTM(50), ' EARLY FAILURE'
END IF
```

The following diagram illustrates the output produced for a particular array FAILTM:

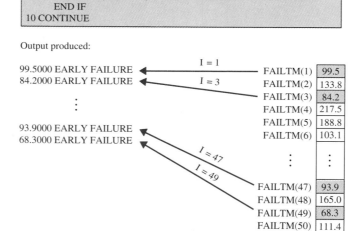

Arrays such as FAILTM involve only a single subscript and are commonly called **one-dimensional arrays.** FORTRAN programs, however, may process arrays of more than one dimension, in which case each element of the array is designated by attaching the appropriate number of subscripts to the array name. In this chapter we consider only one-dimensional arrays; in the next chapter we discuss multidimensional arrays.

The name and the range of subscripts of each one-dimensional array in a program may be declared in a DIMENSION statement of the form

DIMENSION *list*

where *list* is a list of **array declarations** of the form

array-name(l:u)

separated by commas. The pair *l:u* must be a pair of integer constants or parameters specifying the range of values for the subscript to be from the lower limit *l* through the upper limit *u*; for example, the pair $-2:5$ declares that a certain subscript may be any of the integers -2, -1, 0, 1, 2, 3, 4, 5. If the minimum value of the subscript for an array is 1, then only the maximum subscript need be specified. Thus, as we noted earlier, the integer array FAILTM that has a subscript ranging from 1 through 50 may be declared by the statements

```
DIMENSION FAILTM(1:50)
REAL FAILTM
```

or

```
DIMENSION FAILTM(50)
REAL FAILTM
```

Similarly, either

```
DIMENSION COUNT(1:20)
INTEGER COUNT
```

or

```
DIMENSION COUNT(20)
INTEGER COUNT
```

declares COUNT to be a one-dimensional integer array with a subscript ranging from 1 through 20. A single DIMENSION statement can be used to declare both arrays:

```
DIMENSION FAILTM(50), COUNT(20)
REAL FAILTM
INTEGER COUNT
```

As we have noted, the dimension information may also be given in a type statement. Thus,

```
REAL FAILTM(1:50)
INTEGER COUNT(1:20)
```

or

```
REAL FAILTM(50)
INTEGER COUNT(20)
```

can be used in place of the preceding statements. Similarly,

```
REAL ALPHA(20), BETA(20)
```

is acceptable in place of

```
DIMENSION ALPHA(20), BETA(20)
REAL ALPHA, BETA
```

The dimensions in array declarations can also be specified by parameters. For example, the array FAILTM can be declared by

```
INTEGER LLIM, ULIM
PARAMETER (LLIM = 1, ULIM = 50)
REAL FAILTM(LLIM:ULIM)
```

or

```
INTEGER ULIM
PARAMETER (ULIM = 50)
REAL FAILTM(ULIM)
```

Similarly, the arrays COUNT, ALPHA, and BETA can be declared by

```
INTEGER LIMIT
PARAMETER (LIMIT = 20)
INTEGER COUNT(LIMIT)
REAL ALPHA(LIMIT), BETA(LIMIT)
```

This is, in fact, the preferred method for declaring arrays because it makes programs more flexible; to modify a program to process arrays of some other size, only the PARAMETER statement needs to be changed.

The subscripts used in our examples of arrays have been positive valued, ranging from 1 through some upper limit. This is probably the most common subscript range, but as we noted earlier, FORTRAN does allow a subscript to be any integer value, positive, negative, or zero, provided that it does not fall outside the range specified in the array declaration. For example, the array declarations

```
INTEGER LLIM1, ULIM1, LLIM2, ULIM2
PARAMETER (LLIM1 = -1, ULIM1 = 3, LLIM2 = 0, ULIM2 = 5)
INTEGER GAMMA(LLIM1:ULIM1)
REAL DELTA(LLIM2:ULIM2)
```

establish two one-dimensional arrays. The integer array GAMMA may have subscripts ranging from -1 through 3; thus, the following subscripted variables may be used: GAMMA(-1), GAMMA(0), GAMMA(1), GAMMA(2), GAMMA(3). The real array DELTA has subscripts ranging from 0 through 5 so that any of the subscripted variables DELTA(0), DELTA(1), . . . , DELTA(5) may be used.

As we have noted, each component of an array is directly accessible. This direct access is accomplished by means of **address translation.** The first word in the memory block reserved for an array is used to store the first component.

Its address is called the **base address** of the array, and the address of any other component is calculated in terms of this base address. For example, if the base address for the array FAILTM is B and each failure time can be stored in a single memory word, then the address of FAILTM(1) is B, the address of FAILTM(2) is $B + 1$, the address of FAILTM(3) is $B + 2$, and in general, the address of FAILTM(I) is $B + I - 1$.

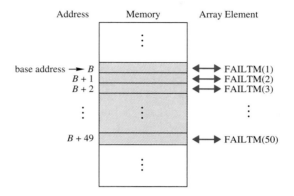

If W memory words are required for each component, then FAILTM(1) is stored in W consecutive words, beginning at the word located at address B, FAILTM(2) in a block beginning at address $B + W$, and in general, FAILTM(I) in a block of size W beginning at address $B + (I - 1)*W$. Each time an array component is accessed using a subscripted variable, this address translation must be performed by the system software and/or hardware to determine the location of that component in memory.

7.2 Input/Output of Arrays

There are three ways in which the entries of a one-dimensional array can be read or displayed:

1. Use a DO loop containing an input/output statement.
2. Use only the array name in an input/output statement.
3. Use an implied DO loop in an input/output statement.

In this section we describe each of these methods.

Input/Output Using a DO Loop. As we noted in the preceding section, one way to process each item in a one-dimensional array is to use an array reference in which the subscript is a variable within a loop that changes the value of the subscript on each pass through the loop. To read or display the elements of an array, therefore, one might simply place an input or output statement containing an array reference with a variable subscript within a DO loop. For example, if VELOC is a one-dimensional array and we wish to read 10 values into this array, the following statements might be used:

```
          INTEGER LIMIT
          PARAMETER (LIMIT = 10)
          REAL VELOC(LIMIT)
          INTEGER I

          DO 10 I = 1, LIMIT
             READ *, VELOC(I)
    10    CONTINUE
```

The DO loop containing the READ statement is equivalent to the following sequence of 10 READ statements:

```
     READ *, VELOC(1)
     READ *, VELOC(2)
     READ *, VELOC(3)
     READ *, VELOC(4)
     READ *, VELOC(5)
     READ *, VELOC(6)
     READ *, VELOC(7)
     READ *, VELOC(8)
     READ *, VELOC(9)
     READ *, VELOC(10)
```

Recall that each execution of a READ statement requires a new line of input data. Consequently, the 10 values to be read into the array VELOC must be entered on 10 separate lines, one value per line.

If we wish to declare a larger array and use only part of it, the statements

```
          INTEGER LIMIT
          PARAMETER (LIMIT = 50)
          REAL VELOC(LIMIT)
          INTEGER NUMVEL, I

          PRINT *, 'ENTER NUMBER OF VELOCITIES'
          READ *, NUMVEL
          DO 10 I = 1, NUMVEL
             READ *, VELOC(I)
    10    CONTINUE
```

might be used. The DO loop here has the same effect as the sequence of statements

```
     READ *, VELOC(1)
     READ *, VELOC(2)
            .
            .
            .
     READ *, VELOC(NUMVEL)
```

Arrays can be displayed in a similar manner by using a PRINT statement within a DO loop. Thus, the first 10 elements of the array VELOC can be displayed with the statements

```
      DO 20 I = 1, 10
         PRINT *, VELOC(I)
   20 CONTINUE
```

This is equivalent to the following sequence of 10 PRINT statements:

```
      PRINT *, VELOC(1)
      PRINT *, VELOC(2)
      PRINT *, VELOC(3)
      PRINT *, VELOC(4)
      PRINT *, VELOC(5)
      PRINT *, VELOC(6)
      PRINT *, VELOC(7)
      PRINT *, VELOC(8)
      PRINT *, VELOC(9)
      PRINT *, VELOC(10)
```

Because each execution of a PRINT statement causes output to begin on a new line, the 10 elements of the array VELOC are printed on 10 lines, one value per line.

The program in Figure 7.1 illustrates this method of reading and displaying the elements of a one-dimensional array. The array declaration specifies that VELOC is a real array whose subscripts may range from 1 through 50; thus, VELOC may have at most 50 elements. A value is then read for the number NUMVEL of velocities to be processed, and a DO loop is used to read this number of values into the array VELOC. These velocities are then displayed by using a PRINT statement within a DO loop.

In the sample run of the program, the value 10 is entered for NUMVEL. The READ statement in the first DO loop is thus executed 10 times, and as we have noted, this requires that the constants to be read appear on 10 lines, one per line. Similarly, because the PRINT statement in the second DO loop is executed 10 times, the entries of VELOC are displayed on 10 lines, one per line. This requirement that data values must be entered on separate lines and are printed on separate lines is one of the disadvantages of using a DO loop for input/output of lists.

```
      PROGRAM VLIST1
***********************************************************************
* Sample program illustrating the use of DO loops to read and display *
* a list of velocities.  NUMVEL is the number of values read into    *
* the array VELOC.                                                    *
***********************************************************************

      INTEGER LIMIT, NUMVEL, I
      PARAMETER (LIMIT = 50)
      REAL VELOC(LIMIT)
```

Figure 7.1

Figure 7.1 (cont.)

```
* Read the list of velocities

      PRINT *, 'ENTER THE NUMBER OF VELOCITIES:'
      READ *, NUMVEL
      PRINT *, 'ENTER THE VELOCITY VALUES, ONE PER LINE:'
      DO 10 I = 1, NUMVEL
          READ *, VELOC(I)
10    CONTINUE

* Print the list of velocities

      PRINT 20
20    FORMAT(/1X, 'LIST OF VELOCITIES:' / 1X, 18('='))
      DO 40 I = 1, NUMVEL
          PRINT 30, I, VELOC(I)
30        FORMAT(1X, I3, '  :', F10.1)
40    CONTINUE
      END
```

Sample run:

```
ENTER THE NUMBER OF VELOCITIES:
10
ENTER THE VELOCITY VALUES, ONE PER LINE:
100.0
 98.5
 99.7
120.6
125.8
 88.7
 99.6
115.0
103.4
 98.6

LIST OF VELOCITIES:
==================
   1  :     100.0
   2  :      98.5
   3  :      99.7
   4  :     120.6
   5  :     125.8
   6  :      88.7
   7  :      99.6
   8  :     115.0
   9  :     103.4
  10  :      98.6
```

Input/Output Using the Array Name. An alternative method of reading or displaying an array is to use an input or output statement containing the array name without subscripts. The effect is the same as listing all of the array elements in the input/output statement. For example, if the array VELOC is declared by

```
INTEGER LIMIT
PARAMETER (LIMIT = 10)
REAL VELOC(LIMIT)
```

the statement

```
READ *, VELOC
```

is equivalent to

```
 READ *, VELOC(1), VELOC(2), VELOC(3), VELOC(4), VELOC(5),
+        VELOC(6), VELOC(7), VELOC(8), VELOC(9), VELOC(10)
```

Because the READ statement is executed only once, the entries for VELOC need not be read from separate lines. All of the entries may be on one line, or seven entries may be on the first line with three on the next, or two entries may be on each of five lines, and so on.

This method can also be used with a formatted READ statement. The number of values to be read from each line of input is then determined by the corresponding format identifier. For example, the statements

```
    READ 20, VELOC
20 FORMAT(5F6.1)
```

read the values for VELOC(1), ..., VELOC(5) from the first line of data and the values for VELOC(6), ..., VELOC(10) from a second line.

An array can be displayed in a similar manner. For example, the statements

```
    PRINT 30, VELOC
30 FORMAT(1X, 5F10.1)
```

are equivalent to

```
    PRINT 30, VELOC(1), VELOC(2), VELOC(3), VELOC(4),
   +          VELOC(5), VELOC(6), VELOC(7), VELOC(8),
   +          VELCO(9), VELOC(10)
30 FORMAT(1X, 5F10.1)
```

and display the entries of the array VELOC on two lines, five entries per line, right justified in fields of width 10 with one digit to the right of the decimal point.

The program in Figure 7.2 illustrates this method of reading and displaying the elements of an array. Note that the array declaration

```
      INTEGER LIMIT
      PARAMETER (LIMIT = 10)
      REAL VELOC(LIMIT)
```

specifies that VELOC is to have 10 elements. One disadvantage of this method of array input/output is that the entire array must be used; that is, the total number of entries specified in the array declaration must be read or displayed. Thus it is not possible to read or display only part or an array; for example, if the dimension of VELOC is 50, this method cannot be used to read or display values for only VELOC(1), . . . , VELOC(10).

```
      PROGRAM VLIST2
*************************************************************************
* Sample program illustrating input/output of a list of velocities    *
* by using the array name.                                            *
*************************************************************************

      INTEGER LIMIT
      PARAMETER (LIMIT = 10)
      REAL VELOC(LIMIT)

* Read the list of velocities

      PRINT *, 'ENTER THE VELOCITY VALUES AS MANY PER LINE AS DESIRED:'
      READ *, VELOC

* Print the list of velocities

      PRINT 20
20    FORMAT(/1X, 'LIST OF VELOCITIES:' / 1X, 18('=')/)
      PRINT 30, VELOC
30    FORMAT(1X, 5F10.1)
      END
```

Sample run:

```
ENTER THE VELOCITY VALUES AS MANY PER LINE AS DESIRED:
100.0  98.5  99.7 120.6 125.8
 88.7  99.6 115.0 103.4  98.6

LIST OF VELOCITIES:
===================
    100.0      98.5      99.7     120.6     125.8
     88.7      99.6     115.0     103.4      98.6
```

Figure 7.2

Input/Output Using Implied DO Loops. An implied DO loop in an input/output statement provides the most flexible method for reading or displaying the elements of an array. It allows the programmer to specify that only a portion of the array be transmitted and to specify the arrangement of the values to be read or displayed.

An **implied DO loop** has the form

(i/o-list, control-variable = initial-value, limit)

or

(i/o-list, control-variable = initial-value, limit, step-size)

The effect of such an implied DO loop is exactly that of a DO loop—as if the left parenthesis were a DO, with indexing information immediately before the matching right parenthesis and the i/o-list constituting the body of the DO loop. The control variable, the initial value, the limit, and the step size are as in a DO statement. The i/o-list may, in general, be a list of variables (subscripted or simple), constants, arithmetic expressions, or other implied DO loops, separated by commas, with a comma at the end of the list.

An implied DO loop may be used in a READ, PRINT, or WRITE statement, or in a DATA statement, as illustrated in Section 7.4. For example, if the array VELOC is declared by

```
INTEGER LIMIT
PARAMETER (LIMIT = 50)
REAL VELOC(LIMIT)
```

and the first 10 entries are to be read, we can use the statement

```
READ *, (VELOC(I), I = 1, 10)
```

which is equivalent to

```
 READ *, VELOC(1), VELOC2), VELOC(3), VELOC(4), VELOC(5),
+        VELOC(6), VELOC(7), VELOC(8), VELOC(9), VELOC(10)
```

or if we also want to read the number NUMVEL of array elements,

```
READ *, NUMVEL, (VELOC(I), I = 1, NUMVEL)
```

which has the same effect as

```
READ *, NUMVEL, VELOC(1), VELOC(2), . . . . , VELOC(NUMVEL)
```

In a similar manner, we can display the entries:

```
PRINT *, (VELOC(I), I = 1, NUMVEL)
```

This has the same effect as

```
PRINT *, VELOC(1), VELOC(2), . . . . , VELOC(NUMVEL)
```

The program in Figure 7.3 illustrates the use of implied DO loops to read and display the elements of a list.

```
      PROGRAM VLIST3
************************************************************************
* Sample program illustrating the use of an implied DO loop to read   *
* and display a list of velocities.  NUMVEL is the number of values   *
* read into the array VELOC.                                          *
************************************************************************

      INTEGER LIMIT, NUMVEL, I
      PARAMETER (LIMIT = 50)
      REAL VELOC(LIMIT)

* Read the list of velocities

      PRINT *, 'ENTER THE NUMBER OF VELOCITIES:'
      READ *, NUMVEL
      PRINT *, 'ENTER THE VELOCITY VALUES AS MANY PER LINE AS DESIRED:'
      READ *, (VELOC(I), I = 1, NUMVEL)

* Print the list of velocities

      PRINT 20, NUMVEL
20    FORMAT(/1X, 'LIST OF', I3, ' VELOCITIES:' / 1X, 21('='))
      PRINT 30, (VELOC(I), I = 1, NUMVEL)
30    FORMAT(1X, 5F10.1)
      END
```

Sample run:

```
ENTER THE NUMBER OF VELOCITIES:
10
ENTER THE VELOCITY VALUES AS MANY PER LINE AS DESIRED:
100.0  98.5  99.7 120.6 125.8
 88.7  99.6 115.0 103.4  98.6

LIST OF 10 VELOCITIES:
=====================
      100.0       98.5       99.7      120.6      125.8
       88.7       99.6      115.0      103.4       98.6
```

Figure 7.3

7.3 Example: Processing a List of Failure Times

Many problems involve processing lists, a list of test scores, a list of temperature readings, a list of employee records, and so on. Such processing includes displaying all the items in the list, inserting new items, deleting items, searching the list for a specified item, and sorting the list so that the items are in a certain order. Because most programming languages do not provide a predefined list type (LISP, an acronym for LISt Processing, is one exception), lists must be processed using some other structure. This is commonly done using an array to store the list, storing the *I*th list item in the *I*th position of the array.

To illustrate, suppose we wish to process a list of failure times using an array, as described in the example of Section 7.1. First we must read the failure times and store them in an array. For this, we can use any of the methods described in the preceding section. To make the program flexible, we might declare the array FAILTM by

```
INTEGER LIMIT
PARAMETER (LIMIT = 50)
REAL FAILTM(LIMIT)
INTEGER NTIMES, I
```

read the number of failure times to be processed, and use an implied DO loop to read these values:

```
READ *, NTIMES
READ *, (FAILTM(I), I = 1, NTIMES)
```

Next we want to calculate the mean time to failure. For this, we must first sum the values stored in the first NTIMES locations of the array FAILTM, which is easily done by varying a subscript I from 1 to NTIMES in a DO loop, and adding the Ith element of the array to a running sum:

```
      SUM = 0
      DO 10 I = 1, NTIMES
         SUM = SUM + FAILTM(I)
  10  CONTINUE
      MEANFT = SUM / NTIMES
```

A list of failure times greater than the mean can then be displayed by using another DO loop to examine each element of the array FAILTM, comparing it with the mean MEANFT, and printing it if it is greater than MEANFT:

```
      DO 20 I = 1, NTIMES
         IF (FAILTM(I) .GT. MEANFT) THEN
            PRINT *, FAILTM(I)
         END IF
  20 CONTINUE
```

The program in Figure 7.4 does this much of the processing of a collection of failure times. The last part of the problem posed in Section 7.1, that of sorting this collection, is considered in Section 7.5.

```
         PROGRAM FAIL
*****************************************************************************
* Program to read a list of failure times, calculate the mean time    *
* to failure, and then print a list of failure times that are greater *
* than the mean.  Identifiers used are:                               *
*      FAILTM  :  one-dimensional array of failure times              *
*      LIMIT   :  parameter: size of the array                        *
*      NTIMES  :  number of failure times to be processed             *
*      I       :  subscript                                           *
*      SUM     :  sum of failure times                                *
*      MEANFT  :  mean time to failure                                *
*****************************************************************************

         INTEGER LIMIT, NTIMES, I
         PARAMETER (LIMIT = 50)
         REAL FAILTM(LIMIT), SUM, MEANFT
         INTEGER NTIMES, I

* Read the failure times and store them in array FAILTM

         PRINT *, 'HOW MANY FAILURE TIMES ARE TO BE PROCESSED?'
         READ *, NTIMES
         PRINT *, 'ENTER THE FAILURE TIMES, AS MANY PER LINE AS DESIRED'
         READ *, (FAILTM(I), I = 1, NTIMES)

* Calculate the mean time to failure

         SUM = 0
         DO 10 I = 1, NTIMES
            SUM = SUM + FAILTM(I)
10       CONTINUE
         MEANFT = SUM / REAL(NTIMES)
         PRINT 100, NTIMES, MEANFT
100      FORMAT(// 1X, I3, ' FAILURE TIMES WITH MEAN =', F6.1)

* Print list of failure times greater than the mean

         PRINT 101
101      FORMAT(// 1X, 'LIST OF FAILURE TIMES GREATER THAN THE MEAN:')
         DO 20 I = 1, NTIMES
            IF (FAILTM(I) .GT. MEANFT) THEN
               PRINT 102, FAILTM(I)
102            FORMAT(1X, F9.1)
            END IF
20       CONTINUE
         END
```

Sample run:

```
HOW MANY FAILURE TIMES ARE TO BE PROCESSED?
10
ENTER THE FAILURE TIMES, AS MANY PER LINE AS DESIRED
 99.5, 133.8, 84.2, 217.5, 188.8
103.1, 93.9, 165.0, 68.3, 111.4

 10 FAILURE TIMES WITH MEAN = 126.6
```

Figure 7.4

Figure 7.4 (cont.)

```
LIST OF FAILURE TIMES GREATER THAN THE MEAN:
    133.8
    217.5
    188.8
    165.0
```

7.4 Array Processing

In the preceding sections we considered array declarations and the input/output of arrays. In this section we describe how other kinds of array processing are carried out in FORTRAN: assignment of arrays, use of arrays as arguments, and arrays in common.

Assigning Values to Arrays. As we know, a value can be assigned to a simple variable by an assignment statement of the form *variable = expression.* The value of an array, however, is a collection of values, and in FORTRAN, each array element must be assigned a value by a separate assignment statement. For example, if the array NUMBER is declared by

```
INTEGER NUMBER(10)
```

and we wish to assign it the sequence consisting of the squares of the first 10 positive integers, 1, 4, 9, 16, 25, 36, 49, 64, 81, 100, we can use a DO loop:

```
      DO 10 I = 1, 10
         NUMBER(I) = I**2
   10 CONTINUE
```

An array may be initialized during compilation using a DATA statement. If all the entries of the array are to be assigned values, the array name together with the set of values may appear in the DATA statement. In this case the number of constants must be equal to the size of the array. For example, if ALPHA is a one-dimensional real array having 10 entries, the statements

```
      REAL ALPHA(10)
      DATA ALPHA /5*0.0, 4*1.0, 2.0/
```

initialize ALPHA(1), . . . , ALPHA(5) to have the value 0.0, ALPHA(6), . . . , ALPHA(9) the value 1.0, and ALPHA(10) the value 2.0. Also, since parameters may be used as values and/or repetition indicators in DATA statements, a parameter used to declare the dimension of an array may also be used in the list of values used to initialize that array. For example, the statements

```
      INTEGER LIMIT
      PARAMETER (LIMIT = 10)
      REAL ALPHA(LIMIT)
      DATA ALPHA /LIMIT*0.0/
```

initialize each of the 10 positions of ALPHA to 0.0.

Several variables and arrays may appear in a single DATA statement, as the following example illustrates:

```
INTEGER N
REAL X, ALPHA(10), BETA(25)
DATA N, X, ALPHA, BETA /10, 3.14, 5*1.0, 30*0.0/
```

Here N is assigned the value 10; X is assigned the value 3.14; the value 1.0 is assigned to ALPHA(1), ... , ALPHA(5); and the value of each of ALPHA(6), ... , ALPHA10), BETA(1), ... , BETA(25) is 0.0.

Implied DO loops may also appear in the list of a DATA statement. For example, to assign 10 to N and 0.0 to the first five entries of the one-dimensional array ALPHA, the following statements can be used:

```
INTEGER N, I
REAL ALPHA(10)
DATA N, (ALPHA(I), I = 1, 5) /10, 5*0.0/
```

Arrays as Arguments. Arrays may also be used as arguments in functions and subroutine subprograms. In this case, *the actual array argument must be declared in the calling program unit, and the corresponding formal array argument must be declared in the subprogram.* When the subprogram is referenced, the first element of the actual array argument is associated with the first element of the corresponding formal array argument. Successive actual array elements are then associated with the corresponding formal array elements.

The program in Figure 7.5 illustrates the use of array arguments. It reads a list of numbers and then calls a function to calculate the mean of the numbers.

```
      PROGRAM AVE
************************************************************************
* Program to read a list of numbers ITEM(1), ITEM(2), ... , ITEM(NUM) *
* and to calculate their mean using the function subprogram MEAN.     *
* Identifiers used are:                                               *
*      ITEM    : one-dimensional array of numbers                     *
*      LIMIT   : size of array ITEM (parameter)                       *
*      I       : subscript                                            *
*      NUM     : number of items                                      *
*      MEAN    : function that finds the mean of a set of numbers     *
************************************************************************

      INTEGER LIMIT
      PARAMETER (LIMIT = 50)
      REAL ITEM(LIMIT), MEAN
      INTEGER NUM, I

      PRINT *, 'ENTER NUMBER OF ITEMS AND THE ITEMS'
      READ *, NUM, (ITEM(I), I = 1, NUM)
      PRINT 100, NUM, MEAN(ITEM, NUM)
100   FORMAT(1X, 'MEAN OF THE ', I3, ' NUMBERS IS ', F6.2)
      END
```

Figure 7.5

Figure 7.5 (cont.)

```
**MEAN*************************************************************
* Function to find the mean of the first N elements of the array X of  *
* dimension XLIMIT.  Local variables used are:                         *
*     SUM    : sum of the numbers                                      *
*     I      : subscript                                               *
*******************************************************************

      FUNCTION MEAN(X, N)

      INTEGER XLIMIT
      PARAMETER (XLIMIT = 50)
      REAL MEAN, X(XLIMIT), SUM
      INTEGER N, I

      SUM = 0
      DO 10 I = 1, N
          SUM = SUM + X(I)
10    CONTINUE
      MEAN = SUM / REAL(N)
      END
```

Sample run:

```
ENTER NUMBER OF ITEMS AND THE ITEMS
10
55, 88.5, 90, 71.5, 100, 66.5, 70.3, 81.2, 93.7, 41
MEAN OF THE   10 NUMBERS IS   75.77
```

Execution of this program associates the actual array ITEM with the formal array X so that corresponding pairs of elements refer to the same memory locations:

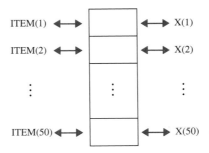

Thus if any of the array elements $X(1), \ldots, X(50)$ are assigned a value in the subprogram, the corresponding elements of the array ITEM are also changed.

If the array X in the subprogram were dimensioned by

```
      REAL X(-5:44)
```

then the first element ITEM(1) of the actual array ITEM and the first element

$X(-5)$ of the formal array X would be associated; that is, they would refer to the same memory location. The successive elements of the array ITEM would then be associated in order with the elements in the array X:

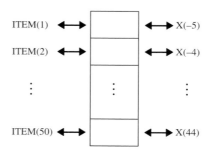

As we noted earlier, when an array is used as a formal argument, it must be declared in the subprogram, and the corresponding actual array argument must be declared in the calling program unit. To make it possible to design subprograms that can be used to process arrays of various sizes, FORTRAN allows both the array and its dimension to be passed to the subprogram. Such an array is said to have **adjustable dimensions**. For example, the program in Figure 7.5 that used the function subprogram MEAN to calculate the mean of a list of numbers can be rewritten as shown in Figure 7.6. Note that the formal argument XLIM is used to specify the dimension of the formal array X in this subprogram. The actual dimension 50 and the actual array ITEM are passed to the subprogram from the main program when the function is referenced.

```
      PROGRAM AVE
*********************************************************************
* Program to read a list of numbers ITEM(1), ITEM(2), ... , ITEM(NUM)  *
* and to calculate their mean using the function subprogram MEAN.      *
* Identifiers used are:                                                *
*      ITEM    : one-dimensional array of numbers                      *
*      LIMIT   : size of array ITEM (parameter)                        *
*      I       : subscript                                             *
*      NUM     : number of items                                       *
*      MEAN    : function that finds the mean of a set of numbers      *
*********************************************************************

      INTEGER LIMIT
      PARAMETER (LIMIT = 50)
      REAL ITEM(LIMIT), MEAN
      INTEGER NUM, I

      PRINT *, 'ENTER NUMBER OF ITEMS AND THE ITEMS'
      READ *, NUM, (ITEM(I), I = 1, NUM)
      PRINT 100, NUM, MEAN(ITEM, LIMIT, NUM)
100   FORMAT(1X, 'MEAN OF THE ', I3, ' NUMBERS IS ', F6.2)
      END
```

Figure 7.6

Figure 7.6 (cont.)

```
**MEAN***********************************************************
* Function to find the mean of first N elements of the array X of    *
* dimension XLIM.  The actual dimension is passed to the subprogram   *
* by the actual argument corresonding to XLIM.  Local variables       *
* used are:                                                           *
*      SUM    : sum of the numbers                                    *
*      I      : subscript                                             *
*****************************************************************

      FUNCTION MEAN(X, XLIM, N)

      INTEGER XLIM, N, I
      REAL MEAN, X(XLIM), SUM

      SUM = 0
      DO 10 I = 1, N
         SUM = SUM + X(I)
10    CONTINUE
      MEAN = SUM / REAL(N)
      END
```

In a subprogram, it is also possible to specify that a one-dimensional formal array have the same size as the corresponding actual array by using an asterisk (∗) to specify the dimension. In this case, it is not permissible to use the array name in any statement that requires information about the array size. Thus, one would not be allowed to give only the array name in an input/output statement.

Arrays in Common. To illustrate the use of arrays in COMMON statements, suppose that the statements

```
      REAL A(5)
      COMMON A
```

appear in one program unit and that the statements

```
      REAL ALPHA(5)
      COMMON ALPHA
```

appear in another program unit. These COMMON statements allocate the first five memory locations of blank common to both of the arrays A and ALPHA so that the array elements are associated in the following manner:

Array Element	Blank Common Location	Array Element
A(1)	#1	ALPHA(1)
A(2)	#2	ALPHA(2)
A(3)	#3	ALPHA(3)
A(4)	#4	ALPHA(4)
A(5)	#5	ALPHA(5)

7.5   Examples: Frequency Distributions, Averages of Grouped Data, Sorting, Searching

EXAMPLE 1: Frequency Distributions. A quality control engineer monitors a machine by recording each hour the number of defective parts produced by that machine. This information is to be summarized in a *frequency distribution* that shows the number of one-hour periods in which there were no defective parts, one defective part, two defective parts, . . . , five or more defective parts.

To solve this problem, we use the array:

COUNT: COUNT(I) is the number of one-hour periods during which I defective parts were produced, I = 0, 1, . . . , 5.

An appropriate algorithm is

ALGORITHM TO GENERATE A FREQUENCY DISTRIBUTION

```
*  Algorithm to read several values for DEFECT, the number of      *
*  defective parts produced by a machine in a given one-hour period, *
*  and to determine COUNT(I) = the number of periods in which       *
*  there were I defective parts.                                    *
```

1. Initialize array COUNT to all zeros.
2. Read first value for DEFECT
3. While there is more data, do the following:
   a. If DEFECT > 5, set DEFECT to 5.
   b. Increase COUNT(DEFECT) by 1.
   c. Read next value for DEFECT

The program in Figure 7.7 implements this algorithm. Also shown is a listing of the data file used in the sample run.

```
      PROGRAM FREQ1
*******************************************************************
* Program to generate a frequency distribution of the number of 1-hour *
* periods in which there were 0, 1, 2, ... defective parts produced by *
* a machine.  The data is read from a file.  Identifiers used are:   *
*     MAXDEF  :  parameter representing maximum # of defective parts  *
*     COUNT   :  COUNT(I) = # of 1-hour periods with I defective parts *
*     DEFECT  :  # of defective parts read from file                 *
*     FNAME   :  name of the data file                               *
*     EOF     :  end of file indicator                               *
*     I       :  index                                               *
*******************************************************************
      INTEGER MAXDEF
      PARAMETER (MAXDEF = 5)
      INTEGER DEFECT, COUNT(0:MAXDEF), I, EOF
      CHARACTER*20 FNAME
      DATA COUNT/0, MAXDEF*0/
```

Figure 7.7

Figure 7.7 (cont.)

```
* Get file name, open the file as unit 15

      PRINT *, 'ENTER NAME OF DATA FILE'
      READ *, FNAME
      OPEN (UNIT = 15, FILE = FNAME, STATUS = 'OLD')

* While there is more data, read # of defective parts and
* increment appropriate counter
      READ (15, *, IOSTAT = EOF) DEFECT
10    IF (EOF .GE. 0) THEN
          IF (DEFECT .GT. MAXDEF) THEN
              DEFECT = MAXDEF
          END IF
          COUNT(DEFECT) = COUNT(DEFECT) + 1
          READ (15, *, IOSTAT = EOF) DEFECT
      GO TO 10
      END IF

* Print the frequency distribution

      PRINT 101
      PRINT 102
101   FORMAT(1X, '# OF DEFECTIVES   # OF HOURS')
102   FORMAT(1X, '===============   ==========')
      DO 20 I = 0, MAXDEF
          PRINT 103, I, COUNT(I)
103       FORMAT(1X, I9, I15)
20    CONTINUE

      CLOSE (15)
      END
```

Listing of DEFECTS-FILE used in sample run:

```
0
1
0
2
2
0
1
6
3
0
3
1
2
0
1
2
0
```

Figure 7.7 (cont.)

Sample run:

```
ENTER NAME OF DATA FILE
DEFECTS-FILE
# OF DEFECTIVES     # OF HOURS
===============     ==========
              0              6
              1              4
              2              4
              3              2
              4              0
              5              1
```

A **bar graph** or **histogram** is often used to display frequency distributions graphically. Each of the categories whose frequency is being determined is displayed by a bar whose length corresponds to the number of items in that category. Thus, the frequency distribution produced by the sample run in Figure 7.7 could be represented by the bar graph

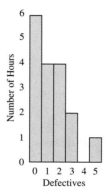

The program in Figure 7.8 is a modification of the preceding program that displays a similar bar graph.

```
      PROGRAM FREQ2
*****************************************************************************
* Program to plot a bar graph of the number of 1-hour periods in which *
* there were 0, 1, 2, ... defective parts produced by a machine.       *
* The data is read from a file.  Identifiers used are:                 *
*     MAXDEF  :  parameter representing maximum # of defective parts    *
*     COUNT   :  COUNT(I) = # of 1-hour periods with I defective parts  *
*     DEFECT  :  # of defective parts read from file                    *
*     FNAME   :  name of the data file                                  *
*     EOF     :  end-of-file indicator                                  *
*****************************************************************************
```

Figure 7.8

Figure 7.8 (cont.)

```
      INTEGER MAXDEF
      PARAMETER (MAXDEF = 5)
      INTEGER DEFECT, COUNT(0:MAXDEF), EOF
      CHARACTER*20 FNAME
      DATA COUNT /0, MAXDEF*0/

* Get file name, open the file as unit 15

      PRINT *, 'ENTER NAME OF DATA FILE'
      READ '(A)', FNAME
      OPEN (UNIT = 15, FILE = FNAME, STATUS = 'OLD')

* While there is more data, read # of defective parts and
* increment appropriate counter

      READ (15, *, IOSTAT = EOF) DEFECT
10    IF (EOF .GE. 0) THEN
          IF (DEFECT .GT. MAXDEF) THEN
              DEFECT = MAXDEF
          END IF
          COUNT(DEFECT) = COUNT(DEFECT) + 1
          READ (15, *, IOSTAT = EOF) DEFECT
      GO TO 10
      END IF

      CALL BGRAPH(COUNT, MAXDEF, 'DEFECTIVES', 'NUMBER OF HOURS')

      CLOSE (15)
      END

**BGRAPH****************************************************************
* Subroutine to plot a bar graph representation of a frequency        *
* distribution.  Variables used are:                                  *
*      FREQ    :  array of frequencies                                *
*      NFREQ   :  number of frequencies                               *
*      VLABEL  :  label for vertical axis                             *
*      HLABEL  :  label for horizontal axis                           *
*      LIMBAR  :  parameter giving the size of the array BAR          *
*      BAR     :  character array used to print one bar of bar graph  *
*      LARGE   :  largest of FREQ(0), FREQ(1), ...                    *
*      I, J    :  indices                                             *
***********************************************************************

      SUBROUTINE BGRAPH(FREQ, NFREQ, VLABEL, HLABEL)

      INTEGER NFREQ, FREQ(0:NFREQ), LIMBAR, LARGE, I, J
      PARAMETER (LIMBAR = 20)
      CHARACTER*(*), VLABEL, HLABEL
      CHARACTER*3 BAR(LIMBAR)

* Find largest count

      LARGE = FREQ(0)
      DO 10 I = 1, NFREQ
          LARGE = MAX(LARGE, FREQ(I))
10    CONTINUE
```

Figure 7.8 (cont.)

```
* Print the bar graph
      PRINT 100, VLABEL
100   FORMAT(//1X, A)
      DO 40 I = 0, NFREQ
          DO 20 J = 1, LIMBAR
              BAR(J) = ' '
20        CONTINUE
          DO 30 J = 1, FREQ(I)
              BAR(J) = 'XXX'
30        CONTINUE
          PRINT 101, I, ':', BAR
101       FORMAT(1X, I10, 21A)
40    CONTINUE
      PRINT 102, ('.', I = 0, 3 * LARGE)
      PRINT 103, (I, I = 0, LARGE)
      PRINT 104, HLABEL
102   FORMAT(11X, 80A)
103   FORMAT(9X, 20I3)
104   FORMAT(11X, A)

      END
```

Sample run:

```
ENTER NAME OF DATA FILE
DEFECTS-FILE


DEFECTIVES
        0:XXXXXXXXXXXXXXXXX
        1:XXXXXXXXXXX
        2:XXXXXXXXXXX
        3:XXXXX
        4:
        5:XXX
        .................
        0   1   2   3   4   5   6
        NUMBER OF HOURS
```

EXAMPLE 2: Averages of Grouped Data. Four kinds of rocket propellant are being tested. A collection of data pairs consisting of propellant codes and burn rates from test firing the rocket have been recorded. The average burn rate for each of the four kinds of propellants is to be calculated.

In solving this problem, we use two one-dimensional arrays:

COUNT: COUNT(PROPEL) is the number of burn rates for propellant PROPEL = 1, 2, 3, 4.

SUM: SUM(PROPEL) = sum of the burn rates for all test firings with propellant PROPEL = 1, 2, 3, 4.

An appropriate algorithm is the following:

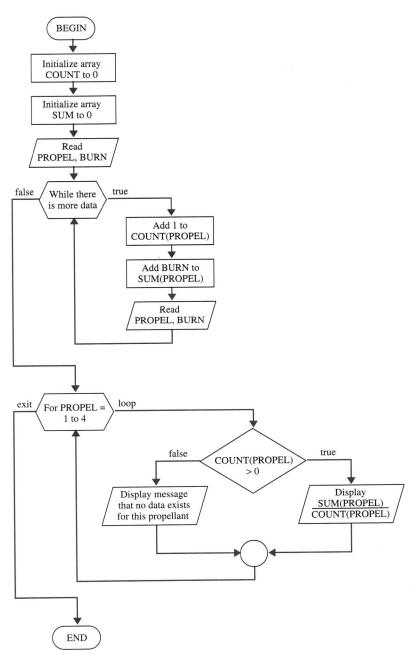

Figure 7.9

ALGORITHM FOR THE BURN RATE PROBLEM

* Algorithm to find the average burn rate for each of four kinds of   *
* propellants. The arrays COUNT and SUM store the number and   *
* sum of the burn rates.   *

1. Initialize the arrays COUNT and SUM to 0.

2. Read the kind of PROPELlant and BURN rate.
3. While there is more data, do the following:
    a. Add 1 to COUNT(PROPEL).
    b. Add BURN to SUM(PROPEL).
    c. Read the kind of PROPELlant and BURN rate.
4. Do the following for PROPEL ranging from 1 through 4:
    If COUNT(PROPEL) > 0 then
        Display SUM(PROPEL) / COUNT(PROPEL).
    Else
        Display a message that there was no data for this
        type of propellant.

The structure of this algorithm is shown in flowchart form in Figure 7.9.

The program in Figure 7.10 implements this algorithm. Note the use of PARAMETER and DATA statements to declare and initialize arrays COUNT and SUM.

```
      PROGRAM ROCKET
*************************************************************************
* Program to find the average burn rate for each of several kinds of  *
* propellants, using data consisting of a propellant type and burn    *
* rate observed during test firing of a rocket with that type of      *
* propellant.  Identifiers used are:                                  *
*     PROPEL : kind of propellant                                     *
*     NUMPRO : parameter specifying number of kinds of propellants    *
*     COUNT  : COUNT(I) = number of burn rates for propellant I       *
*     SUM    : SUM(I) = sum of burn rates for propellant I            *
*     BURN   : current burn rate being processed                      *
*************************************************************************

      INTEGER NUMPRO
      PARAMETER (NUMPRO = 4)
      INTEGER COUNT(NUMPRO), PROPEL
      REAL SUM(NUMPRO), BURN
      DATA COUNT, SUM /NUMPRO*0, NUMPRO*0.0/

      PRINT *, 'ENTER PROPELLANT TYPES AND BURN RATES (0,0 TO STOP)'
      READ *, PROPEL, BURN

* While there is more data, read a propellant type and burn rate,
* increment the appropriate counter, and add the burn rate to the
* appropriate sum.

10    IF (PROPEL .GT. 0) THEN
          IF (PROPEL .LE. NUMPRO) THEN
              COUNT(PROPEL) = COUNT(PROPEL) + 1
              SUM(PROPEL) = SUM(PROPEL) + BURN
          ELSE
              PRINT *, '*** ILLEGAL PROPELLANT TYPE:', PROPEL
          END IF
          READ *, PROPEL, BURN
      GO TO 10
      END IF
```

Figure 7.10

Figure 7.10 (cont.)

```
* Calculate and print average burn rates

      PRINT 100
100   FORMAT(//1X, 'FOR PROPELLANT')
      DO 20 PROPEL = 1, NUMPRO
         IF (COUNT(PROPEL) .GT. 0) THEN
            PRINT 101, PROPEL, SUM(PROPEL) / COUNT(PROPEL)
101         FORMAT(1X, I14, ':  AVERAGE BURN RATE IS', F6.2)
         ELSE
            PRINT 102, PROPEL
102         FORMAT(1X, I14, ':  THERE WERE NO BURN RATES RECORDED')
         END IF
20    CONTINUE
      END
```

Sample run:

```
ENTER PROPELLANT TYPES AND BURN RATES (0,0 TO STOP)
1 34.0
1 32.7.
2 30.1
5 29.8
*** ILLEGAL PROPELLANT TYPE:   5
3 29.8
2 32.8
1 32.0
3 28.1
1 29.4
2 28.9
3 27.4
0 0


FOR PROPELLANT
        1:   AVERAGE BURN RATE IS 32.02
        2:   AVERAGE BURN RATE IS 30.60
        3:   AVERAGE BURN RATE IS 28.43
        4:   THERE WERE NO BURN RATES RECORDED
```

EXAMPLE 3: Sorting. A common programming problem is **sorting,** that is, arranging the items in a list so that they are in either ascending or descending order. There are many sorting methods, most of which assume that arrays are used to store the items to be sorted. In this section we describe one of the simplest sorting methods known as **simple selection sort**. Although it is not an efficient sorting method for large lists, it does perform reasonably well for small lists, and it is easy to understand. More efficient sorting schemes are described in the exercises at the end of this section.

The basic idea of a selection sort of a list is to make a number of passes through the list, or a part of the list, and on each pass to select one item to be correctly positioned. For example, on each pass through a sublist, the smallest item in this sublist might be found and then moved to its proper location.

As an illustration, suppose that the following list is to be sorted into ascending order:

$$67, 33, 21, 84, 49, 50, 75$$

We scan the list to locate the smallest item and find it in position 3:

$$67, 33, 21, 84, 49, 50, 75$$

We interchange this item with the first item and thus properly position the smallest item at the beginning of the list:

$$21, 33, 67, 84, 49, 50, 75$$

We now scan the sublist consisting of the items from position 2 on to find the smallest item

$$21, 33, 67, 84, 49, 50, 75$$

and exchange it with the second item (itself in this case) and thus properly position the next-to-smallest item in position 2:

$$21, 33, 67, 84, 49, 50, 75$$

We continue in this manner, locating the smallest item in the sublist of items from position 3 on and interchanging it with the third item, then properly positioning the smallest item in the sublist of items from position 4 on, and so on until we eventually do this for the sublist consisting of the last two items:

$$21, 33, 49, 84, 67, 50, 75$$

$$21, 33, 49, 50, 67, 84, 75$$

$$21, 33, 49, 50, 67, 84, 75$$

$$21, 33, 49, 50, 67, 75, 84$$

Positioning the smallest item in this last sublist obviously also positions the last item correctly and thus completes the sort.

An algorithm for this simple selection sort is

SIMPLE SELECTION SORT ALGORITHM

* Algorithm to sort the list of items X(l), X(2), . . . , X(N) so they are *
* in ascending order.   *

For I ranging from 1 to N − 1, do the following:

    * On the Ith pass, first find the smallest item in the sublist X(I),   *
    * . . . , X(N).   *

   1. Set LOCSM equal to I.
   2. Set SMALL equal to X(LOCSM).
   3. For J ranging from I + 1 to N do the following:
      If X(J) < SMALL then
        * Smaller item found *
      a. Set SMALL equal to X(J).
      b. Set LOCSM equal to J.

```
    * Now interchange this smallest item with the item at the          *
    * beginning of this sublist.                                        *
```

  4. Set X(LOCSM) equal to X(I).
  5. Set X(I) equal to SMALL.

This algorithm sorts the items into ascending order. To sort them into descending order, one need only change $>$ to $<$ in the comparison of X(J) with SMALL in step 3.

One problem that requires sorting is determining the median value of a set of data items. The **median** of a set of numbers $X_1, \ldots, X_n$ is the middle value when these numbers have been arranged in ascending order. It should be clear that one half of the numbers are greater than or equal to this median value and that one half are smaller. After the list of numbers has been sorted, the median value is in position $(n + 1)/2$ if n is odd and is the average of the numbers in positions $n/2$ and $n/2 + 1$ if n is even.

To illustrate, suppose that a company is planning to build a new manufacturing facility and that one of the factors in selecting the site is the cost of labor in the various cities under consideration. To analyze this data, it may be helpful to sort the labor costs for these cities so that they can be displayed in order and so that the median cost can be computed. The program in Figure 7.11 calls subroutine RDCOST to read a list of costs, calls subroutine SORT to sort them using the selection sort algorithm, and then calls subroutine OUTPUT to display the sorted list and the median cost.

```
      PROGRAM SORTER
*****************************************************************
* This program reads and counts a list of labor costs, sorts them in   *
* ascending order and finds the median cost.  For more costs, change   *
* the value of the parameter LIMIT.  Identifiers used are:             *
*     LIMIT   :  parameter representing maximum # of costs             *
*     COST    :  list of labor costs (in millions).                    *
*     N       :  number of labor costs                                 *
*****************************************************************

      INTEGER LIMIT
      PARAMETER (LIMIT = 100)
      INTEGER COST(LIMIT), N

      CALL RDCOST (COST, LIMIT, N)
      CALL SORT (COST, LIMIT, N)
      CALL OUTPUT (COST, LIMIT, N)

      END
```

Figure 7.11

Figure 7.11 (cont.)

```
**RDCOST************************************************************
* Subroutine to read a list of up to LIMIT costs, store them in array  *
* COST, return this list and a count N of the number of values read.   *
* Local variables:                                                     *
*      INDATA  : data value read (an actual cost or end-of-data signal) *
*******************************************************************

         SUBROUTINE RDCOST (COST, LIMIT, N)

         INTEGER LIMIT, COST(LIMIT), N, INDATA

         PRINT *, 'ENTER LABOR COSTS IN MILLIONS (0 OR NEGATIVE TO STOP).'
         N = 0
         READ *, INDATA

* While there is another data value, count it, store it in
* the next location of array COST, and read another value.

10       IF (INDATA .GT. 0) THEN
              N = N + 1
              COST(N) = INDATA
              READ *, INDATA
         GO TO 10
         END IF

         END


**SORT**************************************************************
* Subroutine to sort ITEM(1), ..., ITEM(N) into ascending order using  *
* the simple selection sort algorithm.  LIM is the upper limit on the   *
* size of the array ITEM.  For descending order change .LT. to .GT. in  *
* the logical expression ITEM(I) .LT. SMALL. Local variables used:      *
*      SMALL   : smallest item in current sublist                       *
*      LOCSM   : location of SMALL                                      *
*      I, J    : subscripts                                             *
*******************************************************************

         SUBROUTINE SORT(ITEM, LIM, N)

         INTEGER LIM, ITEM(LIM), N, I, SMALL

         DO 20 I = 1, N - 1

*            Find smallest item in sublist ITEM(I), ..., ITEM(N)

             SMALL = ITEM(I)
             LOCSM = I
             DO 10 J = I + 1, N
                  IF (ITEM(J) .LT. SMALL) THEN
*                      Smaller item found
                       SMALL = ITEM(J)
                       LOCSM = J
                  END IF
10           CONTINUE
```

Figure 7.11 (cont.)

```
*          Interchange smallest item with ITEM(I) at
*          beginning of sublist

           ITEM(LOCSM) = ITEM(I)
           ITEM(I) = SMALL

20      CONTINUE
        END


**OUTPUT***************************************************************
* Subroutine to display the sorted list of N COSTs and the median    *
* cost.  LIMIT is the upper limit on the array COST.  Local variables: *
*     I      : subscript                                             *
**********************************************************************

        SUBROUTINE OUTPUT (COST, LIMIT, N)

        INTEGER LIMIT, COST(LIMIT), N, I

        PRINT 100, 'SORTED LIST', '====== ===='
100     FORMAT(2(/, 1X, A))
        DO 10 I = 1, N
           PRINT 101, COST(I)
101        FORMAT(1X, I6)
10      CONTINUE
        IF (MOD(N,2) .NE. 0) THEN
           PRINT 102, COST((N + 1)/2)
        ELSE
           PRINT 102, (COST(N/2) + COST(N/2 + 1)) / 2.0
        END IF
102     FORMAT(/1X, 'MEDIAN = ', I6, ' MILLION DOLLARS')
        END
```

Sample run:

```
ENTER LABOR COSTS IN MILLIONS (0 OR NEGATIVE TO STOP).
870
778
655
640
956
538
1050
529
689
0
```

Figure 7.11 (cont.)

```
SORTED LIST
====== ====
   529
   538
   640
   655
   689
   778
   870
   956
  1050

MEDIAN =    689 MILLION DOLLARS
```

EXAMPLE 4: Searching. Another important problem is **searching** a collection of data for a specified item and retrieving some information associated with that item. For example, one searches a telephone directory for a specific name in order to retrieve the phone number listed with that name. A **linear search** begins with the first item in a list and searches sequentially until either the desired item is found or the end of the list is reached. The following algorithm describes this method of searching:

LINEAR SEARCH ALGORITHM

```
* Algorithm to linear search a list X(1), X(2), . . . , X(N) for a      *
* specified ITEM. The logical variable FOUND is set to true and        *
* LOC to the position of ITEM if the search is successful; otherwise,  *
* FOUND is set to false.                                               *
```

1. Initialize LOC to 1 and FOUND to false.
2. While LOC $\leq$ N and not FOUND, do the following:
   If ITEM = X(LOC), then
       Set FOUND to true.
   Else
       Increment LOC by 1.

Although linear search may be an adequate method for small data sets, a more efficient technique is needed for large collections. If the list to be searched has been sorted, the **binary search** algorithm may be used. With this method, we first examine the middle element in the list, and if this is the desired entry, the search is successful. Otherwise we determine whether the item being sought is in the first half or the second half of the list and then repeat this process, using the middle entry of that list.

To illustrate, suppose the list to be searched is

> 1279
> 1331
> 1373
> 1555
> 1824
> 1898
> 1991
> 2002
> 2335
> 2665
> 3103

and we are looking for 1991. We first examine the middle number 1898 in the sixth position. Because 1991 is greater than 1898, we can disregard the first half of the list and concentrate on the second half.

> 1991
> 2002
> 2335
> 2665
> 3103

The middle number in this sublist is 2335, and the desired item 1991 is less than 2335, so we discard the second half of this sublist and concentrate on the first half.

> 1991
> 2002

Because there is no middle number in this sublist, we examine the number immediately preceding the middle position, that is, the number 1991. In this case, we have located the desired entry with three comparisons rather than seven, as would be required in a linear search.

In general, the algorithm for a binary search is as follows:

BINARY SEARCH ALGORITHM

```
* Algorithm to binary search a list X(1), X(2), . . . , X(N) that has    *
* been ordered so the elements are in ascending order. The logical       *
* variable FOUND is set to true and LOC to the position of the           *
* ITEM being sought if the search is successful; otherwise, FOUND        *
* is set to false.                                                       *
```

1. Initialize FIRST to 1 and LAST to N. These values represent the positions of the first and last items of the list or sublist being searched.
2. Initialize the logical variable FOUND to false.

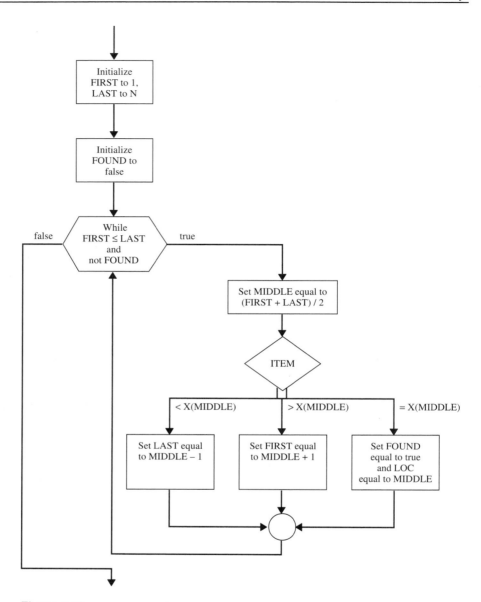

Figure 7.12

3. While FIRST ≤ LAST and not FOUND, do the following:
   a. Find the middle position in the sublist by setting MIDDLE equal to the integer quotient (FIRST + LAST) / 2.
   b. Compare the ITEM being searched for with X(MIDDLE). There are three possibilities:

(i) ITEM < X(MIDDLE):	Item is in the first half of the sublist; set LAST equal to MIDDLE − 1.
(ii) ITEM > X(MIDDLE):	ITEM is in the second half of the sublist; set FIRST equal to MIDDLE + 1.
(iii) ITEM = X(MIDDLE):	ITEM has been found; set LOC equal to MIDDLE and FOUND to true.

Figure 7.12 shows the structure of this algorithm in flowchart form. The program in Figure 7.13 uses this binary search algorithm to search a file in which each record contains the chemical formula and name of an inorganic compound and its specific heat (the ratio of the amount of heat required to raise the temperature of a body 1°C to that required to raise an equal mass or water 1°C). The file is assumed to be sorted so that the chemical formulas are in alphabetical order. A formula is entered during program execution; the list is searched using a binary search; and if the formula is found, the name and specific heat are displayed.

```
      PROGRAM CHEM
************************************************************************
* Program to read a file containing the chemical formula, name, and   *
* specific heat for various inorganic compounds and store these in    *
* parallel arrays.  File is sorted so that the formulas are in        *
* alphabetical order.  The user enters a formula, the list of formulas *
* is searched using the binary search algorithm, and if the formula is *
* found, its name and specific heat are displayed.   Identifiers used  *
* are:                                                                *
*      LIMIT   :  parameter specifying maximum # of array elements    *
*      LENGTH  :  parameter specifying length of character strings    *
*      FORMUL  :  array of formulas                                   *
*      NAME    :  array of names                                      *
*      SPHEAT  :  array of specific heats                             *
*      N       :  number of records in the file                      *
************************************************************************

      INTEGER LIMIT, LENGTH, N
      PARAMETER (LIMIT = 100, LENGTH = 10)
      CHARACTER*(LENGTH) FORMUL(LIMIT), NAME(LIMIT)*(2*LENGTH)
      REAL SPHEAT(LIMIT)

      CALL RDDATA(FORMUL, NAME, SPHEAT, LIMIT, N)
      CALL LOOKUP(FORMUL, NAME, SPHEAT, LIMIT, N)

      END
```

Figure 7.13

Figure 7.13 (cont.)

```
**RDDATA*************************************************************
* Subroutine to read a list of up to LIM chemical formulas, names,    *
* and specific heats, store them in parallel arrays FORMUL, NAME, and *
* SPHEAT, and count (N) how many sets of readings are stored.  FNAME  *
* is the name of the file from which data is read and EOF is an       *
* end-of-file indicator.                                              *
********************************************************************

        SUBROUTINE RDDATA(FORMUL, NAME, SPHEAT, LIM, N)
        INTEGER LIM, N, EOF
        CHARACTER*(*) FORMUL(LIM), NAME(LIM)
        REAL SPHEAT(LIM)
        CHARACTER*20 FNAME

* Open the file, then read, count, and store the items

        PRINT *, 'ENTER NAME OF FILE'
        READ '(A)', FNAME
        OPEN (UNIT = 15, FILE = FNAME, STATUS = 'OLD')
        N = 0

*       While there is more data in the file, read it and
*       store it in the parallel arrays

        READ (UNIT = 15, FMT = 100, IOSTAT = EOF)
     +        FORMUL(N), NAME(N), SPHEAT(N)
100     FORMAT(2A, F5.0)
10      IF (EOF .GE. 0) THEN
            N = N + 1
            READ (UNIT = 15, FMT = 100, IOSTAT = EOF)
     +            FORMUL(N), NAME(N), SPHEAT(N)
        GO TO 10
        END IF

        END
```

Figure 7.13 (cont.)

```
**LOOKUP*************************************************************
* Subroutine that allows user to enter formulas.  The array FORMUL   *
* having N chemical formulas is then searched for this formula, and  *
* if found, the corresponding entries of the parallel arrays NAME and*
* SPHEAT are displayed.  User enters QUIT to stop searching. LIM     *
* dimensions the arrays, and LENGTH is used to specify the lengths of *
* the formulas and names.  Local identifiers used are:               *
*     UFORM   :  formula entered by the user                         *
*     FOUND   :  signals if UFORM found in array FORMUL              *
*     LOC     :  location of time in FORMUL if found                 *
*     LENGTH  :  parameter used to specify length of UFORM           *
*********************************************************************

      SUBROUTINE LOOKUP(FORMUL, NAME, SPHEAT, LIM, N)

      INTEGER LIM, N, LOC, LENGTH
      PARAMETER (LENGTH = 10)
      CHARACTER*(*) FORMUL(LIM), NAME(LIM)
      CHARACTER*(LENGTH) UFORM
      REAL SPHEAT(LIM)
      LOGICAL FOUND

      PRINT *
      PRINT *, 'ENTER FORMULA TO SEARCH FOR, (QUIT TO STOP)'
      READ '(A)', UFORM

* While UTIME not equal to 'QUIT',  search FORMUL array for it,
* display information found, and read next UFORM

10    IF (UFORM.NE. 'QUIT') THEN
          CALL SEARCH(FORMUL, LIMIT, N, LENGTH, UFORM, FOUND, LOC)
          IF (FOUND) THEN
              PRINT 100, 'HAS SPECIFIC HEAT', SPHEAT(LOC)
100           FORMAT(6X, A, F7.4)
          ELSE
              PRINT 100, ' NOT FOUND'
          END IF
          PRINT *
          PRINT *, 'ENTER FORMULA TO SEARCH FOR, (QUIT TO STOP)'
          READ '(A)', UFORM
      GO TO 10
      END IF

      CLOSE (15)
      END
```

Figure 7.13 (cont.)

```
**SEARCH***********************************************************
* Subroutine to search the list ITEM For UITEM using binary search.   *
* If UITEM is found in the list, FOUND is returned as true and the    *
* LOCation of the item is returned; otherwise FOUND is false.  LIM is *
* the limit on the size of ITEM.  In this version of binary search,   *
* UITEM and the elements of ITEM are character strings of length LEN. *
* Local variables used are:                                           *
*     FIRST   :  first item in (sub)list being searched               *
*     LAST    :  last   "    "    "      "     "                       *
*     MIDDLE  :  middle "    "    "      "     "                       *
*********************************************************************

         SUBROUTINE SEARCH(ITEM, LIM, N, LEN, UITEM, FOUND, LOC)

         INTEGER LIM, N, LOC, FIRST, LAST, MIDDLE
         CHARACTER*(*) ITEM(LIM), UITEM
         LOGICAL FOUND

         FIRST = 1
         LAST = N
         FOUND = .FALSE.

*        While FIRST less than or equal to LAST and not FOUND do

10       IF ((FIRST .LE. LAST) .AND. .NOT. FOUND) THEN
             MIDDLE = (FIRST + LAST) / 2
             IF (UITEM .LT. ITEM(MIDDLE)) THEN
                 LAST = MIDDLE - 1
             ELSE IF (UITEM .GT. ITEM(MIDDLE)) THEN
                 FIRST = MIDDLE + 1
             ELSE
                 FOUND = .TRUE.
                 LOC = MIDDLE
             END IF
         GO TO 10
         END IF

         END
```

Listing of SPECHEAT-FILE used in sample run:

```
AGCL        SILVER CHLORIDE      .0804
ALCL3       ALUMINUM CHLORIDE    .188
AUI         GOLD IODIDE          .0404
BACO3       BARIUM CARBONATE     .0999
CACL2       CALCIUM CHLORIDE     .164
CACO3       CALCIUM CARBONATE    .203
FE2O3       FERRIC OXIDE         .182
H2O2        HYDROGEN PEROXIDE    .471
KCL         POTASSIUM CHLORIDE   .162
LIF         LITHIUM FLOURIDE     .373
NABR        SODIUM BROMIDE       .118
NACL        SODIUM CHLORIDE      .204
PBBR2       LEAD BROMIDE         .0502
SIC         SILICON CARBIDE      .143
SNCL2       STANNOUS CHLORIDE    .162
ZNSO4       ZINC SULFATE         .174
```

Figure 7.13 (cont.)

Sample run:

```
ENTER NAME OF FILE
SPECHEAT-FILE

ENTER FORMULA TO SEARCH FOR, (QUIT TO STOP)
AGCL
        HAS SPECIFIC HEAT 0.0804

ENTER FORMULA
NACL
      HAS SPECIFIC HEAT 0.2040

ENTER FORMULA
FECO3
      *** NOT FOUND ***

ENTER FORMULA
FE2O3
      HAS SPECIFIC HEAT 0.1820

ENTER FORMULA
ZNSO4
      HAS SPECIFIC HEAT 0.1740

ENTER FORMULA
QUIT
```

Exercises

1. Assume that the following declarations have been made:

```
INTEGER NUMBER(10), I
REAL POINT(-5:5)
LOGICAL TORF(5)
CHARACTER*1 SYMBOL(5)
```

Assume also that the following format statements are given,

```
100 FORMAT(10(1X, I1))
110 FORMAT(5(L1, 1X, L2))
120 FORMAT(5L2)
130 FORMAT(5(A2, A1))
140 FORMAT(5A1)
```

and that the following data is entered:

```
T1F2F3T4T5T6F7F8F9T0
```

For each of the following, tell what value (if any) is assigned to each array element, or explain why an error occurs.

(a)
```
     DO 10 I = 1, 10
          NUMBER(I) = I / 2
  10 CONTINUE
```

(b)
```
      DO 10 I = 1, 6
          NUMBER(I) = I * I
   10 CONTINUE
      DO 20 I = 7, 10
          NUMBER(I) = NUMBER(I - 5)
   20 CONTINUE
```

(c)
```
      I = 1
   10 IF (I .NE. 10) THEN
          IF (MOD(I,3) .EQ. 0) THEN
              NUMBER(I) = 0
          ELSE
              NUMBER(I) = I
          END IF
          I = I + 1
      GO TO 10
      END IF
```

(d)
```
      NUMBER(1) = 1
      I = 2
   10 CONTINUE
          NUMBER(I) = NUMBER(I - 1)
          I = I + 1
      IF (I .LT. 10) GO TO 10
```

(e)
```
      DO 10 I = 1, 10
          READ 100, NUMBER(I)
   10 CONTINUE
```

(f)
```
      READ 100, NUMBER
```

(g)
```
      READ 100, (NUMBER(I), I = 1, 10)
```

(h)
```
      READ 100, (POINT(I), I = -5, 5)
```

(i)
```
      READ 110, (TORF(I), I = 1, 5)
```

(j)
```
      READ 120, TORF
      DO 10 I = 1, 5
          IF (TORF(I)) THEN
              POINT(I - 4) = -1.1 * I
              POINT(I) = 1.1 * I
          ELSE
              POINT(I - 4) = 0
              POINT(I) = 0
          END IF
   10 CONTINUE
```

(k)
```
      READ 130, (SYMBOL(I), I = 1, 5)
```

```
(l)     READ 140, SYMBOL
        DO 10 I = 1, 5
           IF (('A' .LE. SYMBOL(I)) .AND.
      +        (SYMBOL(I) .LE. 'Z')) THEN
              POINT(I-4) = -1.1 * I
              POINT(I) = 1.1 * I
           ELSE
              POINT(I-4) = 0
              POINT(I) = 0
           END IF
     10 CONTINUE
```

2. For each of the following, write appropriate declarations and statements to create the specified array:

   (a) An array whose subscripts are the integers from 0 through 5 and in which each element is the same as the subscript.
   (b) An array whose subscripts are the integers from -5 through 5 and in which the elements are the subscripts in reverse order.
   (c) An array whose subscripts are the integers from 1 through 20 and in which an array element has the value true if the corresponding subscript is even, and false otherwise.
   (d) An array whose subscripts are the integers from 0 through 359 and whose elements are the values of the sine function at the angles $0°, 1°, \ldots, 359°$.

3. Assuming that integer and logical values are stored in one memory word, that real values require two memory words, and that character values are packed two per word, indicate with a diagram like that in Section 7.1 where each component of an array A declared as follows is stored if the base address of A is B. Also, give the general address translation formula for A(I):

   (a) `INTEGER A(5)`
   (b) `REAL A(5)`
   (c) `LOGICAL A(5)`
   (d) `CHARACTER*8 A(5)`
   (e) `INTEGER A(-5:5)`
   (f) `REAL A(5:15)`
   (g) `LOGICAL A(0:9)`
   (h) `CHARACTER A(0:9)`

4. Assuming a list of N real numbers representing noise levels has been read and stored in an array NOISE, write a program segment to implement the linear search algorithm to find a given real number NVALUE in this list or to determine that it is not in the list.

5. In general, one need not linear search an entire list to determine that it does not contain a given item if the list has been previously sorted. Write a modified linear search algorithm for such an ordered list.

6. The following data was collected by a company and represents discrete values of a function for which an explicit formula is not known:

x	f(x)
1.123400	167.5600
2.246800	137.6441
3.370200	110.2523
4.493600	85.38444
5.617000	63.04068
6.740400	43.22099
7.863800	25.92535
8.987200	11.15376
10.11060	-1.093781
11.23400	-10.81726
12.35740	-18.01665
13.48080	-22.69202
14.60420	-24.84334
15.72760	-24.47060
16.85100	-21.57379
17.97440	-16.15295
19.09780	-8.208008
20.22120	2.260895
21.34460	15.25394
22.46800	30.77100
23.59140	48.81213
24.71480	69.37738
25.83820	92.46655
26.96160	118.0799
28.08500	146.2172

One can, however, use *linear interpolation* to approximate the $f(x)$ value for any given x value between the smallest and the largest x values. First, find the two x values x_i and x_{i+1} in the list that bracket the given x value, using a modified linear search procedure similar to that in Exercise 5, and then interpolate to find the corresponding $f(x)$ value:

$$f(x) = f(x_i) + \frac{f(x_{i+1}) - f(x_i)}{x_{i+1} - x_i}(x - x_i)$$

(If the x value is out of range, print a message.) Test your program with the following x values: -7.8, 1.1234, 13.65, 22.5, 23.5914, 25, 25.085, and 33.8.

7. If **a** and **b** are *n-dimensional vectors* given by

$$\mathbf{a} = (a_1, a_2, \ldots, a_n)$$

$$\mathbf{b} = (b_1, b_2, \ldots, b_n)$$

then

$$|\mathbf{a}| = \sqrt{a_1^2 + a_2^2 + \cdots + a_n^2}$$

is the *norm* (or *length* or *magnitude*) of **a**, and

$$\frac{1}{|\mathbf{a}|}\,\mathbf{a} = \left(\frac{a_1}{|\mathbf{a}|}, \frac{a_2}{|\mathbf{a}|}, \ldots, \frac{a_n}{|\mathbf{a}|}\right)$$

is a *unit vector* in the same direction as **a**. The *sum* and *difference* of **a** and **b** are defined by

$$\mathbf{a} + \mathbf{b} = (a_1 + b_1, a_2 + b_2, \ldots, a_n + b_n)$$

$$\mathbf{a} - \mathbf{b} = (a_1 - b_1, a_2 - b_2, \ldots, a_n - b_n)$$

and the *dot* (or *scalar*) *product* of **a** and **b** is defined by

$$\mathbf{a} \cdot \mathbf{b} = \sum_{i=1}^{n} a_i b_i = a_1 b_1 + a_2 b_2 + \cdots + a_n b_n$$

(a) Write a function subprogram that accepts a value for n and an n-dimensional vector and that calculates the norm of that vector.

(b) Write a subroutine subprogram that accepts a value for n and an n-dimensional vector and that returns a unit vector having the same direction as that vector.

(c) Write a subroutine subprogram that accepts a value for n and two n-dimensional vectors and that returns the sum, the difference, and the dot product of the vectors.

Use these subprograms in a main program that reads several pairs of n-dimensional vectors for various values of n and displays their norms, unit vectors in the same direction as the vectors, the sum, the difference, the dot product of each pair of vectors, and the cosine of the angle θ between the vectors, calculated using

$$\cos\theta = \frac{\mathbf{a} \cdot \mathbf{b}}{|\mathbf{a}|\,|\mathbf{b}|}$$

8. The Cawker City Candy Company records the number of cases of candy produced each day over a four-week period. Write a program that reads these production numbers and stores them in an array. The program should then accept from the user a week number and a day number and should display the production level for that day. Assume that each week consists of five workdays.

9. The Cawker City Candy Company manufactures different kinds of candy, each identified by a product number. Write a program that reads two arrays, NUMBER and PRICE, in which NUMBER(1) and PRICE(1) are the product number and the unit price for the first item, NUMBER(2) and PRICE(2) are the product number and the unit price for the second item, and so on. The program should then allow the user to select one of the following options:

1. Retrieve and display the price of a product whose number is entered by the user.

2. Print a table displaying the product number and the price of each item.

Make the program modular by using subprograms to perform the various tasks.

10. The Cawker City Candy Company maintains two warehouses, one in Chicago and one in Detroit, each of which stocks at most 25 different items. Write a program that first reads the product numbers of the items stored in the Chicago warehouse and stores them in an array, and then repeats this for the items stored in the Detroit warehouse, storing these product numbers in another array. The program should then find and display the *intersection* of these two lists of numbers, that is, the collection of product numbers common to both lists. The lists should not be assumed to have the same number of elements.

11. Repeat Exercise 10, but find and display the *union* of the two lists, that is, the collection of product numbers that are elements of at least one of the lists.

12. A hardware store sells lawn sprinklers. Past experience has indicated that the selling season is only six months long, lasting from April 1 through September 30. The sales division has forecast the following sales for next year:

Month	Demand
April	40
May	20
June	30
July	40
August	30
September	20

All sprinklers are purchased from an outside source at a cost of $8.00 per sprinkler. However, the supplier sells them only in lots of 10, 20, 30, 40, or 50; monthly orders for fewer than 10 sprinklers or more than 50 are not accepted. Discounts based on the size of the lot ordered are as follows:

Lot Size	Discount (percent)
10	5
20	5
30	10
40	20
50	25

For each order placed, the store is charged a fixed cost of $15.00 to cover shipping costs, insurance, packaging, and so on, regardless of the number ordered (except that there is no charge for a month when none is ordered). Assume that orders are placed on the first of the month and are received immediately. The store also incurs a carrying charge of $1.80 for each sprinkler remaining in stock at the end of any one month.

Write a program to calculate the total seasonal cost, the price that must be charged per sprinkler in order for the hardware store to break even, and the price that must be charged to realize a profit of 30 percent. Run your program with each of the following six ordering policies and determine which is the best:

Policy Number	Number Ordered/Month					
	April	May	June	July	August	September
1	40	20	30	40	30	20
2	50	50	50	30	0	0
3	40	50	0	40	50	0
4	50	50	40	40	0	0
5	50	10	50	20	50	0
6	50	50	0	50	30	0

13. Write a program that reads two lists of integers that have been sorted so that they are in ascending order and then calls a subroutine to *merge* these lists into a third list in which the integers are also in ascending order. Run the program for at least the following lists:

(a) List-1: 1, 3, 5, 7, 9
   List-2: 2, 4, 6, 8, 10

(b) List-1: 1, 4, 5, 6, 9, 10
   List-2: 2, 3, 7, 8

(c) List-1: 1, 2, 3, 4, 5, 6, 7
   List-2: 8, 9, 20

(d) List-1: 10
   List-2: 1, 2, 3, 4, 5, 6, 7, 8, 9

14. Write a program that calls subprograms to read and count a list of numbers and to calculate their mean, variance, and standard deviation. Print how many numbers there are and their mean, variance, and standard deviation with appropriate labels. If $\bar{x}$ denotes the mean of the numbers $x_1, \ldots, x_n$, the *variance* is the average of the squares of the deviations of the numbers from the mean:

$$\text{variance} = \frac{1}{n} \sum_{i=1}^{n} (x_i - \bar{x})^2$$

and the *standard deviation* is the square root of the variance.

15. Letter grades are sometimes assigned to numeric scores by using the grading scheme commonly called *grading on the curve*. In this

scheme, a letter grade is assigned to a numeric score, according to the following table:

x = Numeric Score	Letter Grade
$x < m - \dfrac{3}{2}\sigma$	F
$m - \dfrac{3}{2}\sigma \leq x < m - \dfrac{1}{2}\sigma$	D
$m - \dfrac{1}{2}\sigma \leq x < m + \dfrac{1}{2}\sigma$	C
$m + \dfrac{1}{2}\sigma \leq x < m + \dfrac{3}{2}\sigma$	B
$m + \dfrac{3}{2}\sigma \leq x$	A

where m is the mean score and σ is the standard deviation. Extend the program of Exercise 14 to read a list of real numbers representing numeric scores, calculate their mean and standard deviation, and then find and display the letter grade corresponding to each numeric score.

16. *Insertion sort* is an efficient sorting method for small data sets. It consists of beginning with the first item $X(1)$, then inserting $X(2)$ into this one-item list in the correct position to form a sorted two-element list, then inserting $X(3)$ into this two-element list in the correct position, and so on. For example, to sort the list 7, 1, 5, 2, 3, 4, 6, 0, the steps are as follows (the element being inserted is underlined):

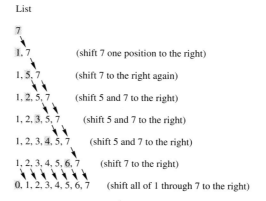

List

7

1, 7   (shift 7 one position to the right)

1, 5, 7   (shift 7 to the right again)

1, 2, 5, 7   (shift 5 and 7 to the right)

1, 2, 3, 5, 7   (shift 5 and 7 to the right)

1, 2, 3, 4, 5, 7   (shift 5 and 7 to the right)

1, 2, 3, 4, 5, 6, 7   (shift 7 to the right)

0, 1, 2, 3, 4, 5, 6, 7   (shift all of 1 through 7 to the right)

Write a subroutine to sort a list of items using this insertion sort method, and then write a main program that reads a set of values and calls this subroutine to sort them.

17. Insertion sort (see Exercise 16) performs best for small lists and for partially sorted lists. *Shell sort* (named after Donald Shell) uses insertion sort to sort small sublists to produce larger partially ordered sublists. Specifically, one begins with a "gap" of a certain size g

and then uses insertion sort to sort sublists of elements that are g apart, first, $X(1)$, $X(1 + g)$, $X(1 + 2g)$, ... , then the sublist $X(2)$, $X(2 + g)$, $X(2 + 2g)$, ... , then $X(3)$, $X(3 + g)$, $X(3 + 2g)$, ... , and so on. Next the size of the gap g is reduced, and the process repeated. This continues until the gap g is 1, and the final insertion sort results in the sorted list.

Write a subroutine to sort a list of items using this Shell sort method, beginning with a gap g of the form $(3^k - 1)/2$ for some integer k, and dividing it by 3 at each stage. Then write a main program that reads a set of values and calls this subroutine to sort them.

18. The investment firm of Shyster and Shyster has been recording the trading price of a particular stock over a 15-day period. Write a program that reads these prices and sorts them into increasing order, using the insertion sort scheme described in Exercise 16. The program should display the trading range, that is, the lowest and highest prices recorded, and also the median price.

19. A *prime number* is an integer greater than 1 whose only positive divisors are 1 and the integer itself. One method for finding all the prime numbers in the range 2 through n is known as the *Sieve of Eratosthenes*. Consider the list of numbers from 2 through n. Here 2 is the first prime number, but the multiples of 2 (4, 6, 8, ...) are not, and so they are "crossed out" in the list. The first number after 2 that was not crossed out is 3, the next prime. We then cross out all higher multiples of 3 (6, 9, 12, ...) from the list. The next number not crossed out is 5, the next prime; we cross out all higher multiples of 5 (10, 15, 20, ...). We repeat this procedure until we reach the first number in the list that has not been crossed out and whose square is greater than n. Then all the numbers that remain in the list are the primes from 2 through n. Write a program that uses this sieve method to find all the prime numbers from 2 through n. Run it for $n = 50$ and for $n = 500$.

20. Write a subroutine to add two large integers of any length, say up to 300 digits. A suggested approach is as follows: Treat each number as a list, each of whose elements is a block of digits of that number. For example, the integer 179,534,672,198 might be stored with $N(1) = 198$, $N(2) = 672$, $N(3) = 534$, $N(4) = 179$. Then add the two integers (lists) element by element, carrying from one element to the next when necessary. Test your subroutine with a program that reads two large integers and calls the subroutine to find their sum.

21. Proceed as in Exercise 20, but write a subroutine to multiply two large integers, say, of length up to 300 digits.

22. Peter the postman became bored one night, and to break the monotony of the night shift, he carried out the following experiment with a row of mailboxes in the post office: These mailboxes were numbered 1

through 150, and beginning with mailbox 2, he opened the doors of all the even-numbered mailboxes. Next, beginning with mailbox 3, he went to every third mail box, opening its door if it were closed and closing it if it were open. Then he repeated this procedure with every fourth mailbox, then every fifth mailbox, and so on. When he finished, he was surprised at the distribution of closed mailboxes. Write a program to determine which mailboxes these were.

23. Write a program to investigate the *birthday problem:* If there are n persons in a room, what is the probability that two or more of them have the same birthday? You might consider values of n, say from 10 through 40, and for each value of n, generate n random birthdays, and then scan the list to see whether two of them are the same. To obtain some approximate probabilities, you might do this 100 times for each value of n.

24. Write a program to read the files STUDENT-FILE and STUDENT-UPDATE (see Appendix B) and produce an updated grade report. This grade report should show

    (a) The current date.
    (b) The student's name and student number.
    (c) A list of the names, grades and credits for each of the current courses under the headings COURSE, GRADE, and CREDITS.
    (d) Current GPA (multiply the credits by the numeric grade— $A = 4.0$, $A- = 3.7$, $B+ = 3.3$, $B = 3.0$, ..., $D- = 0.7$, $F = 0.0$—for each course to find honor points earned for that course; sum these to find the total new honor points, then divide the total new honor points by the total new credits to give the current GPA, rounded to two decimal places).
    (e) Total credits earned (old credits from STUDENT-FILE plus total new credits).
    (f) New cumulative GPA (first, calculate old honor points = old credits times old cumulative GPA, then new cumulative GPA = sum of old honor points and new honor points divided by updated total credits).

25. Write a subprogram to evaluate a polynomial $a_0 + a_1 x + a_2 x^2 + \cdots + a_n x^n$ for any degree n, coefficients $a_0, a_1, \ldots, a_n$, and values of x that are supplied to it as arguments. Then write a program that reads a value of n, the coefficients, and various values of x and then uses this subprogram to evaluate the polynomial at x.

26. Proceed as in Exercise 25, but use *nested multiplication* (also known as *Horner's method*) to evaluate the polynomial; that is, use the fact that

$$a_0 + a_1 x + a_2 x^2 + \cdots + a_n x^n =$$
$$a_0 + (a_1 + (a_2 + \cdots + (a_{n-1} + a_n x)x) \cdots x)x$$

For example:

$$7 + 6x + 5x^2 + 4x^3 + 3x^4 = 7 + (6 + (5 + (4 + 3x)x)x)x$$

27. A data structure that is sometimes implemented using an array is a *stack*. A stack is a list in which elements may be inserted or deleted at only one end of the list, called the *top* of the stack. Because the last element added to a stack will be the first one removed, a stack is called a *Last-In-First-Out (LIFO)* structure. A stack can be implemented as an array STACK, with STACK(1) representing the bottom of the stack and STACK(TOP) the top, where TOP is the position of the top element of the stack. Write subprograms PUSH and POP to implement insertion and deletion operations for a stack. Use these subprograms in a program that reads a command I (Insert) or D (Delete); for I, an integer is then read and inserted into (''pushed onto'') the stack; for D, an integer is deleted (''popped'') from the stack and displayed.

28. Another data structure that can be implemented using an array is a *queue*. A queue is a list in which elements may be inserted at one end, called the *rear*, and removed at the other end, called the *front*. Because the first element added is the first to be removed, a queue is called a *First-In-First-Out (FIFO)* structure. Write subprograms to implement insertion and deletion operations for a queue. Use these subprograms in a program like that in Exercise 27 to insert integers into or delete integers from a queue. (*Note:* The most efficient representation of a queue as an array is obtained by thinking of the array as being circular, with the first array element immediately following the last array element.)

29. (Project) A problem from the area of *artificial intelligence:* The game of *Nim* is played by two players. There are three piles of objects, and each player is allowed to take any number (at least one) of objects from any pile on his or her turn. The player taking the last object wins. Write a program in which the computer ''learns'' to play Nim. One way to ''teach'' the computer is to have the program assign a value to each possible move based on experience gained from playing games. The value of each possible move is stored in some array, and each value is set to 0. The program then keeps track of each move the computer makes as it plays the game. At the end of each game that the computer wins, the value of each move the computer made is increased by 1. At the end of any game lost by the computer, 1 is subtracted from the value of each move made. The computer plays by selecting, from all legal moves, the one that has the largest value. When there are several possible moves having this same largest value, some strategy must be chosen. (One possibility is to have it select a move randomly.)

30. (Project) The spread of a contagious disease and the propagation of a

rumor have a great deal in common. Write a program to simulate the spread of a disease or a rumor. You might proceed as follows: Establish a population of N individuals, and assign to each individual three parameters (perhaps different numbers to various individuals):

(a) A "resistance" parameter: the probability that the individual will be infected by the disease (rumor) upon transmission from a carrier.

(b) A "recovery" (or "forgetting") parameter: the probability that the infected individual will recover from the disease (forget the rumor) before transmitting it to others in the population.

(c) An "activity" parameter: the probability that the individual will in fact transmit the disease (rumor) to another person he or she contacts.

(d) A "transmission" parameter: the probability that the individual will in fact transmit the disease (rumor) to another person he or she contacts.

A person who comes in contact with an infected person either becomes infected or does not; a random number can be compared with his or her resistance parameter to determine the result.

Once a person is infected, that is, becomes a carrier, another random number can be compared with his or her recovery (forgetting) parameter to determine whether or not he or she will recover from the disease (forget the rumor) before contacting other persons.

The activity parameter of a person who does not recover from the disease (forget the rumor) before contacting other persons determines how many persons he or she will contact, and the transmission parameter determines the actual number of persons to whom the disease (rumor) will be transmitted. The specific individuals can then be selected at random from the population and the disease (rumor) transmitted to them.

Select one individual to initiate the process. You might keep track of the number of persons infected in each stage; the "degrees of exposure (credibility)," that is, the number of persons exposed once, twice, and so on; the effect of building in certain percentages to indicate the decreased chances of reinfection; and so on.

Programming Pointers

In this chapter we discussed arrays. It is quite common for beginning programmers to have some difficulty when using arrays. The following are some of the major points to remember:

1. *All arrays in a FORTRAN program must be dimensioned.* If, for example, ALPHA has been declared by

```
REAL ALPHA
```

but has not been dimensioned, the compiler may interpret a reference to an element of ALPHA, as in

```
     X = ALPHA(1)
```

as a reference to a function named ALPHA, which is an error.

2. *Arrays must be declared in each program unit in which they are used.* The dimension can be specified by constants or parameters, and in subprograms, adjustable dimensions are allowed.

3. *Subscripts must be integer valued and must stay within the range specified in the array declarations.* Related to this requirement are two kinds of errors that can easily arise when using arrays. The first error results from forgetting to declare a subscript to be of integer type. For example, consider the program segment

```
     INTEGER ALPHA(10)
     DO 10 ELM = 1, 10
        ALPHA(ELM) = 0
 10  CONTINUE
        .
        .
        .
```

Because the type of ELM has not been declared, the FORTRAN naming convention implies that it is of real type. Consequently, an error results when the array ALPHA is referenced by the statement

```
     ALPHA(ELM) = 0
```

because the subscript is not of integer type.

Another error results from allowing a subscript to get "out of bounds," that is, to have a value less than the lower bound or greater than the upper bound specified in the array declaration. The result of an out-of-range subscript is compiler dependent. If a compiler does range checking, an error results, and execution is usually terminated. For some compilers, however, no such range checking is done, and the memory location that is accessed is determined simply by counting forward or backward from the memory location associated with the first array element. This is illustrated by the program in Figure 7.14. Here A, B, and C are arrays declared by

```
     INTEGER A(4), B(4), C(4)
```

and the illegal array references B($-$2) and B(7) access the memory locations associated with A(2) and C(3):

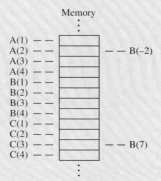

> Thus modifying B(-2) and B(7) changes A(2) and C(3), respectively. This change is obviously undesirable. An array reference such as B(500) that is very much out of range may even cause a program instruction to be modified! Consequently, *it is important to ensure that subscripts do not get out of range.*

```
      PROGRAM ARRAYS
*********************************************************************
* Program to demonstrate what may result when subscripts get out of  *
* bounds.  Variables used are                                        *
*     A, B, C : one-dimensional arrays of integers                   *
*********************************************************************

      INTEGER A(4), B(4), C(4)
      DATA A /1,2,3,4/, B /5,6,7,8/, C /9,10,11,12/

* Display the original arrays

      PRINT 100, 'A =', A
      PRINT 100, 'B =', B
      PRINT 100, 'C =', C
 100  FORMAT(1X, A, 4I5)

* Reference array B with a subscript that is out of bounds

      B(-2) = -999
      B(7) = 999

* Print each of the arrays again

      PRINT *
      PRINT 100, 'A =', A
      PRINT 100, 'B =', B
      PRINT 100, 'C =', C
      END
```

Sample run:

```
A =    1    2    3    4
B =    5    6    7    8
C =    9   10   11   12

A =    1 -999    3    4
B =    5    6    7    8
C =    9   10  999   12
```

Figure 7.14

FORTRAN 90 Features

- Assignment of one array to another is permitted, provided that the arrays have the same number of elements.

- Array constants of the form

    (/ *value-1*, *value-2*, . . . , *value-k* /)

    where each *value-i* is a constant expression or an *implied-do constructor* of the form

    (*value-list*, *implied-do-control*)

    are permitted. For example, if A is declared by

    ```
    INTEGER A(10)
    ```

    it can be assigned the sequence 1, 2, 3, . . . , 10 by any of the following statements:

    ```
    A = (/ 1, 2, 3, 4, 5, 6, 7, 8, 9, 10 /)
    A = (/ I, I = 1, 10 /)
    A = (/ 1, (I, I = 2, 9), 10 /)
    ```

- Operators and functions normally applied to simple expressions may also be applied to arrays having the same number of elements and to arrays and simple expressions. In this case, operations applied to an array are carried out elementwise. To illustrate, consider the following declarations:

    ```
    INTEGER A(4), B(4), C(0:3), D(6:9)
    LOGICAL P(4)
    ```

    If A and B are assigned values

    ```
    A = (/ 1, 2, 3, 4 /)
    B = (/ 5, 6, 7, 8 /)
    ```

    The statement

    ```
    A = A + B
    ```

    assigns to A the sequence 6, 8, 10, 12. If C is assigned a value

    ```
    C = (/ -1, 3, -5, 7 /)
    ```

    the statement

    ```
    D = 2 * ABS(C) + 1
    ```

    assigns to D the sequence 3, 7, 11, 15. Logical operations are also allowed. For example, the statement

    ```
    P = (C > 0) .AND. (MOD(B, 3) = 0)
    ```

    assigns to P the sequence of truth values .FALSE., .TRUE., .FALSE., .FALSE.

● Array sections, which are arrays consisting of selected elements from a parent array, are allowed. Such array sections are defined by specifications of the form

   array-name(subscript-triplet)

or

   array-name(vector-subscript)

A subscript triplet has the form

   lower : upper : stride

and specifies the elements in positions *lower, lower + stride, lower + 2 * stride, . . .* going as far as possible without going beyond *upper* if *stride* > 0, or below *upper* if *stride* < 0. If *stride* is omitted it is taken to be 1. For example, if A, B, and I are arrays dimensioned by

```
INTEGER A(10), B(5), I(5), J
```

and A is assigned a value by

```
A = (/ 11, 22, 33, 44, 55, 66, 77, 88, 99, 110 /)
```

then the statement

```
B = A(2:10:2)
```

assigns to B the section of array A consisting of the elements 22, 44, 66, 88, 110. The statement

```
A(1:10:2) = (/ I**2, I = 1, 5 /)
```

changes the elements in the odd positions of A to be 1, 4, 9, 16, 25.

A vector subscript is a sequence of subscripts of the parent array. For example, if A is the array considered earlier,

```
A = (/ 11, 22, 33, 44, 55, 66, 77, 88, 99, 110 /)
```

and I is the vector subscript

```
I = (/ 6, 5, 3, 9, 1 /)
```

then the assignment statement

```
B = A(I)
```

assigns B the section of array A consisting of the elements 66, 55, 33, 99, and 11, whereas the assignment statement

```
B = A((/ 5, 3, 3, 4, 3/))
```

assigns to B the sequence of elements 55, 33, 33, 44, and 33.

● A WHERE construct of the form

   WHERE (*logical-array-expression*)
      sequence-1 of array-assignment-statements

```
ELSEWHERE
```
sequence-2 of array-assignment-statements
```
END WHERE
```

(where the ELSEWHERE part is optional) may be used to assign values to arrays, depending on the value of a logical array expression. For example, if arrays A and B are declared by

```
INTEGER A(5)
REAL B(5)
```

and A is assigned the value

```
A = (/ 0, 2, 5, 0, 10 /)
```

the WHERE construct

```
WHERE (A > 0)
   B = 1.0 / REAL(A)
ELSEWHERE
   B = -1.0
END WHERE
```

assigns to B the sequence −1.0, 0.5, 0.2, −1.0, 0.1.
- Formal array arguments in subprograms may be *assumed-shape arrays* in which the dimension of the array is taken to be the dimension of the corresponding actual array argument. In this case, the declaration of the formal array in the subprogram has the form

  array-name(*lower*:)

  or

  array-name(:)

  In the second case, the lowest subscript is taken to be 1.
- The dimension of local arrays in subprograms may be specified by formal arguments or by the values of the array inquiry functions SIZE, LBOUND, and UBOUND for the corresponding actual array argument. For example, the subroutine

```
      SUBROUTINE SWAP(A, B)
 *    Subroutine to interchange elements of A and B *

      REAL DIMENSION(:) :: A, B    !assumed-size arrays
      REAL DIMENSION SIZE(A) :: TEMP!local array

      TEMP = A
      A = B
      B = TEMP
      END SUBROUTINE
```

- The value returned by a function may be an array.
- Several new predefined functions for processing arrays have been added. These include:

DOTPRODUCT(A, B):	Returns the dot product of A and B.
MAXVAL(A):	Returns the maximum value in array A.
MAXLOC(A):	Returns the locations of a maximum value in A.
MINVAL(A):	Returns the minimum value in array A.
MINLOC(A):	Returns the locations of a minimum value in A.
PRODUCT(A):	Returns the product of the elements of A.
SUM(A):	Returns the sum of the elements of A.

● Arrays may be *allocatable arrays*, which means that space is not allocated to them at compile time but rather by an ALLOCATE statement during execution; their bounds are also specified at that time. Such arrays are useful in applications where their sizes are known only after some data has been read or some calculation performed.

An array is declared to be allocatable by including the ALLO-CATABLE attribute in its type declaration. For example, the type specification statement

```
REAL, DIMENSION (:), ALLOCATABLE :: A, B
```

declares A and B to be one-dimensional allocatable arrays. The actual bounds are determined by an ALLOCATE statement, for example,

```
ALLOCATE (A(N), B(1:N+1))
```

where N is an integer variable. When this statement is executed, sufficient memory is allocated for the arrays A and B.

8

Multidimensional Arrays

Yea, from the table of my memory
I'll wipe away all trivial fond records.

WILLIAM SHAKESPEARE, *Hamlet*

In the preceding chapter we considered one-dimensional arrays and used them to process lists of data. We also observed that FORTRAN allows arrays of more than one dimension and that two-dimensional arrays are useful when the data being processed can be arranged in rows and columns. Similarly, a three-dimensional array is appropriate when the data can be arranged in rows, columns, and ranks. When several characteristics are associated with the data, still higher dimensions may be appropriate, with each dimension corresponding to one of these characteristics. In this chapter we consider how such multidimensional arrays are processed in FORTRAN programs.

8.1 Introduction to Multidimensional Arrays and Multiply Subscripted Variables

There are many problems in which the data being processed can be naturally organized as a table. For example, suppose that water temperatures are recorded four times each day at each of three locations near the discharge outlet of a nuclear power plant's cooling system. These temperature readings can be arranged in a table having four rows and three columns:

Time	Location 1	Location 2	Location 3
1	65.5	68.7	62.0
2	68.8	68.9	64.5
3	70.4	69.4	66.3
4	68.5	69.1	65.8

In this table, the three temperature readings at time 1 are in the first row, the three temperatures at time 2 are in the second row, and so on.

These twelve data items can be conveniently stored in a two-dimensional array. The array declaration

```
DIMENSION TEMTAB(1:4, 1:3)
REAL TEMTAB
```

or

```
DIMENSION TEMTAB(4,3)
REAL TEMTAB
```

reserves twelve memory locations for these data items. This dimensioning information can also be included in the type statement:

```
REAL TEMTAB(1:4, 1:3)
```

or

```
REAL TEMTAB(4,3)
```

The doubly subscripted variable

```
TEMTAB(2,3)
```

then refers to the entry in the second row and third column of the table, that is, to the temperature 64.5 recorded at time 2 at location 3. In general,

```
TEMTAB(I,J)
```

refers to the entry in the Ith row and Jth column, that is, to the temperature recorded at time I at location J.

To illustrate the use of an array with more than two dimensions, suppose that the temperature readings are made for one week so that seven such tables are collected:

Time	Location 1	2	3	
1	66.5	69.4	68.4	
2	68.4	71.2	69.3	Day 7
3	70.1	71.9	70.2	
4	69.5	70.0	69.4	

Time	Location 1	2	3	
1	63.7	66.2	64.3	
2	64.0	68.8	64.9	Day 2
			66.3	
			65.8	

Time	Location 1	2	3	
1	65.5	68.7	62.0	
2	68.8	68.9	64.5	Day 1
3	70.4	69.4	66.3	
4	68.5	69.1	65.8	

A three-dimensional array TEMP declared by

```
DIMENSION TEMP(1:4, 1:3, 1:7)
REAL TEMP
```

or

```
DIMENSION TEMP(4,3,7)
REAL TEMP
```

or

```
REAL TEMP(1:4, 1:3, 1:7)
```

or

```
REAL TEMP(4,3,7)
```

can be used to store these eighty-four temperature readings. The value of the triply subscripted variable

```
TEMP(1,3,2)
```

is the temperature recorded at time 1 at location 3 on day 2, that is, the value 64.3 in the first row, third column, second rank. In general,

```
TEMP(TIME,LOC,DAY)
```

is the temperature recorded at time TIME at location LOC on day DAY.

The general form of an **array declaration** is

$$array\text{-}name(l_1:u_1, l_2:u_2, \ldots, l_k:u_k)$$

where the number k of dimensions is at most seven, and each pair $l_i:u_i$ must be a pair of integer constants or parameters specifying the range of values for the ith subscript to be from l_i through u_i. There must be one such array declaration for each array used in a program, and these declarations may appear in DIMENSION or type statements. For example, the statements

```
DIMENSION GAMMA(1:2, -1:3), KAPPA(5:12),
+        BETA(0:2, 0:3, 1:2)
REAL GAMMA, BETA
INTEGER KAPPA
```

or

```
REAL GAMMA(1:2, -1:3), BETA(0:2, 0:3, 1:2)
INTEGER KAPPA(5:12)
```

establish three arrays. The array GAMMA is a two-dimensional 2×5 real array, with the first subscript either 1 or 2 and the second subscript ranging from −1 through 3. Thus, the doubly subscripted variables GAMMA(1, −1), GAMMA(1,0), GAMMA(1,1), GAMMA(1,2), GAMMA(1,3), GAMMA(2, −1), GAMMA(2,0), GAMMA(2,1), GAMMA(2,2), and GAMMA(2,3) may be used. The first subscript in the three-dimensional 3 × 4 × 2 real array BETA is equal to 0, 1, or 2; the second subscript ranges from 0 through 3; and the third subscript is equal to 1 or 2. The one-dimensional integer array KAPPA has subscripts ranging from 5 through 12.

8.2 Processing Multidimensional Arrays

In the preceding section we gave several examples of multidimensional arrays and showed how such arrays are declared in a FORTRAN program. We also noted that each element of the array can be accessed directly by using a multiply subscripted variable consisting of the array name followed by the subscripts that specify the location of that element in the array. In this section we consider the processing of multidimensional arrays, including the input and output of arrays or parts of arrays.

As we observed in the preceding chapter, the most natural order for processing the elements of a one-dimensional array is the usual sequential order, from first item to last. For multidimensional arrays, however, there are several orders in which the subscripts may be varied when processing the array elements.

Two-dimensional arrays are often used when the data can be organized as a table consisting of rows and columns. This suggests two natural orders for processing the entries of a two-dimensional array: **rowwise** and **columnwise.** Rowwise processing means that the array elements in the first row are processed first; then those in the second row are processed next; and so on, as shown in Figure 8.1(a) for the 3 × 4 array A, which has three rows and four columns. In columnwise processing, the entries in the first column are processed first; then those in the second column are processed next; and so on, as illustrated in Figure 8.1(b). In most cases, the user can select one of these orderings by controlling the manner in which the subscripts vary. *If this is not done, the FORTRAN convention is that two-dimensional arrays will be processed columnwise.*

To illustrate these two ways of processing a two-dimensional array, we reconsider the table of temperature readings described in the preceding section:

Time	Location 1	Location 2	Location 3
1	65.5	68.7	62.0
2	68.8	68.9	64.5
3	70.4	69.4	66.3
4	68.5	69.1	65.8

Suppose that these twelve temperatures are to be read and stored in the two-dimensional 4 × 3 real array TEMTAB declared by

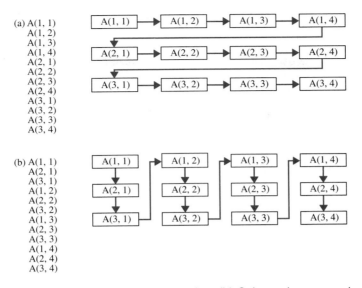

Figure 8.1 (a) Rowwise processing. (b) Columnwise processing.

```
REAL TEMTAB(4,3)
```

so that TEMTAB has the value

$$\begin{bmatrix} 65.5 & 68.7 & 62.0 \\ 68.8 & 68.9 & 64.5 \\ 70.4 & 69.4 & 66.3 \\ 68.5 & 69.1 & 65.8 \end{bmatrix}$$

If these twelve temperatures are to be entered in the order 65.5, 68.7, 62.0, 68.8, 68.9, 64.5, 70.4, 69.4, 66.3, 68.5, 69.1, 65.8, then rowwise processing is required. We must first read the three temperatures recorded at time 1; that is, we must read the values for the first row of TEMTAB:

Row 1 of TEMTAB: 65.5 68.7 62.0

After these values are read, the three temperatures recorded at time 2 must be entered and stored in the second row of TEMTAB:

Row 2 of TEMTAB: 68.8 68.9 64.5

We then enter the three temperatures recorded at time 3 and store them in the third row of TEMTAB:

Row 3 of TEMTAB: 70.4 69.4 66.3

Finally, the three values recorded at time 4 are read and stored in the fourth row of TEMTAB:

Row 4 of TEMTAB: 68.5 69.1 65.8

On the other hand, if the twelve temperature readings are to be entered in the order 65.5, 68.8, 70.4, 68.5, 68.7, 68.9, 69.4, 69.1, 62.0, 64.5, 66.3, 65.8, then columnwise processing is required. The four temperatures recorded at location 1 must be read and stored in the first column of TEMTAB:

Column 1 of TEMTAB:

```
65.5
68.8
70.4
68.5
```

After these four values have been read, the four temperatures at location 2 must be read and stored in the second column of TEMTAB:

Column 2 of TEMTAB:

```
68.7
68.9
69.4
69.1
```

Finally, the four temperatures recorded at location 3 are read and stored in the third column of TEMTAB:

Column 3 of TEMTAB:

```
62.0
64.5
66.3
65.8
```

In the list of array elements shown in Figure 8.1(a), we observe that in rowwise processing of a two-dimensional array, the second subscript varies first and the first subscript varies second; that is, the second subscript must vary over its entire range of values before the first subscript changes. It is just the opposite for columnwise processing, as we see from Figure 8.1(b): The first subscript varies first and the second subscript second; that is, the first subscript must vary over its entire range before the second subscript changes.

For arrays of three or more dimensions, the elements can be processed in many ways. One of the more common is the analog of columnwise processing for the two-dimensional case; that is, the first subscript varies first, followed by the second subscript, then by the third, and so on. This method is illustrated in Figure 8.2 for the $2 \times 4 \times 3$ array B, which has two rows, four columns, and three ranks.

In Section 7.2 we considered three ways in which data could be input or output for one-dimensional arrays:

1. Use a DO loop containing an input/output statement.
2. Use only the array name in an input/output statement.
3. Use an implied DO loop in an input/output statement.

Each of these three techniques can also be used for the input and output of

B(1, 1, 1)
B(2, 1, 1)
B(1, 2, 1)
B(2, 2, 1)
B(1, 3, 1)
B(2, 3, 1)
B(1, 4, 1)
B(2, 4, 1)
B(1, 1, 2)
B(2, 1, 2)
B(1, 2, 2)
B(2, 2, 2)
B(1, 3, 2)
B(2, 3, 2)
B(1, 4, 2)
B(2, 4, 2)
B(1, 1, 3)
B(2, 1, 3)
B(1, 2, 3)
B(2, 2, 3)
B(1, 3, 3)
B(2, 3, 3)
B(1, 4, 3)
B(2, 4, 3)

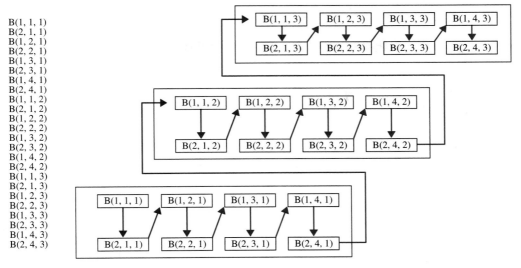

Figure 8.2

multidimensional arrays, and we consider each in turn, paying particular attention to the order in which the values are processed.

Input/Output Using DO Loops. When DO loops are used to read or display a multidimensional array, the input/output statement is placed within a set of nested DO loops, each of which controls one of the array's subscripts. For example, reconsider the problem of reading temperature values into the 4 × 3 real array TEMTAB declared by

```
REAL TEMTAB(4,3)
```

so that it has the value

$$\begin{bmatrix} 65.5 & 68.7 & 62.0 \\ 68.8 & 68.9 & 64.5 \\ 70.4 & 69.4 & 66.3 \\ 68.5 & 69.1 & 65.8 \end{bmatrix}$$

Suppose we use the following statements:

```
      DO 20 TIME = 1, 4
         DO 10 LOC = 1, 3
            READ *, TEMTAB(TIME,LOC)
   10    CONTINUE
   20 CONTINUE
```

Here the outer DO loop sets the value of the control variable TIME to 1, and the inner DO loop is then executed using 1 as the value for TIME. The effect, therefore, is the same as executing

```
    DO 10 LOC = 1, 3
        READ *, TEMTAB(1,LOC)
10 CONTINUE
```

which is equivalent to the following three READ statements:

```
READ *, TEMTAB(1,1)
READ *, TEMTAB(1,2)
READ *, TEMTAB(1,3)
```

The first pass through the outer DO loop thus reads values for the first row of TEMTAB, so that the first three values entered must be

```
65.5
68.7
62.0
```

Note that they must be entered on separate lines, one per line, because the READ statement is executed three times and each execution requires a new line of input.

Now the outer DO loop sets the value of TIME to 2, and the inner DO loop is executed again,

```
    DO 10 LOC = 1, 3
        READ *, TEMTAB(2,LOC)
10 CONTINUE
```

which is equivalent to the three READ statements

```
READ *, TEMTAB(2,1)
READ *, TEMTAB(2,2)
READ *, TEMTAB(2,3)
```

so that the next three values entered must be

```
68.8
68.9
64.5
```

again on separate lines. The outer DO loop then causes the inner DO loop to be executed again, with TIME set equal to 3

```
    DO 10 LOC = 1, 3
        READ *, TEMTAB(3,LOC)
10 CONTINUE
```

which is equivalent to

```
READ *, TEMTAB(3,1)
READ *, TEMTAB(3,2)
READ *, TEMTAB(3,3)
```

so that the values for the third row of TEMTAB must be entered on separate lines:

```
70.4
69.4
66.3
```

Finally, the value of TIME is set to 4, and the inner DO loop is executed again,

```
    DO 10 LOC = 1, 3
        READ *, TEMTAB(4,LOC)
10 CONTINUE
```

which has the same effect as

```
READ *, TEMTAB(4,1)
READ *, TEMTAB(4,2)
READ *, TEMTAB(4,3)
```

for which the values for the fourth row of TEMTAB must be entered:

```
68.5
69.1
65.8
```

Columnwise input is also possible; we need only reverse the order of the two DO loops:

```
    DO 20 LOC = 1, 3
        DO 10 TIME = 1, 4
            READ *, TEMTAB(TIME,LOC)
10      CONTINUE
20 CONTINUE
```

These statements are equivalent to the following sequence of twelve READ statements:

```
READ *, TEMTAB(1,1)
READ *, TEMTAB(2,1)
READ *, TEMTAB(3,1)
READ *, TEMTAB(4,1)
READ *, TEMTAB(1,2)
READ *, TEMTAB(2,2)
READ *, TEMTAB(3,2)
READ *, TEMTAB(4,2)
READ *, TEMTAB(1,3)
READ *, TEMTAB(2,3)
READ *, TEMTAB(3,3)
READ *, TEMTAB(4,3)
```

Because the READ statement is encountered twelve times, the data values must be entered on twelve separate lines, one per line:

```
65.5
68.8
70.4
68.5
68.7
68.9
69.4
69.1
62.0
64.5
66.3
65.8
```

Because the data values must appear on separate lines, one value per line, this method of input is cumbersome for large arrays. A similar problem also occurs with output, since each execution of a PRINT or WRITE statement within nested DO loops such as

```
      DO 20 TIME = 1, 4
         DO 10 LOC = 1, 3
            PRINT *, TEMTAB(TIME,LOC)
10       CONTINUE
20 CONTINUE
```

causes output to begin on a new line. Thus, the entries of the array are displayed on separate lines, one entry per line, rather than in a tabular format.

Input/Output Using the Array Name. In this method of reading or displaying an array, the array name without subscripts appears in the input/output statement. As we observed for one-dimensional arrays, this is equivalent to listing a *complete* set of array elements in the input/output list. The total number of entries as specified in the array declaration must be read or displayed, and therefore, it is not possible to read or display only part of an array using this method.

Another disadvantage of this method is the order in which multidimensional arrays are read or displayed. Because the order in which the subscripts vary is not specified by the programmer, the standard columnwise order (or its analog for arrays of more than two dimensions) is used. For example, the statements

```
      INTEGER MAT(3,4)
      READ *, MAT
```

cause values to be read columnwise into the array MAT. Thus, for the input data

```
77, 56, 32, 25, 99, 10
100, 46, 48, 89, 77, 33
```

the value assigned to MAT is

$$\begin{bmatrix} 77 & 25 & 100 & 89 \\ 56 & 99 & 46 & 77 \\ 32 & 10 & 48 & 33 \end{bmatrix}$$

The output statement

```
PRINT '(1X, 4I5/)', MAT
```

displays the elements in columnwise order and so produces the output

```
   77   56   32   25

   99   10  100   46

   48   89   77   33
```

We note that in contrast with the first method for input/output of arrays, the form in which the data is prepared for input or displayed by output may be specified. The number of items on each line of input or output is determined by the programmer.

Input/Output Using Implied DO Loops. An implied DO loop, introduced in Section 7.2, has the form

(i/o-list, control-variable = initial-value, limit)

or

(i/o-list, control-variable = initial-value, limit, step-size)

The fact that the input/output list may contain other implied DO loops makes it possible to use implied DO loops to read or display multidimensional arrays. For example, the statement

```
READ *, ((MAT(ROW,COL), COL = 1, 4), ROW = 1, 3)
```

is equivalent to the statement

```
READ *, (MAT(ROW,1), MAT(ROW,2),
+        MAT(ROW,3), MAT(ROW,4), ROW = 1, 3)
```

which has the same effect as

```
READ *, MAT(1,1), MAT(1,2), MAT(1,3), MAT(1,4),
+       MAT(2,1), MAT(2,2), MAT(2,3), MAT(2,4),
+       MAT(3,1), MAT(3,2), MAT(3,3), MAT(3,4)
```

and thus reads the entries of the array MAT in rowwise order. Note that because the READ statement is encountered only once, all the data values can be entered on the same line, or with four values on each of three lines, or with seven values on one line, four on the next, and one on another line, and so on.

By interchanging the indexing information in the nested implied DO loops, columnwise input is possible. Thus, the statement

```
READ *, ((MAT(ROW,COL), ROW = 1, 3), COL = 1, 4)
```

which is equivalent to

```
READ *, (MAT(1,COL), MAT(2,COL), MAT(3,COL), COL = 1, 4)
```

or

```
 READ *, MAT(1,1), MAT(2,1), MAT(3,1),
+        MAT(1,2), MAT(2,2), MAT(3,2),
+        MAT(1,3), MAT(2,3), MAT(3,3),
+        MAT(1,4), MAT(2,4), MAT(3,4)
```

may be used if the entries of MAT are to be entered in columnwise order. Similarly, the statement

```
READ *, (((B(I,J,K), I = 1, 2), J = 1, 4), K = 1, 3)
```

reads values into the three-dimensional array B in the standard order indicated in Figure 8.2.

Note the use of parentheses and commas in these statements. They should be used exactly as indicated, or an error message may result. Each implied DO loop must be enclosed within parentheses, and a comma must separate the list from the indexing information.

In contrast with the two preceding methods of array input/output, using an implied DO loop in an input/output list permits the programmer to determine the form of the input/output data and to read or display only part of an array. For example, if ALPHA is a 3 × 10 real array, the statements

```
    PRINT 50, ((ALPHA(K,L), L = 4, 10, 3), K = 1, 3, 2)
50 FORMAT(1X, 3F12.4)
```

will display ALPHA(1,4), ALPHA(1,7), ALPHA(1,10), ALPHA(3,4), ALPHA(3,7), AND ALPHA(3,10) in this order, with three numbers per line.

The program in Figure 8.3 illustrates this flexibility of implied DO loops. It reads the number NTIMES of times at which temperatures are recorded and the number NLOCS of locations at which these readings are made, and then uses implied DO loops to read NTIMES * NLOCS values into the two-dimensional array TEMTAB declared by

```
REAL TEMTAB(MAXTIM,MAXLOC)
```

where MAXTIM and MAXLOC are integer parameters with values 24 and 10, respectively, and to display these temperatures in tabular format.

```
      PROGRAM TEMPS
**************************************************************************
* Program illustrating the use of nested implied DO loops to read and  *
* print the elements of a two-dimensional array. Identifiers used are:  *
*      TEMTAB : two-dimensional array of temperatures                   *
*      MAXTIM : parameter specifying maximum # of times                 *
*      MAXLOC : parameter specifying maximum # of locations             *
*      NTIMES : # of times temperatures are recorded                    *
*      NLOCS  : # of locations at which temperatures are recorded       *
*      TIME   : row subscript for the table                             *
*      LOC    : column subscript for the table                          *
**************************************************************************

      INTEGER MAXTIM, MAXLOC, NTIMES, NLOCS, TIME, LOC
      PARAMETER (MAXTIM = 24, MAXLOC = 10)
      REAL TEMTAB(MAXTIM,MAXLOC)

      PRINT *, 'ENTER # OF TIMES TEMPERATURES ARE RECORDED'
      PRINT *, 'AND # OF LOCATIONS WHERE RECORDED:'
      READ *, NTIMES, NLOCS
      PRINT *, 'ENTER THE TEMPERATURES AT THE FIRST LOCATION,'
      PRINT *, 'THEN THOSE AT THE SECOND LOCATION, AND SO ON:'
      READ *, ((TEMTAB(TIME,LOC), LOC = 1, NLOCS), TIME = 1, NTIMES)
      PRINT *
      PRINT 100, (LOC, LOC = 1, NLOCS)
100   FORMAT(1X, T13, 'LOCATION' / 1X, 'TIME', 10I6)
      DO 130 TIME = 1, NTIMES
          PRINT 110, TIME, (TEMTAB(TIME,LOC), LOC = 1, NLOCS)
110       FORMAT(/1X, I3, 2X, 10F6.1/)
130   CONTINUE
      END
```

Sample run:

```
ENTER # OF TIMES TEMPERATURES ARE RECORDED
AND # OF LOCATIONS WHERE RECORDED:
4, 3
ENTER THE TEMPERATURES AT THE FIRST LOCATION,
THEN THOSE AT THE SECOND LOCATION, AND SO ON:
65.5, 68.7, 62.0
68.8, 68.9, 64.5
70.4, 69.4, 66.3
68.5, 69.1, 65.8

          LOCATION
TIME    1     2     3

  1    65.5  68.7  62.0

  2    68.8  68.9  64.5

  3    70.4  69.4  66.3

  4    68.5  69.1  65.8
```

Figure 8.3

The following examples exhibit some of the additional flexibility available with implied DO loops. In these examples the integer variable NTOT has the value 152; NUM is the one-dimensional integer array containing the four numbers 16, 37, 76, and 23; and RATE is a 3 × 4 real array having the value

$$
\begin{bmatrix}
16.1 & 7.3 & 18.4 & 6.5 \\
0.0 & 1.0 & 1.0 & 3.5 \\
18.2 & 16.9 & 0.0 & 0.0
\end{bmatrix}
$$

Input/output statement:

```
    READ *, N, (NUM(I), I = 1, N), M,
   +         ((RATE(I,J), J = 1, N), I = 1, M)
```

Possible lines of input data:

```
4
16, 37, 76, 23
3
16.1,  7.3, 18.4, 6.5
0.0,   1.0,  1.0, 3.5
18.2, 16.9,  0.0, 0.0
```

Input/output statement:

```
    PRINT 5, ('ROW', I, (RATE(I,J), J = 1, 4), I = 1, 3)
  5 FORMAT(1X, A, I2, '--', 4F6.1/)
```

Output produced:

```
ROW 1--  16.1   7.3  18.4   6.5
-------------------------------
ROW 2--   0.0   1.0   1.0   3.5
-------------------------------
ROW 3--  18.2  16.9   0.0   0.0
-------------------------------
```

Input/output statement:

```
    PRINT 6, (J, (RATE(I,J), I = 1,3), NUM(J), J = 1,4),
   +          'TOTAL', NTOT
  6 FORMAT(4(1X, I4, 5X, 3F6.1, I10/), 1X, A, T35, I3)
```

Output produced:

```
   1         16.1   0.0  18.2        16
   2          7.3   1.0  16.9        37
   3         18.4   1.0   0.0        76
   4          6.5   3.5   0.0        23
TOTAL                               152
```

Multidimensional Arrays as Arguments. In the preceding chapter we noted that one-dimensional arrays may be used as arguments in function and subroutine subprograms. Much of the discussion there also applies to multi-dimensional arrays. In particular, an actual multidimensional array argument must be declared in the calling program unit, and the corresponding formal array argument must be declared in the subprogram.

When higher-dimensional arrays are used as arguments, the elements are associated in the standard columnwise order. Suppose, for example, that the array ALPHA declared by

```
REAL ALPHA(3,4)
```

is used as the actual argument and that the corresponding formal argument is declared in the subprogram by

```
REAL TABLE(3,4)
```

Then the first elements of the arrays ALPHA and TABLE are associated, and successive elements are associated in columnwise order as follows:

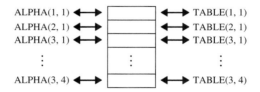

The same method of establishing the correspondence between the elements of two arrays is used even if they are of different dimensions. For example, if the array ALPHA is associated with the array T declared by

```
REAL T(2,6)
```

then the array elements are associated as follows:

$$
\begin{array}{ccc}
\text{ALPHA}(1,1) \longleftrightarrow & \boxed{} & \longleftrightarrow T(1,1) \\
\text{ALPHA}(2,1) \longleftrightarrow & & \longleftrightarrow T(2,1) \\
\text{ALPHA}(3,1) \longleftrightarrow & & \longleftrightarrow T(1,2) \\
\text{ALPHA}(1,2) \longleftrightarrow & & \longleftrightarrow T(2,2) \\
\text{ALPHA}(2,2) \longleftrightarrow & & \longleftrightarrow T(1,3) \\
\text{ALPHA}(3,2) \longleftrightarrow & & \longleftrightarrow T(2,3) \\
\vdots & \vdots & \vdots \\
\text{ALPHA}(3,4) \longleftrightarrow & & \longleftrightarrow T(2,6)
\end{array}
$$

If ALPHA is associated with a one-dimensional array Y declared by

```
REAL Y(12)
```

then the association of array elements is the following:

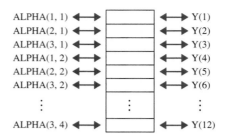

Normally, when two arrays are associated as arguments, the first element of the actual array is associated with the first element of the formal array. It is possible, however, to specify that some other element of the actual array be matched with the first element of the formal array. This is accomplished by using that array element name as the actual argument. For example, consider the actual array GAMMA declared by

```
REAL GAMMA(4,5)
```

and the formal array CONST declared by

```
SUBROUTINE EXTRAC(CONST)
REAL CONST(4)
```

To associate the last column of the array GAMMA with the array CONST, we could use the statement

```
CALL EXTRAC(GAMMA(1,5))
```

The association of array elements is as follows:

```
GAMMA(1, 5) ⟷ [ ] ⟷ CONST(1)
GAMMA(2, 5) ⟷ [ ] ⟷ CONST(2)
GAMMA(3, 5) ⟷ [ ] ⟷ CONST(3)
GAMMA(4, 5) ⟷ [ ] ⟷ CONST(4)
```

Like one-dimensional arrays, multidimensional arrays may have adjustable dimensions; that is, the dimensions used to declare the formal array argument in a subprogram may be arguments of the subprogram whose values are passed from the calling program unit. However, *some care must be exercised to ensure that the dimensions of the formal arrays match those of the corresponding actual arrays.* To illustrate, suppose that GRID is a 10×10 array declared by

```
INTEGER ROWLIM, COLLIM
PARAMETER (ROWLIM = 10, COLLIM = 10)
INTEGER GRID(ROWLIM,COLLIM), NROWS, NCOLS
```

but that the actual number of rows and columns are NROWS = 3 and NCOLS = 4, respectively, and that the value of GRID is

$$\text{GRID} = \begin{bmatrix} 90 & 80 & 0 & 40 \\ 60 & 55 & 95 & 83 \\ 72 & 71 & 93 & 89 \end{bmatrix}$$

Suppose also that a subroutine MATPRN to print this array uses adjustable dimensions for the corresponding formal array argument:

```
SUBROUTINE MATPRN(G, M, N)

INTEGER M, N, G(M,N), I, J

DO 10 I = 1, M
    PRINT '(10I5)', (G(I,J), J = 1, N)
10 CONTINUE
    END
```

If the subroutine is called with the statement

```
CALL MATPRN(GRID, NROWS, NCOLS)
```

the formal array G is considered to be a 3×4 array, since it is dimensioned as an $M \times N$ array and the values passed to M and N are NROWS = 3 and NCOLS = 4, respectively. And since actual arrays and formal arrays are associated in a columnwise manner, the elements of GRID and G are associated as follows:

GRID(1, 1) ◄►	90	◄► G(1, 1)
GRID(2, 1) ◄►	60	◄► G(2, 1)
GRID(3, 1) ◄►	72	◄► G(3, 1)
GRID(4, 1) ◄►	??	◄► G(1, 2)
GRID(5, 1) ◄►	??	◄► G(2, 2)
GRID(6, 1) ◄►	??	◄► G(3, 2)
GRID(7, 1) ◄►	??	◄► G(1, 3)
GRID(8, 1) ◄►	??	◄► G(2, 3)
GRID(9, 1) ◄►	??	◄► G(3, 3)
GRID(10, 1) ◄►	??	◄► G(1, 4)
GRID(1, 2) ◄►	80	◄► G(2, 4)
GRID(2, 2) ◄►	55	◄► G(3, 4)

Thus, the 3×4 array displayed by the subroutine is

$$\begin{bmatrix} 90 & ?? & ?? & ?? \\ 60 & ?? & ?? & 80 \\ 72 & ?? & ?? & 55 \end{bmatrix}$$

where ?? denotes an undefined value, which undoubtedly is not what was intended.

The desired association can be achieved by *passing the declared dimensions of an actual array to the subprogram and using them to dimension the corresponding formal array:*

```
       CALL MATPRN(GRID, ROWLIM, COLLIM, NROWS, NCOLS)
                  .
                  .
                  .
       SUBROUTINE MATPRN(G, RLIM, CLIM, M, N)

       INTEGER RLIM, CLIM, G(RLIM,CLIM), M, N, I, J

       DO 10 I = 1, M
          PRINT '(10I5)', (G(I,J), J = 1, N)
    10 CONTINUE
       END
```

Multidimensional Arrays in Common. To illustrate the use of multidimensional arrays in COMMON statements, suppose that the statements

```
    REAL A(3,3)
    COMMON A
```

appear in one program unit and that the statements

```
    REAL ALPHA(3,3)
    COMMON ALPHA
```

appear in another program unit. These COMMON statements allocate the first nine memory locations of blank common to both of the arrays A and ALPHA in a columnwise order so that the array elements are associated in the following manner:

Array Element	Blank Common Location	Array Element
A(1,1)	#1	ALPHA(1,1)
A(2,1)	#2	ALPHA(2,1)
A(3,1)	#3	ALPHA(3,1)
A(1,2)	#4	ALPHA(1,2)
A(2,2)	#5	ALPHA(2,2)
A(3,2)	#6	ALPHA(3,2)
A(1,3)	#7	ALPHA(1,3)
A(2,3)	#8	ALPHA(2,3)
A(3,3)	#9	ALPHA(3,3)

8.3   Examples: Pollution Table, Oceanographic Data Analysis

EXAMPLE 1: Pollution Table. Suppose that in a certain city, the pollution level is measured at two-hour intervals, beginning at midnight. These measurements were recorded for a one-week period and stored in the file POLLUTION-FILE, the first line of which contains the pollution levels for day 1, the second line for day 2, and so on. For example, suppose the pollution file for a certain week contains the following data:

```
30 30 31 32 35 40 43 44 47 45 40 38
33 32 30 34 40 48 46 49 53 49 45 40
38 35 34 37 44 50 51 54 60 58 51 49
49 48 47 53 60 70 73 75 80 75 73 60
55 54 53 65 70 80 90 93 95 94 88 62
73 70 65 66 71 78 74 78 83 75 66 58
50 47 43 35 30 33 37 43 45 52 39 31
```

A program is to be written to produce a weekly report that displays the pollution levels in a table of the form

```
                              TIME
DAY:    1    2    3    4    5    6    7    8    9   10   11   12
     - - - - - - - - - - - - - - - - - - - - - - - - - - - - - -
  1 :   30   30   31   32   35   40   43   44   47   45   40   38
  2 :   33   32   30   34   40   48   46   49   53   49   45   40
  3 :   38   35   34   37   44   50   51   54   60   58   51   49
  4 :   49   48   47   53   60   70   73   75   80   75   73   60
  5 :   55   54   53   65   70   80   90   93   95   94   88   62
  6 :   73   70   65   66   71   78   74   78   83   75   66   58
  7 :   50   47   43   35   30   33   37   43   45   52   39   31
```

and that also displays the average pollution level for each day and the average pollution level for each sampling time.

The input to the program is to be a file of pollution levels, as previously described, and the output is to be a report of the indicated form. The required algorithm is as follows:

ALGORITHM FOR POLLUTION REPORT

```
* Algorithm to read a two-dimensional array POLTAB from a file      *
* containing pollution levels measured at selected times for several *
* days. These measurements are displayed in tabular form. The        *
* average pollution level for each day and the average pollution level *
* for each sampling time are then calculated.                        *
```

1. Read the contents of the pollution file into the 7 × 12 array POLTAB so that each of the 7 rows contains the pollution measurements for a given day and each of the 12 columns contains the pollution measurements for a given time.
2. Print the array POLTAB with appropriate headings.
3. Calculate the average pollution level for each day, that is, the average of each of the rows, as follows:
   a. For DAY ranging from 1 through the number NDAYS of days, do the following:
      (i) Set SUM equal to 0.
      (ii) For TIME ranging from 1 through the number NTIMES of sampling times
             Add POLTAB(DAY, TIME) to SUM.
   b. Display SUM/NTIMES.

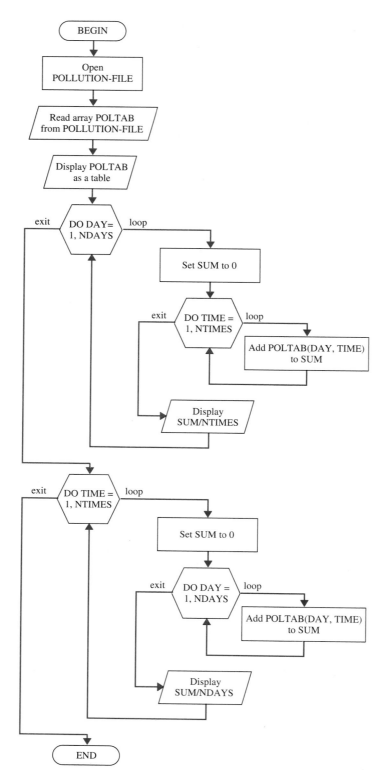

Figure 8.4

4. Calculate the average pollution level for each sampling time, that is, the average of each of the columns, as follows:
   a. For TIME ranging from 1 through NTIMES, do the following:
      (i) Set SUM equal to 0.
      (ii) For DAY ranging from 1 through NDAYS
            Add POLTAB(DAY,TIME) to SUM.
   b. Display SUM/NDAYS.

Figure 8.4 shows the structure of this algorithm in flowchart form, and the program in Figure 8.5 implements this algorithm and uses the data file described previously.

```
        PROGRAM POLLUT
***********************************************************************
* This program reads the entries of the two-dimensional array  POLTAB  *
* from the file  POLLUTION-FILE  and produces a report showing a table *
* of pollution levels, the average pollution level for each day, and   *
* the average pollution level for each sampling time.  Identifiers      *
* used are:                                                            *
*     NDAYS   : parameter giving the number of rows (days)             *
*     NTIMES  : parameter giving the number of columns (times)         *
*     POLTAB  : an NDAYS X NTIMES array of pollution levels            *
*     DAY,TIME: row, column subscripts                                 *
*     SUM     : variable used in accumulating row & column sums        *
***********************************************************************

        INTEGER NDAYS, NTIMES
        PARAMETER (NDAYS = 7, NTIMES = 12)
        INTEGER POLTAB(NDAYS,NTIMES), DAY, TIME
        REAL SUM

* Read in the pollution levels and display them in a table
* of the required form.

        OPEN (UNIT = 15, FILE = 'POLLUTION-FILE', STATUS = 'OLD')
        READ (15,*) ((POLTAB(DAY,TIME), TIME = 1, NTIMES), DAY = 1, NDAYS)
        PRINT 100, (TIME, TIME = 1, NTIMES)
100     FORMAT(T30, 'TIME' / 1X, 'DAY:', 12I4 / 1X, 53('-'))
        PRINT 110,
     +       (DAY, (POLTAB(DAY,TIME), TIME = 1, NTIMES), DAY = 1, NDAYS)
110     FORMAT(1X, I2, ' :', 12I4)

* Calculate average pollution level for each day (row averages)

        PRINT *
        DO 20 DAY = 1, NDAYS
            SUM = 0
            DO 10 TIME = 1, NTIMES
                SUM = SUM + POLTAB(DAY,TIME)
10          CONTINUE
            PRINT 120, 'FOR DAY', DAY, SUM / REAL(NTIMES)
120         FORMAT(1X, 'AVERAGE POLLUTION LEVEL ', A7, I3, ':', F6.1)
20      CONTINUE
```

Figure 8.5

Figure 8.5 (cont.)

```
* Calculate average pollution level for each time (column averages)

        PRINT *
        DO 40 TIME = 1, NTIMES
            SUM = 0
            DO 30 DAY = 1, NDAYS
                SUM = SUM + POLTAB(DAY,TIME)
30          CONTINUE
            PRINT 120, 'AT TIME', TIME, SUM / REAL(NDAYS)
40      CONTINUE
        CLOSE (15)
        END
```

Sample run:

```
                                TIME
DAY:   1   2   3   4   5   6   7   8   9  10  11  12
------------------------------------------------------
 1 :  30  30  31  32  35  40  43  44  47  45  40  38
 2 :  33  32  30  34  40  48  46  49  53  49  45  40
 3 :  38  35  34  37  44  50  51  54  60  58  51  49
 4 :  49  48  47  53  60  70  73  75  80  75  73  60
 5 :  55  54  53  65  70  80  90  93  95  94  88  62
 6 :  73  70  65  66  71  78  74  78  83  75  66  58
 7 :  50  47  43  35  30  33  37  43  45  52  39  31

AVERAGE POLLUTION LEVEL FOR DAY   1:   37.9
AVERAGE POLLUTION LEVEL FOR DAY   2:   41.6
AVERAGE POLLUTION LEVEL FOR DAY   3:   46.8
AVERAGE POLLUTION LEVEL FOR DAY   4:   63.6
AVERAGE POLLUTION LEVEL FOR DAY   5:   74.9
AVERAGE POLLUTION LEVEL FOR DAY   6:   71.4
AVERAGE POLLUTION LEVEL FOR DAY   7:   40.4

AVERAGE POLLUTION LEVEL AT TIME   1:   46.9
AVERAGE POLLUTION LEVEL AT TIME   2:   45.1
AVERAGE POLLUTION LEVEL AT TIME   3:   43.3
AVERAGE POLLUTION LEVEL AT TIME   4:   46.0
AVERAGE POLLUTION LEVEL AT TIME   5:   50.0
AVERAGE POLLUTION LEVEL AT TIME   6:   57.0
AVERAGE POLLUTION LEVEL AT TIME   7:   59.1
AVERAGE POLLUTION LEVEL AT TIME   8:   62.3
AVERAGE POLLUTION LEVEL AT TIME   9:   66.1
AVERAGE POLLUTION LEVEL AT TIME  10:   64.0
AVERAGE POLLUTION LEVEL AT TIME  11:   57.4
AVERAGE POLLUTION LEVEL AT TIME  12:   48.3
```

EXAMPLE 2: Oceanographic Data Analysis. A petroleum exploration company has collected some depth readings for a square section of the ocean. The diagonal of this square is parallel to the equator. The company has divided the square into a grid with each intersection point (node) of the grid separated by five miles. The entire square is fifty miles on each side. Two separate crews did exploratory drilling in this area, one in the northern half (above the diagonal) and the other in the southern half. A program is to be written to find the approximate average ocean depth for each crew and the overall average for the entire square. The depth data (in feet) collected by the crews was

301.3	304.5	312.6	312.0	325.6	302.0	299.8	297.6	304.6	314.7	326.8
287.6	294.5	302.4	315.6	320.9	315.7	300.2	312.7	308.7	324.5	322.8
320.8	342.5	342.5	323.5	333.7	341.6	350.5	367.7	354.2	342.8	330.9
312.6	312.0	325.6	301.3	304.5	302.0	314.7	326.8	299.8	297.6	304.6
302.4	308.7	324.5	315.6	287.6	294.5	320.9	315.7	300.2	312.7	322.8
320.8	333.7	341.6	350.5	367.7	354.2	342.8	342.5	342.5	323.5	330.9
312.0	325.6	326.8	302.0	299.8	297.6	304.6	314.7	301.3	304.5	312.6
294.5	302.4	315.6	320.9	315.7	300.2	312.7	308.7	324.5	287.6	322.8
320.8	342.5	323.5	333.7	341.6	350.5	367.7	342.5	354.2	342.8	330.9
312.0	304.6	314.7	326.8	301.3	304.5	312.6	325.6	302.0	299.8	297.6
312.7	308.7	324.5	322.8	287.6	294.5	302.4	315.6	320.9	315.7	300.2

NORTH

The following algorithm calculates the desired averages, using a two-dimensional array DEPTH to store the depth readings:

ALGORITHM FOR OCEANOGRAPHIC DATA ANALYSIS

```
* Algorithm to find the average ocean depth in each half (separated   *
* by the diagonal) of a square section of the ocean and the overall   *
* average. The depth readings are stored in the N × N two-            *
* dimensional array DEPTH.                                            *
```

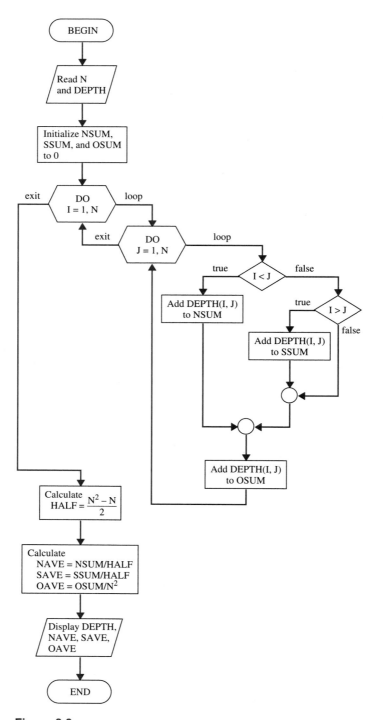

Figure 8.6

1. Read N and the array DEPTH.
2. Initialize the north, south, and overall sums NSUM, SSUM, and OSUM to 0.
3. Do the following for I ranging from 1 to N:
    Do the following for J ranging from 1 to N:
    a. If I < J then
        Add DEPTH(I,J) to NSUM
        Else if I > J then
        Add DEPTH(I,J) to SSUM.
    b. Add DEPTH(I,J) to OSUM.
4. Set HALF equal to $(N^2 - N) / 2$; this is the number of entries in each half.
5. Calculate the north, south, and overall average depths by
    NAVE = NSUM / HALF, SAVE = SSUM / HALF, and
    OAVE = OSUM / N^2.
6. Display DEPTH, NAVE, SAVE, and OAVE.

Figure 8.6 shows the structure of this algorithm in flowchart form, and the program in Figure 8.7 implements the algorithm.

```
      PROGRAM OCEAN
************************************************************************
* Program to find the average ocean depth in each half (separated by  *
* the diagonal) of a square section of the ocean.  Identifiers used:  *
*     DEPTH  : a two-dimensional array of depth readings              *
*     FNAME  : name of the file containing depth readings             *
*     LIMIT  : limit on the size of DEPTH (parameter)                 *
*     N      : the number of rows (or columns)                        *
*     NSUM   : the sum of the northern depths                         *
*     NAVE   : the average of the northern depths                     *
*     SSUM   : the sum of the southern depths                         *
*     SAVE   : the average of the southern depths                     *
*     OSUM   : the overall sum                                        *
*     OAVE   : the overall average                                    *
*     HALF   : number of elements in each half                        *
* Note: It is assumed that the elements on the diagonal are           *
*       included in the overall average but not in either half.       *
************************************************************************

      INTEGER LIMIT
      PARAMETER (LIMIT = 11)
      CHARACTER*20 FNAME
      INTEGER HALF
      REAL DEPTH(LIMIT,LIMIT), NSUM, NAVE, SSUM, SAVE, OSUM, OAVE
      DATA NSUM, SSUM, OSUM /3*0.0/

      PRINT *, 'ENTER NAME OF DATA FILE:'
      READ '(A)', FNAME
      OPEN (UNIT = 10, FILE = FNAME, STATUS = 'OLD')
      READ (10,*) N, ((DEPTH(I,J), J = 1, N), I = 1, N)
```

Figure 8.7

Figure 8.7 (cont.)

```
      DO 20 I = 1,N
         DO 10 J = 1, N
            IF (I .LT. J) THEN
               NSUM = NSUM + DEPTH(I,J)
            ELSE IF (I .GT. J) THEN
               SSUM = SSUM + DEPTH(I,J)
            END IF
            OSUM = OSUM + DEPTH(I,J)
10       CONTINUE
20    CONTINUE

      HALF = (N**2 - N) / 2
      NAVE = NSUM / REAL(HALF)
      SAVE = SSUM / REAL(HALF)
      OAVE = OSUM / REAL(N**2)

      PRINT 100
      PRINT 110, ((DEPTH(I,J), J = 1, N), I = 1, N)
100   FORMAT(1X, T29, 'OCEAN DEPTHS')
110   FORMAT(/1X, 11F6.1)

      PRINT 120, NAVE, SAVE, OAVE
120   FORMAT(// 1X,'NORTHERN HALF AVERAGE DEPTH', T30, F6.2, ' FEET',
     +         // 1X, 'SOUTHERN HALF AVERAGE DEPTH', T30, F6.2, ' FEET',
     +         // 1X, 'OVERALL AVERAGE DEPTH', T30, F6.2, ' FEET')
      END
```

Sample run:

```
ENTER NAME OF DATA FILE:
OCEAN
                      OCEAN DEPTHS

 301.3 304.5 312.6 312.0 325.6 302.0 299.8 297.6 304.6 314.7 326.8

 287.6 294.5 302.4 315.6 320.9 315.7 300.2 312.7 308.7 324.5 322.8

 320.8 342.5 342.5 323.5 333.7 341.6 350.5 367.7 354.2 342.8 330.9

 312.6 312.0 325.6 301.3 304.5 302.0 314.7 326.8 299.8 297.6 304.6

 302.4 308.7 324.5 315.6 287.6 294.5 320.9 315.7 300.2 312.7 322.8

 320.8 333.7 341.6 350.5 367.7 354.2 342.8 342.5 342.5 323.5 330.9

 312.0 325.6 326.8 302.0 299.8 297.6 304.6 314.7 301.3 304.5 312.6

 294.5 302.4 315.6 320.9 315.7 300.2 312.7 308.7 324.5 287.6 322.8

 320.8 342.5 323.5 333.7 341.6 350.5 367.7 342.5 354.2 342.8 330.9

 312.0 304.6 314.7 326.8 301.3 304.5 312.6 325.6 302.0 299.8 297.6

 312.7 308.7 324.5 322.8 287.6 294.5 302.4 315.6 320.9 315.7 300.2

NORTHERN HALF AVERAGE DEPTH 318.31 FEET

SOUTHERN HALF AVERAGE DEPTH 318.63 FEET

OVERALL AVERAGE DEPTH       318.02 FEET
```

8.4 Matrix Applications: Matrix Multiplication, Solving Linear Systems, Least Squares Curve Fitting

A two-dimensional array with numeric entries having m rows and n columns is called an $\boldsymbol{m} \times \boldsymbol{n}$ **matrix**. Matrices arise naturally in many problems in engineering and applied mathematics, and in this section we consider three examples.

EXAMPLE 1: Matrix Multiplication. One important operation of matrix algebra is matrix multiplication, defined as follows: Suppose that MAT1 is an L $\times$ M matrix and MAT2 is an M $\times$ N matrix. Note that the number of columns (M) in MAT1 is equal to the number of rows in MAT2, which must be the case for the product of MAT1 with MAT2 to be defined. The product PROD of MAT1 with MAT2 is an L $\times$ N matrix with the entry PROD(I,J), which appears in the Ith row and Jth column, given by

PROD(I,J) = The sum of the products of the entries in row I of
   MAT1 with the entries of column J of MAT2

= MAT1(I,1) * MAT2(1,J) + MAT1(I,2) * MAT2(2,J)
   + $\cdots$ + MAT1(I,M) * MAT2(M,J).

For example, suppose that MAT1 is the 2 $\times$ 3 matrix

$$\begin{bmatrix} 1 & 0 & 2 \\ 3 & 0 & 4 \end{bmatrix}$$

and MAT2 is the 3 $\times$ 4 matrix

$$\begin{bmatrix} 4 & 2 & 5 & 3 \\ 6 & 4 & 1 & 8 \\ 9 & 0 & 0 & 2 \end{bmatrix}$$

Because the number of columns (3) in MAT1 equals the number of rows in MAT2, the product matrix PROD is defined. The entry in the first row and the first column, PROD(1,1), is

$$1 * 4 + 0 * 6 + 2 * 9 = 22$$

Similarly, the entry PROD(1,2) in the first row and the second column is

$$1 * 2 + 0 * 4 + 2 * 0 = 2$$

The complete product matrix PROD is the 2 $\times$ 4 matrix given by

$$\begin{bmatrix} 22 & 2 & 5 & 7 \\ 48 & 6 & 15 & 17 \end{bmatrix}$$

In general, the algorithm for multiplying matrices is as follows:

MATRIX MULTIPLICATION ALGORITHM

```
* Algorithm to calculate the matrix product PROD of the          *
* ROWS1 × COLS1 matrix MAT1 with the ROWS2 × COLS2               *
```

* matrix MAT2. COLS1 must equal ROWS2 for the product to be   *
* defined.   *

1. If COLS1 does not equal ROWS2, the number of columns in MAT1
   is not equal to the number of rows in MAT2, and the product PROD
   = MAT1 * MAT2 is not defined; terminate the algorithm. Otherwise
   proceed with the following steps:
2. For I ranging from 1 to the number of rows ROWS1 of MAT1, do
   the following:
   For J ranging from 1 to the number of columns COLS2 of MAT2,
   do the following:
   (a) Set SUM equal to 0.

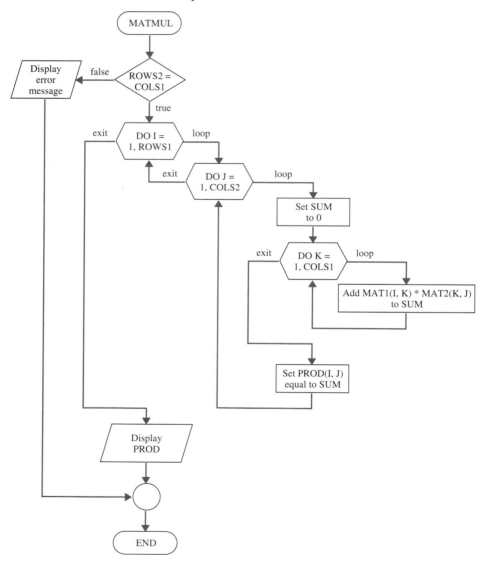

Figure 8.8

(b) For K ranging from 1 to the number of columns COLS1 of MAT1 (which is equal to the number of rows ROWS2 of MAT2):

Add MAT1(I,K) * MAT2(K,J) to SUM.

(c) Set PROD(I,J) equal to SUM.

Figure 8.8 displays the structure of this algorithm as a flowchart.

The program in Figure 8.9 reads two matrices and calls the subroutine MATMUL, which uses this algorithm to calculate their product. The three two-dimensional arrays MAT1, MAT2, and PROD used in this subroutine have adjustable dimensions, making MATMUL a general subprogram that can be used with two-dimensional arrays of any size. The parameter SIZE, used to dimension the arrays A, B, and C in the main program that correspond to MAT1, MAT2, and PROD, respectively, is also used as an actual argument corresponding to the formal argument LIMIT used to dimension the arrays MAT1, MAT2, and PROD in the subroutine. This is the recommended way of using adjustable dimensions for multidimensional arrays, as described in Section 8.2.

```
      PROGRAM MATRIX
***********************************************************************
* This program reads in a ROWS1 X COLS1 matrix and a ROWS2 X COLS2   *
* matrix, calls the subroutine MATMUL to multiply them, and displays *
* the product.  Identifiers used are:                                *
*      SIZE    :  parameter giving maximum dimensions of matrices     *
*      A, B    :  the two matrices being multiplied                   *
*      C       :  the product of A and B                              *
*      ROWS1   :  # of rows in first matrix                           *
*      COLS1   :  # of columns in first matrix                        *
*      ROWS2   :  # of rows in second matrix                          *
*      COLS2   :  # of columns in second matrix                       *
*      I, J    :  subscripts                                          *
*      MATCH   :  true if product defined (COLS1 = ROWS2) else false  *
***********************************************************************

      INTEGER SIZE
      PARAMETER (SIZE = 10)
      REAL A(SIZE,SIZE), B(SIZE,SIZE), C(SIZE,SIZE)
      INTEGER ROWS1, COLS1, ROWS2, COLS2, I, J
      LOGICAL MATCH

* Read the two matrices A and B

      PRINT *,'ENTER THE DIMENSIONS OF MATRIX 1'
      READ *, ROWS1, COLS1
      PRINT *, 'ENTER THE ELEMENTS OF MATRIX 1 ROWWISE'
      READ *, ((A(I,J), J = 1, COLS1), I = 1, ROWS1),
      PRINT *,'ENTER THE DIMENSIONS OF MATRIX 2'
      READ *, ROWS2, COLS2
      PRINT *, 'ENTER THE ELEMENTS OF MATRIX 2 ROWWISE'
      READ *, ((B(I,J), J = 1, COLS2), I = 1, ROWS2),
```

Figure 8.9

Figure 8.9 (cont.)

```
* Calculate C = A * B and display C

      CALL MATMUL(A, B, C, SIZE, ROWS1, COLS1, ROWS2, COLS2, MATCH)
      IF (MATCH) THEN
          PRINT *, 'PRODUCT MATRIX IS:'
          DO 10 I = 1, ROWS1
              PRINT 100, (C(I,J), J = 1, COLS2)
100           FORMAT(1X, 10F8.2)
10        CONTINUE
      ELSE
          PRINT *, 'PRODUCT NOT DEFINED -- # OF COLUMNS IN FIRST'
          PRINT *, 'MATRIX IS NOT EQUAL TO # OF ROWS IN SECOND'
      END IF
      END




**MATMUL***********************************************************
* Subroutine to calculate the product of an M X N matrix with a P X Q  *
* matrix.  N must equal P for the product to be defined (MATCH =       *
* .TRUE.), and the product PROD is then an M X Q matrix.  Variables    *
* used are:                                                            *
*     LIMIT   :  limit on dimensions of the matrices                   *
*     M       :  # of rows in first matrix                             *
*     N       :  # of columns in first matrix                          *
*     P       :  # of rows in second matrix                            *
*     Q       :  # of columns in second matrix                         *
*     MAT1    :  the first matrix                                      *
*     MAT2    :  the second matrix                                     *
*     PROD    :  the product of MAT1 and MAT2                          *
*     I, J, K :  subscripts                                            *
*     SUM     :  used to calculate the product matrix                  *
******************************************************************

      SUBROUTINE MATMUL(MAT1, MAT2, PROD, LIMIT, M, N, P, Q, MATCH)

      INTEGER LIMIT, M, N, P, Q
      REAL MAT1(LIMIT,LIMIT), MAT2(LIMIT,LIMIT), PROD(LIMIT,LIMIT),
      INTEGER I, J, K
      REAL SUM
      LOGICAL MATCH

      IF (N .EQ. P) THEN
          MATCH = .TRUE.
          DO 30 I = 1, M
              DO 20 J = 1, Q
                  SUM = 0
                  DO 10 K = 1, N
                      SUM = SUM + MAT1(I,K) * MAT2(K,J)
10                CONTINUE
                  PROD(I,J) = SUM
20            CONTINUE
30        CONTINUE
      ELSE
          MATCH = .FALSE.
      END IF
      END
```

Figure 8.9 (cont.)

Sample run:

```
ENTER THE DIMENSIONS OF MATRIX 1
2,2
ENTER THE ELEMENTS OF MATRIX 1 ROWWISE
2 0
0 2
ENTER THE DIMENSIONS OF MATRIX 2
2,3
ENTER THE ELEMENTS OF MATRIX 2 ROWWISE
1 2 3
4 5 6
PRODUCT MATRIX IS:
     2.00    4.00    6.00
     8.00   10.00   12.00
```

EXAMPLE 2: Solving Linear Systems—Electrical Networks. Consider the following electrical network containing six resistors and a battery:

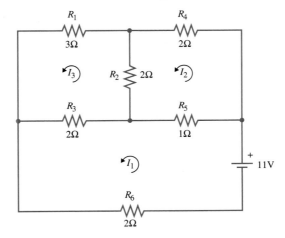

If the currents in the three loops are denoted by I_1, I_2, and I_3 (where current is considered positive when the flow is in the direction indicated by the arrows), then the current through resistor R_1 is I_3, the current through resistor R_2 is $I_2 - I_3$, and so on. The voltage drop across a resistor is $R * I$, where R is the resistance in ohms and I is the current in amperes. One of Kirchhoff's laws states that the algebraic sum of the voltage drops around any loop is equal to the applied voltage. This law gives rise to the following **system of linear equations** for the loop currents I_1, I_2, and I_3:

$$2I_1 + 1(I_1 - I_2) + 2(I_1 - I_3) = 11$$

$$2I_2 + 2(I_2 - I_3) + 1(I_2 - I_1) = 0$$

$$3I_3 + 2(I_3 - I_1) + 2(I_3 - I_2) = 0$$

Collecting terms gives the simplified linear system

$$5I_1 - 1I_2 - 2I_3 = 11$$
$$-1I_1 + 5I_2 - 2I_3 = 0$$
$$-2I_1 - 2I_2 + 7I_3 = 0$$

To find the loop currents, we must solve this linear system; that is, we must find the values for I_1, I_2, and I_3 that satisfy these equations simultaneously.

One method for solving the linear system is called **Gaussian elimination.** To use this method, we first eliminate I_1 from the second equation by adding 1/5 times the first equation to the second equation. Similarly, we eliminate I_1 from the third equation by adding 2/5 times the first equation to the third equation. This yields the linear system

$$5I_1 - 1I_2 - 2I_3 = 11$$
$$4.8I_2 - 2.4I_3 = 2.2$$
$$-2.4I_2 + 6.2I_3 = 4.4$$

which is equivalent to the original system in that they will have the same solution. We then eliminate I_2 from the third equation by adding $2.4/4.8 = 1/2$ times the second equation to the third, yielding the new equivalent linear system

$$5I_1 - 1I_2 - 2I_3 = 11$$
$$4.8I_2 - 2.4I_3 = 2.2$$
$$5I_3 = 5.5$$

Once the original system has been reduced to such a *triangular* form, it is easy to find the solution. It is clear from the last equation that the value of I_3 is

$$I_3 = \frac{5.5}{5} = 1.100$$

Substituting this value for I_3 in the second equation and solving for I_2 gives

$$I_2 = \frac{2.2 + 2.4(1.1)}{4.8} = 1.008$$

and substituting these values for I_2 and I_3 in the first equation gives

$$I_1 = \frac{11 + 1.008 + 2(1.100)}{5} = 2.842$$

To demonstrate how matrices can be used to simplify these computations, we rewrite the original linear system as the single vector equation

$$\mathbf{Ax} = \mathbf{b}$$

where A is the **coefficient matrix**

$$A = \begin{bmatrix} 5 & -1 & -2 \\ -1 & 5 & -2 \\ -2 & -2 & 7 \end{bmatrix}$$

b is the **constant vector**

$$\mathbf{b} = \begin{bmatrix} 11 \\ 0 \\ 0 \end{bmatrix}$$

and **x** is the **vector of unknowns**

$$\mathbf{x} = \begin{bmatrix} I_1 \\ I_2 \\ I_3 \end{bmatrix}$$

The operations performed in reducing the original linear system to triangular form use only the coefficient matrix A and the constant vector **b**. It is convenient therefore to combine these into a single matrix by adjoining the constant vector to the coefficient matrix as a last column. This new matrix is called the **augmented matrix**, and for this example, the augmented matrix is

$$\text{AUG} = \begin{bmatrix} 5 & -1 & -2 & 11 \\ -1 & 5 & -2 & 0 \\ -2 & -2 & 7 & 0 \end{bmatrix}$$

The first step in the reduction process was to eliminate I_1 from the second and third equations by adding multiples of the first equation to these equations. This corresponds to adding multiples of the first row of the augmented matrix to the second and third rows so that all entries in the first column except AUG(1,1) are zero. Thus we added $-\text{AUG}(2,1)/\text{AUG}(1,1) = 1/5$ times the first row of AUG to the second row and $-\text{AUG}(3,1)/\text{AUG}(1,1) = 2/5$ times the first row of AUG to the third row to obtain the new matrix

$$\text{AUG} = \begin{bmatrix} 5 & -1 & -2 & 11 \\ 0 & 4.8 & -2.4 & 2.2 \\ 0 & -2.4 & 6.2 & 4.4 \end{bmatrix}$$

The variable I_2 was then eliminated from the third equation. The corresponding operation on the rows of the preceding matrix was to add $-\text{AUG}(3,2)/\text{AUG}(2,2) = 1/2$ times the second row to the third row. The resulting matrix, which corresponds to the final triangular system, thus is

$$\text{AUG} = \begin{bmatrix} 5 & -1 & -2 & 11 \\ 0 & 4.8 & -2.4 & 2.2 \\ 0 & 0 & 5 & 5.5 \end{bmatrix}$$

From this example, we see that the basic row operation performed at the ith step of the reduction process is:

For $k = i + 1, i + 2, \ldots, n$

$$\text{Replace row}_k \text{ by row}_k - \frac{\text{AUG}(k, i)}{\text{AUG}(i, i)} \times \text{row}_i$$

Clearly, for this to be possible, the element AUG(i, i), called a **pivot element,** must be nonzero. If it is not, we must interchange the ith row with a later row to produce a nonzero pivot.

To illustrate, suppose we wish to solve the linear system

$$4x_1 + 4x_2 - 5x_3 + 2x_4 = 7$$
$$3x_1 + 3x_2 + 5x_3 - x_4 = 9$$
$$2x_1 + x_2 - x_3 + x_4 = 4$$
$$-x_1 + x_2 - x_3 + x_4 = 1$$

The corresponding augmented matrix for this system is

$$AUG = \begin{bmatrix} 4 & 4 & -5 & 2 & 7 \\ 3 & 3 & 5 & -1 & 9 \\ 2 & 1 & -1 & 1 & 4 \\ -1 & 1 & -1 & 1 & 1 \end{bmatrix}$$

The first three row operations are:

$$\text{row}_2 = \text{row}_2 - \frac{3}{4} \times \text{row}_1$$

$$\text{row}_3 = \text{row}_3 - \frac{2}{4} \times \text{row}_1$$

$$\text{row}_4 = \text{row}_4 + \frac{1}{4} \times \text{row}_1$$

giving the new matrix

$$AUG = \begin{bmatrix} 4.000 & 4.000 & -5.000 & 2.000 & 7.000 \\ 0 & 0 & 8.750 & -2.500 & 3.750 \\ 0 & -1.000 & 1.500 & 0 & 0.500 \\ 0 & 2.000 & -2.250 & 1.500 & 2.750 \end{bmatrix}$$

Since AUG(2,2) is zero, we must interchange the second row with either the third or the fourth row. To minimize the effect of roundoff error in the computations, it always is best to rearrange the rows to obtain as a pivot that element which is largest in absolute value. In this example, therefore, we interchange the second and fourth rows to obtain 2.000 as the next pivot element:

$$AUG = \begin{bmatrix} 4.000 & 4.000 & -5.000 & 2.000 & 7.000 \\ 0 & 2.000 & -2.250 & 1.500 & 2.750 \\ 0 & 0 & 8.750 & -2.500 & 3.750 \\ 0 & -1.000 & 1.500 & 0 & 0.500 \end{bmatrix}$$

The next row operation in the reduction process is

$$\text{row}_4 = \text{row}_4 + \frac{1}{2} \times \text{row}_2$$

yielding the matrix

$$AUG = \begin{bmatrix} 4.000 & 4.000 & -5.000 & 2.000 & 7.000 \\ 0 & 2.000 & -2.250 & 1.500 & 2.750 \\ 0 & 0 & 8.750 & -2.500 & 3.750 \\ 0 & 0 & 0.375 & 0.750 & 1.875 \end{bmatrix}$$

Since the element AUG(3,3) = 8.750 is greater than AUG(4,3) = 0.375, we use it as the next pivot element. The last row operation in the reduction process is

$$\text{row}_4 = \text{row}_4 - \frac{0.375}{8.75} \times \text{row}_3$$

and this gives the final triangular matrix

$$\text{AUG} = \begin{bmatrix} 4.000 & 4.000 & -5.000 & 2.000 & 7.000 \\ 0 & 2.000 & -2.250 & 1.500 & 2.750 \\ 0 & 0 & 8.750 & -2.500 & 3.750 \\ 0 & 0 & 0 & 0.857 & 1.714 \end{bmatrix}$$

The solution of the corresponding linear system is then easily seen to be

$$\mathbf{x} = \begin{bmatrix} 1 \\ 1 \\ 1 \\ 2 \end{bmatrix}$$

The following algorithm, which summarizes the method of Gaussian elimination to solve a linear system, uses the pivoting strategy of the preceding example. Note that if it is not possible to find a nonzero pivot element at some stage, then the linear system is said to be a **singular** system and does not have a unique solution.

GAUSSIAN ELIMINATION ALGORITHM

```
* Algorithm to solve the linear system AX = B, using Gaussian      *
* elimination. A is the N × N coefficient matrix, B is the N × 1    *
* constant vector, and X is the N × 1 vector of unknowns.           *
```

1. Form the N × (N + 1) augmented matrix AUG by adjoining B to A:

$$\text{AUG} = [A \mid B]$$

2. For I ranging from 1 to N, do the following:
    a. Find the entry AUG(K, I), K = I, I + 1, ... , N that has the largest absolute value.
    b. Interchange row I and row K.
    c. If AUG(I,I) = 0, display a message that the matrix A is singular.
    d. For J ranging from I + 1 to N, do the following:
    Add $-\dfrac{\text{AUG(J,I)}}{\text{AUG(I,I)}}$ times the Ith row of AUG to the Jth row of AUG to eliminate X(I) from the Jth equation.
3. Set X(N) equal to $\dfrac{\text{AUG(N, N + 1)}}{\text{AUG(N, N)}}$.
4. For J ranging from N − 1 to 1 in steps of − 1, do the following:
    Substitute the values of X(J + 1), ... , X(N) in the Jth equation and solve for X(J).

The program in Figure 8.10 implements this algorithm for Gaussian elimination. Because real numbers cannot be stored exactly, the statement implementing step 2c checks if ABS(AUG(I,I)) is less than some small positive number EPSIL rather than if AUG(I,I) is exactly 0.

```
        PROGRAM LINSYS
*********************************************************************
* Program to solve a linear system  using Gaussian elimination.    *
* Identifiers used are:                                            *
*      LIMIT  : parameter giving maximum dimensions of matrix      *
*      LIMAUG : parameter (LIMIT + 1) for maximum # columns in AUG *
*      N      : number of equations and unknowns                   *
*      I, J   : indices                                            *
*      AUG    : augmented matrix for the linear system             *
*      X      : solution vector                                    *
*      SINGUL : indicates if matrix is (nearly) singular           *
*********************************************************************

        INTEGER LIMIT, LIMAUG
        PARAMETER (LIMIT = 10, LIMAUG = LIMIT + 1)
        REAL AUG(LIMIT,LIMAUG), X(LIMIT)
        INTEGER N, I, J
        LOGICAL SINGUL

* Read coefficient matrix and constant vector

        PRINT *, 'ENTER NUMBER OF EQUATIONS'
        READ *, N
        PRINT *, 'ENTER COEFFICIENT MATRIX ROWWISE'
        READ *, ((AUG(I,J), J = 1, N), I = 1, N)
        PRINT *, 'ENTER CONSTANT VECTOR'
        READ *, (AUG(I, N + 1), I = 1, N)

* Use subroutine GAUSS to find the solution A,
* and then display X.

        CALL GAUSS(AUG, LIMIT, LIMAUG, N, X, SINGUL)
        IF (.NOT. SINGUL) THEN
            PRINT *, 'SOLUTION VECTOR IS'
            DO 10 I = 1, N
                PRINT 100, I, X(I)
100             FORMAT(1X, 'X(', I2, ') =', F8.3)
10          CONTINUE
        ELSE
            PRINT *, 'MATRIX IS (NEARLY) SINGULAR'
        END IF
        END
```

Figure 8.10

Figure 8.10 (cont.)

```
**GAUSS******************************************************************
* Subroutine to find solution of linear system AX = B using Gaussian  *
* elimination, provided a unique solution exists.  If the matrix is   *
* (nearly) singular, SINGUL is returned as true, and the solution X   *
* is undefined.   Local identifiers are:                              *
*     I,J,K  : indices                                                *
*     MULT    : multiplier used to eliminate an unknown               *
*     ASBPIV : absolute value of pivot element                        *
*     PIVROW : row containing pivot element                           *
*     EPSIL  : a small positive real value ("almost zero")            *
*     TEMP   : used to interchange rows of matrix                     *
***********************************************************************


          SUBROUTINE GAUSS(AUG, LIM, LIMAUG, N, X, SINGUL)

          REAL AUG(LIM, LIMAUG), X(LIM), TEMP, MULT, EPSIL
          PARAMETER (EPSIL = 1E-6)
          INTEGER N, PIVROW
          LOGICAL SINGUL

          SINGUL = .FALSE.
          DO 50 I = 1, N

*         Locate pivot element

          ABSPIV = ABS(AUG(I,I))
          PIVROW = I
          DO 10 K = I + 1, N
              IF (ABS(AUG(K,I)) .GT. ABSPIV) THEN
                  ABSPIV = ABS(AUG(K,I))
                  PIVROW = K
              END IF
10        CONTINUE

*         Check if matrix is (nearly) singular

          IF (ABSPIV .LT. EPSIL) THEN
              SINGUL = .TRUE.
              RETURN
          END IF

*         It isn't, so interchange rows PIVROW and I if necessary

          IF (PIVROW .NE. I) THEN
              DO 20 J = 1, N + 1
                  TEMP = AUG(I,J)
                  AUG(I,J) = AUG(PIVROW,J)
                  AUG(PIVROW,J) = TEMP
20            CONTINUE
          END IF
```

Figure 8.10 (cont.)

```
*          Eliminate Ith unknown from equations I + 1, ..., N

           DO 40 J = I + 1, N
               MULT = -AUG(J,I)  / AUG(I,I)
               DO 30 K = I, N + 1
                   AUG(J,K) = AUG(J,K) +  MULT * AUG(I,K)
30                 CONTINUE
40             CONTINUE

50     CONTINUE

* Find the solutions by back substitution

       X(N)  = AUG(N, N + 1) / AUG(N,N)
       DO 70 J = N - 1, 1, -1
           X(J) = AUG(J, N + 1)
           DO 60 K = J + 1, N
               X(J)  = X(J)  - AUG(J,K) * X(K)
60         CONTINUE
           X(J)  = X(J)  / AUG(J,J)
70     CONTINUE
       END
```

Sample runs:

```
ENTER NUMBER OF EQUATIONS
3
ENTER COEFFICIENT MATRIX ROWWISE
 5 -1 -2
-1  5 -2
-2 -2  7
ENTER CONSTANT VECTOR
11
0
0
SOLUTION VECTOR IS
X( 1) =  2.842
X( 2) =  1.008
X( 3) =  1.100

ENTER NUMBER OF EQUATIONS
4
ENTER COEFFICIENT MATRIX ROWWISE
 4  4 -5  2
 3  3  5 -1
 2  1 -1  1
-1  1 -1  1
ENTER CONSTANT VECTOR
7
9
4
1
SOLUTION VECTOR IS
X( 1) =  1.000
X( 2) =  1.000
X( 3) =  1.000
X( 4) =  2.000
```

Figure 8.10 (cont.)

```
ENTER NUMBER OF EQUATIONS
3
ENTER COEFFICIENT MATRIX ROWWISE
1 1 1
2 3 4
3 4 5
ENTER CONSTANT VECTOR
1
2
3
MATRIX IS (NEARLY) SINGULAR
```

EXAMPLE 3: Least Squares Curve Fitting. In Example 3 of Section 4.11, we described the method of least squares for finding the equation of a line that best fits a set of data points. This method can also be used to find best-fitting curves of higher degree. For example, to find the equation of the parabola

$$y = A + Bx + Cx^2$$

that best fits a set of n data points, the values of A, B, and C must be determined for which the sum of the squares of the deviations of the observed y values from the predicted y values (using the equation) is as small as possible. These values are found by solving the linear system

$$nA + (\Sigma x)B + (\Sigma x^2)C = \Sigma y$$
$$(\Sigma x)A + (\Sigma x^2)B + (\Sigma x^3)C = \Sigma xy$$
$$(\Sigma x^2)A + (\Sigma x^3)B + (\Sigma x^4)C = \Sigma x^2 y$$

This system can be solved using the program in Example 2.

Similar linear systems must be solved to find least squares curves of higher degrees. For example, for a least squares cubic

$$y = A + Bx + Cx^2 + Dx^3$$

the coefficients A, B, C, and D can be found by solving the system of equations

$$nA + (\Sigma x)B + (\Sigma x^2)C + (\Sigma x^3)D = \Sigma y$$
$$(\Sigma x)A + (\Sigma x^2)B + (\Sigma x^3)C + (\Sigma x^4)D = \Sigma xy$$
$$(\Sigma x^2)A + (\Sigma x^3)B + (\Sigma x^4)C + (\Sigma x^5)D = \Sigma x^2 y$$
$$(\Sigma x^3)A + (\Sigma x^4)B + (\Sigma x^5)C + (\Sigma x^6)D = \Sigma x^3 y$$

Exercises

1. Assume that the following declarations have been made

```
INTEGER MAT(3,3), NUM(6), I, J
```

and that the following data is entered for those of the following statements that involve input:

```
1, 2, 3, 4, 5, 6, 7, 8, 9
```

For each of the following, tell what value (if any) is assigned to each array element, or explain why an error results:

(a)
```
      DO 20 I = 1, 3
          DO 10 J = 1, 3
              MAT(I,J) = I + J
   10     CONTINUE
   20 CONTINUE
```

(b)
```
      DO 20 I = 1, 3
          DO 10 J = 3, 1, -1
              IF (I .EQ. J) THEN
                  MAT(I,J) = 0
              ELSE
                  MAT(I,J) = 1
              END IF
   10     CONTINUE
   20 CONTINUE
```

(c)
```
      DO 20 I = 1, 3
          DO 10 J = 1, 3
              IF (I .LT. J) THEN
                  MAT(I,J) = -1
              ELSE IF (I .EQ. J) THEN
                  MAT(I,J) = 0
              ELSE
                  MAT(I,J) = 1
              END IF
   10     CONTINUE
   20 CONTINUE
```

(d)
```
      DO 30 I = 1, 3
          DO 10 J = 1, I
              MAT(I,J) = 0
   10     CONTINUE
          DO 20 J = I + 1, 3
              MAT(I,J) = 2
   20     CONTINUE
   30 CONTINUE
```

(e)
```
      DO 20 I = 1, 3
          DO 10 J = 1, 3
              READ *, MAT(I,J)
   10     CONTINUE
   20 CONTINUE
```

(f) `READ *, MAT`

(g) `READ *, ((MAT(I,J), J = 1, 3), I = 1, 3)`

(h) `READ *, ((MAT(J,I), I = 1, 3), J = 1, 3)`

(i) `READ *, ((MAT(I,J), I = 1, 3), J = 1, 3)`

(j)
```
      DO 10 I = 1, 3
         READ *, (MAT(I,J), J = 1, 3)
   10 CONTINUE
```

(k)
```
      READ *, NUM
      DO 20 I = 1, 3
         DO 10 J = 1, 3
            MAT(I,J) = NUM(I) + NUM(J)
   10    CONTINUE
   20 CONTINUE
```

(l)
```
      READ *, NUM, (MAT(1,J), J = 1, 3)
      DO 20 I = 1, 2
         DO 10 J = 1, 3
            MAT(NUM(I + 1), NUM(J)) = NUM(I + J)
   10    CONTINUE
   20 CONTINUE
```

2. Modify the following program so that when the square array A is displayed, it has been changed into its transpose. The *transpose* of an $m \times n$ matrix A is the $n \times m$ matrix whose rows are the columns of A.

```
          PROGRAM MAT2
     **************************************************
     * Program to read matrix A, replace it by its    *
     * transpose, and display it.                     *
     **************************************************

          INTEGER N, I, J
          REAL A(10,10)

          PRINT *, 'ENTER THE # OF ROWS (= # of COLUMNS)'
          READ *, N

          READ 100, ((A(I,J), J = 1, N), I = 1, N)
     100  FORMAT(10F10.3)

     *
     * Place your statements to replace A by its
     * transpose here
     *

          PRINT 110
     110  FORMAT(///, T30, 'THE TRANSPOSE OF A' //)
          PRINT 120, ((A(I,J), J = 1, N), I = 1, N)
     120  FORMAT(1X, 10F10.3)
          END
```

3. Given the following program:

a. Write declarations for all the arrays and other variables used in the program.

b. Calculate (by hand) the values stored in arrays A, B, and C.

c. Add statements to create array D = A * B + C. (The sum of two matrices is obtained by adding corresponding entries. See also Exercise 5.)

d. Add statements to create array E, the transpose of array D (see the preceding exercise).

```
          PROGRAM MAT3
     ********************************************
     * Program to do various matrix calculations.*
     ********************************************

     *
     * Place your declaration statements here.
     *
          DO 20 I = 1, 3
              DO 10 J = 1, 3
                  A(J,I) = I + J
                  B(I,J) = I - J
10            CONTINUE
20        CONTINUE
          DO 40 I = 1, 3
              DO 30 J = 1, 3
                  C(I,J) = 5
30            CONTINUE
40        CONTINUE

     *
     * Place your statements to calculate D here.
     *
          DO 50 I = 1, 3
              PRINT 60, (D(I, J), J = 1, 3)
60            FORMAT (1X, 3I7)
50        CONTINUE
     *
     * Place your statements to find E here.
     *
          PRINT *
          DO 70 I = 1, 3
              PRINT 60, (E(I,J), J = 1, 3)
70        CONTINUE
          END
```

4. A car manufacturer has collected some data on the noise level (measured in decibels) produced at seven different speeds by six different models of cars that it produces. This data is summarized in the following table:

Car	20	30	40	Speed(MPH) 50	60	70	80
1	88	90	94	102	111	122	134
2	75	77	80	86	94	103	113
3	80	83	85	94	100	111	121
4	68	71	76	85	96	110	125
5	77	84	91	98	105	112	119
6	81	85	90	96	102	109	120

Write a program that will display this table in a nice format and that will calculate and display the average noise level for each car model, the average noise level at each speed, and the overall average noise level.

5. A number of students from three different engineering sections, 1, 2, and 3, performed the same experiment to determine the tensile strength of sheets made from two different alloys. Each of these strength measurements is a real number in the range 0 through 10. Write a program to read several lines of data, each consisting of a section number and the tensile strength of the two types of sheets recorded by a student in that section, and calculate

(a) For each section, the average of the tensile strengths for each type of alloy.

(b) The number of persons in a given section who recorded strength measures of 5 or higher.

(c) The average of the tensile strengths recorded for alloy 2 by students who recorded a tensile strength lower than 3 for alloy 1.

6. Write and test a subroutine to add two matrices. If A_{ij} and B_{ij} are the entries in the ith row and jth column of $m \times n$ matrices A and B, respectively, then $A_{ij} + B_{ij}$ is the entry in the ith row and jth column of the *sum*, which will also be an $m \times n$ matrix. For example,

$$\begin{bmatrix} 1 & 0 & 2 \\ -1 & 3 & 5 \end{bmatrix} + \begin{bmatrix} 4 & 2 & 1 \\ 7 & 0 & 3 \end{bmatrix} = \begin{bmatrix} 5 & 2 & 3 \\ 6 & 3 & 8 \end{bmatrix}$$

7. A certain company manufactures four electronic devices using five different components that cost $10.95, $6.30, $14.75, $11.25, and $5.00, respectively. The number of components used in each device is given in the following table:

Device Number	Component Number 1	2	3	4	5
1	10	4	5	6	7
2	7	0	12	1	3
3	4	9	5	0	8
4	3	2	1	5	6

Write a program to

(a) Calculate the total cost of each device.

(b) Calculate the total cost of producing each device if the estimated labor cost for each device is 10 percent of the cost in part (a).

8. An electronics firm manufactures four types of radios. The number of capacitors, resistors, and transistors (denoted by C, R, and T) in each of these is given in the following table:

Radio Type	C	R	T
1	2	6	3
2	6	11	5
3	13	29	10
4	8	14	7

Each capacitor costs 35 cents, a resistor costs 20 cents, and a transistor costs $1.40. Write a program that uses the subroutine MATMUL in Section 8.4 to find the total cost of the components for each of the types of radios.

9. A company produces three different products. They are processed through four different departments, A, B, C, and D, and the following table gives the number of hours that each department spends on each product:

Product	A	B	C	D
1	20	10	15	13
2	18	11	11	10
3	28	0	16	17

The cost per hour of operation in each of the departments is as follows:

Department	A	B	C	D
Cost per hour	$140	$295	$225	$95

Write a program that uses the subroutine MATMUL in Section 8.4 to find the total cost of each of the products.

10. The vector-matrix equation

$$\begin{bmatrix} N \\ E \\ D \end{bmatrix} = \begin{bmatrix} \cos\alpha & -\sin\alpha & 0 \\ \sin\alpha & \cos\alpha & 0 \\ 0 & 0 & 1 \end{bmatrix} \begin{bmatrix} \cos\beta & 0 & \sin\beta \\ 0 & 1 & 0 \\ -\sin\beta & 0 & \cos\beta \end{bmatrix} \begin{bmatrix} 1 & 0 & 0 \\ 0 & \cos\gamma & -\sin\gamma \\ 0 & \sin\gamma & \cos\gamma \end{bmatrix} \begin{bmatrix} I \\ J \\ K \end{bmatrix}$$

is used to transform local coordinates (I, J, K) for a space vehicle to inertial coordinates (N, E, D). Write a program that reads values for α, β, and γ and a set of local coordinates (I, J, K) and then uses the subroutine MATMUL in Section 8.4 to determine the corresponding inertial coordinates.

11. Write a program to calculate and print the first ten rows of *Pascal's triangle*. The first part of the triangle has the form

$$
\begin{array}{ccccccccc}
& & & & 1 & & & & \\
& & & 1 & & 1 & & & \\
& & 1 & & 2 & & 1 & & \\
& 1 & & 3 & & 3 & & 1 & \\
1 & & 4 & & 6 & & 4 & & 1
\end{array}
$$

in which each row begins and ends with 1s and each other entry in a row is the sum of the two entries just above it. If the preceding form for the output seems too challenging, you might have it appear as follows:

```
1
1 1
1 2 1
1 3 3 1
1 4 6 4 1
```

12. A *magic square* is an $n \times n$ matrix in which all of the integers 1, 2, 3, . . . , n^2 appear exactly once, and all the column sums, row sums, and diagonal sums are equal. For example, the following is a 5 × 5 magic square in which all rows, columns, and diagonals sum to 65:

17	24	1	8	15
23	5	7	14	16
4	6	13	20	22
10	12	19	21	3
11	18	25	2	9

The following is a procedure for constructing an $n \times n$ magic square for any odd integer n. Place 1 in the middle of the top row. Then after placing integer k, move up one row and to the right one column to place the next integer $k + 1$, unless one of the following occurs:

(a) If a move takes you above the top row in the jth column, move to the bottom of the jth column and place the integer there.
(b) If a move takes you outside to the right of the square in the ith row, place the integer in the ith row at the left side.
(c) If a move takes you to an already filled square or if you move out of the square at the upper right-hand corner, place $k + 1$ immediately below k.

Write a program to construct a magic square for any odd value of n.

13. Suppose that each of the four edges of a thin square metal plate is maintained at a constant temperature and that we wish to determine the steady-state temperature at each interior point of the plate. To do this, we divide the plate into squares (the corners of which are called

nodes) and find the temperature at each interior node by averaging the four neighboring temperatures; that is, if T_{ij} denotes the old temperature at the node in row i and column j, then

$$\frac{T_{i-1,j} + T_{i,j-1} + T_{i,j+1} + T_{i+1,j}}{4}$$

will be the new temperature.

To model the plate, we can use a two-dimensional array, with each array element representing the temperature at one of the nodes. Write a program that first reads the four constant temperatures (possibly different) along the edges of the plate, and some guess of the temperature at the interior points, and uses these values to initialize the elements of the array. Then determine the steady-state temperature at each interior node by repeatedly averaging the temperatures at its four neighbors, as just described. Repeat this procedure until the new temperature at each interior node differs from the old temperature by no more than some specified small amount. Then print the array and the number of iterations used to produce the final result. (It may also be of interest to print the array at each stage of the iteration.)

14. Write a program similar to that in Exercise 13 to find steady-state temperatures in a fireplace, a diagram of which follows. The north, west, and east wall temperatures are held constant, and the south wall is insulated. The steady-state temperatures at each interior node are to be calculated using the averaging process described in Exercise 13, but those for the nodes along the south wall are to be calculated using the formula

$$\frac{2T_{i-1,j} + T_{i,j-1} + T_{i,j+1}}{4}$$

Your program should read the constant north, west, and east temperatures and a constant fire wall temperature (e.g., 10, 50, 40, 1500), the number of rows and columns in the grid (e.g., 4, 7), the numbers of the fire's first and last rows and the first and last columns (e.g., 3, 4, and 3, 6), a small value to be used as a termination criterion (e.g., .0001), and an initial guess for the interior temperatures (e.g., 500).

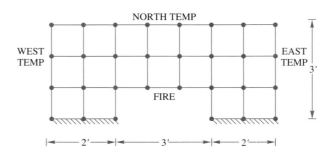

15. The game of *Life*, invented by the mathematician John H. Conway, is intended to model life in a society of organisms. Consider a rectangular array of cells, each of which may contain an organism. If the array is assumed to extend indefinitely in both directions, each cell will have eight neighbors, the eight cells surrounding it. Births and deaths occur according to the following rules:

(a) An organism is born in an empty cell that has exactly three neighbors.

(b) An organism dies from isolation if it has fewer than two neighbors.

(c) An organism dies from overcrowding if it has more than three neighbors.

The following display shows the first five generations of a particular configuration of organisms:

Write a program to play the game of Life and investigate the patterns produced by various initial configurations. Some configurations die off rather quickly; others repeat after a certain number of generations; others change shape and size and may move across the array; and still others may produce "gliders" that detach themselves from the society and sail off into space.

16. A *Markov chain* is a system that moves through a discrete set of states in such a way that when the system is in state i there is probability P_{ij} that it will next move to state j. These probabilities are given by a *transition matrix* P, whose (i, j) entry is P_{ij}. It is easy to show that the (i, j) entry of P^n then gives the probability of starting in state i and ending in state j after n steps.

One model of gas diffusion is known as the *Ehrenfest urn model*. In this model, there are two urns A and B containing a given number of balls (molecules). At each instant, a ball is chosen at random and is transferred to the other urn. This is a Markov chain if we take as a state the number of balls in urn A and let P_{ij} be the probability that a ball is transferred from A to B if there are i balls in urn A. For example, for four balls, the transition matrix P is given by

$$\begin{bmatrix} 0 & 1 & 0 & 0 & 0 \\ 1/4 & 0 & 3/4 & 0 & 0 \\ 0 & 1/2 & 0 & 1/2 & 0 \\ 0 & 0 & 3/4 & 0 & 1/4 \\ 0 & 0 & 0 & 1 & 0 \end{bmatrix}$$

Write a program that reads a transition matrix P for such a Markov chain and calculates and displays the value of n and P^n for several values of n. (See Example 1 of Section 8.4 for a description of matrix multiplication.)

17. A *directed graph,* or *digraph,* consists of a set of *vertices* and a set of *directed arcs* joining certain of these vertices. For example, the following diagram pictures a directed graph having five vertices numbered 1, 2, 3, 4, and 5, and seven directed arcs joining vertices 1 to 2, 1 to 4, 1 to 5, 3 to 1, 3 to itself, 4 to 3, and 5 to 1:

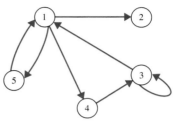

A directed graph having n vertices can be represented by its *adjacency matrix,* which is an $n \times n$ matrix, with the entry in the ith row and jth column a 1 if vertex i is joined to vertex j, and 0 otherwise. The adjacency matrix for this graph is

$$\begin{bmatrix} 0 & 1 & 0 & 1 & 1 \\ 0 & 0 & 0 & 0 & 0 \\ 1 & 0 & 1 & 0 & 0 \\ 0 & 0 & 1 & 0 & 0 \\ 1 & 0 & 0 & 0 & 0 \end{bmatrix}$$

If A is the adjacency matrix for a directed graph, the entry in the ith row and jth column of A^k gives the number of ways that vertex j can be reached from the vertex i by following k edges. Write a program to read the number of vertices in a directed graph and a collection of ordered pairs of vertices representing directed arcs, to construct the adjacency matrix, and then to find the number of ways that each vertex can be reached from every other vertex by following k edges for some value of k.

18. Consider the following material balance problem: A solution that is 80 percent oil, 15 percent usable by-products, and 5 percent impurities enters a refinery. One output is 92 percent oil and 6 percent usable by-products. The other output is 60 percent oil and flows at the rate of 1000 L/h.

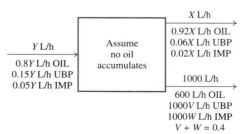

We thus have the following material balance equations:

Total:	$Y =$	$X + 1000$
Oil:	$0.8Y =$	$0.92X + 600$
Usable by-products:	$0.15Y =$	$0.06X + 1000V$
Impurities:	$0.05Y =$	$0.02X + 1000W$
Also:	$V + W = 0.4$	

Use the program in Example 2 of Section 8.4 to find a solution of the first four equations. Check that your solution also satisfies the last equation.

19. Write a program to find the equation of the least squares parabola (see Example 3 of Section 8.4) for the following set of data points:

x	y
0.05	0.957
0.12	0.851
0.15	0.832
0.30	0.720
0.45	0.583
0.70	0.378
0.84	0.295
1.05	0.156

20. Write a program to find the equation of the least squares cubic (see Example 3 of Section 8.4) for the set of data points in Exercise 19.

21. The *inverse* of an $n \times n$ matrix A is a matrix A^{-1} for which both the products $A * A^{-1}$ and $A^{-1} * A$ are equal to the *identity matrix* having 1s on the diagonal from the upper left to the lower right and 0s elsewhere. An approximate inverse for matrix A can be calculated by solving the linear systems $Ax = b$ for each of the following constant vectors b:

$$\begin{bmatrix} 1 \\ 0 \\ 0 \\ \vdots \\ 0 \end{bmatrix} \begin{bmatrix} 0 \\ 1 \\ 0 \\ \vdots \\ 0 \end{bmatrix} \begin{bmatrix} 0 \\ 0 \\ 1 \\ \vdots \\ 0 \end{bmatrix} \cdots \begin{bmatrix} 0 \\ 0 \\ 0 \\ \vdots \\ 1 \end{bmatrix}$$

These solutions give the first, second, third, ... , nth column of A^{-1}. Write a program that uses Gaussian elimination (see Example 2 of Section 8.4) to solve these linear systems and thus calculate the inverse of a matrix.

22. In Example 3 and Exercise 23 of Section 4.10, and in Example 3 of Section 8.4, we considered the problem of *least squares curve fitting* for a set of data points. A general three-term equation for fitting a curve is

$$y = A + Bf(x) + Cg(x)$$

where f and g can be any functions of x. The least squares curve of this type can then be found by solving the linear system

$$nA + (\Sigma f(x))B + (\Sigma g(x))C = \Sigma y$$

$$(\Sigma f(x))A + (\Sigma f(x)^2)A + (\Sigma f(x)g(x))C = \Sigma f(x)y$$

$$(\Sigma g(x))A + (\Sigma f(x)g(x))B + (\Sigma g(x)^2)C = \Sigma g(x)y$$

for A, B, and C. Write a subprogram whose arguments are the functions f and g and a set of data points and that finds the coefficients A, B, and C, for this least squares curve.

Programming Pointers

The difficulties encountered when using multidimensional arrays are similar to those for one-dimensional arrays, considered in the preceding chapter. The following first three programming pointers are simply restatements of some of the programming pointers in Chapter 7, and the reader should refer to those pointers for an expanded discussion.

1. *All arrays in a FORTRAN program must be dimensioned.*

2. *Arrays must be declared using constants or parameters to specify the dimensions.*

3. *Subscripts must be integer valued and must stay within the range specified in the array declarations.*

4. *Unless some other order is specified, two-dimensional arrays are processed columnwise.* In general, the FORTRAN convention for processing multidimensional arrays is to vary each subscript over its entire range before varying the subscript that follows it. Any other processing order must be established by the programmer.

   To illustrate, suppose that the two-dimensional array TABLE is declared by

       INTEGER TABLE(3,4)

   and the following data is to be read into the array:

       11, 22, 27, 35, 39, 40, 48, 51, 57, 66, 67, 92

   If these values are to be read and assigned in a rowwise manner so that the value of TABLE is

$$\begin{bmatrix} 11 & 22 & 27 & 35 \\ 39 & 40 & 48 & 51 \\ 57 & 66 & 67 & 92 \end{bmatrix}$$

the following READ statement is appropriate:

```
READ *, ((TABLE(I,J), J = 1, 4), I = 1, 3)
```

If the values are to be read and assigned in a columnwise manner so that the value of TABLE is

$$\begin{bmatrix} 11 & 35 & 48 & 66 \\ 22 & 39 & 51 & 67 \\ 27 & 40 & 57 & 92 \end{bmatrix}$$

the statements should be

```
READ *, ((TABLE(I,J), I = 1, 3), J = 1, 4)
```

or

```
READ *, TABLE
```

FORTRAN 90 Features

The FORTRAN 90 features described at the end of the preceding chapter for one-dimensional arrays apply to multidimensional arrays as well. In particular:

- Assignment of one array to another is permitted, provided that the arrays have the same dimension and the same extent (number of subscripts) in each dimension.
- A reference to the intrinsic function RESHAPE of the form

    RESHAPE(*shape, source-array, pad-array, order*)

returns an array with the specified *shape*, with values obtained from the specified *source-array,* followed by elements of the array *pad-array;* and *order* is a one-dimensional array that specifies the order in which the subscripts are to be varied when filling in the resulting array. The arguments *pad-array* and *order* are optional. For example, if A and B are declared by

```
INTEGER A(3,2), B(6)
```

and B has been assigned a value by

```
B = (/ 11, 22, 33, 44, 55, 66 /)
```

then the statement

```
A = RESHAPE((/ 2, 3 /), B)
```

assigns to A the array

$$\begin{bmatrix} 11 & 33 & 55 \\ 22 & 44 & 66 \end{bmatrix}$$

The statement

```
A = RESHAPE((/2, 3/), (/11, 22, 33, 44/), &
            (/0, 0/), (/2, 1/))
```

assigns to A the array

$$\begin{bmatrix} 11 & 22 & 33 \\ 44 & 0 & 0 \end{bmatrix}$$

- Operators and functions normally applied to simple expressions may also be applied to arrays having the same number of elements and to arrays and simple expressions. In this case, operations applied to an array are carried out elementwise. To illustrate, consider the following declarations:

```
INTEGER A(2,2), B(2,2)
DATA A /11, 22, 33, 44/
```

so that A is initialized as the 2×2 array

$$A = \begin{bmatrix} 11 & 33 \\ 22 & 44 \end{bmatrix}$$

The statement

```
B = 2*A + 1
```

assigns to B the array

$$B = \begin{bmatrix} 23 & 67 \\ 45 & 89 \end{bmatrix}$$

and the statement

```
B = A * A
```

assigns to B the array

$$B = \begin{bmatrix} 121 & 1089 \\ 484 & 1936 \end{bmatrix}$$

Note that this is the elementwise product of A with itself, and not the usual matrix product as described in Section 8.4.

- Array sections, which are arrays consisting of selected elements from a parent array, are allowed. Such array sections are defined by specifications of the form

array-name(*section-subscript-list*)

where each item in the *section-subscript-list* is a subscript, or a subscript triplet, or a vector subscript. (See the FORTRAN 90 features of Chapter 7 for a description of subscript triplet and vector subscripts.) For example, if A is an array declared by

```
INTEGER A(2, 3)
```

with value

$$A = \begin{bmatrix} 11 & 22 & 33 \\ 44 & 55 & 66 \end{bmatrix}$$

the array section A(1:2:1, 2:3:1), or simply A(:, 2:3), is the 2×2 subarray

$$\begin{bmatrix} 22 & 33 \\ 55 & 66 \end{bmatrix}$$

and the value of the array section A(2, 1:3:1), or simply A(2, :), is the one-dimensional array consisting of the last row of the array:

$$[44 \quad 55 \quad 66]$$

The value of the array section A((/ 2, 1 /), 2:3), in which the first item in the section subscript list is the subscript vector (/ 2, 1 /) and the second item is the subscript triplet 2:3 with stride 1, is the 2×2 array

$$\begin{bmatrix} 55 & 66 \\ 22 & 33 \end{bmatrix}$$

- The WHERE construct described in the FORTRAN 90 Features section of Chapter 7 for one-dimensional arrays may also be used with multi-dimensional arrays.
- Formal array arguments in subprograms may be *assumed-shape arrays* in which the dimension of the array is taken to be the dimension of the corresponding actual array argument. In this case the declaration of the formal array in the subprogram has the form

  array-name(lower-1:, lower-2:, . . .)

  or

  array-name(:, :, . . .)

  In the second case, the lowest subscript in each dimension is taken to be 1.
- The dimensions of local arrays in subprograms may be specified by formal arguments or by the values of the array inquiry functions SIZE, LBOUND, and UBOUND for the corresponding actual array argument. When used with a single array argument, the functions LBOUND and UBOUND return vectors specifying the array's lower bounds and upper bounds, respectively. They may also be used with a second argument specifying a given dimension for which the lower or upper bound is desired. For example, if array TEMP is declared by

  ```
  REAL TEMP(0:9, 1:5, -2:2)
  ```

  the value of LBOUND(TEMP) is the one-dimensional integer array (/ 0, 1, -2 /), and the value of LBOUND(TEMP, 3) is -2. Similarly, SIZE may be called with a single array argument and returns the number of elements in the array, or with a second argument to find the size along a single dimension. Thus SIZE(TEMP) returns the value 250, and SIZE(TEMP, 1) returns the value 10.

- As several examples have indicated, the value returned by a function may be an array.
- Several new predefined functions for processing arrays have been added, including

MAXVAL(A, D):	Returns the maximum values in array A along dimension D. If D is omitted, the maximum value in the entire array is returned.
MAXLOC(A):	Returns the locations of a maximum value in A.
MINVAL(A, D):	Returns the minimum values in array A along dimension D. If D is omitted, the minimum value in the entire array is returned.
MINLOC(A):	Returns the locations of a minimum value in A.
PRODUCT(A, D):	Returns the products of the elements of A along dimension D. If D is omitted, the elementwise product of the elements in the entire array is returned.
SUM(A, D):	Returns the sums of the elements of A along dimension D. If D is omitted, the sum of the elements in the entire array is returned.
SPREAD(A, D, N):	Returns an array of dimension one more than the dimension of A obtained by broadcasting N copies of A along dimension D. For example, SPREAD ((/ 11, 22, 33 /), 1, 2) returns the array

$$\begin{bmatrix} 11 & 22 & 33 \\ 11 & 22 & 33 \end{bmatrix}$$

and SPREAD((/ 11, 22, 33 /), 2, 2) returns the array

$$\begin{bmatrix} 11 & 11 \\ 22 & 22 \\ 33 & 33 \end{bmatrix}$$

MATMUL(A, B):	Returns the matrix product of A and B.
TRANSPOSE(A):	Returns the transpose of the two-dimensional array A.

- Arrays may be *allocatable arrays* for which space is not allocated at compile time but rather by an ALLOCATE statement during execution; their bounds are also specified at that time. An array is declared to be allocatable by including the ALLOCATABLE attribute in its type declaration which must also specify the number of dimensions in the array, but not the bounds in each dimension. For example, the type specification statement

```
REAL, DIMENSION (:, :), ALLOCATABLE :: A, B
```

declares A and B to be two-dimensional allocatable arrays. The actual bounds in each dimension are determined by an ALLOCATE statement, for example,

```
ALLOCATE (A(N, N), B(N, 1:N+1))
```

where N is an integer variable. When this statement is executed, sufficient memory is allocated for the $N \times N$ real array A and the $N \times (N + 1)$ real array B.

9

Double Precision and Complex Data Types

Ten decimals are sufficient to give the circumference of the earth to the fraction of an inch.

S. NEWCOMB

All such expressions as $\sqrt{-1}$, $\sqrt{-2}$, . . . are neither nothing, nor greater than nothing, nor less than nothing, which necessarily constitutes them imaginary or impossible.

L. EULER

There are two types of numeric data that we have not yet explored, double precision and complex, and they are the focus of this chapter.

Real data values are commonly called **single precision** data, because each real constant is usually stored in a single memory location. In a machine that has 32-bit words, for example, this provides approximately seven significant digits for each real value. In many computations, particularly those involving iteration or long sequences of calculations, single precision is not adequate to express the precision required. To overcome this limitation, FORTRAN provides the **double precision** data type. Each double precision value is usually stored in two consecutive memory locations, thus providing approximately twice as many significant digits as does single precision.[1]

The second data type considered in this chapter is the complex type. A **complex number** is a number of the form

$$a + bi$$

---

[1] In machines with a smaller word length, single precision values may be stored in two or more memory words. For example, in a 16-bit machine, each real value is stored in two consecutive memory words, and double precision values are stored in four consecutive words.

440

where *a* and *b* are real numbers and

$$i^2 = -1$$

The first real number, *a*, is called the **real part** of the complex number, and the second real number, *b*, is called the **imaginary part.** In FORTRAN a complex number is represented as a pair of real numbers, and thus each complex data value is usually stored in a pair of memory locations.

9.1 Double Precision Type

In Chapter 1 we considered the internal representation of data and noted that because of the finite length of memory words, most real (floating point) numbers cannot be stored exactly. Even such "nice" decimal fractions as .1 do not have terminating binary representations and thus cannot be represented exactly in the computer's memory. In this connection, we observed in Sections 4.2 and 4.4 that because of this approximate representation, logical expressions formed by comparing two real quantities with .EQ. often are evaluated as false, even though the quantities are algebraically equal. In particular, we observed in Figure 4.1 that even though

```
X * (1.0 / X)
```

is algebraically equal to 1 for all nonzero values of X, the logical expression

```
X * (1.0 / X) .EQ. 1
```

is false for most real values of X. Many other familiar algebraic equalities fail to hold for real data values; for example, values of the real variables A, B, and C can be found for which the values of the following real expressions are not equal:

(A + B) + C and A + (B + C)
(A * B) * C   and A * (B * C)
A * (B + C)   and (A * B) + (A * C)

As another example of the effect of approximate representation, consider the following short program:

```
PROGRAM DEMO1
REAL A, B, C

READ *, A, B
C = ((A + B) ** 2 - 2 * A * B - B ** 2) / A ** 2
PRINT *, C
END
```

The following table shows the output produced by one computer system for various values of A and B:

A	B	C
0.5	888.0	1.00000
0.1	888.0	− 12.5000
0.05	888.0	− 50.0000
0.003	888.0	− 13888.9
0.001	888.0	− 125000.0

These results are rather startling, since the algebraic expression

$$\frac{(A + B)^2 - 2AB - B^2}{A^2}$$

can be written as

$$\frac{A^2 + 2AB + B^2 - 2AB - B^2}{A^2}$$

which simplifies to

$$\frac{A^2}{A^2}$$

and thus is identically 1 (provided $A \neq 0$).

For computations in which more precision is needed than is available using the real data type, FORTRAN provides the double precision data type. When the preceding program with A, B, and C declared to be double precision was executed with the given values for A and B, the value displayed for C in each case differed from 1 by less than 0.017.

The names of variables, arrays, or functions that are double precision may be any legal FORTRAN names, but their types must be declared using the **DOUBLE PRECISION type statement.** For example, the statement

```
DOUBLE PRECISION Z, BETA(5,5)
```

declares the variable Z and the 5 × 5 array BETA to be double precision. The statements

```
DOUBLE PRECISION FUNCTION F(X, Y)
DOUBLE PRECISION X, Y
```

or

```
FUNCTION F(X, Y)
DOUBLE PRECISION F, X, Y
```

declare F to be a double precision–valued function of two double precision arguments X and Y.

Double precision constants are written in scientific notation with a D used to indicate the exponent. Thus,

```
3.1415926535898D0
1D-3
0.2345678D+05
```

are double precision constants.

All variables, arrays, and functions that are to have double precision values must be declared double precision. If R is a double precision variable and A has not been declared to be double precision, the computation in the statement

```
A = 3.1415926535898D0 * R ** 2
```

will be carried out in double precision, but the resulting value will then be assigned to the single precision variable A, thus losing approximately half of the significant digits.

Similarly, values assigned to double precision variables should be double precision values. For example, consider the following program:

```
PROGRAM DEMO2

REAL X
DOUBLE PRECISION A, B

X = 0.1
B = 0.1D0
A = X
PRINT *, A
A = B
PRINT *, A
END
```

On some systems the values displayed for A by the first two PRINT statements resemble the following:

```
0.99999994039536D-01
0.10000000000000D+00
```

Here the value 0.1 of the single precision variable X is stored in only one memory location (actually, a binary approximation of 0.1 is stored), but the value 0.1D0 of the double precision variable B is stored with more precision in two memory locations. This accounts for the discrepancy between the two printed values of A.

Although mixed-mode expressions involving double precision, real, and integer constants and variables are permitted and are evaluated to produce double precision values, accuracy may be lost because of the use of single precision constants or variables. For example, consider the following statements:

```
DOUBLE PRECISION A, B
      .
      .
      .
A = (B + 3.7) ** 2
```

Because of the presence of the single precision constant 3.7, the value for A is limited to single precision accuracy. To ensure double precision accuracy for the value of A, the assignment statement

```
A = (B + 3.7D0) ** 2
```

should therefore be used.

Double precision variables and arrays may be assigned initial values in a DATA statement. In this case, a double precision form for the constants being assigned must be used.

Formatted input and output of double precision data can be accomplished with a D descriptor of the form

$rDw.d$

where

    D   indicates that the data is to be input or output in D form.

    w is an integer constant indicating the total width of the field from which the data is to be read, in the case of input, or displayed, in the case of output.

    d is an integer constant indicating the number of digits to the right of the decimal point.

    r is an integer constant indicating the number of times the field is to be repeated.

For example, the statements

```
      DOUBLE PRECISION A, B, C
      READ 10, A, B, C
   10 FORMAT(2D15.0, D7.0)
```

can be used to read values from the input data line

```
1.66932506172D0___-.7325379D-02__1.1D0
```

When double precision values are displayed using a D descriptor, they usually appear in a *normalized form:* a negative sign, if necessary, followed by one leading zero; then the decimal point followed by the specified number of digits to the right of the decimal point; and finally D with the appropriate exponent displayed in the next four spaces. The F, G, and E descriptors may also be used for the input and output of double precision values. For example, for the variables A, B, and C assigned values by the preceding READ statement, the statements

```
      PRINT 20, A, B, C
      PRINT 30, A, B, C
      PRINT 40, A, B, C
   20 FORMAT(1X, D20.12, 2D20.6)
   30 FORMAT(1X, F20.12, 2F20.6)
   40 FORMAT(1X, E20.12, 2E20.6)
```

produce output resembling the following:

```
__0.166932506172D+01_____-0.732538D-02_____0.110000D+01
_____1.669325061720_____-0.007325_____1.100000
__0.166932506172E+01_____-0.732538E-02_____0.110000E+01
```

Most of the library functions listed in Table 5.1, such as ABS, COS, and LOG, may also be used with double precision arguments. Three other library functions are especially useful for processing double precision data:

DBLE(x)   Transforms the value of the integer or real argument
                   x or the real part of the complex argument x to
                   double precision form.
DPROD(x_1, x_2)   Calculates the double precision product of the real
                   arguments x_1, x_2.
REAL(x)   Converts the double precision argument x to a sin-
                   gle precision number.

One problem in which double precision arithmetic may be required is in solving certain systems of linear equations. For example, consider the linear system

$$\text{(I)} \quad 2x + 6y = 8$$
$$2x + 5.999999y = 8.000002$$

for which the solution is

$$x = 10$$
$$y = -2$$

This linear system is an example of an *ill-conditioned system*. One characteristic of such systems is that they are very sensitive to perturbations of the coefficients and constant terms. Small changes in one or more of these coefficients or constants may produce large changes in the solution. For example, if this linear system is changed to

$$\text{(II)} \quad 2x + 6y = 8$$
$$2x + 6.000001y = 8.000001$$

the solution becomes

$$x = 1$$
$$y = 1$$

When these linear systems were solved using the program in Figure 8.10 for solving linear systems with Gaussian elimination, the results were

$$x = 7.000$$
$$y = -1.000$$

for system (I) and

$$x = 4.000$$

$$y = 0.000$$

for system (II).

The program in Figure 9.1 uses double precision arithmetic to carry out the computations involved in Gaussian elimination. Note that in the sample runs, the correct solutions to these linear systems are obtained.

```
      PROGRAM LINSYS
*****************************************************************************
* Program to solve a linear system using Gaussian elimination with   *
* double precision arithmetic.  Identifiers used are:                *
*      LIMIT  : parameter giving maximum dimensions of matrix        *
*      LIMAUG : parameter (LIMIT + 1) for maximum # columns in AUG   *
*      N      : number of equations and unknowns                     *
*      I, J   : indices                                              *
*      AUG    : augmented matrix for the linear system               *
*      X      : solution vector                                      *
*      SINGUL : indicates if matrix is (nearly) singular             *
*****************************************************************************

      INTEGER LIMIT, LIMAUG
      PARAMETER (LIMIT = 10, LIMAUG = LIMIT + 1)
      DOUBLE PRECISION AUG(LIMIT,LIMAUG), X(LIMIT)
      INTEGER N, I, J
      LOGICAL SINGUL

* Read coefficient matrix and constant vector

      PRINT *, 'ENTER NUMBER OF EQUATIONS'
      READ *, N
      PRINT *, 'ENTER COEFFICIENT MATRIX ROWWISE'
      READ *, ((AUG(I,J), J = 1, N), I = 1, N)
      PRINT *, 'ENTER CONSTANT VECTOR'
      READ *, (AUG(I, N + 1), I = 1, N)

* Use subroutine GAUSS to find the solution A,
* and then display X.

      CALL GAUSS(AUG, LIMIT, LIMAUG, N, X, SINGUL)
      IF (.NOT. SINGUL) THEN
          PRINT *, 'SOLUTION VECTOR IS'
          DO 10 I = 1, N
              PRINT 100, I, X(I)
100           FORMAT(1X, 'X(', I2, ') =', F8.3)
10        CONTINUE
      ELSE
          PRINT *, 'MATRIX IS (NEARLY) SINGULAR'
      END IF
      END
```

Figure 9.1

Figure 9.1 (cont.)

```
**GAUSS*******************************************************************
* Subroutine to find solution of linear system AX = B using Gaussian    *
* elimination, provided a unique solution.  If the matrix is (nearly)    *
* singular, SINGUL is returned as true, and the solution X is            *
* is undefined.   Local identifiers are:                                 *
*     I,J,K  : indices                                                   *
*     MULT   : multiplier used to eliminate an unknown                   *
*     ASBPIV : absolute value of pivot element                          *
*     PIVROW : row containing pivot element                             *
*     EPSIL  : a small positive real value ("almost zero")              *
*     TEMP   : used to interchange rows of matrix                        *
*************************************************************************

        SUBROUTINE GAUSS(AUG, LIM, LIMAUG, N, X, SINGUL)

        DOUBLE PRECISION AUG(LIM, LIMAUG), X(LIM), TEMP, MULT, EPSIL
        PARAMETER (EPSIL = 1D-15)
        INTEGER N, PIVROW
        LOGICAL SINGUL

        SINGUL = .FALSE.
        DO 50 I = 1, N

*         Locate pivot element.

          ABSPIV = ABS(AUG(I,I))
          PIVROW = I
          DO 10 K = I + 1, N
              IF (ABS(AUG(K,I)) .GT. ABSPIV) THEN
                  ABSPIV = ABS(AUG(K,I))
                  PIVROW = K
              END IF
10        CONTINUE

*         Check if matrix is (nearly) singular.

          IF (ABSPIV .LT. EPSIL) THEN
              SINGUL = .TRUE.
              RETURN
          END IF

*         It isn't, so interchange rows PIVROW and I if necessary.

          IF (PIVROW .NE. I) THEN
              DO 20 J = 1, N + 1
                  TEMP = AUG(I,J)
                  AUG(I,J) = AUG(PIVROW,J)
                  AUG(PIVROW,J) = TEMP
20            CONTINUE
          END IF
```

Figure 9.1 (cont.)

```
*          Eliminate Ith unknown from equations I + 1, ..., N

           DO 40 J = I + 1, N
              MULT = -AUG(J,I) / AUG(I,I)
              DO 30 K = I, N + 1
                 AUG(J,K) = AUG(J,K) +  MULT * AUG(I,K)
30            CONTINUE
40         CONTINUE

50     CONTINUE

* Find the solutions by back substitution.

       X(N) = AUG(N, N + 1) / AUG(N,N)
       DO 70 J = N - 1, 1, -1
          X(J) = AUG(J, N + 1)
          DO 60 K = J + 1, N
             X(J) = X(J) - AUG(J,K) * X(K)
60        CONTINUE
          X(J) = X(J) / AUG(J,J)
70     CONTINUE

       END
```

Sample runs:

```
ENTER NUMBER OF EQUATIONS
2
ENTER COEFFICIENT MATRIX ROWWISE
2 6
2 5.999999
ENTER CONSTANT VECTOR
8
8.000002
SOLUTION VECTOR IS
X( 1) =   10.000
X( 2) =   -2.000

ENTER NUMBER OF EQUATIONS
2
ENTER COEFFICIENT MATRIX ROWWISE
2 6
2 6.000001
ENTER CONSTANT VECTOR
8
8.000001
SOLUTION VECTOR IS
X( 1) =    1.000
X( 2) =    1.000
```

It should be noted, however, that although double precision reduces the effects of limited precision, it is not a panacea. Simply declaring everything in the program to be double precision does not avoid all of the problems caused by single precision, because double precision representations of most real numbers still are only approximate.

9.2 Complex Type

Complex numbers arise in many problems in science and engineering, especially in physics and electrical engineering. As noted in the introduction to this chapter, a complex number has the form

$$a + bi$$

where a and b are real numbers called the **real part** and the **imaginary part**, respectively, and

$$i^2 = -1$$

Complex numbers can be plotted in a plane by taking the horizontal axis to be the real axis and the vertical axis to be the imaginary axis, so that the complex number $a + bi$ is represented as the point $P(a, b)$:

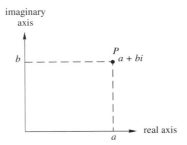

An alternative geometric representation is to associate the complex number $z = a + bi$ with the vector $\overrightarrow{OP}$ from the origin to the point $P(a, b)$:

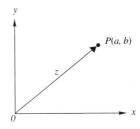

In FORTRAN, a complex constant is represented as a pair of real constants

$$(a, b)$$

where a and b are single precision constants representing the real part and the imaginary part of the complex number, respectively. For example,

```
(1.0,1.0)
(-6.0,7.2)
(-5.432,-1.4142)
```

are complex constants equivalent to

$$1.0 + 1.0i$$
$$-6.0 + 7.2i$$
$$-5.432 - 1.4142i$$

respectively.

The names of variables, arrays, or functions that are complex may be any legal FORTRAN names, but their types must be declared using the **COMPLEX type statement.** For example, the statement

```
COMPLEX A, RHO(10,10)
```

declares the variable A and the 10×10 array RHO to be complex. The statements

```
COMPLEX FUNCTION GAMMA(Z, W)
COMPLEX Z, W
```

or

```
FUNCTION GAMMA(Z, W)
COMPLEX GAMMA, Z, W
```

declare GAMMA to be a complex-valued function of two complex arguments Z and W.

The **sum** of two complex numbers $z = a + bi$ and $w = c + di$ is

$$z + w = (a + c) + (b + d)i$$

If the vector representation is used for complex numbers, this corresponds to the usual sum of vectors; that is, the vector representing $z + w$ is the sum of the vectors representing z and w:

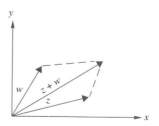

Similarly, the **difference** of z and w defined by

$$z - w = (a - c) + (b - d)i$$

corresponds to vector subtraction.

The **product** of two complex numbers $z = a + bi$ and $w = c + di$ is

$$z \cdot w = (ac - bd) + (ad + bc)i$$

This complex number is represented by a vector whose magnitude is the product of the magnitudes of the vectors representing z and w and whose angle of inclination is the sum $\theta_1 + \theta_2$ of the angles of inclination of the vectors:

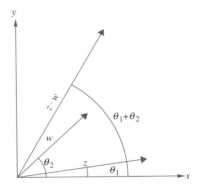

The **quotient** of z and w is

$$\frac{z}{w} = \frac{ac + bd}{c^2 + d^2} + \frac{bc - ad}{c^2 + d^2} i \text{ (provided } c^2 + d^2 \neq 0)$$

This quotient corresponds to a vector whose magnitude is the quotient of the magnitudes of the vectors representing z and w and whose angle of inclination is the difference $\theta_1 - \theta_2$ of the angles of inclination of the vectors.

These four basic arithmetic operations for complex numbers are denoted in FORTRAN by the usual operators $+$, $-$, $*$, and $/$. The exponentiation operation $**$ is defined for a complex number only when the exponent is an integer.

Mixed-mode expressions and assignments involving integer, real, and complex values are allowed, but *double precision values may not be combined with complex values, nor may a double precision value be assigned to a complex variable or a complex value to a double precision variable.* For example, suppose that C and Z are complex variables with the value of C given by

```
C = (6.2,2.4)
```

Then the assignment statement

```
Z = 4.0 * C / 2
```

assigns the complex value (12.4, 4.8) to Z. If this same expression is assigned to the real variable X

```
X = 4.0 * C / 2
```

only the real part of the expression's value is assigned to X; thus, X has the value 12.4. Similarly, if N is an integer variable, the statement

```
N = 4.0 * C / 2
```

assigns the integer part of this value to N, so that N has the value 12.

The only relational operators that may be used with complex values are .EQ. and .NE.. Two complex values are **equal** if and only if their real parts are equal and their imaginary parts are equal.

Some of the mathematical functions commonly used with complex numbers are the absolute value, conjugate, and complex exponential functions. For the complex number $z = a + bi$, these functions are defined as follows:

Absolute value: $|z| = \sqrt{a^2 + b^2}$
Conjugate: $\bar{z} = a - bi$
Complex exponential: $e^z = e^a(\cos b + i \sin b)$

If the vector representation is used for complex numbers, $|z|$ is the magnitude of the vector representing z; $\bar{z}$ is represented by the vector obtained by reflecting the vector representing z in the x axis; and the complex exponential e^z is associated with the polar representations of z (see Exercise 11 at the end of this section).

These three functions are implemented in FORTRAN by the library functions ABS, CONJG, and EXP, respectively. Several of the other library functions listed in Table 5.1, such as SIN, COS, and LOG, may also be used with complex arguments. Three library functions that are useful in converting from real type to complex type, and vice versa, are

AIMAG(*z*)   Gives the imaginary part of the complex argument *z* as a single precision number.

CMPLX(*x,y*)   Converts the two integer, real, or double precision arguments *x* and *y* into a complex number. The first
or   argument *x* becomes the real part of the complex num-
CMPLX(*x*)   ber, and the second argument *y* becomes the imaginary part. The second form is equivalent to CMPLX(*x*, 0).

REAL(*z*)   Gives the real part of the complex argument *z*.

Complex values may be read using a list-directed READ statement, with the complex numbers entered as a pair of real numbers enclosed in parentheses. They may also be read using a formatted READ statement. In this case, a pair of F, E, or G descriptors may be used for each complex value to be read, and parentheses are not used to enclose the parts of the complex number when it is entered. Complex values displayed using a list-directed output statement appear as a pair of real values separated by a comma and enclosed in parentheses. For formatted output of complex values, a pair of F, E, or G descriptors is used for each complex value.

The following program illustrates the input and output of complex numbers and complex arithmetic:

```
      PROGRAM DEMO3

      COMPLEX X, Y, W, Z, A

      READ *, X, Y
      READ 5, W
    5 FORMAT(2F2.0)
      PRINT *, X, Y, W
      PRINT 10, X, Y, W
   10 FORMAT(1X, F6.2, ' +' F8.2, 'I')
      Z = (X + Y) / (1.0,2.2)
      A = X * Y
      PRINT 10, Z, A
      END
```

If the following data is entered,

```
(3,4), (.75,-2.23)
 5 7
```

the output produced is

```
(3.00000,4.00000)   (0.750000,-2.23000)   (5.00000,7.00000)
  3.00 +    4.00I
  0.75 +   -2.23I
  5.00 +    7.00I
  1.31 +   -1.11I
 11.17 +   -3.69I
```

In Section 4.3 we considered the problem of solving quadratic equations

$$Ax^2 + Bx + C = 0$$

and noted that if the discriminant $B^2 - 4AC$ is negative, there are no real roots. In this case, the quadratic equation has two complex solutions, which can be found by using the quadratic formula. For example, for the equation

$$x^2 + 2x + 5 = 0$$

the discriminant is

$$2^2 - 4 \cdot 1 \cdot 5 = -16$$

so the roots are complex. The quadratic formula gives the roots

$$\frac{-2 \pm \sqrt{-16}}{2} = \frac{-2 \pm 4i}{2} = -1 \pm 2i$$

The program in Figure 9.2 reads the complex coefficients A, B, and C of a quadratic equation, uses the quadratic formula to calculate the roots, and displays them as complex numbers.

```
        PROGRAM CQUAD
**********************************************************************
* Program to solve a quadratic equation having complex coefficients: *
* using the quadratic formula.  Variables used are:                  *
*    A, B, C : the coefficients of the quadratic equation            *
*    DISC    : the discriminant, B ** 2 - 4 * A * C                  *
*    ROOT1, ROOT2 : the two roots of the equation                    *
**********************************************************************

        COMPLEX A, B, C, DISC, ROOT1, ROOT2

        PRINT *, 'ENTER THE COEFFICIENTS OF THE QUADRATIC EQUATION'
        READ *, A, B, C
        DISC = SQRT(B ** 2 - 4 * A * C)
        ROOT1 = (-B + DISC) / (2 * A)
        ROOT2 = (-B - DISC) / (2 * A)
        PRINT *, 'THE ROOTS ARE:'
        PRINT 10, ROOT1, ROOT2
10      FORMAT (5X, F7.3, ' +', F7.3, 'I')
        END
```

Sample runs:

```
ENTER THE COEFFICIENTS OF THE QUADRATIC EQUATION
(1,0), (-5,0), (6,0)
THE ROOTS ARE:
      3.000 +  0.000I
      2.000 +  0.000I

ENTER THE COEFFICIENTS OF THE QUADRATIC EQUATION
(1,0), (2,0), (5,0)
THE ROOTS ARE:
     -1.000 +  2.000I
     -1.000 + -2.000I

ENTER THE COEFFICIENTS OF THE QUADRATIC EQUATION
(1,0), (0,0), (1,0)
THE ROOTS ARE:
      0.000 +  1.000I
      0.000 + -1.000I
```

Figure 9.2

In Example 2 of Section 8.4, we considered the problem of determining the loop currents in a direct current circuit and found these currents by solving a system of linear equations. Whereas the current, voltage, and resistance of a dc circuit can be represented by real numbers, these same quantities are represented by complex numbers for alternating current circuits. Consequently, the equations in a linear system for finding loop currents in an ac circuit have coefficients that are complex numbers. Such a system can be solved using Gaussian elimination (or other methods used for solving linear systems) if the real operations are replaced by complex operations.

Exercises

1. Assuming that all values are represented with three significant digits (rounded when necessary), find values for A, B, and C for which

    (a) (A + B) + C does not have the same value as A + (B + C).
    (b) (A * B) * C does not have the same value as A * (B * C).
    (c) A * (B + C) does not have the same value as (A * B) + (A * C).

2. For $z = 1 + 2i$ and $w = 3 - 4i$, calculate

    (a) $z + w$ **(b)** $z - w$ **(c)** $z \cdot w$ **(d)** $\dfrac{z}{w}$

    (e) z^2 **(f)** $\bar{z}$ **(g)** $\bar{w}$ **(h)** $\dfrac{z + \bar{z}}{2}$

    (i) $\dfrac{z - \bar{z}}{2i}$ **(j)** $z \cdot \bar{z}$ **(k)** $\dfrac{1}{z}$ **(l)** $\dfrac{z + w}{z - w}$

3. Repeat Exercise 2 for $z = 6 - 5i$ and $w = 5 + 12i$.

4. Assuming the declarations

    ```
    INTEGER N1, N2
    REAL R1, R2
    DOUBLE PRECISION D1, D2
    COMPLEX C1, C2
    ```

    and the assignment statements

    ```
    N1 = 2
    R1 = 0.5
    D1 = .1D0
    C1 = (6.0,8.0)
    ```

    find the value assigned to the specified variable in each of the following assignment statements or indicate why there is an error:

    (a) `R2 = D1`
    (b) `N2 = D1`
    (c) `R2 = C1`
    (d) `N2 = C1`
    (e) `D2 = C1`
    (f) `D2 = N1`
    (g) `R2 = REAL(C1)`
    (h) `R2 = AIMAG(C1)`
    (i) `C2 = C1 * (0,1)`
    (j) `C2 = 1 / C1`
    (k) `R2 = ABS(C1)`
    (l) `N2 = CONJG(C1)`
    (m) `C2 = C1 ** N1`
    (n) `C2 = C1 ** R1`
    (o) `C2 = CMPLX(N1, R1)`

(p) `C2 = N1 + R1 * D1 + C1`
(q) `C2 = REAL(C1) + AIMAG(C1)`
(r) `C2 = EXP((0,0))`

5. For the sequence of numbers $a_0, a_1, a_2, \ldots$ defined by

$$a_0 = e^1 - 1$$

and

$$a_{n+1} = (n + 1)a_n - 1 \qquad \text{for } n = 0, 1, 2, \ldots$$

it can be shown that for each n,

$$a_n = n! \left[e^1 - \left(1 + 1 + \frac{1}{2!} + \cdots + \frac{1}{n!} \right) \right]$$

so that this sequence converges to 0. Write a program that prints a table of values of a_n for $n = 0, 1, 2, \ldots, 15$, calculated first in single precision and then in double precision.

6. Write a program to find a double precision approximation to the zero of a function using Newton's method (see Example 1 of Section 5.2).

7. Write a program to find a double precision approximation to an integral using the trapezoidal method or Simpson's rule (see Exercises 21 and 22 of Section 4.11).

8. Repeat Exercise 13 of Section 5.1 for calculating values of the hyperbolic sine function sinh by using a subprogram to calculate e^x, but perform all calculations in double precision. In particular, use the series to calculate values for e^x using double precision arithmetic to achieve ten-place accuracy.

9. Write a program that reads three complex numbers P, Q, and R and that then determines whether the triangle whose vertices are the points corresponding to P, Q, and R in the complex plane is a right triangle.

10. The exponentiation operator ** is defined for complex values only when the exponent is an integer. To calculate z^a when z is complex and a is real or complex, we can use

$$z^a = e^{a \log z}$$

Write a function that calculates z^a. Use the function in a program that reads values for z and a and then calls the function to calculate the value of z^a.

11. In Section 9.2 we noted that a complex number $z = a + bi$ can be represented geometrically by the vector $\overrightarrow{OP}$ from the origin to the point P having rectangular coordinates (a, b). Using polar coordinates for *P* gives the following *polar representation* for *z*:

$$z = r(\cos \theta + i \sin \theta)$$

which can be equivalently written as

$$z = re^{i\theta}$$

where *r* is the length of $\overrightarrow{OP}$ and θ is the angle from the positive axis to $\overrightarrow{OP}$. Write a subroutine that converts a complex number from its usual representation to its polar representation. Use the subroutine in a program that reads a complex number *z* and a positive integer *n* and finds the *nth roots of z* as given by

$$z^{1/n} = r^{1/n} \left[\cos \left(\frac{\theta + 2k\pi}{n} \right) + i \sin \left(\frac{\theta + 2k\pi}{n} \right) \right]$$

$$k = 0, 1, \ldots, n - 1$$

12. Suppose that an ac circuit contains a capacitor, an inductor, and a resistor in series:

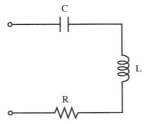

The impedance Z_R for the resistor is simply the resistance *R*, but for inductors and capacitors, it is a function of the frequency. The impedance Z_L of the inductor is the complex value given by

$$Z_L = \omega L i$$

where ω is the frequency (in radians per second) of the ac source and *L* is the self-inductance (in henries). For the capacitor, the impedance is

$$Z_C = \frac{-i}{\omega C}$$

where *C* is the capacitance (in farads). Write a program that reads values for *R*, *L*, and *C*, then reads several pairs of values for the frequency ω (a real number) and the instantaneous voltage *V* (a complex number), and calculates for each pair the total impedance

$$Z = Z_R + Z_L + Z_C$$

and the instantaneous current *I* and its magnitude where

$$I = \frac{V}{Z}$$

13. Repeat Exercise 26 in Section 7.5 for polynomial evaluation using nested multiplication, but allow the coefficients of the polynomial and the value of x to be complex numbers.

Programming Pointers

In this chapter we considered the two numeric data types double precision and complex. The main points to remember when using these data types are the following:

1. *Precision may be lost in double precision expressions and assignments because of the presence of single precision constants and/or variables.*

To illustrate, consider the declarations

```
REAL X
DOUBLE PRECISION A, B
```

In the assignment statement

```
B = 0.1 * A ** 2
```

precision may be lost because of the single precision constant 0.1. This statement should be written as

```
B = 0.1D0 * A ** 2
```

Similarly, in the assignment statement

```
X = (A + B) * (A - B)
```

the expression on the right side is evaluated in double precision, but the resulting value is then assigned to the single precision variable X. Remember, however, that simply declaring everything to be double precision does not solve all of the problems arising from limited precision. For example, the logical expression

```
A * (1.0D0 / A) .EQ. 1.0D0
```

is still false for most double precision values of A.

2. *Double precision and complex values may not both be used in an expression, nor may a double precision (complex) value be assigned to a complex (double precision) variable.*

3. *A pair of real constants representing a complex data value is enclosed in parentheses for list-directed input but not for formatted input.*

4. *Formatted output of complex values requires two real descriptors.*

5. *Complex values may be compared only with the relational operators .EQ. and .NE..* Remember however, the danger of comparing real numbers with these relational operators (see Sections 4.2 and 4.4).

FORTRAN 90 Features

The double precision and complex data types described in this chapter are also supported in FORTRAN 90. The main variations and extensions include the following:

● The precision of a real, double precision, or complex constant or variable may be specified by using KIND type parameters. Every processor must provide at least two kinds of precision, one corresponding to single precision real type and one corresponding to double precision type. A KIND = clause is used in the declaration of parameters and variables to specify their precision:

REAL (KIND = *kind-type-parameter*) *list-of-identifiers*

Two intrinsic functions, SELECTED__REAL__KIND and KIND, are used to determine the kind type parameters. A reference to SELECTED__REAL__KIND has the form

SELECTED__REAL__KIND(N)

where N is an integer, and returns the kind type parameter that will provide at least N decimal digits of precision. For example, the statements

```
INTEGER, PARAMETER :: PREC10 = SELECTED_REAL_KIND(10)
REAL (KIND = PREC10) V, W
```

declare that V and W are real variables whose values are to have at least ten decimal digits of precision. A reference to the KIND function has the form

KIND(X)

and returns the kind type parameter of X. For example, the declaration

```
REAL (KIND = KIND(1.0D0)) A, B
```

is equivalent to

```
DOUBLE PRECISION A, B
```

● The intrinsic function PRECISION can be used to determine the precision of a real or complex value (which may be an array). Thus for the variable W just declared, PRECISION(W) would return the value 10.
● The REAL function can be referenced with a second argument,

REAL(*x*, *kind-type-parameter*)

to convert *x* of type integer, real, or complex to a real value whose precision is specified by the kind type parameter. Similarly, the CMPLX function can be referenced with a kind type parameter

CMPLX(*x*, *y*, *kind-type-parameter*)
CMPLX(*x*, *kind-type-parameter*)

to form the complex number $x + yi$ in the first case, and $x + 0i$ in the second, whose components have the precision specified by the kind type parameter.

- The components of a complex value may have any precision. In particular, they may be double precision values.

10

Advanced Character Data

Everyone knows how laborious the usual Method is of attaining to Arts and Sciences; whereas by this Contrivance, the most ignorant Person at a reasonable Charge, and with a little bodily Labour, may write Books in Philosophy, Poetry, Politicks, Law, Mathematicks, and Theology, without the least Assistance from Genius or Study. He then led me to the Frame, about the sides whereof all his Pupils stood in Ranks. It was Twenty Foot square . . . linked by slender Wires. These Bits . . . were covered on every Square with Paper pasted upon them; and on These Papers were written all the Words of their Language. . . .

The Professor then desired me to observe, for he was going to set his Engine at work. The Pupils at this Command took each of them hold of an Iron Handle, whereof there were Forty fixed round the Edges of the Frame; and giving them a sudden Turn, the whole Disposition of the Words was entirely changed. . . .

JONATHAN SWIFT, *Gulliver's Travels*

The word *compute* usually suggests arithmetic operations performed on numeric data; thus, computers are sometimes thought to be mere "number crunchers," devices whose only function is to process numeric information. In Chapter 1, however, we considered coding schemes used to represent character information in a computer, and in subsequent chapters we introduced some of the character-processing capabilities of FORTRAN. We have discussed character constants, character variables and their declarations, assignment of values to character variables, input and output of character data, and comparison of character values in a logical expression. In this chapter we continue our study of the character data type.

10.1   Character Data and Operations

Recall that a character constant is a string of characters from the FORTRAN character set enclosed in apostrophes (single quotes) and that the number of characters enclosed is the length of the constant.

As we have seen, character variables may be declared using a type statement of the form

CHARACTER*n, *list*

where *list* is a list of variables being typed as character and n is the length of their values. The comma preceding the list may be omitted; the length specification n also may be omitted, in which case it is assumed to be 1. For example, the statement

```
CHARACTER*10 CITY, STATE, COUNTRY
```

declares CITY, STATE, and COUNTRY to be of character type with string values of length 10. The length specification may be overridden for any variable in the list by appending a length descriptor of the form *m to its name; thus

```
CHARACTER*10 CITY*20, STATE, COUNTRY
```

declares STATE and COUNTRY to have values of length 10 and CITY to have values of length 20. In Chapter 5 we also noted that when a formal argument of character type is being declared in a function or subroutine subprogram, a declaration of the form

CHARACTER*(*) *list-of-identifiers*

which contains the **assumed length specifier** *, may be used. In this case, the formal argument will have the same length as the corresponding actual argument.

For character data there is one binary operation that can be used to combine two character values. This operation is **concatenation** and is denoted by //. Thus

```
'CENTI' // 'METERS'
```

produces the string

```
'CENTIMETERS'
```

and if SQUNIT is a variable declared by

```
CHARACTER*7 SQUNIT
```

and is assigned a value by

```
SQUNIT = 'SQUARE'
```

then

```
SQUNIT // 'CENTI' // 'METERS'
```

yields the string

```
'SQUARE CENTIMETERS'
```

Another operation commonly performed on character strings is accessing a sequence of consecutive characters from a given string. Such a sequence is called a **substring** of the given string. For example, the substring consisting of the fourth through the seventh characters of the character constant

```
'CENTIMETERS'
```

is the string

```
'TIME'
```

In FORTRAN a substring can be extracted from the value of a character variable by specifying the name of the variable followed by the positions of the first and last characters of the substring, separated by a colon (:) and enclosed in parentheses. For example, if character variable UNITS has the value

```
'CENTIMETERS'
```

then

```
UNITS(4:7)
```

has the value

```
'TIME'
```

The initial and final positions of the substring may be specified by integer constants, variables, or expressions. If the initial position is not specified, it is assumed to be 1, and if the final position is not specified, it is assumed to be the last position in the value of the character variable. To illustrate, consider the following statements:

```
CHARACTER*15 COURSE, NAME*20
COURSE = 'MATHEMATICS'
```

Then

```
COURSE(:5)
```

has the value

```
'MATHE'
```

and the value of

```
COURSE(8:)
```

is

```
'TICSƀƀƀƀ'
```

where ƀ denotes a blank. If N has the value 3, then

```
COURSE(N:N + 2)
```

has the value

```
'THE'
```

Care must be taken to ensure that the first position specified for a substring is positive and that the last position is greater than or equal to the first position but not greater than the length of the given string.

Substring references may be used to form character expressions just as character variables are used. For example, they may be concatenated with other character values, as in

```
COURSE(:4) // '. 141'
```

the value of which is the string

```
'MATH. 141'
```

An assignment statement or an input statement may also be used to modify part of a string by using a substring reference. Only the character positions specified in the substring name are assigned values; the remaining positions are not changed. To illustrate, consider the statements

```
CHARACTER*8 COURSE
COURSE = 'CPSC 141'
```

The assignment statement

```
COURSE(1:4) = 'MATH'
```

or

```
COURSE(:4) = 'MATH'
```

changes the value of COURSE to

```
'MATH 141'
```

Positions to which new values are being assigned may not be referenced, however, in the character expression on the right side of such assignment statements. Thus

```
COURSE(2:4) = COURSE(5:7)
```

is valid, whereas

```
COURSE(2:4) = COURSE (3:5)
```

is not because the substring being modified overlaps the substring being referenced.

Character values can be displayed using either list-directed or formatted output. List-directed output of a character value consists of the string of characters in that value, displayed in a field whose width is equal to the length of that value. For example, if STRA and STRB are declared by

```
CHARACTER*8 STRA, STRB
```

and are assigned values by

```
STRA = 'SQUARE'
STRB = 'CENTIMETERS'
```

the statement

```
PRINT *, '***', STRA, '***', STRB, '***'
```

produces the output

```
***SQUARE  ***CENTIMET***
```

Note the two trailing blanks in the value of STRA that result from the padding that takes place when a string of length 6 is assigned to a character variable of length 8. Note also that the last three characters in the string 'CENTIMETERS' are not displayed because they were truncated in the assignment of the value to STRB.

Character expressions may also appear in the output list of a PRINT statement. For example,

```
PRINT *, STRA(:2) // '. ' // STRB(:1) // STRB(6:6) // '.'
```

produces as output

```
SQ. CM.
```

An A descriptor (see Section 6.1) is used for formatted output of character values. To illustrate, consider the following program segment:

```
      CHARACTER*15 ITEM, COLOR*5

      ITEM = 'MM CAMERA'
      COLOR = 'BLACK'
      PRINT 5, COLOR, 'RED'
    5 FORMAT(1X, A, A4)
      PRINT 10, COLOR
   10 FORMAT(1X, A1)
      PRINT 15, 'MOVIE-' // ITEM(4:9)
   15 FORMAT(1X, A)
      PRINT 20, 35, ITEM
   20 FORMAT(1X, I2, A)
```

These statements produce the following output:

```
BLACK RED
B
MOVIE-CAMERA
35MM CAMERA
```

Character values can be read using either list-directed or formatted input. For list-directed input, character values must be enclosed in single quotes. For formatted input, when a value is read for a character variable, **all** characters in the field associated with the corresponding A descriptor are read. For example, if the line of data

```
SCIENTIFIC FORTRAN
```

is read by the statements

```
      CHARACTER*8 STRA, STRB

      READ 20, STRA, STRB
   20 FORMAT(2A)
```

the value

```
SCIENTIF
```

is assigned to STRA and

```
IC FORTR
```

to STRB.

A substring reference may also appear in an input list. For example, if COURSE has the value

```
'CPSC 141'
```

and the input for the statement

```
READ '(A)', COURSE(2:6)
```

is

```
LAS 3
```

the value of COURSE is changed to

```
'CLAS 341'
```

10.2   The INDEX and LEN Functions

When extracting or modifying substrings, it is often convenient to locate a given pattern within a string. For example, we might wish to search the string

```
'ATOMIC WEIGHT OF KRYPTON'
```

to find the location of the substring

```
'WEIGHT'
```

This can be done using the FORTRAN library function INDEX of the form

INDEX(*string1, string2*)

where *string1* and *string2* are any expressions of character type. The first argument is the string being searched, and the second is the substring whose location is to be determined. The value of the function is the integer value corresponding to the character position at which the first occurrence of that substring begins, or 0 if the substring does not appear in the given string. Thus, the value of

```
INDEX('ATOMIC WEIGHT OF KRYPTON', 'WEIGHT')
```

is 8, whereas the value of

```
INDEX('ATOMIC WEIGHT OF KRYPTON', 'NUMBER')
```

is 0.

The following table gives more examples of the index function. In these examples, UNITS and DIST are assumed to be declared by

```
CHARACTER UNITS*15, DIST*6
```

and to have the values

```
UNITS = 'FEET PER SECOND'
DIST = 'METERS'
```

Expression	Value
INDEX(UNITS, DIST)	0
INDEX(UNITS, 'PER')	6
INDEX(UNITS, DIST(4:5))	7
INDEX(UNITS, 'E')	2
UNITS(INDEX(UNITS, 'S'):)	'SECOND'
DIST(3:INDEX(UNITS, ' '))	'TER'
DIST // UNITS(INDEX(UNITS, ' '):)	'METERS PER SECOND'

Another FORTRAN library function that may be used with character data is the LEN function of the form

LEN(*string*)

where *string* is any character expression. The value of this function is the length of the specified string.

Suppose that NAME has been declared to be of character type by the statement

```
CHARACTER*20 NAME
```

and consider the assignment statement

```
NAME = 'JOHN DOE'
```

The following table shows the results of several uses of the LEN function:

Function	Result
PRINT *, LEN('JOHN DOE')	8 is displayed
PRINT *, LEN(NAME)	20 is displayed
N = LEN('MR. '//NAME)	24 is assigned to N
PRINT *, LEN(NAME(9:))	12 is displayed
DO 10 I = 1, LEN(NAME)	Loop is repeated 20 times

As the preceding examples show, for a character constant, the value of the LEN function is simply the number of characters in that constant, and for a character variable, it is the declared length of that variable. Consequently, this function has a rather limited use. However, a statement such as

```
DO 10 I = 1, LEN(NAME)
```

is preferred to

```
DO 10 I = 1, 20
```

because it does not have to be changed if the program is modified by changing the declared length of NAME. The LEN function is also useful in subprograms in which an assumed length specifier is used to declare arguments of character type.

The preparation of textual material such as research papers, books, and computer programs often involves the insertion, deletion, and replacement of parts of the text. The software of most computers systems includes an **editing** package that makes it easy to carry out these operations. As an example showing the text-processing capabilities of FORTRAN, we consider the editing problem of replacing a specified substring in a given line of text with another string. A solution to this problem is given in the program in Figure 10.1. The sample run shows that in addition to string replacements, the program can be used to make insertions and deletions. For example, changing the substring

```
A N
```

in the line of text

```
A NATION CONCEIVED IN LIBERTY AND AND DEDICATED
```

to

```
A NEW N
```

yields the edited line

```
A NEW NATION CONCEIVED IN LIBERTY AND AND DEDICATED
```

Entering the edit change

```
AND //
```

changes the substring

```
AND♭
```

(where ♭ denotes a blank) in the line of text to an *empty* or *null* string containing no characters, and so the edited result is

```
A NEW NATION CONCEIVED IN LIBERTY AND DEDICATED
```

```
       PROGRAM EDITOR
***********************************************************************
* Program to perform some basic text-editing functions on lines of    *
* text.  The basic operation is replacing a substring of the text     *
* with another string.  This replacement is accomplished by a command *
* of the form                                                          *
*                         oldstring/newstring/                         *
* where oldstring specifies the substring in the text to be replaced  *
* with newstring; newstring may be an empty string, which then causes *
* oldstring (if found) to be deleted.  The text lines are read from a  *
* file, and after editing, the edited lines are written to another    *
* file.  Identifiers used are:                                         *
*     OLDFIL  : name of the input file                                 *
*     NEWFIL  : name of the output file                                *
*     EOF     : end-of-file indicator                                  *
*     TEXT    : a character string representing a line of text         *
*     LENGTH  : length of text line                                    *
*     CHANGE  : a character string specifying the edit operation       *
*               Value is of the form:                                  *
*                       'oldstring/newstring/'                         *
*     RESPON  : user response (Y or N)                                 *
***********************************************************************

       INTEGER LENGTH, EOF
       PARAMETER (LENGTH = 80)
       CHARACTER*(LENGTH) TEXT, CHANGE, OLDFIL*20, NEWFIL*20, RESPON*1

       PRINT *, 'ENTER THE NAME OF THE INPUT FILE'
       READ '(A)', OLDFIL
       PRINT *, 'ENTER THE NAME OF THE OUTPUT FILE'
       READ '(A)', NEWFIL
       OPEN (UNIT = 15, FILE = OLDFIL, STATUS = 'OLD')
       OPEN (UNIT = 16, FILE = NEWFIL, STATUS = 'NEW')

* While there is more data, read a line of text and edit it.
       READ (15, '(A)', IOSTAT = EOF) TEXT
10     IF (EOF .GE. 0) THEN
          PRINT *, TEXT
          PRINT *, 'EDIT THIS LINE (Y OR N)?'
          READ '(A)', RESPON
```

Figure 10.1

Figure 10.1 (cont.)

```
*           While RESPON <> 'N', get editing change, modify the
*           line of text, and display the edited line.
20          IF (RESPON .NE. 'N') THEN
               PRINT *, 'ENTER EDIT CHANGE'
               READ '(A)', CHANGE
               CALL EDIT(TEXT, CHANGE)
               PRINT *, TEXT
               PRINT *, 'MORE EDITING (Y OR N)'
               READ '(A)', RESPON
            GO TO 20
            END IF
            WRITE (16, '(A)') TEXT
            PRINT *
            READ (15, '(A)', IOSTAT = EOF) TEXT
         GO TO 10
         END IF

         CLOSE(15)
         CLOSE(16)
         END

**EDIT*******************************************************************
* Subroutine to edit a line of TEXT by replacing a substring of the    *
* text by another string as specified by the command CHANGE, which has *
* the form                                                             *
*                     oldstring/newstring/                             *
* newstring (which may be empty) replaces the first occurrence of      *
* oldstring in TEXT.  Local identifiers used are:                      *
*     TXTEND  : last part of edited text                               *
*     SLASH1  : position of first slash (/) in CHANGE                  *
*     SLASH2  : position of second slash (/) in CHANGE                 *
*     OLDSTR  : old string -- to be replaced                           *
*     OLDLEN  : actual length of OLDSTR                                *
*     NEWSTR  : new replacement string                                 *
*     NEWLEN  : actual length of NEWSTR                                *
*     INDOLD  : index of old string in TEXT                            *
***********************************************************************

         SUBROUTINE EDIT(TEXT, CHANGE)

         INTEGER LENGTH, SLASH1, SLASH2, OLDLEN, NEWLEN, INDOLD
         PARAMETER (LENGTH = 80)
         CHARACTER*(LENGTH) TEXT, CHANGE, OLDSTR, NEWSTR, TXTEND

* Attempt to locate slash delimiters in CHANGE
         SLASH1 = INDEX(CHANGE, '/')
         SLASH2 = SLASH1 + INDEX(CHANGE(SLASH1 + 1 : ), '/')
         IF (SLASH1 .LT. 0 .OR. SLASH2 .EQ. SLASH1) THEN
            PRINT *, 'MISSING SLASH'
            RETURN
         END IF
```

Figure 10.1 (cont.)

```
* Slashes were found, so continue with editing
* First extract OLDSTR and NEWSTR from CHANGE, and locate
* OLDSTR in TEXT.

        OLDLEN = SLASH1 - 1
        OLDSTR = CHANGE( : OLDLEN)
        NEWLEN = SLASH2 - SLASH1 - 1
        NEWSTR = CHANGE(SLASH1 + 1: SLASH2 - 1)
        INDOLD = INDEX(TEXT, OLDSTR( : OLDLEN))
        IF (INDOLD .GT. 0) THEN
*           Append text following OLDSTR to NEWSTR.
            TXTEND = NEWSTR( :NEWLEN) // TEXT(INDOLD + OLDLEN : )

*           Prepend text preceding OLDSTR (if any) to form edited TEXT.
            IF (INDOLD .EQ. 1) THEN
                TEXT = TXTEND
            ELSE
                TEXT = TEXT( : INDOLD - 1) // TXTEND
            END IF
        END IF

    END
```

Listing of TEXT-FILE used in sample run:

```
FOURSCORE AND FIVE YEARS AGO, OUR MOTHERS
BROUGHT FORTH ON CONTINENT
A NATION CONCEIVED IN LIBERTY AND AND DEDICATED
TO THE PREPOSITION THAT ALL MEN
ARE CREATED EQUAL.
```

Sample run:

```
ENTER THE NAME OF THE INPUT FILE
TEXT-FILE
ENTER THE NAME OF THE OUTPUT FILE
NEW-TEXT-FILE
FOURSCORE AND FIVE YEARS AGO, OUR MOTHERS
EDIT THIS LINE (Y OR N)?
Y
ENTER EDIT CHANGE
FIVE/SEVEN/
FOURSCORE AND SEVEN YEARS AGO, OUR MOTHERS
MORE EDITING (Y OR N)
Y
ENTER EDIT CHANGE
MO/FA/
FOURSCORE AND SEVEN YEARS AGO, OUR FATHERS
MORE EDITING (Y OR N)
N

BROUGHT FORTH ON CONTINENT
EDIT THIS LINE (Y OR N)?
Y
```

Figure 10.1 (cont.)

```
ENTER EDIT CHANGE
ON/ON THIS
MISSING SLASH
BROUGHT FORTH ON CONTINENT
MORE EDITING (Y OR N)
Y
ENTER EDIT CHANGE
ON/ON THIS/
BROUGHT FORTH ON THIS CONTINENT
MORE EDITING (Y OR N)
N

A NATION CONCEIVED IN LIBERTY AND AND DEDICATED
EDIT THIS LINE (Y OR N)?
Y
ENTER EDIT CHANGE
A N/A NEW N/
A NEW NATION CONCEIVED IN LIBERTY AND AND DEDICATED
MORE EDITING (Y OR N)
Y
ENTER EDIT CHANGE
AND //
A NEW NATION CONCEIVED IN LIBERTY AND DEDICATED
MORE EDITING (Y OR N)
N

TO THE PREPOSITION THAT ALL MEN
EDIT THIS LINE (Y OR N)?
Y
ENTER EDIT CHANGE
PRE/PRO/
TO THE PROPOSITION THAT ALL MEN
MORE EDITING (Y OR N)
N

ARE CREATED EQUAL.
EDIT THIS LINE (Y OR N)?
N
```

Listing of NEW-TEXT-FILE produced by sample run:

```
FOURSCORE AND SEVEN YEARS AGO, OUR FATHERS
BROUGHT FORTH ON THIS CONTINENT
A NEW NATION CONCEIVED IN LIBERTY AND DEDICATED
TO THE PROPOSITION THAT ALL MEN
ARE CREATED EQUAL.
```

10.3 Character Comparison

In Section 4.2 we stated that a collating sequence is used to define the ordering of characters in the FORTRAN character set. Character strings are compared using the encoding schemes (such as ASCII and EBCDIC) that represent character information in a computer, as described in Chapter 1. Each such encoding scheme assigns a unique integer to each character that the machine can process. These characters can then be arranged in an order in which one character precedes another if its numeric code is less than the numeric code of the other. This ordering of characters based on their numeric codes is called a **collating sequence** and varies from one computer to another. The ANSI FORTRAN 77 standard, however, partially specifies this sequence. It requires that the upper-case letters A through Z and the digits 0 through 9 be ordered in the usual way and that the letters and digits not overlap. The blank character must precede both A and 0 in the ordering. The standard does not, however, specify any particular order for special characters or their relation to other characters.

When characters are compared in a logical expression, this collating sequence is used. Thus,

```
'C' .LT. 'D'
'Z' .GT. 'W'
```

are true logical expressions, since C must precede D and Z must follow W in every collating sequence. However, the truth or falsity of the logical expressions

```
'1' .LT. 'A'
'*' .GT. ')'
```

depends on the encoding scheme used in a particular computer. Both logical expressions are true for ASCII but false for EBCDIC.

Similarly, the logical expressions

```
'HCL' .LT. 'NACL'
'CO2' .GT. 'C'
```

are true, since strings are compared character by character using the collating sequence and in the first case, H must precede N, and in the second case, O must follow a blank character. (Recall that for strings of different lengths, the shorter string is blank padded so that two strings of equal length are compared.) However, the truth or falsity of such logical expressions as

```
'A3' .LT. 'AB'
'PDQ+123' .GT. 'PDQ*123'
```

depends on the collating sequence used in a particular computer.

The variation in collating sequences may cause the same program to execute differently on one machine than it does on another. This difficulty can be circumvented, however, by using the special functions LLT, LLE, LGT, and LGE. The LLT function has the form

LLT(*string1, string2*)

where *string1* and *string2* are character expressions. The value of this function is true if *string1* precedes *string2* using the collating sequence *determined by ASCII encoding* and is false otherwise. Thus,

```
LLT('1', 'A')
```

is true, *regardless* of which collating sequence is in effect.

Similarly,

```
LLE(string1, string2)
```

is true if *string1* precedes or is equal to *string2* using the ASCII collating sequence;

```
LGT(string1, string2)
```

is true if *string1* follows *string2*; and

```
LGE(string1, string2)
```

is true if *string1* follows or is equal to *string2* using the ASCII collating sequence.

The position of a character in the collating sequence can be obtained by using the ICHAR function of the form

```
ICHAR(char)
```

where *char* is an expression whose value is a single character. The value of this function is the integer that corresponds to the character's position in the computer's collating sequence.

The inverse function CHAR has the form

```
CHAR(integer)
```

and produces a single character whose position in the collating sequence is the specified integer, provided, of course, that this integer is in the appropriate range. Thus, if X has a single character as its value,

```
CHAR(ICHAR(X))
```

is equal to X, and if K is an integer variable whose value is in the appropriate range,

```
ICHAR(CHAR(K))
```

is equal to K.

The program in Figure 10.2 uses these character functions to implement a simple cryptographic scheme for coding a message as a scrambled sequence of characters, known as a *cryptogram*. It encodes a message by converting each character to its numeric representation (ASCII or EBCDIC) using the function ICHAR and then adding a key value. Because this sum may be outside the range of legal numeric codes (usually 0–255), the MOD function is used to obtain a legal value, which is then converted to a character using the CHAR function.

```
      PROGRAM CODER
***************************************************************************
* This program scrambles a message by converting each character of the *
* message to its numeric code, adding an integer to this code, and     *
* then converting the resulting number back to a character.  Variables *
* used are the following:                                              *
*     MESS    : message to be scrambled                                *
*     KEY     : integer to be added in scrambling the message          *
*     SYMBOL  : an individual character of the message                 *
*     CODE    : numeric code for SYMBOL                                *
*     I       : counter                                                *
***************************************************************************

      CHARACTER*80 MESS, SYMBOL*1
      INTEGER KEY, I, CODE

      PRINT *, 'ENTER MESSAGE (END WITH #):'
      READ '(A)', MESS
      PRINT *, 'ENTER KEY:'
      READ *, KEY
      I = 1
      SYMBOL = MESS(1:1)

* While not end of string do

10    IF (I .LT. LEN(MESS) .AND. SYMBOL .NE. '#') THEN
          CODE = MOD(ICHAR(SYMBOL) + KEY, 256)
          MESS(I:I) = CHAR(CODE)
          I = I + 1
          SYMBOL = MESS(I:I)
          GO TO 10
      END IF

      PRINT *, 'CODED MESSAGE:'
      PRINT *, MESS
      END
```

Sample run (assuming ASCII):

```
ENTER MESSAGE (END WITH #):
THE REDCOATS ARE COMING#
ENTER KEY:
5
CODED MESSAGE:
YMJ%WJIHTFYX%FWJ%HTRNSL#
```

Figure 10.2

10.4. Examples: Plotting Graphs, Density Plots, and Contour Maps

EXAMPLE 1: Plotting Graphs. The number and quality of software packages and even hand-held calculators that can be used to generate high-resolution graphs of functions is increasing rapidly. For example, Figure 10.3(a)

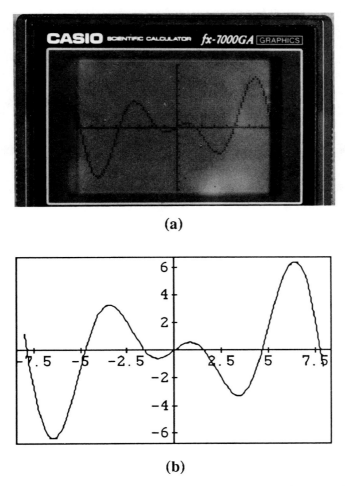

(a)

(b)

Figure 10.3 (a) Plot of $y = x * \cos(x)$ on a CASIO fx-7000GA calculator (Photo by Randal Nyhof, Nyhof School Pictures). (b) Plot of $y = x * \cos(x)$ produced by Mathematica.

shows the graph of $y = x * \cos(x)$ for $-8 \leq x \leq 8$ as plotted on a CASIO fx-7000GA calculator, and Figure 10.3(b) shows the same graph as produced by the powerful software package Mathematica™. In this section, we consider this problem of plotting the graph of a function $y = f(x)$.

The window containing each of the plots shown in Figure 10.3 is simply a two-dimensional array of points (called *pixels*) on the screen, some of which (those corresponding to points on the graph of the function) are "on" (black) and the rest of which are "off" (white). Figure 10.4 shows an enlarged view of the portion of the graphics window near the origin in Figure 10.3; the grid structure of this part of the window is evident.

The subroutine PLOT in the program of Figure 10.5 uses this same approach to plot the graph of a function defined by a function subprogram F and passed as an argument to PLOT. It uses a HORIZ × VERT character array WINDOW, each element of which is a single character corresponding to a

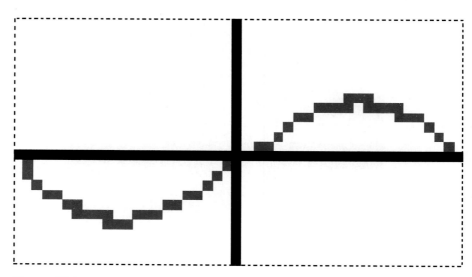

Figure 10.4

point in a graphics window. The user enters values for XMIN and XMAX, the minimum and maximum X values, and for YMIN and YMAX, the minimum and maximum Y values. The rows of the two-dimensional array WINDOW correspond to X values ranging from XMIN to XMAX in increments of DELX = (XMAX − XMIN) / HORIZ, and the columns correspond to Y values ranging from YMIN to YMAX in steps of DELY = (YMAX − YMIN) / VERT. For each X value, the Y value nearest the actual function value Y = F(X) is determined, and the point WINDOW(X, Y) is set to some plotting character such as '*' (''on''); all other elements of WINDOW are blank (''off'').

```
      PROGRAM GRAPH
*******************************************************************
* Program to plot the graph of a function Y = F(X).  F is defined by a  *
* function subprogram and passed to subroutine PLOT.  Identifiers  *
* used are:                                                        *
*      F          : function to be plotted                         *
*      XMIN, XMAX : minimum and maximum X values                   *
*      YMIN, YMAX : minimum and maximum Y values                   *
*******************************************************************
      REAL F, XMIN, XMAX, YMIN, YMAX
      EXTERNAL F

      PRINT *, 'ENTER MINIMUM AND MAXIMUM X VALUES AND'
      PRINT *, 'THE MINIMUM AND MAXIMUM Y VALUES:'
      READ *, XMIN, XMAX, YMIN, YMAX
      CALL PLOT(F, XMIN, XMAX, YMIN, YMAX)

      END
```

Figure 10.5

Figure 10.5 (cont.)

```
**F****************************************************************
*                 Function whose graph is to be plotted          *
******************************************************************

        FUNCTION F(X)

        REAL X, F

        F = X * COS(X)
        END


**PLOT*************************************************************
* Subroutine to plot the graph of a function Y = F(X) for X ranging from *
* XMIN to XMAX; Y is allowed to range from YMIN to YMAX.  Local   *
* identifiers used are:                                           *
*      FNAME  : name of file containing the output                *
*      HLIMIT,                                                    *
*      VLIMIT : parameters:  limits on the size of the plotting WINDOW  *
*      WINDOW : two-dimensional character array -- the graphics window  *
*      SYMBOL : plotting character -- represents a point on the graph   *
*      DELX   : X increment                                       *
*      DELY   : Y increment                                       *
*      X, Y   : a point on the graph                              *
*      XLOC,                                                      *
*      YLOC   : location of a point in the window                 *
*      COUNT  : counts units on Y axis for labeling purposes      *
******************************************************************

        SUBROUTINE PLOT(F, XMIN, XMAX, YMIN, YMAX)

        REAL F, XMIN, XMAX, YMIN, YMAX, DELX, DELY, X, Y
        INTEGER HLIMIT, VLIMIT, XLOC, YLOC, COUNT
        PARAMETER (HLIMIT = 70, VLIMIT = 20)
        CHARACTER*1 WINDOW(0: HLIMIT, 0:VLIMIT), SYMBOL, FNAME*20
        PARAMETER (SYMBOL = '*')

        PRINT *, 'ENTER NAME OF FILE TO CONTAIN THE GRAPH'
        READ '(A)', FNAME
        OPEN (UNIT = 20, FILE = FNAME, STATUS = 'NEW')

        DELX = (XMAX - XMIN) / REAL(HLIMIT)
        DELY = (YMAX - YMIN) / REAL(VLIMIT)

        DO 20 YLOC = 0, VLIMIT
            DO 10 XLOC = 0, HLIMIT
                WINDOW(XLOC, YLOC) = ' '
10          CONTINUE
20      CONTINUE
```

Figure 10.5 (cont.)

```
* Turn on points in WINDOW corresponding to points on graph.

      X = XMIN
      DO 30 XLOC = 0, HLIMIT
          Y = F(X)
          IF (Y .GE. YMIN  .AND.  Y .LE. YMAX) THEN
              YLOC = NINT((Y - YMIN)/ DELY)
              WINDOW(XLOC, YLOC) = SYMBOL
          END IF
          X = X + DELX
30    CONTINUE

* Draw the WINDOW in the file together with labeled Y axis.

      Y = YMAX
      COUNT = 5 * (VLIMIT / 5)
      DO 40 YLOC = VLIMIT, 0, -1
          IF (MOD(COUNT, 5) .EQ. 0) THEN
              WRITE(20, 100) Y, (WINDOW(XLOC,YLOC), XLOC = 0, HLIMIT)
100           FORMAT(1X, F8.2, ':', 200A)
          ELSE
              WRITE(20, 101) (WINDOW(XLOC,YLOC), XLOC = 0, HLIMIT)
101           FORMAT(9X, ':', 200A)
          END IF
          COUNT = COUNT - 1
          Y = Y - DELY
40    CONTINUE

* Draw a labeled X axis in the file.

      WRITE (20, 102), ('.', XLOC = 0, HLIMIT)
102   FORMAT(9X, 200A)
      WRITE(20, 103) (XMIN + XLOC*DELX, XLOC = 0, HLIMIT, 10)
103   FORMAT(3X, 50F10.3)

      END
```

A sample run with XMIN $= -8.0$, XMAX $= 8.0$, YMIN $= -7.0$, and YMAX $= 7.0$ produced the output shown in Figure 10.6. Using twice as many rows and columns (VLIMIT $= 40$ and HLIMIT $= 140$) to increase the resolution resulted in the plot shown in Figure 10.7. Modifying the program in Figure 10.5 to plot graphs of parameteric equations of the form

$$X = X(T), \quad Y = Y(T), \quad A \leq T \leq B$$

is straightforward and is left as an exercise.

EXAMPLE 2: Density Plots and Contour Maps. In Example 1 we showed how a function $y = f(x)$ of a single variable x can be plotted. Graphs of functions $z = f(x, y)$ of two variables x and y are surfaces in three dimensions and are considerably more difficult to display on a two-dimensional screen.

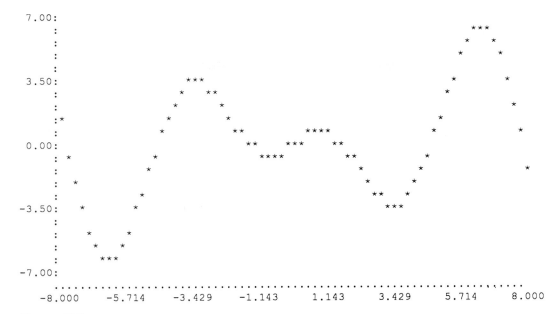

Figure 10.6

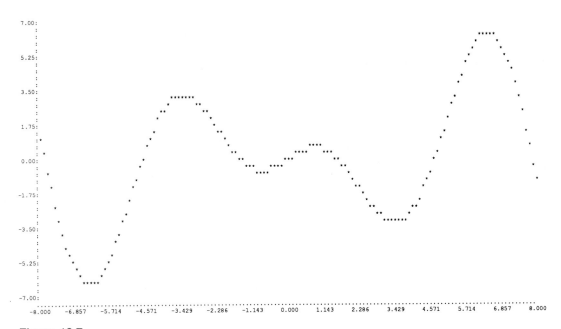

Figure 10.7

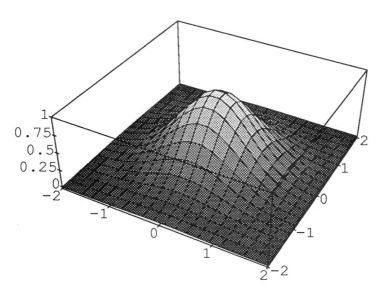

Figure 10.8

Some software packages are able to generate good two-dimensional representations of many three-dimensional surfaces. For example, Figure 10.8 shows a graph produced by Mathematica of the surface defined by the function

$$z = e^{-(x^2 + y^2)}$$

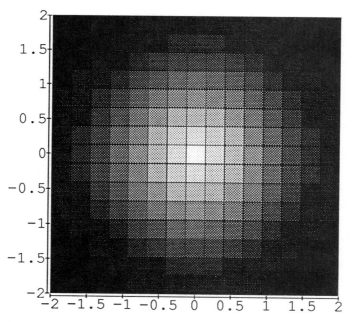

Figure 10.9

Note that in this representation, shading is used to represent the height of the function, with lighter shades for larger values and darker shades for smaller values. This shading, together with the curved grid lines and the enclosing box produces a visual illusion of a three-dimensional surface. Another representation of a surface that also uses shading but not perspective is a **density plot** obtained by projecting a representation like that in Figure 10.8 onto a plane. Figure 10.9 shows the density plot generated by Mathematica for this surface. The various densities of gray again indicate different heights of the function.

The program in Figure 10.10 produces a density plot for a function F. It uses a character array WINDOW of NUMLEV = 10 different characters, with WINDOW(X, Y) representing the height of the function at point (X, Y). The order of the characters in the DATA statement corresponds to increasing Z values, beginning with ZMIN, the minimum Z value. The sample run shows the output produced for the function $f(x, y) = e^{-(x^2 + y^2)}$ with ZMIN = 0 and ZMAX = 1, using the characters '0', '1', . . . , '9'.

```
      PROGRAM DENSTY
*********************************************************************
* Program to produce a density plot of a function Y = F(X).  F is   *
* defined by a function subprogram and is passed to subroutine DNPLOT. *
* Identifiers used are:                                             *
*      F           : function to be plotted                         *
*      XMIN, XMAX : minimum and maximum X values                    *
*      YMIN, YMAX : minimum and maximum Y values                    *
*      ZMIN, ZMAX : minimum and maximum Z values                    *
*********************************************************************

      REAL F, XMIN, XMAX, YMIN, YMAX, ZMIN, ZMAX
      EXTERNAL F

      PRINT *, 'ENTER MINIMUM AND MAXIMUM X VALUES, THEN Y VALUES'
      READ *, XMIN, XMAX, YMIN, YMAX
      PRINT *, 'ENTER MINIMUM AND MAXIMUM VALUES OF FUNCTION'
      READ *, ZMIN, ZMAX
      CALL DNPLOT(F, XMIN, XMAX, YMIN, YMAX, ZMIN, ZMAX)

      END

**F****************************************************************
*                Function whose graph is to be plotted.           *
*****************************************************************

      FUNCTION F(X,Y)

      REAL F, X, Y

      F = EXP(-(X**2 + Y**2))
      END
```

Figure 10.10

Figure 10.10 (cont.)

```
**DNPLOT********************************************************************
* Subroutine to generate a density plot of a function Z = F(X, Y) for    *
* X ranging from XMIN to XMAX and Y ranging from YMIN to YMAX; Z is       *
* allowed to range from ZMIN to ZMAX.  Local identifiers used are:        *
*      FNAME  : name of file containing the output                        *
*      HLIMIT,                                                            *
*      VLIMIT : parameters:  limits on the size of the plotting WINDOW    *
*      WINDOW : two-dimensional character array -- the graphics window    *
*      LGRAY  : parameter: largest index in array GRAY                    *
*      GRAY   : array of NGRAYS symbols representing shades of gray       *
*      DELX   : X increment                                               *
*      DELY   : Y increment                                               *
*      DELZ   : Z increment                                               *
*      X, Y   : a point on the graph                                      *
*      XLOC,                                                              *
*      YLOC   : location of a point in the window                         *
*      ZSHADE : shade of gray used to represent height Z                  *
****************************************************************************


      SUBROUTINE DNPLOT (F, XMIN, XMAX, YMIN, YMAX,ZMIN, ZMAX)

      REAL F, XMIN, XMAX, YMIN, YMAX, ZMIN, ZMAX, DELX, DELY, DELZ
      INTEGER HLIMIT, VLIMIT, XLOC, YLOC, LGRAY, ZSHADE
      PARAMETER (HLIMIT = 75, VLIMIT = 45, LGRAY = 9)
      CHARACTER*1 WINDOW(0: HLIMIT, 0:VLIMIT), GRAY(0:LGRAY), FNAME*20

*     Initialize array of characters to indicate "densities of gray"
*     that in turn represent heights of function F

      DATA GRAY /'0','1','2','3','4','5','6','7','8','9'/


      PRINT *, 'ENTER NAME OF FILE TO CONTAIN THE DENSITY PLOT'
      READ '(A)', FNAME
      OPEN (UNIT = 20, FILE = FNAME, STATUS = 'NEW')

      DELX = (XMAX - XMIN) / REAL(HLIMIT)
      DELY = (YMAX - YMIN) / REAL(VLIMIT)
      DELZ = (ZMAX - ZMIN) / REAL(LGRAY)
```

Figure 10.10 (cont.)

```
*  "Shade" each element of WINDOW with appropriate gray

        Y = YMIN
        DO 20 YLOC = 0, VLIMIT
            X = XMIN
            DO 10 XLOC = 0, HLIMIT
                Z = F(X, Y)

*               Find gray shade corresponding to Z value

                IF (Z .GE. ZMAX) THEN
                    ZSHADE = NGRAYS
                ELSE
                    ZSHADE = NINT((Z - ZMIN) / DELZ)
                END IF

                WINDOW(XLOC, YLOC) = GRAY(ZSHADE)
                X = X + DELX
10          CONTINUE

            Y = Y + DELY
20      CONTINUE

*  Draw the WINDOW in the file

        DO 30 YLOC = VLIMIT, 0, -1
            WRITE(20, *)(WINDOW(XLOC,YLOC), XLOC = 0, HLIMIT)
30      CONTINUE

        END
```

Sample run:

```
ENTER MINIMUM AND MAXIMUM X VALUES, THEN Y VALUES
-2 2 -2 2
ENTER MINIMUM AND MAXIMUM VALUES OF FUNCTION
0 1
ENTER NAME OF FILE TO CONTAIN THE DENSITY PLOT
DENSEPLOT
```

Figure 10.10 (cont.)

Listing of DENSEPLOT (reduced:)

```
0000000000000000000000000000000000000000000000000000000000000000000000000000
0000000000000000000000000000000000000000000000000000000000000000000000000000
0000000000000000000000000000000000000000000000000000000000000000000000000000
000000000000000000000000000111111111111111111111000000000000000000000000000
00000000000000000000000001111111111111111111111111111000000000000000000000000
00000000000000000000001111111111111111111111111111111111000000000000000000000
00000000000000000111111111111111222222222222211111111111111111000000000000000
000000000000000011111111111112222222222222222222222211111111111110000000000000
00000000000000111111111112222222222333333333332222222222211111111111000000000000
0000000000000111111111122222222233333333333333333333322222222221111111111000000000000
0000000000011111111222222333333344444444444444433333332222221111111111100000000000
0000000000111111112222233333444444555555554444443333332222211111111100000000000
000000000111111112222333344444555555556665555555544444333322221111111000000000
00000000011111112222333344455556666666666666655554444333322221111111110000000
0000000011111112222333444555666677777777776666555444433322221111111100000000
000000011111112222333445556667777788888777776666555444333222211111111000000000
0000000111111122223334455566677788888888888887776665554443332222111111110000000
0000001111111222233344455566677788888999988887776665544433322221111111100000000
00000011111112222333344455566777888889999999998888777665544433322221111111000000
00000011111112222333344455566777888889999999999888877766655444333222211111110000000
00000011111112222333344455566777888889999999998888777665544433322221111111000000
0000001111111222233344455566677788888999988887776665544433322221111111100000000
000000011111112222333445556667777788888777776666555444333222211111111000000000
0000000111111122223334455566677777777777766665555444433322221111111100000000
00000000111111122223334445556666666666666666655554444333322221111111110000000
000000000111111112222333344444555555556665555555544444333322221111111000000000
0000000000111111112222233333444444555555554444443333332222211111111100000000000
0000000000011111111222222333333344444444444444433333332222221111111111100000000000
0000000000000111111111122222222233333333333333333333322222222221111111111000000000000
00000000000000111111111112222222222333333333332222222222211111111111000000000000
000000000000000011111111111112222222222222222222222211111111111110000000000000
000000000000000000000000000111111111111111222222222222211111111111111111000000000000
00000000000000000000000001111111111111111111111111111000000000000000000000000
00000000000000000000000000001111111111111111111111111100000000000000000000000
0000000000000000000000000000000000000000000000000000000000000000000000000000
0000000000000000000000000000000000000000000000000000000000000000000000000000
0000000000000000000000000000000000000000000000000000000000000000000000000000
0000000000000000000000000000000000000000000000000000000000000000000000000000
```

Characters other than '0', '1', . . . , '9' can be used simply by changing the DATA statement in this program. For example, if "gray-scale characters" were available, a density plot similar to that in Figure 10.9 could be generated. Figure 10.11 shows the result obtained when ordinary characters such as '#', '@', and '+' are used to achieve various densities and the output is reduced still more than that in Figure 10.10.

Another common two-dimensional representation of a three-dimensional surface $z = f(x, y)$ is obtained by displaying its **level curves** or **contour maps.** A level curve consists of all points (x, y) where the function has a particular constant value. For example, if $f(x, y)$ represents the temperature at point (x, y), the level curve $f(x, y) = 30$ is an isothermal curve consisting of all points where the temperature is 30.

The level curves for $f(x, y) = e^{-(x^2+y^2)}$ can be seen in the density plots produced by the program in Figure 10.10 as the circles that separate one level from another. Figure 10.12 shows the level curves for this function as produced

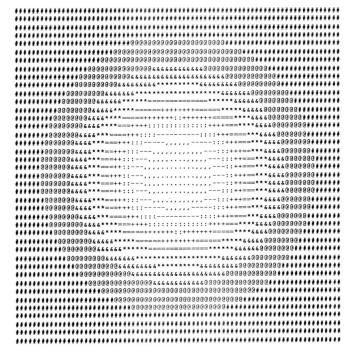

Figure 10.11

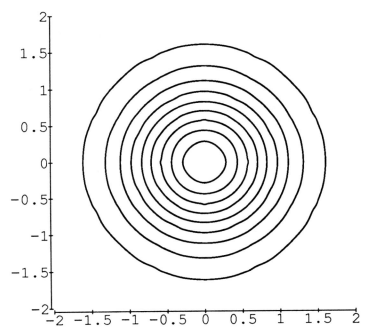

Figure 10.12

by Mathematica. The largest circle is the level curve $e^{-(x^2+y^2)} = 0.1$, or equivalently $x^2 + y^2 = |\ln (0.1)|$; the smallest circle is the level curve $e^{-(x^2+y^2)} = 0.9$, which can also be written $x^2 + y^2 = |\ln (0.9)|$; the other circles are level curves corresponding to 0.8, 0.7, . . . , 0.2.

The ideas in this example can be modified to display an image that is represented in digitized form and to enhance this image. This digitized representation might be a table of light intensities transmitted from a remote sensor such as a television camera in a satellite. This problem of visual image processing and enhancement is described in the exercises.

10.5 Examples: Lexical Analysis; Reverse Polish Notation

EXAMPLE 1: Lexical Analysis. In our discussion of system software in Chapter 1, we mentioned compilers, which are programs whose function is to translate a source program written in some high-level language such as FORTRAN into an object program written in machine code. This object program is then executed by the computer.

The basic phases of the compiler are summarized in the following diagram:

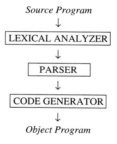

Source Program
↓
LEXICAL ANALYZER
↓
PARSER
↓
CODE GENERATOR
↓
Object Program

The input to a compiler is a stream of characters that comprise the source program. Before the translation can actually be carried out, this stream of characters must be broken up into meaningful groups, such as identifiers, key words, constants, and operators. For example, for the assignment statement

```
ALPHA = 200*BETA + 500
```

or as a "stream" of characters

```
ALPHAƀ=ƀ200*BETAƀ+ƀ500
```

(where ƀ is a blank), the following units must be identified:

ALPHA	---------	identifier
=	---------	assignment operator
200	---------	integer constant
*	---------	arithmetic operator
BETA	---------	identifier
+	---------	arithmetic operator
500	---------	integer constant

These units are called **tokens,** and the part of the compiler that recognizes these tokens is called the **lexical analyzer.**

It is the task of the **parser** to group these tokens together to form the basic **syntactic structures** of the language as determined by the syntax rules. For example, it must recognize that the three consecutive tokens

$$\begin{array}{ccc} \text{integer-constant} & \text{arithmetic-operator} & \text{identifier} \\ \downarrow & \downarrow & \downarrow \\ 200 & * & \text{BETA} \end{array}$$

can be grouped together to form a valid arithmetic expression, that

$$\begin{array}{ccc} \text{arithmetic-expression} & \text{arithmetic-operator} & \text{integer-constant} \\ \downarrow & \downarrow \\ & + & 500 \end{array}$$

constitute a valid arithmetic expression, and then that

$$\begin{array}{ccc} \text{identifier} & \text{assignment-operator} & \text{arithmetic-expression} \\ \downarrow & \downarrow \\ \text{ALPHA} & = \end{array}$$

form a valid assignment statement. The complete **parse tree** constructed during compilation of the preceding statement is

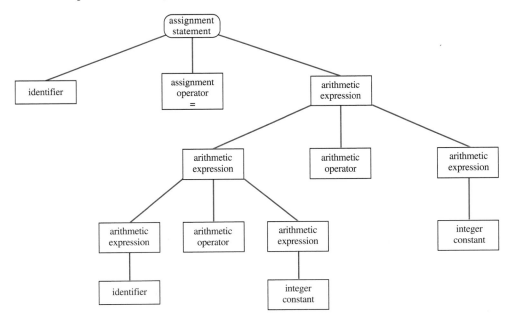

Later phases of the compiling process generate the machine code for this assignment statement.

When designing a lexical analyzer to recognize various tokens, one can begin by representing each token by a **finite automaton** (also called a **finite state machine**), which has a finite number of states, and there are transitions from one state to another depending on what the next input symbol is. If the machine is in one of certain states called *accepting states* after an input string is processed, then that string is said to be *recognized* or *accepted* by the automaton. For example, a finite automaton to recognize bit strings that contain 01 is

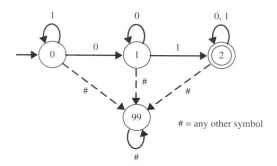

Here, the arrow pointing to state 0 indicates that this is the initial state. The automaton begins processing input symbols in this state and makes transitions from one state to another or remains in the current state as specified by the labels on the arrows.

To illustrate, consider the input string 0011. The finite automaton begins in state 0, and because the first input symbol is 0, it transfers to state 1. Since the next input symbol is a 0, the automaton remains in state 1. However, the third symbol is a 1, which causes a transition to state 2. The final symbol is a 1 and causes no state change. The end of the input string has now been reached, and because the finite automaton is in an accept state as indicated by the double circle, it has accepted the string 0011. It is easy to see that any bit string containing 01 will be processed in a similar manner and lead to the accept state and that only such strings will cause the automaton to terminate in state 2. For example, the string 11000 is not accepted, because the automaton will be in state 1 after processing this string, and state 1 is not an accept state. Neither is the bit string 100201 accepted since the "illegal" symbol 2 causes a transition from state 1 to state 99, which is not an accept state.

State 99 is a "reject" or "dead" state: Once it is entered, it is never exited. The transitions to this state are shown as dashed lines since the existence of such a state is usually assumed and transitions to it are not drawn in the diagram; for any state and any input symbol for which no transition is specified, it is assumed that the transition is to such a reject state. Thus, the finite automaton is usually drawn as

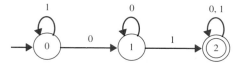

As another example, consider the following finite automaton:

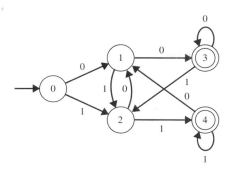

After some analysis and experimentation it should become clear that to terminate processing in one of the accept states 3 or 4, the last two input symbols must both be 0s or both be 1s. This finite automaton thus recognizes bit strings ending in 00 or 11.

To show how a finite automaton can be used to advantage in the design of lexical analyzers, we consider the problem of recognizing FORTRAN integer constants. A finite automaton that does this is

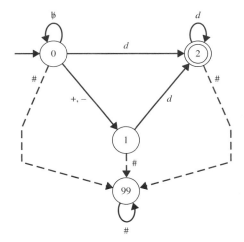

where d denotes one of the digits 0, 1, . . . , 9; ♭ denotes a blank; and state 2 is the only accepting state. The machine begins in state 0, and if the first input symbol is a blank, it stays in state 0, ''gobbling up'' leading blanks; if it is a + or −, it goes to state 1; if it is a digit, it goes to state 2; otherwise, the input character is not valid, and thus the string does not represent a valid integer.

Writing program statements corresponding to such a finite automaton is then straightforward. The program in Figure 10.13 illustrates this. It reads a string of characters and determines whether it represents a valid FORTRAN integer. The part of the program highlighted in color implements the preceding finite automaton.

```
       PROGRAM LEX
*********************************************************************
* This program implements a simple lexical analyzer for FORTRAN    *
* integer constants.  A finite automaton that recognizes integer   *
* constants was used in designing the program.  Identifiers used:  *
*      DEAD   : dead state                                         *
*      STATE  : current state                                      *
*      I      : index                                             *
*      STRING : input string to be checked                        *
*      SYMBOL : a character in STRING                             *
*      MARK   : end-of-string mark                               *
*      RESPON : user response                                     *
*********************************************************************

       INTEGER DEAD
       PARAMETER (DEAD = 99)
       INTEGER STATE, I
       CHARACTER*1 SYMBOL, MARK, RESPON, STRING*80
       DATA MARK /';'/

* Repeat the following until no more strings to check

10     CONTINUE
       PRINT *, 'Enter the string to be checked (end with ', MARK, ')'
       READ '(A)', STRING
       I = 1

*      Begin in initial state
       STATE = 0

*      While Ith symbol in STRING is not the end-of-line mark do
20     IF (STRING(I:I) .NE. MARK) THEN

          SYMBOL = STRING(I:I)
          IF (STATE .EQ. 0) THEN
             IF (SYMBOL .EQ. ' ') THEN
                STATE = 0
             ELSE IF (SYMBOL .EQ. '+' .OR. SYMBOL .EQ. '-') THEN
                STATE = 1
             ELSE IF (SYMBOL .GE. '0' .AND. SYMBOL .LE. '9') THEN
                STATE = 2
             ELSE
                STATE = DEAD
             END IF

          ELSE IF (STATE .EQ. 1 .OR. STATE .EQ. 2) THEN
             IF (SYMBOL .GE. '0' .AND. SYMBOL .LE. '9') THEN
                STATE = 2
             ELSE
                STATE = DEAD
             END IF
          END IF

          I = I + 1
       GO TO 20
       END IF
```

Figure 10.13

Figure 10.13 (cont.)

```
      IF (STATE .EQ. 2) THEN
          PRINT *, 'VALID INTEGER'
      ELSE
          PRINT *, 'NOT A VALID INTEGER'
      END IF

      PRINT *
      PRINT *, 'MORE DATA (Y OR N)'
      READ '(A)', RESPON
   IF (RESPON .EQ. 'Y') GO TO 10

      END
```

Sample run:

```
Enter the string to be checked (end with ;)
1234;
VALID INTEGER

MORE DATA (Y OR N)
Y
Enter the string to be checked (end with ;)
+9999;
VALID INTEGER

MORE DATA (Y OR N)
Y
Enter the string to be checked (end with ;)
-1;
VALID INTEGER

MORE DATA (Y OR N)
Y
Enter the string to be checked (end with ;)
123+4;
NOT A VALID INTEGER

MORE DATA (Y OR N)
Y
Enter the string to be checked (end with ;)
ABCDEF;
NOT A VALID INTEGER

MORE DATA (Y OR N)
N
```

EXAMPLE 2: Reverse Polish Notation. The task of a compiler is to generate the machine language instructions required to carry out the instructions of the source program written in a high-level language (see Section 1.3). One part of this task is to generate the machine instructions for evaluating arithmetic expressions like that in the assignment statement

```
      X = A * B + C
```

The compiler must generate machine instructions to

1. Retrieve the value of A from the memory location where it is stored and load it into the accumulating register.
2. Retrieve the value of B and multiply the value in the accumulating register by this value.
3. Retrieve the value of C and add it to the value in the accumulating register.

Arithmetic expressions are ordinarily written using *infix* notation like the preceding, in which the symbol for each binary operation is placed between the operands. In many compilers, the first step in evaluating such infix expressions is to transform them into *postfix* notation in which the operation symbol follows the operands. Then machine instructions are generated to evaluate these postfix expressions. Likewise, calculators commonly evaluate arithmetic expressions using postfix notation. The reasons for this are that conversion from infix to postfix is straightforward and that postfix expressions are in general easier to evaluate mechanically than are infix expressions.

When infix notation is used for arithmetic expressions, parentheses are often needed to indicate the order in which the operations are to be carried out. For example, parentheses are placed in the expression $2 * (3 + 4)$ to indicate that the addition is to be performed before the multiplication. If the parentheses were omitted, giving $2 * 3 + 4$, the standard priority rules would dictate that the multiplication is to be performed before the addition.

In the early 1950s, the Polish logician Jan Lukasiewicz observed that parentheses are not necessary in postfix notation, also called **Reverse Polish Notation (RPN).** For example, the infix expression

$$2 * (3 + 4)$$

can be written in RPN as

$$2 \ 3 \ 4 + *$$

To demonstrate how such RPN expressions are evaluated, consider

$$1 \ 5 + 8 \ 4 \ 1 - - *$$

which corresponds to the infix expression $(1 + 5) * (8 - (4 - 1))$. This expression is scanned from left to right until an operator is found. At that point, the last two preceding operands are combined, using this operator. In our example, the first operator encountered is $+$, and its operands are 1 and 5, as indicated by the underline in the following:

$$\underline{1 \ 5} + 8 \ 4 \ 1 - - *$$

Replacing this subexpression with its value 6 gives the reduced RPN expression

$$6 \ 8 \ 4 \ 1 - - *$$

Resuming the left-to-right scan, we next encounter the operator $-$ and determine its two operands:

$$6 \ 8 \ \underline{4 \ 1 \ -} - *$$

Applying this operator then yields

$$6 \ 8 \ 3 - *$$

The next operator encountered is another − and its two operands are 8 and 3:

$$6 \underline{\ 8\ 3\ -\ } *$$

Evaluating this difference gives

$$6\ 5\ *$$

The final operator is *,

$$\underline{6\ 5\ *}$$

and the value 30 is obtained for this expression.

This method of evaluating an RPN expression requires that the operands be stored until an operator is encountered in the left-to-right scan. At this point, the last two operands must be retrieved and combined using this operation. Thus, a **Last-In-First-Out (LIFO)** data structure called a *stack*, should be used to store the operands.

A **stack** (or **push-down stack**) is a list in which elements may be inserted or deleted at only one end of the list, called the **top** of the stack. This structure is so named because it functions in the same manner as does a spring-loaded stack of plates or trays used in a cafeteria. Plates are added to the stack by pushing them onto the top of the stack. When a plate is removed from the top of the stack, the spring causes the next plate to pop up. For this reason, the insertion and deletion operations for a stack are commonly called *push* and *pop*, respectively.

The following algorithm for evaluating an RPN expression uses a stack to store the operands in the expression. When an operator is encountered, the top two values are popped from the stack, the operator is applied to them, and the result is pushed back onto the stack.

ALGORITHM TO EVALUATE RPN EXPRESSIONS

* Algorithm to evaluate an expression given in RPN. A stack is   *
* used to store the operands.   *

1. Initialize an empty stack.
2. Repeat the following until the end of the expression is encountered:
   a. Get the next token (constant, variable, arithmetic operator) in the RPN expression.
   b. If the token is an operand, push it onto the stack. If it is an operator, then do the following:
      (i) Pop the top two values from the stack. (If the stack does not contain two items, an error due to a malformed RPN expression has occurred, and evaluation is terminated.)
      (ii) Apply the operator to these two values.
      (iii) Push the resulting value back onto the stack.
3. When the end of the expression is encountered, its value is on top of the stack (and in fact must be the only value in the stack).

Figure 10.14 shows the application of this algorithm to the RPN expression:

$$2\ 4\ *\ 9\ 5\ +\ -$$

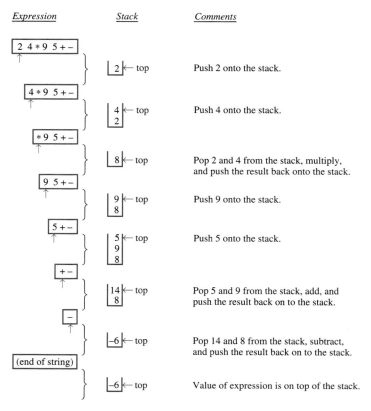

Figure 10.14 Evaluation of the RPN expression 2 4 * 9 5 + −.

The up arrow (↑) indicates the current token.

To illustrate how a stack is also used in the conversion from infix to RPN, consider the infix expression

$$7 + 2 * 3$$

In a left-to-right scan of this expression, 7 is encountered first and may be immediately displayed. Next, the operator + is encountered, but since its right operand has not yet been displayed, it must be stored and thus is pushed onto a stack of operators:

Output	Stack
7	+

Next, the operand 2 is encountered and displayed. At this point, it must be determined whether 2 is the right operand for the preceding operator + or the left operand for the next operator, which is done by comparing the operator + on the top of the stack with the next operator *. Because * has a higher priority than +, the preceding operand 2 that was displayed is the left operand for *, and so we push * onto the stack and search for its right operand:

Output	Stack
7 2	* +

The operand 3 is encountered next and displayed. Because the end of the expression has now been reached, the right operand for the operator * on the top of the stack has been found, so * can now be popped and displayed:

Output	*Stack*
7 2 3 *	$\boxed{+}$

The end of the expression also signals that the right operand for the remaining operator + in the stack has been found, so it too can be popped and displayed, yielding the RPN expression

$$7\ 2\ 3 * +$$

Parentheses within infix expressions present no real difficulties. A left parenthesis indicates the beginning of a subexpression, and when encountered, it is pushed onto the stack. When a right parenthesis is encountered, operators are popped from the stack until the matching left parenthesis rises to the top. At this point, the subexpression originally enclosed by the parentheses has been converted to RPN, and so the parentheses may be discarded, and the conversion continues. All of this is contained in the following algorithm:

ALGORITHM TO CONVERT INFIX EXPRESSION TO RPN

* Algorithm to convert an infix expression to RPN. A stack is used to *
* store the operands.   *

1. Initialize an empty stack.
2. Repeat the following until the end of the infix expression is reached:
   a. Get the next input token (constant, variable, arithmetic operator, left parenthesis, right parenthesis) in the infix expression.
   b. If the token is
      - (i) a left parenthesis: Push it onto the stack.
      - (ii) an operand: Display it.
      - (iii) an operator: If the stack is empty or the operator has a higher priority than the top stack element, push the operator onto the stack.

        Otherwise, pop an operator from the stack and display it; then repeat the comparison of the current token with the new top stack item.

        Note: A left parenthesis in the stack is assumed to have a lower priority than that of operators.

      - (iv) a right parenthesis: Pop and display stack elements until a left parenthesis is on top of the stack. Pop it also, but do not display it.
3. When the end of the infix expression is reached, pop and display stack items until the stack is empty.

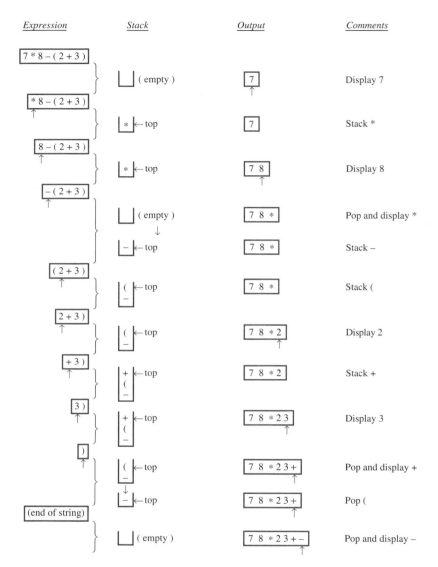

Figure 10.15 Converting infix expression 7 ∗ 8 − (2 + 3) to RPN.

Figure 10.15 illustrates this algorithm for the infix expression

$$7 * 8 - (2 + 3)$$

An up-arrow (↑) has been used to indicate the current input symbol and the symbol displayed by the algorithm. The program in Figure 10.16 implements this algorithm.

```
      PROGRAM POLISH
**MAIN***********************************************************
* Program to read an infix expression, and then call subroutine GENRPN *
* to generate the corresponding expression Reverse Polish Notation.     *
* Identifiers used are:                                                 *
*     RESPON : user response                                            *
*     EXPR   : infix expression                                         *
*     MARK   : end-of-expression marker                                 *
*     RPN    : RPN expression                                           *
*     ERROR  : signals an error in EXPR                                 *
*****************************************************************

      CHARACTER*80, EXPR, RPN, MARK*1, RESPON*1
      LOGICAL ERROR
      DATA MARK /';'/

* Repeat the following until RESPON = 'N'

10    CONTINUE
      PRINT *, 'ENTER INFIX EXPRESSION (END WITH ', MARK, ')'
      READ '(A)', EXPR
      CALL GENRPN(EXPR, MARK, RPN, ERROR)
      IF (.NOT. ERROR) THEN
           PRINT *, 'RPN EXPRESSION IS '
           PRINT *, RPN
      END IF
      PRINT *
      PRINT *, 'MORE (Y OR N)'
      READ '(A)', RESPON
   IF (RESPON .NE. 'N') GO TO 10

      END

**GENRPN*********************************************************
* Subroutine to convert infix expression EXPR to Reverse Polish        *
* Notation.  MARK marks the end of EXPR.  ERROR is returned as true if *
* an error is detected in EXPR.  Other identifiers used are:           *
*     STKLIM : parameter = limit on stack size                         *
*     STACK  : character array used as a stack                         *
*     TOP    : pointer to top of stack                                 *
*     SYMBOL : a symbol in expression EXPR                             *
*     I, R   : indices                                                 *
* Subprograms ISOPER and OPERAT are used to process operators, IDENT   *
* for identifiers and RPAREN for right parentheses.  The basic stack   *
* operations are implemented by subprograms CREATE, EMPTY, PUSH, and   *
* POP.                                                                 *
*****************************************************************

      SUBROUTINE GENRPN(EXPR, MARK, RPN, ERROR)

      CHARACTER*(*) EXPR, MARK, RPN
      INTEGER STKLIM
      PARAMETER (STKLIM = 80)
      CHARACTER*2, STACK(STKLIM), SYMBOL
      INTEGER TOP, I, R
      LOGICAL ISOPER, ERROR, EMPTY
```

Figure 10.16

Figure 10.16 (cont.)

```
* Initialize an empty stack and blank out RPN

      CALL CREATE(STACK, TOP, STKLIM)
      RPN = ' '
      ERROR = .FALSE.

* Begin the conversion to RPN

      I = 1
      R = 1

* While not end of expression do:

10    IF (EXPR(I:I) .NE. MARK) THEN

*         Skip blanks
20        IF (EXPR(I:I) .EQ. ' ') THEN
             I = I + 1
          GO TO 20
          END IF
          SYMBOL = EXPR(I:I)

          IF ((SYMBOL .GE. 'A') .AND. (SYMBOL .LE. 'Z') .OR.
     +        (SYMBOL .GE. '0') .AND. (SYMBOL .LE. '9')) THEN
*         First letter/digit of identifier/constant

              CALL IDENT(EXPR, I, RPN, R)

          ELSE IF (SYMBOL .EQ. '(') THEN
*         Left parenthesis, push it onto stack

              CALL PUSH(STACK, TOP, STKLIM, SYMBOL)

          ELSE IF (SYMBOL .EQ. ')') THEN
*         Right parenthesis

              CALL RPAREN(STACK, TOP, STKLIM, RPN, R, ERROR)

          ELSE IF (ISOPER(SYMBOL)) THEN
*         Operator

*             Check for exponentiation operator
              IF ((SYMBOL .EQ. '*') .AND.
     +            (EXPR(I+1 : I+1) .EQ. '*')) THEN
                  SYMBOL = '**'
                  I = I + 1
              END IF
              CALL OPERAT(STACK, TOP, STKLIM, SYMBOL, RPN, R)

          ELSE
*             Illegal character -- skip it

              PRINT *, SYMBOL , ' IS ILLEGAL CHARACTER -- IGNORED'

          END IF
          I = I + 1
          SYMBOL = EXPR(I:I)
      GO TO 10
      END IF
```

Figure 10.16 (cont.)

```
* End of expression reached.  If no error detected, pop
* any operands on the stack and put them in RPN

      IF (.NOT. ERROR) THEN
40       IF (.NOT. EMPTY(STACK, TOP, STKLIM)) THEN
             CALL POP(STACK, TOP, STKLIM, SYMBOL)
             R = R + 2
             IF (SYMBOL .EQ. '**') THEN
                 RPN(R-1: R+1) = '** '
                 R = R + 1
             ELSE
                 RPN(R-1:R) = SYMBOL // ' '
             END IF
         GO TO 40
         END IF
      END IF

      END

**RPAREN*****************************************************************
* Subroutine to process a symbol that is a right parenthesis by popping *
* symbols from STACK (max size STKLIM, TOP is top of stack) until the   *
* corresponding left parenthesis appears, adding these symbols to the   *
* RPN expression at position R.  ERROR is returned as true if no left   *
* parenthesis is found.  Local identifiers used are:                    *
*     SYMBOL  : a symbol popped from stack                              *
************************************************************************

      SUBROUTINE RPAREN(STACK, TOP, STKLIM, RPN, R, ERROR)

      INTEGER STKLIM, TOP, R
      CHARACTER*2, STACK(1:STKLIM), SYMBOL, RPN*(*)
      LOGICAL ERROR, EMPTY

*     Repeatedly pop symbols until left parenthesis appears
*     or stack becomes empty.

10    CONTINUE
         IF (EMPTY(STACK, TOP, STKLIM)) THEN
             ERROR = .TRUE.
         ELSE
             CALL POP(STACK, TOP, STKLIM, SYMBOL)
             IF (SYMBOL .NE. '(') THEN
                 R = R + 2
                 IF (SYMBOL .EQ. '**') THEN
                     RPN(R-1: R+1) = '** '
                     R = R + 1
                 ELSE
                     RPN(R-1:R) = SYMBOL // ' '
                 END IF
             END IF
         END IF
      IF (.NOT. ERROR .AND. SYMBOL .NE. '(') GO TO 10

      END
```

Figure 10.16 (cont.)

```
**IDENT*******************************************************************
* Subroutine to copy letters and digits from EXPR, beginning at         *
* position I, into RPN, beginning at position R.  Local variables used:*
*     SYMBOL : a symbol in EXPR                                         *
*     L      : an index used to locate last letter/digit                *
*************************************************************************

      SUBROUTINE IDENT(EXPR, I, RPN, R)

      CHARACTER*(*) EXPR, RPN, SYMBOL*2
      INTEGER I, R, L

      L = I + 1
      SYMBOL = EXPR(L:L)

* While L-th character of EXPR is a letter or digit do:
10    IF ((SYMBOL .GE. 'A') .AND. (SYMBOL .LE. 'Z') .OR.
     +    (SYMBOL .GE. '0') .AND. (SYMBOL .LE. '9')) THEN
         L = L + 1
         SYMBOL = EXPR(L:L)
      GO TO 10
      END IF

* Copy identifier/constant into RPN

      R = R + 1
      RPN(R : R + L - I) = EXPR(I:L-1) // ' '
      R = R + L - I
      I = L - 1

      END


**ISOPER******************************************************************
* Logical-valued function that determines if SYMBOL is an operator     *
*************************************************************************

      LOGICAL FUNCTION ISOPER(SYMBOL)

      CHARACTER*(*) SYMBOL, OPER(5)*2
      INTEGER OP
      DATA OPER / '+', '-','*','/', '**' /

      ISOPER = .FALSE.
      DO 10 OP = 1, 5
         IF (SYMBOL .EQ. OPER(OP)) ISOPER = .TRUE.
10    CONTINUE
      END
```

Figure 10.16 (cont.)

```
**OPERAT***************************************************************
* Subroutine to process a symbol OP that is an operator by popping    *
* operators from STACK (max size STKLIM, TOP is top of stack) until   *
* the stack becomes empty or an operator appears on the top of the    *
* stack whose priority is less than or equal to that of OP.  OP is    *
* then pushed onto the stack.  Local identifiers used are:            *
*     TOPOP  : operator on top of stack                               *
*     DONE   : signals completion of stack popping                    *
* The function PRIOR is used to find the priorities of operators.     *
***********************************************************************

      SUBROUTINE OPERAT(STACK, TOP, STKLIM, OP, RPN, R)

      INTEGER STKLIM, TOP, R, PRIOR
      CHARACTER*2, STACK(STKLIM), OP, TOPOP, RPN*(*)
      LOGICAL DONE, EMPTY

      DONE = .FALSE.

* Repeat the following until done popping

10    CONTINUE

          IF (EMPTY(STACK, TOP, STKLIM)) THEN
              DONE = .TRUE.
          ELSE
              CALL POP(STACK, TOP, STKLIM, TOPOP)
              IF (PRIOR(OP) .LE. PRIOR(TOPOP)) THEN
                  R = R + 2
                  IF (TOPOP .EQ. '**') THEN
                      RPN(R-1: R+1) = '** '
                      R = R + 1
                  ELSE
                      RPN(R-1:R) = TOPOP // ' '
                  END IF
              ELSE
                  CALL PUSH(STACK, TOP, STKLIM, TOPOP)
                  DONE = .TRUE.
              END IF
          END IF
      IF (.NOT. DONE) GO TO 10

      CALL PUSH(STACK, TOP, STKLIM, OP)

      END
```

Figure 10.16 (cont.)

```
**PRIOR***********************************************************************
* Function to find the priority of operator or left parenthesis OPER.   *
******************************************************************************

        FUNCTION PRIOR(OPER)

        INTEGER PRIOR
        CHARACTER*2 OPER

        IF (OPER .EQ. '(') THEN
            PRIOR = 0
        ELSE IF ((OPER .EQ. '+') .OR. (OPER .EQ. '-')) THEN
            PRIOR = 1
        ELSE IF ((OPER .EQ. '*') .OR. (OPER .EQ. '/')) THEN
            PRIOR = 2
        ELSE IF (OPER .EQ. '**') THEN
            PRIOR = 3
        ELSE
            PRIOR = -1
        END IF
        END


******************************************************************************
******************************************************************************
************      PACKAGE OF STACK-PROCESSING SUBPROGRAMS      ************
******************************************************************************
******************************************************************************
*                                                                            *
**CREATE**********************************************************************
* Subroutine to create an empty stack of character strings.                *
******************************************************************************

        SUBROUTINE CREATE(STACK, TOP, STKLIM)

        INTEGER TOP, STKLIM
        CHARACTER*(*) STACK(STKLIM)

        TOP = 0

        END

**EMPTY**********************************************************************
* Function to check if a stack of character strings is empty.              *
******************************************************************************

        LOGICAL FUNCTION EMPTY(STACK, TOP, STKLIM)

        INTEGER TOP, STKLIM
        CHARACTER*(*) STACK(STKLIM)

        EMPTY = (TOP .EQ. 0)

        END
```

Figure 10.16 (cont.)

```
**PUSH****************************************************************
* Subroutine to push character symbol onto top of stack.           *
*********************************************************************

      SUBROUTINE PUSH(STACK, TOP, STKLIM, SYMBOL)

      INTEGER TOP, STKLIM
      CHARACTER*(*) STACK(STKLIM), SYMBOL

      IF (TOP .EQ. STKLIM) THEN
          STOP '*** STACK OVERFLOW ***'
      ELSE
          TOP = TOP + 1
          STACK(TOP) = SYMBOL
      END IF
      END

**POP***************************************************************
* Subroutine to pop top symbol from stack.                         *
*********************************************************************

      SUBROUTINE POP(STACK, TOP, STKLIM, SYMBOL)

      INTEGER TOP, STKLIM
      CHARACTER*(*) STACK(STKLIM), SYMBOL

      IF (TOP .EQ. 0) THEN
          PRINT *, '*** EMPTY STACK ***'
      ELSE
          SYMBOL = STACK(TOP)
          TOP = TOP - 1
      END IF
      END
*                                                                  *
*********************************************************************
*********************************************************************
```

Sample run:

```
ENTER INFIX EXPRESSION (END WITH ;)
A + B;
RPN EXPRESSION IS
 A B +

MORE (Y OR N)
Y
ENTER INFIX EXPRESSION (END WITH ;)
A - B - C;
RPN EXPRESSION IS
 A B - C -

MORE (Y OR N)
Y
```

Figure 10.16 (cont.)

```
ENTER INFIX EXPRESSION (END WITH ;)
A - (B - C);
RPN EXPRESSION IS
 A B C - -

MORE (Y OR N)
Y
ENTER INFIX EXPRESSION (END WITH ;)
((A + 525)/BETA - 2)*GAMMA;
RPN EXPRESSION IS
 A 525 + BETA / 2 - GAMMA *

MORE (Y OR N)
Y
ENTER INFIX EXPRESSION (END WITH ;)
(B**2 - 4*A*C)/ %PER;
%  IS ILLEGAL CHARACTER -- IGNORED
RPN EXPRESSION IS
 B 2 ** 4 A * C * - PER /

MORE (Y OR N)
N
```

Exercises

1. Given that the following declarations have been made

```
CHARACTER*10 ALPHA, BETA*5, GAMMA*1, LABEL1*4,
    +              LABEL2*3, STR1*3, STR2*4
```

and that STR1 = 'FOR', STR2 = 'TRAN', LABEL1 = 'FOOT', LABEL2 = 'LBS', find the value assigned to the given variable for each of the following, or indicate why the statement is not valid:

(a) GAMMA = 123
(b) GAMMA = '123'
(c) ALPHA = 'ONE' // 'TWO'
(d) ALPHA = '1' // '2'
(e) BETA = 'ANTIDISESTABLISHMENTARIANISM'
(f) BETA = '1,000,000,000'
(g) BETA = 'ONE' // 23
(h) ALPHA = STR1 // STR2 // '-77'
(i) BETA = STR1 // STR2 // '-77'
(j) ALPHA = LABEL1 // LABEL2
(k) GAMMA = LABEL1
(l) ALPHA = LABEL1 // '-' // LABEL2
(m) BETA = STR1 // STR2(:1)
(n) ALPHA = STR2(2:3) // 'NDOM'
(o) STR2(2:3) = 'UR'
(p) STR2(:2) = STR2(3:)
(q) STR1(:2) = STR1(2:)

2. Given the declarations

```
INTEGER N
REAL A
CHARACTER*40 FORM, S1*10, S2*6
```

show how the data should be entered for each of the following READ statements so that N, A, S1, and S2 are assigned the values 1, 1.1, MODEL-XL11, and CAMERA, respectively.

(a)   READ *, N, A, S1, S2

(b)   READ 10, N, A, S1, S2
    10 FORMAT (I2, F4.1, 2A)

(c)   READ '(I1, A, F2.1, A)', N, S1, A, S2

(d)   FORM = '(25X, I3, T1, F5.0, 1X, A, T18, A)'
     READ FORM, N, A, S1, S2

(e)   FORM = '(I5, F5.0, 2A15)'
     READ FORM, N, A, S1, S2

(f)   READ 20, N, A, S1, S2
    20 FORMAT (T9, I1, TL1, F2.1, T1, 2A)

3. Write a program that reads a character string and prints it in reverse order, beginning with the last nonblank character.

4. Write a program to determine whether a specified string occurs in a given string, and if so, print an asterisk (*) under the first position of each occurrence.

5. Write a program to count the occurrences of a specified character in several lines of text.

6. Write a program to count the occurrences of a specified string in several lines of text.

7. Write a program that permits the input of a name consisting of a first name, a middle name or initial, and a last name, in that order, and then prints the last name followed by a comma and then the first and middle initials, each followed by a period. For example, the input JOHN HENRY DOE should produce DOE, J. H.

8. Write a program to read STUDENT-FILE and display the name and cumulative GPA of all students with a given major that is entered during execution.

9. A file contains grade records for students in a freshman engineering class. Each record consists of several lines of information. The first line contains the student's name in columns 1 through 30 and the letter T or F in column 31 to indicate whether a letter grade is to be assigned (T) or the course is to be graded on a pass/fail basis (F). The next ten lines contain the test scores for this student, one integer score per line in columns 1 through 3. Write a program to read these records and, for each student, to display on a single line his or her name, term average (in the form xxx.x), and final grade. If the student has selected the pass/fail option, the final grade is 'PASS' for a term average of 70.0 or above and 'FAIL' otherwise. If the student has selected the letter grade option, the final grade is 'A' for a term average of 90.0 or above, 'B' for a term average of 80.0 through 89.9, 'C' for a term average of 70.0 through 79.9, 'D' for a term average of 60.0 through 69.9, and 'F' otherwise.

10. The following data file contains for each of several objects its shape (cube or sphere), its critical dimension (edge or radius), its density, and the material from which it is made:

```
sphere      2.0      .00264      aluminum
cube        3.0      .00857      brass
cub         1.5      .0113       lead
sphere      1.85     .0088       nickel
CUBE        13.7     .00035      cedar
SPHERE      2.85     .00075      oak
```

Write a program to read these records and produce a table displaying the following information for each object:

(a) shape
(b) critical dimension
(c) material
(d) volume
(e) mass
(f) whether the object will float when immersed in an oil bath
(g) mass of oil displaced by the object

(An object will float if its density is less than or equal to the density of oil, .00088 kg/cm^3.) Your program should check that each object's shape is one of the strings 'cube', 'CUBE', 'sphere', or 'SPHERE'.

11. The encoding scheme used to produce a cryptogram in the program of Figure 10.2 consists simply of adding a specified integer to the code of each character of the message. This is a special case of the technique known as *keyword* encoding, in which a sequence of integers corresponding to the characters of a specified keyword is added in order to the codes of the message characters. For example, if the keyword is 'ABC' and the message is 'MEETATNOON', the codes for 'A', 'B', and 'C' are added to the codes for 'M', 'E', and 'E', respectively, then added to the codes for 'T', 'A', and 'T', respectively, and so on, producing the cryptogram 'NGHUCWOQRO' (assuming an ASCII machine). Write a program to implement this keyword method of encoding.

12. The Morse code is a standard encoding scheme that uses substitutions similar to the scheme described in Exercise 11. The substitutions used in this case are

A $\cdot$ -	M - -	Y - $\cdot$ - -
B - $\cdot$ $\cdot$ $\cdot$	N - $\cdot$	Z - - $\cdot$ $\cdot$
C - $\cdot$ - $\cdot$	O - - -	1 $\cdot$ - - - -
D - $\cdot$ $\cdot$	P $\cdot$ - - $\cdot$	2 $\cdot$ $\cdot$ - - -
E $\cdot$	Q - - $\cdot$ -	3 $\cdot$ $\cdot$ $\cdot$ - -
F $\cdot$ $\cdot$ - $\cdot$	R $\cdot$ - $\cdot$	4 $\cdot$ $\cdot$ $\cdot$ $\cdot$ -
G - - $\cdot$	S $\cdot$ $\cdot$ $\cdot$	5 $\cdot$ $\cdot$ $\cdot$ $\cdot$ $\cdot$
H $\cdot$ $\cdot$ $\cdot$ $\cdot$	T -	6 - $\cdot$ $\cdot$ $\cdot$ $\cdot$
I $\cdot$ $\cdot$	U $\cdot$ $\cdot$ -	7 - - $\cdot$ $\cdot$ $\cdot$
J $\cdot$ - - -	V $\cdot$ $\cdot$ $\cdot$ -	8 - - - $\cdot$ $\cdot$
K - $\cdot$ -	W $\cdot$ - -	9 - - - - $\cdot$
L $\cdot$ - $\cdot$ $\cdot$	X - $\cdot$ $\cdot$ -	0 - - - - -

Write a program to accept as input a message in plain text or in Morse code and then encode or decode the message, respectively. (For a terminal with a bell or "beep" you might try to output Morse code as sound.)

13. Rev. Zeller developed a formula for computing the day of the week on which a given date fell or will fall. Suppose that we let a, b, c, and d be integers defined as follows:

a = the month of the year, with March = 1, April = 2, and so on, with January and February being counted as months 11 and 12 of the preceding year.

b = the day of the month.

c = the year of the century.

d = the century.

For example, July 31, 1929, gives $a = 5$, $b = 31$, $c = 29$, $d = 19$; January 3, 1988, gives $a = 11$, $b = 3$, $c = 87$, $d = 19$. Now calculate the following integer quantities:

w = the integer quotient $(13a - 1) / 5$.

x = the integer quotient $c / 4$.

y = the integer quotient $d / 4$.

$z = w + x + y + b + c - 2d$.

r = z reduced modulo 7; that is, r is the remainder of z divided by 7; $r = 0$ represents Sunday, $r = 1$ represents Monday, and so on.

Write a program to accept a date as input and then calculate on what day of the week that date fell or will fall.

(a) Verify that December 12, 1960, fell on a Monday and that January 1, 1991, fell on a Tuesday.

(b) On what day of the week did January 25, 1963, fall?

(c) On what day of the week did June 2, 1964, fall?

(d) On what day of the week did July 4, 1776, fall?

(e) On what day of the week were you born?

14. Write a program that will convert ordinary Hindu–Arabic numerals into Roman numerals and/or vice versa. (I = 1, V = 5, X = 10, L = 50, C = 100, D = 500, and M = 1000. Roman numeration also uses a subtraction principle: IV = 5 − 1 = 4, IX = 10 − 1 = 9, XL = 50 − 10 = 40, XC = 100 − 10 = 90, CD = 500 − 100 = 400, CM = 1000 − 100 = 900, but no other cases of a smaller number preceding a larger are allowed.)

15. A string is said to be a *palindrome* if it does not change when the order of the characters in the string is reversed. For example,

```
MADAM
463364
ABLE WAS I ERE I SAW ELBA
```

are palindromes. Write a program to read a string and then determine whether it is a palindrome.

16. Write a simple *text-formatting* program that reads a file of text and produces another file in which blank lines are removed, multiple blanks are replaced with a single blank, and no lines are longer than some given length. Put as many words as possible on the same line. You will have to break some lines of the given file, but do not break any words.

17. Extend the text-formatting program of Exercise 16 to right-justify each line except the last in the new file by adding evenly distributed blanks in lines where necessary.

18. Modify the program in Figure 10.5 to plot graphs of parametric equations of the form

$$x = x(t), \quad y = y(t), \quad a \leq t \leq b$$

19. In Example 2 of Section 10.4, we noted that the ideas in that example can be modified to carry out *visual image processing* and *enhancement*. Make a file that represents light intensities of an image in digitized form, say, with intensities from 0 through 9. Write a program that reads these intensities from the file and then reconstructs and displays them using a different character for each intensity. This image might then be enhanced to sharpen the contrast. For example, "gray" areas might be removed by replacing all intensities in the range 0 through some value by 0 (light) and intensities greater than this value by 9 (dark). Design your program to accept a threshold value that distinguishes light from dark and then enhances the image in the manner described.

20. An alternative method for enhancing an image (see Exercise 19) is to accept three successive images of the same object and, if two or more of the intensities agree, to use that value; otherwise, the average of the three values is used. Modify the program of Exercise 19 to use this technique for enhancement.

21. Design a finite automaton to recognize bit strings

(a) containing 00 or 11.
(b) containing an even number of ones.
(c) containing an even number of zeros and an even number of ones.
(d) in which the remainder when n divided by 3 is 1, where n is the number of ones.

22. A real number in FORTRAN has one of the forms $m.n$, $+m.n$, or $-m.n$, where m and n are nonnegative integers; or it may be expressed in scientific form xEe, $xE+e$, or $xE-e$, where x is an integer or a real number not in scientific form and e is a nonnegative integer. Write a program that reads a string of characters and then checks to see if it represents a valid real constant.

23. (Project) A *rational number* is of the form a/b, where a and b are integers with $b \neq 0$. Write a program to do rational number arithmetic. The program should read and display each rational number in the format a/b, or simply a if the denominator is 1. The following examples illustrate the menu of commands that the user should be allowed to enter:

Input	Output	Comments
3/8 + 1/6	13/24	$a/b + c/d = (ad + bc)/bd$ reduced to lowest terms.
3/8 − 1/6	5/24	$a/b - c/d = (ad - bc)/bd$ reduced to lowest terms.
3/8 * 1/6	1/16	$a/b * c/d = ac/bd$ reduced to lowest terms.
3/8 / 1/6	9/4	$a/b / c/d = ad/bc$ reduced to lowest terms.
3/8 I	8/3	Invert a/b.
8/3 M	2 + 2/3	Write a/b as a mixed fraction.
6/8 R	3/4	Reduce a/b to lowest terms.
6/8 G	2	Greatest common divisor of numerator and denominator.
1/6 L 3/8	24	Lowest common denominator of a/b and c/d.
1/6 < 3/8	true	$a/b < c/d$?
1/6 <= 3/8	true	$a/b \leq c/d$?
1/6 > 3/8	false	$a/b > c/d$?
1/6 >= 3/8	false	$a/b \geq c/d$?
3/8 = 9/24	true	$a/b = c/d$?
2/3 X + 2 = 4/5	X = −9/5	Solution of linear equation $(a/b)X + c/d = e/f$.

24. Write a program for a lexical analyzer to recognize assignment statements of the form

$$variable = constant$$

where *constant* is an integer constant or a real constant.

25. Write a program for a lexical analyzer to recognize assignment statements of the form

$$variable = string\ constant$$

26. Extend the program of Exercise 25 to allow substrings and the concatenation operator.

27. Write a program for a lexical analyzer to process assignment statements of the form

$$logical\text{-}variable = logical\text{-}value$$

Have it recognize the following tokens: variable, logical constant, assignment operator, and logical operator (.NOT., .AND., .OR., .EQV., and .NEQV.).

28. Suppose that A = 7.0, B = 4.0, C = 3.0, and D = −2.0. Evaluate the following RPN expressions:

(a) A B + C / D*   (b) A B C + / D *
(c) A B C D + / *   (d) A B + C + D +
(e) A B + C D + +   (f) A B C + + D +
(g) A B C D + + +   (h) A B − C − D
(i) A B − C D − −   (j) A B C − − D −
(k) A B C D − − −

29. Convert the following infix expressions to RPN:

(a) A * B + C − D   (b) A + B / C + D
(c) (A + B) / C + D   (d) A + B / (C + D)
(e) (A + B) / (C + D)   (f) (A − B) * (C − (D + E))
(g) (((A − B) − C) − D) − E (h) A − (B − (C − (D − E)))

30. Convert the following RPN expressions to infix notation:

(a) A B C + − D *   (b) A B + C D − *
(c) A B C D + − *   (d) A B + C − D E * /
(e) A B / C / D /   (f) A B / C D / /
(g) A B C / D / /   (h) A B C D / / /

31. An alternative to postfix notation is *prefix* notation, in which the symbol for each operation precedes the operands. For example, the infix expression 2 * 3 + 4 would be written in prefix notation as + * 2 3 4, and 2 * (3 + 4) would be written as * 2 + 3 4. Convert each of the infix expressions in Exercise 29 to prefix notation.

32. Suppose that A = 7.0, B = 4.0, C = 3.0, and D = −2.0. Evaluate the following prefix expressions:

(a) ∗ A / + B C D   (b) ∗ / + A B C D
(c) − A − B − C D   (d) − − A B − C D
(e) − A − − B C D   (f) − − − A B C D
(g) + A B ∗ − C D   (h) + ∗ A B − C D
(i) + ∗ − A B C D

33. Convert the following prefix expressions to infix notation:

(a) + A B ∗ − C D   (b) + ∗ A B − C D
(c) − − A B − C D   (d) − − A − B C D
(e) − − − A B C D   (f) / + ∗ A B − C D E
(g) / + ∗ A B C − D E   (h) / + A ∗ B C − D E

34. The symbol − cannot be used for the unary minus operation in prefix or postfix notation because ambiguous expressions result. For example, 5 3 − − can be interpreted as either 5 − (−3) = 8 or −(5 − 3) = −2. Suppose instead that ~ is used for unary minus.

(a) Evaluate the following RPN expressions if A = 7, B = 5, and C = 3:

(i) A ~ B C + −   (ii) A B ~ C + −
(iii) A B C ~ + −   (iv) A B C + ~ −
(v) A B C + − ~   (vi) A B C − − ~ ~ ~

(b) Convert the following infix expressions to RPN:

(i) A ∗ (B + ~C)   (ii) ~(A + B / (C − D))
(iii) (~A) ∗ (~B)   (iv) ~(A − (~B ∗ (C + ~D)))

(c) Convert the infix expressions in (b) to prefix notation.

35. Convert the following logical expressions to RPN:

(a) A .AND. B .OR. C
(b) A .AND. (B .OR. .NOT. C)
(c) .NOT. (A .AND. B)
(d) (A .OR. B) .AND. (C .OR. (D .AND. .NOT. E))
(e) (A .EQ. B) .OR. (C .EQ. D)
(f) ((A .LT. 3) .AND. (A .GT. 9))
    .OR. .NOT. (A .GT. 0)
(g) ((B ∗ B − 4 ∗ A ∗ C) .GE. 0)
    .AND. ((A .GT. 0) .OR. (A .LT. 0))

36. Convert each of the logical expressions in Exercise 35 to prefix notation.

37. Write a program to implement the algorithm in Example 2 of Section 10.5 for evaluating RPN expressions that involve only one-digit integers and the binary operators +, −, ∗, and /.

38. Write a program that converts infix expressions to prefix.

39. Write a program to evaluate prefix expressions containing only one-digit integers and the binary operators $+$, $-$, $*$, and $/$.

40. The program in Figure 10.16 does not check that the infix expression is well formed (parentheses match, each binary operation has two operands, and so on) and thus may not generate a well-formed RPN expression. Write a program that reads an RPN expression and determines whether it is well-formed, that is, whether each binary operator has two operands and the unary operator $\sim$ has one (see Exercise 34).

Programming Pointers

The character data type was introduced in earlier chapters and has been described in more detail in this chapter. Some of the following programming pointers are summaries of earlier programming pointers, and the reader should refer to those for an expanded discussion.

1. *The first position specified in a substring should be no greater than the last position; also, both positions should be positive and no greater than the length of the string.* For a substring consisting of the leftmost characters of a string, the position need not be specified. Thus, if STRING is declared by

```
CHARACTER*10 STRING
```

then the substring reference

```
STRING( :4)
```

is equivalent to

```
STRING(1:4)
```

Similarly, for a substring consisting of the rightmost characters, the last position need not be specified. Thus,

```
STRING(6: )
```

is equivalent to

```
STRING(6:10)
```

2. *In an assignment to a substring, the value being assigned may not be a character expression that references any of the same positions to which values are being assigned.* Thus, for the character variable declared by

```
CHARACTER*10 STRING
```

the following assignment statement is not allowed:

```
STRING(3:7) = STRING(6:10)
```

3. *The collating sequence used to compare characters depends on the encoding system used to store characters.* For example,

```
'123' .LT. 'A23'
```

is true if ASCII coding is used, but it is false for EBCDIC.

4. *Character constants must be enclosed in single quotation marks for list-directed input but not for formatted input.*

5. *In assignment statements and in list-directed input, if the value being assigned or read has a length greater than that specified for the character variable (or substring), the rightmost characters are truncated. If the value has a length less than that of the variable (or substring), blanks are added at the right.* An acronym sometimes used to remember this is

- **APT:** For **A**ssignment (and list-directed input), blank **P**adding and **T**runcation both occur on the right.

See Potential Problem 12 in the Programming Pointer section of Chapter 3 for more details.

6. *For formatted input/output, characters are truncated or blanks are added according to whether the field width is too small or too large. For input, truncation occurs on the left and blank padding on the right; for output, truncation occurs on the right and blank padding on the left.* The acronyms similar to that in Programming Pointer 5 are

- **POT:** **P**adding on the left with blanks occurs for formatted **O**utput, or **T**runcation of rightmost characters occurs.
- **TIP:** **T**runcation of leftmost characters occurs for formatted **I**nput, or **P**adding with blanks on the right occurs.

See Programming Pointer 4 of Chapter 6 for more details.

FORTRAN 90 Features

FORTRAN 90 adds some new features to the character data type. These include the following:

- Character strings may be enclosed either within apostrophes (*'string'*) or within quotation marks (*"string"*). A string that is enclosed in apostrophes may contain quotation marks, and a string that is enclosed in quotation marks may contain apostrophes.

- A string may be empty, thus having a length of 0. A character constant consisting of two consecutive apostrophes or two consecutive quotation marks denotes an empty string.
- A substring specification may be attached to a string constant.
- Character strings to be read by a list-directed input statement need not be enclosed in apostrophes or within quotation marks unless
  1. they contain blanks, commas, or slashes.
  2. they extend over more than one line.
  3. the leading nonblank character is a quotation mark or an apostrophe.
  4. a repetition indicator is used.
  In this case the input value is terminated by the first blank, comma, or end of line that is encountered.
- The OPEN statement may contain a DELIM = 'APOSTROPHE', 'QUOTE', or 'NONE' clause to specify the delimiter used for character strings written with list-directed or NAMELIST formatting.
- Several new instrinsic string-processing functions are provided:

ACHAR(I):	The character whose ASCII code is I.
ADJUSTL(STR):	Returns string obtained from STR by moving leading blanks to the right end.
ADJUSTR(STR):	Returns string obtained from STR by moving trailing blanks to the left end.
IACHAR(CH):	The ASCII code of character CH.
LEN_TRIM(STR):	Length of string STR, ignoring trailing blanks.
REPEAT(STR, N):	Returns string formed by concatenating N copies of STR.
SCAN(STR1, STR2) or SCAN(STR1, STR2, BACK):	Returns position of leftmost character of STR1 that appears in STR2 (or rightmost if the second form is used with BACK = .TRUE.), 0 if none appear in STR2.
TRIM(STR):	Returns initial substring of STR with trailing blanks removed.
VERIFY(STR1, STR2) or VERIFY(STR1, STR2, BACK):	Returns position of leftmost character of STR1 that is not in STR2 (or rightmost if the second form is used with BACK = .TRUE.), 0 if all appear in STR2.

11

File Processing

In Chapter 6 we introduced file processing for those applications involving large data sets that can be processed more conveniently if stored on magnetic tape or disk or some other external media. We considered simple forms of several FORTRAN statements that are used to process files. In this chapter we review these statements, give their complete forms, and introduce some additional file concepts.

The files we have considered thus far are called **sequential files.** These are files in which the lines of data or **records** are written in sequence and must be read in that same order. This means that to read a particular record in a sequential file, all of the preceding records must first be read. In contrast, **direct-access files** are files in which each record may be accessed directly, usually by referring to a record number. This means that a particular record may be accessed without reading (or writing) those records that precede it. All records in a direct-access file must have the same fixed length, whereas records in a sequential file may be of varying lengths.

Another distinction between files is that they may be **formatted** or **unformatted.** All the files we have considered thus far have been formatted, which means that they consist of records in which information is represented in external character form. In contrast, unformatted files are those in which the information is represented in internal binary form. Thus, the precise form of the records in an unformatted file is machine dependent, as it depends on the manner in which values are stored internally in a particular system. For this reason, unformatted files are discussed only briefly in this chapter, and instead we focus our attention on formatted files.

11.1   The OPEN, CLOSE, and INQUIRE Statements

A file must be connected to a unit number using the OPEN statement introduced in Section 6.5 before input from or output to that file can take place. When such input/output is completed, the file should be disconnected from its unit number using the CLOSE statement, also introduced in Section 6.5. In some situations, it may also be convenient to inquire about certain properties of a file, and the INQUIRE statement may be used for this purpose.

Opening Files.   The **OPEN statement** has the general form

> OPEN (*open-list*)

where *open-list* must include

1. A unit specifier indicating a unit number to be connected to the file being opened.

In most cases, it also includes

2. A FILE = clause giving the name of the file being opened.
3. A STATUS = clause specifying whether the file is new, old, or scratch or has an unknown status.

It may also include other specifiers selected from the following list:

4. An IOSTAT = clause indicating whether the file has been successfully opened.
5. An ERR = clause specifying a statement to be executed if an error occurs while attempting to open the file.
6. An ACCESS = clause specifying the type of access as sequential or direct.
7. A FORM = clause specifying whether the file is formatted or unformatted.
8. A RECL = clause specifying the record length for a direct-access file.
9. A BLANK = clause specifying whether blank columns in a numeric field are to be interpreted as zeros or are to be ignored.

The unit specifier has the form

UNIT = *integer-expression*

or simply

integer-expression

where the value of *integer-expression* is a nonnegative integer that designates the unit number to be connected to this file. Reference to this file by subsequent READ or WRITE statements is by means of this unit number. If the second form of the unit specifier is used, it must be the first item in the open list.

The FILE = clause has the form

FILE = *character-expression*

where the value of *character-expression* (ignoring trailing blanks) is the name of the file to be connected to the specified unit number.

The STATUS = clause has the form

STATUS = *character-expression*

where the value of *character-expression* (ignoring trailing blanks) is one of the following:

```
OLD
NEW
SCRATCH
UNKNOWN
```

If the value is OLD or NEW, the name of the file must have been given in the FILE = clause. OLD means that the file already exists in the system, and NEW means that the file does not yet exist and is being created by the program. The OPEN statement creates an empty file with the specified name and changes its status to OLD. If the status is SCRATCH, the file must not be named in a FILE = clause; the OPEN statement creates a work file that is used during execution of this program but that is deleted by a CLOSE statement or by normal termination of the program. A status of UNKNOWN means that none of the preceding applies. In this case, the status of the file depends on the particular system being used. If the STATUS = clause is omitted, the file is assumed to have an UNKNOWN status.

The IOSTAT = clause is of the form

IOSTAT = *status-variable*

where *status-variable* is an integer variable to which a value of zero is assigned if the file is opened successively, and a positive value is assigned otherwise. A positive value usually represents the number of an appropriate error message in a list found in system manuals.

The ERR = clause has the form

ERR = *n*

where *n* is the label of an executable statement that is the next statement executed if an error occurs in attempting to open the file.

The ACCESS = clause is of the form

ACCESS = *access-method*

where *access-method* is a character expression whose value (ignoring trailing blanks) is

SEQUENTIAL   or   DIRECT

If this clause is omitted, the file is assumed to be sequential.

The FORM = clause is of the form

FORM = *form-specifier*

where *form-specifier* is a character expression whose value (ignoring trailing blanks) is either

FORMATTED   or   UNFORMATTED

If this clause is omitted, the file being opened is assumed to be formatted if it is a sequential file or to be unformatted if it is a direct-access file.

The RECL = clause has the form

RECL = *record-length*

where *record-length* is an integer expression whose value must be positive. This clause is used only for direct-access files and specifies the length of the records in the file. For a formatted file, the record length is the number of characters in each record of that file. For an unformatted file, it is a processor-dependent measure of the record length.

The BLANK = clause has the form

BLANK = *blank-specifier*

where *blank-specifier* is a character expression whose value (ignoring trailing blanks) is either

ZERO   or   NULL

The first specification causes blanks in the numeric fields of records in the file being opened to be interpreted as zeros, whereas the NULL specifier causes such blanks to be ignored. In all cases, however, a numeric field consisting only of blanks is interpreted as zero.

As an illustration, suppose that a file has been previously created and saved under the name 'INFO1' and that data values are to be read from this file. A unit number such as 10 must first be connected to this file by an OPEN statement such as

```
OPEN (UNIT = 10, FILE = 'INFO1', STATUS = 'OLD')
```

Alternatively, the name of the file can be read during execution:

```
CHARACTER*10 INFILE

PRINT *, 'ENTER NAME OF INPUT FILE'
READ *, INFILE
OPEN (UNIT = 10, FILE = INFILE, STATUS = 'OLD')
```

Because the ACCESS = and FORM = clauses are not used, the file is assumed to be sequential and formatted. If we wish to specify this explicitly, we can use

```
 OPEN (UNIT = 10, FILE = INFILE, STATUS = 'OLD'),
+      FORM = 'FORMATTED', ACCESS = 'SEQUENTIAL')
```

The statement

```
OPEN (UNIT = 10, FILE = INFILE, STATUS = 'OLD', ERR = 50)
```

also serves the same purpose, but if an error occurs during the opening of the file, the ERR = clause causes execution to continue with the statement labeled 50.

If the program is to create a new file named 'INFO2', we might attach the unit number 11 to it with the statement

```
OPEN (UNIT = 11, FILE = 'INFO2', STATUS = 'NEW')
```

Execution of this statement changes the status of this file to OLD, so that it will exist after execution of the program is completed. On the other hand, if a temporary work file is needed only during execution, we might use a statement such as

```
OPEN (UNIT = 12, STATUS = 'SCRATCH')
```

This temporary file will then be deleted if it is closed by a CLOSE statement or when execution terminates.

Closing Files. The **CLOSE statement** is used to disconnect a file from its unit number. This statement is of the form

CLOSE (*close-list*)

where *close-list* must include

1. A unit specifier.

It may also include items selected from the following:

2. An IOSTAT = clause.
3. An ERR = clause.
4. A STATUS = clause specifying whether the file is to be kept or deleted.

The IOSTAT = and ERR = clauses are used to detect errors that may occur when attempting to close the file and have the same form as the corresponding clauses in the OPEN statement. The STATUS = clause has the form

STATUS = *character-expression*

where the value of *character-expression* (ignoring trailing blanks) is

```
KEEP    or    DELETE
```

depending on whether the file is to continue to exist or not exist after the CLOSE statement is executed. KEEP may not be used for a SCRATCH file. If the STATUS = clause is omitted, scratch files are deleted, but all other types are kept. Thus, to close the file INFO2 with the unit number 11 referred to earlier so that it is saved after execution, we could use any of the following statements:

```
CLOSE (11)
CLOSE (UNIT = 11)
CLOSE (UNIT = 11, STATUS = 'KEEP')
```

A file that has been closed by a CLOSE statement may be reopened by an OPEN statement; the same unit number may be connected to it, or a different one may be used. All files that are not explicitly closed with a CLOSE statement are automatically closed when execution of the program is terminated (except when termination is caused by an error).

The INQUIRE Statement. The **INQUIRE statement** may be used to ascertain the properties of a file or of its connection to a unit number. It has the form

INQUIRE (*inquiry-list*)

where *inquiry-list* must include a unit specifier or a file specifier, but not both, and may include an IOSTAT = clause and/or an ERR = clause. The inquiry list may also contain a number of other clauses, each of which serves as a question concerning some property of the file. When the INQUIRE statement is executed, a value that answers the question is assigned to the variable in each clause. A complete list of the clauses and their meanings is given in Table 11.1.

TABLE 11.1 Clauses Allowed in an INQUIRE Statement

Clause	Variable Type	Values and Their Meanings
IOSTAT = *variable*	Integer	Zero if no error condition exists; positive if an error exists.
EXIST = *variable*	Logical	True if the file with the specified name or unit number exists; false otherwise.
OPENED = *variable*	Logical	True if the specified file or unit number has been connected to a unit number or file, respectively; false otherwise.
NUMBER = *variable*	Integer	Either the file's unit number or undefined.
NAMED = *variable*	Logical	True if the file has a name; false otherwise.
NAME = *variable*	Character	Either the name of the file or undefined if file has no name.
ACCESS = *variable*	Character	SEQUENTIAL if file is open for sequential access; DIRECT if it is open for direct access; undefined otherwise.
SEQUENTIAL = *variable*	Character	YES if file can be connected for sequential access; NO if it cannot; UNKNOWN if the file's suitability for sequential access cannot be determined.
DIRECT = *variable*	Character	YES if file can be connected for direct access; NO if it cannot; UNKNOWN if the file's suitability for direct access cannot be determined.
FORM = *variable*	Character	FORMATTED if the file is open for formatted data transfer; UNFORMATTED if the file is open for unformatted data transfer; undefined if the file is not open.
FORMATTED = *variable*	Character	YES if the file is formatted; NO if the file is unformatted; UNKNOWN if the record type cannot be determined.
UNFORMATTED = *variable*	Character	YES if the file is unformatted; NO if the file is formatted; UNKNOWN if the record type cannot be determined.
RECL = *variable*	Integer	Record length for a direct-access file; undefined if the file is not connected for direct access.
NEXTREC = *variable*	Integer	One plus the number of the last record read from or written to a direct-access file; undefined if the file is not connected for direct access or the record number cannot be determined.
BLANK = *variable*	Character	ZERO if the blanks in numeric fields are to be interpreted as zeros; NULL if they are to be ignored; undefined if the file is not connected.

11.2 File Input/Output and Positioning

File input/output is accomplished using the general READ and WRITE statements introduced in Chapter 6. The complete forms of these statements are considered in this section. Some file positioning is also carried out by these statements. Other positioning statements that may be used for sequential files are the REWIND, BACKSPACE, and ENDFILE statements.

File Input. Data can be read from a file using a **READ statement** of the general form

> READ (*control-list*) *input-list*

The *input-list* is a list of variable names, substring names, array names, or implied DO loops, separated by commas. The *control-list* must include

1. A unit specifier indicating the unit number connected to the file.

It may also include one or more of the following:

2. A format specifier describing the format of the information to be read.
3. An IOSTAT = clause to check the status of the input operation, in particular, to detect an end-of-file condition or an input error.
4. An END = clause specifying a statement to be executed when the end of a sequential file is reached.
5. An ERR = clause specifying a statement to be executed if an input error occurs.
6. A REC = clause indicating the number of the record to be read for a direct-access file.

The forms of the unit specifier, format specifier, the IOSTAT = clause, and the END = clause were described in detail in Chapter 6.
The ERR = clause has the form

> ERR = *n*

where *n* is the label of a statement to be executed if an input error occurs. For example, suppose that NUMBER and NAME are declared by

```
INTEGER NUMBER
CHARACTER*20 NAME
```

For the READ statement

```
    READ (15, 10, ERR = 20) NUMBER, NAME
10 FORMAT(I5, A20)
```

if the following data is read from the file with unit number 15

```
123 JOHN HENRY DOE
```

an input data error occurs because the character J in the fifth column is read as part of the value for the integer variable NUMBER. The ERR = clause then causes execution to continue with the statement numbered 20, which might be a statement to print an error message such as

```
20 PRINT *, 'INPUT DATA ERROR'
```

In Chapter 6 we noted that when a READ statement containing an IOSTAT = clause of the form

IOSTAT = *integer-variable*

is executed, the variable in this clause is assigned

1. A positive value (usually the number of an error message in a list found in system manuals) if an error occurs.
2. A negative value if the end of data is encountered but no input error occurs.
3. Zero if neither an input error nor the end of data occurs.

Up to now we have used the IOSTAT = clause only to detect the end of data. However, it also provides an alternative to the ERR = clause for detecting input errors. For example, if ERROR is an integer variable, the preceding statements could also be written

```
    READ (15, 10, IOSTAT = ERROR) NUMBER, NAME
10  FORMAT(I5, A20)
    IF (ERROR .GT. 0) THEN
        PRINT *, 'INPUT DATA ERROR'
    END IF
```

The REC = clause has the form

REC = *integer-expression*

where the value of the *integer-expression* is positive and indicates the number of the record to be read from a direct-access file. The clause must be used if input is to be from a file connected for direct access. The control list may not contain both a REC = clause and an END = clause.

All the files used in the example programs in this text have thus far been sequential files. The program in Figure 11.1 uses a direct-access file to retrieve information in a parts inventory file. The name FNAME of the file is read during execution and is then opened with the statement

```
  OPEN (UNIT = 10, FILE = FNAME, STATUS = 'OLD',
 +      ACCESS = 'DIRECT', FORM = 'FORMATTED',
 +      RECL = RECLEN)
```

The user then enters a part number, which is used to access a record of the file:

```
  READ (10, '(A)', REC = PARTNO, IOSTAT = BADNUM) INFO
```

The information in this record INFO is then displayed to the user.

```
      PROGRAM INVEN
************************************************************************
* Program to read a part number during execution, access a record in  *
* a direct-access parts inventory file, and display this record.       *
* Identifiers used are:                                                *
*     RECLEN : a parameter specifying record length                    *
*     PARTNO : part number                                             *
*     FNAME  : name of the file                                        *
*     INFO   : a record in the file                                    *
*     BADNUM : 0 if valid part number, otherwise nonzero               *
* Note:  The compiler used for this program requires that the          *
* end-of-line character in a file record be counted in determining     *
* the record length; therefore, RECLEN is set at 31.                   *
************************************************************************

      INTEGER PARTNO, RECLEN, BADNUM
      PARAMETER (RECLEN = 31)
      CHARACTER*20 FNAME, INFO*(RECLEN)

* Get the name of the file and open it for direct access

      PRINT *, 'ENTER NAME OF FILE'
      READ '(A)', FNAME
      OPEN (UNIT = 10, FILE = FNAME, STATUS = 'OLD',
     +      ACCESS = 'DIRECT', FORM = 'FORMATTED', RECL = RECLEN)

      PRINT *, 'ENTER PART NUMBER (0 TO STOP)'
      READ *, PARTNO

* While there are more part numbers to process do the following

10    IF (PARTNO .NE. 0) THEN
          READ (10, '(A)', REC = PARTNO, IOSTAT = BADNUM) INFO
          IF (BADNUM .EQ. 0) THEN
              PRINT '(1X, ''PART'', I3, '': '', A)', PARTNO, INFO
          ELSE
              PRINT '(1X, ''INVALID PART NUMBER: '', I3)', PARTNO
          END IF
          PRINT *
          PRINT *, 'PART NUMBER?'
          READ *, PARTNO
      GO TO 10
      END IF

      CLOSE(10)
      END
```

Listing of test file used in sample run:

```
CHROME-BUMPER...$152.95.....15
SPARK-PLUG........$1.25....125
DISTRIBUTOR-CAP..$39.95.....57
FAN-BELT..........$5.80.....32
DOOR-HANDLE......$18.85.....84
```

Figure 11.1

Figure 11.1 (cont.)

Sample run:

```
ENTER NAME OF FILE
PARTSFILE
ENTER PART NUMBER (0 TO STOP)
4
PART  4: FAN-BELT..........$5.80.....32

PART NUMBER?
2
PART  2: SPARK-PLUG........$1.25....125

PART NUMBER?
10
INVALID PART NUMBER:  10

PART NUMBER?
0
```

File-positioning Statements. There are three FORTRAN statements that may be used to position a file. Each of these statements has two possible forms:

> REWIND *unit*   or   REWIND (*position-list*)
> BACKSPACE *unit* or   BACKSPACE (*position-list*)
> ENDFILE *unit*   or   ENDFILE (*position-list*)

In the first form, *unit* is the unit number connected to the file. In the second form, *position-list* must contain

1. A unit specifier of the form *unit* or UNIT = *unit*.

It may also contain

2. An ERR = clause specifying the number of a statement to be executed if an error occurs while positioning the file.
3. An IOSTAT = clause specifying a status variable that is assigned zero if the file is successfully positioned or a positive value if an error occurs.

The **REWIND statement** positions the file at its initial point, that is, at the beginning of the file's first record. The **BACKSPACE statement** positions the file at the beginning of the preceding record. If the file is at its initial point, these statements have no effect.

The **ENDFILE statement** writes into the file a special record called an **end-of-file record.** When this record is encountered by a READ statement, an end-of-file condition occurs that can be detected by an IOSTAT = clause or an END = clause in the control list of the READ statement. After the execution of an ENDFILE statement, no more data can be transferred to or from this file until the file is repositioned at some record preceding the end-of-file record.

File Output.   Data is written to a file using a **WRITE statement** of the general form

WRITE *(control-list) output-list*

The *output-list* is a list of expressions, array names, or implied DO loops separated by commas. The *control-list* must include

1. A unit specifier indicating the unit number connected to the file.

It may also include one or more of the following:

2. A format specifier describing the form of the information being output.
3. An ERR = clause specifying a statement to be executed if an output error occurs.
4. An IOSTAT = clause to check the status of the output operation.
5. A REC = clause indicating the number of the record to which the information is to be output for a direct-access file.

The form of each of these items is the same as for a READ statement.

The format of the output to a direct-access file must be supplied by the user. Also, the REC = clause may not appear when the output is list directed (indicated by an asterisk for the format specifier).

EXAMPLE 1: Merging Files.   An important problem in file processing is merging two files that have been previously sorted so that the resulting file is also sorted. To illustrate, suppose that FILE1 and FILE2 have been sorted and contain the following integers:

FILE1: 2 4 5 7 9 15 16 20   FILE2: 1 6 8 10 12

To merge these files to produce FILE3, we read one element from each file, say X from FILE1 and Y from FILE2:

FILE1: [2] 4 5 7 9 15 16 20   FILE2: [1] 6 8 10 12
         ↑   ↑
         X   Y

We write the smaller of these values, in this case Y, into FILE3:

FILE3: 1

and then read another value for Y from FILE2:

FILE1: [2] 4 5 7 9 15 16 20   FILE2: 1 [6] 8 10 12
         ↑   ↑
         X   Y

Now X is smaller than Y, and so it is written to FILE3, and a new value for X is read from FILE1:

FILE1: 2 [4] 5 7 9 15 16 20   FILE2: 1 [6] 8 10 12
           ↑   ↑
           X   Y
FILE3: 1 2

Again, X is less than Y, and so X is written to FILE3, and a new X value is read from FILE1:

FILE1: 2 4 5̲ 7 9 15 16 ~20   FILE 2: 1 6̲ 8 10 12
         ↑   ↑
         X   Y
FILE3: 1 2 4

Continuing in this manner, we eventually reach the value 15 for X and the value 12 for Y:

FILE1: 2 4 5 7 9 1̲5̲ 16 20   FILE2: 1 6 8 10 1̲2̲
             ↑   ↑
             X   Y
FILE3: 1 2 4 5 6 7 8 9 10

Because Y is smaller than X, we write Y to FILE3:

FILE3: 1 2 4 5 6 7 8 9 10 12

Because the end of FILE2 has been reached, we simply copy the remaining values of FILE1 to FILE3 to obtain the final sorted file FILE3:

FILE3: 1 2 4 5 6 7 8 9 10 12 15 16 20

The general algorithm to merge two sorted files is as follows:

ALGORITHM TO MERGE FILES

* Algorithm to merge sorted files FILE1 and FILE2 to produce the   *
* sorted file FILE3.   *

1. Open FILE1, FILE2, and FILE3.
2. Read the first element X from FILE1 and the first element Y from FILE2.
3. While the end of neither FILE1 nor FILE2 has been reached, do the following:
   If X ≤ Y then
      a. Write X to FILE3.
      b. Read a new X value from FILE1.
   Else do the following:
      a. Write Y to FILE3.
      b. Read a new Y value from FILE2.
4. If the end of FILE1 has not been reached, copy the rest of FILE1 into FILE3. If the end of FILE2 has not been reached, copy the rest of FILE2 into FILE3.

In this algorithm, we assumed that the file components are numbers, strings, and so on that can be compared. If the files contain records that are sorted on the basis of some key field in the records, then the key field of X is compared with the key field of Y in step 3. The program in Figure 11.2 implements this modified merge algorithm. It merges two files whose records consist of a student number, student name, and cumulative GPA and that have been sorted so that the student numbers are in ascending order.

```
      PROGRAM MERGE
*****************************************************************************
* Program to read two files of records containing a student number, a     *
* student name, and a cumulative GPA, where the files are sorted so       *
* that student numbers are in ascending order, and merge these two        *
* files to produce another that is also sorted.  Variables used are:      *
*      FNAME1, FNAME2  : names of files to be merged                      *
*      FNAME3          : name of file produced                            *
*      SNAME1, SNAME2  : name of student in FILE1, FILE2                  *
*      SNUMB1, SNUMB2  : number of student in FILE1, FILE2                *
*      GPA1, GPA2      : cumulative GPA of student in FILE1, FILE2        *
*      EOF1, EOF2      : indicator of end of FILE1, FILE2                 *
*****************************************************************************

      CHARACTER*20, FNAME1, FNAME2, FNAME3, SNAME1, SNAME2
      INTEGER SNUMB1, SNUMB2, EOF1, EOF2
      REAL GPA1, GPA2

* Get the names of the files and open them.

      PRINT *, 'ENTER THE NAMES OF THE FILES TO BE MERGED AND THE NAME'
      PRINT *, 'OF THE FILE TO BE PRODUCED ON SEPARATE LINES:'
      READ '(A)', FNAME1, FNAME2, FNAME3
      OPEN (UNIT = 10, FILE = FNAME1, STATUS = 'OLD',
     +      ACCESS = 'SEQUENTIAL')
      OPEN (UNIT = 20, FILE = FNAME2, STATUS = 'OLD',
     +      ACCESS = 'SEQUENTIAL')
      OPEN (UNIT = 30, FILE = FNAME3, STATUS = 'NEW',
     +      ACCESS = 'SEQUENTIAL')

* Read the first two records from each file

      READ (10, 100, IOSTAT = EOF1) SNUMB1, SNAME1, GPA1
      READ (20, 100, IOSTAT = EOF2) SNUMB2,SNAME2, GPA2
100   FORMAT(I5, 1X, A, F4.2)

* While neither the end of FILE1 or FILE2 has been reached,
* do the following:

10    IF (EOF1 .EQ. 0 .AND. EOF2 .EQ. 0) THEN
         IF (SNUMB1 .LE. SNUMB2) THEN
            WRITE (30, 100) SNUMB1, SNAME1, GPA1
            READ (10, 100, IOSTAT = EOF1) SNUMB1, SNAME1, GPA1
         ELSE
            WRITE (30,100) SNUMB2, SNAME2, GPA2
            READ (20, 100, IOSTAT = EOF2) SNUMB2, SNAME2, GPA2
         END IF
      GO TO 10
      END IF

* If more records remain in FILE1, copy them to FILE3

20    IF (EOF1 .EQ. 0) THEN
         WRITE (30,100) SNUMB1, SNAME1, GPA1
         READ (10, 100, IOSTAT = EOF1) SNUMB1, SNAME1, GPA1
      GO TO 20
      END IF
```

Figure 11.2

Figure 11-2 (cont.)

```
* If more records remain in FILE2, copy them to FILE3

30      IF (EOF2 .EQ. 0) THEN
            WRITE (30,100) SNUMB2, SNAME2, GPA2
            READ (20, 100, IOSTAT = EOF2) SNUMB2, SNAME2, GPA2
        GO TO 30
        END IF

        PRINT *
        PRINT *, 'FILE MERGING IS COMPLETE'

        END
```

Sample run:

```
ENTER THE NAMES OF THE FILES TO BE MERGED AND THE NAME
OF THE FILE TO BE PRODUCED ON SEPARATE LINES:
FILE1
FILE2
FILE3

FILE MERGING IS COMPLETE
```

Data files used in sample run:

FILE1:

```
12320 JOHN HENRY DOE      3.50
12346 FRED SAMUEL DOE     3.48
13331 MARY JANE SMITH     3.85
13345 PETER VANDER VAN    2.99
14400 ALFRED E. NEWMAN    1.00
15555 HENRY SMITHSMA      2.05
```

FILE2:

```
12360 ALICE M. VAN DOE    2.15
12365 JANE E. JONES       1.89
13400 JESSE JAMES         1.66
14001 RICHARD VAN VAN     4.00
```

FILE3 produced by the sample run:

```
12320 JOHN HENRY DOE      3.50
12346 FRED SAMUEL DOE     3.48
12360 ALICE M. VAN DOE    2.15
12365 JANE E. JONES       1.89
13331 MARY JANE SMITH     3.85
13345 PETER VANDER VAN    2.99
13400 JESSE JAMES         1.66
14001 RICHARD VAN VAN     4.00
14400 ALFRED E. NEWMAN    1.00
15555 HENRY SMITHSMA      2.05
```

EXAMPLE 2: External Sorting: Mergesort. The sorting algorithms we considered in Chapter 7 are *internal* sorting schemes; that is, the entire collection of items to be sorted must be stored in main memory. In many sorting problems, however, the data sets are too large to store in main memory and so must be stored in external memory. To sort such collections of data, an *external* sorting algorithm is required. One popular and efficient external sorting method is the **mergesort** technique, a variation of which, called **natural mergesort,** we examine here.

As the name *mergesort* suggests, the basic operation in this sorting scheme is merging data files. To see how the merge operation can be used in sorting a file, consider the following file F containing fifteen integers:

    F: 75 55 15 20 80 30 35 10 70 40 50 25 45 60 65

Notice that several segments of F contain elements that are already in order:

    F: | 75 | 55 | 15 20 80 | 30 35 | 10 70 | 40 50 | 25 45 60 65 |

These segments, enclosed by vertical bars, are called *subfiles* or *runs* in F and subdivide F in a natural way.

We begin by reading these subfiles of F and alternately writing them to two other files, F1 and F2

    F1: | 75 | 15 20 80 | 10 70 | 25 45 60 65 |
    F2: | 55 | 30 35 | 40 50 |

and then identifying the sorted subfiles in F1 and F2.

    F1: | 75 | 15 20 80 | 10 70 | 25 45 60 65 |
    F2: | 55 | 30 35 40 50 |

Note that although the subfiles of F1 are the same as those copied from F, two of the original subfiles written into F2 have combined to form a larger subfile.

We now merge the first subfile of F1 with the first subfile of F2, storing the elements back in F.

    F: | 55 75 |

Next the second subfile of F1 is merged with the second subfile of F2 and written to F.

    F: | 55 75 | 15 20 30 35 40 50 80 |

This merging of corresponding subfiles continues until the end of either or both of the files F1 and F2 is reached. If either file still contains subfiles, these are simply copied into F. Thus, in our example, because the end of F2 has been reached, the remaining subfiles of F1 are copied back into F.

    F: | 55 75 | 15 20 30 35 40 50 80 | 10 70 | 25 45 60 65 |

Now file F is again split into files F1 and F2 by copying its subfiles alternately into F1 and F2.

F1: | 55 75 | 10 70 |
F2: | 15 20 30 35 40 50 80 | 25 45 60 65 |

Identifying the sorted subfiles in each of these files, we see that for this splitting, none of the original subfiles written into either F1 or F2 combine to form larger ones. Once again we merge corresponding subfiles of F1 and F2 back into F.

F: | 15 20 30 35 40 50 55 75 80 | 10 25 45 60 65 70 |

When we now split F into F1 and F2, each of the files F1 and F2 contains a single sorted subfile, and each is, therefore, completely sorted.

F1: | 15 20 30 35 40 50 55 75 80 |
F2: | 10 25 45 60 65 70 |

Thus, when we merge F1 and F2 back into F, F will also contain only one sorted subfile and hence will be sorted.

F: | 10 15 20 25 30 35 40 45 50 55 60 65 70 75 80 |

This example shows that the mergesort method has two steps: (1) splitting file F into two other files, F1 and F2, and (2) merging corresponding subfiles in these two files. These steps are repeated until each of the smaller files contains a single sorted subfile; when these are merged, the resulting file is completely sorted. Designing an algorithm to split the file and a program to implement the mergesort scheme is left as an exercise.

Unformatted Files. Information is stored in a formatted file using a standard coding scheme such as ASCII or EBCDIC, and when such a file is listed, these codes are automatically converted to the corresponding characters by the terminal, printer, or other output device. In contrast, information is stored in an **unformatted** or **binary file** using the internal representation scheme for the particular computer being used. This representation usually cannot be correctly displayed in character form by the output device, nor can it be used easily with another computer system.

There are, however, some advantages in using unformatted files. When information in a formatted file is read by a FORTRAN program, two separate processes are involved: (1) the transfer of the information from the file and (2) the conversion of this information to internal form. Similarly, the output of information to a formatted file involves two steps: (1) conversion to external form and (2) the actual transfer of this information to the file. Because such conversion is time-consuming, it may be desirable to eliminate it, especially when a file is to be read and processed only by the computer and not displayed to the user. Another advantage in using unformatted files is that data items are usually stored more compactly using their internal representation rather than their external representation in one of the standard coding schemes.

Unformatted file input/output is accomplished by using a READ or WRITE statement in which the format specification is omitted. For example, the statement

```
WRITE (UNIT = 10, ERR = 100) NUM, RATE, TIME
```

writes values of NUM, RATE, and TIME to the unformatted file having unit number 10.

The variables in the input list of a READ statement used to read information from an unformatted file should match in number and type the variables in the output lists of the WRITE statements that produced that file. Also, both formatted and unformatted input/output statements cannot be used with the same file.

Internal Files. An **internal file** is a sequence of memory locations containing information stored in character form and named by a character variable, a character array or array element, or a character substring. Such internal files are useful in converting information from character form to numeric form.

For example, suppose the character variable DATE is assigned the value

```
DATE = 'JULY 4, 1776'
```

and we wish to extract the year 1776 from this character string and convert it to a numeric form suitable for computations. To do this, we first use a substring reference to extract the substring to be converted:

```
YEAR = DATE(9:12)
```

The value of the character variable YEAR is the character string '1776', and thus YEAR can be viewed as an internal file. The information

```
1776
```

stored in this file can be read and assigned to a numeric variable NYEAR by using a READ statement in which the name YEAR of this internal file is used as the unit specifier:

```
READ (UNIT = YEAR, FMT = '(I4)') NYEAR
```

or simply

```
READ (YEAR, '(I4)') NYEAR
```

The integer 1776 can also be read and assigned to NYEAR by using the character substring name DATE (9:12) as the name of the internal file:

```
READ (DATE(9:12), '(I4)') NYEAR
```

or by considering DATE as the name of the internal file and using the appropriate positioning descriptors in the format identifier:

```
READ (DATE, '(8X, I4)') NYEAR
```

In no case, however, is list-directed input allowed.

Conversely, a numeric constant can be converted to the corresponding character string and assigned to a character variable by considering that character variable to be an internal file and writing to it. For example, suppose the integer variable N has been assigned the value

```
N = 1776
```

and we wish to concatenate the corresponding character string '1776' to the character constant 'JULY 4,'. To do this, we first convert the value of N to character form and assign the resulting string to the character variable REVOL by the statement

```
WRITE (UNIT = REVOL, FMT = '(I4)') N
```

or simply

```
WRITE (REVOL, '(I4)') N
```

in which REVOL is viewed as an internal file. The value of REVOL can then be concatenated with 'JULY 4, ' and assigned to the character variable DATE by

```
DATE = 'JULY 4, ' // REVOL
```

When a character array is viewed as an internal file, the number of records in that file is equal to the number of elements in the array, and the length of each record is equal to the declared length of the array elements. Each READ and WRITE statement using this array as an internal file begins transfering data with the first array element.

List-directed input/output is not allowed for internal files, nor may the auxiliary input/output statements

```
OPEN
CLOSE
INQUIRE
BACKSPACE
ENDFILE
REWIND
```

be used for such files.

11.3   Example: Inventory Update

To illustrate some of the file concepts discussed in this chapter, we consider the problem of maintaining an inventory file. A program must be written that accepts as input an order number followed by a list of item numbers and order quantities for several items. For each of these items, the appropriate record in the inventory file must be read to determine whether there is sufficient stock of this item to fill the order. If there is, the quantity ordered is subtracted from the number in stock and a message is displayed indicating this fact. If the number remaining in stock is less than the reorder point for that item, an appropriate message must be displayed. If there are not enough items to fill the order, a message indicating how much of the order can be filled at this time must be displayed.

Because an inventory file typically contains a large number of records and because a large number of transactions is processed using this file, sequential access to such a file is inefficient. Consequently, the inventory file will be organized as a direct-access file, which allows one to access a specific record directly rather than to search sequentially through all the records preceding it. In order to access a specific record in a direct-access file, it is necessary to know its record number. Thus, a correspondence must be established between the item number and the number of the record in the inventory file that contains the information relevant to this item. This is accomplished by constructing an array INDEX, consisting of a list of item numbers arranged in the same order as in the file. Thus, the position of a given item number in this array is the same as the number of the corresponding record in the file. When the program is executed, the elements of the array INDEX are read from a file that contains the item numbers. This file is unformatted, because it is read only by the program and is not intended for display to the user.

There are two major tasks that the program must carry out. The first is the initialization task, which consists of opening the necessary files and constructing the array INDEX. The second task is the transaction processing, which consists of accepting the order information from the user, searching the index file to determine the appropriate record number, and carrying out the necessary processing using the order information and the information found in this record. The structure diagram in Figure 11.3 displays these tasks and subtasks and the relationship between them.

The program and sample run in Figure 11.4 represent an early stage in the development of the program to solve this problem. The main program calls the subroutine INIT and then repeatedly calls the subroutine TRANS until the user indicates that there are no more transactions to process. INIT opens the inventory file and the index file by calling the subroutine OPENER, which is designed to generate a unit number and attach it to a specified file whose name is passed to it as an argument; the appropriate character strings to be used in the FORM =, STATUS =, and ACCESS = clauses of the OPEN statement are also to be passed as arguments. In this early version of the program, the subroutine OPENER is a program stub that merely displays some of the information passed to it.

The subroutine INIT also calls CONST to construct the array INDEX of

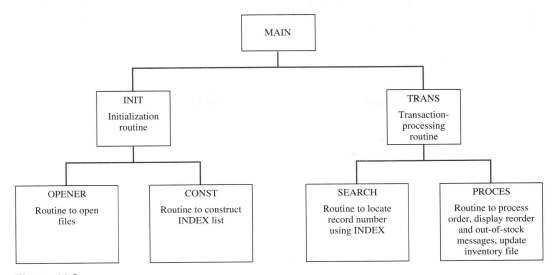

Figure 11.3

item numbers. In Figure 11.4 this is also a program stub that displays a message that the subroutine has been called.

After the files are opened and the array INDEX is constructed, the transaction processing begins. Subroutine TRANS accepts an order for a certain item and calls subroutine SEARCH to search the array INDEX in order to find the position of this item in the inventory file. If the item is found, subroutine PROCES then processes the order. In the program in Figure 11.4, these two subroutines are also implemented as program stubs.

```
      PROGRAM INVEN
**MAIN***************************************************************
* This program accepts an order from the terminal, searches an inven- *
* tory file to see if the item ordered is in stock, updates the file, *
* and displays an out-of-stock message and reorder message when      *
* necessary.  The search of the inventory file uses an index of stock *
* numbers.  This index is read into main memory from an unformatted   *
* file.  Identifiers used are:                                        *
*     LIMIT  :  Upper limit on the number of items in inventory file  *
*     LREC   :  Length of records in inventory file                   *
*     INUNIT :  Unit number of INFILE                                 *
*     INDEX  :  Array of item numbers (INDEX(0) = # of items)         *
*     RESPON :  Response from user (Y or N) re more orders to process *
* Note:  The compiler used for this program requires that the         *
* end-of-line character in a file record be counted in determining    *
* the record length; therefore, RECLEN is set at 45.                  *
*********************************************************************

      INTEGER LREC, LIMIT
      PARAMETER (LIMIT = 1000, LREC = 45)
      CHARACTER*1 RESPON
      INTEGER INUNIT, INDEX(0:LIMIT)

      CALL INIT(INUNIT, INDEX, LIMIT, LREC)
```

Figure 11.4

Figure 11.4 (cont.)

```
* Repeat the following until there are no more transactions

10      CONTINUE
           CALL TRANS(INUNIT, INDEX, LIMIT)
           PRINT *, 'MORE TRANSACTIONS (Y OR N)?'
           READ '(A)', RESPON
        IF (RESPON .EQ. 'Y') GO TO 10

        END


**INIT*****************************************************************
* This subroutine opens the inventory file and the index file and con- *
* structs the array INDEX of item numbers.  Identifiers used:          *
*      INUNIT, INDEX, LIMIT, LREC as in MAIN                           *
*      INFILE        : Name of inventory file                         *
*      IXFILE, IXUNIT  : Name and unit number of index file           *
***********************************************************************

        SUBROUTINE INIT(INUNIT, INDEX, LIMIT, LREC)

        CHARACTER*20 INFILE, IXFILE
        INTEGER INUNIT, INDEX(0:LIMIT), IXUNIT, LREC, LIMIT

        PRINT *, 'ENTER NAME OF INVENTORY FILE:'
        READ '(A)', INFILE
        CALL OPENER(INFILE, INUNIT, 'FORMATTED', 'OLD', 'DA', LREC)
        PRINT *, 'ENTER NAME OF INDEX FILE:'
        READ '(A)', IXFILE
        CALL OPENER(IXFILE, IXUNIT, 'UNFORMATTED', 'OLD', 'SE', 0)
        CALL CONST(IXUNIT, INDEX, LIMIT)
        END


**OPENER***************************************************************
* Subroutine to open a file and assign it a unit number.  Successive   *
* calls to this subroutine assign unit numbers 10, 11, 12, ... A call  *
* to OPENER with TYPE = 'SE' open a sequential file, and a call with    *
* TYPE = 'DA' opens a direct-access file.  Variables used are:         *
*      FNAME  :  Name of file to be opened                            *
*      NUNIT  :  Unit number to be connected to file (integer)        *
*      FORMSP :  'FORMATTED' or 'UNFORMATTED' depending on whether file *
*             :  is formatted or unformatted                          *
*      STAT   :  Status of file ('OLD', 'NEW', 'SCRATCH', etc.)       *
*      TYPE   :  Indicates whether file is sequential or direct access *
*      LREC   :  Length of records for direct access files            *
***********************************************************************

        SUBROUTINE OPENER(FNAME, NUNIT, FORMSP, STAT, TYPE, LREC)

        CHARACTER*(*) FNAME, FORMSP, STAT, TYPE
        INTEGER LREC, NUNIT

        IF (TYPE .EQ. 'SE') THEN
           PRINT *, FNAME, ' IS OPENED FOR SEQUENTIAL ACCESS'
        ELSE
           PRINT *, FNAME, ' IS OPENED FOR DIRECT ACCESS'
        END IF
        END
```

Figure 11.4 (cont.)

```
**CONST*********************************************************************
* This subroutine constructs the array INDEX of item numbers from the   *
* (unformatted) file IXFILE.  IXFILE, IXUNIT, INDEX, and                *
* LIMIT are as in MAIN.                                                 *
***************************************************************************

      SUBROUTINE CONST(IXUNIT, INDEX, LIMIT)

      INTEGER LIMIT, INDEX(0:LIMIT), IXUNIT

      PRINT *, 'INDEX CONSTRUCTED'
      END


**TRANS*********************************************************************
* This subroutine processes a transaction by accepting an order for     *
* a certain item from the terminal, searching the array INDEX to find   *
* the number of the record in the inventory file describing this item,  *
* and then updating this record (displaying out-of-stock and/or reorder*
* messages at the terminal when necessary).  Variables used:            *
*     INUNIT, INDEX, LIMIT as in MAIN and INIT                          *
*     NUMORD  :  Order number                                           *
*     INDEX   :  Item number                                            *
*     QUANT   :  Number of items ordered                                *
*     NUMREC  :  Number of record containing information re INDEX       *
*             :  (VALUE 0 indicates item not found)                     *
***************************************************************************

      SUBROUTINE TRANS(INUNIT, INDEX, LIMIT)

      INTEGER LIMIT, INDEX (0:LIMIT), INUNIT, NUMORD, ITNUM, QUANT,
     +        NUMREC

      CALL SEARCH(INDEX, ITNUM, LIMIT, NUMREC)
      CALL PROCES(NUMREC, QUANT, NUMORD, INUNIT)
      END


**SEARCH********************************************************************
* This subroutine searches the array INDEX of item numbers to locate    *
* the number NUMREC of the record in the inventory file containing      *
* information re the item with item number INDEX.  LIMIT is as in MAIN.*
***************************************************************************

      SUBROUTINE SEARCH(INDEX, ITNUM, LIMIT, NUMREC)

      INTEGER LIMIT, INDEX(0:LIMIT), ITNUM, NUMREC

      PRINT *, 'SEARCHING INDEX'
      END
```

Figure 11.4 (cont.)

```
**PROCES**********************************************************************
* This subroutine processes an order (order # NUMORD) for QUANT items. *
* The NUMREC-th record of the inventory file (unit number INUNIT) is   *
* examined to determine whether the number in stock is sufficient to   *
* fill the order.  If not, an out-of-stock message will be displayed   *
* at the terminal.  In either case, this record will be updated.       *
* Also, if the new number in stock is below the reorder point, a       *
* reorder message will be displayed at the terminal.                   *
**********************************************************************

      SUBROUTINE PROCES(NUMREC, QUANT, NUMORD, INUNIT)

      INTEGER NUMREC, QUANT, NUMORD, INUNIT

      PRINT *, 'PROCESSING ORDER'
      END
```

Sample run:

```
ENTER NAME OF INVENTORY FILE:
TEST-FILE
TEST-FILE               IS OPENED FOR DIRECT ACCESS
ENTER NAME OF INDEX FILE:
INDEX-FILE
INDEX-FILE              IS OPENED FOR SEQUENTIAL ACCESS
INDEX CONSTRUCTED
SEARCHING INDEX
PROCESSING ORDER
MORE TRANSACTIONS (Y OR N)?
N
```

Figure 11.5 shows the final program in which the subroutines OPENER, CONST, SEARCH, and PROCES have been developed. Also shown is a small test file used in a sample run and a listing of the updated test file produced by this run.

```
        PROGRAM INVEN
**MAIN***************************************************************
* This program accepts an order from the terminal, searches an inven- *
* tory file to see if the item ordered is in stock, updates the file, *
* and displays an out-of-stock message and reorder message when       *
* necessary.  The search of the inventory file uses an index of stock *
* numbers.  This index is read into main memory from an unformatted   *
* file.  Identifiers used are:                                        *
*     LIMIT   :  Upper limit on the number of items in inventory file *
*     LREC    :  Length of records in inventory file                  *
*     INUNIT  :  Unit number of INFILE                                *
*     INDEX   :  Array of item numbers (INDEX(0) = # of items)        *
*     RESPON  :  Response from user (Y or N) re more orders to process *
* Note: The compiler used for this program requires that the          *
* end-of-line character in a file record by counted in determining    *
* the record length; therefore, RECLEN is set at 45.                  *
*********************************************************************

        INTEGER LREC, LIMIT
        PARAMETER (LIMIT = 1000, LREC = 45)
        CHARACTER*1 RESPON
        INTEGER INUNIT, INDEX(0:LIMIT)

        CALL INIT (INUNIT, INDEX, LIMIT, LREC)

* Repeat the following until there are no more transactions

10      CONTINUE
            CALL TRANS(INUNIT, INDEX, LIMIT)
            PRINT *, 'MORE TRANSACTIONS (Y OR N)'
            READ '(A)', RESPON
        IF (RESPON .EQ. 'Y') GO TO 10

        END

**INIT****************************************************************
* This subroutine opens the inventory file and the index file and con- *
* structs the array INDEX of item numbers.  Variables used:           *
*     INUNIT, INDEX, LIMIT, LREC as in MAIN                           *
*     INFILE          :  Name of inventory file                       *
*     IXFILE, IXUNIT  :  Name and unit number of index file           *
*********************************************************************

        SUBROUTINE INIT(INUNIT, INDEX, LIMIT, LREC)

        CHARACTER*20 INFILE, IXFILE
        INTEGER INUNIT, LIMIT, INDEX(0:LIMIT), IXUNIT, LREC

        PRINT *, 'ENTER NAME OF INVENTORY FILE:'
        READ '(A)', INFILE
        CALL OPENER(INFILE, INUNIT, 'FORMATTED', 'OLD', 'DA', LREC)
        PRINT *, 'ENTER NAME OF INDEX FILE:'
        READ '(A)', IXFILE
        CALL OPENER(IXFILE, IXUNIT, 'UNFORMATTED', 'OLD', 'SE', 0)
        CALL CONST(IXUNIT, INDEX, LIMIT)
        END
```

Figure 11.5

Figure 11.5 (cont.)

```
**OPENER*************************************************************
* Subroutine to open a file and assign it a unit number.  Successive  *
* calls to this subroutine assign unit numbers 10, 11, 12, ... A call  *
* to OPENER with TYPE = 'SE' opens a sequential file, and a call with  *
* TYPE = 'DA' opens a direct access file.  Variables used are:         *
*     FNAME  :  Name of file to be opened                              *
*     NUNIT  :  Unit number to be connected to file (integer)          *
*     N      :  Last unit number assigned by subroutine                *
*     FORMSP :  'FORMATTED' or 'UNFORMATTED' depending on whether file  *
*            :  is formatted or unformatted                            *
*     STAT   :  Status of file ('OLD', 'NEW', 'SCRATCH', etc.)         *
*     TYPE   :  Indicates if file is sequential or direct access       *
*     LREC   :  Length of records for direct-access files              *
*********************************************************************

      SUBROUTINE OPENER(FNAME, NUNIT, FORMSP, STAT, TYPE, LREC)

      CHARACTER*(*) FNAME, FORMSP, STAT, TYPE
      INTEGER LREC, NUNIT, N
      SAVE N
      DATA N/10/

      IF(TYPE .EQ. 'SE') THEN
          OPEN(UNIT = N, FILE = FNAME, FORM = FORMSP, STATUS = STAT,
     +         ERR = 10)
      ELSE
          OPEN(UNIT = N, FILE = FNAME, FORM = FORMSP, STATUS = STAT,
     +         ACCESS = 'DIRECT', RECL = LREC, ERR = 10)
      END IF
      NUNIT = N
      N = N + 1
      RETURN
10    PRINT *, FNAME, ' CANNOT BE OPENED'

      END


**CONST*************************************************************
* This subroutine constructs the array INDEX of item numbers from the  *
*(unformatted) file IXFILE.  IXFILE, IXUNIT, INDEX, and LIMIT are as   *
* in MAIN.  Other variables used are:                                  *
*     I      :  Count of records in inventory file (stored in           *
*            :  INDEX(0) before return)                                 *
*     ITNUM  :  Item number                                             *
*********************************************************************

      SUBROUTINE CONST(IXUNIT, INDEX, LIMIT)

      INTEGER LIMIT, INDEX(0:LIMIT), IXUNIT, I, ITNUM

      I = 0
```

Figure 11.5 (cont.)

```
* While there is more data, do the following:

10      CONTINUE
            READ (IXUNIT, END = 20) ITNUM
            I = I + 1
            INDEX(I) = ITNUM
        GO TO 10
20      CONTINUE

* Store the count in INDEX(0)

        INDEX(0) = I
        END

**TRANS**********************************************************
* This subroutine processes a transaction by accepting an order for   *
* a certain item from the terminal, searching the array INDEX to find  *
* the number of the record in the inventory file describing this item, *
* and then updating this record (displaying out-of-stock and/or reorder*
* messages at the terminal when necessary).  Variables used:           *
*      INUNIT, INDEX, LIMIT as in MAIN and INIT                        *
*      NUMORD  :  Order number                                         *
*      ITNUM   :  Item number                                          *
*      QUANT   :  Number of items ordered                              *
*      NUMREC  :  Number of record containing information re ITNUM     *
*              :  (VALUE 0 indicates item not found)                   *
*****************************************************************

        SUBROUTINE TRANS(INUNIT, INDEX, LIMIT)

        INTEGER LIMIT, INDEX (0:LIMIT), INUNIT, NUMORD, ITNUM, QUANT,
       +          NUMREC
        PRINT *, 'ENTER ORDER #'
        READ *, NUMORD
        PRINT *, '(ENTER 0/ FOR ITEM # TO TERMINATE ORDER)'
        PRINT *, 'ITEM #, QUANTITY'
        READ *, ITNUM, QUANT

* While ITNUM not equal to 0 do the following:

10      IF (ITNUM .NE. 0) THEN
            CALL SEARCH(ITNUM, INDEX, LIMIT, NUMREC)
            IF (NUMREC .NE. 0)
       +        CALL PROCES(NUMREC, QUANT, NUMORD, INUNIT)
            PRINT *, 'ITEM #, QUANTITY'
            READ *, ITNUM, QUANT
        GO TO 10
        END IF
        END
```

Figure 11.5 (cont.)

```
**SEARCH********************************************************************
* This subroutine searches the array INDEX of item numbers to locate   *
* the number NUMREC of the record in the inventory file containing      *
* information re the item with item number ITNUM.  LIMIT is as in MAIN  *
* and FOUND is a boolean indicating whether the item has been found.    *
***************************************************************************

       SUBROUTINE SEARCH(ITNUM, INDEX, LIMIT, NUMREC)

       INTEGER LIMIT, INDEX(0:LIMIT), ITNUM, NUMREC, I
       LOGICAL FOUND

       I = 1
       FOUND = .FALSE.

* While FOUND is false and I is less than or equal to the
* number of items in the array INDEX do the following:

10     IF ((.NOT. FOUND) .AND. (I .LE. INDEX(0))) THEN
          IF (ITNUM .EQ. INDEX(I)) THEN
             NUMREC = I
             FOUND = .TRUE.
          ELSE
             I = I + 1
          END IF
       GO TO 10
       END IF
       IF (.NOT. FOUND) THEN
          PRINT *, 'BAD ITEM NUMBER'
          NUMREC = 0
       END IF
       END


**PROCES*******************************************************************
* This subroutine processes an order (order # NUMORD) for QUANT items.  *
* The NUMREC-th record of the inventory file (unit number INUNIT) is    *
* examined to determine whether the number in stock is sufficient to    *
* fill the order.  If not, an out-of-stock message will be displayed    *
* at the terminal.  In either case, this record will be updated.        *
* Also, if the new number in stock is below the reorder point, a        *
* reorder message will be displayed at the terminal.  New variables     *
* used are:                                                             *
*     INFO   :  Unused information in a record                          *
*     REORD  :  Reorder point                                           *
*     INSTOK :  Number of items in stock                                *
*     INLEV  :  Desired inventory level                                 *
*     STOCK  :  INSTOK - QUANT (# remaining in stock)                   *
*     FORM   :  An i/o format                                           *
***************************************************************************

       SUBROUTINE PROCES(NUMREC, QUANT, NUMORD, INUNIT)

       CHARACTER*29 INFO, FORM
       INTEGER NUMREC, QUANT, NUMORD, INUNIT, REORD, INSTOK, INLEV, STOCK
       SAVE FORM
       DATA FORM / '(I4, A29, 3I3 /)'/
```

Figure 11.5 (cont.)

```
READ (INUNIT, FORM, REC = NUMREC) ITNUM, INFO, REORD, INSTOK,
+      INLEV
STOCK = INSTOK - QUANT
IF (STOCK .LT. 0) THEN
     PRINT *, 'OUT OF STOCK ON ITEM #', ITNUM
     PRINT *, 'BACK ORDER', -1*STOCK, ' FOR ORDER #', NUMORD
     PRINT *, 'ONLY', INSTOK,' UNITS CAN BE SHIPPED AT THIS TIME'
     PRINT *, 'THE DESIRED INVENTORY LEVEL IS', INLEV
     INSTOK = 0
ELSE
     INSTOK = STOCK
     PRINT *, 'DONE'
END IF
WRITE (INUNIT, FORM, REC = NUMREC) ITNUM, INFO, REORD, INSTOK,
+      INLEV
IF ((STOCK .GE. 0) .AND. (STOCK .LE. REORD)) THEN
     PRINT *, 'ONLY',INSTOK,' UNITS OF',ITNUM,' REMAIN IN STOCK'
     PRINT *, 'REORDER POINT IS', REORD
     PRINT *, 'DESIRED INVENTORY LEVEL IS', INLEV
END IF
END
```

Sample run:

```
ENTER NAME OF INVENTORY FILE:
TEST-FILE
ENTER NAME OF INDEX FILE:
INDEX-FILE
ENTER ORDER #
11111
(ENTER 0/ FOR ITEM # TO TERMINATE ORDER)
ITEM #, QUANTITY
1023, 2
DONE
ITEM #, QUANTITY
1023, 5
DONE
ITEM #, QUANTITY
1023, 8
DONE
ONLY      0 UNITS OF 1023 REMAIN IN STOCK
REORDER POINT IS      5
DESIRED INVENTORY LEVEL IS      15
ITEM #, QUANTITY
1011, 12
DONE
ONLY      8 UNITS OF 1011 REMAIN IN STOCK
REORDER POINT IS      15
DESIRED INVENTORY LEVEL IS      25
ITEM #, QUANTITY
1011, 10
OUT OF STOCK ON ITEM # 1011
BACK ORDER      2 FOR ORDER #  11111
ONLY       8 UNITS CAN BE SHIPPED AT THIS TIME
THE DESIRED INVENTORY LEVEL IS      25
ITEM #, QUANTITY
0/
MORE TRANSACTIONS (Y OR N)
Y
```

Figure 11.5   (cont.)

```
ENTER ORDER #
22222
(ENTER 0/ FOR ITEM # TO TERMINATE ORDER)
ITEM #, QUANTITY
1012, 15
OUT OF STOCK ON ITEM # 1012
BACK ORDER       3 FOR ORDER #  22222
ONLY      12 UNITS CAN BE SHIPPED AT THIS TIME
THE DESIRED INVENTORY LEVEL IS       20
ITEM #, QUANTITY
0/
MORE TRANSACTIONS (Y OR N)
N
```

Listing of original file TEST-FILE used in sample run:

```
1011TELEPHOTO POCKET CAMERA  5495 15 20 25
1012MINI POCKET CAMERA       2495 15 12 20
1021POL. ONE-STEP CAMERA     4995 10 20 20
1022SONAR 1-STEP CAMERA     18995 12 13 15
1023PRONTO CAMERA            7495  5 15 15
10318MM ZOOM MOVIE CAMERA   27999 10  9 15
```

Listing of updated TEST-FILE produced by sample run:

```
1011TELEPHOTO POCKET CAMERA  5495 15  0 25
1012MINI POCKET CAMERA       2495 15  0 20
1021POL. ONE-STEP CAMERA     4995 10 20 20
1022SONAR 1-STEP CAMERA     18995 12 13 15
1023PRONTO CAMERA            7495  5  0 15
10318MM ZOOM MOVIE CAMERA   27999 10  9 15
```

Exercises

1. Write a program to concatenate two files, that is, to append one file to the end of the other.

2. Following the example of the text, show the various splitting–merging stages of mergesort for the following lists of numbers:

   (a) 1, 5, 3, 8, 7, 2, 6, 4
   (b) 1, 8, 2, 7, 3, 6, 5, 4
   (c) 1, 2, 3, 4, 5, 6, 7, 8
   (d) 8, 7, 6, 5, 4, 3, 2, 1

3. (a) Design an algorithm to perform the file splitting required by mergesort.

(b) Write a program to read records from USERSFILE (described in Appendix B) and sort them using mergesort so that the resources used to date are in increasing order.

4. Information about computer terminals in a computer network is maintained in a direct-access file. The terminals are numbered 1 through 100, and information about the nth terminal is stored in the nth record of the file. This information consists of a terminal type (string), the building in which it is located (string), the transmission rate (integer), an access code (character), and the date of last service (month, day, year). Write a program to read a terminal number, retrieve and display the information about that terminal, and modify the date of last service for that terminal.

5. (Project) Some text formatters allow command lines to be placed in the file of unformatted text. These command lines might have forms such as the following:

.P m n Insert m blank lines before each paragraph, and indent each paragraph n spaces.

.W n Page width (line length) is n.

.L n Page length (number of lines per page) is n.

.I n Indent by n spaces all lines following this command line.

.U   Undent all following lines, and reset to the previous left margin.

Write a program to read a file containing lines of text and some of these command lines throughout, and produce a new file in which these formatting commands have been implemented.

6. (Project) Modify and extend the text-editor program of Section 10.2 so that other editing operations can be performed. Include commands of the following forms in the menu of options:

Fn Find and display the nth line of the file.

Pn Print n consecutive lines, beginning with the current line.

Mn Move ahead n lines from the current line.

T   Move to the top line of the file.

C/*string1*/*string2*/   Change the current line by replacing *string1* with *string2*.

L *string*   Search the file starting from the current line to find a line containing *string*.

Dn Delete n consecutive lines, beginning with the current line.

I *line*   Insert the given *line* after the current line.

7. (Project) A *pretty printer* is a special kind of text formatter that reads a file containing a source program and then prints it in a "pretty"

format. For example, a pretty printer for FORTRAN might insert blank lines between subprograms, indent and align statements within other statements such as IF constructs and DO loops, and so on, to produce a format similar to that used in the sample programs in this text. Write a pretty print program for FORTRAN programs to indent and align statements in a pleasing format.

8. (Project) Write a menu-driven program that uses STUDENT-FILE and STUDENT-UPDATE (see Appendix B) and allows (some of) the following options. For each option, write a separate subprogram so that options and corresponding subprograms can be easily added or removed.

1. Locate a student's permanent record when given the student's number and print it in a nicer format than that in which it is stored.
2. Same as option 1, but locate the record when given the student's name.
3. Print a list of all student names and numbers in a given class (1, 2, 3, 4, 5).
4. Same as option 3 but for a given major.
5. Same as option 3 but for a given range of cumulative GPAs.
6. Find the average cumulative GPAs for (a) all females, (b) all males, (c) all students with a specified major, and (d) all students.
7. Produce updated grade reports with the following format:

```
          GRADE REPORT — SEMESTER 2   5/29/91

                   DISPATCH UNIVERSITY

     10103        JAMES L. JOHNSON


                            GRADE                CREDITS
                            =====                =======
     ENGL 176                 C                      4
     EDUC 268                 B                      4
     EDUC 330                 B+                     3
     P E 281                  C                      3
     ENGR 317                 D                      4

     CUMULATIVE CREDITS:    28
     CURRENT GPA:          1.61
     CUMULATIVE GPA:       2.64
```

Here, letter grades are assigned according to the following scheme: A = 4.0, A− = 3.7, B+ = 3.3, B = 3.0, B− = 2.7, C+ = 2.3, C = 2.0, C− = 1.7, D+ = 1.3, D = 1.0, D− = 0.7, and F = 0.0. (See Exercise 24 at the end of Chapter 7 for details on the calculation of GPAs.)

8. Same as option 7, but instead of producing grade reports, produce a new file containing the updated total credits and new cumulative GPAs.
9. Produce an updated file when a student (a) drops or (b) adds a course.
10. Produce an updated file when a student (a) transfers into or (b) withdraws from the university.

FORTRAN 90 Features

The new file-processing features added in FORTRAN 90 consist mainly of new clauses that may be included in the OPEN, CLOSE, INQUIRE, READ, and WRITE statements.

● New clauses that may be used in an OPEN statement are

POSITION = 'REWIND' or 'APPEND', or 'ASIS': Positions the file at its initial point, at the end of the file, or leaves its position unchanged, respectively.

ACTION = 'READ' or 'WRITE', or 'READWRITE': Opens the file for reading only, for writing only, or both, respectively.

DELIM = 'APOSTROPHE', 'QUOTE', or 'NONE': Character strings to be written to the file by list-directed output or by name-list formatting are enclosed in apostrophes or quotation marks or with no enclosing delimiters, respectively.

PAD = 'YES' or 'NO': Specifies whether or not an input value is to be padded with blanks.

● New clauses that may be used in READ and WRITE statements are

NML = *name-list-group-name*: See the FORTRAN 90 section in Chapter 6 for a description of NAMELIST input/output.

NULLS = *integer-variable*: Used in a list-directed input statement to count the null values read.

ADVANCE = 'NO' or 'YES': Enables or disables nonadvancing input/output.

SIZE = *integer-variable*: Used in nonadvancing input statements to count the characters read.

EOR = *label*: Transfers control to the specified statement if an end-of-record condition is encountered in a nonadvancing input/output statement.

● New clauses that may be used in the INQUIRE statement are

POSITION = *character-variable*: Assigns 'REWIND', 'APPEND', or 'ASIS' to the specified character variable, according to the file position specified in the OPEN statement for that file.

ACTION = *character-variable*: Assigns 'READ', 'WRITE', or 'READWRITE' to the specified character variable, according to the action specified in the OPEN statement for that file.

READ = *character-variable*: Assigns 'YES', 'NO', or 'UNKNOWN' to the specified character variable, according to whether READ is allowed, not allowed, or undetermined for the specified file.

WRITE = *character-variable*: Assigns 'YES', 'NO', or 'UNKNOWN' to the specified character variable, according to whether WRITE is allowed, not allowed, or undetermined for the specified file.

READWRITE = *character-variable*: Assigns 'YES', 'NO', or 'UN-KNOWN' to the specified character variable, according to whether READWRITE is allowed, not allowed, or undetermined for the specified file.

DELIM = *character-variable*: Assigns 'APOSTROPHE', 'QUOTE', or 'NONE' to the specified character variable, according to the de-limiter specified in the OPEN statement for that file.

PAD = *character-variable*: Assigns 'YES' or 'NO' to the specified character variable, according to whether or not padding is specified in the OPEN statement for that file.

IOLENGTH = *integer-variable*: Assigns to the specified integer var-iable the length of an unformatted output list in processor-dependent units. This value may be used in a RECL = clause in an OPEN statement for unformatted direct-access files.

12

Additional FORTRAN Features

We have more useless information than ignorance of what is useful.

Vauvenargues

There are a number of FORTRAN features that we have not yet discussed, as they are not commonly used and in some cases are not consistent with the principles of structured programming. But because they are part of the standard FORTRAN language, we examine these miscellaneous topics in this chapter.

12.1 The STOP and PAUSE Statement

The END statement in a FORTRAN program serves to terminate execution of the program. In more complex programs it may be necessary to stop execution before the END statement is reached. In such cases, execution can be terminated with a **STOP statement,** which has the form

    STOP

or

    STOP *constant*

where *constant* is an integer constant with five or fewer digits or is a character constant. Usually the constant is displayed when execution is terminated by a STOP statement of the second form, but the precise form of the termination message depends on the compiler.

In some cases, it may be desirable to interrupt program execution and then either terminate or continue it after examining some of the results produced.

A **PAUSE statement** may be used for this purpose. This statement has the form

PAUSE

or

PAUSE *constant*

where *constant* is an integer constant with five or fewer digits or a character constant that is usually displayed when execution is interrupted; the exact message (if any) depends on the compiler.

When the PAUSE statement is encountered, execution of the program is interrupted, but it may be resumed by means of an appropriate command. Execution resumes with the first executable statement following the PAUSE statement that caused execution to be suspended. The action required to resume execution depends on the system.

12.2 The IMPLICIT Statement

The usual FORTRAN naming convention is that unless otherwise specified, all variable names beginning with I, J, K, L, M, *or* N *are integer and that all other variables are real.* The programmer can override this naming convention with an **IMPLICIT statement,** which has the form

IMPLICIT *type1* $(a_1, a_2, \ldots)$, *type2* $(b_1, b_2, \ldots)$, $\ldots$

where each a_i, b_i, $\ldots$ is a letter or a pair of letters separated by a hyphen (-), and each *typei* is one of the following:

INTEGER
REAL
CHARACTER*n
LOGICAL
DOUBLE PRECISION
COMPLEX

The effect of this statement is to declare that all variables whose names begin with one of the letters a_1, a_2, $\ldots$ are *type1* variables, all those whose names begin with one of the letters b_1, b_2, $\ldots$ are *type2* variables, and so on. For example, the statement

IMPLICIT INTEGER (A-F, Z), CHARACTER*10 (L, X, Y)

declares that all variables whose names begin with A, B, C, D, E, F, or Z are of integer type and that all those whose names begin with L, X, or Y are character variables of length 10.

The IMPLICIT statement and all type statements (as well as other declaration statements considered in earlier chapters) must be placed in the specification part of a program, and among these, the IMPLICIT statement must precede all others. All variables whose names begin with letters other than those listed in the IMPLICIT statement have types determined by the naming convention or by subsequent type declarations. Thus, in the following set of statements

```
IMPLICIT CHARACTER*10 (A, L-N, Z), CHARACTER*5 (D-G)
INTEGER NUMBER, ZIP
CHARACTER*20 ADDRESS, LNAME, FNAME*12
REAL ALPHA, LAMBDA
```

the last three type statements override the types specified for the indicated variables by the naming convention established by the IMPLICIT statement or by the default FORTRAN naming convention.

As we have noted, however, it is a good programming practice to declare explicitly the type of each variable, because this encourages the programmer to think carefully about what each variable represents and how it is to be used. It is important that variables of a given type be used in a manner that is consistent with that data type, as the program may not execute correctly otherwise. Consequently, the programmer should not rely on the IMPLICIT statement or the default FORTRAN naming convention to determine the types of variables.

12.3   Other Control Statements: Arithmetic IF, Computed GO TO, Assigned GO TO

In our discussion in Chapter 4 of the three basic control structures—sequential structure, selection structure, and repetition structure—the selection structure was implemented using an IF or IF-ELSE IF construct and the logical IF statement. Three other statements in FORTRAN may also be used to implement selection structures, but they are less commonly used. They are the arithmetic IF statement, the computed GO TO statement, and the assigned GO TO statement.

The Arithmetic IF Statement.   The **arithmetic IF statement** has the form

IF $(expression)$ n_1, n_2, n_3

where the expression enclosed in parentheses is an arithmetic expression and n_1, n_2, and n_3 are labels of executable statements, not necessarily distinct. When this statement is executed, the value of the expression is calculated, and execution will continue with statement n_1 if this value is negative, with statement n_2 if it is zero, and with statement n_3 if it is positive. For example, consider the arithmetic IF statement

```
IF (X ** 2 - 10.5) 10, 15, 20
```

If X has the value 3.1, statement 10 will be executed next.

The program in Figure 12.1 is a modification of the program in Figure 4.9 to solve quadratic equations:

$$A x^2 + B x + C = 0$$

An arithmetic IF statement is used in place of an IF-ELSE IF construct to select the appropriate statements for execution, depending on whether the value of the discriminant $B^2 - 4AC$ is negative, zero, or positive.

```
      PROGRAM QUAD4
*************************************************************************
* Program to solve a quadratic equation using the quadratic formula.   *
* It uses an arithmetic IF statement to select the appropriate action  *
* depending on whether the discriminant DISC is negative, zero, or     *
* positive.  Variables used are:                                       *
*    A, B, C       : the coefficients of the quadratic equation        *
*    DISC          : the discriminant, B ** 2 - 4 * A * C              *
*    ROOT1, ROOT2 : the two roots of the equation                      *
*************************************************************************

      REAL A, B, C, DISC, ROOT1, ROOT2

      PRINT *, 'ENTER THE COEFFICIENTS OF THE QUADRATIC EQUATION'
      READ *, A, B, C
      DISC = B ** 2 - 4 * A * C
      IF (DISC) 10, 20, 30

* No real roots

10    PRINT *, 'DISCRIMINANT IS', DISC
      PRINT *, 'THERE ARE NO REAL ROOTS'
      STOP

* Repeated real root

20    ROOT1 = -B / (2 * A)
      PRINT *, 'REPEATED ROOT IS', ROOT1
      STOP

* Distinct real roots

30    DISC = SQRT(DISC)
      ROOT1 = (-B + DISC) / (2 * A)
      ROOT2 = (-B - DISC) / (2 * A)
      PRINT *, 'THE ROOTS ARE', ROOT1, ROOT2
      END
```

Figure 12.1

The Computed GO TO Statement.

The **computed GO TO statement** has the form

GO TO $(n_1, n_2, \ldots, n_k)$, *integer-expression*

where $n_1, n_2, \ldots, n_k$ are labels of executable statements, not necessarily distinct. The comma preceding the integer expression is optional. When this statement is executed, the value of the expression is computed. If this value is the integer i, execution will continue with the statement whose label is n_i. The computed GO TO statement can thus be used to implement a multialternative selection structure. For example, if J and K are integer variables, the statement

```
GO TO (50, 10, 5, 50, 80, 100), J - K
```

selects one of the statements 5, 10, 50, 80, 100 for execution, depending on the value of the expression J − K. If J − K has the value 5, statement 80 is executed next.

The Assigned GO TO Statement.

The **assigned GO TO statement** uses an integer variable to select the statement to be executed next. It has the form

GO TO *integer-variable*

or

GO TO *integer-variable*, $(n_1, \ldots, n_k)$

where $n_1, \ldots, n_k$ are labels of executable statements. The comma following the integer variable in the second form is optional.

Before execution of this statement, a statement label must be assigned to the integer variable by an **ASSIGN statement** of the form

ASSIGN *statement-label* TO *integer-variable*

The assigned GO TO statement then causes execution to continue with the statement whose label has been assigned to the specified integer variable.

In the second form of the assigned GO TO statement, a check is made at the time of execution to determine whether the statement label assigned to the integer variable is in the list $n_1, \ldots, n_k$. If it is not, an error message results. In the first form of the assigned GO TO statement, no such validation of the value of the integer variable takes place; if it is out of range, execution continues with the next executable statement in the program.

12.4 More About COMMON and Block Data Subprograms

Other COMMON Features. In Section 5.6 we described how the COMMON statement can be used to establish common regions for simple variables and in Sections 7.4 and 8.2 for arrays with the same dimensions. It is also possible to use the COMMON statement to establish common regions for arrays of different dimensions. For example, the statements

```
INTEGER B(3,4)
COMMON B
```

in one program unit and the statements

```
INTEGER BETA(2,6)
COMMON BETA
```

in another allocate the first twelve memory locations of the blank common region to both B and BETA, resulting in the following associations:

Array Element	Blank Common Location	Array Element
B(1,1)	#1	BETA(1,1)
B(2,1)	#2	BETA(2,1)
B(3,1)	#3	BETA(1,2)
B(1,2)	#4	BETA(2,2)
B(2,2)	#5	BETA(1,3)
B(3,2)	#6	BETA(2,3)
B(1,3)	#7	BETA(1,4)
B(2,3)	#8	BETA(2,4)
B(3,3)	#9	BETA(1,5)
B(1,4)	#10	BETA(2,5)
B(2,4)	#11	BETA(1,6)
B(3,4)	#12	BETA(2,6)

A COMMON statement may be used to associate two or more arrays with a single array. If the statements

```
REAL A(3,3), CONS(3)
COMMON A, CONS
```

appear in one program unit and

```
REAL AUG(3,4)
COMMON AUG
```

appear in another, the following associations will be established:

Array Element	Blank Common Location	Array Element
A(1,1)	#1	AUG(1,1)
A(2,1)	#2	AUG(2,1)
A(3,1)	#3	AUG(3,1)
A(1,2)	#4	AUG(1,2)
A(2,2)	#5	AUG(2,2)
A(3,2)	#6	AUG(3,2)
A(1,3)	#7	AUG(1,3)
A(2,3)	#8	AUG(2,3)
A(3,3)	#9	AUG(3,3)
CONS(1)	#10	AUG(1,4)
CONS(2)	#11	AUG(2,4)
CONS(3)	#12	AUG(3,4)

It also is possible to mix both simple variables and arrays in COMMON statements. For example, if the statements

```
REAL COEFF(2,2), C,D
COMMON COEFF, C, D
```

appear in one program unit and the statements

```
REAL GAUSS(2,3)
COMMON GAUSS
```

appear in another, these variables and array elements are associated as follows:

Array Element	Blank Common Location	Array Element
COEFF(1,1)	#1	GAUSS(1,1)
COEFF(2,1)	#2	GAUSS(2,1)
COEFF(1,2)	#3	GAUSS(1,2)
COEFF(2,2)	#4	GAUSS(2,2)
C	#5	GAUSS(1,3)
D	#6	GAUSS(2,3)

When arrays are listed in a COMMON statement, it is possible to dimension the arrays in the COMMON statement itself. For example, the preceding two pairs of statements can be written as

```
REAL COEFF, C, D
COMMON COEFF(2,2), C, D
```

and

```
REAL GAUSS
COMMON GAUSS(2,3)
```

In our examples thus far, the association established between items has been complete; that is, there is a one-to-one correspondence between the items. It also is possible to establish a partial correspondence, in which some of the items listed in one of the COMMON statements are not associated with items in the other COMMON statement. For example, the statements

```
REAL A, X(3)
COMMON A, X
```

in one program unit and

```
REAL B(6)
COMMON B
```

in another program unit establish a partial association, as follows:

$$
\begin{array}{ll}
A & \leftrightarrow B(1) \\
X(1) & \leftrightarrow B(2) \\
X(2) & \leftrightarrow B(3) \\
X(3) & \leftrightarrow B(4) \\
& B(5) \\
& B(6)
\end{array}
$$

Numeric and character type variables may not be allocated memory locations from the same common region. Named common regions, however, are separate regions. Consequently, numeric variables may be allocated to one named region and character variables to another, with both regions established in the same COMMON statement. Thus, the statements

```
REAL X, Y
INTEGER M, N
CHARACTER*10 A, B, C
COMMON /NUMER/ X, Y, M, N /CHARAC/ A, B, C
```

may appear in one program unit, and the statements

```
REAL X, Z
INTEGER I, J
CHARACTER*10 ALPHA, BETA, GAMMA
COMMON /NUMER/ X, Z, I, J /CHARAC/ ALPHA, BETA, GAMMA
```

in another.

Block Data Subprograms. We noted in Section 5.6 that items that are allocated memory locations in blank common may not be initialized in DATA statements. However, items allocated memory locations from a named common region may be initialized in a DATA statement, provided that this initialization is done in a special kind of subprogram called a **block data subprogram.**

The first statement of a block data subprogram is

BLOCK DATA

or

BLOCK DATA *name*

A program may contain more than one block data subprogram, but at most one of these may be unnamed. A *block data subprogram contains no executable statements.* Only comments and the following statements may appear in block data subprograms:

IMPLICIT
PARAMETER
DIMENSION
COMMON
SAVE
EQUIVALENCE
DATA
END
Type statements

The last statement of the subprogram must, of course, be an END statement.

A block data subprogram initializes items in named common regions by listing these items in COMMON statements and specifying their values in DATA statements. Suppose, for example, that variables A and B and the array LIST are allocated memory locations in common region BLOCK1 and that the character variable CODE and character array NAME are allocated locations in common region BLOCK2. The following block data subprogram could be used to initialize A, B, LIST(1), . . . , LIST(5), CODE, and the entire array NAME:

```
BLOCK DATA
INTEGER M, N
PARAMETER (M = 20, N = 50)
REAL A, B
INTEGER LIST(M)
CHARACTER*10 CODE, NAME(N)
COMMON /BLOCK1/ A, B, LIST /BLOCK2/ CODE, NAME
DATA A, B, (LIST(I), I = 1, 5) /2.5, 3.5, 5*0/
DATA CODE, NAME /'&', N*' '/
END
```

12.5 The EQUIVALENCE Statement

The **EQUIVALENCE statement** makes it possible to associate variables and arrays in the *same* program unit so that they refer to the same memory locations. This statement is of the form

EQUIVALENCE (*list1*), (*list2*), . . .

where each of *list1*, *list2*, ... is a list of variables, arrays, array elements, or substring names separated by commas, which are to be allocated the same memory locations. Each of the sets of items that constitute one of the lists in parentheses is said to be an **equivalence class.** *The EQUIVALENCE statement is nonexecutable and must appear in the specification part of the program.*

As an illustration, consider the statements

```
INTEGER M1, M2, NUM
REAL X, Y, ALPHA(5), BETA(5)
EQUIVALENCE (X, Y), (M1, M2, NUM), (ALPHA, BETA)
```

The variables and elements of the arrays that appear in the EQUIVALENCE statement are allocated in the following manner:

$$X \leftrightarrow Y$$
$$M1 \leftrightarrow M2 \leftrightarrow NUM$$
$$ALPHA(1) \leftrightarrow BETA(1)$$
$$ALPHA(2) \leftrightarrow BETA(2)$$
$$ALPHA(3) \leftrightarrow BETA(3)$$
$$ALPHA(4) \leftrightarrow BETA(4)$$
$$ALPHA(5) \leftrightarrow BETA(5)$$

Because associated variables refer to the same memory locations, changing the value of one of these variables also changes the value of all variables in the same equivalence class.

The following rules govern the use of EQUIVALENCE statements:

1. Two (or more) items may not be equivalenced if they *both* appear in a COMMON statement(s) in the same program unit.
2. Formal arguments may not be equivalenced.
3. Items of character type may be equivalenced only with other items of character type. Numeric items of different types may be equivalenced, but extreme care must be exercised because of the different internal representations used for different numeric types.

The EQUIVALENCE statement is most often used to make efficient use of memory by associating the elements of large arrays. Suppose, for example, a program processes a 100×100 array BIG and a 40×250 array TABLE. If the array BIG is no longer needed when the processing of TABLE begins, the two arrays can be equivalenced by the statement

```
EQUIVALENCE (BIG, TABLE)
```

In the preceding examples, arrays have been equivalenced by specifying the array names in the same equivalence class. This has the effect of associating the first elements in these arrays and successive elements. For example, the statements

```
REAL A(5), B(5)
EQUIVALENCE (A, B)
```

associate the elements of the arrays A and B in the following manner:

A(1)   A(2)   A(3)   A(4)   A(5)
↕   ↕   ↕   ↕   ↕
B(1)   B(2)   B(3)   B(4)   B(5)

The name of an array element may also be used in specifying the items of an equivalence class. The statement

```
EQUIVALENCE (A(1), B(1))
```

establishes the same associations as in the preceding example. This same association can also be established with the statement

```
EQUIVALENCE (A(3), B(3))
```

or

```
EQUIVALENCE (A(4), B(4))
```

and so on. The array elements listed in an equivalence class indicate the elements at which the association is to begin, with the remaining elements in the arrays associated in the natural way. Thus, the statement

```
EQUIVALENCE (A(2), B(3))
```

establishes the following associations:

                A(1)   A(2)   A(3)   A(4)   A(5)
                ↕   ↕   ↕   ↕
        B(1)   B(2)   B(3)   B(4)   B(5)

Similarly, the statements

```
REAL P, X(3), Y(5), Z(7)
EQUIVALENCE (P, X, Y(3), Z(4))
```

establish the following associations

                                P
                                ↕
                                X(1)   X(2)   X(3)
                                ↕   ↕   ↕
                Y(1)   Y(2)   Y(3)   Y(4)   Y(5)
                ↕   ↕   ↕   ↕   ↕
        Z(1)   Z(2)   Z(3)   Z(4)   Z(5)   Z(6)   Z(7)

If variables of character type are equivalenced, association begins with the first character position of each variable and continues with successive positions. If substrings are equivalenced, association begins with the first positions of the specified substrings with the remaining character positions associated in the natural way. For example, the statements

```
CHARACTER*5 F, G, H, I, J*7, K*8
EQUIVALENCE (F, G), (H, J), (I(2: ), K(4: ))
```

establish the following associations:

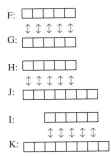

When character arrays are equivalenced using the array names, association begins with the first character position of the first elements of each array and continues with successive character positions of successive array elements. For example, the statements

```
CHARACTER*4 A(3), B(6)*2
EQUIVALENCE (A, B)
```

establish the following associations:

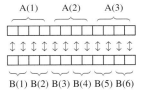

Specifying an array element or a substring of an array element in an equivalence class is also possible. In this case, association begins with the first character position of the array element or substring indicated and continues in the manner described for arrays and substrings.

It is possible for a variable or an array to appear in both an EQUIVALENCE statement and a COMMON statement. To illustrate, suppose that one program unit contains the statements

```
REAL BIG(100,100), LARGE(40, 250)
EQUIVALENCE (BIG, LARGE)
COMMON BIG
```

and another program unit contains the statements

```
REAL X(10000)
COMMON X
```

Each of the following triples of array elements then refers to the same memory location:

BIG(1,1),	LARGE(1, 1),	X(1)
BIG(2,1),	LARGE(2, 1),	X(2)
.	.	.
.	.	.
.	.	.
BIG(100,1),	LARGE(20, 3),	X(100)
BIG(1,2),	LARGE(21, 3),	X(101)
.	.	.
.	.	.
.	.	.
BIG(100,100),	LARGE(40, 250),	X(10000)

Some care must be exercised, however, when using such a combination of EQUIVALENCE and COMMON statements. When an array appears in an EQUIVALENCE statement, it may imply an extension of a common region. For example, the statements

```
REAL X, Y, Z, A(5)
COMMON X, Y, Z
EQUIVALENCE (Y, A(2))
```

establish the following associations:

Variable	Blank Common Location	Array Element
X	#1	A(1)
Y	#2	A(2)
Z	#3	A(3)
	#4	A(4)
	#5	A(5)

with the implied extension of blank common by the addition of memory locations #4 and #5. Such an extension "in the direction of increasing locations" is allowed, but an extension to locations preceding the first one is not. Thus, replacement of the preceding EQUIVALENCE statement by

```
EQUIVALENCE (Y, A(3))
```

is not allowed, since this statement would require the following extension:

Variable	Blank Common Location	Array Element
		A(1)
X	#1	A(2)
Y	#2	A(3)
Z	#3	A(4)
	#4	A(5)

12.6   Alternate Entries and Returns

The ENTRY Statement.   The normal entry point of a subprogram is the first executable statement following the FUNCTION or SUBROUTINE statement. In some cases, some other entry may be convenient. For example, it may be necessary to assign values to certain variables the first time a subprogram is referenced but not on subsequent references.

Multiple entry points in subprograms are introduced by using **ENTRY statements** of the form

ENTRY *name(argument-list)*

where *name* is the name of the entry point and *argument-list* is similar to the argument list in a FUNCTION or SUBROUTINE statement.

ENTRY statements are *nonexecutable* and thus have no effect on the normal execution sequence in the subprogram. Entry into the subprogram can be directed to the first executable statement following an ENTRY statement.

Suppose we wish to prepare a function subprogram to evaluate $Ax^2 + Bx + C$ for various values of x. In this case, we could use the following function subprogram:

```
FUNCTION QUAD(X)
REAL QUAD, X, A, B, C, POLY
SAVE A, B, C

READ *, A, B, C

ENTRY POLY(X)

QUAD = A * X ** 2 + B * X + C

END
```

The first reference to this function in the main program would be with a statement such as

```
VAL = QUAD(Z)
```

which would cause values for A, B, and C in the subprogram to be read and the function evaluated at Z. Subsequent references to this function might be by a statement such as

```
Y = POLY(Z)
```

In such cases, entry into the subprogram would be at the first statement following the ENTRY statement; thus, the function would be evaluated at Z using the values for A, B, and C read previously.

Different entry points in a subprogram may have different argument lists. In this case, care must be taken to ensure that the actual argument list in a reference agrees with the formal argument list in the corresponding ENTRY statement.

Normally, all entry names in a function subprogram are the same type as that of the function name. In this case, any of these names may be used to assign the function value to be returned. Thus, the statement

```
POLY = A * X ** 2 + B * X + C
```

could be used in place of the statement

```
QUAD = A * X ** 2 + B * X + C
```

in the function subprogram QUAD.

If any entry name is of character type, then all entry names, including the function name, must be of character type, and all must have the same lengths. For numeric-valued functions, entry names may be of different types, but for each reference to some entry name, there must be at least one statement that assigns a value to an entry name having the same type as the name being referenced.

Alternate Returns. In certain situations, it may be convenient to return from a subroutine at some point other than the normal return point (the first executable statement following the CALL statement). This can be accomplished as follows:

1. In the CALL statement, specify the alternate points of return by using arguments of the form

    $*n$

    where n denotes a statement label indicating the statement to be executed upon return from the subprogram.
2. Use asterisks (*) as the corresponding formal arguments in the SUBROUTINE statement.
3. Use a statement in the subroutine of the form

    RETURN k

where *k* is an integer expression whose value indicates which of the alternate returns is to be used.

The following example illustrates:

Main Program:

```
      .
      .
      .
      CALL SUBR(A, B, C, *30, *40)
   20 D = A * B
      .
      .
      .
   30 D = A + B
      .
      .
      .
   40 D = A - B
      .
      .
      .
      END

      SUBROUTINE SUBR(X, Y, TERM, *, *)
      .
      .
      .
      IF (TERM .LT. 0) RETURN 1
      IF (TERM .GT. 0) RETURN 2
      END
```

The return to the main program from the subroutine SUBR is to statement 30 if the value of TERM is less than 0, to statement 40 if it is greater than zero, and to statement 20 (normal return) if it is equal to zero.

FORTRAN 90 Features

For several of the FORTRAN features described in this chapter, better alternatives are already available in FORTRAN 77, and these features have therefore been declared to be "obsolescent" in FORTRAN 90, which means that they are candidates for deletion in a future FORTRAN language standard. These obsolescent features are

- The PAUSE statement
- The arithmetic IF statement
- The ASSIGN statement
- The assigned GO TO statement
- Alternate returns

13

New Directions in FORTRAN 90

Great things can be reduced to small things, and small things can be reduced to nothing.

CHINESE PROVERB

*Yea, from the table of my memory
I'll wipe away all trivial fond records.*

WILLIAM SHAKESPEARE, *Hamlet*

[Pointers] are like little jumps, leaping wildly from one part of a data structure to another. Their introduction into high-level languages has been a step backward from which we may never recover.

C. A. R. HOARE

I've got a little list, I've got a little list.

GILBERT AND SULLIVAN, *The Mikado*

At the ends of most of the preceding chapters we have included sections entitled *FORTRAN 90 Features* in which we have described some of the variations of and extensions to FORTRAN 77 that are provided in FORTRAN 90, including improved source form features, new data type declarations, additional selection and repetition structures, internal procedures, additional input/output facilities, and array operations. There are also several fundamental additions to FORTRAN that extend the language in more modern directions by supporting important new software-engineering concepts and techniques. These include user-defined data types, pointer types that may be used to implement linked data structures, and modules, which facilitate modular programming. In this chapter we describe each of these FORTRAN 90 features.

13.1 Modules

In many applications there are parameters, variables, types, and subprograms that must be shared by several program units or by separate programs. FORTRAN 90 provides a program unit called a **module**, which is a package of declarations and definitions that can be imported into other program units. This makes it possible to reuse these declarations and definitions in separate programs or program units without rewriting them in each unit in which they are needed.

The simplest form of a module consists only of a heading, a specification part, and an END statement:

MODULE *module-name*
    specification part
END MODULE *module-name*

where the specification part has the same form as for other program units, and the word MODULE and the module name are optional in the END statement. For example, the module

```
MODULE CIRCLE

! Module containing definitions and declarations
! for processing circles with known radii.

    REAL, PARAMETER :: PI = 3.141592
    REAL RADIUS

END MODULE CIRCLE
```

defines the real parameter PI and declares RADIUS to be a real variable.

Once a module has been compiled, its parameters, variables, types, and subprograms are ready to be *exported* to programs, subprograms, and other modules. They must be *imported* into these program units by placing a USES statement of the form

USES *module-name*

or

USES *module-name*, ONLY : *item-list*

at the beginning of the specification part of that unit. The first form makes available all of the items in the specified module (except those that have been declared to be private items), while the second form makes available only those items specified in *item-list*. The following program with an attached external function illustrates:

```
PROGRAM PROCESS_CIRCLES

   USES CIRCLE
   REAL AREA

   PRINT *, 'ENTER RADIUS OF CIRCLE:'
   READ *, RADIUS
   PRINT *, 'AREA = ', AREA(RADIUS)

END PROGRAM PROCESS_CIRCLES

REAL FUNCTION AREA(RADIUS)

   USES CIRCLE

   AREA = PI * RADIUS**2

END FUNCTION AREA
```

Besides definitions and declarations of parameters, variables, and types, modules may also contain procedures. In this case, the form of the module is

MODULE *module-name*
   specification part
CONTAINS
   module procedures
END MODULE *module-name*

For example, we could package the function AREA with the declarations of PI and RADIUS in the module CIRCLE:

```
MODULE CIRCLE

! Module containing definitions, declarations,
! and a function AREA for processing circles
! with known radii.

   REAL, PARAMETER :: PI = 3.141592
   REAL RADIUS

CONTAINS
   REAL FUNCTION AREA(RADIUS)

     AREA = PI * RADIUS**2

   END FUNCTION AREA

END MODULE CIRCLE
```

The program PROCESS__CIRCLES could now be written:

```
PROGRAM PROCESS_CIRCLES

   USES CIRCLE

   PRINT *, 'ENTER RADIUS OF CIRCLE:'
   READ *, RADIUS
   PRINT *, 'AREA = ', AREA(RADIUS)

END PROGRAM PROCESS_CIRCLES
```

The USES statement imports the definitions and declarations of the real parameter PI, the real variable RADIUS, and the real-valued function AREA from module CIRCLE.

In the same way, these items can be imported into and used in any other program unit in which it is necessary to find the area of a circle with a given radius:

```
PROGRAM PROCESS_CIRCLES2

   USES CIRCLE
   REAL DIAMETER

   PRINT *, 'ENTER DIAMETER OF CIRCLE:'
   READ *, DIAMETER
   RADIUS = DIAMETER / 2.0
   PRINT *, 'AREA = ', AREA(RADIUS)

END PROGRAM PROCESS_CIRCLES2
```

As described in the FORTRAN 90 Features of Chapter 5, interface blocks may be used to specify functions used to define or overload operators, to specify subroutines used to extend the assignment operator, and to specify a collection of subprograms that may be referenced by a single generic subprogram name. When the functions or subroutines are procedures contained in a module, a special form of the interface block must be used to specify these procedures:

> INTERFACE *specifier*
> > MODULE PROCEDURE *list-of-procedures*
>
> END INTERFACE

where *specifier* has one of the forms

> OPERATOR (*operator*)
> ASSIGNMENT (=)
> *generic-name*

This is especially useful when using modules to define new data types, as described in the next section.

In the preceding examples of modules, all of the items defined and declared in a module are *public* items, which means that they all can be imported from such a module into a program unit. It is also possible to specify that certain items within a module are *private* to that module; that is, they can be used only within that module and are not accessible outside it. This may be done by listing these items in a PRIVATE statement or by specifying the attribute PRIVATE in the type statements used to declare those items. For example, the parameter PI can be declared to be private to the module CIRCLE by inserting the statement

```
PRIVATE PI
```

in the specification part of the module or by modifying the declaration of PI as

```
REAL, PRIVATE, PARAMETER :: PI = 3.141592
```

A PUBLIC statement and the attribute PUBLIC are also available for explicitly specifying those items that are exported from the module.

13.2 Derived Data Types

FORTRAN 77 provides the six simple data types—INTEGER, REAL, DOUBLE PRECISION, COMPLEX, CHARACTER, and LOGICAL—and one structured data type, the array, but it makes no provision for user-defined types. FORTRAN 90 refers to the aforementioned types as *intrinsic* data types, and to these can be added user-defined types that are *derived* from these intrinsic types. These new types are called **derived types,** and an item of such a type is called a **structure**.

Arrays are used to store elements of the same type. In many situations, however, we need to process items that are related in some way but that are not all of the same type. For example, a date consists of a month name (of character type), a day (of integer type), and a year (of integer type); a record of computer usage might contain, among other items, a user's name and password (character strings), identification number (integer), and resources used to date (real). In FORTRAN 90, a derived data type can be used to declare a structure, which can be used to store such related data items of possibly different types. The positions in the structure in which these data items are stored are called the **components** of the structure. Thus, a structure for storing computer usage information might contain a name component, a password component, an identification number component, and a resources used component.

A simple form of a derived type definition is

TYPE *type-name*
   type specification statement for component-list-1
   type specification statement for component-list-2
     .
     .
     .

END TYPE *type-name*

where *type-name* is a valid FORTRAN identifier that names the derived type and each of the type specification statements declares the type of one or more components. For example, the type definition

```
TYPE COMPUTER_USER
    CHARACTER (LEN = 20) :: NAME, PASSWORD
    INTEGER ID_NUMBER
    REAL RESOURCES_USED
END TYPE COMPUTER_USER
```

defines the derived type COMPUTER_USER. A structure of this type will have four components: NAME and PASSWORD, which are of character type with values of length 20; ID_NUMBER of integer type; and RESOURCES_USED of real type. The components of a structure need not be of different types. For example, the type definition

```
TYPE POINT
    REAL X, Y
END TYPE POINT
```

defines the derived type POINT, and a structure of type POINT will have two components named X and Y, each of which is of real type.

Such type definitions are placed in the specification part of a program unit. The type identifiers they define can then be used in a type specification statement of the form

TYPE (*type-name*) *list-of-identifiers*

to declare the types of structures. For example, the type specification statement

```
TYPE (POINT) P, Q
```

declare structures P and Q of type POINT;

```
TYPE (COMPUTER_USER) PERSON
```

declares a structure PERSON of type COMPUTER_USER; and

```
TYPE (COMPUTER_USER) USER(50)
```

or

```
TYPE (COMPUTER_USER) DIMENSION (50) :: USER
```

declares a one-dimensional array USER, each of whose elements is a structure of type COMPUTER_USER.

Values of a derived type are sequences of values for the components of that derived type. Their form is

type-name(*list of component values*)

For example,

```
POINT(2.5, 3.2)
```

is a value of type POINT and can be assigned to the variable P of type POINT

```
P = POINT(2.5, 3.2)
```

or associated with a parameter ORIGIN of type POINT,

```
TYPE (POINT), PARAMETER :: ORIGIN = POINT(2.5, 3.2)
```

Similarly,

```
COMPUTER_USER('John Q. Doe', 'SECRET', 12345, 234.98)
```

is a value of type COMPUTER__USER and can be assigned to the variable PERSON or to a component of the array USER:

```
PERSON = COMPUTER_USER('John Q. Doe', 'SECRET', 12345, 234.98)
USER[1] = PERSON
```

The values of the components in such *derived-type constructors* may also be variables or expressions. For example, if A is a real variable with value 1.1, the assignment statement

```
P = POINT(A, 2.0*A)
```

assigns the structure having real components 1.1 and 2.2 to the variable P.
A reference to an individual component of a structure has the form

structure-name%component-name

For example, P%X is the first component of the structure P of type POINT, and P%Y is the second component; USER[1]%NAME, USER[1]%PASS-WORD, USER[1]%ID__NUMBER, and USER[1]%RESOURCES__USED refer to the four components of the structure USER[1].
The components of a structure may be of any type; in particular, they may be other structures. For example, the declarations

```
TYPE POINT
    REAL X, Y
END TYPE POINT

TYPE CIRCLE
    TYPE (POINT) CENTER
    REAL RADIUS
END TYPE CIRCLE

TYPE (CIRCLE) C
```

declare C to be a structure whose values are of type CIRCLE. Such a structure has two components: The first component CENTER is of type POINT and is itself a structure having two real components named X and Y; the second component RADIUS is of type REAL.

The components within such a **nested structure** may be accessed by simply affixing a second component identifier to the name of the larger structure. Thus, if C is assigned a value by

```
C = CIRCLE(POINT(2.5, 3.2), 10)
```

representing a circle of radius 10, centered at (2.5, 3.2), the value of C%CENTER%X is 2.5, the value of C%CENTER%Y is 3.2, and the value of C%RADIUS is 10.0.

Each component of a structure has a specified type, and any reference to that component of the form *structure-name%component-name* may be used in the same way as is any item of that type. For example, since PERSON%NAME is of character type, it may be assigned a value in an assignment statement

```
PERSON%NAME = 'MARY Q. SMITH'
```

or by an input statement

```
READ '(A)', PERSON%NAME
```

Its value can be displayed by using an output statement

```
PRINT *, PERSON%NAME
```

and its value can be modified by a substring reference:

```
PERSON%NAME(1:4) = 'JOAN'
```

The only intrinsic operation provided for structures is the assignment operation (=); all other processing must be carried out using the individual components. As we noted in the preceding section, however, it is possible to define new operations on any data type, and in particular, operations on derived types. For example, suppose that two circles are said to be equal if they have the same center and the same radius, and we wish to extend the relational operator = = to include this meaning for structures of type CIRCLE. An interface block of the following form can be used to overload = =:

```
INTERFACE OPERATOR (==)
   MODULE PROCEDURE EQUALS
END INTERFACE
```

A function EQUALS to implement = = for structures of type CIRCLE is

```
FUNCTION EQUALS (C1, C2)

! Function to determine if two circles C1 and C2 are
! equal, which means that they have the same center and
! equal radii.

TYPE (CIRCLE) C1, C2
LOGICAL EQUALS

EQUALS = C1%CENTER%X == C2%CENTER%X &
   .AND. C1%CENTER%Y == C2%CENTER%Y &
   .AND. C1%RADIUS == C2%RADIUS

END FUNCTION EQUALS
```

Packaging the type definitions of CIRCLE, the preceding interface block,
and the function EQUALS in a module like the following makes it possible to
use this new data type in much the same way as intrinsic data types:

```
MODULE CIRCLE_TYPE

! Module to define the derived data type CIRCLE for
! processing circles with given centers and radii. It also
! extends the relational operator == to type CIRCLE.
! Two circles are equal if they have the same center and
! equal radii.

   TYPE POINT
      REAL X, Y
   END TYPE POINT

   TYPE CIRCLE
      TYPE (POINT) CENTER
      REAL RADIUS
   END TYPE CIRCLE

   INTERFACE OPERATOR (==)
      MODULE PROCEDURE EQUALS
   END INTERFACE

CONTAINS
   FUNCTION EQUALS(C1, C2)

      ! Function to determine if two circles C1 and C2 are
      ! equal, which means that they have the same center and
      ! equal radii.

      TYPE (CIRCLE) C1, C2
      LOGICAL EQUALS
      EQUALS = C1%CENTER%X == C2%CENTER%X &
         .AND. C1%CENTER%Y == C2%CENTER%Y &
         .AND. C1%RADIUS == C2%RADIUS

   END FUNCTION EQUALS

END MODULE CIRCLE_TYPE
```

This new data type may then be used in any other program unit by simply importing it from this module:

```
PROGRAM CIRCLE_DEMO

    USES CIRCLE_TYPE
    TYPE (CIRCLE) UNITCIRCLE, CIR
          .
          .
          .
    UNITCIRCLE = CIRCLE(POINT(0.0, 0.0), 1.0)
    IF (CIR == UNITCIRCLE) THEN
          .
          .

END PROGRAM CIRCLE_DEMO
```

13.3 Pointers and Linked Structures

Variables are symbolic addresses of memory locations. This relationship between a variable and the memory location it names is a static one that is established when the program is compiled and remains fixed throughout the execution of the program. Although the contents of a memory location associated with a variable may change, variables themselves can be neither created nor destroyed during execution. Consequently, these variables are called **static variables.**

In some situations, however, the memory requirements are known only while the program is executing, so that static variables are not adequate. In such cases, a method for acquiring additional memory locations as needed during execution and for releasing them when they are no longer needed is required. Variables that are created and disposed of during execution are called **dynamic variables.** At one point during execution, there may be a particular memory location associated with a dynamic variable, and at a later time, no memory location or a different one may be associated with it.

Unlike **static data structures** such as arrays whose sizes and associated memory locations are fixed at compile time, **dynamic data structures** expand or contract as required during execution, and their associated memory locations change. A dynamic data structure is a collection of elements called **nodes** of the structure that are linked together. This linking is established by associating with each node a pointer that points to the next node in the structure. One of the simplest linked structures is a *linked list* that might be pictured as follows:

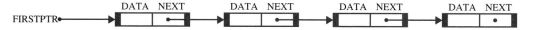

Dynamic data structures are especially useful for storing and processing data sets whose sizes change during program execution, for example, the collection of jobs that have been entered into a computer system and are awaiting execution or the collection of passenger names and seat assignments on a given airplane flight.

Construction of a dynamic data structure requires the ability to allocate memory locations as needed during program execution. Because the number of locations is not known in advance, they cannot be allocated in the usual manner using variable declarations, since such allocations are made at compile time. Instead, an ALLOCATE statement is used for this purpose. When it is executed, it returns the address of a memory location (possibly consisting of several memory words) in which a node of the data structure can be stored. To access this memory location so that data can be stored in it or retrieved from it, a special kind of variable called a **pointer variable,** or simply **pointer,** is used. The value of a pointer is thus the address of some memory location.

The nodes of a dynamic data structure may be of any type but are most often structures. A pointer used to reference the memory location storing one of these nodes must be declared to have the POINTER attribute in a type statement of the form

TYPE (*type-name*), POINTER :: *pointer-variable*

where *type-name* specifies the type of the nodes. For example, the declarations

```
TYPE INVENTORY_INFO
   INTEGER NUMBER
   REAL PRICE
END TYPE INVENTORY_INFO

TYPE (INVENTORY_INFO), POINTER :: INVPTR
```

can be used to declare a pointer INVPTR to nodes of type INVEN-TORY__INFO.

The ALLOCATE statement may then be used during program execution to acquire memory locations in which inventory records can be stored. The statement has the form

ALLOCATE (*list-of-pointer-variables*)

which assigns addresses of distinct memory locations to the specified pointer variables. Thus the statement

```
ALLOCATE (INVPTR)
```

assigns to INVPTR a memory address, say 1074; that is, the value of INVPTR is this memory address:

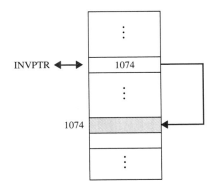

This is the address of a memory location where a value of type INVEN-TORY__INFO can be stored. We say that INVPTR "points" to this memory location and picture this by a diagram like the following:

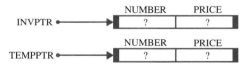

The contents of boxes representing components of a structure of type INVEN-TORY_INFO are shown here as question marks to indicate that these components are initially undefined.

Each execution of an ALLOCATE statement acquires new memory locations for each of the pointer variables in it. This means that any of these pointer variables are disassociated from any other memory locations to which they may have pointed and they are now associated with new locations; the other memory locations are no longer accessible (unless pointed to by some other pointer variables). It also means that the ALLOCATE statement will never cause two different pointer variables to be associated with the same memory locations. Thus, if TEMPPTR is also a pointer of the same type as INVPTR, the statement

```
ALLOCATE (TEMPPTR)
```

will acquire a new memory location pointed to by TEMPPTR:

The value of a pointer is the address of a memory location. Whenever a pointer name is used in an expression or on the left side of an assignment statement, however, it refers to the value stored in this memory location. Thus, for the most part, a pointer variable like INVPTR can be used in a program unit as though it were a structure of type INVENTORY__INFO. For example, the statement

```
INVPTR = INVENTORY_INFO(3511, 7.50)
```

is legal and copies the values 3511 and 7.50 into the memory location pointed to by INVPTR:

Similarly, if ITEM is a static variable of type INVENTORY__INFO, the assignment statement

```
ITEM = INVPTR
```

is legal and copies the contents of the memory location pointed to by INVPTR into the memory location associated with ITEM, just as though INVPTR were itself a structure of type INVENTORY__INFO.

One consequence of this convention is that an assignment statement involving two pointers such as

```
TEMPPTR = INVPTR
```

is treated as an assignment involving two structures and copies the structure pointed to by INVPTR into the location pointed to by TEMPPTR:

It does *not* assign the value of INVPTR (which is a memory address) to TEMPTR. A special assignment operator ($=>$) is used to copy the value (memory address) of a pointer variable and assign it to another pointer variable. Thus, the statement

```
TEMPPTR => INVPTR
```

assigns the value of INVPTR to TEMPPTR so that both point to the same memory location:

	NUMBER	PRICE
INVPTR ●──────→	3511	7.50
	NUMBER	PRICE
TEMPPTR ●	3511	7.50

The previous location (if any) pointed to by TEMPPTR can no longer be accessed unless pointed to by some other pointer.

In some situations it is necessary to assign a special value called a **nil** value to a pointer variable that indicates that it does not point to any memory location. This can be done by using a NULLIFY statement of the form

NULLIFY (*list-of-pointer-variables*)

The intrinsic function ASSOCIATED can be used to test whether a pointer is nil. A reference of the form

ASSOCIATED(*pointer-variable*)

returns false if the specified pointer variable has been nullified and true otherwise; it is undefined if the pointer variable has been neither allocated nor nullified.

If the memory locations pointed to by certain pointer variables are no longer needed, they may be released and made available for later allocation by using a DEALLOCATE statement of the form

DEALLOCATE (*list-of-pointer-variables*)

This statement frees the memory locations pointed to by the specified pointers and nullifies these pointer variables.

One of the important properties of pointer variables is that they make it possible to implement dynamic data structures such as linked lists. A **linked list** consists of a collection of elements called **nodes** linked together by pointers, together with a pointer to the first node in the list. The nodes contain two different kinds of information: (1) the actual data item being stored and (2) a **link** or pointer to the next node in the list. A linked list containing the integers 95, 47, and 83 with 95 as the first element might thus be pictured as follows:

In this diagram, FIRSTPTR is a pointer to the first node in the list. The DATA component of each node stores one of the integers, and the NEXT component is a pointer to the next node. The dot in the last node having no arrow emanating from it represents a nil pointer and indicates that there is no next node.

The nodes in a linked list are represented in FORTRAN 90 as structures having two kinds of components, **data components** and **link components.** The data components have types that are appropriate for storing the necessary information, and the link components are pointers. For example, the type of the nodes in the preceding linked list may be defined by

```
TYPE LIST_NODE
    INTEGER DATA
    TYPE (LIST_NODE), POINTER :: NEXT
END TYPE LIST_NODE
```

Each node in this list is a structure of type LIST_NODE, consisting of two components. The first component DATA is of integer type and is used to store the data. The second component NEXT is a pointer and points to the next node in the list.

In addition to the nodes of the list in which to store the data items, a pointer to the first node is needed. Thus we declare a pointer variable FIRSTPTR by

```
TYPE (LIST_NODE), POINTER :: FIRSTPTR
```

To illustrate the basic steps in the construction of a linked list, suppose that the integers 83 and 47 have already been stored in a linked list:

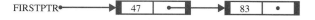

and that we wish to add 95 to this list. In the construction, we use two pointers, FIRSTPTR to point to the first node in the list and TEMPPTR as a temporary pointer:

```
TYPE (LIST_NODE), POINTER :: FIRSTPTR, TEMPPTR
```

We first acquire a new node temporarily pointed to by TEMPPTR,

```
ALLOCATE (TEMPPTR)
```

and store 95 in the data component of this structure:

```
TEMPPTR%DATA = 95
```

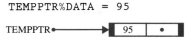

This node can then be joined to the list by setting its link component so that it points to the first node:

```
TEMPPTR%NEXT => FIRSTPTR
```

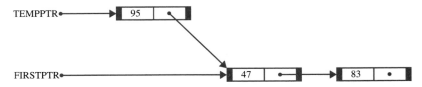

The pointer FIRSTPTR is then updated to point to this new node:

```
FIRSTPTR => TEMPPTR
```

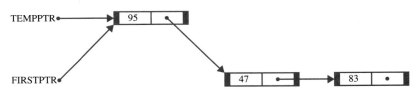

To construct the entire list, we could first initialize an empty list:

```
NULLIFY (FIRSTPTR)
```

and then repeat the preceding four statements three times, replacing 95 by 83 in the second assignment statement, then by 47, and finally using the value 95. In practice, however, such linked lists are usually constructed by reading the data values rather than assigning them by means of assignment statements. In this example, the linked list could be constructed by using the following program segment, where ITEM is an integer variable:

```
! Initially the list is empty
  NULLIFY (FIRSTPTR)

! Read the data values and construct the list
  READ *, ITEM
  DO WHILE (ITEM .NE. END_DATA_FLAG)
     ALLOCATE (TEMPPTR)
     TEMPPTR%DATA = ITEM
     TEMPPTR%NEXT => FIRSTPTR
     FIRSTPTR => TEMPPTR
     READ *, ITEM
  END DO
```

Once a linked list has been constructed, we may want to **traverse** the list from beginning to end, displaying each element in it. To traverse a list stored in an array, we can easily move through the list from one element to the next by varying an array subscript in some repetition structure. The analog for a linked list is to move through the list by varying a pointer variable in a repetition structure.

To illustrate, suppose we wish to display the integers stored in the linked list:

We begin by initializing a pointer variable CURRPTR to point to the first node:

```
CURRPTR => FIRSTPTR
```

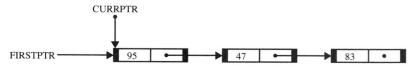

and display the integer stored in this node:

```
PRINT *, CURRPTR%DATA
```

To move to the next node, we follow the link from the current node:

```
CURRPTR => CURRPTR%NEXT
```

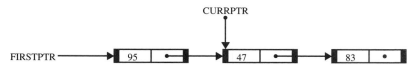

After displaying the integer in this node, we move to the next node:

```
CURRPTR => CURRPTR%NEXT
```

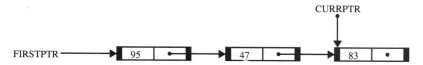

and display its data. Since we have now reached the last node, we need some way to signal this condition. But this is easy, for if we attempt to move to the next node, CURRPTR becomes nil:

The function ASSOCIATED can be used to determine when this occurs:

```
CURRPT => FIRSTPTR
DO WHILE (ASSOCIATED(CURRPTR))
   PRINT *, CURRPTR%DATA
   CURRPTR => CURRPTR%NEXT
END DO
```

In general, linked lists are preferred over arrays for processing dynamic lists—whose sizes vary as items are added and deleted—because the number of nodes in a linked list is limited only by the available memory and because the insertion and deletion operations are easy to implement.

To insert an element into a linked list, we first obtain a new node temporarily accessed via a pointer TEMPPTR:

```
ALLOCATE (TEMPPTR)
```

and store the element in its data component:

```
TEMPPTR%DATA = ELEMENT
```

There are now two cases to consider: (1) inserting the element at the beginning of the list and (2) inserting it after some specified element in the list. The first case has already been illustrated. For the second case, suppose that the new node is to be inserted between the nodes pointed to by PREDPTR and CURRPTR:

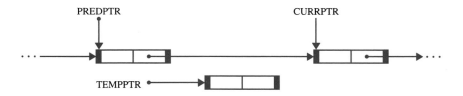

The node is inserted by setting the pointer in the link component of the new node to point to the node pointed to by CURRPTR:

```
TEMPPTR%NEXT => CURRPTR
```

and then resetting the pointer in the link component of the node pointed to by PREDPTR to point to the new node:

```
PREDPTR%NEXT => TEMPPTR
```

The following diagram illustrates:

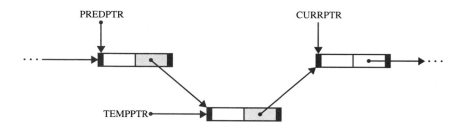

For deletion, there also are two cases to consider: (1) deleting the first element in the list and (2) deleting an element that has a predecessor. The first case is easy and consists of the following steps, assuming that CURRPTR points to the node to be deleted:

1. Set FIRSTPTR to point to the second node in the list:

```
FIRSTPTR => CURRPTR%NEXT
```

2. Release the node pointed to by CURRPTR:

```
DEALLOCATE (CURRPTR)
```

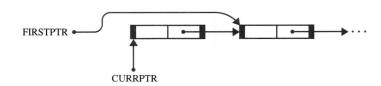

For the second case, suppose that the predecessor of the node to be deleted is pointed to by PREDPTR:

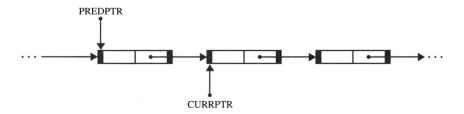

The node is deleted by setting the link component of the node pointed to by PREDPTR so that it points to the successor of the node to be deleted,

```
PREDPTR%NEXT => CURRPTR%NEXT
```

and then releasing the node pointed to by CURRPTR:

```
DEALLOCATE (CURRPTR)
```

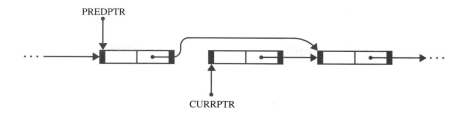

In this section we have shown how pointers and structures can be used to implement linked lists. Other useful dynamic data structures include linked stacks, linked queues, and trees, and these can also be implemented using techniques similar to those for linked lists.

"Where shall I begin, please Your Majesty?" he asked. "Begin at the beginning," the King said, gravely, "and go on till you come to the end; then stop."

LEWIS CARROLL, *Alice's Adventures in Wonderland*

ASCII and EBCDIC

Decimal	Binary	Octal	Hexadecimal	ASCII	EBCDIC
32	00100000	040	20	SP (Space)	
33	00100001	041	21	!	
34	00100010	042	22	``	
35	00100011	043	23	#	
36	00100100	044	24	$	
37	00100101	045	25	%	
38	00100110	046	26	&	
39	00100111	047	27	' (Single quote)	
40	00101000	050	28	(	
41	00101001	051	29	)	
42	00101010	052	2A	*	
43	00101011	053	2B	+	
44	00101100	054	2C	, (Comma)	
45	00101101	055	2D	- (Hyphen)	
46	00101110	056	2E	. (Period)	
47	00101111	057	2F	/	
48	00110000	060	30	0	
49	00110001	061	31	1	
50	00110010	062	32	2	
51	00110011	063	33	3	
52	00110100	064	34	4	
53	00110101	065	35	5	
54	00110110	066	36	6	
55	00110111	067	37	7	
56	00111000	070	38	8	
57	00111001	071	39	9	
58	00111010	072	3A	:	
59	00111011	073	3B	;	
60	00111100	074	3C	<	
61	00111101	075	3D	=	
62	00111110	076	3E	>	
63	00111111	077	3F	?	
64	01000000	100	40	@	SP (Space)
65	01000001	101	41	A	
66	01000010	102	42	B	
67	01000011	103	43	C	
68	01000100	104	44	D	
69	01000101	105	45	E	

Decimal	Binary	Octal	Hexadecimal	ASCII	EBCDIC
70	01000110	106	46	F	
71	01000111	107	47	G	
72	01001000	110	48	H	
73	01001001	111	49	I	
74	01001010	112	4A	J	¢
75	01001011	113	4B	K	. (Period)
76	01001100	114	4C	L	>
77	01001101	115	4D	M	(
78	01001110	116	4E	N	+
79	01001111	117	4F	O	|
80	01010000	120	50	P	&
81	01010001	121	51	Q	
82	01010010	122	52	R	
83	01010011	123	53	S	
84	01010100	124	54	T	
85	01010101	125	55	U	
86	01010110	126	56	V	
87	01010111	127	57	W	
88	01011000	130	58	X	
89	01011001	131	59	Y	
90	01011010	132	5A	Z	!
91	01011011	133	5B	[	$
92	01011100	134	5C	\	*
93	01011101	135	5D	]	)
94	01011110	136	5E	∧	;
95	01011111	137	5F	_ (Underscore)	¬ (Negation)
96	01100000	140	60	`	- (Hyphen)
97	01100001	141	61	a	/
98	01100010	142	62	b	
99	01100011	143	63	c	
100	01100100	144	64	d	
101	01100101	145	65	e	
102	01100110	146	66	f	
103	01100111	147	67	g	
104	01101000	150	68	h	
105	01101001	151	69	i	
106	01101010	152	6A	j	|
107	01101011	153	6B	k	, (Comma)
108	01101100	154	6C	l	%
109	01101101	155	6D	m	_ (Underscore)
110	01101110	156	6E	n	>
111	01101111	157	6F	o	?
112	01110000	160	70	p	
113	01110001	161	71	q	
114	01110010	162	72	r	
115	01110011	163	73	s	
116	01110100	164	74	t	
117	01110101	165	75	u	
118	01110110	166	76	v	
119	01110111	167	77	w	
120	01111000	170	78	x	
121	01111001	171	79	y	
122	01111010	172	7A	z	:
123	01111011	173	7B	{	#
124	01111100	174	7C	|	@
125	01111101	175	7D	}	' (Single quote)

Decimal	Binary	Octal	Hexadecimal	ASCII	EBCDIC
126	01111110	176	7E	~	=
127	01111111	177	7F		"
128	10000000	200	80		
129	10000001	201	81		a
130	10000010	202	82		b
131	10000011	203	83		c
132	10000100	204	84		d
133	10000101	205	85		e
134	10000110	206	86		f
135	10000111	207	87		g
136	10001000	210	88		h
137	10001001	211	89		i
.	.	.	.		.
.	.	.	.		.
.	.	.	.		.
145	10010001	221	91		j
146	10010010	222	92		k
147	10010011	223	93		l
148	10010100	224	94		m
149	10010101	225	95		n
150	10010110	226	96		o
151	10010111	227	97		p
152	10011000	230	98		q
153	10011001	231	99		r
.	.	.	.		.
.	.	.	.		.
.	.	.	.		.
162	10100010	242	A2		s
163	10100011	243	A3		t
164	10100100	244	A4		u
165	10100101	245	A5		v
166	10100110	246	A6		w
167	10100111	247	A7		x
168	10101000	250	A8		y
169	10101001	251	A9		z
.	.	.	.		.
.	.	.	.		.
.	.	.	.		.
192	11000000	300	C0		}
193	11000001	301	C1		A
194	11000010	302	C2		B
195	11000011	303	C3		C
196	11000100	304	C4		D
197	11000101	305	C5		E
198	11000110	306	C6		F
199	11000111	307	C7		G
200	11001000	310	C8		H
201	11001001	311	C9		I
.	.	.	.		.
.	.	.	.		.
.	.	.	.		.
208	11010000	320	D0		}
209	11010001	321	D1		J
210	11010010	322	D2		K
211	11010011	323	D3		L
212	11010100	324	D4		M

Decimal	Binary	Octal	Hexadecimal	ASCII	EBCDIC
213	11010101	325	D5		N
214	11010110	326	D6		O
215	11010111	327	D7		P
216	11011000	330	D8		Q
217	11011001	331	D9		R
.	.	.	.		.
.	.	.	.		.
.	.	.	.		.
224	11100000	340	E0		\
225	11100001	341	E1		
226	11100010	342	E2		S
227	11100011	343	E3		T
228	11100100	344	E4		U
229	11100101	345	E5		V
230	11100110	346	E6		W
231	11100111	347	E7		X
232	11101000	350	E8		Y
233	11101001	351	E9		Z
.	.	.	.		.
.	.	.	.		.
.	.	.	.		.
240	11110000	360	F0		0
241	11110001	361	F1		1
242	11110010	362	F2		2
243	11110011	363	F3		3
244	11110100	364	F4		4
245	11110101	365	F5		5
246	11110110	366	F6		6
247	11110111	367	F7		7
248	11111000	370	F8		8
249	11111001	371	F9		9
.	.	.	.		.
.	.	.	.		.
.	.	.	.		.
255	11111111	377	FF		

B

Sample Files

Several exercises in the text use the files INVENTORY-FILE, STUDENT-FILE, USERS-FILE, INVENTORY-UPDATE, STUDENT-UPDATE, and USER-UPDATE. This appendix describes the contents of the records in these files and gives a sample listing for each.

INVENTORY FILE

Columns	Contents
1–4	Item number
5–28	Item name
29–33	Unit price (no decimal point, but three digits before and two after the decimal point are assumed)
34–36	Reorder point
37–39	Number currently in stock
40–42	Desired inventory level

The file is sorted so that the item numbers of the records are in increasing order.

INVENTORY-FILE

```
1011TELEPHOTO POCKET CAMERA   5495 15 20 25
1012MINI POCKET CAMERA        2495 15 12 20
1021POL. ONE-STEP CAMERA      4995 10 20 20
1022SONAR 1-STEP CAMERA      18995 12 13 15
1023PRONTO CAMERA             7495  5 15 15
10318MM ZOOM MOVIE CAMERA    27999 10  9 15
1032SOUND/ZOOM 8MM CAMERA    31055 10 15 15
104135MM SLR XG-7 MINO. CAM.38900 12 10 20
104235MM SLR AE-1 PENT. CAM.34995 12 11 20
104335MM SLR ME CAN. CAM.   31990 12 20 20
```

```
104435MM HI-MATIC CAMERA       11995 12 13 20
104535MM COMPACT CAMERA         8999 12 20 20
1511ZOOM MOVIE PROJECTOR       12995  5  7 10
1512ZOOM-SOUND PROJECTOR       23999  5  9 15
1521AUTO CAROUSEL PROJECTOR    21999  5 10 10
1522CAR. SLIDE PROJECTOR       11495  5  4 10
2011POCKET STROBE               1495  5  4 15
2012STROBE SX-10                4855 10 12 20
2013ELEC.FLASH SX-10            2899 15 10 20
3011TELE CONVERTER              3299 15 13 30
301228MM WIDE-ANGLE LENS        9799 15 14 25
3013135MM TELEPHOTO LENS        8795 15 13 25
301435-105 MM ZOOM LENS        26795  5  8 10
301580-200 MM ZOOM LENS        25795  5  7 10
3111HEAVY-DUTY TRIPOD           6750  5  4 10
3112LIGHTWEIGHT TRIPOD          1995  5 10 10
351135MM ENLARGER KIT          15999  5 10 10
401140X40 DELUXE SCREEN         3598  5  4 15
401250X50 DELUXE SCREEN         4498  5 10 10
5011120-SLIDE TRAY               429 25 17 40
5012100-SLIDE TRAY               295 25 33 40
5021SLIDE VIEWER                 625 15 12 25
5031MOVIE EDITOR                5595 10 12 20
6011CONDENSER MICROPHONE        5995  5 10 10
6111AA ALKALINE BATTERY           89100 80200
7011GADGET BAG                  1979 20 19 35
8011135-24 COLOR FILM            149 50 45100
8021110-12 COLOR FILM             99 50 60100
8022110-24 COLOR FILM            145 50 42100
8023110-12 B/W FILM               59 25 37 75
8024110-24 B/W FILM               95 25 43 75
8031126-12 COLOR FILM             89 50 44100
8032126-12 B/W FILM               59 25 27 50
80418MM FILM CASSETTE            689 50 39100
804216MM FILM CASETTE           1189 50 73100
9111COMBINATION CAMERA KIT     95999 10  8 15
```

INVENTORY UPDATE

Columns	Contents
1–7	Order number (three letters followed by four digits)
8–11	Item number (same as those used in INVENTORY-FILE)
12	Transaction code (S = sold, R = returned)
13–15	Number of items sold or returned

The file is sorted so that item numbers are in increasing order. (Some items in INVENTORY-FILE may not have update records; others may have more than one.)

INVENTORY UPDATE

```
CCI75431012S   2
LTB34291012S   7
DJS67621021S   9
NQT18501022S   1
WYP64251023S   4
YOK22101023R   2
QGM31441023S   1
NPQ86851031S   5
MAP81021031S  13
JRJ63351031S   1
UWR93861032S   3
TJY19131032S  11
YHA94641041S   5
SYT74931041S   3
FHJ16571042S   7
OJQ12211043S   8
UOX77141043S   2
ERZ21471043S   7
MYW25401044S   1
UKS35871045S   2
AAN37591045S   2
WZT41711045S  12
TYR94751511S   1
FRQ41841511S   1
TAV36041512S   2
DCW93631522S   1
EXN39641522R   1
OIN55241522S   1
EOJ82181522S   1
YFK06832011S   2
PPX47432012S   4
DBR17092013S   4
JOM54082013S   3
PKN06712013S   1
LBD83913011S   9
DNL63263012S   9
BTP53963013S   1
GFL49133013S   8
EHQ75103013S   7
QQL64723013S   5
SVC65113014S   4
XJQ93913014S   4
ONO52513111S   3
CXC77803111S   1
VGT81693112S   8
IMK58613511S   2
QHR19443511S   1
ZPK62114011S   2
VDZ29704012S   6
BOJ90695011S   6
MNL70295011S   9
MRG87035021S  10
DEM92895021S   1
BXL16515031S   2
VAF87336111S  65
```

```
UYI03687011S   2
VIZ68798011S  16
GXX90938011S  19
HHO56058021S  41
BOL23248021S  49
PAG92898023S  15
MDF55578023S  17
IQK33888024S  12
OTB13418024S  28
SVF56748031S  24
ZDP94848031S  15
OSY81778032S  15
GJQ01858032S   8
VHW01898041S  20
WEU92258041S   6
YJO37558041S   8
```

STUDENT-FILE

Columns	Contents
1–5	Student number
6–20	Student's last name
21–35	Student's first name
36	Student's middle initial
37–59	Address
60–66	Phone number
67	Sex (M or F)
68	Class level (1, 2, 3, 4, or 5 for special)
69–72	Major (four-letter abbreviation)
73–75	Total credits earned to date (an integer)
76–78	Cumulative GPA (no decimal point, but one digit before and two after the decimal point are assumed)

The file is sorted so that the student numbers are in increasing order.

STUDENT-FILE

```
10103JOHNSON         JAMES        LWAUPUN, WISCONSIN       7345229M1ENGR 15315
10104ANDREWS         PETER        JGRAND RAPIDS, MICHIGAN 9493301M2CPSC 42278
10110PETERS          ANDREW       JLYNDEN, WASHINGTON      3239550M5ART  63205
10113VANDENVANDER    VANNESSA     VFREMONT, MICHIGAN       5509237F4HIST110374
10126ARISTOTLE       ALICE        ACHINO, CALIFORNIA       3330861F3PHIL 78310
10144LUCKY           LUCY         LGRANDVILLE, MICHIGAN    7745424F5HIST 66229
10179EULER           LENNIE       LTHREE RIVERS, MICHIGAN 6290017M1MATH 15383
10191NAKAMURA        TOKY         OCHICAGO, ILLINOIS       4249665F1SOCI 12195
10226FREUD           FRED         ELYNDEN, WASHINGTON      8340115M1PSYC 15185
10272SPEARSHAKE      WILLIAM      WGRAND RAPIDS, MICHIGAN 2410744M5ENGL102295
10274TCHAIKOVSKY     WOLFGANG     ABYRON CENTER, MICHIGAN 8845115M3MUSC 79275
10284ORANGE          DUTCH        VGRAAFSCHAAP, MICHIGAN   3141660M2ENGR 42298
10297CAESAR          JULIE'       SDENVER, COLORADO        4470338F4HIST117325
10298PSYCHO          PRUNELLA     EDE MOTTE, INDIANA       5384609F4PSYC120299
```

```
10301BULL            SITTING      UGALLUP, NEW MEXICO      6632997M1EDUC 14195
10302CUSTER          GENERAL      GBADLANDS, SOUTH DAKOTA 5552992M3HIST 40195
10303FAHRENHEIT      FELICIA      OSHEBOYGAN, WISCONSIN    5154997F2CHEM 40385
10304DEUTSCH         SPRECHEN     ZSPARTA, MICHIGAN        8861201F5GERM 14305
10307MENDELSSOHN     MOZART       WPEORIA, ILLINOIS        2410744M3MUSC 76287
10310AUGUSTA         ADA          BLAKEWOOD, CALIFORNIA    7172339F2CPSC 46383
10319GAUSS           CARL         FYORKTOWN, PENNSYLVANIA 3385494M2MATH 41400
10323KRONECKER       LEO          PTRAVERSE CITY, MICHIGAN6763991M3MATH 77275
10330ISSACSON        JACOB        ASILVER SPRINGS, MD      4847932M5RELI 25299
10331ISSACSON        ESAU         BSILVER SPRINGS, MD      4847932M5RELI 25298
10339DEWEY           JOHANNA      ASALT LAKE CITY, UTAH    6841129F2EDUC 41383
10348VIRUS           VERA         WSAGINAW, MICHIGAN        6634401F4CPSC115325
10355ZYLSTRA         ZELDA        ADOWNS, KANSAS           7514008F1ENGL 16195
10377PORGY           BESS         NCOLUMBUS, OHIO          4841771F2MUSC 44278
10389NEWMANN         ALFRED       ECHEYENNE, WYOMING       7712399M4EDUC115099
10395MEDES           ARCHIE       LWHITINSVILLE, MA        9294401M3ENGR 80310
10406MACDONALD       RONALD       BSEATTLE, WASHINGTON     5582911M1CPSC 15299
10415AARDVARK        ANTHONY      AGRANDVILLE, MICHIGAN    5325912M2ENGR 43279
10422GESTALT         GLORIA       GWHEATON, ILLINOIS       6631212F2PSYC 42248
10431GOTODIJKSTRA    EDGAR        GCAWKER CITY, KANSAS     6349971M1CPSC 15400
10448REMBRANDT       ROBERTA      ESIOUX CENTER, IOWA      2408113F1ART  77220
10458SHOEMAKER       IMELDA       MHONOLULU, HAWAII        9193001F1POLS 15315
10467MARX            KARL         ZHAWTHORNE, NEW JERSEY   5513915M3ECON 78275
10470SCROOGE         EBENEZER     TTROY, MICHIGAN          8134001M4SOCI118325
10482NIGHTINGALE     FLORENCE     KROCHESTER, NEW YORK     7175118F1NURS 15315
10490GAZELLE         GWENDOLYN    DCHINO, CALIFORNIA       3132446F2P E  43278
10501PASTEUR         LOUISE       AWINDOW ROCK, ARIZONA    4245170F1BIOL 16310
10519ELBA            ABLE         MBOZEMAN, MONTANA        8183226M3SPEE 77340
10511LEWIS           CLARK        NNEW ERA, MICHIGAN       6461125M4GEOG114337
10515MOUSE           MICHAEL      EBOISE, IDAHO            5132771M5EDUC 87199
10523PAVLOV          TIFFANY      TFARMINGTON, MICHIGAN    9421753F1BIOL 13177
10530CHICITA         JUANITA      AOKLAHOMA CITY, OK       3714377F5ENGL 95266
10538BUSCH           ARCH         EST LOUIS, MISSOURI      8354112M3ENGR 74275
10547FAULT           PAIGE        DPETOSKEY, MICHIGAN      4543116F5CPSC 55295
10553SANTAMARIA      NINA         PPLYMOUTH, MASSACHUSETTS2351881F1HIST 15177
10560SHYSTER         SAMUEL       DEVERGLADES, FLORIDA     4421885M1SOCI 13195
10582YEWLISS         CAL          CRUDYARD, MICHIGAN       3451220M3MATH 76299
10590ATANASOFF       ENIAC        CSPRINGFIELD, ILLINOIS   6142449F1CPSC 14188
10597ROCKNE          ROCKY        KPORTLAND, OREGON        4631744M4P E  116198
10610ROOSEVELT       ROSE         YSPRING LAKE, MICHIGAN   9491221F5E SC135295
10623XERXES          ART          ICINCINATTI, OHIO        3701228M4GREE119325
10629LEIBNIZ         GOTTFRIED    WBOULDER, COLORADO       5140228M1MATH 13195
10633VESPUCCI        VERA         DRIPON, CALIFORNIA       4341883F5GEOG 89229
10648PRINCIPAL       PAMELA       PALBANY, NEW YORK        7145513F1EDUC 14175
10652CICERO          MARSHA       MRAPID CITY, SD          3335910F3LATI 77287
10657WEERD           DEWEY        LDETROIT, MICHIGAN       4841962M4PHIL115299
10663HOCHSCHULE      HORTENSE     CLINCOLN, NEBRASKA       7120111F5EDUC100270
10668EINSTEIN        ALFRED       MNEWARK, NEW JERSEY      3710225M2ENGR 41278
10675FIBONACCI       LEONARD      ONASHVILLE, TENNESSEE    4921107M4MATH115325
10682ANGELO          MIKE         LAUSTIN, TEXAS           5132201M4ART  117374
10688PASCAL          BLAZE        RBROOKLYN, NEW YORK      7412993M1CPSC 15198
```

STUDENT-UPDATE

Columns	Contents
1–5	Student number (same as those used in STUDENT-FILE)
6–12	Name of course #1 (e.g., CPSC141)
13–14	Letter grade received for course #1 (e.g., A−, B+, C$\flat$)
15	Credits received for course #1
16–22	Name of course #2
23–24	Letter grade received for course #2
25	Credits received for course #2
26–32	Name of course #3
33–34	Letter grade received for course #3
35	Credits received for course #3
36–42	Name of course #4
43–44	Letter grade received for course #4
45	Credits received for course #4
46–52	Name of course #5
53–54	Letter grade received for course #5
55	Credits received for course #5

The file is sorted so that the student numbers are in increasing order. There is one update record for each student in STUDENT-FILE.

STUDENT-UPDATE

```
10103ENGL176C 4EDUC268B 4EDUC330B+3P E 281C 3ENGR317D 4
10104CPSC271D+4E SC208D-3PHIL340B+2CPSC146D+4ENGL432D+4
10110ART 520D 3E SC259F 1ENGL151D+4MUSC257B 4PSYC486C 4
10113HIST498F 3P E 317C+4MUSC139B-3PHIL165D 3GEOG222C 3
10126PHIL367C-4EDUC420C-3EDUC473C 3EDUC224D-3GERM257F 4
10144HIST559C+3MATH357D 3CPSC323C-2P E 246D-4MUSC379D+4
10179MATH169C-4CHEM163C+4MUSC436A-3MATH366D-2BIOL213A-4
10191SOCI177F 4POLS106A 4EDUC495A-3ENGR418B+2ENGR355A 4
10226PSYC116B 3GERM323B-4ART 350A 4HIST269B+4EDUC214C+3
10272ENGL558A-4EDUC169D+3PSYC483B+4ENGR335B+2BIOL228B 4
10274MUSC351B 4PSYC209C-4ENGR400F 1E SC392A 4SOCI394B-3
10284ENGR292D 4PSYC172C 4EDUC140B 4MATH274F 4MUSC101D+4
10297HIST464F 1HIST205F 1ENGR444F 1MATH269F 1EDUC163F 1
10298PSYC452B 3MATH170C+4EDUC344C-2GREE138C-2SPEE303A-3
10301EDUC197A 4P E 372B 3ENGR218D 4MATH309C 4E SC405C-4
10302CHEM283F 1P E 440A 2MATH399A-3HIST455C-4MATH387C-3
10303HIST111D-3ART151 C+3ENGL100C-3PSYC151D+3PE104  A-1
10304GERM526C-2CHEM243C 4POLS331B-4EDUC398A 3ENGR479D+4
10307MUSC323B+3MATH485C 4HIST232B+4EDUC180A 3ENGL130B+4
10310CPSC264B 2POLS227D+3ENGR467D-3MATH494D-4ART 420C+4
10319MATH276B 2E SC434A 3HIST197B-4GERM489B-2ART 137C-3
10323MATH377D-4EDUC210D 4MATH385D-4ENGR433C 2HIST338A-4
10330HIST546C+3E SC440B+3GREE472C+3BIOL186B 4GEOG434C+2
10331HIST546C 3E SC440B+3GREE472C 3BIOL186B+4GEOG434C+2
10339EDUC283B 3CPSC150B 3ENGR120D 4CPSC122F 4ART 216B 4
10348CPSC411C-3HIST480C+4PSYC459B 4BIOL299B+4ECON276B+3
10355ENGL130C-3CPSC282C+4CPSC181A-4CPSC146C-4SOCI113F 1
10377SOCI213D+3PSYC158D 4MUSC188C 3PSYC281D-4ENGR339B+4
```

```
10389EDUC414D+4PSYC115C-2PSYC152D-4ART 366D-3ENGR366F 4
10395ENGR396B 4HIST102F 3ENGL111A 4PSYC210D-2GREE128A 4
10406CPSC160C+4CPSC233C 1LATI494C+3ENGL115C-3MATH181A 3
10415ENGR287C 4EDUC166B-4EDUC106A-3P E 190F 3MATH171B-3
10422PSYC275A-4MATH497A 4EDUC340F 1GERM403C-4MATH245D+4
10431CPSC187D-4CPSC426F 4ENGR476B-4BIOL148B+3CPSC220F 3
10448ART 171D+3CPSC239C-3SOCI499B-4HIST113D+3PSYC116C 4
10458POLS171F 1CPSC187C+4CHEM150B 2PHIL438D-4PHIL254D 4
10467ECON335D-3E SC471B+4MATH457C+3MATH207C 2BIOL429D 4
10470MUSC415C+3POLS177C 3CPSC480A 4PSYC437B 3SOCI276D 4
10482ENGL158D-4EDUC475B 3HIST172B-2P E 316F 4ENGR294A-3
10490P E 239F 4ENGL348F 3LATI246F 4CPSC350F 4MATH114F 1
10501BIOL125F 4CPSC412F 3E SC279F 4ENGR153F 2ART 293F 1
10519SPEE386B+4HIST479C 4PSYC249B-2GREE204B-4P E 421A 1
10511E SC416B 3MATH316D-4MATH287C 2MATH499A-4E SC288D 3
10515EDUC563D+3PHIL373D-3ART 318B 4HIST451F 1ART 476C+3
10523BIOL183D-2HIST296D+4HIST380B+4ENGR216C 4MATH412B-2
10530ENGL559F 1EDUC457D+4CPSC306A 3ENGR171B+1CPSC380A 4
10538ENGR328A-4ENGR336C 3EDUC418D+3PHIL437B+4CPSC475D 4
10547CPSC537A-4ART 386D 4HIST292D-4ENGR467A-4P E 464B+4
10553HIST170A-4SOCI496D-3PHIL136B+4CPSC371D-4CPSC160A-1
10560SOCI153D+3MATH438D+4CPSC378C 4BIOL266F 3EDUC278D+3
10582MATH388A-3P E 311B 3ECON143D 4MATH304C+3P E 428C+4
10590CPSC134B-3E SC114B+3CPSC492C 4ENGL121C 4ENGR403A-4
10597P E 423A-3BIOL189D+3PHIL122D-4ENGL194C-4SOCI113D+3
10610E SC594C-3PHIL344F 4CPSC189B+2ENGR411D-3MATH241A 4
10623GREE412B-4ENGL415D-3ENGL234D-4MATH275F 1SOCI124B+3
10629MATH137D 2MATH481F 3E SC445F 1MATH339D 4ART 219B+4
10633GEOG573B 4ENGL149C+4EDUC113B+4ENGR458C-2HIST446D+4
10648EDUC132D+4MUSC103D-4ENGL263C 4ENGL134B+4E SC392A 3
10652LATI363F 3BIOL425F 1CPSC267C 4EDUC127C+3MATH338B 4
10657PHIL429F 1ART 412D-4MUSC473B-4SOCI447C-4MATH237D+2
10663EDUC580B-4ENGR351B+4SOCI283D 4ART 340C 4PSYC133D+3
10668ENGR274B+4SOCI438C 1P E 327C 4BIOL158A 4EDUC457A-4
10675MATH457A 4ENGR114C 4CPSC218C 3E SC433C-3PSYC243C+1
10682ART 483D+3GERM432C 3ENGL103B+4MUSC169C-3SOCI381C-2
10688CPSC182F 1HIST371C+4PSYC408F 1MUSC214B+4MATH151C 3
```

USERS–FILE

Columns	Contents
1–15	User's last name
16–30	User's first name
31–35	Identification number
36–40	Password
41–44	Resource limit (in dollars)
45–49	Resources used to date (no decimal point, but three digits before and two after the decimal point are assumed)

The file is sorted so that the identification numbers of the records are in increasing order.

USERS-FILE

```
MILTGEN        JOSEPH       10101MOE   75038081
SMALL          ISAAC        10102LARGE 65059884
SNYDER         SAMUEL       10103R2-D2 25019374
EDMUNDSEN      EDMUND       10104ABCDE 25017793
BRAUNSCHNEIDER CHRISTOPHER  10105BROWN 85019191
PIZZULA        NORMA        10106PIZZA 35022395
VANDERVAN      HENRY        10107VAN   75016859
FREELOADER     FREDDIE      10108RED   450 7661
ALEXANDER      ALVIN        10109GREAT 65040504
MOUSE          MICHAEL      10110EARS   50 4257
LUKASEWICZ     ZZZYK        10111RPN   350 7350
CHRISTMAS      MARY         10112NOEL  850 3328
SINKE          CJ           10113TRAIN 75032753
NIJHOFF        LARAN        10114KKID  55038203
LIESTMA        STAN         10115SAAB  550 2882
ZWIER          APOLLOS      10116PJ    95025618
JAEGER         TIM          10117BIKE  45033701
VANZWALBERG    JORGE        10118EGYPT 35024948
JESTER         COURTNEY     10119JOKER 45028116
MCDONALD       RONALD       10120FRIES 250 3500
NEDERLANDER    BENAUT       10121DUTCH 650 3836
HAYBAILER      HOMER        10122FARM  850 3732
SPEAR          WILLIAM      10123SHAKE 25024673
ROMEO          JULIET       10124XOXOX 15010019
GREEK          JIMMY        10125WAGER 250    3
VIRUS          VERA         10126WORM  750 6735
BEECH          ROCKY        10127BOAT  55039200
ENGEL          ANGEL        10128WINGS 150 1639
ABNER          LIL          10129DAISY 950 8957
TRACY          DICK         10130CRIME 85046695
MCGEE          FIBBER       10131MOLLY 75033212
BELL           ALEXANDER    10132PHONE 85033743
COBB           TYRUS        20101TIGER  50 3281
GEORGE         RUTH         20102BABE  25010934
DESCARTES      RONALD       20103HORSE 35026993
EUCLID         IAN          20104GREEK 95018393
DANIELS        EZEKIEL      20105LIONS 35012869
TARZAN         JANE         20106APES  15010031
HABBAKUK       JONAH        20107WHALE 350 6363
COLOMBUS       CHRIS        20108PINTA 85020224
BYRD           RICHARD      20109NORTH 55016849
BUNYON         PAUL         20110BABE  55033347
CHAUCER        JEFF         20111POEM  950 3702
STOTLE         ARI          20112LOGIC 75033774
HARRISON       BEN          20113PRES  55026297
JAMES          JESSE        20114GUNS  250 5881
SCOTT          FRANCINE     20115FLAG  35016811
PHILLIPS       PHYLLIS      20116GAS66 65032222
DOLL           BARBARA      20117KEN   350 2634
FINN           HUCK         20118TOM   350 2286
SAWYER         TOM          20119HUCK  95046030
NEWMANN        ALFRED       20120MAD   45011600
SIMON          SIMPLE       20121SAYS  55048605
SCHMIDT        MESSER       20122PLANE 250 3531
LUTHER         CALVIN       20124REF   77766666
YALE           HARVARD      20125IVY   15012770
```

USER UPDATE

Columns	Contents
1–5	Account number
6	Blank
7–10	Resources used (no decimal point, but three digits before and two after the decimal point are assumed)

The file is sorted so that the account numbers are in increasing order.

USER-UPDATE

```
10101   732
10101  2133
11003  3502
10105   555
10105   329
10105    89
10105  1053
10109  8934
10116  1234
10116   583
10116  1563
10117  5023
10117  9823
10118  4523
10118   234
10118  8993
10120  2331
10122   345
10122   679
10122    78
10122  3402
10122   222
10122   328
10123  3409
10130    45
10130    89
10130   328
10132  4412
10132  1210
20101  1122
20101   534
20101  1001
20101   634
20111  1164
20111   154
20111  3226
20111  9923
20121  5545
20121  6423
20121  3328
```

C

Program Composition

This diagram indicates the correct placement of the various types of FORTRAN statements in a program unit. The arrows indicate the order in which the statements may be used. For example, the arrow from the PARAMETER statements block to the DATA statements block indicates that all PARAMETER statements must precede all DATA statements in a program unit. The horizontal two-headed arrows indicate that these types of statements may be interspersed. For example, comment lines may appear anywhere in a program unit before the END statement.

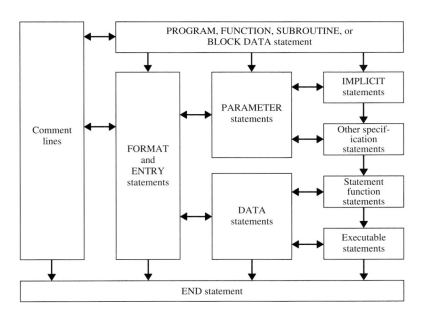

Function Description	Generic Name	Specific Name	Number of Arguments	Type of Arguments	Type of Function
Conversion of numeric to integer	INT	—	1	Integer	Integer
		INT		Real	Integer
		IFIX		Real	Integer
		IDINT		Double	Integer
		—		Complex	Integer
Conversion of numeric to real	REAL	REAL	1	Integer	Real
		FLOAT		Integer	Real
		—		Real	Real
		SNGL		Double	Real
		—		Complex	Real
Conversion of numeric to double precision	DBLE	—	1	Integer	Double
		—		Real	Double
		—		Double	Double
		—		Complex	Double
Conversion of numeric to complex	CMPLX	—	1	Integer	Complex
		—		Real	Complex
		—		Double	Complex
		—		Complex	Complex
Conversion of integer to character	—	CHAR	1	Integer	Character
Conversion of character to integer	—	ICHAR	1	Character	Integer
Truncation	AINT	AINT	1	Real	Real
		DINT		Double	Double
Rounding to nearest integer	ANINT	ANINT	1	Real	Real
		DNINT		Double	Double
Rounding to nearest integer	NINT	NINT	1	Real	Integer
		IDNINT		Double	Integer

Function Description	Generic Name	Specific Name	Number of Arguments	Type of Arguments	Type of Function
Absolute value	ABS	IABS	1	Integer	Integer
		ABS		Real	Real
		DABS		Double	Double
		CABS		Complex	Real
Remaindering	MOD	MOD	2	Integer	Integer
		AMOD		Real	Real
		DMOD		Double	Double
Transfer of sign	SIGN	ISIGN	2	Integer	Integer
		SIGN		Real	Real
		DSIGN		Double	Double
Positive difference	DIM	IDIM	2	Integer	Integer
		DIM		Real	Real
		DDIM		Double	Double
Double precision product		DPROD	2	Real	Double
Maximum value	MAX	MAX0	≥ 2	Integer	Integer
		AMAX1		Real	Real
		DMAX1		Double	Double
	—	AMAX0		Integer	Real
	—	MAX1		Real	Integer
Minimum value	MIN	MIN0	≥ 2	Integer	Integer
		AMIN1		Real	Real
		DMIN1		Double	Double
	—	AMIN0		Integer	Real
	—	MIN1		Real	Integer
Length of character item	—	LEN	1	Character	Integer
Index of a substring	—	INDEX	2	Character	Integer
Imaginary part of a complex value	—	AIMAG	1	Complex	Real
Conjugate of a complex value	—	CONJG	1	Complex	Complex
Square root	SQRT	SQRT	1	Real	Real
		DSQRT		Double	Double
		CSQRT		Complex	Complex
Exponential	EXP	EXP	1	Real	Real
		DEXP		Double	Double
		CEXP		Complex	Complex
Natural logarithm	LOG	ALOG	1	Real	Real
		DLOG		Double	Double
		CLOG		Complex	Complex
Common logarithm	LOG10	ALOG10	1	Real	Real
		DLOG10		Double	Double
Sin	SIN	SIN	1	Real	Real
		DSIN		Double	Double
		CSIN		Complex	Complex
Cosine	COS	COS	1	Real	Real
		DCOS		Double	Double
		CCOS		Complex	Complex
Tangent	TAN	TAN	1	Real	Real
		DTAN		Double	Double
Arcsine	ASIN	ASIN	1	Real	Real
		DASIN		Double	Double
Arccosine	ACOS	ACOS	1	Real	Real
		DACOS		Double	Double

Function Description	Generic Name	Specific Name	Number of Arguments	Type of Arguments	Type of Function
Arctangent	ATAN	ATAN	1	Real	Real
		DATAN		Double	Double
	ATAN2	ATAN2	2	Real	Real
		DATAN2		Double	Double
Hyperbolic sine	SINH	SINH	1	Real	Real
		DSINH		Double	Double
Hyperbolic cosine	COSH	COSH	1	Real	Real
		DCOSH		Double	Double
Hyperbolic tangent	TANH	TANH	1	Real	Real
		DTANH		Double	Double
Lexically greater than or equal to	—	LGE	2	Character	Logical
Lexically greater than	—	LGT	2	Character	Logical
Lexically less than or equal to	—	LLE	2	Character	Logical
Lexically less than	—	LLT	2	Character	Logical

Answers to Selected Exercises

Section 1.3 (p. 22)

5. (a) 9   (c) 64   (e) 1.5

6. (a) 83   (c) 4096   (e) 7.25

7. (a) 18   (c) 2748   (e) 8.75

8. (a) 1010011   (c) 1000000000000   (e) 111.01

9. (a) 10010   (c) 101010111100   (e) 1000.11

10. (a) 11   (c) 100   (e) 1.4

11. (a) 9   (c) 40   (e) 1.8

12. (a) (i) 11011_2 (ii) 33_8 (iii) $1B_{16}$
     (c) (i) 100111010_2 (ii) 472_8 (iii) $13A_{16}$

13. (a) (i) 0.1_2 (ii) 0.4_8 (iii) 0.8_{16}
     (d) (i) 10000.0001_2 (ii) 20.04_8 (iii) 10.1_{16}

14. (a) (i) $0.0\overline{1001}_2$ (ii) $0.\overline{23146}_8$ (iii) $0.4\overline{C}_{16}$
     (c) (i) $0.000\overline{011}_2$ (ii) $0.0\overline{3146}_8$ (iii) $0.0\overline{C}_{16}$

15. (a) 64   (c) -65 (e) -256

16. (a) 0000000011111111
     (c) 1111111100000001
     (e) 1100011010001001

18. (a) (i) 0110000000010001   **(ii)** Same as (i)
   (c) (i) 0101000000010001   **(ii)** Same as (i)
   (e) (i) 0110011001111101   **(ii)** Same as (i)

19. (a) (i)

0	1	0	1	0	1	0	0	0	1	0	0	1	1	1	1

        T   O

(ii)

1	1	1	0	0	0	1	1	1	1	0	1	0	1	1	0

        T   O

(d) (i)

0	1	0	0	0	1	0	1	0	1	0	1	0	1	0	0

        E   T

0	1	0	0	0	0	1	1	0	0	1	0	1	1	1	0

        C   .

(ii)

1	1	0	0	0	1	0	1	1	1	1	0	0	0	1	1

        E   T

1	1	0	0	0	0	1	1	0	1	0	0	1	0	1	1

        C   .

Section 2.5 (p. 47)

6. Given information: Two temperature scales. Celsius and Fahrenheit, with 0° Celsius corresponding to 32° Fahrenheit, 100° Celsius corresponding to 212° Fahrenheit, and a linear relationship of the form $F = aC + b$ that holds in general. Also given some temperature C on the Celsius scale.

To find: The corresponding number F of degrees on the Fahrenheit scale.

We first must find the specific linear relationship between the two scales. In general, $C°$ Celsius corresponds to $F°$ Fahrenheit, where $F = aC + b$ for some constants a and b. Because 0° Celsius corresponds to 32° Fahrenheit, we must have

$$32 = a \cdot 0 + b$$

so that $b = 32$. This means, then, that

$$F = aC + 32$$

Because 100° Celsius corresponds to 212° Fahrenheit, we must have

$$212 = a\,100 + 32$$

which gives $a = 9/5$, so that our equation becomes

$$F = \frac{9}{5}C + 32$$

The algorithm for solving the problem is now straightforward:

```
* This algorithm converts a temperature of DEGC degrees     *
* on the Celsius scale to the corresponding DEGF degrees on  *
* the Fahrenheit scale.                                      *
```

1. Enter DEGC.
2. Calculate

$$DEGF = \frac{9}{5} DEGC + 32$$

3. Display DEGF.

Expressed in flowchart form, the algorithm is

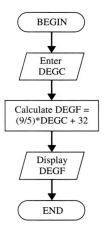

9. Input—Pollution Index: INDEX
   Output—Air quality description: Pleasant, unpleasant, or hazardous

ALGORITHM

```
* Algorithm for air quality based on pollution index. Indices  *
* are classified until a negative value for INDEX is entered.   *
```

1. Enter INDEX.
2. While INDEX $\geq$ 0 do the following:
   a. If INDEX $<$ 35 then display 'Pleasant'
      else if INDEX $\leq$ 60 display 'Unpleasant'
      else display 'Hazardous',
   b. Enter INDEX.

22.
```
      PROGRAM TEMPS
*********************************************************
* Program to convert a temperature of DEGC degrees  *
* on the Celsius scale to the corresponding         *
* temperature DEGF on the Fahrenheit scale.         *
*********************************************************
      REAL DEGC, DEGF

      PRINT *, 'ENTER TEMPERATURE IN DEGREES CELSIUS:'
      READ *, DEGC
      DEGF = (9.0/5.0) * DEGC + 32.0
      PRINT *, 'FAHRENHEIT TEMPERATURE IS', DEGF
      END
```

Section 3.3 (p. 62)

2. (a) 12 is integer.
  (b) 12. is real.
  (c) '12' is neither.
  (d) 8 + 4 is neither.

3. (a) 'X' is legal.
  (b) RATE' is not legal.
  (c) '$1.98' is legal.

4. (a) `REAL TEMP, PRESS, VOLUME`
  (b) `INTEGER ZETA`
  (f) `CHARACTER*20 NAME1, NAME2, NAME3*10`

5. (a) GAUSS is of real type.
  (b) FORTRAN is not a legal variable (name is too long).
  (c) H is of real type.
  (d) I is of integer type.

6. (a) `REAL RATE`
      `PARAMETER (RATE = 1.25)`
  (b) `INTEGER GRAV`
      `PARAMETER (GRAV = 32)`
  (f) `CHARACTER*8 COURSE`
      `PARAMETER (COURSE = 'CPSC141')`

7. (a) `REAL RATE1, RATE2`
      `DATA RATE1, RATE2 /1.25, 2.33/`
  (b) `INTEGER NUM1, NUM2`
      `DATA NUM1, NUM2 /10, 20/`
  (f) `CHARACTER*4 DEPT`
      `INTEGER COURS1, COURS2`
      `DATA DEPT, COURS1, COURS2 /'CPSC', 141, 142/`

Section 3.4 (p. 68)

1. **(a)** 1   **(c)** .5   **(e)** 25
   (g) 729   **(i)** 6561   **(k)** -9.0
   (m) 5   **(o)** 1   **(q)** 3.0

2. **(a)** 11.0   **(c)** 12.25   **(e)** 4.0
   (g) 3.0

3. **(a)** $10 + 5 * B - 4 * A * C$ **(c)** $SQRT(A + 3 * B ** 2)$
   (e) $A ** 2 + B ** 2 - 2 * A * B * COS(T)$

Section 3.5 (p. 73)

1. **(a)** Valid
   (c) Valid
   (e) Valid

2. **(a)** 125.0   **(c)** 6.1   **(e)** 0.0
   (g) 10   **(i)** 1

3. **(a)** Not valid—1 is not of   **(c)** 'ONETWObbbb'
   character type
   (e) Not valid—illegal character   **(g)** 'ABCDE'
   constant
   (i) 'FOURbbbbbb'

4. **(a)** `DIST = RATE * TIME`
   (d) `VALUE = P * (1 + R) ** N`
   (g) `RANGE = 2 * V ** 2 * SIN(A) * COS(A) / G`

5. **(a)** `I = 3, J = 4, K = 6`

Section 3.8 (p. 87)

3.
```
        PROGRAM TRIANG
***********************************************************
* Program to read three sides of a triangle and then     *
* calculate its perimeter and area. Variables used:      *
* A, B, C : three sides of a triangle                    *
* S : One-half the perimeter                             *
* AREA : Area of the triangle                            *
***********************************************************
        REAL A, B, C, S, AREA

        PRINT *, 'ENTER THREE SIDES OF TRIANGLE:'
        READ *, A, B, C
        S = (A + B + C) / 2.0
        AREA = SQRT(S * (S - A) * (S - B) * (S - C))
        PRINT *, 'PERIMETER = ', 2.0 * S
        PRINT *, 'AREA = ', AREA
        END
```

Section 4.3 (p. 110)

1. (a) .TRUE.
   (d) .TRUE.
   (g) .FALSE.
   (j) .FALSE.

2. (a)

A	B	A .OR. .NOT. B	
T	T	**T**	F
T	F	**T**	T
F	T	**F**	F
F	F	**T**	T

   (c)

A	B	.NOT. A .OR. .NOT. B		
T	T	F	**F**	F
T	F	F	**T**	T
F	T	T	**T**	F
F	F	T	**T**	T

   (e)

A	B	C	A .AND. (B .OR. C)	
T	T	T	**T**	T
T	T	F	**T**	T
T	F	T	**T**	T
T	F	F	**F**	F
F	T	T	**F**	T
F	T	F	**F**	T
F	F	T	**F**	T
F	F	F	**F**	F

3. (a) X .GT. 3
   (d) (ALPHA .GT. 0) .AND. (BETA .GT. 0)
   (g) (A .LT. 6) .OR. (A .GT. 10)

4. (a) A .AND. B .AND. .NOT. C

6. (a) (i) SUM1 = (A .OR. B) .AND. .NOT. (A .AND. B)
            CARRY1 = A .AND. B
     (ii) SUM = (SUM1 .OR. CIN) .AND.
                .NOT. (SUM1 .AND. CIN)
            CARRY = CARRY1 .OR. (SUM1 .AND. CIN)

Section 4.4 (p. 126)

1. (a) IF (CODE .EQ. 1) THEN
           READ *, X, Y
           PRINT *, 'SUM = ', X + Y
      END IF

2. (a) IF (0 .LE. T .AND. T .LE. 1.0/60.0) THEN
           V = 100.0 * ABS(SIN(120 * 3.1416 * T))
      END IF

Section 4.11 (p. 167)

3. (a)

```
        DO 10 I = 1, 100
              PRINT *, I
    10  CONTINUE
```

(b)

```
        IF (X .LT. 0 .OR. X .GT. 10) GO TO 50
```

5. (a) 1. Initialize COUNT to 0.
2. Read NUMBER.
3. Repeat the following until NUMBER = 0:
   a. Increment COUNT by 1.
   b. Set NUMBER = NUMBER / 10 (integer division).

Section 5.1 (p. 198)

1.

```
     RANGE(NUM1, NUM2) = ABS(NUM1 - NUM2)
```

9. (a)

```
          FUNCTION NGRADE(LETTER)
    ************************************
    * Function returns the numeric grade *
    * corresponding to a LETTER grade.    *
    ************************************

          REAL NGRADE
          CHARACTER*1 LETTER

          IF (LETTER .EQ. 'A') THEN
              NGRADE = 4.0
          ELSE IF (LETTER .EQ. 'B') THEN
              NGRADE = 3.0
          ELSE IF (LETTER .EQ. 'C') THEN
              NGRADE = 2.0
          ELSE IF (LETTER .EQ. 'D') THEN
              NGRADE = 1.0
          ELSE
              NGRADE = 0
          END IF
          END
```

Section 5.3 (p. 229)

```
2.            SUBROUTINE SWITCH(A,B)
       ********************************
       * Subroutine to interchange the *
       * values of variables A and B.  *
       ********************************

              INTEGER A, B, TEMP

              TEMP = A
              A = B
              B = TEMP
              END
```

Section 6.2 (p. 289)

1. (a) C̲O̲M̲P̲U̲T̲E̲R̲_̲S̲C̲I̲E̲N̲C̲E̲-̲E̲X̲E̲R̲C̲I̲S̲E̲_̲6̲.̲2̲

(d) blank line

(g) C̲O̲M̲P̲U̲T̲E̲R̲_̲S̲C̲I̲E̲N̲C̲E̲_̲6̲.̲2̲

(j)
```
-------------------------------------------------
__12345__12346__87.65430____88.654_____90._____
```

(m) _____1̲2̲3̲4̲5̲____8̲7̲.̲6̲5̲4̲
      _____1̲2̲3̲4̲6̲____8̲8̲.̲6̲5̲4̲

(p) 1̲_̲=̲_̲0̲_̲I̲S̲_̲F̲

Section 6.7 (p. 318)

1. (a) 77, 550, 123.77, 6.0

(c) ƀ77ƀ123.77ƀƀƀƀ550ƀƀƀƀ6.0 (ƀ denotes a blank)

(e) ƀƀƀ77123.77
      ƀƀ550ƀƀƀ6.0

(g) 12377ƀ6ƀ550

(j) 12377ƀ77Tƀƀ6.0550F

(m) FORTRAN77.TRUE.

Section 7.5 (p. 367)

1. (a) NUMBER(1) = 0
        NUMBER(2) = 1
        NUMBER(3) = 1
        NUMBER(4) = 2
        NUMBER(5) = 2
        NUMBER(6) = 3
        NUMBER(7) = 3
        NUMBER(8) = 4
        NUMBER(9) = 4
        NUMBER(10) = 5

(d) NUMBER(1), ... , NUMBER(9) are all equal to 1, but NUMBER(10) is not assigned a value.

(g) NUMBER(1) = 1
NUMBER(2) = 2
NUMBER(3) = 3
NUMBER(4) = 4
NUMBER(5) = 5
NUMBER(6) = 6
NUMBER(7) = 7
NUMBER(8) = 8
NUMBER(9) = 9
NUMBER(10) = 0

2. (a)
```
      INTEGER X(0:5), I
      DO 10 I = 0, 5
          X(I) = I
 10 CONTINUE
```

(c)
```
      LOGICAL L(20)
      INTEGER I
      DO 10 I = 1, 20
          L(I) = (MOD(I,2) .EQ. 0)
 10 CONTINUE
```

3. (a) $A(I) \rightarrow B + (I - 1)$

(d) $A(I) \rightarrow B + (I + 5)$

Section 8.4 (p. 423)

1. (a) $\begin{bmatrix} 2 & 3 & 4 \\ 3 & 4 & 5 \\ 4 & 5 & 6 \end{bmatrix}$

(d) $\begin{bmatrix} 0 & 2 & 2 \\ 0 & 0 & 2 \\ 0 & 0 & 0 \end{bmatrix}$

(g) $\begin{bmatrix} 1 & 2 & 3 \\ 4 & 5 & 6 \\ 7 & 8 & 9 \end{bmatrix}$

(j) First Row of MAT is 1 2 3, but all other entries are undefined.

3. (a) ```
        INTEGER I, J, K, A(3,3), B(3,3), C(3,3)
       +   D(3,3), E(3,3)
```

(b) $A = \begin{bmatrix} 2 & 3 & 4 \\ 3 & 4 & 5 \\ 4 & 5 & 6 \end{bmatrix}, C = \begin{bmatrix} 5 & 5 & 5 \\ 5 & 5 & 5 \\ 5 & 5 & 5 \end{bmatrix}$

7. (a)
```
          FUNCTION NORM(V,N)
      ****
      * Function returns the norm of the   *
      * N-dimensional vector V. SUM is the   *
      * sum of the squares of the components *
      * and I is an index.   *
      ****
          INTEGER I, N
          REAL NORM, SUM, V(N)

          SUM = 0
          DO 10 I = 1, N
              SUM = SUM + V(I) ** 2
   10   CONTINUE
          NORM = SQRT(SUM)
          END
```

## Section 9.2 (p. 455)

1. (a) $A = 12.3, B = .049, C = 0.41$

2. (a) $4 - 2i$          (c) $11 + 2i$
   (e) $-3 + 4i$          (g) $3 + 4i$
   (i) $2$                (k) $\dfrac{1}{5} - \dfrac{2}{5}i$
```

4. **(a)** .1
   (c) 6.0
   (e) Not valid. Complex value may not be assigned to a double precision variable.
   (g) 6.0
   (i) $(-8.0, 6.0)$
   (k) 10.0
   (m) $(-28.0, 96.0)$
   (o) (2.0, 0.5)
   (q) (14.0, 0.0)

Section 10.5 (p. 506)

1. **(a)** Not valid—123 is not of character type.
   (d) '12ᵇᵇᵇᵇᵇᵇᵇᵇ' (ᵇ denotes a blank)
   (g) Not valid—23 is not of character type
   (j) 'FOOTLBSᵇᵇᵇ'
   (m) 'FORTᵇ'
   (p) 'ANAN'

2. **(a)** `1, 1.1, 'MODEL-XL11', 'CAMERA'`
   (c) `1MODEL-XL1111CAMERA`
   (e) `ᵇᵇᵇᵇ1ᵇᵇ1.1MODEL-XL11ᵇᵇᵇᵇᵇCAMERAᵇᵇᵇᵇᵇᵇᵇ`

21. **(b)**

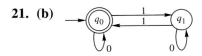

28. **(a)** $-7.\overline{3}$ **(d)** 12.0   **(g)** 12.0   **(j)** 8.0

29. **(a)** A B * C + D −   **(d)** A B C D + / +
    (g) A B − C − D − E −

30. **(a)** (A − (B + C)) * D   **(d)** ((A + B) − C) / (D * E)
    (g) A / ((B / C) / D)

31. **(a)** − + * A B C D   **(d)** + A / B + C D
    (g) − − − − A B C D E

32. **(a)** −24.5   **(d)** 2.0   **(g)** 55.0

33. **(a)** (A + B) * (C − D)   **(d)** A − (B − C) − D
    (g) (A * B + C) / (D − E)

34. **(a)** **(i)** −15   **(iv)** 15
    (b) **(i)** A B C ~ + *   **(iii)** A ~ B ~ *
    (c) **(i)** * A + B ~ C   **(iii)** * ~ A ~ B

35. (a) A B .AND. C .OR.   **(e)** A B .EQ. C D .EQ. .OR.

36. (a) .OR. .AND. A B C   **(e)** .OR. .EQ. A B .EQ. C D

Section 11.3 (p. 546)

2. (a) F: | 1 5 | 3 8 | 7 | 2 6 | 4 |
      F1: | 1 5 7 | 4 |
      F2: | 3 8 | 2 6 |
      F: | 1 3 5 7 8 | 2 4 6 |
      F1: | 1 3 5 7 8 |
      F2: | 2 4 6 |
      F: | 1 2 3 4 5 6 7 8 |

Index of
Programming
Exercises

Chapter 4

Section 4.3

Section 4.4

Section 4.11

Chapter 5

Chapter 10

Section 10.5

Reversing a string (Ex. 3, p. 507)
Locating a string in a given string (Ex. 4, p. 507)
Counting occurrences of characters and strings in lines of text (Ex. 5, 6, p. 507)
Reversing a name (Ex. 7, p. 507)
File processing using STUDENT-FILE (Ex. 8, p. 507)
Processing grade information (Ex. 9, p. 507)
Mass and oil displacement caused by various shapes (Ex. 10, p. 508)
Keyword encoding (Ex. 11, p. 508)
Morse code (Ex. 12, p. 508)
Determining day on which a date falls (Ex. 13, p. 509)
Hindu–arabic and roman numeral conversion (Ex. 14, p. 510)
Palindromes (Ex. 15, p. 510)
Text formatting (Ex. 16, 17, p. 510)
Plotting graphs of parametric equations (Ex. 18, p. 510)
Visual image processing and enhancement (Ex. 19, 20, p. 510)
Lexical analysis of FORTRAN real numbers (Ex. 22, p. 511)
Rational number arithmetic (Ex. 23, p. 511)
Lexical analysis of assignment statements (Ex. 24, 25, 26, 27, p. 512)
Evaluation of RPN expressions (Ex. 37, p. 513)
Conversion of infix to prefix (Ex. 38, p. 514)
Evaluation of prefix expressions (Ex. 39, p. 514)
Determining if RPN expressions are well formed (Ex. 40, p. 514)

Chapter 11

Section 11.3

Concatenation of files (Ex. 1, p. 546)
Mergesort (Ex. 3, p. 546)
Processing a direct access file (Ex. 4, p. 547)
Text formatting (Ex. 5, p. 547)
Text editing (Ex. 6, p. 547)
Pretty printer (Ex. 7, p. 547)
Menu-driven operations using STUDENT-FILE (Ex. 8, p. 548)

INDEX

Examples and Sample Programs